FOR
STUDENTS

Over the past four years we have spent time in classrooms across Canada, speaking to students just like you.

We've asked what you want to see in a textbook, how you learn, how many hours a week you spend online, and what you find most valuable when preparing for a test. Based on your feedback, we've developed a new hybrid learning solution—**PSYCH**. Your textbook, the Chapter in Review cards, and our online resources present a new, exciting, and fresh approach to learning. Check out the website at **www.icanpsych.com** for an unrivalled set of learning tools.

- Interactive e-book
- Flashcards
- Build a Summary activities
- Multi
- Pow
- Gam
- Intera
- **And**

D0709933

NELSON / EDUCATION

PSYCH, Canadian Edition

by Spencer A. Rathus, Shannon J. Maheu, and Scott G. Veenvliet

Vice President, Editorial Director:
Evelyn Veitch

Editor-in-Chief, Higher Education:
Anne Williams

Senior Acquisitions Editor:
Lenore Taylor-Atkins

Marketing Manager:
Ann Byford

Senior Developmental Editor:
Sandy Matos

Photo Researcher and Permissions Coordinator:
Jessie Coffey

Senior Content Production Manager:
Natalia Denesiuk Harris

Production Service:
Bill Smith Group

Copy Editor:
Valerie Adams

Proofreader:
Jennifer Hwo

Indexer:
Nancy Ball

Manufacturing Manager:
Joanne McNeil

Design Director:
Ken Phipps

Managing Designer:
Franca Amore

Interior Design:
Beckmeyer Design

Cover Design:
Martyn Schmoll

Cover Image:
Masterfile

Compositor:
Bill Smith Group

Printer:
RRDonnelley

Library and Archives Canada Cataloguing in Publication Data

Rathus, Spencer A.
     Psych / Spencer A. Rathus, Shannon J. Maheu, Scott G. Veenliet. — 1st Canadian ed.

Includes indexes.
ISBN 978-0-17-650346-8

     1. Psychology—Textbooks. I. Maheu, Shannon J., 1974– II. Veenvliet, Scott G., 1976– III. Title.

BF121.R335 2011
150   C2011-901343-6

ISBN-13: 978-0-17-650346-8
ISBN-10: 0-17-650346-3

PSYCH
Brief Contents

M.C. Escher's "Relativity" © 2010 The M.C. Escher Company - Holland. All rights reserved. www.mcescher.com

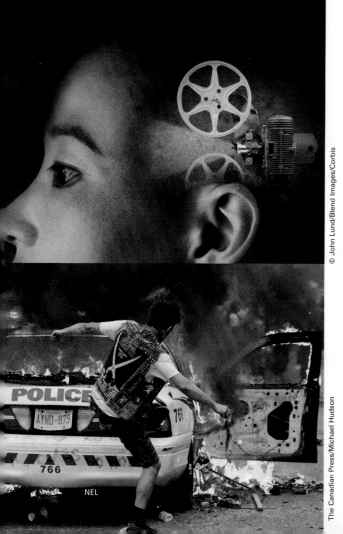

© John Lund/Blend Images/Corbis

The Canadian Press/Michael Hudson

NEL

LOG IN!

PSYCH Contents

David Buffington/Getty Images

Penelope Breese/Liaison/Getty Images

Photodisc/Getty Images

Image Source/Getty Images

Lev Olkha/Shutterstock.com

Jupiterimages

Kevin Arnold/Brand X Pictures/Jupiterimages

Elyse Lewin/Brand X Pictures/Jupiterimages

Christa Renee/The Image Bank/Getty Images

RubberBall/Alamy

Keith Brofsky/Getty Images

plainpicture/FirstLight.com

Gabriela Medina/Blend Images/Jupiterimages

Guelph Mercury/The Canadian Press/Dave Carter

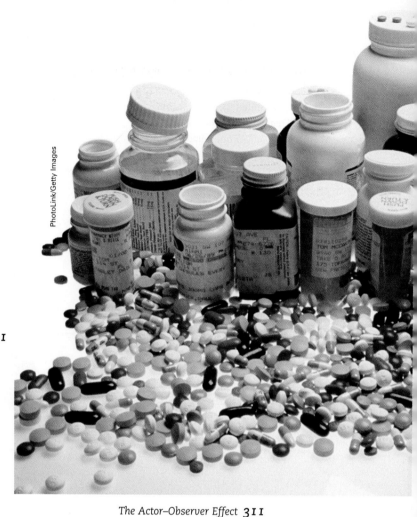

PhotoLink/Getty Images

Julian Finney/Getty Images

Chapter Features in the Canadian Edition

Chapter 1

- Expanded section on the learning perspective overview includes psychologist Albert Bandura.
- A new table explains experimental method terminology (e.g., dependent and independent variables, experimental and control groups).
- A section about Canada's National Council on Ethics in Human Research was added.

Chapter 2

- The chapter begins with the story of a ski accident, which intends to lead the reader to try to predict what influence the brain damage had on later behaviour.
- The important topics of biology and psychology are covered. The chapter presents, in a clear and concise way, the cellular structure and function of neurons, the structures of the brain and their functions, the broader endocrine system, and current trends in evolutionary psychology.
- A section on neurological plasticity is included.
- Canadian research and researchers are highlighted, including Wilder Penfield and his neuroscience work at McGill, Brian Kolb and his work on neuroplasticity at the University of Lethbridge, and James Olds and Peter Milner's accidental discovery of the pleasure centre of the hypothalamus in rats.

Chapter 3

- Visual perceptual systems, such as Gestalt organization and perceptual constancies, are discussed immediately following the discussion of how the eye works. This integration of sensation and perception should help students understand how the systems are intricately related.
- Canadian content added includes a discussion of new groundbreaking research from Mel Goodale at the University of Western Ontario that investigates the dual processing routes of the visual system, and how one is fooled by optical illusions, and the other is not.
- Detail on the paranormal million-dollar challenge is included. This current contest, run by Canadian James Randi, will get students thinking critically about extra sensory perception and why people believe it.

Chapter 4

- The chapter begins with a popular case of Kenneth Parks (from the Toronto area), who murdered his in-laws while sleepwalking and was acquitted based on evidence.
- Canadian statistics regarding sleep patterns and sleep disorders are included.
- Examples are provided from popular culture—blockbuster movies—to highlight our views of consciousness and what our minds may (or may not) be capable of doing.
- Some common myths about hypnosis are included.

Chapter 5

- A new feature box on behaviour modification highlights our Canadian inclusive education for autism and PDD in the classroom.

- Additional practical examples explain negative reinforcement and schedules of reinforcement.

Chapter 6

- Many "Try It!" boxes are included to allow students to practise the concepts they are learning.
- Information was added on reconstructing memory based on Loftus' experiments to demonstrate inaccuracies in our memory.

Chapter 7

- Canadian focus on bilingual language acquisition (English and French) is highlighted at the end of the chapter.
- More examples of insight problems that will interest/challenge students' cognition were added.
- Gardner's theory of multiple intelligences is featured.

Chapter 8

- The chapter was reorganized to discuss the different aspects of development across the lifespan.
- More focus is put on prenatal and child physical and cognitive development and on social development in adolescence.
- A summary of Kübler-Ross's death and dying stages was added.
- Canadian highlights of age and illness were added—e.g., related to osteoporosis.

Chapter 9

- Motivation can be linked to the Vancouver 2010 Olympics and Sidney Crosby's game-winning overtime goal.
- "Try It!" boxes bring to life the research on achievement motivation and the facial-feedback hypothesis.
- Canadian content was added, including a discussion of new groundbreaking research from Tony Bogaert at Brock University that investigates the effect of fraternal birth order on sexual orientation.
- Statistics on the sexuality of Canadian youth and the life satisfaction of Canadians in various cities are included.
- The section on positive psychology discusses what makes Canadians happy.

Chapter 10

- The chapter includes Canadian statistics related to stress, health, and adjustment.
- The Montreal college bombing is featured as an introductory example of stress and PTSD.
- "Try It!" box allows students to assess their stress level.
- Particular interests of Canadian researchers in stress and illness were highlighted by adding information about HIV/AIDS.

Chapter 11

- The chapter begins with references to several Canadian personalities (e.g., musicians, actors) and should serve to draw Canadian students into the topic of personality, including how it forms and how we measure it.
- "Try It!" boxes illustrate the concepts for the student and can be incorporated into the classroom to explore topics such as cultural individualism and collectivism's influence on personality, and the Rorschach inkblot test.
- The section on the "Big Five" personality trait research was expanded to suggest that there may be a sixth personality trait (or perhaps more) that is important to understanding personality.

- The details and criticisms of Freudian personality theory; the important neo-Freudians; trait theory; the behaviourist, humanistic, sociocultural, and social-cognitive perspectives; and how personality is measured are covered in a clear, concise, and relevant way for Canadian students.
- All Canadian statistics are current and relevant. Canadian students will recognize (or learn about) information about Canadian identity and newsworthy current issues.

Chapter 12

- The chapter begins with a story about a student who suffers from Seasonal Affective Disorder (SAD). SAD is a disorder that many Canadians suffer from, especially during much of the winter term of the school year.
- The section on depression and suicide has significant detail and will be helpful and necessary for the current student population. Canadian college and university students are at more risk for suicide than their similarly aged non-college peers.
- The biopsychosocial explanation for psychological disorders is introduced, emphasizing that biology, cognition, and the social environment all have a role to play in the manifestation and maintenance of various psychological disorders.
- The nature and causes of many psychological disorders, including schizophrenia, mood, anxiety, somatoform, dissociative, and personality disorders, are described in under 25 pages!
- All Canadian statistics on prevalence rates of the various disorders and suicide are current and relevant. Canadian celebrities and infamous personalities who suffer from psychological disorders are introduced to aid in memory recall.

Chapter 13

- All Canadian statistics on prevalence rates of the various therapies are current and relevant.
- Multiculturalism information was updated, and issues related to the psychological treatment of visible minority groups in Canada.
- The history of psychotherapy in Canada is described, as well as psychoanalysis, psychodynamic therapy, humanistic therapies, behavioural therapy, cognitive therapy, group therapies, and drug therapies.
- A new feature box gives guidance to students who may need help for mental health issues and some resource suggestions to help them find assistance.
- Information is provided about modern technological advances in therapy, including virtual reality, systematic desensitization, internet counselling, and telephone therapy. The benefits and challenges of each are discussed.

Chapter 14

- The chapter begins with a narrative of the 2008 Montreal hockey riot and should serve to draw Canadian students into the topic of social psychology and how a situation can influence our behaviour.
- "Try It!" boxes illustrate the concepts for the student and can be incorporated into the classroom to explore topics such as door-in-the-face and low-ball sales techniques.
- Milgram's obedience study and Asch's conformity study are described in depth.
- Canadian students will recognize (or learn about) the social influences involved in current Canadian issues.

1

What *is* Psychology?

Learning Outcomes

LO1   Define psychology and its goals

LO2   Describe the various fields and sub-fields of psychology

LO3   Describe the origins of psychology and identify those who made significant contributions to the field

LO4   Identify theoretical perspectives of modern psychologists toward behaviour and mental processes

LO5   Describe modern approaches to research and practice—critical thinking, the scientific method, and ethical considerations

> # "The most popular misperception about psychology is that it stems from common sense. "

S.M.: When the topic of psychology comes up in my house, it's funny how members of my family—and friends—laugh off that I study psychology. They make comments like "Oh, great, so are you going to analyze me now?" or (my husband's favourite) "Why do I have to tell you what I'm thinking, can't you read my mind?" Ha! If only I could—I wonder what he would really think about that.

Like my family and friends, many of you likely know *something* about psychology—right? In fact, if I were to ask you the question, "What is psychology?" what would you tell me? *Intuition? Common sense? Behaviour analysis? Mind reading?*

Take a moment and complete the Try It! Test of Common Beliefs on the next page. You may be surprised by how much you know about psychology.

We'll find out how you did on the common belief statements shortly, but first, here are a few things you should know about psychologists. Psychologists cannot read minds (although we like to convince you otherwise—see Chapter 4). Not all psychologists can "analyze" you (or even want to) with accuracy, but they do know a lot about how and why we think and behave in certain ways. Psychologists use scientific, measurable methods to explain our behaviour and thinking processes—and it is to this point that we turn our attention.

DID YOU KNOW?

- More than 2000 years ago, Aristotle wrote a book on psychology, with contents similar to the book you are now holding.

- Kissing on the lips, as a greeting, is used by chimpanzees.

- Men who *thought* they were drinking alcohol behaved more aggressively even though they weren't given alcohol.

- The first Canadian psychology lab was opened in 1891 at the University of Toronto.

- Deception is still used in many experiments; in these experiments, neither the subjects nor the researchers know who is receiving the real treatment and who is not.

LO1 Psychology as a Science

Psychology is the scientific study of behaviour and mental processes. Topics of interest to psychologists include the nervous system, sensation and perception, learning and memory, intelligence, language, thought, growth and development, personality, stress and health, psychological disorders, ways of treating those disorders, and the behaviour of people in social settings such as groups and organizations.

The questions you answered in the Try It! text include some of the questions that Griggs and Ransdell (1987) asked students

psychology
the science that studies behaviour and mental processes

theory
a formulation of relationships underlying observed events

pure research
research conducted without concern for immediate applications; purely for research's sake

applied research
research conducted in an effort to find solutions to particular problems

in introductory psychology classes. How did you do? If you responded "false" to all of the items, then you did very well! If you responded "true" in some cases, we are excited for you (even though you got the answers wrong)—you especially will be learning about the science of psychology throughout this course! You have been taken prisoner to the power of common sense, which has led you to believe some popular misconceptions about our behaviour and thinking processes.

What are the goals of psychology? Psychology, like other sciences, seeks to describe, explain, predict, and control the events it studies. Psychology thus seeks to describe, explain, predict, and control behaviour and mental processes. "Controlling" behaviour and mental processes doesn't mean to psychologists

---

Try It!

Test of Common Beliefs

Instructions: Read each item carefully and then circle "T" or "F" to indicate whether you believe the statement to be *true* or *false*.

T F 1. To change people's behaviour toward members of ethnic minority groups, we must first change their attitudes.

T F 2. Children memorize much more easily than adults.

T F 3. The more you memorize by rote (e.g., poems), the better you will become at memorizing.

T F 4. The best way to ensure that a desired behaviour will persist after training is completed is to reward the behaviour every single time it occurs throughout training (rather than intermittently).

T F 5. Fortunately for babies, human beings have a strong maternal instinct.

T F 6. Psychiatrists are defined as medical people who use psychoanalysis.

T F 7. Genius is akin to insanity.

T F 8. In love and friendship, more often than not, opposites attract one another.

Source: Griggs, R.A., and Ransdell, S.E. (1987). "Misconception tests or misconceived tests?" *Teaching of Psychology, 14*(4): 210–214. Reprinted by permission of the publisher, Taylor & Francis Group, http://www.informaworld.com.

---

what it may sound like to most people. Psychologists are committed to a belief in the dignity of human beings, and human dignity requires that people be free to make their own decisions and choose their own behaviour. Psychologists study the influences on human behaviour, but they use this knowledge only on request and to help people meet their own goals. For example, a psychologist would wish to help someone who is suffering from anxiety and who asks for help.

When possible, descriptive terms such as *a threat* and concepts such as *anxiety* are interwoven into **theories**. Theories propose reasons for relationships among events, as in perception of *a threat* can arouse feelings of *anxiety*. They allow us to derive *explanations* and *predictions*, as in "Dwayne will feel *anxious* if he perceives *a threat*." A theory of hunger should allow us to predict when people will or will not eat. Many psychological theories combine statements about behaviour (such as *avoiding a threat*), mental processes (such as *thinking that the threat may be harmful*), and biological processes (such as *rapid heart and respiration rates*). If our observations are not adequately explained by or predicted from a theory, we should consider revising or replacing it.

The remainder of this chapter presents an overview of psychology as a science. You will see that psychologists have diverse interests and fields of specialization. We discuss the history of psychology and the perspectives from which today's psychologists view behaviour and mental processes. Finally, we consider the research methods used by psychologists.

LO2 What Psychologists Do

Psychologists share a keen interest in behaviour and thinking; but, in other ways, they may differ markedly. *Just what do psychologists do?* Psychologists engage in research, practice, and teaching. Some researchers engage primarily in basic, or **pure research**. Pure research has no immediate application to personal or social problems and, therefore, has been characterized as research for its own sake. Others engage in **applied research**, which is designed to find solutions to specific personal or social problems. Although pure research is sparked by curiosity and the desire to know and understand, today's pure research frequently enhances tomorrow's way of life. For example, pure research on learning and motivation in pigeons, rats, and monkeys done early in the 20th century has found applications in school systems. The research has shown, for example, that learning often takes time and repetition and profits from "booster shots" (that is, repetition even after the learning goal has been reached). Pure research into the workings of the nervous system has enhanced knowledge of disorders such as epilepsy, Parkinson's disease, and Alzheimer's disease.

Many psychologists *practise* psychology by applying psychological knowledge to help individuals change their behaviour or their thinking process so that they can meet their own goals more effectively. Still other psychologists primarily teach. They share psychological knowledge in classrooms, seminars, and workshops. Some psychologists engage in all three: research, practice, and teaching.

Fields of Psychology

Psychologists are found in different specialties. Although some psychologists wear more than one hat, most of them carry out their functions in the following fields:

- *Clinical psychologists* help people with psychological disorders adjust to the demands of life. Clinical psychologists evaluate problems such as anxiety and depression through interviews and psychological tests. They help clients resolve problems and change self-defeating behaviour. For example, they may help clients face "threats," such as public speaking, by exposing the clients gradually to situations in which they make presentations to actual or virtual groups (see *virtual therapy* in Chapter 13). Clinical psychologists are the largest subgroup of psychologists in Canada.

- *Counselling psychologists*, like clinical psychologists, use interviews and tests to define their clients' problems. Their clients typically have adjustment problems but not serious psychological disorders. For example, clients may have trouble making academic or vocational decisions or making friends in college or university. Counselling psychologists most often work in a variety of social services areas.

- *School and educational psychologists* help school systems identify and assist students who have problems that interfere with learning. They help schools make decisions about placing students in special classes. These psychologists research theoretical issues related to learning, measurement, and child development. They study how learning is affected by psychological factors such as motivation and intelligence, sociocultural factors such as poverty and acculturation, and teacher behaviour. Some educational psychologists prepare standardized tests such as the SATs.

- *Developmental psychologists* study the changes—physical, cognitive, social, and emotional—that occur across the life span. They try to sort out the effects of heredity and the environment on development.

- *Personality psychologists* identify and measure human traits and determine influences on human thought processes, feelings, and behaviour. They are particularly concerned with issues such as anxiety, aggression, and gender roles.

- *Social psychologists* are concerned with the nature and causes of individuals' thoughts, feelings, and behaviour in social situations. Whereas personality psychologists tend to look within the person for explanations of behaviour, social psychologists tend to focus on social influences.

- *Environmental psychologists* study the ways in which people and the environment—the natural environment and the human-made environment—influence one another. For example, we know that extremes of temperature and loud noises interfere with learning in school. Environmental psychologists also study ways to encourage people to recycle and to preserve our natural landscapes.

- *Experimental psychologists* specialize in basic processes such as the nervous system, sensation and perception, learning and memory, thought, motivation, and emotion. For example, experimental psychologists study which areas of the brain are involved in solving math problems or listening to music. They use people or animals such as pigeons and rats to study learning.

- *Industrial/organizational psychologists* focus on the relationships between people and work. They study the behaviour of people in organizations such as businesses.

- *Cognitive psychologists* study our thought processes involved in behaviour. For example, a cognitive psychologist uses cognitive therapy to help people change the way they think in order to change the way they behave. Cognitive psychologists focus on self-esteem and self-efficacy as important factors in behaviour.

- *Health psychologists* examine the ways in which behaviour and attitudes are related to physical health. They study the effects of stress on health problems such as headaches, cardiovascular disease, and cancer. Health psychologists also guide clients toward healthier behaviour patterns, such as exercising and quitting smoking.

- *Sport psychologists* help athletes concentrate on their performance and not on the crowd, use cognitive strategies such as positive visualization (imagining themselves making the right moves) to enhance performance, and avoid choking under pressure.

PA Photos/Landov

This researcher measures electrical activity of participants' brains while they kiss.

introspection deliberate looking into one's own cognitive processes to examine one's thoughts and feelings

• *Forensic psychologists* apply psychology to the criminal justice system. They deal with legal matters such as whether a defendant was sane when he or she committed a crime. Forensic psychologists may also treat psychologically ill offenders, consult with lawyers on matters such as picking a jury, and analyze criminals' behaviour and mental processes. Forensic psychologists, like other psychologists, may choose to conduct research on matters ranging from evaluation of eyewitness testimony to interrogation methods.

LO3 Where Psychology Comes From: A History

The ancient Greek philosopher Aristotle (384–322 BCE) argued that human behaviour, like the movements of the stars and the seas, is subject to rules and laws. Then he delved into his subject matter, topic by topic, in his book *Peri Psyches*: personality, sensation and perception, thought, intelligence, needs and motives, feelings and emotion, and memory. And so began the history of psychological thought and historical views of the mind and behaviour.

Have you heard the expression "Know thyself"? It was suggested by the ancient Greek philosopher Socrates (c. 470–399 BCE) more than 2000 years ago. He expressed that psychology is in large part the endeavour to know ourselves. Knowledge of the history of psychology allows us to appreciate its theoretical conflicts, its place among the sciences, the evolution of its methods, and its social and political roles. Socrates suggested that we should rely on rational thought and **introspection**—careful examination of one's own thoughts and emotions—to achieve self-knowledge. He also pointed out that people are social creatures who influence one another.

Had we room enough and time, we could trace psychology's roots to thinkers even farther back in time than the ancient Greeks, and we could trace its development through the great thinkers of the Renaissance. As it is, we must move on to the development of psychology as a laboratory science during the second half of the 19th century. Some historians set the marker date at 1860. It was then that Gustav Theodor Fechner (1801–1887) published his landmark book *Elements of Psychophysics*, which showed how physical events (such as lights and sounds) are related to psychological sensation and perception. Fechner also showed how we can scientifically measure the effect of these events. Most historians set the debut of modern psychology as a laboratory science in the year 1879, when German psychologist Wilhelm Wundt (1832–1920) established the first psychological laboratory in Leipzig, Germany. Let's look at the early history of psychology, which was brought to Canada in 1891.

Structuralism

Like Aristotle, Wundt saw the mind as a natural event that could be studied scientifically, like light, heat, and the flow of blood. Wundt used introspection to try to discover the basic elements of experience.

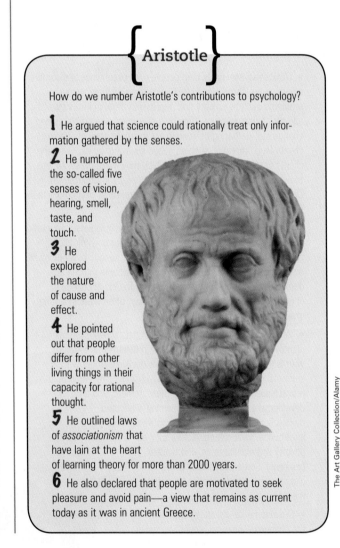

{Aristotle}

How do we number Aristotle's contributions to psychology?

1 He argued that science could rationally treat only information gathered by the senses.

2 He numbered the so-called five senses of vision, hearing, smell, taste, and touch.

3 He explored the nature of cause and effect.

4 He pointed out that people differ from other living things in their capacity for rational thought.

5 He outlined laws of *associationism* that have lain at the heart of learning theory for more than 2000 years.

6 He also declared that people are motivated to seek pleasure and avoid pain—a view that remains as current today as it was in ancient Greece.

The Art Gallery Collection/Alamy

Wundt and his students founded the school of psychology called **structuralism**. *What is structuralism?* Structuralism attempted to break conscious experience down into objective sensations, such as sight or taste, and subjective feelings, such as emotional responses, will, and mental images like memories or dreams. Structuralists believed that the mind functions by combining objective and subjective elements of experience.

Despite its use of observation and experimentation, structuralism is most criticized for it use of introspection—which was often ruled as subjective.

Functionalism

Toward the end of the 19th century, William James became a major figure in the development of psychology in North America. He focused on the relation between conscious experience and behaviour. He argued, for example, that the stream of consciousness is fluid and continuous. Introspection convinced him that experience cannot be broken down into objective sensations and subjective feelings as the structuralists maintained.

James was a founder of the school of **functionalism**. *What is functionalism?* The school of functionalism focused on behaviour in addition to the mind or consciousness. Functionalists looked at how our experience helps us function more adaptively in our environments—for example, how habits help

us cope with common situations. (When eating with a spoon, we do not create an individual plan to bring each morsel of food to our mouths.) They also turned to the laboratory for direct observations as a way to supplement introspection. The structuralists tended to ask, "What are the pieces that make up thinking and experience?" In contrast, the functionalists tended to ask, "How do behaviour and mental processes help people adapt to the requirements of their lives?"

James was also influenced by Charles Darwin's (1809–1882) theory of evolution. Earlier in the 19th century, British naturalist Darwin had argued that organisms with adaptive features—that is, the "fittest"—survive and reproduce. Functionalists adapted Darwin's theory and proposed that adaptive behaviour patterns are learned and maintained. Maladaptive behaviour patterns tend to drop out; only the "fittest" behaviour survives. Adaptive behaviours tend to be repeated and become habits. James wrote, "habit is the enormous flywheel of society." Habit keeps the engine of civilization running.

structuralism
the school of psychology that argues that the mind consists of three basic elements— sensations, feelings, and images—that combine to form experience

functionalism
the school of psychology that emphasizes the uses or functions of the mind rather than the elements of experience

{ Psychology in Canada }

1891—James Mark Baldwin established the first psychology lab in Canada at the University of Toronto. Although he left shortly thereafter to teach at Princeton, his landmark research on the cognitive development of children began the work of many developmental psychologists today.

Behaviourism

Imagine you have placed a hungry rat in a maze. It meanders down a pathway that ends in a T. It can turn left or right. If you consistently reward the rat with food for turning right, it will learn to turn right when it arrives there, at least when it is hungry. But what does the rat *think* when it is learning to turn right?

Does it seem absurd to try to place yourself in the "mind" of a rat? So it seemed to John Broadus Watson (1878–1958), the founder of American behaviourism. Watson was asked to consider the contents of a rat's "mind" as one of the requirements for his doctoral degree, which he received from the University of Chicago in 1903. Watson (1913) believed that if psychology was to be a natural science, like physics or chemistry, it must limit itself to observable,

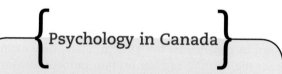

Wilhelm Wundt   William James

measurable events—that is, to behaviour alone—hence, the term *behaviourism*.

What is behaviourism? **Behaviourism** is the school of psychology that focuses on the study of observable behaviour. The term "observable" includes behaviours that are observable by means of instruments, such as the heart rate, blood pressure, and brain waves. These behaviours are *public* in that they can be measured easily and multiple observers would agree about their existence and features. Given their focus on behaviour, behaviourists define psychology as the scientific study of *behaviour*, not of *behaviour and mental processes*.

B.F. Skinner (1904–1990) also contributed to behaviourism. He believed that organisms learn to behave in certain ways based on **reinforcement** for doing so—that is, their behaviour has a positive outcome. He demonstrated that laboratory animals can be trained to carry out behaviours through strategic use of reinforcers, such as food. He trained rats to turn in circles, climb ladders, and push toys across the floor. Because Skin-

J.B. Watson

B.F. Skinner

© Bettmann/CORBIS

ner showed that he could teach animals remarkable combinations of behaviours by means of reinforcement, many psychologists adopted the view that, in principle, one could explain complex human behaviour in terms of thousands of instances of learning through reinforcement.

Gestalt Psychology

In the 1920s, another school of psychology—Gestalt psychology—was prominent in Germany. In the 1930s, the three founders of the school—Max Wertheimer (1880–1943), Kurt Koffka (1886–1941), and Wolfgang Köhler (1887–1967)—left Europe to escape the Nazi threat. They carried on their work in North America, giving further impetus to the growing interest in psychology.

What is Gestalt psychology? Gestalt psychologists focused on perception and on how perception influences thinking and problem solving. The German word *Gestalt* translates as "pattern" or "organized whole." In contrast to the behaviourists, Gestalt psychologists argued that we cannot understand human nature by focusing only on observable behaviour. In contrast to the structuralists, they claimed that we cannot explain human perceptions, emotions, or thought processes in terms of basic units. Perceptions are *more* than the sums of their parts: Gestalt psychologists saw our perceptions as wholes that give meaning to parts, as we see in Figure 1.1.

Gestalt psychologists showed that we tend to perceive separate pieces of information as integrated wholes, depending on the contexts in which they occur. In part A of Figure 1.1, the dots in the centres of the drawings are the same size, yet we may perceive them as being different in size because of their surroundings. The second symbol in each line in part B is identical, but in the top row we may perceive it as a B and in the bottom row as the number 13. The symbol has not changed, but its context has. The inner squares in part C are equally bright, but

© Underwood & Underwood/CORBIS

they do not appear so because of their contrasting backgrounds.

Gestalt psychologists believed that learning could be active and purposeful, not merely responsive and mechanical as in Watson's and Skinner's experiments. They found that much learning, especially in problem solving, is accomplished by insight, not by mechanical repetition.

Consider Wolfgang Köhler's research with chimpanzees, as shown in Figure 1.2. At first, the chimpanzee is unsuccessful in reaching for bananas suspended from the ceiling. Then he suddenly stacks the boxes and climbs up to reach the bananas.

It seems the chimp has experienced a sudden reorganization of the mental elements of the problem—that is, he has had a "flash of insight." Köhler's findings suggest that people too often manipulate the elements of problems until we group them in such a way that we believe we will be able to reach a goal. The manipulations may take quite some time as mental trial and error proceeds. But once the solution has been found, we seem to perceive it all of a sudden.

psychoanalysis
the school of psychology that emphasizes the importance of unconscious motives and conflicts as determinants of human behaviour

Psychoanalysis

What is psychoanalysis? Psychoanalysis—another school of psychology—is the name of the theory of personality and of the method of therapy developed by Sigmund Freud (1856–1939). As a theory of personality, psychoanalysis

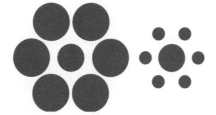
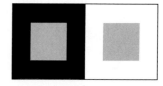

FIGURE 1.1

The Importance of Context

A. Are the dots in the centre of the configurations the same size? Why not take a ruler and measure them?

B. Is the second symbol in each line the letter *B* or the number *13*?

C. Which of the grey squares is brighter?

FIGURE 1.2

Some Insight into Insight

At first, the chimpanzee cannot reach the bananas hanging from the ceiling. After some time has passed, the chimp has an apparent "flash of insight" and piles the boxes on top of one another to reach the fruit.

was based on the idea that much of our lives is governed by unconscious ideas and impulses that originate in childhood conflicts.

Psychoanalytic theory proposes that most of the mind is unconscious—a seething cauldron of conflicting impulses, urges, and wishes. People are motivated to satisfy these impulses, ugly as some of them are. But at the same time, people are motivated to see themselves as decent, and hence may delude themselves about their true motives. As a physician, Freud's goal was to help individuals who were suffering from various psychological and social problems. His method of psychotherapy, psychoanalysis, aims to help patients gain insight into many of their deep-seated conflicts and to find socially acceptable ways of expressing wishes and gratifying needs.

Imagno/Getty Images

Sigmund Freud

LO4 How Today's Psychologists View Behaviour and Mental Processes

Today we no longer find psychologists who describe themselves as structuralists or functionalists. And, although the school of Gestalt psychology gave birth to current research approaches in perception and problem solving, few would label themselves Gestalt psychologists. But we do find Gestalt therapists who help clients integrate conflicting parts of their personality (making themselves "whole"). The numbers of behaviourists and psycho-

analysts have been declining (Robins et al., 1999). Many contemporary psychologists in the behaviourist tradition look on themselves as social-cognitive theorists, and many psychoanalysts consider themselves neoanalysts or ego analysts rather than traditional Freudians.

The history of psychological thought has taken many turns, and contemporary psychologists differ in their approaches. Today there are several broad, influential perspectives in psychology: evolutionary, biological, cognitive, humanistic–existential, psychodynamic, learning, and sociocultural. Each emphasizes different topics of investigation. Each approaches its topics in its own way.

The Evolutionary Perspective

What is the evolutionary perspective? Evolutionary psychologists focus on the evolution of behaviour and mental processes. Charles Darwin argued that in the age-old struggle for existence, only the "fittest" (most adaptive) organisms reach maturity and reproduce. For example, fish that swim faster or people who are naturally immune to certain diseases are more likely to survive and transmit their *genes* to future generations. Individuals die, but species tend to evolve in adaptive directions. Evolutionary psychologists suggest that much human social behaviour, such as aggressive behaviour and mate selection, has a hereditary basis. People may be influenced by social rules, cultural factors, even personal choice, but evolutionary psychologists believe that inherited tendencies move us in certain directions.

The Biological Perspective

When we ask the question "What evolves?" our answer is biological processes and structures. Psychologists assume that thoughts, fantasies, and dreams—and the inborn or *instinctive* behaviour patterns of various species—are made possible by the nervous system and especially by the brain. *What is the biological perspective?* Psychologists with a biological perspective seek the links between the activity of the brain, the activity of hormones, and heredity, on the one hand, and behaviour and mental processes on the other.

Psychologists who look at the activity of the brain seek links between how various brain systems influence our behaviour.

PASIEKA/SPL/Getty Images

The Cognitive Perspective

What is the cognitive perspective? Psychologists with a **cognitive** perspective focus on mental processes to understand human nature. They investigate the ways in which we perceive and mentally represent the world, how we learn, remember the past, plan for the future, solve problems, form judgments, make decisions, and use language. Cognitive psychologists, in short, study those things we refer to as the *mind*.

The Humanistic–Existential Perspective

The humanistic–existential perspective is cognitive in flavour, yet it emphasizes more the role of subjective (personal) experience. *What is the humanistic–existential perspective?* Let us consider each of the parts of this perspective: *humanism* and *existentialism*.

Humanism stresses the human capacity for self-fulfillment and the central roles of consciousness, self-awareness, and decision making. Humanists believe that self-awareness, experience, and choice permit us, to a large extent, to "invent ourselves" as we progress through life. Consciousness—our sense of being in the world—is seen as the force that unifies our personalities. *Existentialism* views people as free to choose and as being responsible for choosing ethical conduct. Grounded in the work of Carl Rogers (1951) and Abraham Maslow (1970), the humanistic–existential perspective has many contemporary adherents (Moss, 2002; Schneider et al., 2003).

The Psychodynamic Perspective

In the 1940s and 1950s, psychodynamic theory dominated the field of psychotherapy and influenced scientific psychology and the arts. Renowned artists and writers consulted psychodynamic therapists to liberate the expression of their unconscious ideas. Today, Freud's influence is still felt, although it no longer dominates psychotherapy. Contemporary psychologists who follow theories derived from Freud are likely to call themselves *neoanalysts*. Famous neoanalysts such as Karen Horney (1885–1952) and Erik Erikson (1902–1994) focused less on the unconscious and more on conscious choice and self-direction.

Perspectives on Learning

Many contemporary psychologists study the effects of experience on behaviour. Learning, to them, is the essential factor in describing, explaining, predicting, and controlling behaviour. The term *learning* has different meanings to psychologists of different persuasions, however. Some students of learning find roles for consciousness and insight. Others do not. This distinction is found today among those who adhere to the behavioural and social-cognitive perspectives.

What are the two major perspectives on learning? Early proponents of the behavioural perspective, like John B. Watson, viewed people as doing things because of their learning histories, their situations, and rewards, not because of conscious choice. Like Watson, contemporary behaviourists emphasize environmental influences and the learning of habits through repetition and reinforcement. **Social-cognitive theorists**, in contrast, suggest that people can modify and create their environments. They note that people engage in intentional learning by observing others. Albert Bandura (1999) maintains that our personal factors (such as feelings, expectations), our behaviour, and the external environment mutually influence one another—a concept known as *reciprocal determinism*. We will look at Bandura's contributions to psychology later when discussing learning theories (Chapter 5), and revisit his concept of reciprocal determinism in understanding personality (Chapter 11). Since the 1960s, social-cognitive theorists have gained influence in the areas of personality development, psychological disorders, and psychotherapy.

The Sociocultural Perspective

Many psychologists today believe we cannot understand people's behaviour and mental processes without reference to their diversity.

What is the sociocultural perspective? The **sociocultural perspective** addresses many of the ways in which people differ from one another. It studies the influences of ethnicity, gender, culture, and socioeconomic status on behaviour and mental processes. Studying cultures other than their own

cognitive
having to do with mental processes such as sensation and perception, memory, intelligence, language, thought, and problem solving

social-cognitive theory
a school of psychology in the behaviourist tradition that includes cognitive factors in the explanation and prediction of behaviour; formerly termed *social learning theory*

sociocultural perspective
the view that focuses on the roles of ethnicity, gender, culture, and socioeconomic status in behaviour and mental processes

helps psychologists understand the roles of culture in behaviour, beliefs, values, and attitudes.

LO5 How Psychologists Study Behaviour and Mental Processes

Does alcohol cause aggression? Does watching violence on TV cause children to be violent? Why do some people hardly ever think of food, whereas others are obsessed with it and snack all day? Why do some unhappy people attempt suicide, whereas others don't? How does having people of different ethnic backgrounds collaborate in their work affect feelings of prejudice?

The experiences of various ethnic groups in Canada highlight the impact of social, political, and economic factors on human behaviour and development.

David Buffington/Getty Images

Many of us have expressed opinions—maybe strong opinions—on questions like these. But as we discussed earlier in the chapter (and may now understand), scientists insist on evidence. Psychologists, like other scientists, use careful means to observe and measure behaviour and the factors that influence behaviour.

The need for evidence is one of the keys to critical thinking. Critical thinking is a life tool for all of us, as well as a pathway toward scientific knowledge.

Critical Thinking

What is critical thinking? Critical thinking has many meanings. On one level, it means taking nothing for granted. It means not believing things just because they are in print or because they were uttered by authority figures or celebrities. It means not necessarily believing that it is healthful to express all of your feelings just because a friend in "therapy" urges you to do so. On another level, critical thinking refers to a process of thoughtfully analyzing and probing the questions, statements, and arguments of others.

Principles of Critical Thinking

1 *Be skeptical.* Keep an open mind. Politicians and advertisers try to persuade you. Are some of your own attitudes and beliefs superficial or unfounded? Accept nothing as the truth until you have examined the evidence.

2 *Insist on evidence.* It is not sufficient that an opinion is traditional, that it appears in print or on the Internet, or it is expressed by a doctor or a lawyer. Ask for evidence.

3 *Examine definitions of terms.* Some statements are true when a term is defined in one way but not when it is defined in another way. Consider the statement, "Montessori programs have raised children's IQs." The correctness of the statement depends on the definition of "IQ." (You will see later in Chapter 7 that *IQ* is not the same thing as *intelligence*.)

4 *Examine the assumptions or premises of arguments.* Consider the statement that one cannot learn about human beings by engaging in research with animals. One premise in the statement seems to be that human beings are not animals. We are, of course.

5 *Be cautious in drawing conclusions from evidence.* For many years, studies had shown that most clients who receive psychotherapy improve. It was therefore generally assumed that psychotherapy worked. Then a psychologist named Hans Eysenck pointed out that most psychologically troubled people who did *not* receive psychotherapy also improved. The question thus becomes whether people receiving psychotherapy are *more* likely to improve than

those who do not. Current research on the effectiveness of psychotherapy therefore carefully compares the benefits of therapy techniques to the benefits of other techniques or of no treatment at all. Be especially skeptical of anecdotes. When you hear "I know someone who…," ask yourself whether this one person's reported experience is satisfactory as evidence.

6 *Consider alternative interpretations of research evidence.* Does alcohol cause aggression? Later in the chapter we will report evidence that there is a clear *connection*, or correlation, between alcohol and aggression. For example, many people who commit violent crimes have been drinking. But does the evidence show that drinking causes aggression? Might other factors, such as gender, age, or willingness to take risks, account for both drinking and aggressive behaviour?

7 *Do not oversimplify.* Most human behaviour involves complex interactions of genetic and environmental influences. Also consider the issue of whether psychotherapy helps people with psychological problems. A broad answer to this question—a simple yes or no—might be oversimplifying. It is more worthwhile to ask, What *type* of psychotherapy, practised by *whom*, is most helpful for *what kind of problem*?

8 *Do not overgeneralize.* Consider the statement that one cannot learn about human beings by engaging in research with nonhuman animals. Is the truth of the matter an all-or-nothing issue? Are there certain kinds of information we can obtain about people from research with animals? What kinds of things are you likely to be able to learn only through research with people?

9 *Apply critical thinking to all areas of life.*

The Scientific Method

What is the scientific method? The scientific method is an organized way of using experience and testing ideas in an effort to expand and refine knowledge. Psychologists do not necessarily follow the steps of the scientific method as we might follow a recipe in a cookbook, but research is guided by certain principles.

Psychologists usually begin by *formulating a research question.* Our daily experiences, psychological theory, even folklore all help generate questions for research. Consider some questions that may arise from daily experience. Daily experience in using day-care centres may motivate us to conduct research on whether day care affects the development of social skills or the bonds of attachment between children and mothers. Social-cognitive principles of observational learning may prompt research on the effects of TV violence. Research questions may also arise from common knowledge. Consider adages such as "misery loves company," "opposites attract," and "seeing is believing." Psychologists may ask, Does

Does misery love company? *Do* opposites attract? *Can* people believe what they see?

misery love company? *Do* opposites attract? *Can* people believe what they see?

A research question may be reworded as a hypothesis (see Figure 1.3). A **hypothesis** is a statement about behaviour or mental processes that is tested through research. One hypothesis about day care might be that preschoolers who are placed in day care will acquire greater social skills in relating to peers than preschoolers who are cared for in the home.

Psychologists next examine the research question or *test the hypothesis* through controlled methods such as the experiment. For example, we could take a group of preschoolers who attend day care and another group who do not, and introduce each to a new

hypothesis
in psychology, a specific statement about behaviour or mental processes that is tested through research

FIGURE 1.3

The Scientific Method

The scientific method is a systematic way of organizing and expanding scientific knowledge.

Go to www.icanpsych.com to access an interactive version of this figure.

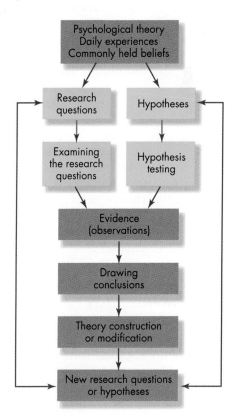

correlation
an association or relationship among variables, as we might find between height and weight or between study habits and school grades

selection factor
a source of bias that may occur in research findings when subjects are allowed to choose for themselves a certain treatment in a scientific study

sample
part of a population

population
a complete group of organisms or events

random sample
a sample drawn so that each member of a population has an equal chance of being selected to participate

stratified sample
a sample drawn so that identified subgroups in the population are represented proportionately in the sample

volunteer bias
a source of bias or error in research reflecting the prospect that people who offer to participate in research studies differ systematically from people who do not

child in a controlled setting such as a child research centre. We could then observe how children in each group interact with the new acquaintance.

Psychologists draw conclusions on the basis of their observations or findings.

When their observations do not bear out their hypotheses, they may modify the theories from which the hypotheses were derived. Research findings often suggest refinements to psychological theories and, consequently, new avenues of research. In our research on day care, we would probably find that children in day care show greater social skills than children who are cared for in the home (Belsky et al., 2001).

As psychologists draw conclusions from research evidence, they are guided by principles of critical thinking. For example, they try not to confuse **correlations**—or associations—between findings with cause and effect. Although more aggressive children apparently spend more time watching violent TV shows, it may be erroneous to conclude from this kind of evidence that TV violence *causes* aggressive behaviour. A **selection factor** may be at work because the children studied choose (select) for themselves what they will watch. Perhaps more aggressive children are more likely than less aggressive children to tune in to violent TV shows.

Problems in Generalizing from Psychological Research

Many factors must be considered in interpreting the accuracy of the results of scientific research. One is the nature of the research **sample**. Later in the chapter we consider research in which the subjects were drawn from a **population** of college men who were social drinkers. That is, they tended to drink at social gatherings but not when alone. Who do college

men represent, other than themselves? To whom can we extend, or generalize, the results? For one thing, the results may not extend to women, not even to college women. In Chapter 4, for example, we see that alcohol often affects women more quickly than men.

Also, compared to the general adult male population, college men tend to be younger and score higher on intelligence tests. We cannot be certain that the findings extend to older men or to those with lower intelligence test scores. Social drinkers may even differ biologically and psychologically from alcoholics, who have difficulty controlling their drinking.

Random and Stratified Sampling

One way to achieve a representative sample is by means of **random sampling**. In a random sample, each member of a population has an equal chance of being asked to participate. Researchers can also use a stratified sample, which is selected so that known subgroups in the population are represented proportionately in the sample. For instance, suppose that 13 percent of the Canadian population is unemployed. A **stratified sample** would thus need to include 13 percent unemployed. As a practical matter, a large randomly selected sample will show accurate stratification. For example, a random sample of 1500 people will represent the broad Canadian population reasonably well, a sample of 20 000 Irish Canadians or only men will not.

Large-scale magazine surveys of sexual behaviour have asked readers to fill out and return questionnaires. Although many thousands of readers completed the questionnaires and sent them in, did the survey respondents represent the true Canadian population? Probably not. These studies and similar ones may have been influenced by **volunteer bias**. People who offer or volunteer to participate in research studies differ systematically from people who do not. In the case of research on sexual behaviour, volunteers may represent subgroups of the population—or of readers of the magazines in question—who are willing to disclose intimate information and therefore may also be likely to be more liberal in their sexual behaviour (Rathus et al., 2008). Volunteers may also be more interested in research than other people, as well as have more spare time. How might such volunteers differ from the population at large? How might such differences slant or bias the research outcomes?

Descriptive Methods of Research

Many people consider themselves experts in psychology. How many times have you or someone else been eager to share a life experience that "proves" some point about human nature?

We see much during our lifetimes—our personal observations tend to be fleeting and unsystematic. We sift through experience for the things that interest us. We often ignore the obvious because it does not fit our assumptions about the way things ought to be. Scientists, however, have devised more controlled ways of observing others—called *descriptive methods*. **What methods of observation are used by psychologists?** In this section we consider three methods of observation widely used by psychologists and other behavioural scientists: the case study, the survey, and naturalistic observation.

Case Study

Case studies collect information about individuals and small groups. Many case studies are clinical; that is, they are detailed descriptions of a person's psychological problems and how a psychologist treated the problems. Case studies are sometimes used to investigate rare occurrences, as in the case of Chris Sizemore, who was diagnosed with multiple personalities (technically termed *dissociative identity disorder*). A psychiatrist identified three distinct personalities in Chris. Her story was made into a more theatrical movie called *The Three Faces of Eve*. One personality, "Eve White," was a mousy, well-meaning woman who had two other "personalities" inside her. One was "Eve Black," a promiscuous personality who emerged now and then to take control of her behaviour. The third personality, "Jane," was a well-adjusted woman who integrated parts of Eve White and Eve Black.

Case studies have various sources of inaccuracy. People's memories have gaps and factual inaccuracies (Loftus, 2004). People may also distort their pasts to please the interviewer or because they want to remember things in certain ways. Interviewers may also have certain expectations and subtly encourage subjects to fill in gaps in ways that are consistent with these expectations. Psychoanalysts, for example, have been criticized for guiding people who seek their help into viewing their own lives from the Freudian perspective (Hergenhahn, 2005). No wonder, then, that many people provide "evidence" that is consistent with psychodynamic theory—such as, "My parents' strictness during toilet training is the source of my compulsive neatness." However, interviewers and other kinds of researchers who hold *any* theoretical viewpoint run the risk of indirectly prodding people into saying what they want to hear.

The Survey

Just as computers and pollsters predict election results and report provincial opinions on the basis of scientifically selected samples, psychologists conduct **surveys** to learn about behaviour and mental processes that cannot be observed in the natural setting or studied experimentally. Psychologists conducting surveys may employ questionnaires and interviews or examine public records. One of the advantages of the survey is that by distributing questionnaires and analyzing answers with a computer, psychologists can study many thousands of people at a time.

Surveys, like case studies, also have sources of inaccuracy. People may recall their behaviour inaccurately or lie about it. Some people try to ingratiate themselves with their interviewers by answering in what they think to be the socially desirable direction. Others may disclose information differently based on the interviewer. For example, women may report more openly about their sexuality if a female is the interviewer rather than male. Similar problems may occur when interviewers and the people surveyed are from different ethnic backgrounds. Other people may falsify their attitudes and exaggerate their problems to draw attention to themselves or to intentionally foul up the results.

Another bias in the case study and survey methods is *social desirability*. That is, many people involved in research studies tend to tell the interviewer what they think the interviewer would like to hear and not what they really think. For example, if people brushed their teeth as often as they

case study
a carefully drawn biography that may be obtained through interviews, questionnaires, and psychological tests

survey
a method of scientific investigation in which a large sample of people answer questions about their attitudes or behaviour

Freefall Images/Alamy

claimed, and used the amount of toothpaste they indicated, three times as much toothpaste would be sold in Canada than is actually sold!

Naturalistic Observation

You use **naturalistic observation**—that is, you observe people in their natural habitats—every day. So do psychologists and other scientists. Naturalistic observation has the advantage of allowing psychologists and other scientists to observe behaviour where it happens, or "in the field." Observers use unobtrusive measures to avoid interfering with the behaviours they are observing. For example, Jane Goodall has observed the behaviour of

chimpanzees in their natural environment to learn about their social behaviour, sexual behaviour, use of tools, and other facts of chimp life. Her observations have shown us that (1) we were incorrect to think that only humans use tools; and (2) kissing on the lips, as a greeting, is apparently used by chimpanzees as well as by humans (Goodall, 2000).

The Experimental Method

What is the experimental method? Most psychologists agree that the preferred method for answering questions about cause and effect is the **experimental method**. In an experiment, a group of participants receives a *treatment,* such as a dose of alcohol, a change in room temperature, perhaps an injection of a drug. The participants are then observed carefully to determine whether the treatment makes a difference in their behaviour. Does alcohol alter the ability to take tests, for example? What about differences in room temperatures and level of background noise?

The experimental method is used when possible because it allows psychologists to control the experiences of participants and draw conclusions about cause and effect. A psychologist may theorize that alcohol leads to aggression because it reduces fear of consequences. She or he may then hypothesize that a treatment in which subjects receive a specified dosage of alcohol will lead to increases in aggression. Let us follow the example of the effects of alcohol on aggression to further our understanding of the experimental method.

Independent and Dependent Variables

In an experiment to determine whether alcohol causes aggression, participants are given an amount of alcohol and its effects are measured. In this case, alcohol is an **independent variable (IV)**. The presence of an independent variable is manipulated by the experimenters so that its effects may be determined. The independent variable of alcohol may be administered at different levels, or doses, from none or very little to enough to cause intoxication or drunkenness.

The measured result, or outcome, in an experiment is called a **dependent variable (DV)**. The presence of dependent variables presumably depends on the independent variable used. In an experiment to determine whether alcohol influences aggression, a participant's aggressive behaviour would be a dependent variable. The amount of aggression is said to be *dependent* on how much alcohol is given to the participant. Other dependent variables of interest to a researcher on the effects of alcohol might include sexual arousal, visual–motor coordination, and performance on cognitive tasks.

Jane Goodall's naturalistic observations revealed that chimpanzees—like humans—use tools and greet one another with a kiss.

Bruce Coleman Inc./Alamy

In an experiment on the relationships between temperature and aggression, temperature would be an independent variable and aggressive behaviour would be a dependent variable. We could set temperatures from below freezing to blistering hot, and study its effects on aggression. We could also use a second independent variable such as social provocation; we could insult some subjects but not others and see whether insults affect their level of aggression. This method would allow us to study the ways in which two independent variables—temperature and social provocation—affect aggression, by themselves and together.

Using an experimental group and a control group enhances a researcher's ability to draw conclusions about cause and effect.

Experimental and Control Groups

The experimental method usually involves two or more groups of participants. Participants are randomly assigned to an "experimental group" or a "control group." Participants in the **experimental group** obtain the treatment; in other words, the experimental group is given the independent variable (IV). Participants in the **control group** do not get exposed to the IV. Every effort is made to ensure that all other conditions are held constant for both groups. This method enhances the researchers' ability to draw conclusions about cause and effect. The researchers can be more confident that

© Dean Mitchell/Dreamstime.com

outcomes of the experiment are caused by the treatments and not by chance factors or chance fluctuations in behaviour.

For example, in an experiment on the effects of alcohol on aggression, the experimental group would ingest alcohol, and the control group would not. The researcher would then measure how much aggression was expressed by each group. Review Table 1.1, which illustrates the key concepts of the experimental method.

experimental groups
in experiments, groups whose members obtain the treatment

control groups
in experiments, groups whose members do not obtain the treatment, while other conditions are held constant

Blinds and Double Blinds

One classic experiment on the effects of alcohol on aggression (Boyatzis, 1974) reported that men at parties where beer and liquor were served acted more aggressively than men at parties where only nonalcoholic drinks were served. But subjects in the experimental group *knew* they had drunk alcohol, and those in the control group *knew* they had not. Aggression that appeared to result from alcohol might thus have reflected the subjects' *expectation* about the effects of alcohol. People tend to act in stereotypical ways

Blind and double-blind experiments minimize both researchers' and participants' expectation biases.

Experimental Method: Key Concepts

Key Term	Description	Example: Effects of Alcohol on Aggression
Independent Variable (IV)	Variable that is controlled or manipulated by the experimenter. It can be modified or changed in order to study its effects on behaviour	Giving alcohol to participants
Dependent Variable (DV)	Variable that is measured. It is the resulting behaviour/outcome of the effects of the IV	Amount of aggressive behaviour after drinking alcohol
Experimental Group	The group of participants that are exposed to the IV	Group of participants that drink alcohol during the experiment
Control Group	The group of participants that are not exposed to the IV. Used to compare the results of the IV on the behaviour of participants	Group of participants that do not drink alcohol during the experiment—perhaps they are just given water

placebo
a bogus treatment that has the appearance of being genuine

blind
in experimental terminology, unaware of whether or not one has received a treatment

double-blind study
a study in which neither the subjects nor the observers know who has received the treatment

when they believe they have been drinking alcohol. For instance, men tend to become less anxious in social situations, more aggressive, and more sexually aroused. To what extent do these behaviour patterns reflect the direct effects of alcohol on the body, and to what extent do they affect people's *beliefs* about the effects of alcohol?

In medicine, physicians sometimes give patients **placebos** (a fake treatment, often sugar pills, that has the appearance of being genuine) when the patient insists on a medical cure but the physician does not believe that one is necessary. When patients report that placebos have helped them, it is because they expected the pills to be of help and not because of the biochemical effects of the pills. Placebos are not limited to pills made of sugar. As we will see, subjects in psychological experiments can be given placebos such as tonic water, but if the subjects think they have drunk alcohol, we can conclude that changes in their behaviour stem from their beliefs about the effects of alcohol, not from the alcohol itself—this is called the *placebo effect*.

Well-designed experiments control for the effects of expectations by creating conditions under which subjects are unaware of, or **blind** to, the treatment. Placebos are one way of keeping subjects blind to whether they have received a treatment. Yet researchers may also have expectations. They may be "rooting for" a certain treatment. This

is known as *experimenter bias*. For example, tobacco company executives may wish to show that cigarette smoking is harmless. In such cases, it is useful if the people measuring the experimental outcomes are unaware of which subjects have received the treatment.

Studies in which neither the subjects nor the experimenters know who has obtained the treatment are called **double-blind** studies. A double-blind study to market safe, new drugs would be certain that the drug and the placebo administered to participants and the observers look and taste alike. In a double-blind experiment, experimenters assign the drug or placebo to participants at random. Neither the participants nor the observers know who is taking the drug and who is taking the placebo. After the final measurements have been made, a neutral panel (a group of people who have no personal stake in the outcome of the study) judges whether the effects of the drug differed from those of the placebo.

In one classic double-blind study on the effects of alcohol, Alan Lang and his colleagues (1975 pretested a cocktail of vodka and tonic water to make certain that it could not be discriminated by taste from tonic water alone. They recruited college male social drinkers as subjects. Some of the men drank vodka and tonic water. Others drank tonic water only. Of those who drank vodka, half were misled into believing they had drunk tonic water only (see Figure 1.4). Of those who drank tonic water only, half were misled into believing their drink contained vodka. Thus, half the subjects were blind to their treatment. Experimenters who measured the men's aggressive responses were also blind concerning which subjects had drunk vodka.

The research team found that men who believed that they had drunk vodka responded "more aggressively" (that is, they chose a higher level of shock and

---

FIGURE 1.4

The Experimental Conditions in the Lang Study

The taste of vodka cannot be discerned when vodka is mixed with tonic water. For this reason, it was possible for subjects in the Lang study on the effects of alcohol to be kept "blind" as to whether or not they had actually drunk alcohol. Blind studies allow psychologists to control for the effects of subjects' expectations.

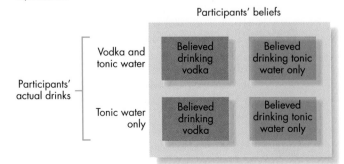

pressed a lever to deliver it) to a provocation than men who believed that they had drunk tonic water only. The actual content of the drink was immaterial. That is, the men's *belief* about what they drank affected their aggressive behaviour more than what they actually consumed. The results of the Lang study differ dramatically from those reported by Boyatzis, perhaps because the Boyatzis study did not control for the effects of expectations or beliefs about alcohol.

> The **men's** *belief* about what they drank affected their aggressive behaviour more than what they actually consumed.

Correlational Research

Are people with higher intelligence more likely to do well in school? Are people with a stronger need for achievement likely to climb higher up the corporate ladder? What is the relationship between stress and health?

Not all questions can be answered by experimental methods. Often factors cannot be manipulated (such as IQ) or are harmful to administer (such as stress). In such cases, researchers rely on the correlational method. *What is the correlational method?* By using the correlational method, psychologists investigate whether an observed behaviour or a measured trait is related to, or correlated with, another. Consider the variables of intelligence and academic performance. To determine whether a relationship exists between them, these variables are assigned numbers such as intelligence test scores and academic averages. Then the numbers are mathematically related and expressed as a correlation coefficient. A **correlation coefficient** is a number that varies between +1.00 and −1.00.

Studies report *positive correlations* between intelligence test scores and academic achievement, as measured, for example, by grade point averages. Generally speaking, the higher people score on intelligence tests, the better their academic performance is likely to be. The scores attained on intelligence tests tend to be *positively correlated* (about +0.60 to +0.70) with academic achievement (see the first panel in Figure 1.5). But factors *other* than performance on intelligence tests may also contribute to academic success—such as achievement motivation and adjustment.

The second panel in Figure 1.5 shows a *negative correlation*; that is, as one variable increases, the other variable decreases. There is a *negative correlation* between stress and health. As the amount of stress affecting us increases, the functioning of our immune system decreases. Under high levels of stress, many people show poorer health.

Correlational research may suggest that two variables are related, but it does not prove cause and

> **correlation coefficient**
> a number between +1.00 and −1.00 that expresses the strength and direction (positive or negative) of the relationship between two variables

FIGURE 1.5

Positive and Negative Correlations

When there is a positive correlation between variables, as there is between intelligence and achievement, one increases as the other increases. By and large, the higher people score on intelligence tests, the better their academic performance is likely to be, as in the diagram on the left. (Each dot represents an individual's intelligence test score and grade point average.) But there is a negative correlation between stress and health. As the amount of stress we experience increases, the functioning of our immune system tends to decrease.

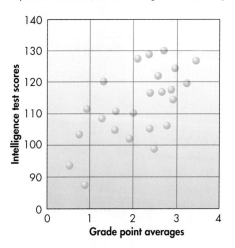

Positive correlation, as found between intelligence and academic achievement

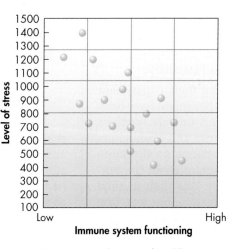

Negative correlation, as found between stress and functioning of the immune system

effect. Correlations are also useful in making predictions. For example, it may seem logical to assume that high intelligence makes it possible for children to profit from education.

Research has also shown, however, that education contributes to higher scores on intelligence tests. Preschoolers who are placed in stimulating Montessouri programs later attain higher scores on intelligence tests than same-age preschoolers who did not have this experience. The relationship between intelligence and academic performance may not be as simple as we might think. What of the link between stress and health? Does stress impair health, or is it possible that people in poorer health encounter more stress?

> Correlational research may suggest that two variables are related, but does not prove cause and effect.

Try It!

Correlational Relationships

What kinds of correlations (positive or negative) would you expect to find among behaviour patterns for each of the following?

1. Churchgoing and crime?
2. Language ability and musical ability?
3. Level of education and incidence of teenage pregnancy?
4. Grades in school and delinquency?

Why? Be careful to use your critical thinking skills.

Ethics of Research with Humans

If the Lang group were running their experiment today rather than in the 1970s, they might have been denied permission to do so by a university ethics review committee. Why? Because the researchers in the Lang study gave some participants alcohol to drink and deceived the entire group about the purposes and methods of the study. Was their method ethical? We'll return to this question, but let's first address a broader one. *What ethical issues affect research and practice with humans?*

Psychologists in Canada must adhere to a number of ethical standards that are intended to promote indi-

vidual dignity, human welfare, and scientific integrity. The standards are also intended to ensure that psychologists do not engage in harmful research methods or treatments. Because in virtually all institutional settings, including universities and colleges, hospitals, and research foundations, ethics review committees help researchers consider the potential harm of their methods and review proposed studies according to ethical guidelines. When the committees find that proposed research might be unacceptably harmful to subjects, they may withhold approval. The committees also weigh the potential benefits of the research against the potential harm.

The National Council on Ethics in Human Research is the governing body in Canada that provides a set of ethical guidelines regarding the participation of human participants in research—the Tri-Council Policy Statement: *Ethical Conduct for Research Involving Humans.*

The Canadian Code of Ethics for Psychologists (2000) includes the following four principles:

1 *Respect for the dignity of persons.* This includes basic human rights, fair treatment, informed consent, privacy, and confidentiality of participants.

2 *Responsible caring.* This includes competence and self-knowledge, maximizing benefits, and minimizing risks/harm analysis for participants.

3 *Integrity in relationships.* This includes honesty, objectivity, and avoidance of conflict of interest. (See the box entitled "Deception.")

4 *Responsibility to society.* This includes respect and development of society through psychological research.

Return to the Lang (Lang et al., 1975) study on alcohol and aggression. In this study, the researchers (1) misinformed subjects about the beverage they were drinking and (2) misled them into believing they were giving other subjects electric shock when they were actually pressing switches on an unconnected control board. (*Aggression* was defined as pressing these switches.) In the study, students who believed they had drunk vodka selected higher levels of shock than students who believed they had not.

Ethics of Research with Animals

Psychologists and other scientists may use animals to conduct research that cannot be carried out with humans. For example, experiments on the effects of early separation from the mother have been done with monkeys and other animals. Such research has helped psychologists investigate the formation of attachment bonds between parent and child (See Chapter 8).

What ethical issues affect research with animals? Experiments with infant monkeys highlight some of the ethical issues faced

BonkersAboutScience/Alamy

by psychologists and other scientists who contemplate potentially harmful research. Psychologists and biologists who study the workings of the brain destroy sections of the brains of laboratory animals to learn how they influence behaviour. For example, a lesion in one part of a brain structure causes a rat to overeat. A lesion elsewhere causes the rat to go on a crash diet. Psychologists generalize to humans from experiments such as these in the hope of finding solutions to problems such as eating disorders. Proponents of the use of animals in research argue that many advances in medicine and psychology could not have taken place without them (Bekoff, 2002). For example, we would know less about how drugs affect tumours or the brain.

Researchers in Canada must abide by the ethical guidelines set out in the CCEP and the guidelines of the Canadian Council on Animal Care (CCAC), which promotes good animal care in science. According to the CCAC (2008), animals may be harmed only when there is no alternative and when researchers believe that the benefits of the research justify the harm.

Now that we have an overview of psychology as a science, we will move on to the connections between psychology and biology in Chapter 2. Psychologists assume that our behaviours and our mental processes are related to biological events. In Chapter 2 we consider the evidence for this assumption.

debriefing
providing participants with an explanation of their role in an experiment and explaining the purposes and methods of the research following completion of the study

Biology
and
Psychology

Learning Outcomes

LO 1 Describe the nervous system, including neurons, neural impulses, and neurotransmitters

LO 2 List the structures of the brain and their functions

LO 3 Explain the role of the endocrine system and list the endocrine glands

LO 4 Describe evolutionary psychology and the connections between heredity, behaviour, and mental processes

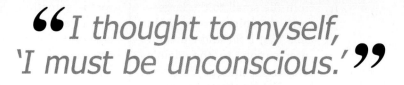

❝I thought to myself, 'I must be unconscious.'❞

S.V.: I remember hearing a loud "thunk," much like the sound of a watermelon hitting the floor, and then suddenly everything was purple and spinning. I thought to myself, "I must be unconscious," which was quickly followed by the thought, "Can I be unconscious if I'm still thinking?"

There I lay, halfway down the slope of a ski hill in Ellicottville, New York, with a massive head injury, struggling to regain consciousness. I was 14 years old and my first across-the-border ski trip had come to a sudden stop when I fell headfirst into a fluffy snow bank. Unfortunately, under the powdery snow was a very hard and jagged tree stump that shattered the top of my head and drove parts of my skull into my brain. I had inadvertently joined the exclusive group of people who have suffered from brain injury, and it immediately affected my behaviours and mental processes.

With a diameter of roughly six centimetres and a depth of three centimetres, the injury was localized on the right side of the top part of my head. If I had hit the front, back, or side of my head near my ears, the resulting effects on my memories, abilities and even personality would have been markedly different. Generations of researchers—psychologists, physicians, biologists, neuroscientists—have investigated how damage in the brain relates to immediate and very real behavioural, sensory, and even personality changes in victims. Much of what we have learned about the human brain comes from investigating those who have suffered from damage to particular areas of the brain.

In this chapter, we will learn about the distinct structures of the brain, their respective functions, and much more. We will travel

DID YOU KNOW?

- Your brain weighs approximately 1.45 kg and makes up 2 percent of your body weight.
- A single cell can stretch all the way from your spine to your toe.
- Messages travel in the brain by means of electricity.
- A brain cell can send out hundreds of messages each second—and manage to catch some rest in between.
- Fear can give you indigestion.
- If a surgeon were to stimulate a certain part of your brain electrically, you might swear that someone had stroked your leg.
- Charles Darwin was nearly excluded from the voyage that led to the development of his theory of evolution because the captain of the ship did not like the shape of his nose.

Bernard Weil/GetStock.com

neuron
a nerve cell

glial cells
cells that nourish and insulate neurons, direct their growth, and remove waste products from the nervous system

dendrites
root-like structures, attached to the cell body of a neuron, that receive impulses from other neurons

axon
a long, thin part of a neuron that transmits impulses to other neurons from branching structures called *terminal buttons*

from the small to the large—from the microscopic brain cells that hold and transmit information, to the visible structures that provide the basis for functions such as memory, speech, sensation, thought, planning, and voluntary movement. As you read and learn about the brain, keep in mind the injury that I suffered as a young teenager, and try to predict what effect, both short- and long-term, the injury might have had on my behaviour and mental processes.

LO1 The Nervous System: On Being Wired

The nervous system is a system of nerves involved in thought processes, heartbeat, visual–motor coordination, and so on. The nervous system contains the brain, the spinal cord, and other parts that make it possible for us to receive information from the world outside and to act on that world.

Some people believe that the human nervous system is more complex than that of any other animal and that our brains are larger than those of any other animal. Now, this last piece of business is not quite true. A human brain weighs about 1.45 kilograms (3 pounds), but the brains of elephants and whales may be four times as heavy. Still, our brains account for a greater part of our body weight than do those of elephants or whales. Our brains weigh about 1/60 of our body weight. Elephant brains weigh about 1/1000 of their total weight, and whale brains are a paltry 1/10 000 of their weight. However, before we get too impressed with our brain-to-weight ratio, we should remember that the shrew, a small mouse-like mammal, has a brain that accounts for nearly 1/10 of its body weight.

The nervous system is composed of cells, most of which are neurons, which is where we will begin our study of the nervous system.

Neurons: Into the Fabulous Forest

Within our brains lies a fabulous forest of nerve cells, or neurons. *What are neurons?* **Neurons** are cells that can be visualized as having branches, trunks, and

roots—something like trees. As we voyage through this forest, we see that many nerve cells lie alongside one another like a thicket of trees. But neurons can also lie end to end, with their "roots" intertwined with the "branches" of the neurons that lie below. Trees receive sunlight, water, and nutrients from the soil. Neurons receive "messages" from a number of sources such as light, other neurons, and pressure on the skin, and they can pass these messages along in a complex biological dance.

We are born with more than 100 billion neurons. Most of them are found in the brain. The nervous system also contains **glial cells**. Glial cells remove dead neurons and waste products from the nervous system, nourish and insulate neurons, and direct their growth. But neurons occupy centre stage in the nervous system. The messages transmitted by neurons somehow account for phenomena ranging from the perception of an itch from a mosquito bite to the coordination of a skier's vision and muscles to the composition of a concerto to the solution of an algebraic equation.

Neurons vary according to their functions and their location. Neurons in the brain may be only a fraction of a centimetre, whereas others in the legs are metres long. Most neurons include a cell body, dendrites, and an axon (see Figure 2.1). The cell body contains the core or *nucleus* of the cell. The nucleus uses oxygen and nutrients to generate the energy needed to carry out the work of the cell. Anywhere from a few to several hundred short fibres, or **dendrites**, extend like roots from the cell body to receive incoming messages from thousands of adjoining neurons. Each neuron has an axon that extends like a trunk from the cell body. Axons are very thin, but those that carry messages from the toes to the spinal cord are almost a meter long.

Like tree trunks, axons can branch off in different directions. **Axons** end in small bulb-shaped structures called *terminals* or *terminal buttons*. Neurons carry messages in one direction only: from the dendrites or cell body through the axon to the axon terminals. The messages are then transmitted from the terminal buttons to other neurons, muscles, or glands.

As a child matures, the axons of neurons become longer, and the dendrites and terminals proliferate, creating vast interconnected networks for the transmission of complex messages. The number of glial cells also increases as the nervous system develops, contributing to its dense appearance.

Gary Paul Lewis/Shutterstock.com

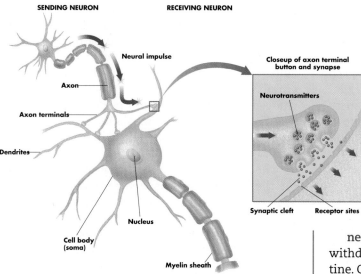

Figure labels:
SENDING NEURON   RECEIVING NEURON
Neural impulse
Axon
Axon terminals
Dendrites
Nucleus
Cell body (soma)
Myelin sheath
Closeup of axon terminal button and synapse
Neurotransmitters
Synaptic cleft   Receptor sites

FIGURE 2.1

The Anatomy of a Neuron

"Messages" enter neurons through dendrites, are transmitted along the trunk-like axon, and then are sent from axon terminal buttons to muscles, glands, and other neurons. Axon terminal buttons contain sacs of chemicals called *neurotransmitters*. Neurotransmitters are released into the synaptic cleft, where many of them bind to receptor sites on the dendrites of the receiving neuron.

Go to www.icanpsych.com to access an interactive version of this figure.

Myelin

The axons of many neurons are wrapped tightly with white, fatty myelin that makes them look like strings of sausages under the microscope. The fat insulates the axon from electrically charged atoms, or ions, found in the fluids that surround the nervous system. The **myelin** sheath minimizes leakage of the electrochemical current being carried along the axon, thereby allowing messages to be conducted more efficiently.

Myelination is part of the maturation process that leads to the child's ability to crawl and walk during the first year. Infants are not physiologically "ready" to engage in visual–motor coordination and other activities until the coating process reaches certain levels. In people with the disease multiple sclerosis, myelin is replaced with a hard fibrous tissue that throws off the timing of nerve impulses and disrupts muscular control.

Sensory and Motor Neurons

If someone steps on your toes, the sensation is registered by receptor neurons near the surface of your skin. Then it is transmitted to the spinal cord and brain through **sensory neurons**, which are up to a metre long. In the brain, subsequent messages might be conveyed by associative neurons (called **interneurons**) that are only a few hundredths of a centimetre long. You experience the pain through this process and perhaps entertain some rather nasty thoughts about the perpetrator, who is now apologizing and begging

for understanding. Long before you arrive at any logical conclusions, however, **motor neurons** send messages to your foot so that you withdraw it and begin an impressive hopping routine. Other efferent neurons stimulate glands so that your heart is beating more rapidly, you are sweating, and the hair on the back of your arms has become erect! Being a good sport, you say, "Oh, it's nothing." But considering all the neurons involved, it really is something, isn't it?

The Neural Impulse: "The Body Electric"[1]

In the 18th century, the Italian physiologist Luigi Galvani (1737–1798) conducted a shocking experiment in a rainstorm. While his neighbours had the sense to remain indoors, Galvani and his wife were out on the porch connecting lightning rods to the heads of dissected frogs whose legs were connected by wires to a well of water. When lightning blazed above, the frogs' muscles contracted. Galvani was demonstrating that the messages (neural impulses) that travel along neurons are electrochemical in nature.

What are neural impulses? Neural impulses are messages that travel within neurons at somewhere between 3 kilometres an hour (in nonmyelinated neurons) and 360 kilometres an hour (in myelinated neurons).

---
[1]From Walt Whitman's *Leaves of Grass*.

myelin
a fatty substance that encases and insulates axons, facilitating transmission of neural impulses

sensory neurons
neurons that transmit messages from sensory receptors to the spinal cord and brain (also called *afferent neurons*)

interneurons
neurons that connect sensory and motor neurons

motor neurons
neurons that transmit messages from the brain or spinal cord to muscles and glands (also called *efferent neurons*)

neural impulse
the electrochemical discharge of a nerve cell, or neuron

polarize
to ready a neuron for firing by creating an internal negative charge in relation to the body fluid outside the cell membrane

resting potential
the electrical potential across the neural membrane when it is not responding to other neurons

depolarize
to reduce the resting potential of a cell membrane from about 70 millivolts toward zero

action potential
the electrical impulse that provides the basis for the conduction of a neural impulse along an axon of a neuron

This speed is not impressive when compared with that of an electrical current in a toaster oven or a lamp, which can travel at close to the speed of light—nearly 300 000 kilometres per second. Distances in the body are short, however, and a message will travel from a toe to the brain in perhaps 1/50 of a second.

An Electrochemical Voyage

The process by which neural impulses travel is electrochemical. Chemical changes take place within neurons that cause an electrical charge to be transmitted along their lengths. Neurons and body fluids contain ions—positively or negatively charged atoms. In a resting state—that is, when a neuron is not being stimulated by its neighbours—negatively charged chloride (Cl–) ions are plentiful within the neuron, contributing to an overall negative charge in relation to the outside. The difference in electrical charge readies (**polarizes**) a neuron for firing by creating an internal negative charge in relation to the body fluid outside the cell membrane. The electrical potential across the neural membrane when it is not responding to other neurons—its **resting potential**—is about –70 millivolts

in relation to the body fluid outside the cell membrane.

When an area on the surface of the resting neuron is adequately stimulated by other neurons, the cell membrane in the area changes its permeability to allow positively charged sodium ions to enter. Thus the area of entry becomes positively charged, or **depolarized**, with respect to the outside (see Figure 2.2A). The permeability of the cell membrane then changes again, allowing no more sodium ions to enter (see Figure 2.2B).

The electrical impulse that provides the basis for the conduction of a neural impulse along an axon of a neuron is termed its **action potential**. The inside of the cell axon at the disturbed area has an action potential of 110 millivolts. This action potential, added to the –70 millivolts that characterize the resting potential, brings the membrane voltage to a positive charge of about +30 to +40 millivolts (see Figure 2.3). This inner change causes the next section of the cell to become permeable to sodium ions. At the same time, other positively charged (potassium) ions are being pumped out of the area of the cell that was previously affected, which returns the area to its resting potential. In this way, the neural impulse is transmitted continuously along an axon. Because the impulse is created anew as it progresses, its strength does not change.

Firing: How Messages Voyage from Neuron to Neuron

The conduction of the neural impulse along the length of a neuron is what is meant by *firing*. When a rifle fires, it sends a bullet speeding through its barrel and discharges it at more than 300 metres per second. *What happens when a neuron fires?* Neurons also fire, but instead of a barrel, a neuron has an axon. Instead of discharging a bullet, it releases neurotransmitters.

Some neurons fire in less than 1/1000 of a second. When they fire, neurons transmit messages to other neurons, muscles, or glands. However, neurons will not fire unless the incoming messages combine to reach a certain strength, which is defined as the *threshold* at which a neuron will fire. A weak message may cause a temporary shift in electrical charge at some point along the

FIGURE 2.2

The Neural Impulse

When a section of a neuron is stimulated by other neurons, the cell membrane becomes permeable to sodium ions so that an action potential of about 40 millivolts is induced. This action potential is transmitted along the axon.

A. During an action potential, sodium gates in the neuron membrane open and sodium ions enter the axon, bringing a positive charge with them.

B. After an action potential occurs, the sodium gates close at that point, and open at the next point along the axon. When the sodium gates close, potassium gates open and potassium ions flow out of the axon, carrying a positive charge with them.

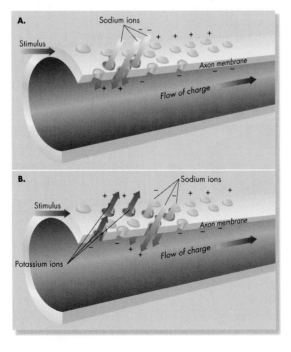

A.
Sodium ions
Stimulus
Axon membrane
Flow of charge

B.
Sodium ions
Stimulus
Axon membrane
Flow of charge
Potassium ions

FIGURE 2.3

Changes in Electrical Charges as a Neural Impulse Is Transmitted Across an Axon

The resting potential of a segment of a cell axon is about −70 millivolts. But the inside of the cell axon at the disturbed area has an action potential of about 110 millivolts. When we add this figure to the −70 millivolts that characterize the resting potential, we bring the membrane voltage to a positive charge of about +30 to +40 millivolts. This inner change causes the next section of the cell to become permeable to sodium ions. In this way, the neural impulse is transmitted continuously along an axon.

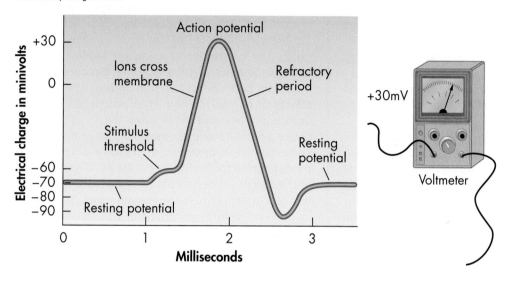

all-or-none principle
the fact that a neuron fires an impulse of the same strength whenever its action potential is triggered

refractory period
a phase following firing during which a neuron is less sensitive to messages from other neurons and will not fire

synapse
a junction between the axon terminals of one neuron and the dendrites or cell body of another neuron

neurotransmitters
chemical substances involved in the transmission of neural impulses from one neuron to another

cell membrane, but this charge will dissipate if the neuron is not stimulated to its threshold.

Not only can a neuron fire in less than 1/1000 of a second, but a neuron may also transmit several hundred messages each second. Every time a neuron fires, it transmits an impulse of the same strength. This occurrence is known as the **all-or-none principle**. That is, either a neuron fires or it doesn't. Neurons fire more often when they have been stimulated by a large number of other neurons (remember, a neuron's dendrites are often linked to thousands of other neurons). Stronger stimuli cause more frequent firing, but again, the strength of each firing remains the same.

For a few thousandths of a second after firing, a neuron is in a **refractory period**; that is, it is insensitive to messages from other neurons and will not fire. This period is a time of recovery during which sodium is prevented from passing through the neuronal membrane. Because such periods of "recovery" might occur hundreds of times per second, it seems a rapid recovery and a short rest indeed.

The Synapse: On Being Well-Connected

A neuron relays its message to another neuron across a junction called a **synapse**. *What is a synapse?* A synapse consists of an axon terminal button from the transmitting neuron, a dendrite or the body of a receiving neuron, and a fluid-filled gap between the two that is called the *synaptic cleft* (see Figure 2.1 on page 25). Although the neural impulse is electrical, it does not jump across the synaptic cleft like a spark. Instead, when a nerve impulse reaches the axon terminal, the electrochemical pulse forces stored chemicals through the cell membrane into the synaptic cleft like myriad ships being cast into the sea. Scientists have identified a few dozen of these often-released chemicals to date. In the following section, we consider a few of them that are usually of the greatest interest to psychologists.

Neurotransmitters: The Chemical Keys to Communication

Sacs called *synaptic vesicles* in the axon terminals contain neurotransmitters (see Figure 2.4 on the next page). When a neural impulse (action potential) reaches the axon terminal, the vesicles are forced toward the cell membrane and release varying amounts of **neurotransmitters**—the chemical keys to communication—into the synaptic cleft. From there, they influence the receiving neuron. *Which neurotransmitters are of interest to psychologists? What do they do?*

Dozens of neurotransmitters have been identified. Each has its own chemical structure,

receptor site
a location on a dendrite of a receiving neuron tailored to receive a neurotransmitter

reuptake
reabsorption of the released neurotransmitter by the releasing neuron

acetylcholine (ACh)
a neurotransmitter that controls muscle contractions

hippocampus
a part of the limbic system of the brain that is involved in memory formation

dopamine
a neurotransmitter that is involved in Parkinson's disease and that appears to play a role in schizophrenia

and each can fit into a specifically tailored harbour, or **receptor site**, on the receiving cell. The analogy of a key fitting into a lock is often used to describe this process. Once released, not all molecules of a neurotransmitter find their way into receptor sites of other neurons. "Loose" neurotransmitters are usually either broken down or reabsorbed by the axon terminal they came from (a process called **reuptake**).

Some neurotransmitters act to *excite* other neurons—that is, to cause other neurons to fire. Other neurotransmitters act to *inhibit* receiving neurons. That is, they prevent the neurons from firing. The sum of the stimulation—excitatory and inhibitory—determines whether a neuron will fire and, if so, when neurotransmitters will be released.

FIGURE 2.4

Neurotransmitters and the Synaptic Gap

Neurotransmitters are released from the synaptic vesicles into the synaptic gap. The neurotransmitters bind to receptor sites on the neighbouring neuron's dendrites that can either increase or decrease the activity of the receiving neuron. Remaining neurotransmitters that do not bind to receptor sites are either broken down in the synaptic gap, or reabsorbed into releasing neuron in a process called *reuptake*.

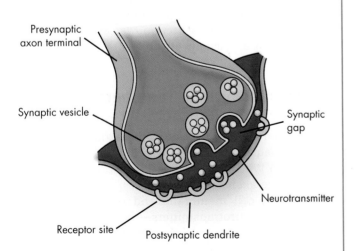

Presynaptic axon terminal

Synaptic vesicle

Synaptic gap

Neurotransmitter

Receptor site

Postsynaptic dendrite

Neurotransmitters are involved in physical processes such as muscle contraction and psychological processes such as thoughts and emotions. Excesses or deficiencies of neurotransmitters have been linked to psychological disorders such as depression and schizophrenia. Let us consider the effects of some neurotransmitters of interest to psychologists: acetylcholine (ACh), dopamine, norepinephrine, serotonin, GABA, and endorphins.

Acetylcholine (ACh) controls muscle contractions. It is excitatory at synapses between nerves and muscles that involve voluntary movement but inhibitory at the heart and some other locations. The effects of curare highlight the functioning of ACh. Curare is a poison that is extracted from plants by native South Americans and used in hunting. If an arrow tipped with curare pierces the skin and the poison enters the body, it prevents ACh from binding to the receptor sites on neurons. Because ACh helps muscles move, curare causes paralysis. The victim is prevented from contracting the muscles used in breathing and therefore dies from suffocation. Botulism, a disease that stems from food poisoning, prevents the release of ACh and has the same effect as curare.

ACh is also normally prevalent in a part of the brain called the **hippocampus**, a structure involved in the formation of memories (Louie & Wilson, 2001). When the amount of ACh available to the brain decreases, as in Alzheimer's disease, memory formation is impaired (Chu et al., 2005). In one experiment, researchers (Egawa et al., 2002) decreased the ACh available to the hippocampus of laboratory rats. As a result, the rats could not learn to navigate a maze, apparently because they could not remember which way to turn at the choice points.

Dopamine acts in the brain and affects ability to perceive pleasure, voluntary movement, and learning and memory (Davis et al., 2004; Heinz, 2004). Deficiencies of dopamine are linked to Parkinson's disease, in which people progressively lose control over their muscles (Olanow, 2000; Swerdlow et al., 2003). They develop muscle tremors and jerky, uncoordinated movements.

The psychological disorder *schizophrenia* is characterized by confusion and false perceptions, and it has been linked to dopamine. People with schizophrenia may have more receptor sites for dopamine in an area of the brain that is involved in emotional responding. For this reason, they may "overutilize" the dopamine available in the brain (Butcher, 2000; Kapur, 2003). Overutilization is connected with hallucinations and disturbances of thought and emotion. The phenothiazines, a group of drugs used in the treatment of schizophrenia, inhibit the action of dopamine by blocking some dopamine receptors (Lidow et al., 2001). Because of their action, phenothiazines may have Parkinson's-like side effects, which are usually treated by lowering the dose, prescribing additional drugs, or switching to another drug.

Norepinephrine is produced largely by neurons in the brain stem, and acts both as a neurotransmitter and as a hormone. It is an excitatory neurotransmitter that speeds up the heartbeat and other body processes and is involved in general arousal, learning and memory, and eating. Excesses and deficiencies of norepinephrine have been linked to mood disorders. Deficiencies of both ACh and norepinephrine particularly impair memory formation (Egawa et al., 2002).

The stimulants cocaine and amphetamines ("speed") boost norepinephrine (as well as dopamine) production, increasing the firing of neurons and leading to persistent arousal. Amphetamines both facilitate the release of these neurotransmitters and prevent their reuptake. Cocaine also blocks reuptake.

Serotonin is involved in emotional arousal and sleep. Deficiencies of serotonin have been linked to eating disorders, alcoholism, depression, aggression, and insomnia. The drug LSD decreases the action of serotonin and may also influence the utilization of dopamine. With LSD, "two no's make a yes."

norepinephrine
a neurotransmitter whose action is similar to that of the hormone epinephrine and that may play a role in depression

serotonin
a neurotransmitter, deficiencies of which have been linked to affective disorders, anxiety, and insomnia

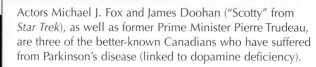

Actors Michael J. Fox and James Doohan ("Scotty" from *Star Trek*), as well as former Prime Minister Pierre Trudeau, are three of the better-known Canadians who have suffered from Parkinson's disease (linked to dopamine deficiency).

gamma-aminobutyric acid (GABA)
an inhibitory neurotransmitter that apparently helps calm anxiety

endorphins
neurotransmitters that are composed of amino acids and that are functionally similar to morphine

nerve
a bundle of axons from many neurons

central nervous system
the brain and spinal cord

peripheral nervous system
the part of the nervous system consisting of the somatic nervous system and the autonomic nervous system

By inhibiting an inhibitor, it increases brain activity, in this case often producing hallucinations.

Gamma-aminobutyric acid (GABA) is another neurotransmitter of great interest to psychologists. One reason is that GABA is an inhibitory neurotransmitter that may help calm anxiety reactions (Stroele et al., 2002). Tranquilizers and alcohol may lower anxiety by binding with GABA receptors and amplifying the effects. One class of antianxiety drug may also increase the sensitivity of receptor sites to GABA. Other studies link deficiencies of GABA to depression (Clénet et al., 2005).

Endorphins are inhibitory neurotransmitters. The word *endorphin* is the contraction of *endogenous morphine*. *Endogenous* means "developing from within." Endorphins occur naturally in the brain and in the bloodstream and are similar to the narcotic morphine in their functions and effects. They lock into receptor sites for chemicals that transmit pain messages to the brain. Once the endorphin "key" is in the "lock," the pain-causing chemicals are locked out. Endorphins may also increase our sense of competence, enhance the functioning of the immune system, and be connected with the pleasurable "runner's high" reported by many long-distance runners (Jonsdottir et al., 2000; Oktedalen et al., 2001).

There you have it—a fabulous forest of neurons in which billions upon billions of axon terminals are pouring armadas of neurotransmitters into synaptic clefts at any given time. The combined activity of all these neurotransmitters determines which messages will be transmitted and which

ones will not. You experience your sensations, your thoughts, and your control over your body as psychological events, but the psychological events come from billions upon billions of electrochemical events. Table 2.1 provides an overview of these neurotransmitters and their functions.

We can think of neurons as the microscopic building blocks of the nervous system. Millions upon millions of these neurons gather together to form larger, visible structures that we think of as the parts of the nervous system. We discuss those parts next.

The Parts of the Nervous System

What are the parts of the nervous system? The nervous system consists of the brain, the spinal cord, and the **nerves** linking them to the sensory organs, muscles, and glands. As shown in Figure 2.5, the brain and spinal cord make up the **central nervous system**. If you compare your nervous system to a computer, your central nervous system would be your central processing unit (CPU).

The sensory neurons, which receive and transmit messages to the brain and spinal cord, and the motor neurons, which transmit messages from the brain or spinal cord to the muscles and glands, make up the peripheral nervous system. In the comparison of the nervous system to a computer, the **peripheral nervous system** makes up the nervous system's peripheral devices—keyboard, mouse, DVD drive, and so on. You would not be able to feed information

TABLE 2.1

Common Neurotransmitters and Some of Their Functions

Neurotransmitter	Functions and Characteristics
Acetylcholine (ACh)	Activates motor neurons controlling skeletal muscles
	Contributes to the regulation of attention, arousal, and memory
	Some ACh receptors stimulated by nicotine
Dopamine (DA)	Contributes to control of voluntary movement, pleasurable emotions
	Decreased levels associated with Parkinson's disease
	Overactivity at DA synapses associated with schizophrenia
	Cocaine and amphetamines elevate activity at DA synapses
Norepinephrine (NE)	Contributes to modulation of mood and arousal
	Cocaine and amphetamines elevate activity at NE synapses
Serotonin	Involved in regulation of sleep and wakefulness, eating, and aggression
	Abnormal levels may contribute to depression and obsessive-compulsive disorder
	Prozac and similar antidepressant drugs affect serotonin circuits
GABA	Serves as widely distributed inhibitory transmitter
	Valium and similar antianxiety drugs work at GABA synapses
Endorphins	Resemble opiate drugs in structure and effects
	Contribute to pain relief and perhaps to some pleasurable emotions

FIGURE 2.5

The Divisions of the Nervous System

The nervous system contains two main divisions: the central nervous system and the peripheral nervous system. The central nervous system consists of the brain and spinal cord. The peripheral nervous system contains the somatic and autonomic systems. In turn, the autonomic nervous system has sympathetic and parasympathetic divisions.

Go to www.icanpsych.com to access an interactive version of this figure.

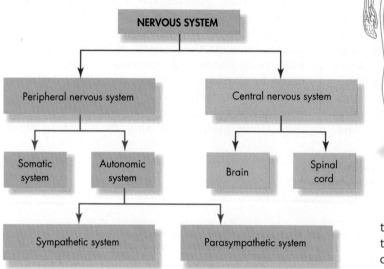

somatic nervous system
the division of the peripheral nervous system that connects the central nervous system with sensory receptors, skeletal muscles, and the surface of the body

autonomic nervous system (ANS)
the division of the peripheral nervous system that regulates glands and activities such as heartbeat, respiration, digestion, and dilation of the pupils

sympathetic
the branch of the ANS that is most active during emotional responses, such as fear and anxiety, that spend the body's reserves of energy

parasympathetic
the branch of the ANS that is most active during processes (such as digestion) that restore the body's reserves of energy

to your computer's central processing unit without these *peripheral* devices. Other peripheral devices, such as your monitor and printer, allow you to follow what is happening inside your CPU and see what it has done.

The Peripheral Nervous System: The Body's Peripheral Devices

What are the divisions and functions of the peripheral nervous system? The peripheral nervous system consists of sensory and motor neurons that transmit messages to and from the central nervous system. Without the peripheral nervous system, our brains would be like isolated CPUs. There would be no keyboards, mouses, CDs, or other ways of inputting information. There would be no monitors, printers, modems, or other ways of displaying or transmitting information. We would be detached from the world: We would not be able to perceive it; we would not be able to act on it. The two main divisions of the peripheral nervous system are the *somatic nervous system* and the *autonomic nervous system*.

The **somatic nervous system** contains sensory and motor neurons. It transmits messages about sights, sounds, smells, temperature, body positions, and so on, to the central nervous system. Messages

> *Autonomic means "automatic."*

transmitted from the brain and spinal cord to the somatic nervous system control purposeful body movements such as raising a hand, winking, or running, as well as the tiny, almost imperceptible movements that maintain our balance and posture.

Autonomic means "automatic." The **autonomic nervous system (ANS)** regulates the glands and the muscles of internal organs. Thus, the ANS controls activities such as heartbeat, respiration, digestion, and dilation of the pupils of the eyes. These activities can occur automatically, while we are asleep. But some of them can be overridden by conscious control. You can breathe at a purposeful pace, for example. Methods like biofeedback and yoga also help people gain voluntary control of functions such as heart rate and blood pressure.

The ANS also has two branches, or divisions: **sympathetic** and **parasympathetic**. These branches have largely opposing effects. Many organs and glands are stimulated by both branches of the ANS (see Figure 2.6 on page 32). When organs and glands are simultaneously stimulated by both divisions, their effects can average out to some degree. In general, the sympathetic division is most active during processes that involve spending body energy from stored reserves, such as when you are threatened by someone and you must choose to fight or run away. The parasympathetic division is

spinal cord
a column of nerves within the spine that transmits messages from sensory receptors to the brain and from the brain to muscles and glands throughout the body

spinal reflex
a simple, unlearned response to stimulation that may involve only two neurons

grey matter
in the spinal cord, the greyish neurons and neural segments that are involved in spinal reflexes

white matter
in the spinal cord, axon bundles that carry messages from and to the brain

most active during processes that replenish reserves of energy, such as eating. When we are afraid, the sympathetic division of the ANS accelerates the heart rate. When we relax, the parasympathetic division decelerates the heart rate. The parasympathetic division stimulates digestive processes, but the sympathetic branch inhibits digestion. The ANS is of particular interest to psychologists because its activities are linked to various emotions such as anxiety and love.

The Central Nervous System: The Body's Central Processing Unit

What are the divisions and functions of the central nervous system? The central nervous system consists of the spinal cord and the brain. The **spinal cord** is a true "information superhighway"—a column of nerves as thick as a thumb. It transmits messages from sensory receptors to the brain and from the brain to muscles and glands throughout the body. The spinal cord also responds to some sources of external stimulation through spinal reflexes. A **spinal reflex** is an unlearned response to a stimulus that may require only two neurons—a sensory neuron and a motor neuron (see Figure 2.7). Therefore, some reflexive responses occur without the message travelling up to the brain first.

The spinal cord and brain contain grey matter and white matter. **Grey matter** consists of nonmyelinated neurons. Some of these are involved in spinal reflexes. Others send their axons to the brain. **White matter** is composed of bundles of longer, myelinated (and thus whitish) axons that carry messages to and from the brain. A cross section of the spinal cord shows that the grey matter, which includes cell bodies, is distributed in a butterfly pattern (see Figure 2.7).

We have many reflexes. We blink in response to a puff of air in our faces.

We swallow when food accumulates in the mouth. A physician may tap below the knee to elicit the knee-jerk reflex, a sign that the nervous system is operating adequately. Sexual response involves many reflexes. Urinating and defecating are reflexes that occur in response to pressure in the bladder and the rectum. It is your central nervous system that makes you so special. Other species see more sharply, smell more keenly, and hear more acutely. Other species run faster, or fly through the air, or swim underwater—without the benefit of artificial devices such as airplanes and submarines. But, as recognized by Canadian psychologist Albert Bandura, it is your central nervous system that enables you to use symbols and language, the abilities that allow people not only to adapt to their

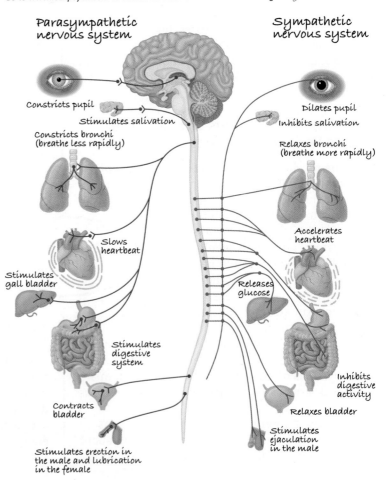

FIGURE 2.6

The Parasympathetic and Sympathetic Branches of the Autonomic Nervous System (ANS)

The parasympathetic branch of the ANS generally acts to replenish stores of energy in the body. The sympathetic branch is most active during activities that expend energy. The two branches of the ANS frequently have antagonistic (opposite and competing) effects on the organs they service.

Go to www.icanpsych.com to access an interactive version of this figure.

Parasympathetic nervous system

Constricts pupil
Stimulates salivation
Constricts bronchi (breathe less rapidly)
Slows heartbeat
Stimulates gall bladder
Stimulates digestive system
Contracts bladder
Stimulates erection in the male and lubrication in the female

Sympathetic nervous system

Dilates pupil
Inhibits salivation
Relaxes bronchi (breathe more rapidly)
Accelerates heartbeat
Releases glucose
Inhibits digestive activity
Relaxes bladder
Stimulates ejaculation in the male

FIGURE 2.7

The Reflex Arc

Reflexes are inborn, stereotyped behaviour patterns that have apparently evolved because they help individuals adapt to the environment even before they can understand and purposefully manipulate the environment. Here we see a cross section of the spinal cord, highlighting a sensory neuron and a motor neuron, which are involved in the knee-jerk reflex. In some reflexes, interneurons link sensory and motor neurons.

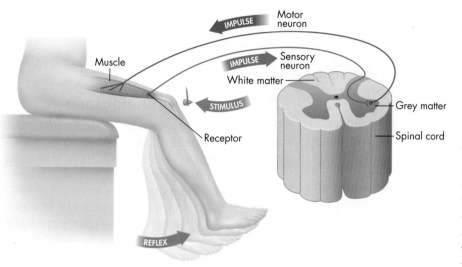

environment but to create new environments and give them names (1999).

LO2 The Brain: Wider Than the Sky

Philosophers and scientists have wondered about the functions of the brain throughout history. Scientists today generally agree that the mind is a function of the brain (Bogen, 1998; Dietrich, 2004; Hohwy & Frith, 2004; Roser & Gazzaniga, 2004). Some engage in research that attempts to pinpoint exactly what happens in certain parts of the brain when we are listening to music or trying to remember someone's face. At other times, knowledge has almost literally fallen into their laps. From injuries to the head—some of them minimal, some horrendous—we have learned that brain damage can impair consciousness, perception, memory, and abilities to make plans and decisions. In some cases, the loss of large portions of the brain may result in little loss of function. But the loss of smaller portions in particular locations can cause language problems, memory loss, or death. It has been known for about two centuries that damage to the left side of the brain is connected with loss of sensation or movement on the right side of the body, and vice versa. Thus it has been assumed that the brain's control mechanisms cross over from right to left, and vice versa, as they descend into the body. *How do researchers learn about the functions of the brain?*

Experimenting with the Brain

We have learned much of how the brain is linked to behaviour and mental process from those who have suffered from disease and accidents. For example, in 1848 Phineas Gage was involved in a railroad accident that blasted a three-centimetre-thick metal tamping rod up through his head. It travelled straight through his head from below his left cheek up and out the top of his skull just behind his forehead. Miraculously, Gage survived the accident, and although he was still able to work, his personality had changed dramatically. Before the accident he was considerate of others, well spoken, and efficient, but afterward, he was rude, frequently profane, and obstinate. It was as if his moral self had been blown out of the top of his head (Harlow, 1868). My own skiing accident resulted in no marked personality changes, but some very real

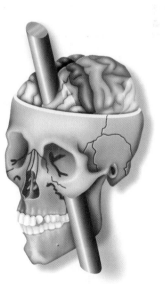

This image shows the tamping rod that shot through Phineas Gage's head, destroying a portion of his frontal lobe. Shockingly, Gage survived. Until the advent of modern neuroimaging techniques, much of what we learned about the relation between the brain and behaviour came from dramatic brain injury patients such as Gage.

Reprinted with permission from Damasio H., Grabowski T., Frank R., Galaburda A.M., Damasio A.R. The return of Phineas Gage: Clues about the brain from a famous patient. *Science*, 264: 1102–1105, © 1994. Dornsife Neuroscience Imaging Center and Brain and Creativity Institute, University of Southern California.

> The Brain—is wider than the Sky—
> For—put them side by side—
> The one the other will contain
> With ease—and you—beside—
>
> —Emily Dickinson

electroencephalograph (EEG) a method of detecting brain waves by means of measuring the current between electrodes placed on the scalp

behavioural effects. Accidents provide unplanned—and uncontrolled—opportunities of studying the brain. Nevertheless, they remain useful (e.g., Baldo et al., 2004; Eslinger et al., 2004). Still, scientists learn more about the brain through methods like experimentation, electroencephalography, and brain scans.

Scientists have also purposefully damaged part of the brain in laboratory animals to observe the results. For example, damaging one part of the hypothalamus causes rats to overeat. Damaging another part of the hypothalamus causes them to stop eating. It is as if parts of the brain contain on–off switches for certain kinds of behaviour, at least in lower animals.

Because the brain has no receptors for pain, Canadian surgeon Wilder Penfield (1969) was able to stimulate parts of human brains with electrical probes. As a result, his patients reported perceiving certain memories. Electrical stimulation of the brain has also shown that parts of the brain are connected with specific kinds of sensations (as of light or sound) or motor activities (such as movement of an arm or leg).

The Electroencephalograph

Penfield stimulated parts of the brain with an electrical current and asked people to report what they experienced. Researchers have also used the **electroencephalograph (EEG)** to record the natural electrical activity of the brain. The EEG (see Figure 2.8) detects minute amounts of electrical activity—called *brain waves*—that pass between the electrodes. Certain brain waves are associated with feelings of relaxation, with various stages of sleep, and with neurological problems such as epilepsy.

Brain-Imaging Techniques

When Phineas Gage had his fabled accident, the only ways to look into the brain were to drill holes or crack it open, neither of which would have contributed to

{ Wilder Penfield }

During his lifetime, Wilder Penfield was called "the greatest living Canadian," and was invited to be a Member of the Order of Canada (the highest civilian honour available in Canada) based on his pioneering neuroscience research at McGill University in Montreal. You may recall the depiction of his work in one of the Canadian *Historica Minute* one-minute movies that ran on television and sometimes before movies. In the commercial, Penfield is shown probing part of a woman's brain and she reports what she is experiencing. At one point he stimulates an area and she responds, "Burnt toast! Dr. Penfield, I can smell burnt toast!" Penfield had found the area of her brain that was associated with her epileptic seizures, and now could work to alleviate them (www.histori.ca/minutes).

The Electroencephalograph (EEG)

The EEG detects brain waves that pass between electrodes that are attached to the scalp. It has been used to reveal electrical activity associated with relaxation and the stages of sleep.

© Richard T. Nowitz/Corbis

the well-being of the subject. But in the latter years of the 20th century, researchers developed imaging techniques that tap the computer's capacity to generate images of the parts of the brain from sources of radiation.

Computerized axial tomography (CAT or CT scan), shown in Figure 2.9A (p. 36), passes X-rays through the head and measures the structures that reflect the beams from various angles, generating a three-dimensional image. The CAT scan reveals deformities in shape and structure that are connected with blood clots, tumours, and other health problems.

A second method, **positron emission tomography (PET scan)**, shown in Figure 2.9B, forms a computer-generated image of the activity of parts of the brain by tracing the amount of glucose used (or metabolized) by these parts. More glucose is metabolized in more active parts of the brain. To trace the metabolism of glucose, a harmless amount of a radioactive compound, called a *tracer,* is mixed with glucose and injected into the bloodstream. When the glucose reaches the brain, the patterns of activity are revealed by measurement of the positrons—positively charged particles—that are given

off by the tracer. The PET scan has been used by researchers to see which parts of the brain are most active when we are, for example, listening to music, working out a math problem, using language, or playing chess.

A third imaging technique is **magnetic resonance imaging (MRI)**, which is shown in Figure 2.9C. In MRI, the person lies in a powerful magnetic field and is exposed to radio waves that cause parts of the brain to emit signals, which are measured from multiple angles. MRI relies on subtle shifts in blood flow. (More blood flows to more active parts of the brain, supplying them with oxygen.) MRI can be used to show which parts of the brain are active when we are, say, solving math problems (Rickard et al., 2000) or speaking (Dogil et al., 2002). **Functional MRI (fMRI)** enables researchers to observe the brain "while it works" by taking repeated scans while subjects engage in activities such as mental processes and voluntary movements.

Some researchers consider the prefrontal cortex to be the "executive centre" of the brain, where decisions are made to keep information in working memory and to solve problems. Research with the PET scan and MRI supports the view that the prefrontal cortex is where we process much of the information involved in making plans and solving problems (Kroger et al., 2002; Rowe et al., 2001).

A Voyage Through the Brain

What are the structures and functions of the brain? Let us begin our tour of the brain with the hindbrain, where the spinal cord rises to meet the brain (refer to Figure 2.10, p. 37). Here we find three major structures: the medulla, the pons, and the cerebellum. Many pathways pass through the **medulla** to connect the spinal cord to higher levels of the brain. The medulla

computerized axial tomography (CAT or CT scan) a method of brain imaging that passes a narrow X-ray beam through the head and measures structures that reflect the rays from various angles, enabling a computer to generate a three-dimensional image

positron emission tomography (PET scan) a method of brain imaging that injects a radioactive tracer into the bloodstream and assesses activity of parts of the brain according to the amount of glucose they metabolize

magnetic resonance imaging (MRI) a method of brain imaging that places a person in a magnetic field and uses radio waves to cause the brain to emit signals that reveal shifts in the flow of blood which, in turn, indicate brain activity

functional MRI (fMRI) a form of MRI that enables researchers to observe the brain "while it works" by taking repeated scans

medulla an oblong area of the hindbrain involved in regulation of heartbeat and respiration

FIGURE 2.9

Brain Imaging Techniques

Part A shows a CAT scan, part B shows a PET scan, and part C shows an MRI.

A. Computerized axial tomography (the CAT scan) passes a narrow X-ray beam through the head and measures structures that reflect the rays from various angles, enabling a computer to generate a three-dimensional image.

B. Positron emission tomography (the PET scan) injects a radioactive tracer into the bloodstream and assesses activity of parts of the brain according to the amount of glucose they metabolize.

C. Magnetic resonance imaging (MRI) places a person in a magnetic field and uses radio waves to cause the brain to emit signals that reveal shifts in the flow of blood which, in turn, indicate brain activity.

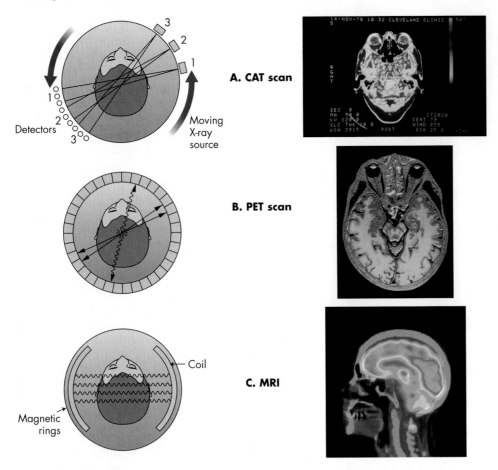

A. CAT scan

B. PET scan

C. MRI

Top: Ohio-Nuclear Corporation/Science Photo Library; centre: Jean Perrin, ISM/Science Photo Library; bottom: Pasieka/Science Photo Library

---

ment and is involved in functions related to regulation of movement, sleep and alertness, and respiration.

Behind the pons lies the **cerebellum** ("little brain" in Latin). The cerebellum has two hemispheres that are involved in maintaining balance and in controlling motor (muscle) behaviour. You may send a command from your forebrain to get up and walk to the refrigerator, but your cerebellum is key to organizing the information that enables you to engage in these movements. The cerebellum allows you to place one leg in front of the other and reach your destination without tipping over. If I had struck the lower back portion of my head in my skiing accident, damaging my cerebellum, my coordination would have been severely disrupted, causing stumbling and loss of muscle tone.

As we tour the hindbrain, we also find the lower part of the **reticular activating system (RAS)**. That is where the

regulates basic functions such as heart rate, blood pressure, and respiration. (In fact, Gage and I both survived our brain injuries because our medullas escaped injury.) The medulla also plays roles in sleeping, sneezing, and coughing. The **pons** is a bulge in the hindbrain that lies forward of the medulla. *Pons* is the Latin word for "bridge." The pons is so named because of the bundles of nerves that pass through it. The pons transmits information about body move-

RAS begins, but it ascends through the midbrain into the lower part of the forebrain. The RAS is vital in the functions of attentiveness, sleep, and arousal. Injury to the RAS may result in a coma. Stimulation of the RAS causes it to send messages to the cerebral cortex (the large wrinkled mass that you think of as your brain), making us more alert to sensory information. In classic neurological research, Guiseppe Moruzzi and Horace Magoun (1949) discovered that electrical stimulation of the reticular formation of a sleeping cat caused it to awaken at once. But when the reticular formation was severed from higher parts of the brain, the animal fell into a coma from which it would not awaken. Drugs known as central nervous system depressants, such as alcohol, are thought to work, in part, by lowering RAS activity.

pons
a structure of the hindbrain involved in respiration, sleep, and arousal

cerebellum
a part of the hindbrain involved in muscle coordination and balance

reticular activating system (RAS)
a part of the brain involved in attentiveness, sleep, and arousal

FIGURE 2.10

The Parts of the Human Brain

The view of the brain, split top to bottom, shows some of the most important structures. The "valleys" in the cerebrum are called *fissures*.

Go to www.icanpsych.com to access an interactive version of this figure.

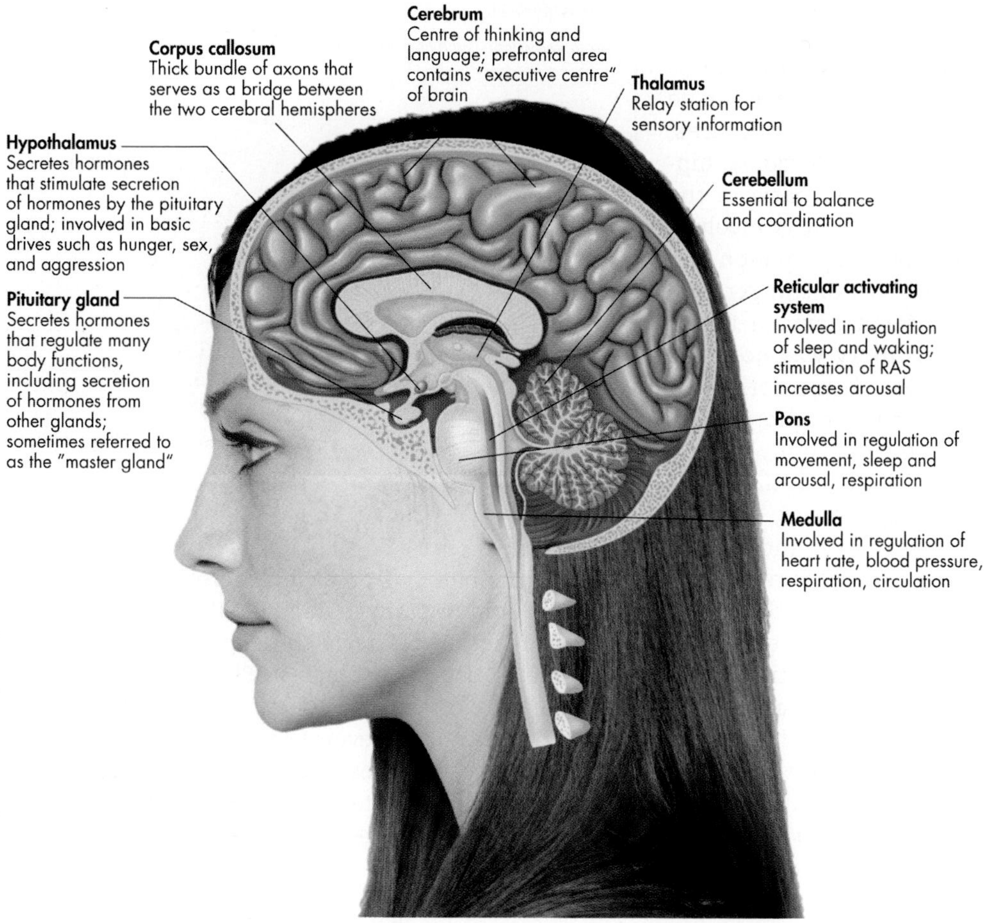

Corpus callosum
Thick bundle of axons that serves as a bridge between the two cerebral hemispheres

Cerebrum
Centre of thinking and language; prefrontal area contains "executive centre" of brain

Thalamus
Relay station for sensory information

Hypothalamus
Secretes hormones that stimulate secretion of hormones by the pituitary gland; involved in basic drives such as hunger, sex, and aggression

Pituitary gland
Secretes hormones that regulate many body functions, including secretion of hormones from other glands; sometimes referred to as the "master gland"

Cerebellum
Essential to balance and coordination

Reticular activating system
Involved in regulation of sleep and waking; stimulation of RAS increases arousal

Pons
Involved in regulation of movement, sleep and arousal, respiration

Medulla
Involved in regulation of heart rate, blood pressure, respiration, circulation

Image Source Black/Jupiterimages

thalamus
an area near the centre of the brain involved in the relay of sensory information to the cortex and in the functions of sleep and attentiveness

hypothalamus
a bundle of nuclei below the thalamus involved in body temperature, motivation, and emotion

Key areas of the forward-most part of the brain, or forebrain, are the thalamus, the hypothalamus, the limbic system, and the cerebrum (see Figure 2.10). The **thalamus** is located near the centre of the brain. It consists of two joined egg-shaped structures. The thalamus serves as a relay station for sensory stimulation. Nerve fibres from sensory systems enter from below; their information is then transmitted to the cerebral cortex by fibres that exit from above. For example, the thalamus relays sensory input from the eyes to the visual areas of the cerebral cortex. The thalamus also regulates sleep and attentiveness in coordination with other brain structures, including the RAS.

The **hypothalamus** lies beneath the thalamus and above the pituitary gland. It weighs only 4 grams, yet it is vital in the regulation of body temperature, concentration of fluids, storage of nutrients, and motivation and emotion. Experimenters learn many of the functions of the hypothalamus by implanting electrodes in parts of it and observing the effects of electrical stimulation. They have found that the hypothalamus is involved in hunger, thirst, sexual behaviour, caring for offspring, and aggression. Among lower animals, stimulation of various areas of the hypothalamus can trigger instinctual behaviours such as fighting, mating, or nest building.

Canadian psychologists James Olds and Peter Milner (1954) made a splendid mistake in the 1950s. They were attempting to implant an electrode in a rat's reticular formation to see how stimulation of the area might affect learning. Olds, however, was primarily a social psychologist and not a biological psychologist. He missed his target and found a part of the animal's hypothalamus instead. Olds and Milner dubbed this area the "pleasure centre" because the animal would repeat whatever it was doing when it was stimulated. The term *pleasure centre* is not used too frequently, because it appears to attribute human emotions to rats. Yet the "pleasure centres" must be doing something right, because rats stimulate themselves in these centres by pressing a pedal several thousand times an hour, until they are exhausted (Olds, 1969).

The hypothalamus is important to humans as well as lower animals. Unfortunately (or fortunately), our "pleasure centres" are not as clearly defined as those of the rat. Then, too, our responses to messages from the hypothalamus are less automatic and

limbic system
a group of structures involved in memory, motivation, and emotion that forms a fringe along the inner edge of the cerebrum

hippocampus
part of brain associated with long-term memory and mental mapping

amygdala
a part of the limbic system that apparently facilitates stereotypical aggressive responses

relatively more influenced by higher brain functions—that is, cognitive factors such as thought, choice, and value systems.

The **limbic system** forms a fringe along the inner edge of the cerebrum and is fully evolved only in mammals (see Figure 2.11). It is made up of several structures, including the amygdala, hippocampus, and parts of the hypothalamus. It is involved in memory and emotion and in the drives of hunger, sex, and aggression. If I had suffered damage to my **hippocampus** (thankfully, my injury was not deep enough), I'd be able to retrieve old memories but unable to permanently store any new information. As a result, I would have lived the rest of my life as a 14-year-old boy, continuously shocked at the image that presented itself to me in the mirror, and surprised each time I saw how my parents and siblings had aged years seemingly overnight (Squire, 2004).

The **amygdala** is near the bottom of the limbic system and looks like two little almonds. Studies using lesioning and electrical stimulation show that the amygdala is connected with aggressive behaviour in monkeys, cats, and other animals. Early in the 20th century, Heinrich Klüver and Paul Bucy (1939) lesioned part of the amygdala of a rhesus monkey. Rhesus monkeys are normally a scrappy lot

FIGURE 2.11

The Limbic System

The limbic system is made up of structures that include the amygdala, the hippocampus, and parts of the hypothalamus. It is evolved fully only in mammals and forms a fringe along the inner edge of the cerebrum. The limbic system is involved in memory and emotion, and in the drives of hunger, sex, and aggression.

Go to www.icanpsych.com to access an interactive version of this figure.

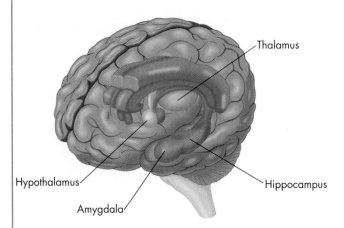

and try to bite or grab at intruders, but destruction of this animal's amygdala made it docile. No longer did it react aggressively to people. It even allowed people to poke and pinch it. Electrical stimulation of the part of the amygdala that Klüver and Bucy had destroyed, however, triggers a "rage response." For example, it causes a cat to hiss and arch its back in preparation to attack. The amygdala is also connected with a fear response (LeDoux, 1998). If you

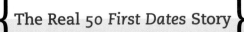

The Real 50 First Dates Story

Perhaps you saw the movie *50 First Dates* (Segal, 2004), with actors Drew Barrymore and Adam Sandler, in which Barrymore's character relives the same day over and over due to a brain injury she suffered in a car accident. The idea for this movie seems to have been based on the real-life struggles of Henry Molaison (Singer, 2009). Henry suffered from debilitating epileptic seizures and underwent aggressive brain surgery where portions of his temporal lobe, including his hippocampus, were removed. Fortunately, this surgery was successful in curing the seizures, but the effect of the missing hippocampus was devastating. As a result of having no hippocampus, Henry was unable to store any new memories. He lived in a short 15-minute interval of time, and any new information following the day of the surgery was never remembered. He was frequently surprised at how old he (and his wife) looked, he would enjoy the same conversations day after day, and he would cheerfully meet new doctors and researchers every day, even those who had been working with him for years. Until the day he passed away

at the age of 82, he greeted each new day still believing that he was 27 years old and just waking up from the surgery for his epilepsy.

electrically stimulate another part of the amygdala, the cat cringes in fear when you cage it with a mouse.

The amygdala is also connected with vigilance. It is involved in emotions, learning, and memory, and it sort of behaves like a spotlight, focusing attention on matters that are novel and important to know more about.

Only in humans does the **cerebrum** make up such a large part of the brain. The cerebrum is responsible for thinking and language. The surface of the cerebrum—the **cerebral cortex**—is wrinkled, or convoluted, with ridges and valleys. The convolutions allow a great deal of surface area to be packed into the brain. If you take a piece of paper and crumple it up, it still has the same amount of total surface area, but it now can be fit into a much smaller area. It is similar with the wrinkled and convoluted cerebral cortex within your skull, and surface area is apparently connected with cognitive ability. Valleys in the cortex are called *fissures*. A key fissure almost divides the cerebrum in half, creating two hemispheres with something of the shape of a walnut. The hemispheres are connected by the **corpus callosum** (Latin for "hard body"), a bundle of some 200 million nerve fibres.

The Cerebral Cortex

The cerebral cortex is the part of the brain that you usually think of as your brain. *Cortex* is a Latin word meaning "bark," as in the bark of a tree. Just as the bark is the outer coating of a tree, the cerebral cortex is the outer coating of the cerebrum. Despite its extreme importance and its creation of a world of civilization and culture, it is only about two to four millimetres thick.

The cerebral cortex is involved in almost every bodily activity, including most sensa-

tions and most responses. It is also the part of the brain that frees people from the tyranny of genetic dictates and instinct. It is the seat of thinking and language, and it enables humans to think deeply about the world outside and to make decisions. *What are the parts of the cerebral cortex?*

FIGURE 2.12

The Geography of the Cerebral Cortex

The cortex has four lobes: frontal, parietal, temporal, and occipital. The visual area of the cortex is in the occipital lobe. The hearing or auditory cortex lies in the temporal lobe. The motor and somatosensory areas—shown below—face each other across the central fissure. Note that the face and the hands are "super-sized" in the motor and somatosensory areas. Why do you think this is so?

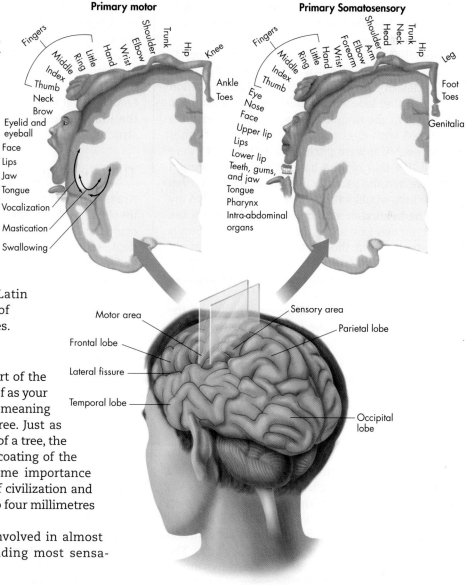

The cerebral cortex has two hemispheres, left and right. Each of the hemispheres is divided into four lobes, as shown in Figure 2.12. The *frontal lobe* lies in front of the central fissure and the *parietal lobe* behind it. The *temporal lobe* lies below the side, or lateral, fissure—across from the frontal and parietal lobes. The *occipital lobe* lies behind the temporal lobe and behind and below the parietal lobe.

Just to remind you, when I hit the tree stump on that ill-fated afternoon, I destroyed the top part of my brain, only on the right side, at the topmost part of my head. As you read the next few sections, and look at Figure 2.12, see if you can predict what effect the injury had on my sensations and behaviour.

When light strikes the eyes, neurons in the occipital lobe fire, and as a result, we "see" (that is, the image is projected in the brain). Direct artificial stimulation of the occipital lobe also produces visual sensations. If neurons in the occipital region of the cortex were stimulated with electricity, you would "see" flashes of light even if it were pitch black or your eyes were covered. If I had hit the back of my head skiing, I may have become partially or completely blind (even though there would have been no damage at all to my eyes). The hearing or auditory area of the cortex lies in the temporal lobe along the lateral fissure. Sounds cause structures in the ear to vibrate. Messages are relayed from those structures to the auditory area of the cortex, and, when you hear a noise, neurons in this area are firing.

Just behind the central fissure at the top of the brain in the parietal lobe lies an area called the somatosensory cortex, which receives messages from skin senses all over the body. These sensations include warmth and cold, touch, pain, and movement. Neurons in different parts of the sensory cortex fire, depending on whether you wiggle your finger or raise your leg. Any guesses about the effects of my injury yet?

Many years ago it was discovered that patients with injuries to one hemisphere of the brain would show sensory or motor deficits on the opposite side of the body below the head. This led to the recognition that sensory and motor nerves cross in the brain and elsewhere. The left hemisphere controls, acts on, and receives inputs from the right side of the body. The right hemisphere controls, acts on, and receives inputs from the left side of the body. The **motor cortex** lies in the frontal lobe at the top of the brain, just across the valley of the central fissure from the somatosensory cortex. Neurons firing in the motor cortex cause parts of our body to move. More than 100 years ago, German scientists electrically stimulated the motor cortex in dogs and observed that muscles contracted in response (Fritsch & Hitzig, 1870/1960). Since then, neuroscientists have mapped the motor cortex in people and lower animals by inserting electrical probes and seeing which muscles contract. For example, José Delgado (1969) caused one patient to make a fist even though he tried to prevent his hand from closing. The patient said, "I guess, doctor, that your electricity is stronger than my will" (Delgado, 1969, p. 114).

So now you should have enough information to make a good guess at how my injury affected my abilities and behaviour. The damage had destroyed my somatosensory cortex and my motor cortex, but only on the right half of my brain. Thus, you could draw a line down the centre of my body and everything below my face on the left side (remember the right side of the brain controls the left side of the body and vice versa) was unable to feel anything (no pain, warmth, or pressure), and I was unable to move any muscle on the left side of my body as well. I had my first lesson in neuropsychology that day, on the immediate and inseparable link between brain structure and our sensations and behaviours.

Thinking, Language, and the Cortex

Areas of the cerebral cortex that are not primarily involved in sensation or motor activity are called *association areas*. They make possible the breadth and depth of human learning, thought, memory, and language. *What parts of the cerebral cortex are involved in thinking and language?* The association areas in the *prefrontal* region of the brain—that is, in the frontal lobes, near the forehead—are the brain's executive centre. It appears to be where we solve problems and make plans and decisions (Baldo et al., 2004; Buchanan et al., 2004; Shimamura, 2002).

Executive functions like problem solving also require memory, like the memory in your computer. Association areas also provide the core of your working memory (Chafee & Goldman-Rakic, 2000; Constantinidis et al., 2001). They are connected with various sensory areas in the brain and can tap whatever sensory information is needed or desired. The prefrontal region thus retrieves visual, auditory, and other memories and manipulates them; similarly, a computer retrieves information from files in storage and manipulates it in working memory.

Here is an example of how the association areas of the brain will work with the other parts of the brain, such as the visual area of the occipital lobe.

Certain neurons in the occipital lobe fire in response to the visual presentation of vertical lines. Others fire in response to presentation of horizontal lines. Although one group of cells may respond to one aspect of the visual field and another group of cells may respond to another, the association areas of your brain put it all together. As a result, we see a box or an automobile or a road map and not a confusing array of verticals and horizontals.

Language Functions

In some ways, the left and right hemispheres of the brain duplicate each other's functions. In other ways, they differ. The left hemisphere contains language functions for nearly all right-handed people and for two out of three left-handed people (Pinker, 1994b). Two key language areas lie within the hemisphere of the cortex that contains language functions (usually the left hemisphere): Broca's area and Wernicke's area (see Figure 2.13). Damage to either area is likely to cause **aphasia**—that is, a disruption of the ability to understand or produce language.

Wernicke's area lies in the temporal lobe near the auditory cortex. It responds mainly to auditory information (sounds). As you are reading this page, however, the visual information is registered in the visual cortex of your occipital lobe. It is then recoded as auditory information as it travels to Wernicke's area. Broca's area is located in the frontal lobe, near the section of the motor cortex that controls the muscles of the tongue, throat, and other areas of the face used when speaking. Broca's area processes the information and relays it to the motor cortex. The motor cortex sends the signals that

FIGURE 2.13

Broca's and Wernicke's Areas of the Cerebral Cortex

The areas that are most involved in speech are Broca's area and Wernicke's area.

Broca's area   Wernicke's area

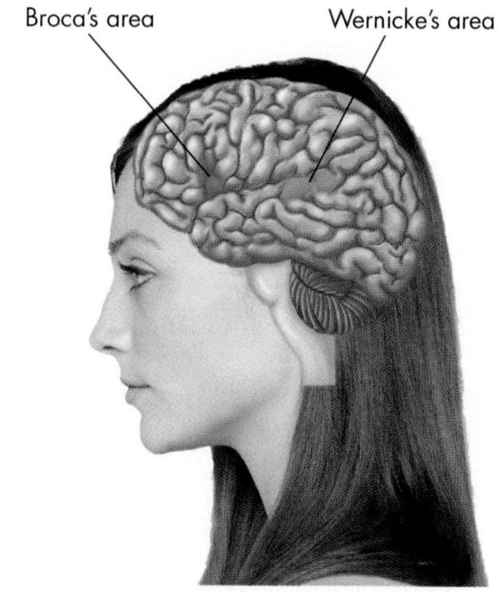

Image Source Black/Jupiterimages

cause muscles in your throat and mouth to contract. If you are "subvocalizing"—saying what you are reading "under your breath"—that is because Wernicke's area transmits information to Broca's area via nerve fibres.

People with damage to Wernicke's area may show **Wernicke's aphasia**, which impairs their abilities to comprehend speech and to think of the proper words to express their own thoughts. Ironically, they usually speak freely and with proper syntax. Wernicke's area is essential to understanding the relationships between words and their meanings. When Broca's area is damaged, people usually understand language well enough but speak slowly and laboriously, in simple sentences. This pattern is termed **Broca's aphasia**.

Some people with Broca's aphasia utter short, meaningful phrases that omit small but important grammatical words such as *is, and,* and *the.* Such an individual may laboriously say "walk dog." The phrase can have various meanings, such as "I want to take the dog for a walk" or "Take the dog out for a walk."

A part of the brain called the *angular gyrus* lies between the visual cortex and Wernicke's area. The angular gyrus "translates" visual information, as in perceiving written words, into auditory information (sounds) and sends it on to Wernicke's area. Brain imaging suggests that problems in the angular gyrus can seriously impair reading ability because it becomes difficult for the reader to segment words into sounds (Milne et al., 2002; Ruff et al., 2003).

Left Brain, Right Brain?

What would it mean to be "left-brained" or "right-brained"? The notion is that the hemispheres of the brain are involved in very different kinds of intellectual and emotional functions and responses. According to this view, left-brained people would be primarily logical and intellectual. Right-brained people would be intuitive, creative, and emotional. Those of us who are fortunate enough to have our brains "in balance" would presumably have the best of it—the capacity for logic combined with emotional richness.

Like many other popular ideas, the left-brain–right-brain notion is exaggerated. Research does suggest that in right-handed individuals, the left hemisphere is relatively more involved in intellectual undertakings that require logical analysis and problem solving, language, and mathematical computation

aphasia
a disruption in the ability to understand or produce language

Wernicke's aphasia
a language disorder characterized by difficulty comprehending the meaning of spoken language

Broca's aphasia
a language disorder characterized by slow, laborious speech

(Corballis et al., 2002; Shenal & Harrison, 2003). The other hemisphere (typically the right hemisphere) is usually superior in visual–spatial functions (it's better at putting puzzles together), recognition of faces, discrimination of colours, aesthetic and emotional responses, understanding metaphors, and creative mathematical reasoning. Despite these differences, the hemispheres of the brain do not act independently such that some people are truly left-brained and others right-brained (Colvin et al., 2005). The functions of the left and right hemispheres overlap to some degree, and they tend to respond simultaneously as we focus our attention on one thing or another.

Whether we are talking about language functions or being "left-brained" or "right-brained," we are talking about people whose hemispheres of the cerebral cortex communicate back and forth.

Handedness

Being left-handed was once seen as a deficiency. Left-handed students were made to learn to write with their right hands. We are usually labelled right-handed or left-handed on the basis of our handwriting preferences, yet some people write with one hand and pass a football with the other.

Being left-handed appears to provide a somewhat-greater-than-average probability of language problems, such as dyslexia and stuttering, and health problems such as migraine headaches and allergies (Andreou et al., 2002; Geschwind & Galaburda, 1987; Habib & Robichon, 2003). But there may also be advantages to being left-handed. Left-handed people are more likely than right-handed people to be numbered among the ranks of gifted artists, musicians, and mathematicians (Kilshaw & Annett, 1983; Ostatníková et al., 2002).

The origin of handedness has a genetic component. If one of your parents is left-handed, your chances of being right-handed drops to about 80 percent. And if both of your parents are left-handed, your chances of also being left-handed are about one in two (Rosenbaum, 2000).

Split-Brain Experiments

A number of people with severe cases of **epilepsy** have split-brain operations in which much of the corpus callosum is severed (refer back to Figure 2.10 on page 37). The purpose of the operation is to confine seizures to one hemisphere of the cerebral cortex rather than allowing a neural tempest to reverberate between both hemispheres. Split-brain operations do seem to help people with epilepsy. *What happens when the brain is split in two?*

FIGURE 2.14

A Divided-Brain Experiment

In the drawing on the left, we see that visual sensations in the left visual field are projected in the occipital cortex of the right hemisphere. Visual sensations from the right visual field are projected in the occipital cortex in the left hemisphere. In the divided-brain experiment diagrammed on the right, a person with a severed corpus callosum handles a key with his left hand and perceives the written word "key" in his left visual field. The word "key" is projected in the right hemisphere. Speech, however, is usually a function of the left hemisphere. The written word "ring," perceived by the right visual field, is projected in the left hemisphere. So, when asked what he is handling, the divided-brain subject reports "ring," not "key."

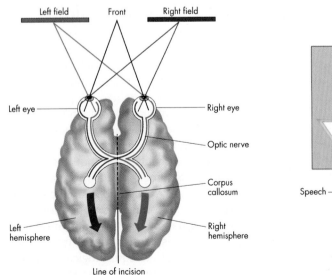
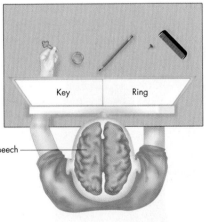

People who have undergone split-brain operations can be thought of as winding up with two brains, yet under most circumstances their behaviour remains ordinary enough. Still, some aspects of hemispheres that have stopped talking to each other are intriguing.

As reported by pioneering brain surgeon Joseph Bogen (1969, 2000), each hemisphere may have a "mind of its own." One split-brain patient reported that her hemispheres frequently disagreed on what she should be wearing. What she meant was that one hand might undo her blouse as rapidly as the other was buttoning it.

Another pioneer of split-brain research, Roger Wolcott Sperry (1982), found that people with split brains whose eyes are closed may be able to verbally describe an object such as a key when they hold it in one hand, but not when they hold it in the other hand. If a person with a split brain handles a key with his left hand behind a screen, tactile impressions of the key are projected into the right hemisphere, which has little or no language ability (see Figure 2.14). Thus, he will not be able to describe the key. If he holds it in his right hand, he will have no trouble describing it because sensory impressions are projected into the left hemisphere of the cortex, which contains language functions. To further confound matters, if the word *ring* is projected into the left hemisphere while the person is asked what he is handling, he will say "ring," not "key."

This discrepancy between what is felt and what is said occurs only in people with split brains. Even so, people who have undergone split-brain operations tend to lead largely normal lives. And for the rest of us, the two hemispheres work together most of the time, such as when we are playing the piano or solving math problems.

Plasticity

What is meant by brain plasticity? The brain remains "plastic," or changeable, throughout the life span. Until recently, it was suspected that after early adolescence the brain was no longer able to change. However, based on the mounting research evidence, Canadian researcher Bryan Kolb suggests that the brain adapts in two distinct ways (Kolb, Gibb, & Robinson, 2003). An example of the first type of **plasticity** comes from research on taxi drivers in London, England. Brain imaging techniques revealed a larger hippocampus (the area of the brain associated with navigational mental mapping) in cab drivers when compared with others. The day-to-day requirements of a London cabbie caused increased growth in the brains of these adults (Maguire et al., 2000). This finding reveals how the environment a person is in forms and changes the "plastic" brain throughout a person's life span.

An example of the second type of brain plasticity was revealed when children who lost the left hemisphere of the brain due to medical problems transferred their speech functions to the right hemisphere (Hertz-Pannier et al., 2002). Thus their brains were able to "reorganize" after the damage, making use of nearby parts of the brain to replace the lost areas. However, this reorganization seems to be age dependent. The older one is, the less swift the reorganization, if it is to happen at all (Stein, Brailowsky, & Will, 1995). Even though the skiing accident rendered the left side of my body senseless and paralyzed, within two weeks I was walking again and learning to sense pressure and pain. How did this occur? Due to plasticity, other parts of my brain took on the role of the destroyed right motor and somatosensory cortex. Thus, I am writing this book using both hands, and able to walk without any aid (although skiing is no longer my favourite sport).

LO3 The Endocrine System

What is the endocrine system? The body contains two types of **glands**: glands with ducts and glands without ducts. A *duct* is a passageway that carries substances to specific locations. Saliva, sweat, tears, and breast milk all reach their destinations through ducts. Psychologists are interested in the substances secreted by a number of *ductless* glands because of their effects on behaviour and mental processes. The ductless glands make up the **endocrine system** (see Figure 2.15 on the next page), and they release **hormones** into the bloodstream. Hormones are then picked up by specific receptor sites and regulate growth, metabolism, and some forms of behaviour. That is, they act only on receptors in certain locations.

Much hormonal action helps the body maintain steady states—fluid levels, blood sugar levels, and so on. Bodily mechanisms measure current levels; when these levels deviate from optimal, they signal glands to release hormones. The maintenance of steady states requires feedback of bodily information to glands. This type of system is referred to as a *negative feedback loop*. When enough of a

plasticity
the brain's ability to adapt and change

gland
an organ that secretes one or more chemical substances such as hormones, saliva, or milk

endocrine system
the body's system of ductless glands that secrete hormones and release them directly into the bloodstream

hormone
a substance secreted by an endocrine gland that regulates various body functions

hormone has been secreted, the gland is signalled to stop.

The Pituitary and the Hypothalamus

The pituitary gland and the hypothalamus work in close cooperation. The **pituitary gland** lies below the hypothalamus. Although the pituitary is only about the size of a pea, it is so central to the body's functioning that it has been dubbed the "master gland." The anterior (front) and posterior (back) lobes of the pituitary gland secrete many hormones. *Growth hormone* regulates the growth of muscles, bones, and glands. Children whose growth patterns are abnormally slow may catch up to their age-mates when they obtain growth hormone. *Prolactin* regulates maternal behaviour in lower mammals such as rats and stimulates production of milk in women. As a water conservation measure, *vasopressin* (also called *antidiuretic hormone*) inhibits production of urine when the body's fluid levels are low. Vasopressin is also connected with stereotypical paternal behaviour in some mammals. *Oxytocin* stimulates labour in pregnant women and

is connected with maternal behaviour (cuddling and caring for young) in some mammals (Insel, 2000; Taylor et al., 2000b). Obstetricians can induce labour by injecting pregnant women with oxytocin. During nursing, stimulation of the nerve endings of the nipples signals the brain to secrete oxytocin, which then causes the breasts to eject milk.

Although the pituitary gland may be the "master gland," the master has a "commander": the hypothalamus. We know today that the hypothalamus regulates much pituitary activity. The hypothalamus secretes a number of releasing hormones, or "factors," that stimulate the pituitary gland to secrete related hormones. For example, growth hormone releasing factor (hGRF) causes the pituitary to produce growth hormone. Blood vessels between the hypothalamus and the pituitary gland provide a direct route for these factors.

The Pineal Gland

The pineal gland secretes the hormone *melatonin,* which helps regulate the sleep–wake cycle and may affect the onset of puberty. Melatonin may also be connected with aging. In addition, it appears that melatonin is a mild sedative and some people use it as a sleeping pill (Arendt, 2000; Nagtegaal et al., 2000). Melatonin may also help people adjust to jet lag (Takahashi et al., 2002).

The Thyroid Gland

The thyroid gland could be considered the body's accelerator. It produces *thyroxin,* which affects the body's *metabolism*—the rate at which the body uses oxygen and produces energy. Some people are overweight because of *hypothyroidism,* a condition that results from too little thyroxin. Thyroxin deficiency in children can lead to *cretinism,* a condition characterized by stunted growth and mental retardation. Adults who secrete too little thyroxin may feel tired and sluggish and may put on weight. People who produce too much thyroxin may develop *hyperthyroidism,* which is characterized by excitability, insomnia, and weight loss.

The Adrenal Glands

The adrenal glands, located above the kidneys, have an outer layer, or cortex, and an inner core, or medulla. The adrenal cortex is regulated by the pituitary hormone ACTH (adrenocorticotrophic hormone). The adrenal cortex secretes hormones known as *corticosteroids,* or cortical steroids. These hormones increase resistance to stress, promote muscle development, and cause the liver to release stored sugar,

FIGURE 2.15

The Endocrine Glands

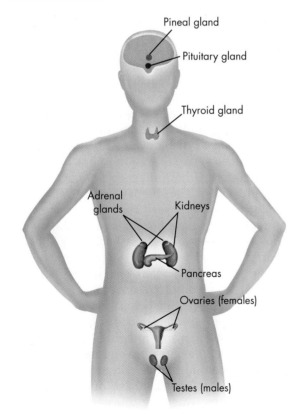

Pineal gland

Pituitary gland

Thyroid gland

Adrenal glands

Kidneys

Pancreas

Ovaries (females)

Testes (males)

Steroids, Behaviour, and Mental Processes

Steroids increase the muscle mass, heighten resistance to stress, and increase the body's energy supply by signalling the liver to release sugar into the bloodstream. The steroid testosterone is connected with the sex drive in both males and females (females secrete some testosterone in the adrenal glands) (Davis, 2000). Anabolic steroids (synthetic versions of the male sex hormone testosterone) have been used, sometimes in tandem with growth hormone, to enhance athletic prowess. Not only do these steroids enhance athletic prowess, they are also connected with self-confidence, aggressiveness, even memory functioning (Janowsky et al., 2000). Anabolic steroids are generally outlawed in sports, and in 2010 the University of Waterloo Warriors' football season was cancelled after nine of the players tested positive for steroid use (Masters, 2010). Even with strict penalties, the lure of steroids is understandable. Sometimes the difference between an acceptable athletic performance and a great one is rather small. Thousands of athletes try to make it in the big leagues, and the edge offered by steroids—even if minor—can spell the difference between a fumbling attempt and a smashing success. If steroids help, why the fuss? Some of it is related to the ethics of competition—the idea that athletes should "play fair." But steroid use is also linked to liver damage and other health problems.

Alex Ardenti/Alamy

making more energy available in emergencies, as when you see another car veering toward your own. Epinephrine and norepinephrine are secreted by the adrenal medulla. *Epinephrine*, also known as adrenaline, is manufactured exclusively by the adrenal glands, but norepinephrine (noradrenaline) is also produced elsewhere in the body. (Norepinephrine acts as a neurotransmitter in the brain.) The sympathetic branch of the autonomic nervous system causes the adrenal medulla to release a mixture of epinephrine and norepinephrine that helps arouse the body to cope with threats and stress. Epinephrine is of interest to psychologists because it has emotional as well as physical effects. It intensifies most emotions and is central to the experience of fear and anxiety.

The Testes and the Ovaries

The testes and ovaries also produce steroids, among them testosterone and estrogen. If it were not for the secretion of the male sex hormone *testosterone* about six weeks after conception, we would all develop the external genital organs of females. Testosterone is produced not only by the testes but in smaller amounts by the ovaries and adrenal glands. A few weeks after conception, testosterone causes the male's sex organs to develop. During puberty, testosterone stokes the growth of muscle and bone and the development of primary and secondary sex characteristics. *Primary sex characteristics* are directly involved in reproduction and include the increased size of the penis and the sperm-producing ability of the testes. *Secondary sex characteristics* such as the presence of a beard and a deeper voice differentiate males from females but are not directly involved in reproduction.

The ovaries produce *estrogen* and *progesterone* as well as small amounts of testosterone. Estrogen is also produced in smaller amounts by the testes. Estrogen fosters female reproductive capacity and secondary sex characteristics such as accumulation of fatty tissue in the breasts and hips. Progesterone stimulates growth of the female reproductive organs and prepares the uterus to maintain pregnancy. Estrogen and testosterone have psychological effects as well as biological effects, which we will explore further in Chapter 8.

natural selection
a core concept of the theory of evolution that holds that adaptive genetic variations among members of a species enable individuals with those variations to survive and reproduce

mutation
a sudden variation in an inheritable characteristic, as distinguished from a variation that results from generations of gradual selection

evolutionary psychology
the branch of psychology that studies the ways in which adaptation and natural selection are connected with mental processes and behaviour

LO4 Evolution and Heredity

Charles Darwin almost missed the boat. Literally. Darwin had volunteered to serve on an expeditionary voyage on the H.M.S. *Beagle,* but the captain, Robert Fitz-Roy, objected to Darwin because of the shape of his nose. Fitz-Roy believed that you could judge a person's character by the outline of his facial features, and Darwin's nose didn't fit the ... bill. But Fitz-Roy relented, and in the 1830s, Darwin undertook the historic voyage to the Galápagos Islands that led to the development of his theory of evolution.

In 1871 Darwin published *The Descent of Man,* which made the case that humans, like other species, were a product of evolution. He argued that the great apes (chimpanzees, gorillas, and so on) and humans shared a common primate ancestor. Evidence from fossil remains suggests that such a common ancestor might have lived about 13 million years ago (Moyà-Solà et al., 2004). Many people ridiculed Darwin's views because they were displeased with the notion that they might share ancestry with apes. Others argued that Darwin's theory contradicted the Bible's book of Genesis, which stated that humans had been created in one day in the image of God.

What is Darwin's theory of evolution? The concept of a *struggle for existence* lies at the core of Darwin's theory of evolution. On the Galápagos Islands, Darwin found himself immersed in the unfolding of a huge game of "Survivor," with animals and plants competing for food, water, territory, even light. But here the game was for real, and the rewards had nothing to do with fame or fortune. The rewards were reaching sexual maturity and transmitting one's genes into subsequent generations.

As described by evolutionary theory, some creatures have adapted successfully to these challenges, and their numbers have increased. Others have not met the challenges and have fallen back into the distant mists of time. Evidence suggests that 99.99 percent of all species that ever existed are now extinct (Gould, 2002). Which species prosper and which fade away is determined by **natural selection**; that is, species that are better adapted to their environment are more likely to survive and reproduce.

When we humans first appeared on Earth, our survival required a different sort of struggle than it does today. We fought or fled from predators such as leopards. We foraged across parched lands for food. But because of the evolution of our intellect, we prevailed. Our numbers have increased. We continue to transmit the traits that led to our selection down through the generations by means of genetic material whose chemical codes are only now being cracked.

Just what is handed down through the generations? The answer is biological structures and processes. Our biology serves as the material base for our behaviours, emotions, and cognitions (our thoughts, images, and plans). Biology somehow gives rise to specific behavioural tendencies in some organisms, such as the chick's instinctive fear of the shadow of the hawk. But the behaviour of many species, especially higher species such as humans, is flexible and affected by experience and choice, as well as by heredity.

According to the theory of evolution, species and individuals compete for the same resources. Small variations—random genetic variations called **mutations**—lead to differences among individuals, differences that affect the ability to adapt to change. Those individuals whose traits are better adapted are more likely to survive (that is, to be "naturally selected"). Survival permits them to reach sexual maturity, to reproduce, and to transmit their features or traits to the next generation. What began as chance variation becomes embedded over the generations—if it fosters survival. Chance variations that hinder survival are likely to disappear from the gene pool.

Evolutionary Psychology: Doing What Comes Naturally

These same concepts of *adaptation* and *natural selection* have also been applied to psychological traits and are key concepts in **evolutionary psychology**. *What is evolutionary psychology?* Evolutionary psychology studies the ways in which adaptation and natural selection are connected with mental processes and behaviour (Buss, 2000; Cory, 2002). Over the eons evolution has provided organisms with advantages such as stronger fins and wings, sharper claws, and camouflage. Human evolution has given rise to various physical traits and also to such diverse activities as language, art, committed relationships, and warfare.

One of the concepts of evolutionary psychology is that not only physical traits but also many

The Evolution of Man

www.CartoonStock.com

patterns of behaviour, including social behaviour, evolve and can be transmitted genetically from generation to generation. Behaviour patterns that help an organism to survive and reproduce may be transmitted to the next generation. Such behaviours are believed to include aggression, strategies of mate selection, even altruism (that is, self-sacrifice of the individual to help perpetuate the family grouping) (Bruene & Ribbert, 2002; McAndrew, 2002). Such behaviour patterns are termed *instinctive* or *species-specific* because they evolved within certain **species**.

What is meant by an "instinct"? An **instinct** is a stereotyped pattern of behaviour that is triggered in a specific situation. Instinctive behaviour is nearly identical among the members of the species in which it appears. It tends to resist modification, even when it serves no purpose (as in the interminable barking of some breeds of dogs) or results in punishment. Instinctive behaviour also appears when the individual is reared in isolation from others of its kind and thus cannot learn the behaviour from experience.

Consider some examples of instinctive behaviour. If you place an egg from the nest of a goose several centimetres in front of her, she will roll it back to the nest with her beak. However, she won't retrieve it if it's farther away—in the "not my egg" zone. If you rear a white-crowned sparrow in isolation from other

sparrows, it will still sing a recognizable species-specific song when it matures. The male stickleback fish instinctively attacks fish (or pieces of painted wood) with the kinds of red bellies that are characteristic of other male sticklebacks. Many psychologists consider language to be "instinctive" among humans. Psychologists are trying to determine what other kinds of human behaviour may be instinctive. However, even instinctive behaviour can be modified to some degree by learning, and most psychologists agree that the richness and complexity of human behaviour are made possible by learning.

Heredity, Genetics, and Behavioural Genetics

What is meant by "heredity"? Heredity defines one's *nature*—which is based on biological structures and processes. *Heredity* refers to the biological transmission of traits that have evolved from generation to generation. Fish are limited in other ways by their natural traits. Chimpanzees and gorillas can understand many spoken words and express some concepts through nonverbal symbol systems such as American Sign Language. Apes cannot speak, however, apparently because of limitations in the speech areas of the brain.

What is meant by "genetics"? The subfield of biology that studies heredity is called *genetics*. The field of **genetics** looks at both species-specific behaviour patterns (instincts) and individual differences among the members of a species. *Behavioural genetics* focuses on individual differences (Plomin & Crabbe, 2000).

Behavioural genetics bridges the sciences of psychology and biology. It is concerned with the genetic transmission of traits that give rise to patterns of behaviour. Psychologists are thinking in terms of behavioural genetics when they ask about the inborn reasons why individuals may differ in their behaviour and mental processes. For example, some children learn language more quickly than others. Part of the reason may lie in behavioural genetics—their heredity. But some children also experience a richer exposure to language at early ages.

species
a category of biological classification consisting of related organisms that are capable of interbreeding; *homo sapiens*—humans—make up one species

instinct
a stereotyped pattern of behaviour that is triggered by a particular stimulus and nearly identical among members of a species, even when they are reared in isolation

heredity
the transmission of traits from parent to offspring by means of genes

genetics
the area of biology that focuses on heredity

gene
a basic unit of heredity, which is found at a specific point on a chromosome

chromosome
a microscopic rod-shaped body in the cell nucleus carrying genes that transmit hereditary traits from generation to generation; humans normally have 46 chromosomes

DNA
acronym for *deoxyribonucleic acid*, the substance that forms the basic material of chromosomes; it takes the form of a double helix and contains the genetic code

Heredity appears to be a factor in almost all aspects of human behaviour, personality, and mental processes (Bouchard & Loehlin, 2001). Examples include sociability, shyness, social dominance, aggressiveness, leadership, thrill seeking, effectiveness as a parent or a therapist, happiness, even interest in arts and crafts (Johnson & Krueger, 2006; Knafo & Plomin, 2006; Leonardo & Hen, 2006).

Heredity also plays a role in psychological disorders ranging from anxiety and depression to schizophrenia, bipolar disorder, alcoholism, and personality disorders (Farmer et al., 2007; Riley & Kendler, 2005). These disorders are discussed in Chapter 12, but here we can note that a study of 794 pairs of female twins by Kendler and his colleagues (2000a) found six aspects of psychological health that were connected with genetic factors: feelings of physical well-being, social relationships, anxiety and depression, substance abuse, use of social support, and self-esteem. Kendler et al. (2000a) also found, however, that the family environment contributed strongly to social relationships, substance abuse, and social support. Although psychological health is influenced by environmental factors, our understanding of the role of heredity continues to expand. Unlocking these mysteries depends on how well we understand genes and chromosomes.

Genes and Chromosomes

Genes are the most basic building blocks of heredity. Genes regulate the development of specific traits. Some traits, such as blood type, are controlled by a single pair of genes. (One gene is derived from each parent.) Other traits are determined by combinations of genes. The inherited component of complex psychological traits, such as intelligence, is believed to be determined by combinations of genes. It is estimated that the cells within your body contain 20 000 to 25 000 genes (Human Genome Sequencing Consortium, 2004).

Genes are segments of **chromosomes**. That is, chromosomes are made up of strings of genes. Each cell in the body contains 46 chromosomes arranged in 23 pairs. Chromosomes are large complex molecules of **DNA** (the acronym for *deoxyribonucleic acid*), which has several chemical components. The tightly wound structure of DNA was first demonstrated in the 1950s by James Watson and Francis Crick. DNA takes the form of a double helix—a twisting molecular ladder (see Figure 2.16). The "rungs" of the ladder are made up of chemicals whose names are abbreviated as A, T, C, and G. A always links up with T to complete a rung, and C always combines with G. Therefore, you can describe the *genetic code* in terms of the nucleotides you find along just one of the rungs—e.g., CTGAGTCAC and so on. A single gene can contain hundreds of thousands of base pairs. So if you think of a gene as a word, it can be a few hundred thousand letters long and completely unpronounceable. A group of scientists working together around the globe—referred to as the Human Genome Project—has learned that the sequencing of your DNA consists of about 3 billion DNA sequences spread throughout your chromosomes (Plomin & Crabbe,

---

FIGURE 2.16

Cells, Chromosomes, and DNA

A. The nuclei of cells contain chromosomes. **B.** Chromosomes are made up of DNA. **C.** Segments of DNA are made up of genes. The genetic code—that is the order of the chemicals A, G, T, and C—determines your species and all those traits that can be inherited, from the colour of your eyes to predispositions toward many psychological traits and abilities, including sociability and musical talent.

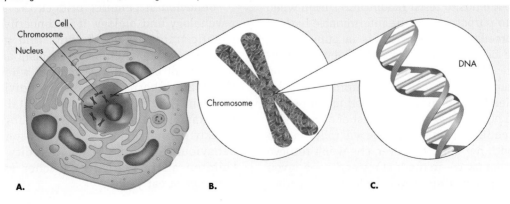

A.   **B.**   **C.**

2000). These sequences—the order of the chemicals we call A, T, C, and G—caused you to grow arms and not wings, and skin rather than scales. Psychologists debate the extent to which genes influence complex psychological traits such as intelligence, aggressiveness, and happiness, and the appearance of psychological disorders such as schizophrenia. Some traits, such as eye colour, are determined by a single pair of genes. Other traits, especially complex psychological traits such as sociability and aggressiveness, are thought to be **polygenic**—that is, influenced by combinations of genes.

Your genetic code provides your **genotype**—that is, your full genetic potential, as determined by the sequencing of the chemicals in your DNA. But the person you see in the mirror was also influenced by your early experiences in the home, injuries, adequacy of nourishment, educational experiences, and numerous other environmental influences. Therefore, you see the outer appearance of your phenotype, including the hairstyles of the day. Your **phenotype** is the manner in which your genetic code manifests itself because of your experiences and environmental circumstances. Your genotype enables you to acquire language. Your phenotype reveals that you are likely to be speaking French if you were reared in Quebec or English if you were reared in British Columbia (or both, if you were raised in a bilingual city such as Montreal or Ottawa).

Your genotype provides what psychologists refer to as your **nature**. Your phenotype represents the interaction of your nature (heredity) and your **nurture** (environmental influences) in the origins of your behaviour and mental processes. Psychologists are especially interested in the roles of nature and nurture in intelligence and psychological disorders. Our genotypes provide us with physical traits that set the stage for certain behaviours. But none of us is the result of heredity alone. Environmental factors such as nutrition, learning opportunities, cultural influences, exercise, and (unfortunately) accident and illness also determine our phenotypes, and whether genetically possible behaviours will be displayed. Behaviour and mental processes represent the interaction of nature and nurture. A potential Shakespeare who is never taught to read or write will not create a *Hamlet*.

We normally receive 23 chromosomes from our father's sperm cell and 23 chromosomes from our mother's egg cell (ovum). When a sperm cell fertilizes an ovum, the chromosomes form 23 pairs. The 23rd pair consists of **sex chromosomes**, which determine whether we are female or male. We all receive an X sex chromosome (so called because of the X shape) from our mother. If we also receive an X sex chromosome from our father, we develop into a female. If we receive a Y sex chromosome (named after the Y shape) from our father, we develop into a male. Chapter 8 will explain further the changes that happen throughout the life span, from conception to death, depending on these initial genetic assignments.

When people do not have the normal number of 46 chromosomes (23 pairs), physical and behavioural abnormalities may result. Most persons with **Down syndrome**, for example, have an extra, or third, chromosome on the 21st pair. Persons with Down syndrome have a downward-sloping fold of skin at the inner corners of the eyes, a round face, a protruding tongue, and a broad, flat nose. They are cognitively impaired and usually have physical problems that cause death by middle age (Schupf, 2000).

polygenic
referring to traits that are influenced by combinations of genes

genotype
one's genetic makeup, based on the sequencing of the nucleotides we term A, C, G, and T

phenotype
one's actual development and appearance, as based on one's genotype and environmental influences

nature
the inborn, innate character of an organism

nurture
the sum total of the environmental factors that affect an organism from conception onward

sex chromosomes
the 23rd pair of chromosomes, whose genetic material determines the sex of the individual

Down syndrome
a condition caused by an extra chromosome on the 21st pair and characterized by mental deficiency, a broad face, and slanting eyes

Kinship Studies

What are kinship studies? Kinship studies are ways in which psychologists compare the presence of traits and behaviour patterns in people who are biologically related or unrelated to help determine the role of genetic factors in their occurrence. The more *closely* people are related, the more *genes* they have in common. Identical twins share 100 percent of their genes. Parents and children have 50 percent of their genes in common, as do siblings (brothers and sisters). Aunts and uncles related by blood have a 25 percent overlap with nieces and nephews. First cousins share 12.5 percent of their genes. If genes are involved in a trait or behaviour pattern, people who are more closely related should be more likely to show similar traits or behaviour. Psychologists and behavioural geneticists are especially interested in running kinship studies with twins and adopted individuals (Plomin, 2002).

Twin Studies

The fertilized egg cell (ovum) that carries genetic messages from both parents is called a *zygote*. Now and then, a zygote divides into two cells that separate, so that instead of developing into a single person, it develops into two people with the same genetic makeup. Such people are identical, or **monozygotic (MZ)**, **twins**. If the woman releases two ova in the same month and they are both fertilized, they develop into fraternal, or **dizygotic (DZ)**, twins. DZ twins, like other siblings, share 50 percent of their genes. MZ twins are important in the study of the relative influences of nature (heredity) and nurture (the environment) because differences between MZ twins are the result of nurture. (They do not differ in their heredity—that is, their nature—because their genetic makeup is the same.)

Twin studies compare the presence of traits and behaviour patterns in MZ twins, DZ twins, and other people to help determine the role of genetic factors in their occurrence. If MZ twins show greater similarity on a trait or behaviour pattern than DZ twins, a genetic basis for the trait or behaviour is suggested.

Twin studies show how strongly genetic factors influence physical features. MZ twins are more likely to look alike and to be similar in height, even to have more similar cholesterol levels than DZ twins. MZ twins also resemble one another more strongly than DZ twins in intelligence and personality traits like sociability, anxiety, friendliness, conformity, and even happiness (Markon et al., 2002; McCourt et al., 1999; McCrae et al., 2000). MZ twins are also more likely than DZ twins to share psychological disorders such as autism, depression, schizophrenia, and even vulnerability to alcoholism (McGue et al., 1992; Plomin, 2000; Veenstra-Vanderweele & Cook, 2003).

Of course, twin studies are not perfect. MZ twins may resemble each other more closely than DZ twins partly because they are treated more similarly. MZ twins frequently are dressed identically, and parents sometimes have difficulty telling them apart.

One way to get around this difficulty is to find and compare MZ twins who were reared in different homes. Then, any similarities between MZ twins reared apart could not be explained by a shared home environment and would appear to be largely a result of heredity. In the fascinating *Minnesota Study of Twins Reared Apart* (Bouchard et al., 1990; DiLalla et al., 1999; Markon et al., 2002), researchers have been measuring the physiological and psychological characteristics of 56 sets of MZ adult twins who were separated in infancy and reared in different homes.

Research shows that MZ twin sisters begin to menstruate about one to two months apart, whereas DZ twins begin to menstruate about a year apart. MZ twins are more alike than DZ twins in their blood pressure, brain wave patterns, even in their speech patterns, gestures, and mannerisms (Hansell et al., 2001; Lensvelt-Mulders & Hettema, 2001; Lykken et al., 1992).

The Canadian Press/Darryl Dyck

Henrik and Daniel Sedin are identical twin brothers who were born in Sweden. The pair are known for their ability to play off each other and have been an asset to the Vancouver Canucks since they joined in 2000.

In sum, MZ twins reared apart are about as similar as MZ twins reared together on a variety of measures of intelligence, personality, temperament, occupational and leisure-time interests, and social attitudes. These traits thus would appear to have a genetic underpinning.

Adoption Studies

The results of kinship studies can be confused when relatives share similar environments as well as genes. Adoption studies overcome some of this problem by comparing children who have been separated from their parents at an early age (or in which identical twins are separated at an early age) and reared in different environments. Psychologists look for similarities between children and their adoptive and biological parents. When children reared by adoptive parents are more similar to their biological parents in a particular trait, strong evidence exists for a genetic role in the development of that trait.

In later chapters we will see that psychologists have been particularly interested in the use of adoption studies to sort out the effects of nature and nurture in the development of personality traits, intelligence, and various psychological disorders. Such traits and disorders apparently represent the interaction of complex groupings of genes as well as environmental influences.

Visit **icanpsych.com** to find the resources you need today!

Located at the back of the textbook are rip-out Chapter in Review cards. Make sure you also go online to check out other tools that PSYCH offers to help you successfully pass your course.

- Flashcards
- Glossary
- Test Yourself
- Videos
- Games
- Interactive Quizzing
- Audio Chapter Reviews

3

Sensation and Perception

Learning Outcomes

LO 1 Define and differentiate between sensation and perception

LO 2 Identify the parts of the eye; explain the properties of light and the theories of colour vision

LO 3 Describe how visual perception is organized

LO 4 Identify the parts of the ear; describe the sense of hearing

LO 5 Describe the chemical senses

LO 6 Explain the properties of the skin senses and theoretical explanations for pain

LO 7 Describe the kinesthetic and vestibular senses

LO 8 Explain why psychologists are skeptical about extra sensory perception

> ## " *The witnesses sensed information with their eyes, but they were unable to perceive what they were seeing.* "

At 7:20 p.m. on November 7, 1990, a woman swimming in a rooftop hotel pool in Montreal saw something puzzling in the sky. Something appeared to be floating above the 17-storey hotel, and it projected beams of light that slowly rotated around it. Confused by what she saw, she calmly asked the lifeguard if he could see the object. He also saw it, so they contacted the hotel security to come and take a look.

Overwhelmed by what he saw in the sky, the security guard called the police, who sent some officers to investigate. A call was also made to *La Presse*, a local Montreal newspaper, which dispatched a reporter to the scene. All who arrived, including the acting police director, were amazed at what they saw. They all gaped at a round metallic object that projected four sets of three beams of light, and was, in the words of one officer, "gigantic." Photos were taken of the object, and then at 10:10 p.m., almost three hours after it was first noticed in the sky, the object vanished.

Calls to the RCMP, the airport, and the military all ended with no explanation for what the score of witnesses had seen that night. One further witness, who was driving on a nearby highway, reported seeing an object at 10:30 p.m. on the same evening, moving from one Montreal landmark to a nearby power station. Strangely, the power station reported a sudden loss of power at the same time given in the witness's account. This witness reported hearing a purring sound as the object moved across the sky.

Four years later after a careful investigation, the conclusion was reached that all the independent witnesses and photographic evidence suggest that something was there, but exactly what it was is still unknown (Canadian Broadcasting Corporation, 2007). What the witnesses and investigators experienced that strange night was sensation with little or no perception. In casual use, the words "sensation" and "perception" are often interchanged, but in psychology they have very specific meanings. The

DID YOU KNOW ?

- People have more than five senses.
- If we could see waves of light with slightly longer wavelengths, warm-blooded animals would glow in the dark.
- People sometimes hear what they want to hear.
- When we mix red and green light, we obtain yellow light. However, mixing red and green paint makes brown paint.
- Many people experience pain "in" limbs that have been amputated.
- After much study, there is no adequate scientific evidence that people can read other people's minds. If you can prove otherwise, you may be $1 000 000 richer.

witnesses of the strange glowing object sensed information with their eyes, and another witness sensed a sound with his ears, but they were unable to understand— that is, to actually perceive—what they were seeing and hearing. Psychologists are interested in studying how these two systems are intimately linked to one another.

sensation
the stimulation of sensory receptors and the transmission of sensory information to the central nervous system

perception
the process by which sensations are organized into an inner representation of the world

absolute threshold
the minimal amount of energy that can produce a sensation

pitch
the highness or lowness of a sound, as determined by the frequency of the sound waves

difference threshold
the minimal difference in intensity required between two sources of energy so that they will be perceived as being different

So now we will explore how we first sense our outside world (sensation), and then organize and understand (perception) what we have just sensed.

LO1 Sensation and Perception

What are sensation and perception? **Sensation** is the stimulation of sensory receptors and the transmission of sensory information to the central nervous system (the spinal cord or brain). Sensory receptors are located in sensory organs such as the eyes and ears, the skin, and elsewhere in the body. Stimulation of the senses is an automatic process. It results from sources of energy, like light and sound, or from the presence of chemicals, as in smell and taste.

Perception is not automatic. Perception is an active process in which sensations are organized and interpreted to form an inner representation of the world. Perception may begin with sensation, but it also reflects our experiences and expectations as it makes sense of sensory stimuli. A person standing five metres away and a 30-centimetre-tall doll right next to you may cast similar-sized images on the back of your eye, but whether you interpret the shape to be a ruler-sized doll or a full-grown person five metres away is a matter of perception that depends on your experience with dolls, people, and distance.

In this chapter you will see that your perception of the world of changing sights, sounds, and other sources of sensory input depends largely on the so-called five senses: vision, hearing, smell, taste, and touch. But touch is just one of several "skin senses," which also include pressure, warmth, cold, and pain. There are also senses that alert you to your own body position without your having to watch every step you take. As we explore each of these senses, we will find that similar sensations may lead to different perceptions in different people—such that strange objects in the sky are perceived as alien visitors to some, and naturally occurring atmospheric activity (the northern lights) to others.

Before we begin our exploration of the senses, let us consider a number of concepts that apply to all of them: *absolute threshold, difference threshold, signal-detection theory,* and *sensory adaptation.* In doing so, we will learn why we can dim the lights gradually to near darkness without anyone noticing. We will also learn why we might become indifferent to the savoury aromas of delightful dinners. *How do we know when something is there? How do we know when it has changed?*

Absolute Threshold

Nineteenth-century German psychologist Gustav Fechner used the term **absolute threshold** to refer to the weakest amount of a stimulus that a person can distinguish from no stimulus at all. For example, the absolute threshold for light would be the minimum brightness (physical energy) required to activate the visual sensory system.

Psychophysicists look for the absolute thresholds of the senses by exposing individuals to progressively stronger stimuli until they find the minimum stimuli that the person can detect 50 percent of the time. These absolute thresholds are not all that absolute, however. Some people are more sensitive than others, and even the same person might have a slightly different response at different times. Nevertheless, under ideal conditions, our ability to detect stimuli is quite sensitive. (See the box feature on the next page.)

How different our lives would be if the absolute thresholds for the human senses differed! If your ears were sensitive to sounds that are lower in **pitch**, you might hear the collisions among molecules of air. If you could see light with slightly longer wavelengths, you would see infrared light waves. Your world would be transformed because heat generates infrared light.

Difference Threshold

How much of a difference in intensity between two lights is required before you will detect one as being brighter than the other? The minimum difference in magnitude of two stimuli required to tell them apart is their **difference threshold**. As with the absolute threshold, psychologists agree to the standard of a difference in strength that can be detected 50 percent of the time.

Psychophysicist Ernst Weber discovered through laboratory research that the threshold for perceiving differences in the intensity of light is about 2 percent (actually closer to 1/60) of their intensity. This fraction, 1/60, is known as **Weber's constant** for light. A related concept is the **just noticeable difference (jnd)**—the minimum difference in stimuli that a person can detect. For example, at least 50 percent of the time, most people can tell if a light becomes just 1/60 brighter or dimmer. Weber's constant for light holds whether we are comparing moderately bright lights or moderately dull lights. But it becomes inaccurate when we compare extremely bright or extremely dull lights.

Weber's constant for noticing differences in lifted weight is 1/53. (Round it off to 1/50, or 2 percent.) That means if you are strong enough to heft a 45-kilogram barbell, you would not notice that it was heavier until about one kilogram was added. Yet if you are a runner who carries two half-kilogram dumbbells, you would definitely notice if someone slipped you another two half-kilogram dumbbells because the increase would be 100 percent.

What about sound? People are most sensitive to changes in the pitch (frequency) of sounds. The Weber constant for pitch is 1/333, meaning that on average, people can tell when a tone rises or falls in pitch by an extremely small one-third of 1 percent. (Even a small error in pitch makes singers sound sharp or flat.) Remember this when friends criticize your singing. The sense of taste is much less sensitive. On average, people cannot detect differences in saltiness of less than 20 percent. That is why "low-salt" chips that have 15 percent less salt than your favourite chips do not taste so bad.

Signal-Detection Theory

From the discussion so far, it might seem that people are simply switched on by certain amounts of stimulation. This is not quite so. People are also influenced by psychological factors. **Signal-detection theory** considers these factors. *What is signal-detection theory?*

According to signal-detection theory, the relationship between a physical stimulus and a sensory response is not fully mechanical. People's ability to detect stimuli such as blips on a radar screen depends not only on the intensity of the blips but also on their training (learning), motivation (desire to perceive blips), and psychological states such as fatigue or alertness.

Weber's constant
the fraction of the intensity by which a source of physical energy must be increased or decreased so that a difference in intensity will be perceived

just noticeable difference (jnd)
the minimal amount by which a source of energy must be increased or decreased so that a difference in intensity will be perceived

signal-detection theory
the view that the perception of sensory stimuli involves the interaction of physical, biological, and psychological factors

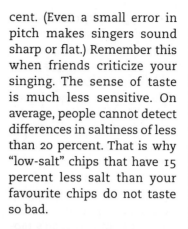

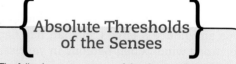

{ **Absolute Thresholds of the Senses** }

The following are measures of the absolute thresholds for the human senses of vision, hearing, taste, smell, and touch:

- *Vision:* a candle flame viewed from about 48 kilometres on a clear, dark night.
- *Hearing:* a watch ticking from about six metres away in a quiet room.
- *Taste:* 1 teaspoon of sugar dissolved in eight litres of water.
- *Smell:* about one drop of perfume diffused throughout a small house (1 part in 500 million).
- *Touch:* the pressure of the wing of a fly falling on a cheek from a distance of about one centimetre.

The intensity of the signal is one factor that determines whether people will perceive sensory stimuli (signals) or a difference between signals. Another is the degree to which the signal can be distinguished from background noise. It is easier to hear a friend speaking in a quiet room than in a room in which people are singing and clinking glasses. The sharpness of a person's biological sensory system is still another factor.

We tend to detect stimuli we are searching for. The place in which you are reading this book may be abuzz with signals. You may even be listening to music, or sitting in front of a television as you read this. If you are focusing your attention on this page, the other signals recede into the background (but if the television show becomes too interesting, or the tune or lyrics of the song catch your attention, your focus will switch and this information will recede to the background, hardly what one wants when trying to study). One psychological factor in signal detection is focusing on signals you consider important.

Feature Detectors in the Brain

Imagine you are walking out of a building on campus and notice a large Canadian flag flapping in the strong wind. When neurons in your sensory organs—in this case, your eyes—are stimulated by the flowing fabric of the flag, they relay information to the sensory cortex in the brain. Windsor, Ontario, native David Hubel and Torsten Wiesel (1979) were awarded the Nobel Prize when they discovered that various neurons in the visual cortex of the brain fire in response to particular features of the visual input. *What are feature detectors?* Many cells in the brain detect (i.e., fire in response to) lines presented at various angles—vertical, horizontal, and in between. Other cells fire in response

I think I can hear a watch on the previous page.

to specific colours. Because they respond to different aspects or features of a scene, these brain cells are termed **feature detectors**. In the example of the flag, visual feature detectors respond to the flag's edges, depth, contours, textures, shadows, and kinds of motion (up, down, forward, and back). There are also feature detectors for other senses. Auditory feature detectors, for example, respond to the pitch, loudness (such as the fabric snapping in the wind), and other aspects of the sounds of the flapping flag.

Sensory Adaptation

Our sensory systems are admirably suited to a changing environment. *How do our sensory systems adapt to a changing environment?* **Sensory adaptation** refers to the processes by which we become more sensitive to stimuli of low magnitude and less sensitive to stimuli that remain the same, such as the background noises outside the window.

Consider how the visual sense adapts to lower intensities of light. When we first walk into a darkened movie theatre, we see little but the images on the screen. As we search for our seats, however, we become increasingly sensitive to the faces around us and to the features of the theatre. The process of becoming more sensitive to stimulation is referred to as **sensitization**, or *positive adaptation*.

But we become less sensitive to constant stimulation. When we live in a city, for example, we become desensitized to sounds of traffic except, perhaps, for the occasional backfire or siren. The process of becoming less sensitive to stimulation is referred to as **desensitization**, or *negative adaptation*.

Our sensitivities to stimulation provide our brains with information that we use to understand and influence the world outside. Therefore, it is not surprising that psychologists study the ways in which

© Carmen Martinez Banus/iStockphoto.com

we sense and perceive this information—through vision, hearing, the chemical senses, and still other senses, as we see throughout the remainder of the chapter.

LO2 Vision

Our eyes are our biological "windows on the world." Because vision is our dominant sense, blindness is considered by many to be the most debilitating sensory loss. To understand vision, let us first "look" at light.

Light

Light is fascinating stuff. It radiates. It illuminates. It dazzles. In almost all cultures, light is a symbol of goodness and knowledge. We speak of genius as "brilliance." People who aren't in the know are said to be "in the dark." *Just what is light?*

It is visible light that triggers visual sensations. Yet visible light is just one small part of a spectrum of electromagnetic energy that surrounds us (see Figure 3.1). All forms of electromagnetic energy move in waves, and different kinds of electromagnetic energy have signature wavelengths:

> **hue**
> the colour of light, as determined by its wavelength

- *Cosmic rays:* The wavelengths of these rays from outer space are only about a *trillionth* of a centimetre long.
- *Radio waves:* Some radio signals extend for many kilometres.
- *Visible light:* Roses are red, and violets are blue. Why? Different colours have different wavelengths, with violet the shortest at about 400 *billionths* of a metre in length and red the longest at 700 billionths of a metre.

Sir Isaac Newton, the British scientist, discovered that sunlight could be broken down into different colours by means of a triangular solid of glass called a *prism* (see Figure 3.1). You can remember the colours of the spectrum, from longest to shortest wavelengths, by using the mnemonic device *Roy G. Biv* (red, orange, yellow, green, blue, indigo, violet). The wavelength of visible light determines its colour, or **hue**. The wavelength for red is longer than the wavelength for orange, and so on, through the spectrum.

FIGURE 3.1

The Visible Spectrum

By passing a source of white light, such as sunlight, through a prism, we break it down into the colours of the visible spectrum. The visible spectrum is just a narrow segment of the electromagnetic spectrum. The electromagnetic spectrum also includes radio waves, microwaves, X rays, cosmic rays, and many others. Different forms of electromagnetic energy have wavelengths that vary from a few trillionths of a metre to thousands of kilometres. Visible light varies in wavelength from about 400 to 700 *billionths* of a metre.

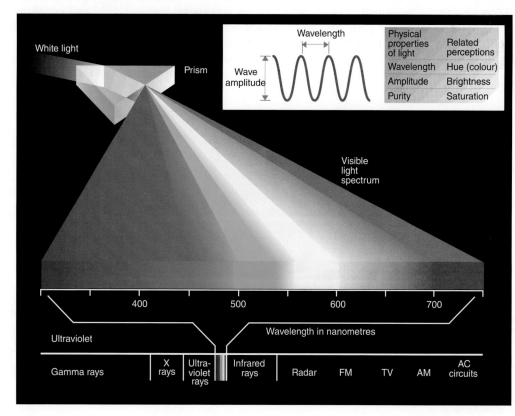

The Eye

How does the eye work? Look at the major parts of the eye, as shown in Figure 3.2. As with a camera, light enters through a narrow opening and is projected onto a sensitive surface. Light first passes through the transparent **cornea**, which covers the front of the eye's surface. (The "white" of the eye, or *sclera*, is composed of hard protective tissue.) The amount of light that passes through the cornea is determined by the size of the opening of the muscle called the iris, which is the coloured part of the eye. The opening in the iris is the pupil. The size of the pupil adjusts automatically to the amount of light present. Therefore, you do not have to purposefully open your eyes farther to see better in low lighting. The more intense the light, the smaller the opening. Pupil size is also sensitive to your emotions: We can be truly "wide-eyed with fear."

Once light passes through the iris, it encounters the **lens**. The lens adjusts or accommodates to the image by changing its thickness. Changes in thickness permit a clear image of the object to be projected onto the retina. These changes focus the light according to the distance of the object from the viewer. If you hold a finger at arm's length and slowly bring it toward your nose, you will feel tension in the eye as the thickness of the lens accommodates to keep the retinal image in focus. When people squint to bring an object into focus, they are adjusting the thickness of the lens.

The **retina** consists of cells called **photoreceptors** that are sensitive to light (photosensitive). There are two types of photoreceptors: *rods* and *cones*. The retina (see Figure 3.2) contains several layers of cells: the rods and cones, **bipolar cells**, and **ganglion cells**. All of these cells are neurons. The rods and cones respond to light with chemical changes that create neural impulses that are picked up by the bipolar cells. These then activate the ganglion cells. The axons of the million or so ganglion cells in our retina converge to form the **optic nerve**. The optic nerve conducts sensory input to the brain, where it is relayed to the visual area of the occipital lobe. As if this were not enough, the eye has additional neurons to enhance this process. Amacrine cells and horizontal cells make sideways connections at a level near the rods and cones and at another level near the ganglion cells. As a result, single bipolar cells can pick up signals from many rods and cones, and, in turn, a single ganglion cell is able to funnel information from multiple bipolar cells. In fact, rods and cones outnumber ganglion cells by more than 100 to 1.

FIGURE 3.2

The Human Eye

In both the eye and a camera, light enters through a narrow opening and is projected onto a sensitive surface. In the eye, the photosensitive surface is called the *retina*, and information concerning the changing images on the retina is transmitted to the brain. The retina contains photoreceptors called *rods* and *cones*. Rods and cones transmit sensory input back through the bipolar neurons to the ganglion neurons. The axons of the ganglion neurons form the optic nerve, which transmits sensory stimulation through the brain to the visual cortex of the occipital lobe.

Go to www.icanpsych.com to access an interactive version of this figure.

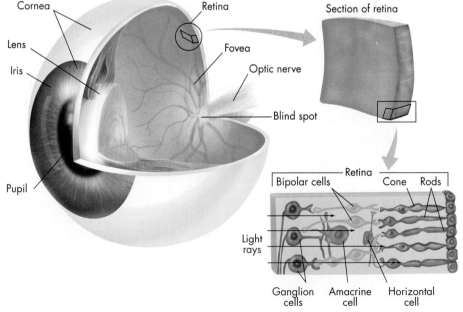

Rods and Cones

Rods and **cones** are the photoreceptors in the retina (see Figure 3.2). About 125 million rods and 6.4 million cones are distributed across the retina. The cones are most densely packed in a small spot at the centre of the retina called the *fovea* (see Figure 3.2). Visual acuity (sharpness and detail) is greatest at this spot. The **fovea** is composed almost exclusively of cones. Rods are most dense just outside the fovea and thin out toward the periphery of the retina.

Rods allow us to see in black and white. Cones provide colour vision. Rods are more sensitive to dim light than cones are. Therefore, as light grows dim during the evening hours, objects appear to lose their colour before their outlines fade from view.

In contrast to the visual acuity of the fovea is the **blind spot**, which is insensitive to visual stimulation. It is the part of the retina where the axons of the ganglion cells converge to form the optic nerve (see Figure 3.2). Figure 3.3 will help you "view" your blind spot.

Visual acuity (sharpness of vision) is connected with the shape of the eye. People who have to be unusually close to an object to discriminate its details are *nearsighted*. People who see distant objects unusually clearly but have difficulty focusing on nearby objects are *farsighted*. Nearsightedness can result when the eyeball is elongated such that the images of distant objects are focused in front of the retina. When the eyeball is too short, the images of nearby objects are focused behind the retina, causing farsightedness. Eyeglasses or contact lenses help nearsighted people focus distant objects on their retinas. Laser surgery can correct vision by changing the shape of the eye. Farsighted people usually see well enough without eyeglasses until they reach their middle years, when they may need glasses for reading.

Beginning in middle age—the late 30s to the mid-40s—the lenses of the eye start to grow brittle, making it more difficult to accommodate to, or focus on, objects. This condition is called **presbyopia**, from the Greek words for "old man" and "eyes." Presbyopia makes it difficult to perceive nearby visual stimuli. People who had normal visual acuity in their youth often require corrective lenses to read in middle adulthood.

Light Adaptation

When we walk out onto a dark street, we may at first not be able to see people, trees, and cars clearly. But as time goes on, we are better able to discriminate the features of people and objects. The process of adjusting to lower lighting is called **dark adaptation**.

The amount of light needed for detection is a function of the amount of time spent in the dark. The cones and rods adapt at different rates. The cones, which permit perception of colour, reach their maximum adaptation to darkness in about 10 minutes. The rods, which allow perception of light and dark only, are more sensitive to dim light and continue to adapt for 45 minutes or so.

Adaptation to brighter lighting conditions takes place more rapidly. For instance, when you emerge from the theatre into the brilliance of the afternoon, you may at first be painfully surprised by the featureless blaze around you. But within a minute or so of entering the street, the brightness of the scene dims and objects regain their edges.

rods
rod-shaped photoreceptors that are sensitive only to the intensity of light

cones
cone-shaped photoreceptors that transmit sensations of colour

fovea
an area near the centre of the retina that is dense with cones and where vision is consequently most acute

blind spot
the area of the retina where axons from ganglion cells meet to form the optic nerve

visual acuity
sharpness of vision

presbyopia
a condition characterized by brittleness of the lens

dark adaptation
the process of adjusting to conditions of lower lighting by increasing the sensitivity of rods and cones

FIGURE 3.3

The Blind Spot

To try a "disappearing act," close your left eye, hold the book close to your face, and look at the boy with your right eye. Slowly move the book away until the pie disappears. The pie disappears because it is being projected onto the blind spot of your retina, the point at which the axons of ganglion neurons collect to form the optic nerve. Note that when the pie disappears, your brain "fills in" the missing checkerboard pattern, which is one reason that you're not usually aware that you have blind spots.

complementary
descriptive of colours of the spectrum that when combined produce white or nearly white light

Colour Vision

For most of us, the world is a place of brilliant colours. Colour is an emotional and aesthetic part of our everyday lives. In this section we explore some of the dimensions of colour and then examine theories about how we manage to convert different wavelengths of light into perceptions of colour. *What are some perceptual dimensions of colour?* These include hue, value, and saturation.

The wavelength of light determines its colour, or *hue*. The value of a colour is its degree of lightness or darkness. The saturation refers to how intense a colour appears to us. A fire-engine red is more saturated than a pale pinkish red.

Colours also have psychological associations within various cultural settings. For example, in Canada a bride may be dressed in white as a sign of purity. In traditional India, the guests would be shocked, because white is the colour for funerals. Here we mourn in black.

If we bend the colours of the spectrum into a circle, we create a colour wheel, as shown in Figure 3.4. The colours on the green–blue side of the colour wheel are considered to be cool in temperature. Those colours on the yellow–orange–red side are considered to be warm.

 FIGURE 3.4

The Colour Wheel

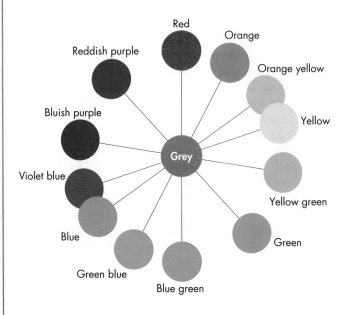

Complementary Colours

The colours across from one another on the colour wheel are labelled **complementary**. Red–green and blue–yellow are the major complementary pairs. If we mix complementary colours together, they dissolve into grey.

"But wait!" you say. "Blue and yellow cannot be complementary because by mixing pigments of blue and yellow we create green, not grey." True enough, but we have been talking about mixing *lights*, not *pigments*. Light is the source of all colour. Pigments reflect and absorb different wavelengths of light selectively. The mixture of lights is an *additive* process. The mixture of pigments is *subtractive*. Figure 3.5 shows mixtures of lights and pigments of various colours.

Pigments gain their colours by absorbing light from certain segments of the spectrum and reflecting the rest. For example, we see most plant life as green because the pigment in chlorophyll absorbs most of the red, blue, and violet wavelengths of light. The remaining green is reflected. A red pigment absorbs most of the spectrum but reflects red. White pigments reflect all colours equally. Black pigments reflect very little light.

Afterimages

Try this experiment: Look at the strangely coloured Canadian flag in Figure 3.6 for at least half a minute. Try not to blink as you are doing so. Then look at a sheet of white or light grey paper. What has

Try It!

You can experience how different vision is with one eye adapted to bright light conditions and one to dark adaptation with this simple exercise. When you wake up tonight to go to the bathroom, place the palm of your hand securely over your left eye before you turn the light on. When the light is turned on, your covered eye will remain adapted to the dark (very little light will penetrate both your palm and your eyelid), whereas your other eye will adjust quickly to the bright light of the bathroom. After you are done and you turn the light out again, remove your palm and your brain will be receiving two very different images. Your one eye will be fully adjusted to bright light conditions and be sending very little information to the brain, whereas your dark-adapted eye will be sending plenty of information, as it is still able to receive the low-light information about the features and details of the dark room you are in (careful getting back into bed; some people find seeing with only one eye disorienting).

FIGURE 3.5

The mixture of lights is an *additive* process.

The mixture of pigments is *subtractive*.

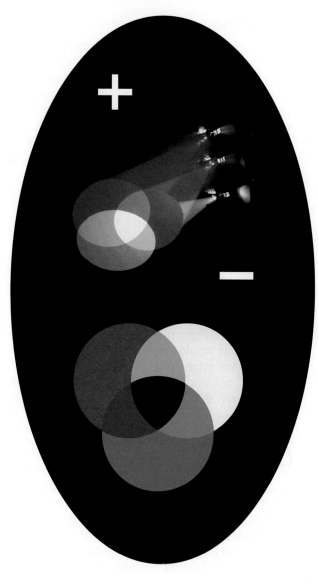

Theories of Colour Vision

Adults with normal colour vision can discriminate thousands of colours across the visible spectrum. Different colours have different wavelengths. Although we can vary the physical wavelengths of light in a continuous manner from shorter to longer, many changes in colour are discontinuous. Our perception of a colour shifts suddenly from blue to green, even though the change in wavelength may be smaller than that between two blues.

How do we perceive colour? Why are roses red and violets blue? Our perception of colour depends on the physical properties of an object and on the eye's transmission of different messages to the brain when lights with different wavelengths stimulate the cones in the retina.

There are two main theories of colour vision: the trichromatic theory and the opponent-process theory (Gegenfurtner & Kiper, 2003). Trichromatic theory is based on an experiment conducted by the British scientist Thomas Young in the early 1800s. As in Figure 3.5, Young projected red, green, and blue-violet lights onto a screen so that they partly overlapped. He found that he could create any colour in the visible spectrum by varying the intensities of the three lights. When all three lights fell on the same spot, they created white light, or the appearance of no colour at all.

The German physiologist Hermann von Helmholtz saw in Young's discovery an explanation of colour vision. Helmholtz suggested that the retina in the eye must have three different types of colour photoreceptors or cones. Some cones must be sensitive to red

afterimage
the lingering visual impression made by a stimulus that has been removed

trichromatic theory
the theory that colour vision is made possible by three types of cones, some of which respond to red light, some to green, and some to blue

FIGURE 3.6

Place a sheet of white paper beneath the book and stare at the black dot in the centre of the flag for at least 30 seconds. Then remove the book. The afterimage on the paper beneath will look familiar.

happened to the flag? If your colour vision is working properly, and if you looked at the miscoloured flag long enough, you should see a flag composed of the familiar red and white. The flag you perceive on the white sheet of paper is an **afterimage** of the first. (If you didn't look at the green and black flag long enough the first time, try it again.) In afterimages, persistent sensations of colour are followed by perception of the complementary colour when the first colour is removed. The same holds true for black and white. Staring at one will create an afterimage of the other. The phenomenon of afterimages has contributed to one of the theories of colour vision, as we will see.

opponent-process theory
the theory that colour vision is made possible by three types of cones, some of which respond to red or green light, some to blue or yellow, and some to the intensity of light

trichromat
a person with normal colour vision

monochromat
a person who is sensitive to black and white only and hence colourblind

dichromat
a person who is sensitive to black–white and either red–green or blue–yellow and hence partially colourblind

light, some to green, and some to blue. We see other colours when various colour receptors are stimulated simultaneously. For example, we perceive yellow when the receptors for red and green are firing.

In 1870, another German physiologist, Ewald Hering, proposed the **opponent-process theory** of colour vision: There are three types of colour receptors, but they are not sensitive only to red, green, and blue, as Helmholtz had claimed. Hering suggested instead that afterimages (such as that of the Canadian flag shown in Figure 3.6) are made possible by three types of colour receptors: red–green, blue–yellow, and a type that perceives differences in brightness. According to Hering, a red–green cone cannot transmit messages for red and green at the same time. Therefore, staring at the green and black flag for 30 seconds will disturb the balance of neural activity. The afterimage of red and white would represent the eye's attempt to re-establish a balance.

Research suggests that each theory of colour vision is partially correct (Li & DeVries, 2004; Shapley & Hawken, 2002). For example, research shows that some cones are sensitive to blue, some to green, and some to red. However, cones appear to be connected by bipolar and ganglion neurons such that the messages produced by the cones are transmitted to the brain in an opponent-process fashion (Hornstein et al., 2004; Suttle et al., 2002).

A neural rebound effect apparently helps explain the occurrence of afterimages. That is, a green-sensitive ganglion that had been excited by green light for half a minute or so might switch briefly to inhibitory activity when the light is shut off. The effect would be to perceive red even though no red light is present (Hornstein et al., 2004).

Colour Blindness

If you can discriminate among the colours of the visible spectrum, you have normal colour vision and are labelled a **trichromat**. This means that you are sensitive to red–green, blue–yellow, and light–dark. *What is colour blindness? Why are some people colourblind?* People who are totally colourblind, called **monochromats**, are sensitive only to lightness and darkness. Total colour blindness is rare. Fully colourblind individuals see the world as trichromats would in a black-and-white movie.

Partial colour blindness is a sex-linked trait that mostly affects males. Partially colourblind people are called **dichromats**. They can discriminate only between two colours—red and green or blue and yellow—and the colours that are derived from mixing these colours (Loop et al., 2003). Figure 3.7 shows the types of tests that are used to diagnose colour blindness.

A dichromat might put on one red sock and one green sock, but would not mix red and blue socks. Monochromats might put on socks of any colour. They would not notice a difference as long as the socks' colours did not differ in intensity—that is, brightness.

LO3 Visual Perception

What do you see in Figure 3.8—meaningless splotches of ink or a rider on horseback? If you perceive a horse and rider, it is not just because of the visual sensations provided by the drawing. Each of the blobs is meaningless in and of itself, and the pattern is vague. Despite the lack of clarity, however, you may still perceive a horse and rider.

FIGURE 3.7

Plates from a Test for Colour Blindness

Can you see the numbers in these plates from a test for colour blindness? A person with red–green colour blindness would not be able to see the 6, and a person with blue–yellow colour blindness would probably not discern the 12. (Caution: These reproductions cannot be used for actual testing of colour blindness.)

FIGURE 3.8

Closure

Meaningless splotches of ink, or a horse and rider? This figure illustrates the Gestalt principle of closure.

Visual perception is the process by which we organize or make sense of the sensory impressions caused by the light that strikes our eyes. Visual perception involves our knowledge, expectations, and motivations. Whereas sensation may be thought of as a mechanical process (e.g., light stimulating the rods and cones of our retina), perception is an active process through which we interpret the world around us.

How do we organize bits of visual information into meaningful wholes? The answer has something to do with your general knowledge and your desire to fit incoming bits and pieces of information into familiar patterns. In the case of the horse and rider, your integration of disconnected pieces of information into a meaningful whole also reflects the principle of closure—that is, the tendency to perceive a complete or whole figure even when there are gaps in the sensory input.

Perceptual Organization

Early in the 20th century, Gestalt psychologists noted certain consistencies in the way we integrate bits and pieces of sensory stimulation into meaningful wholes. They attempted to identify the rules that govern these processes. As a group, these rules are referred to as the *laws of perceptual organization.*

Figure–Ground Perception

If you look out your window, you may see people, buildings, cars, and streets, or perhaps grass, trees, birds, and clouds. These objects tend to be perceived as figures against backgrounds. For instance, individual cars seen against the background of the street are easier to pick out than cars piled on top of one another in a junkyard.

When figure–ground relationships are *ambiguous,* or capable of being interpreted in various ways, our perceptions tend to be unstable and shift back and forth (Bull et al., 2003).

Figure 3.9 shows a Rubin vase, one of psychologists' favourite illustrations of figure–ground relationships. The figure–ground relationship in part

A of the figure is ambiguous. There are no cues that suggest which area must be the figure. For this reason, our perception may shift from seeing the vase to seeing two profiles. There is no such problem in part B. Because it seems that a blue vase has been brought forward against a coloured ground, we are more likely to perceive the vase than the profiles. In part C, we are more likely to perceive the profiles than the vase, because the profiles are complete and the vase is broken against the background. Of course, if we wish to, we can still perceive the vase in part C, because experience has shown us where it is.

closure
the tendency to perceive a broken figure as being complete or whole

proximity
nearness; the perceptual tendency to group together objects that are near one another

similarity
the perceptual tendency to group together objects that are similar in appearance

Other Gestalt Rules for Organization

Gestalt psychologists have noted that our perceptions are also guided by rules or laws of *closure, proximity, similarity, continuity,* and *common fate.*

Let's try a mini-experiment. Without reading further, describe part A of Figure 3.10 (page 64). Did you say it consists of six lines or of three groups of two parallel lines? If you said three sets of lines, you were influenced by the **proximity**, or nearness, of some of the lines. There is no other reason for perceiving them in pairs or subgroups: All lines are parallel and equal in length.

Now describe part B of Figure 3.10. Did you perceive the figure as a six-by-six grid, or as three columns of *x*'s and three columns of *o*'s? According to the law of **similarity**, we perceive similar objects as belonging together. For this reason, you may have been more likely to describe part B in terms of columns than in terms of rows or a grid.

What of part C? Is it a circle with two lines stemming from it, or is it a (broken) line that goes through a circle? If you saw it as a single (broken) line, you

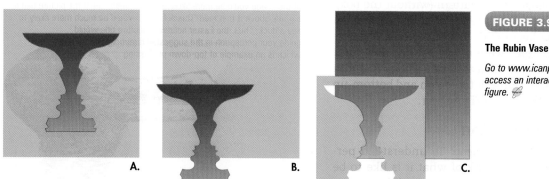

A.   B.   C.

FIGURE 3.9

The Rubin Vase

Go to www.icanpsych.com to access an interactive version of this figure.

texture gradient
a monocular cue for depth based on the perception that closer objects appear to have rougher (more detailed) surfaces

motion parallax
a monocular cue for depth based on the perception that nearby objects appear to move more rapidly in relation to our own motion

binocular cues
stimuli suggestive of depth that involve simultaneous perception by both eyes

retinal disparity
a binocular cue for depth based on the difference in the image cast by an object on the retinas of the eyes as the object moves closer or farther away

convergence
a binocular cue for depth based on the inward movement of the eyes as they attempt to focus on an object that is drawing nearer

size constancy
the tendency to perceive an object as being the same size even as the size of its retinal image changes according to the object's distance

colour constancy
the tendency to perceive an object as being the same colour even though lighting conditions change its appearance

part of Figure 3.12, the left circle is perceived as a two-dimensional circle, but the right circle tends to be perceived as a three-dimensional sphere because of the highlight on its surface and the shadow underneath. In the "sphere," the highlighted central area is perceived as closest to us, with the surface receding to the edges.

Another monocular cue is **texture gradient**. (A gradient is a progressive change.) Closer objects are perceived as having rougher textures.

Motion cues are another kind of monocular cue. If you have ever driven in the country, you have probably noticed that distant objects such as mountains and stars appear to move along with you. Objects at an intermediate distance seem to be stationary, but nearby objects such as roadside markers, rocks, and trees seem to go by quite rapidly. The tendency of objects to seem to move backward or forward as a function of their distance is known as **motion parallax**. We learn to perceive objects that appear to move with us as being at greater distances.

Earlier we noted that nearby objects cause the lens of the eye to accommodate or bend more in order to bring them into focus. The sensations of tension in the eye muscles also provide a monocular cue to depth, especially when we are within about one metre of the object.

Binocular Cues

Binocular cues, or cues that involve both eyes, also help us perceive depth. Two binocular cues are *retinal disparity* and *convergence*.

Try an experiment. Hold your right index finger at arm's length. Now hold your left index finger about 30 centimetres closer, but in a direct line. If you keep

your eyes relaxed as you do so, you will see first one finger and then the other. An image of each finger will be projected onto the retina of each eye, and each image will be slightly different because the finger will be seen from different angles. The difference between the projected images is referred to as **retinal disparity** and serves as a binocular cue for depth perception. Note that in the case of the closer finger, the "two fingers" appear to be farther apart. Closer objects have greater retinal disparity.

If we try to maintain a single image of the closer finger, our eyes must turn inward, or converge on it, making us cross-eyed. **Convergence** causes feelings of tension in the eye muscles and provides another binocular cue for depth. (After convergence occurs, try looking at the finger first with one eye closed, then the other. You will readily see how different the images are in each eye.) The binocular cues of retinal disparity and convergence are strongest when objects are close.

Perceptual Constancies

Think how confusing it would be if you believed that a door was a trapezoid and not a rectangle because it is ajar. Fortunately, perceptual constancies enable us to recognize objects even when their apparent shape or size differs. *What are perceptual constancies?*

Size Constancy

There are a number of perceptual constancies, including that of **size constancy**. The image of a dog seen from seven metres away occupies about the same amount of space on your retina as a three-centimetre-long insect crawling on your hand. Yet you do not perceive the dog to be as small as the insect. Through your visual experiences you have acquired size constancy—that is, the tendency to *perceive* an object as the same size even though the size of its image on your retina varies as a function of its distance. Experience teaches us about perspective—that the same object seen at a distance appears to be smaller than when it is nearby.

Colour Constancy

Colour constancy is the tendency to perceive objects as retaining their colour even though lighting conditions may alter their appearance. Your bright yellow car may edge toward gray as the hours wend their way through twilight. But when you finally locate the car in the parking lot, you may still think of it as yellow. You expect to find a yellow car and still judge it to be "more yellow" than the (twilight-faded) red and green cars on either side of it.

FIGURE 3.13

Brightness Constancy

The orange squares within the blue squares are the same hue, yet the orange within the dark blue square is perceived as brighter. Why?

brightness constancy
the tendency to perceive an object as being just as bright even though lighting conditions change its intensity

shape constancy
the tendency to perceive an object as being the same shape although the retinal image varies in shape as it rotates

Brightness constancy is similar to colour constancy. Consider Figure 3.13. The orange squares within the blue squares are equally bright, yet the one within the dark blue square is perceived as brighter. Why? Again, consider the role of experience. If it were night-time, we would expect orange to fade to grey. The fact that the orange within the dark square stimulates the eye with equal intensity suggests that it must be much brighter than the orange within the lighter square.

Shape Constancy

Shape constancy is the tendency to perceive objects as maintaining their shape, even if we look at them from different angles so that the shape of their image on the retina changes dramatically. You perceive the top of a coffee cup or a glass to be a circle even though it is a circle only when seen from above. When seen from an angle, it is an ellipse. When the cup or glass is seen on edge, its retinal image is the same as that of a straight line. So why do you still describe the rim of the cup or glass as a circle? Perhaps for two reasons: First, experience has taught you that the cup will look circular when seen from above. Second, you may have labelled the cup as circular or round.

Let us return to the door that "changes shape" when it is ajar. The door is a rectangle only when viewed straight on. When we move to the side or open it, the left or right edge comes closer and appears to be larger, changing the retinal image to a trapezoid. Yet we continue to think of doors as rectangles. In the photo on this page, we see a woman with a very large hand, but because of experience, we recognize that the hand only appears to be out of proportion to the rest of her because it is pushed toward us.

Visual Illusions

The principles of perceptual organization make it possible for our eyes to "play tricks" on us. That is, the perceptual constancies trick the eye through *visual illusions*. One such visual illusion can be experienced in Moncton, New Brunswick. The popular tourist destination known as Magnetic Hill confounds travellers when they observe their car start to roll uphill when placed in neutral. This occurs partially because of an obscured horizon, an important cue we use to determine how steep, and in what direction, a slope is. Other famous illusions can be observed in simple drawings, but they are somewhat less spectacular.

The Hering–Helmholtz and Müller–Lyer illusions (see Figure 3.14, p. 68) are named after the people who devised them. In the Hering–Helmholtz illusion (part A), the horizontal lines are straight and parallel. However, the radiating lines cause them to appear to be bent outward near the centre. The two lines in the Müller–Lyer illusion (part B) are the same length, but the line on the right, with its reversed arrowheads, looks longer. The two centre circles in the Ebbinghaus illusion (part C) are the same size, but the one on the

© Enamul Hoque/Getty Images

left appears smaller than the one on the right.

Let us try to explain these illusions. Because of our experience and lifelong use of perceptual cues, we tend to perceive the Hering–Helmholtz drawing as three-dimensional. Because of our tendency to perceive bits of sensory information as figures against grounds, we perceive the blue area in the centre as a circle in front of a series of radiating lines, all of which lie in front of a blue ground. Next, because of our experience with perspective, we perceive the radiating lines as parallel. We perceive the two horizontal lines as intersecting the "receding" lines, and we know that they would have to appear bent out at the centre if they were to be equidistant at all points from the centre of the circle.

Experience probably compels us to perceive the vertical lines in the Müller–Lyer illusion as the corners of a building (see Figure 3.14, part B). We interpret the length of the lines based on our experience with corners of buildings.

The Ebbinghaus illusion (see Figure 3.14, part C) occurs because of the surrounding visual cues. The centre circle on the left is surrounded by large cir-

cles; thus, the relative size of the centre circle is perceived as smaller. Conversely, the centre circle on the right is surrounded by smaller circles, and thus it is comparatively perceived as larger. Close examination will reveal that both centre circles are actually the same size.

Two Visual Systems

Canadian researcher Mel Goodale at the University of Western Ontario has demonstrated that we have two separate, but interacting, visual systems. The first visual system (the **ventral stream**) has the function of creating the mental representation (perception) of everything that we see. All the perceptual rules we have covered so far, such as constancies and cues, would influence this stream of vision. However, there is another important visual system, the dorsal stream of vision. The **dorsal stream** has the role of informing our muscles on how to act toward the objects we perceive (Goodale & Humphrey, 1998). To give an example of how the two systems work together, let's say you are sitting down at a table and in front of you is a nice refreshing beer. The ventral stream would provide information on the meaning of the object as a beverage and the perception that it would be refreshing to drink. The dorsal stream would then provide size, distance, and location information to guide the muscles in your arm, hand, and mouth as you reached out

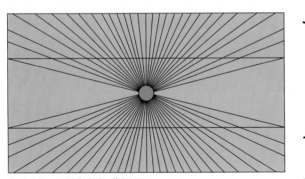

A. The Hering–Helmholtz Illusion

B. The Müller–Lyer Illusion

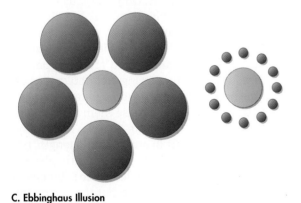

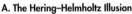

C. Ebbinghaus Illusion

FIGURE 3.14

The Hering–Helmholtz, Müller–Lyer, and Ebbinghaus Illusions

In the Hering–Helmholtz illusion, are the horizontal lines straight or curved? In the Müller–Lyer illusion, are the vertical lines equal in length? In the Ebbinghaus illusion, is the centre circle in the left smaller than the centre circle on the right?

Go to www.icanpsych.com to access an interactive version of this figure.

toward the glass, grasped it, lifted it to your lips, and took a drink.

Further evidence has suggested that only one of the two systems is susceptible to visual illusions. Goodale and his colleagues asked people to grasp objects that were perceived as relatively larger or smaller, depending on other objects in relation to them (see the Ebbinghaus illusion in Figure 3.14). They found that the grasping motion (guided by the dorsal stream) was largely immune to the incorrect perception of one circle as distinctly larger than the other (Haffenden, Schiff, & Goodale, 2001).

LO4 Hearing

Consider the advertising slogan for the classic science fiction film *Alien:* "In space, no one can hear you scream." It's true. Space is an almost perfect vacuum. Hearing requires a medium through which sound can travel, such as air or water. *What is sound?*

Sound, or auditory stimulation, travels through the air like waves. If you could see them, they would look something like the ripples in a pond when you toss in a pebble. You hear the splash even if you can't see the sound of it. The sound of the splash is caused by changes in air pressure. The air is alternately compressed and expanded like the movements of an accordion. If you were listening underwater, you would also hear the splash because of changes in the pressure of the water. In either case, the changes in pressure are vibrations that approach your ears in waves. These vibrations—sound waves—can also be created by a ringing bell, your vocal cords, guitar strings, or the slam of a book thrown down on a desk. A single cycle of compression and expansion is one wave of sound. Sound waves can occur many times in a second. The human ear is sensitive to sound waves with frequencies of from 20 to 20 000 cycles per second.

Pitch and Loudness

Pitch and loudness are two psychological dimensions of sound. The pitch of a sound is determined by its frequency, or the number of cycles per second as expressed in the unit **hertz (Hz)**. One cycle per second is 1 Hz. The greater the number of cycles per second (Hz), the higher the pitch of the sound.

The pitch of women's voices is usually higher than that of men's voices because women's vocal cords are usually shorter and therefore vibrate at a greater frequency. Also, the strings of a violin are shorter than those of a viola or double bass. Pitch detectors in the brain allow us to tell differences in pitch.

The loudness of a sound roughly corresponds to the height, or amplitude, of sound waves. Figure 3.15 shows records of sound waves that vary in frequency and amplitude. Frequency and amplitude are independent. That is, both high and low pitched sounds can be either high or low in loudness. The loudness of a sound is expressed in **decibels (dB)**. Zero dB is equivalent to the threshold of hearing—the lowest sound that the typical person can hear. How loud is that? It's about as loud as the ticking of a watch seven metres away in a very quiet room.

The decibel equivalents of familiar sounds are shown in Figure 3.16 (p. 70). Twenty-five dB is equivalent in loudness to a whisper at 1.5 metres. Thirty dB is roughly the limit of loudness your librarian would like to keep in your school library. You may suffer hearing damage if you are exposed to sounds of 85 to 90 dB for long periods.

The Ear

How does the ear work? The ear is shaped and structured to capture sound waves, vibrate in sympathy with them, and transmit them to the brain. In this way, you not only hear something, you can also figure out what it is. The ear has three parts: the outer ear, middle ear, and inner ear (see Figure 3.17).

The outer ear is shaped to funnel sound waves to the *eardrum,* a thin membrane that vibrates in response to sound waves and thereby transmits them to the middle and inner ears. The middle ear contains

> **hertz (Hz)**
> a unit expressing the frequency of sound waves; 1 Hz equals one cycle per second
>
> **decibel (dB)**
> a unit expressing the loudness of a sound

FIGURE 3.15

Sound Waves of Various Frequencies and Amplitudes

Which sounds have the highest pitch? Which are loudest?

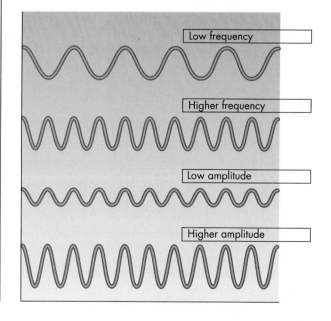

cochlea
the inner ear; the bony tube that contains the basilar membrane and the organ of Corti

basilar membrane
a membrane that lies coiled within the cochlea

organ of Corti
the receptor for hearing that lies on the basilar membrane in the cochlea

auditory nerve
the axon bundle that transmits neural impulses from the organ of Corti to the brain

the eardrum and three small bones, which also transmit sound by vibrating. These bones were given their names, *hammer*, *anvil*, and *stirrup*, because of their shapes. The middle ear functions as an amplifier, increasing the pressure of the air entering the ear.

The stirrup is attached to another vibrating membrane, the *oval window*. The oval window works in conjunction with the round window, which balances the pressure in the inner ear (see Figure 3.17). The round window pushes outward when the oval window pushes in, and is pulled inward when the oval window vibrates outward.

The oval window transmits vibrations into the inner ear, the bony tube called the cochlea (from the Greek word for "snail"). The cochlea, which is shaped like a snail shell, contains two longitudinal membranes that divide it into three fluid-filled chambers. One of the membranes that lies coiled within the cochlea is called the basilar membrane. Vibrations in the fluids within the chambers of the inner ear press against the basilar membrane.

The organ of Corti, sometimes referred to as the "command post" of hearing, is attached to the basilar membrane. Some 25 000 receptor cells—called *hair cells* because they project like hair from the organ of Corti—are found in each ear. Hair cells "dance" in response to the vibrations of the basilar membrane. Their movements generate neural impulses, which are transmitted to the brain via the auditory nerve. Auditory input is then projected onto the hearing areas of the temporal lobes of the cerebral cortex.

Locating Sounds

How do we locate sounds? There is a resemblance between balancing a set of stereo speakers and locating sounds. A sound that is louder in the right ear is perceived as coming from the right. A sound coming from

FIGURE 3.16

Decibel Ratings of Familiar Sounds

Zero dB is the threshold of hearing. You may suffer hearing loss if you incur prolonged exposure to sounds of 85 to 90 dB.

Typical decibel level	Dangerous time exposure	Examples
180		Space shuttle launch
170	Hearing loss certain	
160		Shotgun blast
150		Jet airplane
140	Any exposure dangerous	Siren at 15 metres
		Stereo headset (full volume)
		Threshold of pain
Extremely loud 130	Immediate danger	Thunder, rock concert, basketball or hockey crowd
120		Riveter
110		Factory noise, chain saw
100	Less than 8 hours	Subway, tractor, power mower, screaming child
Very loud 90		Bus, motorcycle, snowmobile
80	More than 8 hours	Loud home stereo, food blender
		Heavy traffic
70		Average automobile
60		Normal conversation
50		Quiet auto
Quiet 40		Quiet office
30		
Very quiet 20		Whisper at 1.5 metres
		Broadcast studio when quiet
10		
Just audible 0		

the right also reaches the right ear first. Both loudness and the sequence in which the sounds reach the ears provide directional cues.

But it may not be easy to locate a sound coming from in front or in back of you or above. Such sounds are equally distant from each ear and equally loud. So what do we do? Simple—we turn our head slightly to determine in which ear the sound increases. If you turn your head to the right and the loudness increases in your left ear, the sound is likely coming from in front.

FIGURE 3.17

The Human Ear

Go to www.icanpsych.com to access an interactive version of this figure.

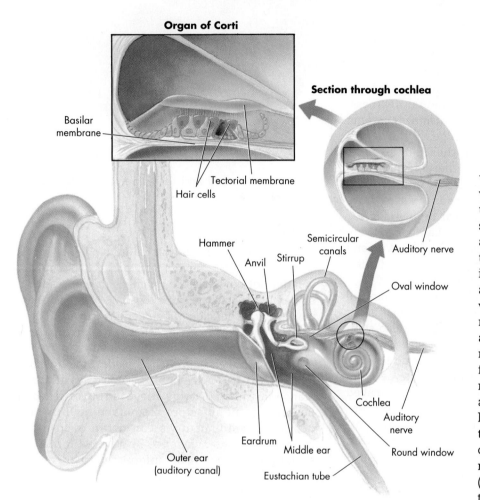

Organ of Corti

Basilar membrane

Tectorial membrane

Hair cells

Section through cochlea

Hammer

Anvil Stirrup

Semicircular canals

Auditory nerve

Oval window

Cochlea

Auditory nerve

Eardrum

Middle ear

Round window

Outer ear (auditory canal)

Eustachian tube

place theory
the theory that the pitch of a sound is determined by the section of the basilar membrane that vibrates in response to the sound

frequency theory
the theory that the pitch of a sound is reflected in the frequency of the neural impulses that are generated in response to the sound

Perception of Loudness and Pitch

Sounds are heard because they cause vibration in parts of the ear and information about these vibrations is transmitted to the brain. *How do we perceive loudness and pitch?* The loudness and pitch of sounds appear to be related to the number of receptor neurons on the organ of Corti that fire and how often they fire. Psychologists generally agree that sounds are perceived as louder when more of these sensory neurons fire.

It takes two processes to explain perception of colour: *trichromatic theory* and *opponent-process theory*. Similarly, it takes at least two processes to explain perception of sound waves that vary in frequency from 20 to 20 000 cycles per second: *place theory* and *frequency theory*.

Hermann von Helmholtz helped develop the **place theory** of pitch discrimination as well as the

trichromatic theory of colour vision. Place theory holds that the pitch of a sound is sensed according to the place along the basilar membrane that vibrates in response to it. In research that led to the award of a Nobel Prize, Georg von Békésy (1957) found that receptors at different sites along the membrane fire in response to tones of differing frequencies. Receptor neurons appear to be lined up along the basilar membrane like piano keys. The higher the pitch of a sound, the closer the responsive neurons lie to the oval window (Larkin, 2000). However, place theory appears to apply only to pitches that are at least 5000 Hz. But what about lower pitches? That's where frequency theory comes in.

Frequency theory notes that for us to perceive lower pitches, we need to match the frequency of the sound waves with our neural impulses. That is, in response to low pitches—say 20 to 1000 cycles per second—hair cells on the basilar membrane fire at the same frequencies as the sound waves. However, neurons cannot fire more frequently. Therefore, frequency theory best explains perception of pitches between 20 and 1000 cycles per second.

It takes at least two processes to explain how people perceive pitch. The perception of sounds between 1000 and 5000 cycles per second depends both on the part of the basilar membrane that vibrates (as in place theory), and the frequency with which it vibrates (as in frequency theory). The processes apparently work together to enable us to hear pitches in the intermediate range (Goldstein, 2004).

flavour
a complex quality of food and other substances that is based on their odour, texture, and temperature as well their taste

olfactory nerve
the nerve that transmits information concerning odours from olfactory receptors to the brain

taste cells
receptor cells that are sensitive to taste

taste buds
the sensory organs for taste; they contain taste cells and are mostly located on the tongue

Deafness

More than 3.1 million Canadians have a hearing impairment, and 310 000 cannot hear at all (Canadian Association of the Deaf, 2007). *What is deafness? What can we do about it?*

Two major types of deafness are conductive deafness and sensorineural deafness. *Conductive deafness* stems from damage to the structures of the middle ear—either to the eardrum or to the bones that conduct (and amplify) sound waves from the outer ear to the inner ear (Canalis & Lambert, 2000). This is the hearing impairment often found among older people. Hearing aids amplify sound and often help people with conductive deafness.

Sensorineural deafness usually stems from damage to the structures of the inner ear, most often the loss of hair cells. Sensorineural deafness can also stem from damage to the auditory nerve, caused by such factors as disease or exposure to very loud sounds. In sensorineural deafness, people tend to be more sensitive to some pitches than others. In so-called Hunter's notch, the loss is limited to the frequencies of the sound waves generated by a gun firing. Prolonged exposure to 85 dB can cause hearing loss. People who attend rock concerts, where sounds may reach around 125 dB, risk damaging their ears, as do workers who run pneumatic drills or drive noisy vehicles. The ringing sensation that often follows exposure to loud sounds probably means that hair cells in the inner ear have been permanently damaged.

Cochlear implants, or "artificial ears," contain microphones that sense sounds and electronic equipment that transmits sounds past damaged hair cells to stimulate the auditory nerve. Such implants have helped many people with sensorineural deafness (Geers et al., 2002), but they cannot assume the functions of damaged auditory nerves.

LO5 The Chemical Senses: Smell and Taste

Smell and taste are the chemical senses. In vision and hearing, physical energy strikes our sensory

Apples and onions are similar in taste, but their flavours differ greatly.

Left: © Gustavo Andrade/iStockphoto.com; right: © Joe Bekinger/Shutterstock.com

receptors. In smell and taste, we sample molecules of substances.

Smell

Smell has an important role in human behaviour. It contributes to the **flavour** of foods, for example. If you did not have a sense of smell, an onion and an apple might taste the same to you. People's sense of smell may be deficient when compared with that of a dog, but we can detect the odour of 1 one-millionth of a milligram of vanilla in a litre of air.

How does the sense of smell work? Smell detects odours. An *odour* is a sample of molecules of a substance in the air. Odours trigger firing of receptor neurons in the olfactory membrane high in each nostril. Receptor neurons can detect even a few molecules of the substance in gaseous form. The receptor neurons transmit information about odours to the brain via the **olfactory nerve**.

Taste

How does the sense of taste work? As in the case of smell, taste samples molecules of a substance. Taste is sensed through **taste cells**—receptor neurons located on **taste buds**. You have about 10 000 taste buds, most of which are located near the edges and back of your tongue. Some taste buds are more responsive to sweetness, whereas others react to several tastes. Other taste receptors are found in the roof, sides, and back of the mouth, and in the throat. Some taste buds are even found only in the stomach, although we perceive tastes only in the mouth and top of the throat. Buds in the mouth are evolutionarily adaptive because they can warn of bad food before it is swallowed (Brand, 2000).

Researchers generally agree on at least four primary taste qualities: sweet, sour, salty, and bitter. Some argue for a fifth basic taste, which is termed

What's that SCENT you're wearing?

umami (pronounced *ooh-mommy*) in Japanese and means "meaty" or "savoury." Regardless of the number of basic tastes, the flavour of a food is more complex than taste alone. *Flavour* depends on odour, texture, and temperature as well as on taste. Apples and onions are similar in taste, but their flavours differ greatly.

Just as some people see better than others, some people taste better than others—but their superiority may be limited to one or more basic tastes. Those of us with low sensitivity for sweetness may require twice the sugar to sweeten our coffee as those who are more sensitive. Those of us who claim to enjoy bitter foods may actually be taste blind to them (Lanier et al., 2005). Sensitivities to various tastes have a genetic component (Bartoshuk, 2000; Duffy et al., 2004).

LO6 The Skin Senses

What are the skin senses? How do they work? The skin senses include touch, pressure, warmth, cold, and pain. We have distinct sensory receptors for pressure, temperature, and pain, but some nerve endings may receive more than one type of sensory input. Here let's focus on touch, pressure, temperature, and pain.

Touch and Pressure

Sensory receptors embedded in the skin fire when the surface of the skin is touched. There may be several kinds of receptors for touch, some that respond to constant pressure, some that respond to intermittent pressure, as in tapping the skin. *Active touching* means continually moving your hand along the surface of an object so that you continue to receive sensory input from the object

(O'Dell & Hoyert, 2002). If you are trying to "get the feel of" a fabric or the texture of a friend's hair, you must move your hand over it. Otherwise the sensations quickly fade. If you pass your hand over the fabric or hair and then hold it still, the sensations of touching will fade. Active touching receives information concerning pressure, temperature, texture, and feedback from the muscles involved in movements of our hands.

Different parts of the body are more sensitive to touch and pressure than others. The parts of the body that "cover" more than their fair share of somatosensory cortex are most sensitive to touch. These parts include the hands, face, and some other regions of the body. Our fingertips, lips, noses, and cheeks are more sensitive than our shoulders, thighs, and calves. Why the difference in sensitivity? First, nerve endings are more densely packed in the fingertips and face than in other locations. Second, more sensory cortex is devoted to the perception of sensations in the fingertips and face (see Figure 2.12 on page 39).

Temperature

The receptors for temperature are neurons located just beneath the skin. When skin temperature increases, the receptors for warmth fire. Decreases in skin temperature cause receptors for cold to fire.

Sensations of temperature are relative. When we are at normal body temperature, we might perceive another person's skin as warm. When we are feverish, though, the other person's skin might seem cool. We also adapt to differences in temperature. When we enter a swimming pool, the water may seem cold because it is below body temperature. Yet after a few moments, a 27°C pool may seem quite warm. In fact, we may chide a newcomer for not diving right in.

Pain

For most people, pain is a frequent visitor. Headaches, backaches, toothaches—these are only a few of the types of pain that most of us encounter from time

vestibular sense the sense of equilibrium that informs us about our bodies' positions relative to gravity

The Vestibular Sense

It is your **vestibular sense** that provides your brain with information as to whether or not you are physically upright.

How does the vestibular sense work? Sensory organs located in the semicircular canals and elsewhere in the ears monitor your body's motion and position in relation to gravity. They tell you whether you are falling and provide cues to whether your body is changing speed, such as when you are in an accelerating airplane or automobile.

LO8 ESP: Is There Perception without Sensation?

Our sensory organs are the peripheral devices that feed information into our central processing units—our brains. What if there were such as thing as extra sensory perception (ESP)? What if sensation were bypassed, and we directly perceived things in the world outside? Although the hard research evidence comes down heavily against ESP, 60 percent of the Canadian public believes that some people have psychic powers or ESP (Bibby, 1990, p. 287). Therefore, it is useful to understand the issue and examine the type of research that psychologists conduct to determine whether it has validity. Let us begin by defining precognition and other topics in ESP.

Precognition, Psychokinesis, Telepathy, and Clairvoyance

Imagine the wealth you could amass if you had *precognition*—that is, if you were able to perceive future events in advance. Perhaps you would check the next week's stock market reports and know what to buy or sell. Or you could bet with confidence on who would win the next Super Bowl or Stanley Cup. Or think of the power you would have if you were capable of *psychokinesis*—that is, of mentally manipulating or moving objects. You may have gotten a

glimpse of the possibilities in films like *The Matrix, The Sixth Sense,* and *Star Wars*. Precognition and psychokinesis are two concepts associated with ESP. Two other theoreical forms of ESP are *telepathy,* or direct transmission of thoughts or ideas from one person to another, and *clairvoyance,* or the perception of objects that do not stimulate the sensory organs. An example of clairvoyance is "seeing" what card will be dealt next, even though it is still in the deck and unseen even by the dealer.

Many psychologists do not believe that ESP is an appropriate area for scientific inquiry. Other psychologists, however, believe that there is nothing wrong with investigating ESP. The issue for them is whether its existence can be demonstrated in the laboratory. *Does ESP really exist?*

A well-known ESP researcher was Joseph Banks Rhine of Duke University, who studied ESP for several decades, beginning in the 1920s. In a typical experiment in clairvoyance, Rhine would use a pack of 25 cards, which contained 5 sets of simple symbols (the opening scene in the movie *Ghostbusters* shows Dr. Peter Venkman, played by Bill Murray, conducting a similar experiment in clairvoyance). Pigeons pecking patterns at random to indicate which one was about to be turned up would be "correct" 20 percent of the time. Rhine found that some people guessed correctly significantly more often than the 20 percent chance rate. He concluded that these people might have some degree of ESP.

A more current method for studying telepathy is the *ganzfeld procedure* (Dalkvist, 2001; Parker, 2001). In this method, one person acts as a "sender" and the other as a "receiver." The sender views randomly selected visual stimuli such as photographs or videotapes, while the receiver, who is in another room and whose eyes are covered and ears are blocked, tries to mentally tune in to the sender. After a session, the receiver is shown four visual stimuli and asked to select the one transmitted by the sender. A person guessing which stimulus was "transmitted" would be correct 25 percent of the time (one time in four) by chance alone. An analysis of 28 experiments using the ganzfeld procedure, however, found that receivers correctly identified the visual stimulus 38 percent of the time (Honorton, 1985), a percentage unlikely to be due to chance. A series of 11 more studies with the ganzfeld procedure obtained similar results (Bem & Honorton, 1994; Honorton et al., 1990).

Overall, however, there are reasons to be skeptical. First is the *file-drawer problem*. Buyers of supermarket tabloids tend to forget the predictions of "psychics" when the predictions fail to come true (that is, they have "filed" them away). Similarly, ESP researchers are more likely to "file away" research results that show failure. Therefore, we would expect unusual findings (for example, a subject with a high success rate on experimental tasks over a few days) to appear in the research literature. In other words, if you flip a coin indefinitely, eventually you will flip ten heads in a row. The odds against it are high, but if you report your eventual success and do not report the weeks of failure, you may give the impression that you have unique coin-flipping ability.

It has also been difficult to replicate experiments in ESP. People who have "demonstrated" ESP with one researcher have failed to do so with another, or they have refused to participate in other studies. Also, the findings in one study are usually absent in follow-ups or under careful analysis. For example, Milton and Wiseman (1999) reviewed the research reported by Bem and Honorton (1994). They weighed the results of 30 ganzfeld ESP studies from seven laboratories. They found no evidence—zero—that subjects in these studies scored above chance levels on the ESP task. From all of these studies, *not one person has emerged who can reliably show ESP from one occasion to another and from one researcher to another*. Research has not identified one single indisputable telepath or clairvoyant. Furthermore, there is currently a reward of $1 000 000 for any who under controlled conditions can demonstrate any paranormal activity (see the James Randi Million-Dollar Challenge feature below). In sum, most psychologists do not grant ESP research much credibility. They prefer to study perception that involves sensation. After all, what is life without sensation?

{ James Randi Million-Dollar Challenge }

The "Amazing" James Randi was born in Toronto, Ontario, and had an early career as a stage magician. Frustrated by the many performers who claimed supernatural powers, Randi has spent a great deal of time challenging and debunking claims of paranormal activity. He publicly challenged several well-known "magicians," "psychics," and "faith healers" including Uri Geller, James Hydrick, Sylvia Browne, and Peter Popoff. Following in the path of another great stage magician (Houdini), Randi offered a reward of $1000 to anyone who could demonstrate, under controlled conditions, a paranormal power of any kind. Since that offer in 1964, the prize money has grown to $1 000 000, and yet it remains unclaimed (www.randi.org). Despite this, there is still widespread acceptance of ESP. Why do you think this is so?

Learning Outcomes

LO1 Define consciousness

LO2 Explain the stages of sleep and sleep cycles

LO3 Explain major sleep disorders

LO4 Explain the use of hypnosis, and forms of meditation, in altering consciousness

LO5 Explain how psychoactive drugs, including substance abuse, alter states of consciousness

Consciousness

> ❝*Conscious experience is at once the most familiar thing in the world and the most mysterious.*❞
>
> —David Chalmers

It's no secret—we are curious about our minds. In fact, we are often most curious about experiences and events that are seemingly unusual or so strangely bizarre that we can only hope to explain why they happen. Take Toronto-area resident Ken Parks, who was a free man after killing his mother-in-law and seriously injuring his father-in-law. *So what happened?* After turning himself in to authorities and confessing that he had killed two people, Ken Parks and his lawyer pleaded "not guilty," arguing that he was sleepwalking and, therefore, committed the crimes while he was unaware (or unconscious) of his brutal actions. Parks testified that sleep disorders run in his family and, following evidence from the testimony of sleep disorder experts, the jury found him not responsible for his actions (Supreme Court of Canada, 1992). Although this example may be an extreme (and irregular) case for the most part, we cannot forget that we all drift in and out of various states of consciousness throughout the day, but (thankfully) most of us do not suffer from a sleep disorder.

The study of consciousness didn't come easily in the history of psychology, but it did begin with a curious need to scientifically unravel some of the mysteries of consciousness. Psychologists for many years banished the topic of consciousness from their field. Both William James and John Watson insisted that consciousness was not a proper area of study for psychologists because scientific methods could not directly observe or measure another person's consciousness.

The past few decades have seen a cognitive revolution, and thousands of psychologists now believe we cannot capture the richness of human experience without referring to consciousness (Schultz & Schultz, 2008). We are flooded with studies of consciousness by psychologists, biologists, neuroscientists, physicists, and even computer scientists. Even though we still cannot directly observe the consciousness of another person, psychologists who study consciousness study it through self-reports and physiological measures, as we observe events such as neural activity in the brain.

DID YOU KNOW?

- Just about everyone dreams while they are sleeping.

- Insomnia is a common sleep disorder that can be caused by trying too hard to fall asleep.

- Sleep deprivation and shift work are key contributors to industrial and automobile accidents.

- Coca-Cola once "added life" to its signature drink through the use of a powerful—but now illegal—stimulant.

- In Ontario, adults may be fined if they are smoking in a motor vehicle if there is a passenger aged 16 or under present.

consciousness
an awareness of our external and internal environment at any given moment

selective attention
the focus of consciousness on a particular stimulus

direct inner awareness
knowledge of one's own thoughts, feelings, and memories

preconscious
in psychodynamic theory, descriptive of material that is not in awareness but can be brought into awareness by focusing one's attention

LO1 What Is Consciousness?

The concept of consciousness has various meanings and psychologists use it in many ways. Sigmund Freud emphasized and differentiated between the conscious, preconscious and unconscious as a way to understand our behaviour. For others, such as William James, the nature of consciousness is influenced by the attention we give to specific issues. Most recently, consciousness has been studied using CT scans and EEG scans of individuals in a sleep or hypnotic state. We will look at **consciousness** as an awareness of our external and internal environment at any given moment.

Consciousness as Awareness

The notion of consciousness as *sensory awareness* of the environment basically emphasizes how our senses enable us to be *conscious* of an object or situation. For example, our sense of vision enables us to see, or be *conscious* of, the sun gleaming on the snow or our sense of hearing allows us to hear, or be *conscious* of, a rock concert. Yet most times we are not aware of all sensory stimulation around us. We may be unaware, or *unconscious*, of sensory stimulation when we do not pay attention to it. For example, we may not be aware (or conscious) of the big crowd of security guards that has gathered behind us to remove a boisterous fan while listening to the rock concert!

This is because we are selective with what we attend to. We pay attention to what is important to us at that very moment. **Selective attention** means focusing one's consciousness on a particular stimulus. When we are focused on the details of a task, for example, trying to drill a hole in the wall to hang a picture, our awareness is much more intentional compared to daydreaming, which is much less intentional.

Adaptation to our environment involves learning which stimuli must be attended to and which can be safely ignored. To keep your car on the road, you must pay more attention to driving conditions than to your hunger pangs or a cellphone call. Selective attention makes our senses keener (Vorobyev et al., 2004). This is why we can pick out the speech of a single person across a room at a cocktail party—a phenomenon aptly termed the *cocktail party effect*.

Our awareness can also be understood through our knowledge of our own thoughts, feelings, and memories—known as **direct inner awareness**. Close your eyes and imagine spilling a can of bright red paint across a black tabletop. Watch it spread across the black, shiny surface and then spill onto the floor. Although this image may be vivid, you did not "see" it literally. Neither your eyes nor any other sensory organs were involved. You were *conscious* of the image through direct inner awareness. Although we may not be able to measure direct inner awareness scientifically, many psychologists argue—if you have it, you know it.

Conscious, Preconscious, Unconscious, and Nonconscious

Sigmund Freud, the founder of psychoanalysis, differentiated between thoughts and feelings of which we are conscious and those that are preconscious and unconscious.

Preconscious material is not currently in awareness but is readily available. If you answer the following questions, you will summon up "preconscious" information: What did you eat for breakfast? What is your phone number? You can make these preconscious bits of information conscious by directing your attention to them.

FINAL EXAM RESULTS

Selective attention makes our senses keener.

Still other mental events are **unconscious**, or unavailable to awareness under most circumstances. Freud believed that some painful memories and sexual and aggressive impulses are unacceptable to us, so we *automatically* (unconsciously) eject them from awareness. That is, we *repress* them. **Repression** allows us to avoid feelings of anxiety, guilt, or shame.

People can also *choose* to stop thinking about unacceptable ideas or distractions. When we consciously eject unwanted mental events from awareness, we are using **suppression**. We may suppress thoughts of an upcoming party when we need to study for a test. We may also try to suppress thoughts of the test while we are at the party!

Some bodily processes, such as the firings of neurons, are **nonconscious**. They cannot be experienced through sensory awareness or direct inner awareness. The growing of hair and the carrying of oxygen in the blood are nonconscious. We can see that our hair has grown, but we have no sense receptors that provide sensations of growing. We feel the need to breathe but do not experience the exchange of carbon dioxide and oxygen.

LO2 Stages of Sleep and Cycles

Sleep is a fascinating topic. After all, we spend about one-third of our adult lives asleep. Sleep experts recommend that adults get eight hours of sleep a night, but according to Statistics Canada's *General Social Survey* (2005) and the Better Sleep Council of Canada (2009), one in four Canadians is sleep-deprived. Factors such as shift work, longer workdays, stress, and family characteristics are associated with lack of sleep for many Canadians (Statistics Canada, 2005).

The Functions of Sleep

Most of us have had the experience of going without sleep for a night and feeling "wrecked" or "out of it" the following day. Perhaps the next evening we went to bed early to "catch up" on our sleep. What happens to you if you do not sleep for one night? Or for several nights?

Many students can pull "all-nighters" in which they cram for a test through the night and perform reasonably

unconscious
in psychodynamic theory, descriptive of ideas and feelings that are not available to awareness; also: without consciousness

repression
in psychodynamic theory, the unconscious ejection of anxiety-evoking ideas, impulses, or images from awareness

suppression
the deliberate, or conscious, placing of certain ideas, impulses, or images out of awareness

nonconscious
descriptive of bodily processes such as the growing of hair, of which we cannot become conscious; for example, we may "recognize" that our hair is growing but cannot directly experience the biological process

circadian rhythm
a biological cycle that is connected with the 24-hour period of the earth's rotation and regulates our bodily functions, including wakefulness and sleep

well the following day (Horowitz et al., 2003). But they begin to show deficits in cognitive functions such as learning and memory if they go sleepless for more than one night (Ohno et al., 2002; Taylor & McFatter, 2003). Shift work has a significant effect on the quality of sleep for many shift workers (Shields, 2002). One-third of shift workers have problems falling asleep or staying asleep, compared to one-quarter of regular workers (Statistics Canada, 2005).

Why do we sleep? Researchers do not have all the answers as to why we sleep, but as you can imagine, sleep seems to serve several purposes: It rejuvenates the body, helps us recover from stress, helps us consolidate learning, and may promote development of infants' brains.

Why do you need the amount of sleep you need? The amount of sleep we need seems to be in part genetically determined. Newborn babies may sleep 16 hours a day, and teenagers may sleep "around the clock" (12 hours or more). It is widely believed that older people need less sleep than younger adults do, but sleep in older people is often interrupted by physical discomfort or the need to go to the bathroom. To make

> Have you ever tossed and turned in bed all night, or noticed changes in your energy level throughout the day? Likely, you have—and typically, you may feel that you have no control over these things.

up for sleep lost at night, older people may "nod off" during the day.

Biological and Circadian Rhythms

There has been an increasing amount of research that links the importance of sleep quality and our body's natural rhythm (De Koninck, 1997). Our lives are connected with the rhythms of the universe at large.

Our alternating periods of wakefulness and sleep reflect an internally generated **circadian rhythm**. *What is a circadian rhythm?* A circadian rhythm is a biological cycle that regulates our body functions throughout a 24-hour period. The cycle influences both our wakefulness and sleep, but the daily cycle also regulates our body temperature, heart rate, blood pressure, hormonal secretions, and other cognitive functions such as alertness and memory (Johnson, Duffy, Dijk, Rhonda, Dyal, & Czeiler, 1992).

How does the circadian rhythm work? Consider how alert you feel at different points in the day. Perhaps as a busy student, you feel more alert and energetic at night (which tends to have you staying up later) and find it difficult to get up in the early morning to make it to class. Circadian patterns tend to regulate a rise in both temperature and alertness in the morning, peak during the day, and decline later in the afternoon and before bed (Kumar, 2004). Research demonstrates that circadian rhythms tend to persist despite environmental cues (Czeiler, Buxton, & Khalsa, 2005). However, disruption of exposure to light seems most likely to influence fluctuations in a circadian cycle. This problem can be easily considered if you have travelled from one time zone to another: You may experience jet lag—challenges associated with your body trying to adjust to day (or night) in a different time zone when it is night (or day) in your time zone. To a smaller extent, you may feel groggy following the return to Daylight Saving Time, when you "lose" an hour of sleep.

The Stages of Sleep

It was not until the 1950s that researchers recognized that the brain's electrical activity was not "dormant" throughout a night of sleep following numerous records of distinct EEG patterns of brain wave activities (Aserinsky & Kleitman, 1955). *How do we record brain activity?* When we are conscious, our brains emit waves characterized by certain *frequencies* (numbers of waves per second) and *amplitudes*

© geotrac/iStockphoto.com

(heights—an index of strength). Brain waves indicate the activity of neurons. The strength or energy of brain waves is expressed in volts (an electrical unit). When we sleep, our brain waves differ from those emitted when we are awake. The electroencephalograph (EEG; see Figure 2.8 on page 35) has enabled researchers to measure brain waves. Figure 4.1 shows EEG patterns that reflect the frequency and strength of brain waves during the waking state, when we are relaxed, and when we are in the various stages of sleep. Brain waves, like other waves, are cyclical. The printouts in Figure 4.1 show what happens during a period of 15 seconds or so.

How do we describe the various stages of sleep? High-frequency brain waves are associated with wakefulness. When we move deeper into sleep, their frequency decreases and their amplitude (strength) increases. When we close our eyes and begin to relax before going to sleep, our brains emit **alpha waves**—low-amplitude brain waves of about 8 to 13 cycles per second.

Stages of Sleep and Dreaming

Figure 4.1 shows five stages of sleep. The first four sleep stages are considered **non–rapid eye movement (NREM)** sleep. These contrast with the fifth stage, **rapid eye movement (REM)** sleep, so called because our eyes dart back and forth beneath our eyelids.

The first sleep cycle begins with stage 1 sleep, called "light sleep." As we enter stage 1 sleep, our brain waves slow down from the alpha rhythm and enter a pattern of theta waves. **Theta waves**, with a frequency of about 6 to 8 cycles per second, are accompanied by slow, rolling eye movements. The transition from alpha waves to theta waves may be accompanied by a *hypnagogic state,* during which we may experience brief but vivid dream-like images. Stage 1 sleep is the lightest stage of sleep. If we are awakened from stage 1 sleep, we may feel we were not sleeping at all.

After 30 to 40 minutes of stage 1 sleep, we undergo a steep descent into stages 2, 3, and 4 (see Figure 4.2, p. 84). During stage 2, brain waves are medium in amplitude with a frequency of about 4 to 7 cycles per second, but these are punctuated by *sleep spindles*. Sleep spindles have a frequency of 12 to 16 cycles per second and represent brief bursts of rapid brain activity.

During deep sleep stages 3 and 4, our brains produce slower **delta waves**, which reach relatively great amplitude. During stage 3, the delta waves

alpha waves
rapid low-amplitude brain waves that have been linked to feelings of relaxation

non–rapid eye movement (NREM) sleep
stages of sleep 1 through 4

rapid eye movement (REM) sleep
a stage of sleep characterized by rapid eye movements, which have been linked to dreaming

theta waves
slow brain waves produced during the hypnagogic state

delta waves
strong, slow brain waves usually emitted during stage 4 sleep

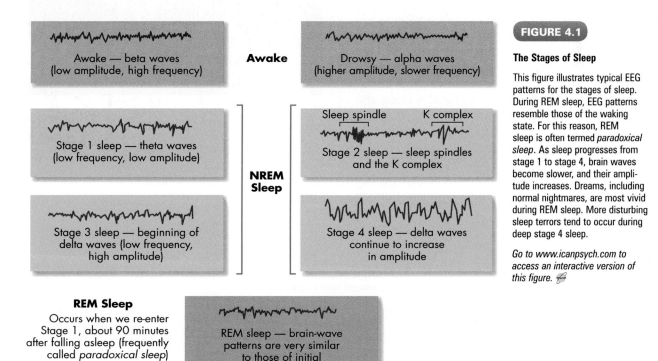

Awake — beta waves
(low amplitude, high frequency)

Awake

Drowsy — alpha waves
(higher amplitude, slower frequency)

Stage 1 sleep — theta waves
(low frequency, low amplitude)

NREM Sleep

Sleep spindle   K complex

Stage 2 sleep — sleep spindles
and the K complex

Stage 3 sleep — beginning of
delta waves (low frequency,
high amplitude)

Stage 4 sleep — delta waves
continue to increase
in amplitude

REM Sleep
Occurs when we re-enter
Stage 1, about 90 minutes
after falling asleep (frequently
called *paradoxical sleep*)

REM sleep — brain-wave
patterns are very similar
to those of initial
NREM stage 1

FIGURE 4.1

The Stages of Sleep

This figure illustrates typical EEG patterns for the stages of sleep. During REM sleep, EEG patterns resemble those of the waking state. For this reason, REM sleep is often termed *paradoxical sleep*. As sleep progresses from stage 1 to stage 4, brain waves become slower, and their amplitude increases. Dreams, including normal nightmares, are most vivid during REM sleep. More disturbing sleep terrors tend to occur during deep stage 4 sleep.

Go to www.icanpsych.com to access an interactive version of this figure.

have a frequency of 1 to 3 cycles per second. Stage 4 is the deepest stage of sleep, from which it is the most difficult to be awakened. During stage 4 sleep, the delta waves slow to about 0.5 to 2 cycles per second, and their amplitude is greatest.

After perhaps half an hour of deep stage 4 sleep, we begin a relatively rapid journey back upward through the stages until we enter REM sleep (see Figure 4.2).

REM Sleep

REM sleep occurs when we re-enter stage 1, about 90 minutes after falling asleep. During REM sleep, we produce relatively rapid, low-amplitude brain waves that resemble those of light stage 1 sleep. REM sleep is also called *paradoxical sleep* because the EEG patterns observed suggest a level of arousal similar to that of the waking state (see Figure 4.1). However, it is difficult to awaken a person during REM sleep. When people are awakened during REM sleep, they report dreaming about 80 percent of the time. (We also dream during NREM sleep but only about 20 percent of the time).

Each night we tend to undergo five cycles through the stages of sleep (see Figure 4.2). Five cycles include five periods of REM sleep. Our first journey through stage 4 sleep is usually longest. Sleep tends to become lighter as the night wears on and periods of REM sleep lengthen. Toward morning, our last period of REM sleep may last about half an hour.

Sleep, Learning, and Memory

REM sleep and deep sleep are both connected with the consolidation of learning and memory (Gais & Born, 2004; Ribeiro & Nicolelis, 2004). In some studies, animals or people have been deprived of REM sleep. Fetuses have periods of waking and sleeping, and REM sleep may foster the development of the brain before birth (Fifer & Moon, 2003). Under deprivation of REM sleep, animals and people learn more slowly and forget what they have learned sooner (Kennedy, 2002; Ribeiro & Nicolelis, 2004). REM-sleep-deprived people and animals tend to show *REM rebound,* meaning that they spend more time in REM sleep during subsequent sleep periods—they "catch up."

Dreams

Dreaming is a source of continuous curiosity. Psychologists study dreams to learn about conscious-

Warner Bros./The Kobal Collection

Can we be manipulated while dreaming? How "real" is Leonardo DiCaprio's ability to enter someone else's dream? Ideas about what we can (or cannot) do with our mind intrigue all of us, which is why media so successfully arouse our curiosity about how our dreams are controlled.

FIGURE 4.2

Sleep Cycles

This figure illustrates the alternation of REM and non-REM sleep for the typical sleeper. There are about five periods of REM sleep during an eight-hour night. Sleep is deeper earlier in the night, and REM sleep tends to become prolonged toward morning.

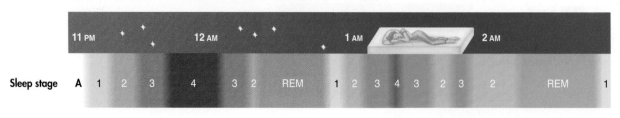

ness and also because dreaming is a universal mental activity (Foulkes, 1996). Even the mass media promote ideas about what we can do with dreams—and we are intrigued. A Warner Bros. release, *Inception* (2010), starring Leonardo DiCaprio, depicts a brilliant thief who steals business information by entering people's dreams. He then must perform the ultimate feat—an inception—planting information into his rival's mind in order to be able to return to his "old life." Can we be manipulated while dreaming?

What are dreams? Dreams are imagery in the absence of external stimulation and can seem real. As a high school cheerleader, I (S.M.) had repeated "anxiety dreams" the night before a big game. I would dream that something had gone wrong with the routine—either I fell, forgot my position, or my skirt was tucked into my bloomers. Imagine my relief when I awakened and realized the big game was still to come!

Dreams are most likely to be vivid during REM sleep. Images are often brief during NREM sleep. If you sleep for eight hours and undergo five sleep cycles, you may have five dreams. Dreams may compress time the way a movie does, by skipping hours or days to a future time, but the actual action tends to take place in "real time." Fifteen minutes of events fills about fifteen minutes of dreaming. Furthermore, your dream theatre is quite flexible. You can dream in black and white or in full colour.

Why do we dream what we dream? There are many theories about why we dream what we dream. Some are psychological and others are more biologically oriented.

Dreams as "the Residue of the Day"

You may recall dreams involving fantastic adventures, but most dreams involve memories of the day gone by—or, poetically, "the residue of the day" (Domhoff, 2001, 2003). In fact, up to 50 percent of our dreams contain some content reflecting the experiences of the day gone by. If we are preoccupied with illness or death, sex or aggression, or moral dilemmas, we are likely to dream about them. The characters in our dreams are more likely to be friends and neighbours than spies, monsters, and princesses. Cartwright's (2004) cognitive problem-solving view proposes that dreams provide us with an opportunity to work through our everyday problems and reflect on unresolved conflict.

Man at desk: John Lund/Heather Hryciw/Blend Images/Getty Images; clouds: Gary Paul Lewis/Shutterstock.com. Photo Illustration by Sam A. Marshall.

Most dreams involve memories of the day gone by—or, poetically, "the residue of the day."

activation–synthesis model the view that dreams reflect activation of cognitive activity by the reticular activating system and synthesis of this activity into a pattern by the cerebral cortex

Traumatic events, however, can spawn nightmares, as reported in the aftermath of the terrorist attacks on the World Trade Center and the Pentagon in 2001 (Gorman, 2001; Singareddy & Balon, 2002). People who have frequent nightmares are more likely than others to also have feelings of anxiety and depression (Blagrove et al., 2004; Levin & Fireman, 2002).

Dreams as the Expression of Unconscious Desires and Wish Fulfillment

In the Disney film *Cinderella,* a song lyric goes, "A dream is a wish your heart makes." Freud theorized that dreams reflect unconscious wishes and urges. He argued that dreams express impulses we would normally censor during the day. Moreover, he said that the content of a dream is symbolic of unconscious fantasized objects, such as the genitals. In his method of psychoanalysis, Freud would interpret his clients' dreams. Freud's *dreamwork* has been criticized by many contemporary researchers as being highly subjective, and it provides little evidence that dreams have hidden unconscious messages.

The Activation–Synthesis Model of Dreams

According to the **activation–synthesis model**, areas of the central nervous system (CNS) stimulate neural responses in the higher brain centres that lead to dreaming (Hobson & McCarley, 1977; Ogawa et al., 2002). One is *activation* of the reticular activating system (RAS; see Figure 2.10 on page 37), which arouses us, but not to waking. During the waking state, firing of these neurons is linked to movement, particularly in walking, running, and other physical acts. But during REM sleep, neurotransmitters tend to inhibit activity so we usually do not thrash about (Bassetti et al., 2000). In this way, we save ourselves—and our bed partners—wear and tear. But the eye muscles are stimulated and show the REM activity associated with dreaming. The RAS also stimulates parts of the cortex involved in memory. The cortex then *synthesizes,* or pieces together, these sources of stimulation to yield the stuff of dreams (Anderson & Horne, 2004). Because recent events are most likely to be reverberating in our brains, we are most likely to dream about them. With the brain cut off from the world outside, learning experiences and memories are replayed and consolidated during sleep (Siegel, 2002; Stickgold et al., 2001). Based on this interpretation of dreams, it is useful to get a night of sleep between studying and test-taking, if you can.

Figure 4.3 outlines the main ideas about dreams according to the three major theories: as wish fulfillment, as problem solving, and as random neuronal firings.

LO3 Major Sleep Disorders

Although nightmares are unpleasant, they do not qualify as sleep disorders. The term *sleep disorder* is reserved for other problems that can seriously interfere with our functioning.

What kinds of sleep disorders are there? Some sleep disorders, like insomnia, are all too familiar; in fact,

Dreams as wish fulfillment (Freud)

The problem-solving view (Cartwright)

Activation–synthesis model (Hobson & McCarley)

The day residue shapes dreams that satisfy unconscious needs.

We think through major problems in our lives.

A story is created to make sense of internal signals.

FIGURE 4.3

Three Theories of Dreaming

Dreams can be explained in a variety of ways. Freud stressed the wish-fulfilling function of dreams. Cartwright emphasizes the problem-solving function of dreams. Hobson and McCarley assert that dreams are merely a byproduct of periodic neural activation. All three theories are speculative and have their critics.

From WEITEN/MCCANN. *Psychology,* 2E. © 2010 Nelson Education Ltd. Reproduced with permission. www.cengage.com/permissions.

Falling asleep at midday may be a sign that you are not getting enough sleep. According to the Better Sleep Council of Canada (2009), one-quarter of Canadians are sleep-deprived.

sleep attacks are dangerous and upsetting. They can occur very randomly, such as while driving or working with sharp tools. They may be accompanied by the collapse of muscle groups or the entire body—a condition called *sleep paralysis*. In sleep paralysis, the person cannot move during the transition

30–40 percent of adults experience insomnia. Other disorders, like apnea (pauses in breathing), affect less than 10 percent of us (Canadian Sleep Society, 2009; National Sleep Foundation, 2008). In this section we discuss insomnia and less common sleep disorders, including narcolepsy, apnea, sleep terrors, and sleepwalking.

Insomnia

According to the Canadian Sleep Society (2009), 30–40 percent of adults are affected by insomnia in any given year, and 10 percent have insomnia problems so severe that the problems interfere with daily functioning. **Insomnia** refers to chronic difficulty in falling asleep, staying asleep, or maintaining restorative sleep. In many cases, trying to get to sleep compounds a person's sleep problems by creating autonomic activity and muscle tension. You cannot force or will yourself to go to sleep. You can only set the stage for sleep by relaxing when you are tired. Some treatment involves *stimulus control* methods to improve sleep quality. By controlling your environment and creating a "sleep routine," you may be able to achieve better sleep. For example, it is not a good idea to drink caffeine or eat before bed, and it is a good idea not to drink, snack, or watch television in bed.

Narcolepsy

A person with **narcolepsy** suddenly falls asleep. The "sleep attack" may last 15 minutes or so, after which the person feels refreshed. Nevertheless,

Breathing strips placed on the nose have become a popular over-the-counter remedy for mild apnea related to blocked airway passages. Football players are often seen wearing these strips to keep their nasal passageways open during game time.

apnea
temporary absence or cessation of breathing

sleep terrors
frightening dream-like experiences that occur during the deepest stage of NREM sleep; nightmares, in contrast, occur during REM sleep

hypnosis
a condition in which people are highly suggestible and behave as though they are in a trance

from consciousness to sleep, and hallucinations (as of a person or object sitting on the chest) occur.

Narcolepsy is thought to be a disorder of REM-sleep functioning. Stimulants and antidepressant drugs have helped many people with the problem (Schwartz, 2004).

Sleep Apnea

Apnea is a dangerous sleep disorder in which the air passages are obstructed while sleeping, such that people stop breathing periodically, up

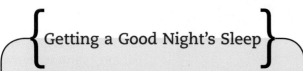

{ **Getting a Good Night's Sleep** }

The College of Family Physicians of Canada (2007) suggests the following tips for sleeping better:

- Go to bed and wake up at the same time every day.
- Develop a routine that is the same every night.
- Use the bedroom for sleeping only—no TV.
- A quiet, dark room is best for sleeping.
- Don't watch the clock if you can't fall asleep.
- Avoid caffeine, decongestants, alcohol, and tobacco.

to several hundred times per night. Obstruction may cause the sleeper to sit up and gasp for air before falling back asleep. People with apnea are stimulated nearly, but not quite, to waking by the build-up of carbon dioxide. Sleep apnea is associated with obesity, hypertension, and chronic snoring, and can lead to high blood pressure, heart attack, and stroke (Yumino & Bradley, 2007).

Causes of apnea include anatomical deformities that clog the air passageways, such as a thick palate, and problems in the breathing centres in the brain. Apnea is treated by such measures as weight loss, surgery, and *continuous positive airway pressure*, which is supplied by a mask that provides air pressure that keeps the airway open during sleep.

Deep-Sleep Disorders: Sleep Terrors and Sleepwalking

Sleep terrors and sleepwalking all occur during deep (stage 3 or 4) sleep. They are more common among children and may reflect immaturity of the nervous system (Kataria, 2004). **Sleep terrors** are

similar to, but more intense than, nightmares, which occur during REM sleep. Sleep terrors usually occur during the first two sleep cycles of the night, whereas nightmares are more likely to occur toward morning. Experiencing a surge in the heart and respiration rates, the person may suddenly sit up, talk incoherently, and thrash about. He or she is never fully awake, returns to sleep, and may recall a vague image as of someone pressing on his or her chest. (Memories of nightmares tend to be more detailed.) Sleep terrors are often decreased by a minor tranquilizer at bedtime, which reduces the amount of time spent in stage 4 sleep.

Sleepwalking typically occurs in stage 3 or 4 sleep. Surveys suggest that some 7–15 percent of children walk in their sleep (Neveus et al., 2002). Only 2 percent of adults do (Ohayon et al., 1999). Sleepwalkers may roam about nightly and can injure themselves accidentally, perhaps by falling down stairs. Sleepwalkers typically do not remember their excursions, although they may respond to questions while they are up and about. Mild tranquilizers and maturity typically decrease the incidence of sleepwalking.

LO4 Altering Consciousness through Hypnosis and Meditation

Perhaps you have watched a classmate try to place a friend in a "trance" after reading a book on hypnosis. Or perhaps you have seen an audience member hypnotized in a nightclub act. If so, chances are the person acted as if he or she had returned to childhood, imagined that a snake was about to strike, or lay rigid between two chairs for a while. Perhaps also, you have tried to interrupt a friend while she was engaged in yoga mediation. In this section we discuss hypnosis and meditation as altered states of consciousness.

Hypnosis

Of these altered states, the one we hear of most is hypnosis. *What is hypnosis?* The word **hypnosis** is derived from *Hypnos*, the Greek god of sleep. It is an altered state of consciousness in which people are suggestible and behave as though they are in a trance. Modern hypnosis evolves from the ideas of Franz Mesmer in the 18th century. Mesmer asserted that everything in the universe was connected by forms of magnetism—which may not be far from the mark. However, he also claimed that people, too, could be drawn to one another by "animal magnetism." Not so. Mesmer used bizarre props to bring people under his "spell" and managed a respectable cure rate for minor ailments. Scientists now attribute his successes to the placebo effect, not animal magnetism.

Today hypnotism is more than a nightclub act. It is also used as an anaesthetic in dentistry, childbirth, and medical procedures (Patterson, 2004; Shenefelt, 2003). Some psychologists use hypnosis to help clients reduce anxiety, overcome fears, or lessen the perception of chronic pain (Jensen et al., 2005; Pinnell & Covino, 2000). A study with 241 surgery patients shows how hypnosis can help people deal with pain and anxiety. The patients had procedures with local anesthetics (Lang et al., 2000). They could use as much pain medication as they wished. Patients who were hypnotized needed less additional pain medication and experienced less anxiety as measured by blood pressure and heart rate. The hypnotized patients focused on pleasant imagery rather than the surgery. Hypnosis helps people relax to cope with stress and enhance the functioning of their immune systems (Kiecolt-Glaser et al., 2001). Hypnosis can also be useful in helping people control their weight and stop smoking (Lynn et al., 2003). Some police departments use hypnosis to prompt the memories of witnesses; however, criticism regarding the use of hypnosis in criminal investigations points to the inconclusiveness of witness recall accuracy (McConkey & Sheehan, 1995).

The state of consciousness called the *hypnotic trance* has traditionally been induced by asking people to narrow their attention to a small light, a spot on the wall, an object held by the hypnotist, or the hypnotist's voice. The hypnotist usually suggests that the person's limbs are becoming warm, heavy, and relaxed. People may also be told that they are becoming sleepy or falling asleep. But hypnosis is *not* sleep, as shown by differences between EEG recordings for the hypnotic trance and the stages of sleep. (Subjects understand that the word *sleep* suggests a hypnotic trance.) Researchers are also studying changes in the brain that result from hypnosis. For example, Rainville and his colleagues (2002) used PET scans on people being hypnotized and found that mental absorption and mental relaxation are associated with changes in blood flow in the cerebral cortex (absorption) and parts of the brain involved in arousal and attention (relaxation).

People who are easily hypnotized are said to have *hypnotic suggestibility*. Part of "suggestibility" is knowledge of what is expected during the "trance state." Generally speaking, suggestible people are prone to fantasy and want to cooperate with the hypnotist (Barber, 2000). As a result, they pay close attention to the instructions. Refer to Table 4.1 (p. 90) to dispel some of the myths regarding hypnosis.

> **Hypnosis is not sleep, as shown by differences between EEG recordings for the hypnotic trance and the stages of sleep.**

Explaining Hypnosis

Hypnotism is no longer explained in terms of animal magnetism, but others have offered explanations. According to Freud, hypnotized adults permit themselves to return to childish modes of responding that emphasize fantasy and impulse rather than fact and logic. Modern views of hypnosis are quite different. *How do psychologists explain the effects of hypnosis?*

The **role theory** view of hypnosis (Sarbin & Coe, 1972) is a *social-cognitive theory* proposing that changes in behaviour attributed to the hypnotic trance can be successfully imitated by people who are motivated to take on the role of being hypnotized (Spanos, 1991). Carleton University researcher Nicholas Spanos recognized that people motivated to play the "role" and who expect to respond to the hypnotist's suggestions develop a perceptual set that makes them ready to "play and respond" to hypnosis. Also, people cannot be hypnotized unless they are familiar with the hypnotic role. This is not to say that participants *fake* the hypnotic role. Researchers suggest that people *allow* themselves to enact this role under the hypnotist's directions (Spanos, 1991; Sarbin & Cole, 1972).

> **role theory**
> a social-cognitive theory that explains hypnotic events in terms of the person's expectations and ability to act (or play the "role") *as though* he or she were hypnotized

imagestopshop/Alamy

transcendental meditation (TM) the simplified form of meditation that focuses on words or sounds to help a person achieve an altered state of consciousness; used as a method for coping with stress

mindfulness meditation (MM) a form of meditation that provides clients with techniques they can use to focus on the present moment rather than ruminate about problems

The social-cognitive theory of hypnosis appears to be supported by research evidence that "suggestible" people want to be hypnotized, are good role players, have vivid imaginations, and know what is expected of them (Barber, 2000; Kirsch, 2000, Spanos, 1991). The fact that the behaviours shown by hypnotized people can be mimicked by people who know what is expected of them means that we need not resort to the concept of the "hypnotic trance"—an unusual and mystifying altered state of awareness—to explain hypnotic events.

Let us now consider another altered state of consciousness that involve different ways of focusing our attention: meditation.

Meditation

What is meditation? The dictionary defines *meditation* as the act or process of thinking. But the concept usually suggests thinking deeply about the universe or about one's place in the world, often within a spiritual context. For psychologists, *meditation* refers to various ways of focusing one's consciousness to alter one's relationship to the world. In this use, ironically, *meditation* can also refer to a process by which people seem to suspend thinking and allow the world to fade away.

The kinds of meditation that helping professionals speak of tend to refer to rituals, exercises, even passive observation—activities that alter the normal relationship between the person and the environment. They are methods of suspending problem solving, planning, worrying, and awareness of the events of the day. These methods alter consciousness—the normal focus of attention—and help people cope with stress by inducing feelings of relaxation.

One common form of meditation, **transcendental meditation (TM)**, is practised by concentrating on *mantras*—words or sounds that are claimed to help the person achieve an altered state of consciousness. TM has some goals that cannot be assessed scientifically, such as expanding consciousness to encompass spiritual experiences, but there are also measurable goals, such as reducing anxiety and blood pressure. For example, Herbert Benson (1975) found that TM lowered the heart and respiration rates and also produced what he labelled a *relaxation response*. The blood pressure of people with hypertension—a risk factor in cardiovascular disease—decreased.

Similarly, studies have compared the effects of TM, muscle relaxation, and a "health education" placebo on high blood pressure (Alexander et al., 1996; Schneider et al., 1995). They found that TM was significantly more effective at reducing blood pressure than relaxation or the placebo. Another form of meditation is the use of **mindfulness meditation (MM)** in cognitive and behaviour therapy. MM, as

TABLE 4.1

Misconceptions Regarding Hypnosis

HYPNOSIS: MYTH AND REALITY	
If you think...	**The reality is...**
Relaxation is an important feature of hypnosis.	It's not. Hypnosis has been induced during vigorous exercise.
It's mostly just compliance.	Many highly motivated subjects fail to experience hypnosis.
It's a matter of willful faking.	Physiological responses indicate that hypnotized subjects generally are not lying.
It has something to do with a sleeplike state.	It does not. Hypnotized subjects are fully awake.
Responding to hypnosis is like responding to a placebo.	Placebo responsiveness and hypnotizability are not correlated.
People who are hypnotized lose control of themselves.	Subjects are perfectly capable of saying no or terminating hypnosis.
Hypnosis can enable people to "relive" the past.	Age-regressed adults behave like adults play-acting as children.
When hypnotized, people can remember more accurately.	Hypnosis may actually muddle the distinction between memory and fantasy and may artificially inflate confidence.
Hypnotized people do not remember what happened during the session.	Posthypnotic amnesia does not occur spontaneously.
Hypnosis can enable people to perform otherwise impossible feats of strength, endurance, learning, and sensory acuity.	Performance following hypnotic suggestions for increased muscle strength, learning, and sensory acuity does not exceed what can be accomplished by motivated subjects outside hypnosis.

opposed to TM, makes no pretence of achieving spiritual goals. Instead, MM provides clients with mantra-like techniques they can use to focus on the present moment rather than ruminate about problems (Heidenreich & Michalak, 2003; Salmon et al., 2004). MM holds promise for helping clients cope with problems such as depression as well as reducing stress (Ramel et al., 2004). Brain imaging also shows that meditation activates neural structures involved in attention and in control of the autonomic nervous system, helping produce feelings of relaxation (Lazar et al., 2000).

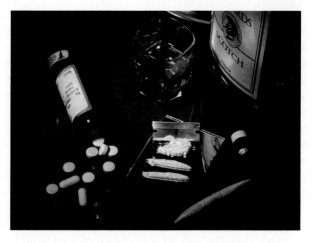

Drugs provide users with an altered state of consciousness. Some drugs give us pleasure; others provide us with a temporary escape from our lives. Nonetheless, all drugs can be dangerous and addictive.

© Craig Cozart/iStockphoto.com

depressant
a drug that lowers the rate of activity of the nervous system

stimulant
a drug that increases activity of the nervous system

substance abuse
persistent use of a substance even though it is causing or compounding problems in meeting the demands of life

LO5 Altering Consciousness through Drugs

It is highly likely that you have known someone who has taken or currently takes drugs. Our world is flooded with drugs that distort our perceptions and change our mood—drugs that take you up, let you down, and move you across town. Some of these drugs are legal; others are illegal. Some are used recreationally; others medically. Some are safe if used appropriately and dangerous if they are not. Some people use drugs because their friends do or because their parents tell them not to. Some are seeking pleasure; others are seeking inner truth or escape.

Young adults often become involved with drugs that impair their ability to learn at school and are often connected with reckless behaviour (Centre for Addiction and Mental Health, 2009). Alcohol is the most popular drug used by youth aged 15 to 24, with 78 percent of youth reporting that they regularly drink (Health Canada, *Canadian Alcohol and Drug Use Monitoring Survey* [CADUMS], 2009). Almost 35 percent of youth have tried marijuana, which is four times higher than adult use; males are twice as likely as females to use marijuana (CADUMS, 2009). The use of **depressants** to get to sleep at night and **stimulants** to get going in the morning

Joe Raedle/Getty Images

has also increased over the past few years, with about one-quarter of Canadians reporting the use of a stimulant to get high (CADUMS, 2009). Use of other illicit drugs, such as cocaine and heroin, has recently decreased among youth and Canadians in general (CADUMS, 2009).

Substance Abuse and Dependence

Where does drug use end and abuse begin? *What are substance abuse and dependence?* Substance abuse is defined as repeated use of a substance despite the fact that it is causing or compounding social, occupational, psychological, or physical problems. If you are missing school or work because you are drunk or "sleeping it off," you are abusing alcohol. The amount you drink is not as crucial as the fact that your pattern of use disrupts your life.

substance dependence
loss of control over use of a substance; biologically speaking, dependence is typified by tolerance, withdrawal symptoms, or both

tolerance
habituation to a drug, with the result that increasingly higher doses of the drug are needed to achieve similar effects

withdrawal symptoms
a characteristic cluster of symptoms that results from sudden decrease in an addictive drug's level of usage

Substance dependence is more severe than substance abuse and has behavioural and biological aspects. Behaviourally, dependence is characterized by loss of control over use of the substance. Dependent people may organize their lives around getting and using a substance. Biological or physiological dependence is typified by tolerance, withdrawal symptoms, or both. **Tolerance** is the body's habituation to a substance so that, with regular usage, higher doses are needed to achieve similar effects. There are **withdrawal symptoms** when the level of usage suddenly drops off. Withdrawal symptoms for alcohol include anxiety, tremors, restlessness, rapid pulse, and high blood pressure.

When going without a drug, people who are *psychologically* dependent show signs of anxiety such as shakiness, rapid pulse, and sweating that may be similar to withdrawal symptoms. Because of these signs, they may believe that they are physiologically dependent on—or addicted to—a drug when they are psychologically dependent. But symptoms of withdrawal from some drugs are unmistakably physiological. One is delirium tremens ("DTs"), experienced when an addict suddenly lowers his or her intake of a drug. People with DTs have heavy sweating, restlessness, disorientation, and frightening hallucinations—often of crawling animals.

Causal Factors in Substance Abuse and Dependence

What are the causes of substance abuse and dependence? Substance abuse and dependence usually begin with experimental use in adolescence (Lewinsohn et al., 2000a). Youth especially experiment with drugs for various reasons, including curiosity, conformity to peer pressure, parental use, rebelliousness, escape from boredom or pressure, and excitement or pleasure (Griffin et al., 2004; Wilkinson & Abraham, 2004). Let's now look at some theories of substance abuse.

Social–cognitive theorists suggest that people often try alcohol and tranquilizers such as Valium (the generic name is diazepam) on the basis of a recommendation or observation of others. Expectations about the effects of a substance predict its use (Cumsille et al., 2000).

Use of a substance may be reinforced by peers or by the drug's positive effects on mood and its reduction of anxiety, fear, and stress (Griffin et al., 2004). Many people use drugs as a form of self-medication for anxiety and depression, even low self-esteem (Dierker et al., 2001). For people who are physiologically dependent, avoidance of withdrawal symptoms is also reinforcing. Carrying a supply of the substance is reinforcing because one need not worry about going without it. Parents who use drugs may increase their children's knowledge of drugs. In effect, they also show their children when to use them—for example, by drinking alcohol to cope with tension or to lessen the anxiety associated with meeting people at parties and other get-togethers (Power et al., 2005).

A large body of research supports that some individuals may have a genetic predisposition toward physiological dependence on certain substances, such as alcohol, opioids, cocaine, and nicotine (Chen et al., 2004; Nurnberger et al., 2004; Radel et al., 2005). For example, the biological children of alcoholics who are reared by nonalcoholic adoptive parents are more likely to develop alcohol-related problems than the biological children of the adoptive parents. An inherited tendency toward alcoholism may involve greater sensitivity to alcohol (that is, greater enjoyment of it) and greater tolerance (Pihl et al., 1990). Greater tolerance is shown by studies in which college students with alcoholic parents show better muscular control and visual–motor coordination when they drink than other college students do (Pihl et al., 1990). Individuals with a family history of alcoholism are also more sensitive to the stimulating effects of alcohol, which occur at lower levels of intoxication (Conrad et al., 2001).

Now that we have learned about substance abuse and dependence, let us turn to a discussion of the different kinds of psychoactive drugs and consider the effects of these drugs on consciousness.

Depressants

Depressants generally act by slowing the activity of the central nervous system (i.e., they slow down our body function; hence, they are often called "downers.") There are also effects specific to each depressant. In this section we consider the effects of alcohol, opiates, and barbiturates.

Alcohol—The Cause of and Solution to All of Life's Problems

Let's face it, for many of us, alcohol is our dinnertime relaxant, our bedtime sedative, and our cocktail-party social facilitator. We use alcohol to celebrate holy days, applaud our accomplishments, and express joyous wishes. The young assert their maturity with alcohol. In fact, in 2008, alcohol was used by 77.3 percent of people over age 15 in the preceding 12 months (CADUMS, 2009), with beer being the most common drink of choice by Canadian college and university students.

Alcohol offers relief from anxiety, depression, or loneliness, and you can drink in public without criticism or stigma (Bonin et al., 2000; Swendsen et al., 2000). But no drug has been so abused as alcohol. Excessive drinking has been linked to lower productivity, loss of employment, and downward movement in social status. In college and university, many students engage in binge drinking. Binge drinking—having five or more drinks in a row for a male, or four or more for a female (Naimi et al., 2003b)—is connected with aggressive behaviour, poor grades, sexual promiscuity, and accidents (Birch et al., 2007; Keller et al., 2007). Nevertheless, 44 percent of college students binge at least twice a month (Hingson et al., 2002).

What are the effects of alcohol? The effects of alcohol vary with the dose and duration of use. Low doses may be stimulating because alcohol dilates blood vessels, which carry sugar through the body. Higher doses have a sedative effect, which is why alcohol is classified as a depressant. Alcohol relaxes people and deadens minor aches and pains. Alcohol also intoxicates: It impairs cognitive functioning, slurs the speech, and impairs coordination.

Alcohol lowers inhibitions. Drinkers may do things they would not do if they were sober, such as having unprotected sex (Donohue et al., 2007). When drunk, people may be less able to foresee the consequences of their behaviour. They may also be less likely to summon up their moral beliefs. Then, too, alcohol induces feelings of elation and euphoria that may wash away doubts. Alcohol is also associated with a liberated social role in our culture. Drinkers may place the blame on alcohol ("It's the alcohol, not me"), even though they choose to drink.

Men are more likely than women to become alcohol-dependent. Why?

> "In 2008, some 77.3 percent of Canadians aged 15 or older reported consuming alcohol in the previous 12 months."
>
> —(CADUMS, 2009)

A cultural explanation is that tighter social constraints are usually placed on women. A biological explanation is that alcohol hits women harder, discouraging them from overindulging. Alcohol "goes to women's heads" faster than to men's, because women metabolize less of it in the stomach (Lieber, 1990). Alcohol reaches women's bloodstreams and brains relatively intact. Asians are less likely than Europeans to drink to excess because they are more likely to show an unpleasant "flushing response" to alcohol, as evidenced by redness of the face, rapid heart rate, dizziness, and headaches (Fromme et al., 2004).

Regardless of how or why one starts drinking, regular drinking can lead to physiological dependence. People are then motivated to drink to avoid withdrawal symptoms. Still, even when alcoholics have "dried out"—withdrawn from alcohol—many return to drinking. Perhaps they still want to use alcohol as a way of coping with stress or as an excuse for failure.

In college and university, many students engage in binge drinking. Binge drinking—having five or more drinks in a row for a male, or four or more for a female—is connected with aggressive behaviour, poor grades, sexual promiscuity, and accidents (Birch et al., 2007; Keller et al., 2007).

opiates
a group of narcotics derived from the opium poppy that provide a euphoric rush and depress the nervous system

narcotics
drugs used to relieve pain and induce sleep; the term is usually reserved for opiates

opioids
chemicals that act on opiate receptors but are not derived from the opium poppy

barbiturate
an addictive depressant used to relieve anxiety or induce sleep

amphetamines
stimulants derived from alpha-methyl-beta-phenyl-ethyl-amine, a colourless liquid consisting of carbon, hydrogen, and nitrogen

Opiates—Narcotics We Get from Opium

Opiates are a group of narcotics derived from the opium poppy, from which they obtain their name. The ancient Sumerians gave the opium poppy its name: It means "plant of joy." Opioids are similar in chemical structure but made in a laboratory. *What are the effects of opiates?* As narcotics, they produce both pain relief and a calming effect. The major medical application of opiates is relief from pain.

One of the most highly addictive opioids is heroin. Heroin can provide a strong euphoric "rush." Users claim that it is so pleasurable it can eradicate thoughts of food or sex. High doses can cause drowsiness and stupor, alter time perception, and impair judgment. With regular use of opiates, the brain stops producing neurotransmitters that are chemically similar to opiates—the pain-relieving endorphins.

As a result, people can become physiologically dependent on opiates, such that going without them can be agonizing. Withdrawal syndromes may begin with flu-like symptoms and progress through tremors, cramps, and chills alternating with sweating, rapid pulse, high blood pressure, insomnia, vomiting, and diarrhea. Heroin was once used as a cure for addiction to morphine. Today, we use methadone, a synthetic (human-made) opioid that is used to treat physiological dependence on heroin. Methadone is slower-acting than heroin and does not provide the thrilling rush, but it does prevent withdrawal symptoms. Methadone maintenance treatment programs are prevalent across Canada and are considered successful in treating opioid addictions (Ontario Addiction Treatment Centre, 2009).

Barbiturates—Sedatives and Tranquilizers

What are the effects of barbiturates? Barbiturates like Nembutal and Ambytal are central nervous system depressants with several medical uses, including relief from anxiety, tension, and pain, as well as treatment of epilepsy, high blood pressure, and insomnia. With regular use, barbiturates lead rapidly to physiological and psychological dependence.

Barbiturates are popular as street drugs because they are relaxing and produce mild euphoria. High doses result in drowsiness, motor impairment, slurred speech, irritability, and poor judgment. A highly physiologically dependent person who is withdrawn abruptly from barbiturates may experience convulsions and die. A milder form of barbiturates is a class of benzodiazapines, such as Valium and Xanax. These are considered more effective and safe for treatment of medical and psychological disorders (Cole & Chiarello, 1990). Because of the additive effects of barbiturates and benzodiazepines, it is dangerous to mix them with alcohol and other depressants.

Stimulants

Stimulants increase the activity of the nervous system (i.e., they make us feel alert, and energetic; hence, they are often called "uppers"). Some of their effects can be positive. For example, amphetamines stimulate cognitive activity and apparently help people control impulses. Some stimulants are appealing as street drugs because they contribute to feelings of euphoria and self-confidence. But they also have their risks. In this section we discuss amphetamines, cocaine, and nicotine.

Amphetamines

What are the effects of amphetamines? Amphetamines were first used by soldiers during World War II to help them stay alert at night. Truck drivers also use them to drive through the night. Students use amphetamines for all-night cram sessions. Dieters use them because they reduce hunger.

Amphetamines are often abused for the euphoric rush that high doses can produce. Some people swallow amphetamines in pill form or inject liquid Methedrine, the strongest form, into their veins. As a result, they may stay awake and high for days on end. But such highs must end. People who have been on prolonged highs sometimes "crash," or fall into a deep sleep or depression. Tolerance for amphetamines develops quickly, and users can become dependent on them, especially when they use them to self-medicate themselves for depression. Whether amphetamines cause physical addiction has been a subject of controversy (Shen et al., 2007). High doses can cause restlessness, insomnia, loss of appetite, hallucinations, paranoid delusions (e.g., false ideas

Ironically, heroin was once used as a cure for addiction to morphine.

that others are eavesdropping or intend them harm), and irritability. Withdrawal symptoms include physical exhaustion, depression, and extreme hunger.

Cocaine—Stimulating Our Pleasure Areas

Cocaine is derived from coca leaves—the plant from which the soft drink Coca-Cola took its name. Do you recall commercials claiming that "Coke adds life"? Given its caffeine and sugar content, "Coke" should provide quite a lift. But Coca-Cola hasn't been "the real thing" since 1906, when the company stopped using cocaine in its formula.

What are the effects of cocaine? The stimulant cocaine produces euphoria, reduces hunger, deadens pain, and boosts self-confidence. As shown in Figure 4.4, cocaine works by binding to sites on sending neurons that normally reuptake molecules of the neurotransmitters norepinephrine, dopamine, and serotonin. As a result, molecules of these transmitters remain longer in the synaptic cleft, enhancing their mood-altering effects and producing a "rush." But when cocaine levels drop, lower absorption of neurotransmitters by receiving neurons causes the user's mood to "crash." Cocaine may be brewed from coca leaves as a "tea," snorted in powder form, or injected in liquid form. Repeated snorting constricts blood

Actor Robert Downey, Jr., the star of *Iron Man 2,* has been arrested and jailed several times for cocaine addiction over the past 15 years. The addiction has landed him in and out of drug rehabilitation centres across the United States. In a recent interview with *Rolling Stone* magazine, Downey admitted to "binging on crack cocaine" for years (*Rolling Stone,* 2010).

vessels in the nose, drying the skin and sometimes exposing cartilage and perforating the nasal septum. The potent cocaine derivatives known as "crack" and "bazooka" are inexpensive because they are unrefined.

Physical dangers include sudden rises in blood pressure, which constricts the coronary arteries and decreases the oxygen supply to the heart, and quickens the heart rate events that can lead to respiratory and cardiovascular collapse, as in the sudden deaths of some young athletes (Mitchell, 2006). Overdoses can cause restlessness and insomnia, tremors, headaches, nausea, convulsions, hallucinations, and delusions. Use of crack has been connected with strokes. Less than 1 percent of adolescents aged 15 to 25 report using cocaine regularly (CADUMS, 2009). Cocaine causes physiological as well as psychological dependence. Best-selling Canadian children's author Robert

---

FIGURE 4.4

How Cocaine Produces Euphoria and Why People "Crash"

A. In the normal functioning of the nervous system, neurotransmitters are released into the synaptic cleft by vesicles in terminal buttons of sending neurons. Many are taken up by receptor sites in receiving neurons.

B. In the process called *reuptake,* sending neurons typically reabsorb excess molecules of neurotransmitters.

C. Molecules of cocaine bind to the sites on sending neurons that normally reuptake molecules of neurotransmitters. As a result, molecules of norepinephrine, dopamine, and serotonin remain longer in the synaptic cleft, increasing their typical mood-altering effects and providing a euphoric "rush." When the person stops using cocaine, the lessened absorption of neurotransmitters by receiving neurons causes the person's mood to "crash."

Go to www.icanpsych.com to access an interactive version of this figure.

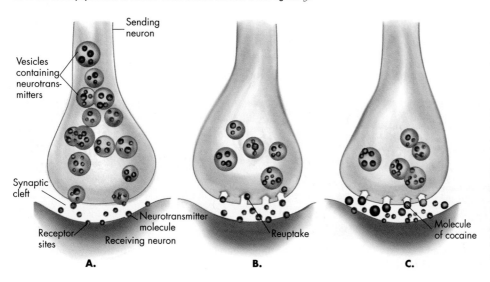

Munsch has even battled both alcohol and cocaine addiction. A number of Hollywood celebrities have battled with cocaine addiction as well, most recently Paris Hilton.

Nicotine

Nicotine is the stimulant in tobacco smoke. *What are the effects of nicotine?* Nicotine stimulates discharge of the hormone adrenaline and the release of neurotransmitters, including dopamine, acetylcholine, GABA, and endorphins (Brody, 2008). Adrenaline creates a burst of autonomic activity that accelerates the heart rate and pours sugar into the blood. Acetylcholine is vital in memory formation, and nicotine appears to enhance memory and attention; improve performance on simple, repetitive tasks; and enhance the mood (Gentry, et al., 2000; Rezvani & Levin, 2001). Although it is a stimulant, because of GABA and endorphins, nicotine has a relaxing effect. It depresses the appetite and raises the metabolic rate. Thus, some people smoke cigarettes to control their weight.

Symptoms of withdrawal from nicotine include nervousness, drowsiness, loss of energy, headaches, irregular bowel movements, light-headedness,

Spencer Platt/Getty Images

The perils of cigarette smoking are widely known today. The Canadian Lung Association (2008) has declared that cigarette smoking is the chief preventable cause of death in Canada. In 2008, approximately 20 percent of Canadians reported that they smoke (CADUMS, 2009), and it is estimated that approximately 45 000 Canadians die each year from cigarette smoking (Health Canada, 2009).

insomnia, dizziness, cramps, palpitations, tremors, and sweating.

The carbon monoxide in cigarette smoke impairs the blood's ability to carry oxygen, causing shortness of breath. The **hydrocarbons** ("tars") in cigarette and cigar smoke lead to lung cancer (Canadian Lung Association, 2008). Cigarette smoking also stiffens arteries (Mahmud & Feely, 2003) and is linked to death from heart disease, chronic lung and respiratory diseases, and other health problems. Women who smoke show reduced bone density, increasing the risk of fracture of the hip and back. Pregnant women who smoke have a higher risk of miscarriage, preterm births, stillborn babies, and children with learning problems (Canadian Lung Association, 2008).

ian nolan/Alamy

WARNING

CIGARETTES ARE HIGHLY ADDICTIVE

Studies have shown that tobacco can be harder to quit than heroin or cocaine.

Health Canada

WARNING

YOU'RE NOT THE ONLY ONE SMOKING THIS CIGARETTE

The smoke from a cigarette is not just inhaled by the smoker. It becomes second-hand smoke, which contains more than 50 cancer-causing agents.

Health Canada

Health Canada, "Cigarettes are highly addictive." Reproduced with permission.

Health Canada, "You're Not the Only One Smoking this Cigarette." Reproduced with permission.

It's no secret. Cigarette packs sold in Canada carry messages like "Warning: cigarettes are highly addictive." Cigarette advertising has been banned on radio and television.

Kuttia - People/GetStock.com

What do you think when you see an adult smoking in a car with a child in the back seat? In some provinces, you can be fined for smoking in a vehicle with a child as a passenger.

Second-hand smoke—smoke inhaled from other people's tobacco products—is also connected with respiratory illnesses, asthma, and other health problems. Prolonged exposure to second-hand smoke during childhood is a risk factor for lung cancer (Canadian Cancer Society, 2009). Because of the effects of second-hand smoke, smoking has been banned from restaurants and bars. Most recently, under the Smoke-Free Ontario Amendment Act (2008), adults can be fined if they are smoking in any motor vehicle with passengers under the age of 16.

Hallucinogens

Hallucinogens are so named because they produce hallucinations—that is, sensations and perceptions in the absence of external stimulation. Hallucinogens may also have additional effects such as relaxation, euphoria, or, in some cases, panic. Marijuana (yes, it has psychedelic properties) and LSD are two known substances that produce hallucinogenic effects.

Marijuana

Marijuana is produced from the *Cannabis sativa* plant, which grows wild in many parts of the world. *What are the effects of marijuana?* Marijuana helps some people relax and can elevate their mood. It also sometimes produces mild hallucinations, which is why we discuss it as a hallucinogen. The major psychedelic substance in marijuana is delta-9-tetrahydrocannabinol, or THC. THC is found in the branches and leaves of the plant, but it is highly concentrated in the resin. *Hashish,* or "hash," is derived from the resin and is more potent than marijuana.

Marijuana has been shown to produce a number of health risks. For example, it impairs the perceptual–motor coordination used in driving and operating machines. It also impairs short-term memory and slows learning (Egerton et al., 2006).

Some users report that marijuana helps them socialize. Moderate to strong intoxication is linked to reports of sharpened perceptions, increases in self-insight, creative thinking, and empathy for others. Time seems to slow. A song might seem to last an hour rather than minutes. There is increased awareness of bodily sensations such as the heartbeat. Marijuana users also report that strong intoxication heightens sexual sensations. Visual hallucinations may occur, and strong intoxication may cause disorientation. If the smoker's mood is euphoric, disorientation may be interpreted as "harmony" with the universe, but some users find disorientation threatening and fear they will not regain their identity (Bonn-Miller et al., 2007). Rapid heart rate and heightened awareness of bodily sensations leads some users to fear their hearts will "run away" with them. Strong intoxication can cause nausea and vomiting. Regular users may experience tolerance and withdrawal symptoms (Budney et al., 2007).

Marijuana is also used for medical purposes. Canada was one of the first countries to approve marijuana for medical use. The first use of medical marijuana was to help cancer patients reduce the nauseating effects of chemotherapy. It is also prescribed for relief of severe pain or persistent muscle spasms for such conditions as multiple sclerosis, spinal cord injury or disease, and epilepsy (Health Canada, 2005a).

LSD (and Other Hallucinogens)

LSD is the abbreviation for lysergic acid diethylamide, a synthetic hallucinogen. *What are the effects of LSD and other kinds of hallucinogens?* Users of "acid" claim that it "expands consciousness" and "opens up new worlds." Sometimes people say they have achieved great insights while using LSD, but when it wears off they cannot apply or recall them. LSD distorts our sensory experiences and produces vivid, colourful hallucinations.

hallucinogen
a substance that causes hallucinations

marijuana
the dried vegetable matter of the Cannabis sativa plant

LSD
lysergic acid diethylamide; a hallucinogen

flashbacks
distorted perceptions or hallucinations that occur days or weeks after LSD usage but mimic the LSD experience

mescaline
a hallucinogen derived from the mescal (peyote) cactus

phencyclidine (PCP)
a hallucinogen; its name is an abbreviation of its chemical structure

Some LSD users have **flashbacks**—distorted perceptions or hallucinations that mimic the LSD "trip" but occur days, weeks, or longer after usage. Research suggests that LSD mimics serotonin in the brain and therefore, decreases serotonin activity in the brain, causing dream-like altered perceptions. Other hallucinogens include **mescaline** (derived from the peyote cactus) and **phencyclidine (PCP)**. PCP was developed as an anesthetic and an animal tranquilizer. It goes by the street names "angel dust," "ozone," "wack," and "rocket fuel." The street terms "killer joints" and "crystal super grass" refer to PCP combined with marijuana.

Regular use of hallucinogens may lead to tolerance and psychological dependence, but it is not known to create physiological dependence. High doses may impair coordination, cloud judgment, change one's mood, and cause frightening hallucinations and delusions. Table 4.2 summarizes the effects of various psychoactive drugs.

LSD is a hallucinogen that can give rise to a vivid parade of colours and visual distortions. Some users claim to have achieved great insights while "tripping," but typically they have been unable to recall or apply them afterward.

TABLE 4.2

Drugs and Their Effects

Drug	Type	How Taken	Desired Effects	Tolerance	Abstinence Syndrome	Side Effects
Alcohol	Depressant	By mouth	Relaxation, euphoria, lowered inhibitions	Yes	Yes	Impaired coordination, poor judgment, hangover*
Heroin	Depressant	Injected, smoked, by mouth	Relaxation, euphoria, relief from anxiety and pain	Yes	Yes	Impaired coordination and mental functioning, drowsiness, lethargy*
Barbiturates and Methaqualone	Depressants	By mouth, Injected	Relaxation, sleep, euphoria, lowered inhibitions	Yes	Yes	Impaired coordination and mental functioning, drowsiness, lethargy*
Amphetamines	Stimulants	By mouth, injected	Alertness, euphoria	Yes	†	Restlessness, loss of appetite, psychotic symptoms
Cocaine	Stimulant	By mouth, snorted, injected	Euphoria, self-confidence	Yes	Yes	Restlessness, loss of appetite, convulsions, strokes, psychotic symptoms
Nicotine (cigarettes)	Stimulant	By tobacco (smoked, chewed, or sniffed)	Relaxation, stimulation, weight control	Yes	Yes	Cancer, heart disease, lung and respiratory diseases
Marijuana	Hallucinogenic	Smoked, by mouth	Relaxation, perceptual distortions, enhancement of experience	†	†	Impaired coordination, learning, respiratory problems, panic
MDMA "Ecstasy"	Stimulant/ Hallucinogenic	By mouth	Alertness, self-confidence, hallucinations	?	?	Impaired memory, increased heart rate, anxiety, confusion, possible depression
LSD, PCP	Hallucinogenic	By mouth	Perceptual distortions, vivid hallucinations	Yes	No	Impaired coordination, psychotic symptoms, panic

*Overdose can result in death.

†Recent research suggests the answer is yes, although some might consider the "jury still to be out"

Learning Outcomes

LO1 Describe the learning process according to classical conditioning

LO2 Describe the learning process according to operant conditioning

LO3 Describe cognitive factors in learning

Learning

© Scott Griessel/Dreamstime.com

"Do violent video games and media really make us more aggressive or think violent thoughts?"

Dylan Klebold and Eric Harris were engrossed in violent video games for hours at a time. They were particularly keen on a game named *Doom*. Harris had managed to reprogram *Doom* so that he, the player, became invulnerable and had an endless supply of weapons. He would "mow down" all the other characters in the game. His program caused some of the characters to ask God why they had been shot as they lay dying. Later on, Klebold and Harris asked some of their shooting victims at Columbine High School in Colorado whether they believed in God. One of the killers also referred to his shotgun as Arlene, the name of a character in *Doom* (Saunders, 2003).

In the small rural town of Bethel, Alaska, Evan Ramsey shot four people, killing two and wounding two. Afterward, he said his favourite video games—*Doom*, *Die Hard*, and *Resident Evil*—taught him that being shot would reduce a player's "health factor" but probably not be lethal.

The debate about whether violence in media such as films, television, and video games fuels violence in the real world has been going on for more than 40 years. Psychologist Craig A. Anderson (2003, 2004), who has carried out extensive research in this area, argues that studies show that media violence is a risk factor for increasing emotional arousal, aggressive behaviour, and violent thoughts. Others, such as the University of Toronto's Jonathan Freedman (2002), maintain that empirical research does not demonstrate that media violence produces violence or aggression in people.

One reason to be particularly concerned about violent video games

DID YOU KNOW?

- A single nauseating meal can give rise to a taste aversion that lasts for years.

- Psychologists once helped a young boy overcome his fear of rabbits by having him eat cookies while a rabbit was brought closer and closer.

- Slot-machine players pop coins into the machines most rapidly when they have no idea when they might win.

- You can train a rat to climb a ramp, cross a bridge, climb a ladder, pedal a toy car, and do several other tasks—all in proper sequence.

- Children who had observed aggressive adults showed significantly more aggressive behaviour than others who had not.

© Raquel Ramirez/PhotoEdit

is that they require audience participation (Anderson et al., 2004). Players don't passively watch; they *participate*. Violent games like *Grand Theft Auto* have grown increasingly popular. Some games reward players for killing police, prostitutes, and bystanders. Virtual weapons include guns, knives, flamethrowers, swords, clubs, cars, hands, and feet. Sometimes the player assumes the role of a hero, but it is also common for the player to assume the role of a criminal. As our technological world expands and our virtual world continues to collide with our real world, we will no doubt remain alarmed and concerned about the effects of interacting and participating in violent games and storylines.

We will return to this controversial issue later in the chapter. For now, we will discuss the contributions from psychologists known as *behaviourists* who focus on the study of observable behaviour, which leads to learning. We will also describe how cognitive psychologists view our behaviour and how their ideas differ from traditional behaviourist theories. Most of what we learn may be helpful and adaptive. But there are exceptions, such as drug addiction or perhaps violent video games.

What is learning? Learning as defined in psychology is more than listening to teachers, honing skateboard jumps, or mastering the use of an iPod. **Learning** is a relatively permanent change in behaviour, capabilities, or knowledge that arises from practice or experience. The definition suggests that players of violent video games went on rampages because they had been rewarded or reinforced for similar behaviour in games or had observed the outcomes of others who play these games.

As we describe the basic perspectives on learning, you will discover that although some behaviours seem to come to us automatically, others we voluntarily choose to engage in. In this way, cognitive psychologists suggest that people choose whether or not to imitate the aggressive and other behaviours they observe, and that people are most likely to imitate behaviours that are consistent with their values.

Sometimes learning experiences are direct, as when we are praised for doing something properly. But we can also learn from the experiences of others—by watching their behaviour and hearing their life stories. We learn, too, from books and media. In this chapter we consider various kinds of learning,

What do we *learn* from violence in video games and other media? Research on media and gaming violence is controversial. A large body of research suggests that we learn a great deal—not only aggressive skills, but also the idea that violence is the normal state of affairs. But others suggest that this is not the case—and that we are not desensitized to violence as a result.

including classical and operant conditioning, and observational learning in which cognition plays a more central role.

LO1 Classical Conditioning: Learning What Is Linked to What

Classical conditioning (also referred to as "respondent conditioning") involves some of the ways in which we learn to associate events with other events. Consider this: We have a distinct preference for a grade of A rather than F. We are also (usually) more likely to stop for a red light than for a green light. Why? We are not born with instinctive attitudes toward the letters A and F. Nor are we born knowing that red means stop and green means go. We learn the meanings of these symbols because they are associated with other events. An A grade is associated with instructor approval and the likelihood of making the Dean's list. Stopping at a red light is associated with avoiding an accident and a traffic citation.

What is classical conditioning? **Classical conditioning** is a simple form of learning that enables organisms to associate specific responses to events, such that following continuous pairing of some neutral event with a **stimulus** is the resulting conditioned behaviour. It is now that we turn to Ivan Pavlov's research on reflex conditioning with dogs to understand one perspective on how we learn.

Ivan Pavlov and Classical Conditioning

Ivan Pavlov (1927) accidentally made his great contribution to the psychology of learning. Pavlov was actually attempting to identify neural receptors in the mouth that triggered a response from the salivary glands. But his efforts were hampered by the dogs' annoying tendency to salivate at undesired times, such as when a laboratory assistant was clumsy and banged the metal food trays.

Just as you salivate after you've taken a big bite of cake (or some other food that you love), a dog salivates if meat powder is placed on its tongue. Pavlov was giving his dogs meat powder for his research because he knew that salivation in response to meat powder is a reflex (i.e., that dogs automatically salivate when they taste food). Pavlov discovered that reflexes can also be learned, or *conditioned,* by association. In his classic research with dogs, his dogs would begin salivating in response to clanging food trays because clanging, in the past, had been repeatedly paired with arrival of food.

He realized that he could train, or condition, his dogs to salivate in response to any stimulus, such as a tone or a bell.

Pavlov termed these trained salivary responses "conditional reflexes." The reflexes were *conditional* on the repeated pairing of a previously neutral stimulus (such as a tone or a bell) and a stimulus (food) that evoked the target response (salivation). Today, conditional reflexes are generally referred to as *conditioned responses*.

Pavlov demonstrated conditioned responses by showing that when meat powder was placed on a dog's tongue, the dog salivated. Pavlov repeated the process several times, with one difference. He preceded the meat powder by half a second or so with the sounding of a bell on each occasion. After several pairings of the meat powder and the bell, Pavlov sounded the bell but did *not* follow it with the meat powder. Still the dog salivated. It had learned to salivate in response to the bell.

Stimuli and Responses in Classical Conditioning

In Pavlov's experiment, the meat powder is an unlearned or **unconditioned stimulus (UCS).**

classical conditioning
a simple form of learning in which a neutral stimulus comes to evoke the response usually evoked by another stimulus by being paired repeatedly with the other stimulus

stimulus
an environmental condition that elicits a response

unconditioned stimulus (UCS)
a stimulus that elicits a response from an organism prior to conditioning

Ivan Pavlov and his associates

© Bettman/Corbis

unconditioned response (UCR)
an unlearned response to an unconditioned stimulus

orienting reflex
an unlearned response in which an organism attends to a stimulus

conditioned stimulus (CS)
a previously neutral stimulus that elicits a conditioned response because it has been paired repeatedly with a stimulus that already elicited that response

conditioned response (CR)
a learned response to a conditioned stimulus

Salivation in response to the meat powder is an unlearned or **unconditioned response (UCR)**. The bell was at first an unassociated or neutral stimulus. It might have caused the dog to look in the direction of the sound—an **orienting reflex**. But the tone was not yet associated with food. Then, through repeated association with the meat powder, the bell became a learned or **conditioned stimulus (CS)** for the salivation response. Salivation in response to the bell (or conditioned stimulus) is a learned or **conditioned response (CR)**. Therefore, salivation can be either a conditioned response or an unconditioned response, depending on the method used to evoke the response (see Figure 5.1).

Taste Aversion

S.M.: On my 19th birthday, my friends took me out for a night at the bar to celebrate my age of majority. It just so happened that the bar we attended had $1 shots. My five friends each spent $10 on shots—that's 50 shots, by the way—that I was to drink! Celebrate! The shots came in an unknown number of varieties; from fruit-flavoured, to milk-flavoured, to who knows what! I had no problem tipping back the first two or three or four, but I slowed up quite quickly after that. I drank as many of those shots as I could (some landed on the floor and were spilled), though, and within less than half an hour, I was home, sick,

FIGURE 5.1

A Schematic Representation of Classical Conditioning

Prior to conditioning, food elicits salivation. The tone, a neutral stimulus, elicits either no response or an orienting response. During conditioning, the tone is rung just before meat powder is placed on the dog's tongue. After several repetitions, the tone, now a CS, elicits salivation, the CR.

Go to www.icanpsych.com to access an interactive version of this figure.

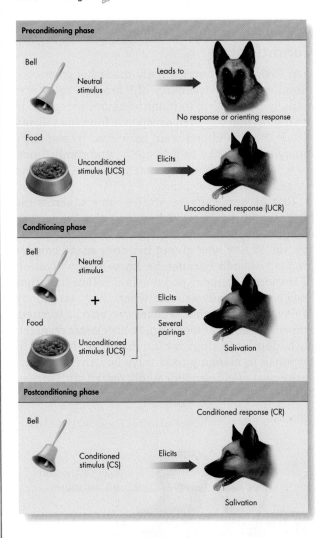

sick, and more sick, and then down and out for the entire next day. When I awoke, the taste and smell of stale milk remained with me—I felt bloated and nauseated. So much so that I could not drink milk (or anything creamy) for a long time. Being near it—just the smell of it—would make me feel nauseated!

The lesson in this story is that my response to milk was a *taste aversion*. *What are taste aversions? Why are they of special interest to psychologists?* A long time has now passed, and the smell of milk still turns my stomach sometimes (but I do drink it again).

Taste aversions are intriguing examples of classical conditioning. They are adaptive because they motivate organisms to avoid harmful foods. Taste aversions differ from other kinds of classical conditioning in a couple of ways. First, only one association may be required. A single evening of milk-flavoured shots left me with a long-time aversion. Second, whereas most kinds of classical conditioning require that the unconditioned stimulus and conditioned stimulus be close together in time, in taste aversion the unconditioned stimulus (in this case, nausea) can occur hours after the conditioned stimulus (in this case, the smell/taste of milk).

The Evolution of Taste Aversion

Research on taste aversion also challenges the view that organisms learn to associate any stimuli that are linked in time. In reality, not all stimuli are created equal. The evolutionary perspective suggests that animals (and humans) would be biologically predisposed to develop aversions that are adaptive in their environments (Garcia et al., 1989). Those of us who acquire taste aversions quickly are less likely to eat bad food, more likely to survive, and more likely to contribute our genes to future generations.

In a classic study, Garcia and Koelling (1966) conditioned two groups of rats. Each group was exposed to the same three-part conditioned stimulus: a taste of sweetened water, a light, and a clicker. Afterward, one group was presented with an unconditioned stimulus of nausea (induced by poison or radiation), and the other group was presented with an unconditioned stimulus of electric shock. After conditioning, the rats who had been nauseated showed an aversion for sweetened water but not to the light or clicker. Although all three stimuli had been presented at the same time, *the rats had acquired only the taste aversion.* After conditioning, the rats that had been shocked avoided both the light and the clicker, *but they did not show a taste aversion to the sweetened water.* For each group of rats, learning was adaptive. In the natural scheme of things, nausea is more likely to

Formation of a Taste Aversion? Taste aversions can be acquired by means of a single pairing of the UCS and the CS. Evolutionary psychologists point out that the rapid acquisition of a taste aversion makes it more likely that a human or an animal will survive and reproduce.

stem from poisoned food than from lights or sounds. So, for nauseated rats, acquiring the taste aversion was appropriate. Sharp pain, in contrast, is more likely to stem from natural events involving lights (e.g., fire, lightning) and sharp sounds (e.g., twigs snapping, things falling). Therefore, it was more appropriate for the shocked animals to develop an aversion to the light and the clicker than for the sweetened water.

In classical conditioning, organisms learn to connect stimuli, such as the sounding of a tone with food. Now let us consider various factors in classical conditioning, beginning with what happens when the connection between stimuli is broken.

Top: Tischenko Irina/Shutterstock.com; bottom: © Kasia Biel/Dreamstime.com

Extinction and Spontaneous Recovery

Extinction and spontaneous recovery are aspects of conditioning that help us adapt by updating our expectations or representations of a changing environment. For example, a child may learn to connect hearing a car pull into the driveway (a conditioned stimulus) with the arrival of his or her parents (an unconditioned stimulus). Thus, the child may squeal with delight when he or she hears the car.

What is the role of extinction in classical conditioning? Extinction enters the picture when times—and the relationships between events—change. After moving to a new house, the child's parents may commute by public transportation. The sound of a car in a nearby driveway may signal a neighbour's, not a parent's, homecoming. When a conditioned stimulus (such as the sound of a car) is no longer followed by an unconditioned stimulus (a parent's homecoming), the conditioned stimulus loses its ability to elicit a conditioned response. The organism adapts to change.

In classical conditioning, **extinction** is the process by which conditioned stimuli lose the ability to elicit conditioned responses, because the conditioned stimuli are no longer associated with unconditioned stimuli. That is, the toddler is no longer gleeful at the sounds of the car in the driveway.

In experiments on the extinction of conditioned responses, Pavlov found that repeated presentations of the conditioned stimulus (the bell) without the unconditioned stimulus (meat powder) led to extinction of the conditioned response (salivation in response to the bell). Basically, the dog stopped salivating at the sound of the bell. Interestingly, Figure 5.2 demonstrates the CS–US pairings over the course of 22 trials

and the associated responses of the dog following extinction. You can see that the dog was conditioned to begin to salivate in response to a sound after two or three pairings of the bell with meat powder. Continued pairings of the stimuli led to increased salivation (measured in number of drops of saliva). After seven or eight trials, salivation levelled off at 11 to 12 drops.

In the next series of experiments, salivation in response to the bell was extinguished by trials in which the bell (CS) was presented without the meat powder. After about ten extinction trials, the dog no longer salivated—it no longer showed the conditioned response when the bell was sounded.

What is the role of spontaneous recovery in classical conditioning? What would happen if we were to allow a day or two to pass after we had extinguished salivation in Pavlov's dog and then again sounded the bell? Would the dog salivate or not?

If you decided that the dog would again show the conditioned response (in this case, salivate in response to the bell), you were correct! Organisms tend to show **spontaneous recovery** of an extinguished conditioned response as a function of the passage of time. For this reason, the term *extinction* may be a bit misleading. Rather, it seems to *inhibit* the response. The response remains available for the future under the "right" conditions.

What would happen if the child in the example referred to earlier heard no car in the driveway for several months? It could be that the next time a car entered the driveway the child would associate the sounds with a parent's homecoming rather than with the arrival of a neighbour. This expectation

FIGURE 5.2

Learning and Extinction Curves

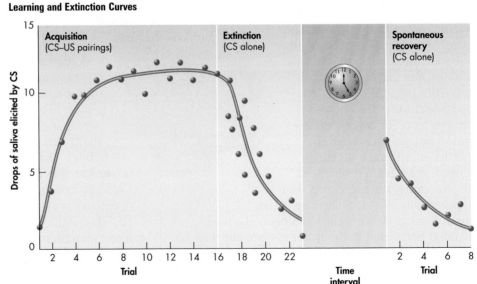

could be appropriate. After all, *something* had changed when no car entered the driveway for so long. Spontaneous recovery helps organisms adapt to situations that recur from time to time.

Generalization and Discrimination

Our ability to adapt to situations becomes important—as no two things are exactly alike, but many things are similar. For example, the barking of two dogs differs, and the sound of the same animal differs slightly from one bark to the next. *Adaptation* requires us to respond similarly (or *generalize*) to stimuli that are equivalent in function and to respond differently to (or *discriminate* between) stimuli that are not.

What is the role of generalization and discrimination in classical conditioning? Pavlov noted that responding to different stimuli as though they are functionally equivalent—*generalizing*—is adaptive for animals. **Generalization** is the tendency for a conditioned response to be evoked by stimuli that are similar to the stimulus to which the response was conditioned. For example, Pavlov demonstrated generalization by getting his dog to salivate when it heard similar tones to the initial bell sound. The more closely the tone resembled the initial bell sound, however, the greater the *strength* of the response (as measured by drops of saliva).

Generalizations involve our knowledge of the world. We know that the general rules of a classroom include coming prepared for class and speaking one at a time. We also likely generalize how we should behave in class as a student. For some of us, a bad experience with a dog off a leash—such as being bitten—may cause us to be fearful of all (or most) dogs that are not on a leash. We may interpret dogs off a leash as a stimuli that promotes being bitten.

In addition to generalizing, organisms must also learn that (1) many stimuli perceived as being similar are functionally different, and (2) they must respond adaptively to each. During the first couple of months of life, for example, babies can discriminate their mother's voice from those of other women. They often stop crying when they hear their mother's voice but not when they hear a stranger's.

Could a dog conditioned to salivate in response to similar bell sounds be trained *not* to salivate in response to horn sounds? After a while, a dog would no longer salivate in response to the horn sounds. Instead, it would show **discrimination**: It would salivate only in response to a bell sound.

Daily life requires generalization and discrimination. Imagine the confusion that would reign if we could not discriminate our friends, partners, or co-workers from other people.

Higher-Order Conditioning

Consider a child who is burned by touching a hot stove. After this experience, the sight of the stove may evoke fear. And because hearing the word *stove* may evoke a mental image of the stove, just hearing the word may evoke fear.

Recall the mini-experiment in the Try It! box on page 104, in which a parent smiles, says "kitchie-coo," and then tickles the bottom of an infant's foot. After a few repetitions, just smiling at the infant may cause the infant to retract his or her foot. In fact, just walking into the room may have the same effect! The experiences with touching the hot stove and tickling the infant's foot are examples of higher-order conditioning. *What is higher-order conditioning?*

In **higher-order conditioning**, a previously neutral stimulus (e.g., hearing the word *stove* or seeing the adult who had done the tickling enter the room) comes to serve as a learned or conditioned stimulus after being paired repeatedly with a stimulus that has already become a learned or conditioned stimulus (e.g., seeing the stove or hearing the phrase "kitchie-coo"). Pavlov demonstrated higher-order conditioning by first conditioning a dog to salivate in response to a tone. He then repeatedly paired the shining of a light with the sounding of the tone. After several pairings, shining the light (the higher-order conditioned stimulus) came to evoke the response (salivation) that had been elicited by the tone (the first-order conditioned stimulus).

Applications of Classical Conditioning

"Little Albert": Classical Conditioning of Fear

In 1920, John B. Watson and Rosalie Rayner published an article describing their study that emotional reactions, such as fears, can be acquired through principles of classical conditioning. The subject of their study was an 11-month-old infant known as "Little Albert."

generalization in conditioning, the tendency for a conditioned response to be evoked by stimuli that are similar to the stimulus to which the response was conditioned

discrimination in conditioning, the tendency for an organism to distinguish between a conditioned stimulus and similar stimuli that do not forecast an unconditioned stimulus

higher-order conditioning a classical conditioning procedure in which a previously neutral stimulus comes to elicit the response brought forth by a *conditioned* stimulus by being paired repeatedly with that conditioned stimulus

Prior to the study, Albert enjoyed playing with a white laboratory rat. To demonstrate whether they could condition Albert to be frightened of a rat, Watson startled Albert by clanging steel bars behind his head when he played with the rat. After repeated pairings, Albert showed fear of the rat even when the clanging was suspended. Albert's fear was also generalized to objects similar in appearance to the rat, such as a rabbit and the fur collar on his mother's coat.

Albert's mother removed him from the laboratory before Watson and Rayner could attempt to *countercondition* the boy's acquired fear. Today, Watson and Rayner's study would be considered unethical and would be unsupported by the Canadian Psychological Association (CPA). The CPA has strict ethical guidelines and standards in place for conducting research on humans and animals.

Chris Stein/Digital Vision/Getty Images

Purestock/Jupiterimages

Watson and Rayner conditioned "Little Albert" to fear a rat by clanging steel bars behind his head when he played with the rat.

Counterconditioning

The reasoning behind counterconditioning is this: If fears, as Watson had shown, could be conditioned by painful experiences like a clanging noise, perhaps fears could be **counterconditioned** by substituting pleasant experiences. In 1924, Watson and a colleague, Mary Cover Jones, attempted to countercondition fear in a two-year-old boy named Peter, who was extremely fearful of rabbits.

In the study, Jones gave Peter candy and cookies to eat. She gradually brought a rabbit closer to Peter while he munched the candy and cookies. Jones first placed the rabbit in a far corner of the room while Peter ate the treats. Peter cast a wary eye, but he continued to consume the treats. As the rabbit was brought closer, Peter simultaneously ate and touched the rabbit. Jones theorized that the joy of eating was incompatible with fear and counterconditioned it.

Mary Cover Jones's technique is called **systematic desensitization**, and it is used as behaviour therapy method for reducing fears. It is based on the classical conditioning principle of extinction and will be discussed in more detail later in Chapter 13.

LO2 Operant Conditioning: Learning What Does What to What

Through classical conditioning, we learn to associate stimuli. As a result, a simple, usually passive, response made to one stimulus is then made in response to the other. In the case of Little Albert, clanging noises were associated with a rat. As a result, the rat came to elicit fear caused by the clanging. However, classical conditioning is only one kind of learning that occurs in these situations. After Little Albert acquired his fear of the rat, his voluntary behaviour changed: He tried to avoid the rat. Thus, Little Albert engaged in another kind of learning—*operant conditioning*. In operant conditioning, organisms learn to do things—or *not* to do things—because of the consequences of their behaviour. For example, I avoided milk to prevent nausea.

Let us now consider the key contributions of B.F. Skinner to operant conditioning.

FIGURE 5.3

Project Pigeon

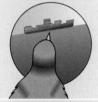

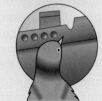

B.F. Skinner and Operant Conditioning

Skinner's earlier (but forgotten) contributions to psychology began with training pigeons during World War II. The pigeons would be **reinforced** with food pellets for pecking at targets projected onto a screen (see Figure 5.3). The plan was that, once trained, the pigeons would be placed in missiles. Their pecking at similar targets displayed on a screen would correct the missile's flight path, resulting in a "hit" and a sacrificed pigeon.

Skinner taught pigeons and other animals to engage in **operant behaviour**, behaviour that operates on, or manipulates, the environment. *What is operant conditioning?* Recall that classical conditioning focuses on how organisms form anticipations about their environments; operant conditioning focuses on what they do about them. **Operant conditioning** is defined as a simple form of learning in which an organism learns to engage in certain behaviour because of the effects that behaviour elicits. In operant conditioning, *voluntary* responses such as pecking at a target to hit it, pressing a lever for food, or developing skills required for playing tennis are acquired, or conditioned. We learn to engage in behaviours that result in presumably desirable consequences such as food, attention, or social approval. Some children learn to conform to social rules to earn the attention and approval of their parents and teachers. Other children, ironically, may learn to "misbehave" because misbehaviour also gets attention. In particular, children may learn to be "bad" when their "good" behaviour is routinely ignored. Some children who do not do well in school seek the approval of deviant peers (Patterson et al., 2000).

> Classical conditioning focuses on how organisms form anticipations about their environments. Operant conditioning focuses on what they do about them.

Methods of Operant Conditioning

To study operant behaviour, Skinner devised an animal cage (or "operant chamber") that has been dubbed the "Skinner box" (see Figure 5.4 on the next page). The cage is ideal for laboratory experimentation because experimental conditions can be carefully introduced and removed, and their effects on laboratory animals can be observed.

The rat in Figure 5.4 was deprived of food and placed in a Skinner box with a lever at one end. At first, it sniffed its way around the cage and engaged in random behaviour. Skinner set up the study such that when the rat pressed the lever a food pellet dropped into the cage. He found that the arrival of the food pellet increased the probability that the rat would press the lever again. The pellet is thus said to have *reinforced* lever pressing.

reinforce
to follow a response with a stimulus that increases the frequency of the response

operant behaviour
involuntary responses that are reinforced

operant conditioning
a simple form of learning in which an organism learns to engage in certain behaviour because it is reinforced

reinforcer
any stimulus that increases the frequency of a behaviour

positive reinforcer
a reinforcer that when *presented* increases the frequency of an operant behaviour

negative reinforcer
a reinforcer that when *removed* increases the frequency of an operant behaviour

In operant conditioning, it matters little why or how the first "correct" response is made. The animal can happen on it by chance or be physically guided to make the response. You may command your dog to "Sit!" and then press its backside down until it is sitting. Finally, you reinforce sitting with food or a pat on the head and a kind word. Animal trainers use physical guiding or coaxing to bring about the first "correct" response. Can you imagine how long it would take to train your dog if you waited for it to sit or roll over and then seized the opportunity to command it to sit or roll over?

People, of course, can be verbally guided into desired responses when they are learning tasks such as spelling, adding numbers, or operating a machine. But they need to be informed when they have made the correct response. Knowledge of results often is all the reinforcement people need to learn new skills.

Types of Reinforcers

A **reinforcer** is any stimulus that increases the probability that responses preceding it—whether pecking a button in a Skinner box or studying for a quiz—will be repeated.

Positive and Negative Reinforcers

Positive reinforcers increase the probability that a behaviour will occur when they are applied. Food and approval usually serve as positive reinforcers. For example, when my children behave (a.k.a. listen to me) while shopping for groceries, they will be able to buy a gumball from the candy machine at the front of the store. The "gumball" is a positive reinforcer for good behaviour—which should increase the likelihood that they will behave the next time we get groceries. **Negative reinforcers** also increase the probability that a behaviour will occur, but they do so when the reinforcers are *removed* (see Figure 5.5). For example, people often take medication to get rid of a headache. In such cases, the medication acts as a negative reinforcer; *removal* of the headache increases the probability that people will take medication again the next time a headache appears.

Immediate versus Delayed Reinforcers

Immediate reinforcers are more effective than delayed reinforcers. Therefore, the short-term consequences of behaviour often provide more of an incentive than the long-term consequences.

It is easy to understand why some students socialize when they should be studying—the pleasure of socializing is immediate. Studying, however, may not pay off until the final exam or graduation. It is difficult to quit smoking cigarettes because the reinforcement of nicotine is immediate and the health hazards of smoking are

FIGURE 5.4

Positive and Negative Reinforcers

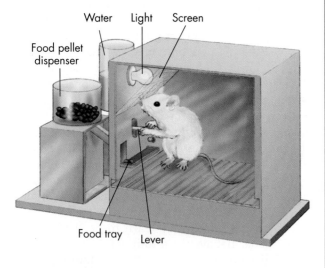

Water Light Screen

Food pellet dispenser

Food tray Lever

FIGURE 5.5

Positive versus Negative Reinforcers

Go to www.icanpsych.com to access an interactive version of this figure.

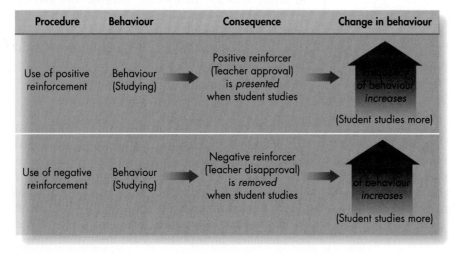

Procedure	Behaviour	Consequence	Change in behaviour
Use of positive reinforcement	Behaviour (Studying)	Positive reinforcer (Teacher approval) is *presented* when student studies	of behaviour *increases* (Student studies more)
Use of negative reinforcement	Behaviour (Studying)	Negative reinforcer (Teacher disapproval) is *removed* when student studies	of behaviour *increases* (Student studies more)

An Example of a Negative Reinforcer
Any behaviour that helps you get rid of your headache is likely to be repeated in the future (such as medication, hot pad to head, acupuncture). These behaviours (medication, hot pad to head, acupuncture) are negative reinforcers.

FIGURE 5.6

Negative Reinforcers versus Punishments

Go to www.icanpsych.com to access an interactive version of this figure.

Procedure	Behaviour	Consequence	Change in behaviour
Use of negative reinforcement	Behaviour (Studying)	Negative reinforcer (Teacher disapproval) is *removed* when student studies	Frequency of behaviour *increases* (Student studies more)
Use of punishment	Behaviour (Talking in class)	Punishment (Detention) is *presented* when student talks in class	Frequency of behaviour *decreases* (Student talks less in class)

more delayed. Focusing on short-term reinforcement is connected with risky behaviours, such as engaging in sexual activity with a stranger or having unprotected sex (Caffray & Schneider, 2000; Fuertes et al., 2002), or abusing alcohol or drugs. Despite our ability to foresee the delayed consequences of our behaviour and to make choices, immediate reinforcers—such as socializing with friends instead of studying—can be powerful temptations indeed.

Primary and Secondary Reinforcers

We can also distinguish between primary and secondary (or conditioned) reinforcers. **Primary reinforcers** are inherent to the organism's biological makeup that fulfills basic survival needs. For example, food, water, warmth (positive reinforcers), and pain (a negative reinforcer) all serve as primary reinforcers—we need to eat, drink, have shelter and have some tolerance for pain. **Secondary reinforcers** are learned through being associated with other, established reinforcers. For example, seeking the attention of our professor before and after a test with the later hopes of obtaining a good grade in a class is a secondary reinforcer.

Punishment

Reinforcers are known by their effects, whereas rewards and punishments are known by how they feel. It may be that most reinforcers—food, hugs, money—feel good, or are pleasant events. Yet things that we might assume would feel bad, such as a slap on the hand or disapproval from a teacher, can be reinforcing, perhaps because they confirm negative feelings toward teachers or one's belonging within a deviant subculture (Atkins et al., 2002).

Punishment is defined as an aversive event that suppresses or decreases the frequency of the behaviour it follows (see Figure 5.6). Punishment can rapidly suppress undesirable behaviour (Gershoff, 2002) by removing a pleasant stimulus or adding an unpleasant stimulus. Punishment examples include

primary reinforcer
an unlearned reinforcer

secondary reinforcer
a stimulus that gains reinforcement value through association with established reinforcers; also termed *conditioned reinforcer*

punishment
an unpleasant stimulus that suppresses the behaviour it follows

scolding, criticism, or paying a fine. In each of these examples, the likelihood of engaging in the behaviour that causes the scolding, criticism, or paying a fine again is reduced. Punishment is different from negative reinforcement. Remember that reinforcement increases the likelihood of continuing a behaviour; punishment decreases the likelihood of a behaviour.

Punishment can encourage *escape* and *avoidance learning. What are escape and avoidance learning?* Based on negative reinforcement, escape learning involves responding to an aversive stimulus in order to end it. Running away from your yelling partner during an argument is an example of escape learning. When you try to smooth things over with your partner by telling little white lies or giving in to avoid the shouting match, you are avoiding the aversive stimulus—and this is known as avoidance learning.

What are some problems with punishment? Let's not be mistaken, effective punishment can rid us of some bad behaviours. But the problems with punishment usually result from several factors, including timing, intensity, and consistency of its application (Parke, 1977):

- *Timing*. Punishment is most effective when it is applied immediately following the misbehaviour. Delaying punishment decreases its effectiveness.

- *Intensity*. The intensity of the punishment should match the misbehaviour in order to be effective. Using the minimum amount of punishment necessary to end the misbehaviour is most important. For example, being charged a $5 parking fine (less than meter-parking) for illegal parking on campus may not be sufficient to deter students from parking illegally, but $20 (more than meter-parking) would be.

- *Consistency*. Applying punishment every time the misbehaviour occurs is most effective in ending the misbehaviour. Inconsistency leads to unclear expectations and weakens the association of the punishment to the misbehaviour.

Extinction and Spontaneous Recovery in Operant Conditioning

If Keisha's teacher writes "Good" on all of her homework assignments before returning them, this can be perceived as a positive reinforcer for Keisha's good work. If one day her teacher no longer writes anything on the assignments—the reinforcement ends. Remember, reinforcers are used to strengthen responses. What happens when reinforcement stops? *What is the role of extinction in operant conditioning?*

Recall in Pavlov's experiment, the meat powder was the event that followed and confirmed the appropriateness of salivation. In Keisha's situation, seeing "Good" written on her assignments confirmed the appropriateness of the way in which she did her homework. In operant conditioning, the ensuing events are reinforcers. When a reinforcer stops (or is no longer appropriate), the likelihood of continuing the operant behaviour may cease. For Keisha, it may be that she will stop doing her homework if she is not reinforced for completing it. In operant conditioning, reinforcers maintain operant behaviour or strengthen habitual behaviour.

With humans, fortunately, we can reinforce ourselves for desired behaviour by telling ourselves we did a good job—or, in Keisha's case, she may tell herself that she is doing the right thing regardless of whether or not her teacher recognizes it.

{ **Nicotine Creates Short-Term Reinforcement** }

It is difficult to quit smoking cigarettes because the reinforcement of nicotine is immediate and the health hazards of smoking more delayed.

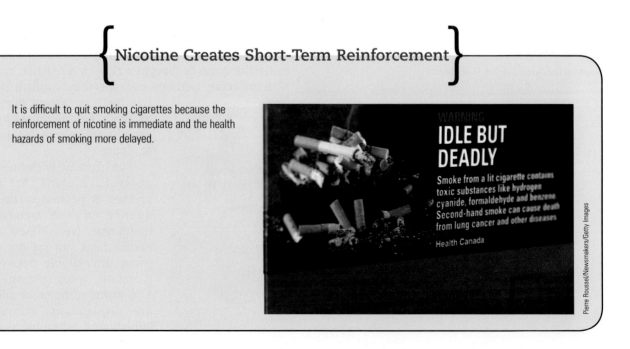

What is the role of spontaneous recovery in operant conditioning? Spontaneous recovery of learned responses occurs in operant conditioning as well. Reinforcers may once again become available after time elapses, which then may strengthen the operant behaviour once again.

What are discriminative stimuli? **Discriminative stimuli**, such as a bell ringing, indicate whether behaviour (students packing up their books) will be reinforced (by the professor's concluding the lecture) or punished (by the professor's disapproval). Behaviours that are punished or not reinforced tend to be extinguished. For the students in this example, the behaviour of packing up before the bell has rung is extinguished by the professor's disapproval. The students would no longer pack up their books if the bell has not rung yet. We learn to discriminate between different stimuli based on a previous reward or nonrewarded response. Police dogs who locate contraband drugs can differentiate between drug types—just like a true wine connoisseur can discriminate between good and bad wine!

Schedules of Reinforcement

In our daily lives, reinforcement does not always occur consistently or frequently with everything that we do. In operant conditioning and in general, some responses are maintained by means of **continuous reinforcement**. You probably become warmer every time you put on heavy clothing. You probably become less thirsty every time you drink water. Yet if you have ever played the slot machines or even the lottery, you know that you are not likely to be reinforced every time you play—but you still might play! Your slot machine or lottery behaviour is maintained by means of **partial reinforcement**. *What are the various schedules of reinforcement? How do they affect behaviour?*

It's no wonder that people can get hooked on gambling—by fixing the game to allow heavy winnings at first. Then gradually space out the winnings (reinforcements) until gambling is maintained by infrequent winning—or even no winning at all. Partial reinforcement schedules can maintain gambling, like other behaviour, for a great deal of time, even though it is not reinforced (Pulley, 1998).

Responses that have been maintained by partial reinforcement are more resistant to extinction than responses that have been maintained by continuous reinforcement (Rescorla, 1999) because people that have been partially reinforced for their behaviour do not expect reinforcement every time they engage in a response. Therefore, they are more likely to persist in the absence of reinforcement. Do you expect to win every time you pull the arm on the slot machine? No! But you do expect that at some point, you might win. This partial reinforcement keeps you pulling the arm on the slot machine.

There are four basic reinforcement schedules: fixed-interval, variable-interval, fixed-ratio, and variable-ratio.

Interval Schedules

In a **fixed-interval schedule**, a fixed amount of time—say, a minute—must elapse before the correct response will result in a reinforcer. With a fixed-interval schedule, an organism's response rate falls off after each reinforcement and then picks up again as the time when reinforcement will occur approaches. For example, in a one-minute fixed-interval schedule, a rat is reinforced with, say, a food pellet for the first operant—for example, the first pressing of a lever—that occurs after a minute has elapsed. After each reinforcement, the rat's rate of lever pressing slows down, but as the end of the one-minute interval draws near, lever pressing increases in frequency, as suggested in Figure 5.7 (p. 114). It is as if the rat has learned that it must wait a while before it is

---

discriminative stimulus
in operant conditioning, a stimulus that indicates whether reinforcement or punishment will follow

continuous reinforcement
a schedule of reinforcement in which every correct response is reinforced

partial reinforcement
one of several reinforcement schedules in which not every correct response is reinforced

fixed-interval schedule
a schedule in which a fixed amount of time must elapse between the previous and subsequent times that reinforcement is available

Try It!

Discriminative Stimuli and Our Behaviour

How do the following discriminative stimuli affect your behaviour?

1. Possibly seeing a police car approaching or travelling on the highway.

2. Waiting for your best friend to text you about plans for going out tonight.

3. Responding to your angry boss about why you were late for work.

4. Spending the day with your grandparents instead of your parents.

variable-interval schedule a schedule in which a variable amount of time must elapse between the previous and subsequent times that reinforcement is available

fixed-ratio schedule a schedule in which reinforcement is provided after a fixed number of correct responses

variable-ratio schedule a schedule in which reinforcement is provided after a variable number of correct responses

shaping a procedure for teaching complex behaviours that at first reinforces approximations of the target behaviour

reinforced. The resultant record on the cumulative recorder shows a typical series of upward waves, or scallops, which are called *fixed-interval scallops*.

Car dealers use fixed-interval reinforcement schedules when they offer incentives for buying up the remainder of the year's line in summer and fall. In a sense, they are suppressing buying at other times, except for consumers whose current cars are in their death throes or those with little self control. Similarly, you learn to check your email only at a certain time of day if your correspondent writes at that time each day.

Reinforcement is more unpredictable in a **variable-interval schedule**. Therefore, the response rate is steadier but lower. If the boss calls us in for a weekly report, we probably work hard to pull things together just before the report is to be given, just as we might cram the night before a weekly quiz. But if we know that the boss might call us in for a report on the progress of a certain project at any time (variable-interval schedule), we are likely to keep things in a state of reasonable readiness at all times. However, our efforts are unlikely to have the intensity they would in a fixed-interval schedule (for example, a weekly report). Similarly, we are less

likely to cram for unpredictable pop quizzes than to study for regular quizzes. But we are likely to do at least some studying on a regular basis. Likewise, if you receive email from your correspondent regularly, you are likely to check your email regularly, but with less eagerness.

Ratio Schedules

In a **fixed-ratio schedule**, reinforcement is provided after a fixed number of correct responses have been made. For example, I will pay you $1 for every three examples of generalization you can come up with. (Okay, not really, but wouldn't you work as quickly as you could to come up with at least three examples?) In a **variable-ratio schedule**, reinforcement is provided after a variable number of correct responses have been made. In a 10:1 ratio schedule, the mean number of correct responses that would have to be made before a subsequent correct response would be reinforced is ten, but the ratio of correct responses to reinforcements might be allowed to vary from, say, 1:1 to 20:1 on a random basis.

Fixed and variable-ratio schedules maintain a high response rate. With a fixed-ratio schedule, it is as if the organism learns that it must make several responses before being reinforced. It then "gets them out of the way" as rapidly as possible. Consider the example of piecework. If a worker must sew five shirts to receive $10, he or she is on a fixed-ratio (5:1) schedule and is likely to sew at a uniformly high rate, although there might be a brief pause after each reinforcement. With a variable-ratio schedule, reinforcement can come at any time. Slot machines tend to pay off on variable-ratio schedules, and players can be seen popping coins into them and yanking their "arms" with barely a pause. Some players do not even stop to pick up their winnings. Instead, they continue to pop in the coins, either from their original stack or from the winnings tray. Table 5.1 illustrates the differences between ratio and interval schedules.

Shaping

If you are teaching hip-hop dancing to people who have never danced, do not wait until they have performed it precisely before telling them they're on the right track. The foxtrot will be back in style before they have learned a thing.

We can teach complex behaviours by **shaping**. Shaping reinforces progressive steps toward the behavioural goal. At first, for example, it may be wise to smile and say, "Good," when a reluctant

FIGURE 5.7

The Fixed-Interval Scallop

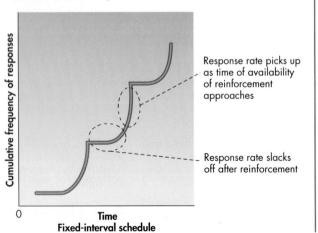

Cumulative frequency of responses

Response rate picks up as time of availability of reinforcement approaches

Response rate slacks off after reinforcement

0

Time
Fixed-interval schedule

Applications of Operant Conditioning

We use both classical and operant conditioning every day in our efforts to influence other people. Parents and peers socialize children (sometimes, unknowingly) to acquire gender-appropriate behaviour patterns through rewards and punishments. Parents also tend to praise their children for sharing their toys and punish them for being too aggressive. Peers participate in the socialization process by playing with children who are generous and nonaggressive and, often, by avoiding those who are not (Warman & Cohen, 2000).

Operant conditioning also plays a role in attitude formation. Adults often reward children for expressing attitudes that coincide with their own and punish or ignore them for expressing contradictory attitudes. Let us now consider some specific applications of operant conditioning.

successive approximations behaviours that are progressively closer to a target behaviour

newcomer gathers the courage to get out on the dance floor, even if your feet are flattened by the dancer's clumsiness. If you are teaching someone to drive a car with a standard shift, at first generously reinforce the learner simply for shifting gears without stalling.

But as training proceeds, we come to expect more before we are willing to provide reinforcement. We reinforce **successive approximations** of the goal. If you want to train a rat to climb a ladder, first reinforce it with a food pellet when it turns toward the ladder. Then wait until it approaches the ladder before giving it a pellet. Then do not drop a pellet into the cage until the rat touches the ladder. In this way, the rat will reach the top of the ladder more quickly than if you had waited for the target behaviour to occur at random.

Biofeedback Training

Biofeedback training (BFT) is based on principles of operant conditioning. BFT has enabled people and lower animals to learn to control autonomic responses to attain reinforcement (Miller, 1969; Vernon et al., 2003).

Through BFT, people can gain control of autonomic functions such as the flow of blood in a finger.

TABLE 5.1

Interval and Ratio Schedules

	Interval	Ratio
Fixed	A fixed (consistent) amount of time elapses between reinforcement	A reinforcement is provided after a fixed number of expected responses
	Predictable; response rate peaks at point of reinforcement	Predictable; response rate is generally the highest
	Example: Tests (have one test every three weeks)	Example: Sales job (paid per number of sales)
Variable	A variable (random) amount of time elapses between reinforcement	A reinforcement is provided after a variable number of expected responses
	Somewhat predictable; steadier response rate	Unpredictable; response rate is high to get to reinforcement quickly
	Example: Pop quiz (may have one on average one or two times per month)	Example: Slot machines (no consistent number or time must elapse before reinforcement)

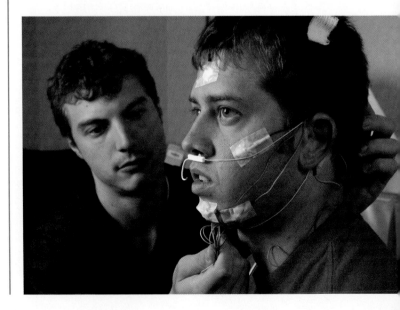

They can also learn to improve their control over functions that can be manipulated voluntarily, such as muscle tension. When people receive BFT, reinforcement is given in the form of *information*. Perhaps a sound changes in pitch or frequency of occurrence to signal that they have modified the autonomic function in the desired direction. For example, we can learn to emit alpha waves—the kind of brain wave associated with feelings of relaxation—through feedback from an electroencephalograph (EEG; an instrument that measures brain waves). People use other instruments to learn to lower their muscle tension, heart rates, and blood pressure.

BFT is also used with people who have lost neuromuscular control of parts of their body as a result of an accident. A "bleep" sound informs them when they have contracted a muscle or sent an impulse down a neural pathway. By concentrating on changing the bleeps, they may gradually regain voluntary control over the damaged function.

Behaviour Modification in the Classroom: Accentuating the Positive

Remember that reinforcers are defined as stimuli that increase the frequency of behaviour—not as pleasant events. Ironically, adults frequently reinforce undesirable behaviour in children by paying attention to them, or punishing them, when they misbehave but ignoring them when they behave in desirable ways. Similarly, teachers who raise their voices when students misbehave may be unintentionally conferring hero status on those pupils in the eyes of their peers. To the teacher's surprise, some children may then go out of their way to earn disapproval.

Teacher preparation and in-service programs show teachers how to use behaviour modification to reverse these response patterns. Teachers are taught to reinforce children when they are behaving appropriately and, when possible, to extinguish misbehaviour by ignoring it. Behaviour modification techniques have been included in teacher training for decades. A more recent focus since the educational movement toward inclusive education now includes assistance for students with disabilities—physical, psychological, and behavioural. Applications of operant conditioning principles play an important role in behavioural intervention techniques (see the box on the next page entitled "Applied Behavioural Analysis" for more information).

Among older children and adolescents, peer approval may be a more powerful reinforcer than teacher approval. Peer approval may maintain misbehaviour, and ignoring misbehaviour may only allow students to become more disruptive. In such cases it may be necessary to separate troublesome children.

Teachers also frequently use *time out* from positive reinforcement to discourage misbehaviour. In this method, children are placed in a quiet, restrictive environment for a specified period, usually about five or ten minutes, when they behave disruptively. While they are isolated, they cannot earn the attention of peers or teachers, and no reinforcers are present.

Focusing on positive consequences for behaviour, some teachers use *token economies*—where desirable behaviours are reinforced with tokens that can be exchanged for rewards. Examples of tokens are money, stickers, more time on the computer, or prizes.

Programmed Learning: Step by Step

B.F. Skinner developed an educational method called *programmed learning* that is based on operant conditioning. This method assumes that any complex task involving conceptual learning as well as motor skills can be broken down into a number of small steps. For example, it may be appropriate to focus on one aspect of a printing exercise for a child, say upper-case letters, rather than printing both upper- and lower-case letters. These steps can be shaped individually and then combined in sequence to form the correct behavioural chain.

Programmed learning does not punish errors. Instead, correct responses are reinforced. A child correctly uses upper- and lower-case letters for one sentence in a paragraph. Programmed learning also assumes it is the task of the teacher (or program) to structure the learning experience in such a way that errors will not be made.

LO3 Cognitive Factors in Learning

Classical and operant conditioning were originally conceived of as relatively simple forms of learning. Much of conditioning's appeal is that it can be said to meet the behaviourist objective of explaining behaviour in terms of *observable events*—in this case, laboratory conditions. Building on this theoretical base, some psychologists have suggested that the most complex human behaviour involves the summation of a series of instances of conditioning. Many psychologists believe, however, that conditioning is too mechanical a process to explain all instances of learned behaviour, even in laboratory rats. They turn to cognitive factors to describe and explain additional findings in the psychology of learning. *How do we explain what happens during conditioning from a cognitive perspective?*

In addition to concepts such as association and reinforcement, cognitive psychologists use concepts such as mental structures, schemas, templates, and information processing. Cognitive psychologists see people as searching for information, weighing evidence, and making decisions. Let us consider some classic research that emphasizes the way in which cognitive factors in learning influence the way we behave.

Latent Learning: Forming Cognitive Maps

Many behaviourists argue that organisms acquire only responses for which they are reinforced. E. C. Tolman, however, showed that rats also learn about their environment in the absence of reinforcement. In doing so, he showed that rats must form **cognitive maps** of their surroundings. *What is the evidence that people and lower animals form cognitive maps of their environments?*

Tolman trained some rats to run through mazes for food goals. Other rats were allowed to explore the same mazes for several days without food goals or other rewards. After the unrewarded rats had been allowed to explore the mazes for ten days, food rewards were placed in a box at the far end of the maze. The previously unrewarded rats reached the food box as quickly as the rewarded rats after only one or two trials (Tolman & Honzik, 1930).

Tolman concluded that the rats had learned about the mazes by exploring them even when they went unrewarded by food. He distinguished between *learning* and *performance*. He demonstrated that learning provided knowledge that led to a cognitive representation about what to expect. In Tolman's study, the rats apparently created a cognitive map of a maze in which they learned to take the fast routes when food was presented. Even though they were not externally motivated to follow a rapid route through the maze, they would learn fast routes just by exploring it. Yet this learning might remain

> Remember that **reinforcers** are defined as stimuli that increase the frequency of behaviour— not just as pleasant events.

cognitive map a mental representation of surroundings

pervasive developmental disorders (PDD) a diagnostic category of the DSM-IV, usually diagnosed in childhood, involving mental disability, learning disorders, and social and communication impairments

autism spectrum disorder (ASD) a neurobiological disorder resulting in developmental impairment and affecting communication, social understanding, and behaviour

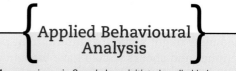

{ Applied Behavioural Analysis }

Many provinces in Canada have initiated applied behavioural analysis (ABA)—behavioural intervention techniques in the education system to assist children with a range of behavioural disabilities, known as *pervasive developmental disorders (PDD)*, including *autism spectrum disorder*. It has been found that ABA has positive outcomes on some aspects of social functioning, and it can improve performance on IQ tests for children with such disorders (McGahan, 2001).

latent
hidden or concealed

contingency theory
the view that learning occurs when stimuli provide information about the likelihood of the occurrence of other stimuli

observational learning
the acquisition of knowledge and skills through the observation of others (who are called *models*) rather than by means of direct experience

model
a person who engages in a response, which serves as an example that is then imitated by another person

hidden, or latent, until food motivated them to take the rapid routes.

Contingency Theory

Robert Rescorla's **contingency theory** suggests that learning occurs only when the conditioned stimulus (CS) provides *information* about the unconditioned stimulus (US).

In classical conditioning of dogs, Rescorla (1967) obtained some results that are difficult to explain without reference to cognitive concepts. Each phase of his work paired a tone (a CS) with an electric shock (a US), but in different ways. With one group of animals, the shock was consistently presented after the tone. The dogs in this group learned to show a fear response when the tone was presented.

A second group of dogs heard an equal number of tones and received an equal number of electric shocks, but the shock did not immediately follow the tone. In other words, the tone and the shock were not paired. Now, from the behaviourist perspective, the dogs should not have learned to associate the tone and the shock, because one did not predict the other. Actually, the dogs learned quite a lot: They learned that they had nothing to fear when the tone was sounded! They showed vigilance and fear when the laboratory was quiet—for the shock might come at any time—but they were calm in the presence of the tone itself.

The third group of dogs also received equal numbers of tones and shocks, but the stimuli were presented at random. Occasionally they were paired, but most often they were not. According to Rescorla, behaviourists might argue that intermittent pairing of the tones and shocks should have brought about some learning. Yet it did not. The animals showed no fear in response to the tone. Rescorla suggests that the animals in this group learned nothing because the tones did not allow them to make predictions about electric shock. Rescorla concluded that learning occurs only when the CS (in this case, the tone) provides information about the UCS (in this case, the shock).

Observational Learning

How many things have you learned from watching other people in real life, in films, and on television? From films and television, you may have gathered vague ideas about how to skydive, snowboard, climb rugged cliffs, score a short-handed goal in the Stanley Cup finals, and even dust for fingerprints, even if you have never tried them yourself. How do people learn by observing others?

Albert Bandura and his colleagues conducted experiments (e.g., Bandura et al., 1963) that show that we can acquire knowledge and skills by **observational learning**—observing the behaviour of others. Observational learning occurs when, for example, as children, we watch our parents cook, clean, or repair a broken appliance or when we see our teachers sliding their fingers along the words of a book while reading to us. Parents and teachers are considered **models** whom their children and students imitate. When we see modelled behaviour being reinforced, we are said to be *vicariously* reinforced. Engaging in the behaviour thus becomes more likely for us as well as for the model. My three-year-old son learned how to cook and scramble an egg in the microwave by watching me. (He served me the scrambled egg—and shell—one morning in bed!) It appears sufficient to pay attention to the behaviour. We may need some practice to refine the skills we acquire (as in the case of my son who didn't remove the shell when scrambling an egg for me).

Observational learning is highly adaptive. I (S.M.) sometimes wonder why my children run away from bees when they have never been stung before, or why they choose not to eat escargot, claiming, "I don't like it!" when they have never even tried it. Well, this is because we learn from watching and listening to others. I always run away from bees and have most definitely turned up my nose in disgust at escargot. Through this, my children have learned to have an adapted fear of bees and aversion to escargot—by watching and listening to me!

Modelling Violence and Aggression: Media Influences

We learn by observing parents and peers, attending school, reading books, and watching media such as television and films. Movies and the Internet are also key sources of informal observational learning. It may be true that children are routinely exposed to violent scenes of murder, beating, and sexual assault—just by turning on the TV set (Huesmann et al., 2003), and over the last two decades, numerous research studies have attempted to conclude what the effects of watching violence in the media really are. When it comes to looking at the effects of violence in the media, parents and others seem to be most concerned about the issue of aggression. Let's face it, children are spending a lot of time watching and engaging with media sources. Children spend approximately 15 hours per week watching television and both children and teens spend up to 44 hours per week engaged with various media, such as video games and Internet games (Roberts, Foehr, & Rideout, 2005).

Bandura: Effects of Violence in the Media

A classic experiment by Bandura, Ross, and Ross (1963) suggests the influence of aggressive models in observational learning. One group of preschool children observed a film of an adult model punching, hitting, and kicking an inflated Bobo doll, while a control group saw a nonaggressive adult model ignore the Bobo doll. The experimental and control groups were then left alone in a room with the same doll, as hidden observers recorded their behaviour. The children who had observed the aggressive model showed significantly more aggressive behaviour toward the doll themselves (see Figure 5.8 on page 120). Many children imitated bizarre attacks they would not have thought up themselves.

Bandura et al.'s (1963) research provided us with interesting insights about observational learning and the media. Part of the problem with observing violence in the media is that violence tends to be glamorized. Superheroes battle villains who are trying to destroy or take over the world, and violence is often portrayed as having only temporary or minimal effects. (How often has Wile E. Coyote fallen from a cliff and been pounded into the ground by a boulder, only to bounce back and pursue the Road Runner once more?) In the great majority of violent TV shows, there is no remorse, criticism, or penalty for violent behaviour. Few TV programs show harmful long-term consequences of aggressive behaviour.

Some researchers suggest that seeing the perpetrator of the violence go unpunished increases the chances that the child will act aggressively (Krcmar & Cooke, 2001) and view violence as an effective way to solve problems (Wood, Wong, & Chachere, 1991). Children may not even view death as much of a problem. As Evan Ramsey said, being shot might reduce a person's "health factor." How often do video-game characters "die"—only to be reborn to fight again?

On the other hand, viewers are more likely to imitate media violence only when they identify with the characters and when the portrayal of violence is realistic (Huesmann et al., 2003). Therefore, viewers may be more likely to imitate violence when the perpetrator looks like them and lives in a similar environment than when it is perpetrated by Wile E. Coyote.

Listening to violent music lyrics increased aggressive thoughts and hostile feelings among 500 college students (Anderson, Carnagey & Eubanks, 2003). Generally, males are relatively more likely than females to act aggressively after playing violent video games and are more likely to see the world as a hostile place (Bartholow & Anderson, 2002). But students who obtain higher grades are less likely than their lower-achieving peers to act aggressively after exposure to violent media games. Thus, gender roles, possible biological gender differences, and psychological factors such as achievement motivation also play a role in the effects of media violence.

Andy Sacks/Stone/Getty Images

FIGURE 5.8

Classic Research on the Imitation of Aggressive Models

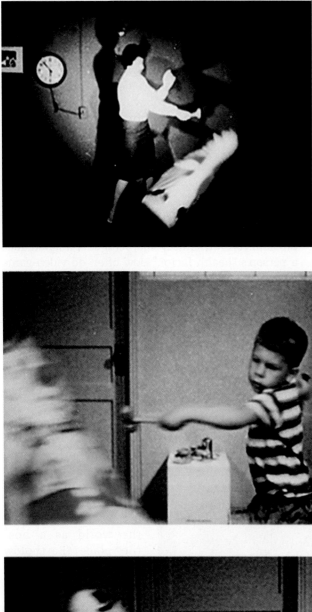

There seems to be a circular relationship between exposure to media violence and aggressive behaviour (Anderson & Dill, 2000; Anderson et al., 2003; Haridakis, 2002). Yes, violence in the media contributes to aggressive behaviour, but aggressive youngsters are also more likely to seek out this kind of entertainment. Figure 5.9 explores the possible connections between media violence and aggressive behaviour.

The family also affects the likelihood that children will imitate media violence. Studies find that parental substance abuse, paternal physical punishments, and single parenting contribute to the likelihood of aggression in early childhood (Brook et al., 2001; Gupta et al., 2001). Parental rejection and use of physical punishment further increase the likelihood of aggression in children (Eron, 1982). These family factors suggest that the parents of aggressive children may be absent or unlikely to help young children understand that the kinds of socially inappropriate behaviours they see in the media are not for them. A harsh home life may also confirm the TV viewer's or game player's vision of the world as a violent place.

If children believe violence to be inappropriate for them, they will be less likely to act aggressively, even if they have acquired aggressive skills from exposure to the media or other sources.

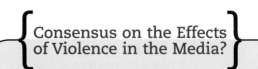

{ Consensus on the Effects of Violence in the Media? }

Most organizations of health professionals agree that media violence contributes to aggression (Anderson, 2004; Huesmann et al., 2003). Consider a number of ways in which depictions of violence make such a contribution:

- *Observational learning.* Children learn from observation. TV violence models aggressive "skills," which children may acquire. Media violence also provides viewers with aggressive scripts—that is, ideas about how to behave in situations like those they have observed.
- *Disinhibition.* Punishment inhibits behaviour. Conversely, media violence may disinhibit aggressive behaviour, especially when media characters "get away" with violence or are rewarded for it.
- *Increased arousal.* Media violence and aggressive video games increase viewers' emotional arousal. That is, media "work them up." We are more likely to be aggressive when we are aroused.
- *Habituation/desensitization.* We become "habituated to," or used to, repeated stimuli. Repeated exposure to TV violence may decrease viewers' sensitivity to real violence. If children come to perceive violence as the norm, they may become more tolerant of it and place less value on restraining aggressive urges.

FIGURE 5.9

What Are the Connections between Media Violence and Aggressive Behaviour?

Does media violence cause aggressive behaviour? Do aggressive children prefer to tune in to violent shows? Or do other factors, such as personality traits that create a disposition toward aggression, contribute both to aggressive behaviour and the interest in media violence?

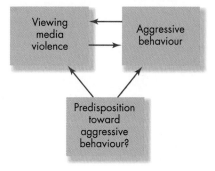

Memory

NEL

© John Lund/Blend Images/Corbis

> ## "Memories of the past that resurface in the future are the ones that we often remember like photographs."

Our memory is very intriguing, isn't it? It can be so frustrating at times when our memory doesn't serve us well—like forgetting the phone number of someone you would really like to go out with. Sometimes, even more frustrating, is when you have studied for an exam and can't recall important information on the exam. On the other hand, we feel great when our memory does serve us well—such as remembering how to get somewhere you haven't been in a long time (like your summer cottage, or to an out-of-town friend's house).

In this chapter, you are probably hoping to find out ways to improve your memory—perhaps so that you can improve your grades by remembering more about the topics you have learned. Well, we hope you will retain some of what you will learn. This chapter is all about the "backup assistant" in your brain—your **memory**—the process by which information is encoded, stored, organized, and later retrieved. Without your memory, there is no past. Without your memory, experience is trivial and learning is lost. Let us see what psychologists have learned about the ways in which we remember things—and why we can forget them.

Let's begin by challenging your memory. This is not an actual memory test to determine whether your memory functioning is within normal limits. Instead, it will provide you with some insight into how your memory works and may also be fun.

Examine the following drawings for one minute. Then copy the *names* of the figures side by side using a piece of paper (or your laptop). Be sure to save the names, because later in the chapter we will be asking you to refer back to them. When you're finished, just keep reading.

DID YOU KNOW?

- A person who suffers from retrograde amnesia may be able to automatically dial a frequently dialled phone number when asked or drive to his or her home.

- You are more likely to retain something if you rehearse it verbally than if you just view it repeatedly.

- If you can see, you have a "photographic memory" (called an *iconic memory*), but it is only brief.

- It may be easier for you to recall the name of your first-grade teacher than the name of someone you just met at a party.

- You may always recall where you were and what you were doing on the morning of September 11, 2001.

- If you study with your iPod (or stereo) on, you would probably do better to write a test with your iPod (or stereo) on.

- Information we hear, like a phone number, can be stored in our short-term memory only briefly (under 30 seconds) before the information is either lost or transferred to long-term memory.

memory
the processes by which information is encoded, stored, and retrieved

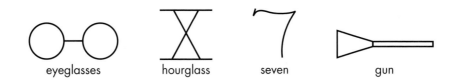

eyeglasses   hourglass   seven   gun

LO1 Processes of Memory

When we think about how we remember something, psychologists and computer scientists speak of processing information; we likely speak of the same. Picture yourself trying to "move" information through your brain to be able to remember something. You may close your eyes to visualize what you are trying to remember. Or if you are trying to remember what someone said, you may try to keep quiet to "hear" the words again. Sometimes, describing memory by considering how a computer works simplifies it. Think of using a computer to write a term paper. Once the system is up and operating, you begin to enter information. You can enter information, for example, by typing alphanumeric characters on a keyboard or—in the case of voice recognition technology—speaking into the microphone. But if you were to take your computer apart to "open up" its memory, you obviously wouldn't find these characters or sounds inside it. This is because the computer is programmed to change the characters or sounds—the information you have entered—into a form that can be placed in its electronic memory where information is stored (sometimes on the hard drive). Similarly, when we perceive information, we must change it into a form that can be remembered if we are to store it in our memory. If the storage system on your computer is organized, you can easily pull up (retrieve) the term paper from one of the files stored on the electronic system. Our memory systems also allow us to recall information—retrieve it—from our storage system in long-term memory (but not always). Let's now discuss the memory process: encoding, storage, retrieval.

Encoding

Information about the outside world first reaches our senses in the form of physical and chemical stimuli. The first stage of information processing is changing information so that we can place it in memory: encoding. *What is the role of encoding in memory?* When we encode information, we change it into psychological formats that can be represented mentally. As you can imagine, the amount of information that enters our sensory system is overwhelming. It would be impossible for us to remember everything that

we feel, hear, smell, taste, and touch—and thank goodness we don't need to remember everything. Important information competes with other information that we sense through **selective attention**. We selectively attend to information that is relevant to what we need to remember and eliminate information that is less important. For example, you may not hear the fans running or the student at the back of the classroom clicking the keyboard while paying attention to the teacher (or you might). By listening to the teacher's voice and ignoring the other sounds around you, you have used selective attention.

To encode information, we commonly use visual, auditory, and semantic codes. The Try It! box illustrates the uses of coding—go ahead and try the exercise presented.

Try It!

Try to recall as many letters in the list as you can after looking at them for only about 20 seconds (then cover the page and try to write the list).

T G I F R C M P T O

How did you do?

If you had used a *visual code* to try to remember the list, you would have mentally represented it as a picture. That is, you would have maintained—or attempted to maintain—a mental image of the letters.

You may also have decided to read the list of letters to yourself—that is, to silently say them in sequence: "t," "g," "i," and so on. By so doing, you would have been using an *acoustic code*, or representing the stimuli as a sequence of sounds. You may also have read the list by attaching meaning to the letters, such as "RCMP." This code has elements of a semantic code.

Semantic codes represent stimuli in terms of their meaning. The ten letters were meaningless in and of themselves. However, they can also serve as three abbreviations—TGIF, for example, stands for "Thank Goodness It's Friday." This observation lends them meaning.

Storage

The second stage of information processing is *storage*. *What is the role of storage in memory?* Storage means maintaining information over time. If you were given the task of storing a list of letters—that is, told to remember it—how would you attempt to place it in storage? (Think about what we just discussed.)

One way would be by **maintenance rehearsal**—by mentally repeating the list, or saying it to yourself over and over again until you can recall the list accurately.

You could also encode the list of letters by relating it to something that you already know. This coding strategy is called **elaborative rehearsal**. You are "elaborating" or extending the semantic meaning of the letters you are trying to remember. "RCMP" is a familiar abbreviation, which makes it more meaningful, and easier to remember.

Our awareness of the functioning of our memory, referred to by psychologists as **metamemory**, becomes more sophisticated as we grow.

Retrieval

The third stage of information processing is *retrieval*. *What is the role of retrieval in memory?* The **retrieval** of stored information means locating it and returning it to consciousness. With well-known information such as our names and occupations, retrieval is effortless and rapid. But when we are trying to remember large amounts of information, or information that is not perfectly understood, retrieval can be difficult or worse—fail. To retrieve information, you must effectively encode and store the information first; otherwise, you will not be able to recall it.

If, in the Try It! box, you recalled the list of letters—good for you; you encoded and stored it effectively. Now, what if you were not able to remember the list of ten letters? What may have gone wrong? In terms of the three processes of memory, it could be that you had (1) not encoded the list in a useful way, (2) not entered the encoded information into storage, or (3) stored the information but forgotten the cues for remembering it—such as the abbreviations within it (e.g., RCMP).

How We Measure Memory

Three basic *memory tasks*—tests of memory—have been used by psychologists to measure it: recognition, recall, and relearning.

Recognition

Having the answers in front of you for a test, as in a multiple-choice test, can be helpful. Having to just recognize terms or concepts on a test can be much easier than having to recall them without any cues. To measure *recognition*, psychologists may ask participants to read a list of nonsense syllables. The participants then read a second list of nonsense syllables and indicate whether they recognize any of the syllables as having appeared on the first list.

Harry Bahrick and his colleagues (1975) studied high-school graduates who had been out of school for various lengths of time. They interspersed photos of the graduates' classmates with four times as many photos of strangers. Recent graduates correctly recognized former classmates 90 percent of the time. Those who had been out of school for 40 years recognized former classmates 75 percent of the time. A chance level of recognition would have been only 20 percent (one photo in five was of an actual classmate). Thus even those who had been out of school for 40 years showed rather impressive recognition ability.

Recall

Unlike recognition tasks, recall tasks require us to supply information without the help of cues (or answers dispersed).

One recall task that psychologists often use involves lists of pairs of nonsense syllables, called **paired associates**. A list of paired associates is shown in Figure 6.1 (p. 126). Participants read through the lists pair by pair. Later they are shown the first member of each pair and asked to recall the second. This is much more

Retrieval of information can be easy. It is easiest to retrieve information stored in a computer by using the name of the file. Similarly, retrieval of information from our memories requires knowledge of the proper cues.

Michael Weber/GetStock.com

method of savings
a measure of memory in which the difference between the number of repetitions originally required to learn a list and the number of repetitions required to relearn the list after a certain amount of time has elapsed is calculated

savings
the difference between the number of repetitions originally required to learn a list and the number of repetitions required to relearn the list after a certain amount of time has elapsed

FIGURE 6.1

Recall Task: Using Paired Associates

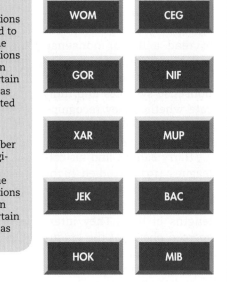

WOM	CEG
GOR	NIF
XAR	MUP
JEK	BAC
HOK	MIB

difficult than simply recognizing the pairs. In this recall task, the participant must retrieve a syllable and attach it with another syllable serving as a cue.

Retrieval is made easier if the two syllables can be meaningfully linked—that is, encoded semantically—even if the "meaning" is stretched. Consider the first pair of nonsense syllables in Figure 6.1. The image of a WOMan smoking a CEG-arette may make CEG easier to retrieve when the person is presented with the cue WOM.

Relearning

Relearning is a third method of measuring memory. Do you remember having to learn all of the provinces and territories of Canada in elementary school? What were the capital cities of Saskatchewan and New Brunswick? (Do you remember?) Even when we cannot recall or recognize information that had

Studies of relearning demonstrate at least one important lesson for students: Relearning material for a final exam takes less time than learning it initially.

once been learned, such as knowing that Regina is the capital of Saskatchewan and Fredericton is the capital of New Brunswick, we can relearn it more rapidly the second time.

To study the efficiency of relearning, Ebbinghaus (1885/1913) devised the **method of savings**. First he recorded the number of repetitions required to learn a list of nonsense syllables or words. Then he recorded the number of repetitions required to relearn the list after a certain amount of time had elapsed. Next he computed the difference in the number of repetitions to determine the **savings**. If a list had to be repeated 20 times before it was learned, and 20 times again after a year had passed, there were no savings. Relearning, that is, was as tedious as the initial learning. If the list could be learned with only ten repetitions after a year had elapsed, however, half the number of repetitions required for learning had been saved.

Figure 6.2 shows Ebbinghaus's classic curve of forgetting. As you can see, there was no loss of memory as measured by savings immediately after a list had been learned. However, recollection dropped quite a bit, by half, during the first hour after learning a list. Losses of learning then became more gradual. It took a month (31 days) for retention to be cut in half again. Forgetting occurred most rapidly right after material was learned.

Studies of relearning demonstrate at least one important lesson for students: Relearning material for a final exam takes less time than learning it initially.

LO2 Stages of Memory (Systems) and Types of Memories

We are all intrigued by the fact that some memories are unreliable. Why, for example, would some memories "go in one ear and out the other,"

FIGURE 6.2

Ebbinghaus's Classic Curve of Forgetting

Recollection of lists of words drops precipitously during the first hour after learning. Losses of learning then becomes more gradual. Retention drops by half within the first hour. It takes a month (31 days), however, for retention to be cut in half again.

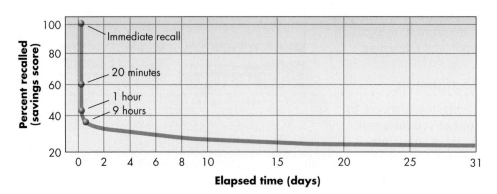

while others stick with us for a lifetime? Psychologists Richard Atkinson and Richard Shiffrin (1968) suggested a model for how some information is lost immediately, other information is held briefly, and still other information is held for a lifetime. *What is the Atkinson–Shiffrin model of memory?* As shown in Figure 6.3, they proposed a three-stage memory system that determines whether (and how long) information is retained: *sensory memory, short-term memory* (STM), and *long-term memory* (LTM).

Sensory Memory

When we look at a visual stimulus, our impressions may seem fluid enough. For example, when lightning flashes, we see it as a stream of light descending from the sky. Actually, however, this visual image consists of a series of eye fixations referred to as *saccadic eye movements.* These movements jump from one point to another about four times each second. Yet the visual sensations seem continuous, or stream-like, because of **sensory memory**. Sensory

sensory memory the type or stage of memory first encountered by a stimulus

---

FIGURE 6.3

Three Stages of Memory: The Atkinson–Shiffrin Model

The Atkinson–Shiffrin model proposes that memory is a three-stage system: (a) sensory memory, (b) short-term memory, and (c) long-term memory. Part A: Sensory information impacts on the registers of sensory memory. Memory traces are held briefly in sensory memory before decaying. If we attend to the information, much of it can be transferred to short-term memory (STM). Part B: Information may be maintained in STM through maintenance rehearsal or elaborative rehearsal. Otherwise, it may decay or be displaced. Part C: Once information is transferred to long-term memory (LTM), it may be filed away indefinitely. However, if the information in LTM is organized poorly, or if we cannot find cues to retrieve it, it can be lost.

Go to www.icanpsych.com to access an interactive version of this figure.

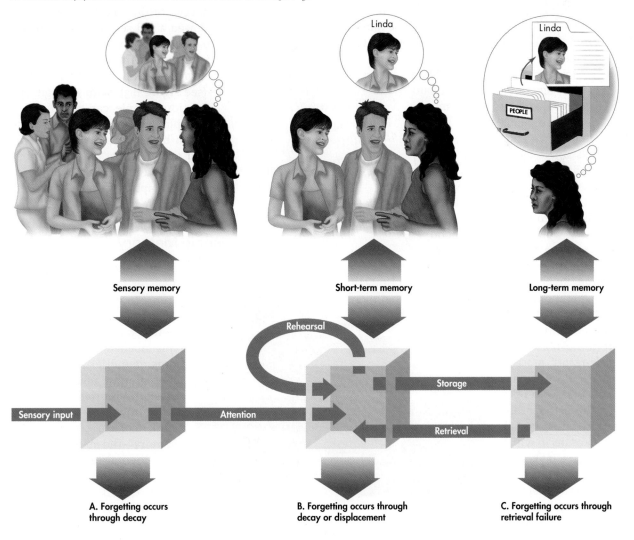

A. Forgetting occurs through decay

B. Forgetting occurs through decay or displacement

C. Forgetting occurs through retrieval failure

memory trace
an assumed change in the nervous system that reflects the impression made by a stimulus

icon
a mental representation of a visual stimulus that is held briefly in sensory memory

iconic memory
the sensory register that briefly holds mental representations of visual stimuli

eidetic imagery
the maintenance of detailed visual memories over several minutes

memory is the type or stage of memory that is first encountered by a stimulus. Although sensory memory holds impressions only briefly, it is long enough so that a series of perceptions (or sensory images) seem to be connected. *How does sensory memory function?*

To explain the functioning of sensory memory, let us return to the list of letters used previously: T G I F R C M P T O. If the list were flashed on a screen for a fraction of a second, the visual image, or **memory trace**, of the stimulus would also last for only a fraction of a second afterward. Psychologists speak of the memory trace of the list as being held in a visual *sensory register.*

If the letters had been flashed on a screen for, say, 1/10 of a second, your ability to remember them on the basis of sensory memory alone would be limited. Your memory would be based on a single eye fixation, and the trace of the image would vanish before a single second had passed. More than a century ago, psychologist William McDougall (1904) engaged in research in which he showed people 1 to 12 letters arranged in rows—just long enough to allow a single eye fixation. Under these conditions, people could typically remember only four or five letters. Thus recollection of T G I F R C M P T O, a list of ten letters arranged in a single row, would probably depend on whether one had encoded it so that it could be processed further.

George Sperling (1960) modified McDougall's classic experimental method and showed that there is a difference between what people can see (sensory memory) and what they can report (retrieval). McDougall had used a *whole-report procedure,* in which people were asked to report every letter they saw in the list. Sperling used a modified *partial-report procedure,* in which people were asked to report the contents of one of three rows of letters. In a typical procedure, Sperling

What most of us usually think of as a photographic memory—the ability to retain exact mental representations of visual stimuli over long periods—is technically termed eidetic imagery.

flashed three rows of letters like the following on a screen for 50 milliseconds (1/20 of a second):

A G R E

V L S B

N K B T

Using the whole-report procedure, people could report an average of four letters from the entire display (one out of three). But if immediately after presenting the display Sperling pointed an arrow at a row he wanted viewers to report, they usually reported most of the letters in the row successfully.

If Sperling presented six letters listed in two rows, people could usually report either row without error. If people were flashed three rows of four letters each—a total of 12—they reported correctly an average of three of four letters in the designated row, suggesting that about 9 of the 12 letters had been perceived. Much more than McDougall initially found.

Sperling also found that the amount of time that elapsed before he pointed to the row to be reported affected people's memory. If he delayed pointing for a few fractions of a second after showing the letters, people were less successful in reporting the letters in the row. If he allowed a full second to elapse, the arrow did not help people remember at all. Sperling concluded that the memory trace of visual stimuli *decays* within a second (see Figure 6.3). With a single eye fixation, people can *see* most of a display of 12 letters clearly, as shown by their ability to immediately read off most of the letters in a designated row. Yet as fractions of a second elapse, the trace of the letters fades. By the time a full second elapses, the trace is gone.

Iconic Memory

Psychologists believe we possess a sensory register for each sense. The mental representations of visual stimuli are referred to as **icons**. The sensory register that holds icons is labelled **iconic memory**. Iconic memories are accurate, photographic memories. But these memories are brief. What most of us usually think of as a photographic memory—the ability to retain exact mental representations of visual stimuli over long periods—is technically termed **eidetic imagery**. Although all

Darrell Young/GetStock.com

people who can see have brief photographic memories (that is, icons), only a few have eidetic imagery.

As mentioned previously, saccadic eye movements occur about four times a second. But iconic memory holds icons up to a second. For this reason, the flow of visual information seems smooth and continuous. Your impression that the words you are reading flow across the page, rather than jumping across in spurts, is a product of your iconic memory. Similarly, motion pictures present 16 to 22 separate frames, or still images, each second, but iconic memory allows you to perceive the imagery in the film as being seamless (G.R. Loftus, 1983).

Echoic Memory

Mental representations of sounds, or auditory stimuli, are called echoes. Echoic memory is the sensory register that holds echoes (sounds).

The memory traces of auditory stimuli—echoes—can last for several seconds, many times longer than the traces of visual stimuli (icons). This difference is one of the reasons that acoustic codes aid in the retention of information that has been presented visually—or why saying the letters or syllables of T G I F R C M P T O makes the list easier to remember.

Short-Term Memory

Imagine that you are completing a writing assignment and you type or speak words and phrases into your word-processing program. They appear on your monitor as a sign that your computer has them in *memory*. Your word-processing program allows you to add words, delete words, check whether they are spelled correctly, add images, and move paragraphs from place to place. Although you can manipulate the information in your computer's memory, it isn't saved. It hasn't been entered into storage. If the program or the computer crashes, the information is lost. To maintain a permanent record of the information, you have to save it. Saving it means naming it—hopefully with a name that you will remember so that you can later find and retrieve the informa-

tion—and instructing your computer to save it (keep it in storage until told otherwise).

If you focus on a stimulus in the sensory register, you will tend to retain it in your own **short-term memory (STM)**—also referred to as **working memory**—for a minute or so after the trace of the stimulus decays. *How does short-term memory function?* As one researcher describes it, "Working memory is the mental glue that links a thought through time from its beginning to its end" (Goldman-Rakic, 1995). When you are given a phone number and write it down or immediately dial the number, you are retaining the number in your short-term memory. When you are told the name of someone at a party and then use that name immediately in addressing that person, you are retaining the name in short-term memory. In short-term memory, the image tends to fade significantly after 10 to 12 seconds if it is not repeated or rehearsed. Short-term memory more easily codes sensory information as auditory information, such as the sound of letters (not

echo
a mental representation of an auditory stimulus (sound) that is held briefly in sensory memory

echoic memory
the sensory register that briefly holds mental representations of auditory stimuli

short-term memory (STM)
the memory system that can hold information only briefly after the trace of the stimulus decays

working memory
another term for *short-term memory*

Memorizing a Script by Rehearsing Echoic Memories
As actors work on memorizing scripts, they first encode visual information (printed words) as echoes (their corresponding sounds within the brain). Then they commit the echoes to memory by rehearsing (repeating) them, referring back to the visual information as necessary. Eventually, the lines of other actors become cues that trigger memory of an actor's own lines.

© Hill Street Studios/Blend Images/Corbis

serial-position effect
the tendency to recall more accurately the first and last items in a series

chunking
encoding (organizing) a stimulus or group of stimuli as a distinct piece of information; grouping stimuli together

long-term memory (LTM)
the type or stage of memory capable of relatively permanent storage

the shape of the letter), so then the sounds can be rehearsed, or repeated. Most people can retain approximately seven (plus or minus two) pieces of information at one time in STM (Miller, 1956).

Once information is in our short-term memories, we can work on it. Like the information in the word-processing program, we can manipulate it. If we don't do something to save—such as write down a new telephone number or key it into a cellphone—it can be lost forever.

To increase the capacity in STM, we need to rehearse the information in order to move it from our short-term memory into a permanent storage area so that we can retrieve it later.

The Serial-Position Effect—One Way We Remember

If asked to recall a seemingly random list of 10 letters (for the first time) T G I F R C M P T O you would be likely to recall the first and last letters in the series, T and O, more accurately than the others. *Why are we most likely to remember the first and last items in a list?* The tendency to recall the first and last items in a series is known as the **serial-position effect**. This effect may occur because we pay more attention to the first (*primacy effect*) and last (*recency effect*) stimuli in a series. They serve as the boundaries for the other stimuli. It may also be that the first items are likely to be rehearsed more frequently (repeated more times) than other items. The last items are likely to have been rehearsed most recently and hence are most likely to be retained in short-term memory.

Chunking—Breaking It Down to Remember It

Rapidly rehearsing ten meaningless letters is not an easy task. With T G I F R C M P T O there are ten distinct elements, or chunks, of information that must be kept in short-term memory. When we encode TGIF RCMP TO as three groups, there are only three chunks to memorize at once—this is called **chunking**.

As Miller (1956) found, most people have little trouble recalling two or three chunks of information, as in a postal code. Some can remember nine, which is, for all but a few, an upper limit. So seven chunks, plus or minus one or two, is a "magic" number in the sense that the typical person can remember that many chunks of information and not much more.

Interference in Short-Term Memory

In a classic experiment with college students, Lloyd and Margaret Peterson (1959) demonstrated how prevention of rehearsal can interfere with short-term memory. They asked students to remember three-letter combinations such as HGB—normally, three easy chunks of information. They then had the students count backward from an arbitrary number, such as 181, by threes (that is, 181, 178, 175, 172, and so on). The students were told to stop counting and to report the letter sequence after the intervals of time. The percentage of correctly recalled letter combinations fell dramatically within seconds (see Figure 6.4). After 18 seconds of counting interference, almost all students' recall of the letter sequences failed.

Psychologists say that the appearance of new information in short-term memory interferes with the old information. *Remember:* Only a few bits of information can be retained in short-term memory at the same time. We will discuss interference theories later in the chapter.

Long-Term Memory

Long-term memory (LTM) is the third memory system (refer back to Figure 6.3 on page 127). Think of your long-term memory as a vast storehouse of information, both general and specific, containing names, dates, places, past experiences and knowledge you have acquired. *How does long-term memory function?*

Some psychologists (Freud was one) believed that nearly all of our perceptions and ideas are stored permanently. We might not be able to retrieve all of them, however.

{ Magic Number 7 }

It makes sense: Businesses pay phone companies hefty premiums so that they can obtain numbers with two or three zeroes or repeated digits—for example, 592-2000 or 277-3333. These numbers include fewer chunks of information and hence are easier to remember. Others use phone numbers with meaningful alpha digits to associate their business and increase customer recall, such as 1-800-EAT-FREE (for restaurant coupons) or 432-HELP (for an IT service desk).

FIGURE 6.4

The Effect of Interference on Short-Term Memory

In this experiment, college students were asked to remember a series of three letters while they counted backward by threes. After just three seconds, retention was cut by half. Ability to recall the words was almost completely lost by 15 seconds.

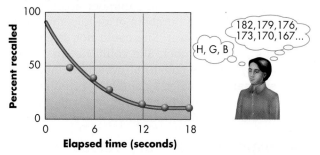

How Much Information Can Be Stored in Long-Term Memory?

How many "gigabytes of storage" are there in your most personal computer—your brain? Unlike a computer, the human ability to store information is, for all practical purposes, unlimited (Goldman-Rakic et al., 2000b). Even the largest hard drives fill up when we save Web pages, photos, songs, and movies. Yet how many "movies" of the past have you saved in your own long-term memory? How many thousands of scenes and stories can you rerun at will? And, assuming that you have an intact sensory system, the movies in your personal storage bins not only have colour and sound, but also aromas, tactile sensations, and more. *Your long-term memory is a biochemical "hard drive" with no known limits on the amount of information it can store.*

New information may replace older information in short-term memory, but there is no evidence that long-term memories—those in "storage"—are lost by displacement. Long-term memories may endure a lifetime. Now and then it may seem that we have forgotten, or "lost," a long-term memory such as the names of elementary school classmates, yet it may be that we cannot find the proper cues to retrieve them. However, if you drive by your elementary school (a cue) you might suddenly recall the long-lost names of schoolteachers.

Explicit versus Implicit Memories

Explicit Memory

What is meant by explicit memory? Explicit memory—also referred to as *declarative memory*—is memory for specific information. Things that are *explicit* are clear, or clearly stated or explained. The use of the term *declarative* indicates that these memories state or reveal (i.e., *declare*) specific information. The information may be autobiographical or refer to general knowledge.

Two kinds of explicit memories are described by psychologist Endel Tulving (1985): episodic and semantic. They are identified according to the type of information they hold.

Episodic Memory (I remember...) Episodic memories are memories of the things that happen to us or take place in our presence. Episodic memory is also referred to as *autobiographical memory*. Your memories of what you ate for breakfast and of what your professor said in class today are episodic memories. We tend to use the phrase "I remember ..." when we are referring to episodic memories, as in "I remember the city bus strike of 2009."

Semantic Memory (I know...) General knowledge that we have (like a "Wikipedia") is referred to as semantic memory—another kind of explicit memory. *Semantics* concerns meanings. You can "know" that Canada has ten provinces and three territories without visiting them and personally adding them up. You may "know" who authored *Hamlet*, although you were not looking over Shakespeare's shoulder as he did so. Your collection of trivia and other pieces of information obtained through learning or hearing about them are part of your semantic memory.

Your future recollection that there are several memory systems is more likely to be semantic than episodic. In other words, you are more likely to "know" that there are several types of memory than to recall where you were and how you were sitting. We are more likely to say "I know ..." in reference to semantic memories, as in "I *know* about—" (or, "I heard about—") "—the War of 1812."

Implicit Memory

What is meant by implicit memory? Implicit memory—also referred to as *nondeclarative memory*—is memory of how to perform a procedure or skill; it is the act

> **Long-term memory is reconstructive rather than photographic.**

explicit memory memory that clearly and distinctly expresses (declares) specific information; also called *declarative memory*

episodic memory memories of events experienced by a person or that take place in the person's presence

semantic memory general knowledge and information we know about, as opposed to episodic memory

implicit memory memory that is suggested (implied) but not plainly expressed, as illustrated in the things that people *do* but do not state clearly; also called *nondeclarative memory*

priming the activation of specific associations in memory, often as a result of repetition and without making a conscious effort to access the memory

retrospective memory memory for past events, activities, and learning experiences, as shown by explicit (episodic and semantic) and implicit memories

prospective memory memory to perform an act in the future, as at a certain time or when a certain event occurs

itself, doing something, like riding a skateboard, accessing your cellphone address book, and texting a message (Schacter et al., 1993). Implicit memories are suggested (or implied) but not plainly stated or verbally expressed. Implicit memories are illustrated by the things that people *do* but not by the things they state clearly. Implicit memories involve procedures and skills, cognitive and physical, and are also referred to as *procedural* or *skill memories*.

Implicit memories can endure even when we have not used them for years. Getting to class "by habit"—without paying attention to landmarks or directions—is another instance of implicit memory. If someone asked you what 2 × 2 is, the number 4 would probably "pop" into mind without conscious calculation. After going over the alphabet or multiplication tables hundreds of times, our memory of them becomes automatic or implicit. We need not focus on them to use them.

Your memory of the alphabet or the multiplication tables reflects repetition that makes associations automatic. This phenomenon is called priming. Brain imaging shows that priming makes it possible for people to carry out mental tasks with less neural activity (Savage et al., 2001; Schacter et al., 2004)—less thinking or processing (see the Try It! box).

Daniel Schacter (1992) illustrates implicit memory with the story of a woman with amnesia who was wandering the streets. The police picked her up and found that she could not remember who she was and that she had no identification. After fruitless interviewing, the police hit on the idea of asking her to dial phone numbers—"any number at all." When asked for the phone numbers of people she knew, she had had no answer. She could not *declare* her mother's phone number. She could not make the number *explicit*. She could not even remember her mother's name, or whether she had a mother. But dialling her mother's phone number was a habit, and she did it "on automatic pilot."

Retrospective Memory versus Prospective Memory

Retrospective memory is the recalling of information that has been previously learned. *Episodic, semantic,* and *implicit memories* involve remembering things that were learned. **Prospective memory** refers to remembering to do things in the future, such as remembering to pay your bills or to take out some cash.

Zaichenko Olga/Shutterstock.com

Most of us have had failures of prospective memory in which we feel we were supposed to do something but can't remember what. Prospective memory may fail when we are preoccupied, distracted or "stressed out" about time (Schacter, 1999).

There are various kinds of prospective memory tasks. *Habitual tasks* such as getting to class on time are easier to remember than occasional tasks such as meeting someone for coffee at an arbitrary time (d'Ydewalle et al., 1999). Motivation also plays a role. You are more likely to remember the coffee date if the person you are meeting excites you. Psychologists also distinguish between event-based and time-based prospective memory tasks (Fortin et al., 2002). *Event-based tasks* are triggered by events, such as remembering to take one's medicine at breakfast or to brush one's teeth after eating. *Time-based tasks* are to be performed at a certain time or after a certain amount of time has elapsed between occurrences, such as tuning in to a favourite news program at 7:30 P.M. or taking a pill every four hours (Marsh et al., 2005).

An age-related decline takes place in retrospective and prospective memories (Brigman & Cherry, 2002; Reese & Cherry, 2002). The decline in older adults may be related to their speed of cognitive processing rather than the "loss" of information per se.

Try It!

Check out these licence plates:

GO LFS GO	WIF N KDS	C ME 4 A DTE
ONTARIO	BRITISH COLUMBIA	NOVA SCOTIA

Did you come up with "Go Leafs Go," "Wife and Kids," and "See me for a date"?

Priming helps us make associations in memory that can assist us in accessing our memory quickly. Even though the cues in the licence plates are limited, you likely made them into words (or phrases).

In the case of prospective memory, older adults take longer to respond to the cues or reminders (West & Craik, 1999).

Moods and attitudes affect prospective memory (Villa & Abeles, 2000). For example, depressed people are less likely to push to remind themselves to do what they intend to do (Rude et al., 1999).

How Accurate Are Long-Term Memories?

Psychologist Elizabeth Loftus (1983) notes that memories are distorted by our biases and needs—by the ways in which we conceptualize our worlds. We represent much of our world in the form of **schemas**. A *schema* is a way of mentally representing the world, such as a belief or expectation, that can influence our perception of persons, objects, and situations.

At the beginning of this chapter you wrote down some labels, each of which described a drawing above it (see page 123). Take a moment now and draw the figures (without looking at the next page) as you recall how they looked. Now look at Figure 6.5 (p. 134). Do your drawings look more like Group 1 or Group 2? It wouldn't be surprising if they were more like those in Group 1. Figure 6.5 is a demonstration of how schemas work. The labels serve as *schemas* for the drawings—ways of organizing your knowledge of them—and these schemas may have influenced your recollections.

Memory as Reconstruction

If schemas influence our memories of some event or, as in the example just given, when recreating drawings, then what does that say about memory? Many researchers believe that what we recall about events is not exactly, perfectly matched to its actual happening. Loftus and Palmer (1974) support that memories are *reconstructed*—that is, that they are influenced by logic, reasoning, and addition of new information. Loftus and Palmer had participants watch a film of a car crash. Following the viewing, the participants were interviewed on the clip they viewed. In particular, participants were asked to estimate how fast the cars were going when the accident happened. One of five different word choices were used: "How fast were the cars going when they _____ [smashed, collided, bumped, hit, or contacted]?" Results showed significant differences in participants' reports of the speed of the cars upon impact. Participants who heard the word "smashed" were also more likely to say that they saw broken glass (even though no glass was broken!). Table 6.1 illustrates these results.

Our reconstruction of memories can cause distortions in how we remember things. This is because of our use of schemas, which allow us to organize and make sense of the world more easily. In the case of the car crash, our perception of two cars "smashing" likely gives us a mental representation of a stronger impact than the word "hit," leading us to believe that glass was broken. This is similar to cases of eyewitness testimonies, where witnesses make false testimony about a potential perpetrator or criminal (Loftus, 1993).

Levels of Processing Information

People who use elaborative rehearsal to remember things are *processing information at a deeper level* than people who use maintenance rehearsal. *What is the levels-of-processing model of memory?* Fergus Craik and Robert Lockhart (1972) pioneered the levels-of-processing model of memory, which holds that memories tend to endure when information is processed

schema
a way of mentally representing the world, such as a belief or an expectation, that can influence perception of persons, objects, and situations

---

TABLE 6.1

Loftus and Palmer (1974) Study

Word Used in Question	Average Speed Estimated*
Smashed	41 mph (66 km/h)
Collided	39 mph (63 km/h)
Bumped	38 mph (61 km/h)
Hit	34 mph (55 km/h)
Contacted	32 mph (52 km/h)

* In miles (and kilometres) per hour.

Source: Adapted from E. Loftus and J.C. Palmer (1974). Reconstruction of automobile destruction: An example of interaction between language and memory, *Journal of Verbal Learning and Verbal Behavior, 13*: 585–589.

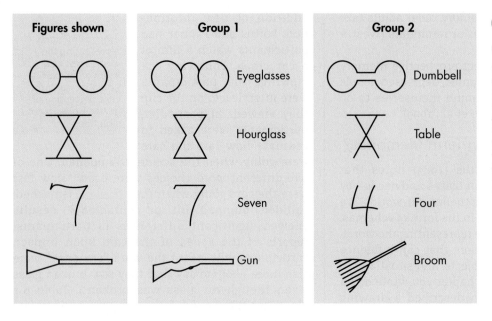

Figures shown	Group 1		Group 2	
		Eyeglasses		Dumbbell
		Hourglass		Table
		Seven		Four
		Gun		Broom

FIGURE 6.5

Memory as a Schema

In their classic experiment, Carmichael, Hogan, and Walter (1932) showed people the figures in the left box and made remarks as suggested in the other boxes. For example, the experimenter might say, "This drawing looks like eyeglasses [or a dumbbell]." When people later reconstructed the drawings, they were influenced by the labels.

deeply—attended to, encoded carefully, pondered, and related to things we already know. Remembering relies on how *deeply* people process information, not on whether memories are transferred from one *stage* of memory to another.

Think of all the math problems we solved in high school. Each problem is an application of a procedure and, perhaps, of certain formulas. By repeatedly applying the procedures and formulas in slightly different contexts, we rehearse them elaboratively. As a result, we are more likely to remember them.

Biologically oriented research connects deep processing with activity in certain parts of the brain, notably the prefrontal area of the cerebral cortex (Constantinidis et al., 2001). One reason that older adults show memory loss is that they tend not to process information quite as deeply as younger people do (Grady et al., 1999). Deep processing requires sustained attention, and older adults, along with people who have suffered brain injuries and strokes, apparently cannot focus as well as they once did (Winocur et al., 2000).

Organization in Long-Term Memory

The storehouse of long-term memory is usually well organized. Items are not just piled on the floor or thrown into closets. *How is knowledge organized in long-term memory?* We tend to gather information about rats and cats into a certain section of the storehouse, perhaps the animal or mammal section. We put information about oaks, maples, and eucalyptus into the tree section. Such categorization of stimuli is a basic cognitive function. It allows us to make predictions about specific instances and to store information efficiently.

We tend to organize information according to a *hierarchical structure,* as shown in Figure 6.6. A *hierarchy* is an arrangement of items (or chunks of information) into groups or classes according to common or distinct features. As we work our way up the hierarchy shown in the figure, we find more encompassing, or *superordinate,* classes to which the items below them belong. For example, all mammals are animals, but there are many types of animals other than mammals.

When items are correctly organized in long-term memory, you are more likely to recall—or know—accurate information about them. For example, do you "remember" whether whales breathe underwater? If you did not know that whales are mammals (or, in Figure 6.6, *subordinate* to mammals), or if you knew nothing about mammals, a correct answer might depend on some remote instance of rote learning. That is, you might be depending on episodic memory rather than on semantic memory. For example, you might recall some details from a TV documentary on whales. If you *did* know that whales are mammals, however, you would also know—or remember—that whales do not breathe underwater. How? You would reconstruct information about whales from knowledge about mammals, the group to which whales are subordinate. Similarly, you would know, or remember, that because they are mammals, whales are warm-blooded, nurse their young, and are a good deal more intelligent than, say, tuna and sharks, which are fish. Had you incorrectly classified whales as fish, you might have searched your memory and constructed the incorrect answer that they do breathe underwater.

FIGURE 6.6

The Hierarchical Structure of Long-Term Memory

Where are whales filed in the hierarchical cabinets of your memory? Your classification of whales may influence your answers to these questions: Do whales breathe underwater? Are they warm-blooded? Do they nurse their young? A note to biological purists: This figure is not intended to represent phyla, classes, orders, and so on, accurately. Rather, it shows how an individual's classification scheme might be organized.

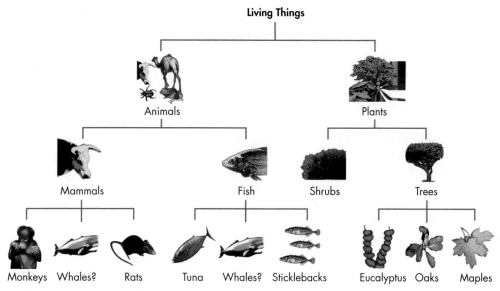

> **tip-of-the-tongue (TOT) phenomenon** the feeling that information is stored in memory although it cannot be readily retrieved

Psychologists term this experience the **tip-of-the-tongue (TOT) phenomenon**, or the *feeling-of-knowing experience. Why do we sometimes feel that the answer to a question is on the tip of our tongue?*

Research provides insight into the TOT phenomenon (Brown & McNeill, 1966; James & Burke, 2000). In classic research, Brown and McNeill (1966) defined some rather unusual words for students, such as *sampan*, a small riverboat used in China and Japan. The students were then asked to recall the words they had learned. Some of the students often had the right word "on the tip of their tongue" but reported words with similar meanings such as *junk, barge,* or *houseboat.* Still other students reported words that sounded similar,

Flashbulb Memories

Why is it that some events, like the attacks of September 11, 2001, can be etched in memory for a lifetime? It appears that we tend to remember events that are surprising, important, and emotionally stirring more clearly. Such events can create "flashbulb memories," which preserve experiences in detail (Finkenauer et al., 1998; Otani et al., 2005). Why is the memory etched when the "flashbulb" goes off? One factor is the distinctness of the memory. It is easier to discriminate stimuli that stand out. Such events are striking in themselves. The feelings caused by them are also special. It is thus relatively easy to pick them out from the storehouse of memories. Major events such as the loss of a close relative, moving away from home, or for hockey fans—Canada winning the gold medal in the Olympics—also tend to have important effects on our lives. We are likely to dwell on them and form networks of associations. That is, we are likely to rehearse them elaboratively. Our rehearsal may include great expectations, or deep fears, for the future.

The Tip-of-the-Tongue Phenomenon

What was the name of the lead actor from *Catch Me If You Can?* You know—the one who recently starred in *Inception* and *Shutter Island?* Having something on the tip of your tongue can be a frustrating experience.

such as *Saipan, Siam, sarong,* and *sanching.* Why?

To begin with, the words were unfamiliar, so elaborative rehearsal did not take place. The students did not have an opportunity to relate the words to other things they knew. Brown and McNeill also suggested that our storage systems are indexed according to cues that include both the sounds and the meanings of words—that is, according to both acoustic and semantic codes. By scanning words similar in sound and meaning to the word on the tip of the tongue, we sometimes find a useful cue and retrieve the word for which we are searching.

Sometimes an answer seems to be on the tip of our tongue because our learning of the topic is incomplete. We may not know the exact answer, but we know something. (As a matter of fact, if we have good writing skills, we may present our incomplete knowledge so forcefully that we earn a good grade on an essay question on the topic!) At such times, the problem lies not in retrieval but in the original processes of learning and memory—that is, encoding and storage.

By the way, the answer to the TOT question at the beginning of this section: Who was the actor that.... is Leonardo DiCaprio!

Context-Dependent Memory

The context in which we acquire information can also play a role in retrieval Have you ever gotten up from the couch to grab something from the kitchen because you were hungry, but when you got there forgot what you went there for? Did you remember once you sat back down on the couch?

This experience is an example of a **context-dependent memory.** Your memory of getting food was particularly clear in the context in which it

was formed. *Why may it be useful to study in the same room in which we will be tested?* One answer is that being in the same context—for example, studying in the exam room or under the same conditions—can dramatically enhance recall (Isarida & Isarida, 1999).

State-Dependent Memory

State-dependent memory is an extension of context-dependent memory. We sometimes retrieve information better when we are in a biological or emotional state similar to the one in which we encoded and stored the information. Feeling the rush of love may trigger other images of falling in love. The grip of anger may prompt memories of incidents of frustration. The research in this area extends to states in which we are sober or inebriated.

LO3 Forgetting

Now that we have talked a lot about memory, how it works, what kinds of memory we can create … what were we going to, uh, talk about next? Oh yes, right, forgetting! We forget for a number of reasons. Some have already been discussed to some extent and others we will discuss here. If you can't remember what we have discussed thus far, it is most likely due to **encoding failure.** We also saw (from Ebbinghaus's studies; see Figure 6.2 on page 126) that memory traces decay over time.

Interference Theory

When we do not attend to, encode, and rehearse sensory input, we may forget it through decay of the trace of the image. Information in short-term memory, like information in sensory memory, can be lost through decay. It can also be lost through displacement, as may happen when we try to remember several new names at a party.

Why can learning French make it harder to remember Spanish? The answer may be found in **interference theory.** According to this view, we also forget material in short-term and long-term memory because newly learned material interferes with it. The two basic types of interference are retroactive

© Digital Vision/Getty Images

interference (also called *retroactive inhibition*) and proactive interference (also called *proactive inhibition*).

Retroactive Interference

In **retroactive interference**, new learning interferes with the retrieval of old learning. For example, a medical student may memorize the names of the bones in the leg through rote repetition. Later he or she may find that learning the names of the bones in the arm makes it more difficult to retrieve the names of the leg bones, especially if the names are similar in sound or in relative location on each limb.

Lev Olkha/Shutterstock.com

Proactive Interference

In **proactive interference**, older learning interferes with the capacity to retrieve more recently learned material. High-school French may pop in when you are trying to retrieve college Spanish or Italian words. All three are Romance languages, with similar roots and spellings. Previously learned Japanese words probably would not interfere with your ability to retrieve more recently learned Spanish or Italian, because the roots and sounds of Japanese differ considerably from those of the Romance languages.

Repression

According to Sigmund Freud, we are motivated to forget painful memories and unacceptable ideas because they produce anxiety, guilt, and shame. *What is the Freudian concept of repression?* Repression, according to Freud, is the automatic ejection of painful memories and unacceptable urges from conscious awareness. It is motivated by the desire to avoid facing painful memories and emotions. Psychoanalysts believe that repression is at the heart of disorders such as **dissociative amnesia** (see Chapter 12).

There is much research on repression, often in the form of case studies that are found in psychoanalytic journals (e.g., Eagle, 2000). Much has been made of case studies in which war veterans have supposedly forgotten traumatic battlefield experiences, developed *post-traumatic stress disorder* (once called "battlefield neurosis"), and then "felt better" once they recalled and discussed the traumatic events (Karon & Widener, 1998). Critics argue that the evidence for such repression and recovery of memories is weak and that this kind of "memory" can be implanted by the suggestions of interviewers (Loftus, 2001). The issue remains controversial, as we see next.

retroactive interference the interference of new learning with the ability to retrieve material learned previously

proactive interference the interference by old learning with the ability to retrieve material learned recently

dissociative amnesia amnesia thought to stem from psychological conflict or trauma

infantile amnesia inability to recall events that occur prior to the age of two or three; also termed *childhood amnesia*

Do People Really Recover Repressed Memories of Childhood?

Despite shaky scientific support, there are cases of so-called recovered memories, especially memories of childhood sexual abuse by a relative, teacher, or friend. The question is whether these memories are induced by therapists who foster beliefs that become so deeply ingrained they seem like authentic memories. "We don't know what percent of these recovered memories are real and what percent are pseudomemories," notes psychiatrist Harold Lief (cited in Brody, 2000), one of the first to challenge such memories.

Psychologist Elizabeth Loftus has engaged in numerous studies that show how easy it is to implant false memories through leading questions. In one study, researchers were able to readily convince half the subjects that they had been lost in a mall or hospitalized with severe pain as children.

Infantile Amnesia

Can children remember events from the first couple of years of life? When he interviewed people about their early experiences, Freud discovered that they could not recall episodes that had happened prior to the age of three or so and that recall was cloudy through the age of five. This phenomenon is referred to as **infantile amnesia**.

Infantile amnesia has little to do with the fact that the episodes occurred in the distant past. Middle-aged and older people have vivid memories from the ages of six through ten, yet the events happened many decades ago. But 18-year-olds show steep declines in memory when they try to recall episodes that occurred earlier than the age of six, even though they happened less than 18 years earlier (Wetzler & Sweeney, 1986).

Freud believed that young children have aggressive impulses and perverse lusts toward their parents. He attributed infantile amnesia to repression of these impulses. The episodes lost to infantile amnesia, however, are not weighted in the direction of such "primitive" impulses. In fact, infantile amnesia probably reflects the interaction of physiological and cognitive factors. For example, a structure of the limbic system (the **hippocampus**) that is involved in the storage of memories does not become mature until we are about two years old (Squire, 2004). Also, myelination of brain pathways is incomplete for the first few years of life, contributing to the inefficiency of information processing and memory formation.

There are also cognitive explanations for infantile amnesia:

- Infants are not particularly interested in remembering the past (Neisser, 1993).
- Infants, in contrast to older children, tend not to weave episodes together into meaningful stories of their own lives. Information about specific episodes thus tends to be lost. Research shows that when parents reminisce about the past with children, the children's memories of being infants are strengthened (Peterson, 2002).
- Infants do not make reliable use of language to symbolize or classify events (Wang, 2003). Their ability to *encode* sensory input—that is, to apply the auditory and semantic codes that facilitate memory formation—is therefore limited. Yet research shows that young infants can recall events throughout the period when infantile amnesia is presumed to occur if they are now and then exposed to objects they played with or photos of events (Rovee-Collier, 1999).

In any event, we are unlikely to remember episodes from early childhood unless we are reminded of them from time to time as we develop. Many early childhood memories that seem so clear today might be reconstructed and hold many inaccuracies. They might also be memories of events that occurred later than we thought. Yet there is no evidence that such early memories are systematically repressed.

Anterograde and Retrograde Amnesia

Adults also experience amnesia, although usually for biological reasons, as in the cases of anterograde and retrograde amnesia (Kopelman, 2002). *Why do people frequently have trouble recalling being in accidents?* In so-called **anterograde amnesia**, there are memory lapses for the period following a trauma such as a blow to the head, an electric shock, or an operation. In some cases the trauma seems to interfere with all the processes of memory. The ability to pay attention, the encoding of sensory input, and rehearsal are all impaired. A number of investigators have linked certain kinds of brain damage—such as damage to the hippocampus—to amnesia (Eichenbaum & Fortin, 2003; Spiers et al., 2001).

In **retrograde amnesia**, the source of trauma prevents people from remembering events that took

We are unlikely to remember episodes from early childhood unless we are reminded of them from time to time.

place before the accident (Wheeler & McMillan, 2001). In one well-known case of retrograde amnesia, a man received a head injury in a motorcycle accident (Baddeley, 1982). When he regained consciousness, he had lost memory for all events that had occurred after the age of 11. In fact, he appeared to believe that he was still 11 years old. During the next few months he gradually recovered more knowledge of his past. He moved toward the present year by year, up until the critical motorcycle ride.

But he never did recover the events just prior to the accident. The accident had apparently prevented the information that was rapidly unfolding before him from being transferred to long-term memory. In terms of stages of memory, it may be that our perceptions and ideas need to consolidate, or rest undisturbed for a while, if they are to be transferred to long-term memory (Nader et al., 2000).

LO4 The Biology of Memory

Psychologists assume that mental processes such as the encoding, storage, and retrieval of information—that is, memory—are accompanied by changes in the brain. Early in the 20th century, many psychologists used the concept of the **engram** in their study of memory. Engrams were viewed as electrical circuits in the brain that corresponded to memory traces—neurological processes that paralleled experiences. Yet biological psychologists such as Karl Lashley (1950) spent many fruitless years searching for such circuits or for the structures of the brain in which they might be housed. Much research on the biology of memory today focuses on the roles of stimulants, neurons, neurotransmitters, hormones, and structures in the brain.

Neural Activity and Memory

What neural events are connected with memory? Rats who are reared in stimulating environments provide some answers. The animals develop more dendrites and synapses in the cerebral cortex than rats reared in impoverished environments (Neisser, 1997a). Moreover, visually stimulating rats increases the number of synapses in their visual cortex (Battaglia et al., 2004; Bilkey, 2004). Therefore, the storage of experience does involve avenues of communication among brain cells.

The hippocampus is not a storage bin. It is involved in relaying sensory information to parts of the cortex.

Information received through other senses is just as likely to lead to corresponding changes in the cortical regions that represent them. For example, sounds may similarly cause changes in the auditory cortex. Experiences perceived by several senses are apparently stored in numerous parts of the cortex. The recall of sensory experiences apparently involves neural activity in related regions of the brain.

Research with sea snails such as *Aplysia* and *Hermissenda* offers more insight into the biology of memory. *Aplysia* has only about 20 000 neurons compared with humans' billions. As a result, researchers have been able to study how experience is reflected at the synapses of specific neurons. The sea snail will reflexively withdraw its gills when it receives electric shock, in the way a person will reflexively withdraw a hand from a hot stove or a thorn. In one kind of experiment, researchers precede the shock with a squirt of water. After a few repetitions, the sea snail becomes conditioned to withdraw its gills when squirted with the water. When sea snails are conditioned, they release more serotonin at certain synapses. As a consequence, transmission at these synapses becomes more efficient as trials (learning) progress (Kandel, 2001). This greater efficiency is termed **long-term potentiation (LTP)**. As shown in Figure 6.8, dendrites can also participate in LTP by sprouting new branches that attach to the transmitting axon. Rats who are given substances that enhance LTP learn mazes with fewer errors; that is, they are less likely to turn down the wrong alley (Uzakov et al., 2005).

Serotonin and many other naturally occurring chemical substances, including adrenaline, noradrenaline, acetylcholine, glutamate, antidiuretic hormone, and even the sex hormones estrogen and testosterone, have been shown to play roles in memory.

Brain Structures and Memory

What structures in the brain are connected with memory? Memory does not reside in a single structure of the

engram
(1) an assumed electrical circuit in the brain that corresponds to a memory trace; (2) an assumed chemical change in the brain that accompanies learning (from the Greek *en-*, meaning "in," and *gramma*, meaning "something that is written or recorded")

long-term potentiation (LTP)
enhanced efficiency in synaptic transmission that follows brief, rapid stimulation

FIGURE 6.7

Hippocampus and Memory

The hippocampus is essential to the formation of new memories. It is vital in storing new information and relaying sensory information to other parts of the brain.

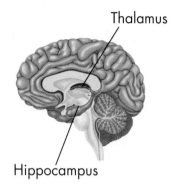

Thalamus

Hippocampus

brain; it relies on complex neural networks that draw on various parts of the brain (Nyberg et al., 2000). However, some parts of the brain play more specific roles in memory. The hippocampus is vital in storing new information even if we can retrieve old information without it (Fields, 2005). But the hippocampus is not a storage bin. Rather, it is involved in relaying sensory information to parts of the cortex. (See the box on p. 38 of Chapter 2 for more information.)

Where are the storage bins? The brain stores parts of memories in the appropriate areas of the sensory cortex. Sights are stored in the visual cortex, sounds in the auditory cortex, and so on. The limbic system is largely responsible for integrating these pieces of information when we recall an event. The frontal lobes apparently store information about where and when events occur (Goldman-Rakic et al., 2000a).

The prefrontal cortex (see Figure 6.9) is the executive centre in memory (Buckner et al., 2001; Wheeler & Treisman, 2002). It appears to empower people with consciousness—the ability to mentally represent and become aware of experiences that occur in the past, present, and future. It enables people to mentally travel back in time to re-experience the personal, autobiographical past. It enables people to focus on the things they intend to do in the future, such as mail a letter on the way to class or brush their teeth before going to bed.

The hippocampus is also involved in the where and when of things (Eichenbaum & Fortin, 2003). The hippocampus does not become mature until we are about two years old. Immaturity may be connected with infantile amnesia. Adults with hippocampal damage may be able to form new procedural memories, even though they cannot form new episodic ("where and when") memories (Fields, 2005). They can develop new skills even though

FIGURE 6.8

One Avenue to Long-Term Potentiation (LTP)

LTP can occur via the action of neurotransmitters such as serotonin and glutamate at synapses. Structurally, LTP can also occur as shown in these illustrations, when dendrites sprout new branches that connect with transmitting axons, increasing the amount of stimulation they receive.

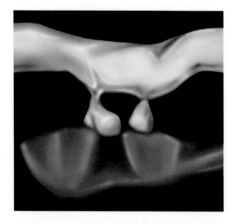

The Prefrontal Cortex of the Brain

The prefrontal cortex comes in pairs. One is found in each hemisphere, a bit above the outer edge of the eyebrow. The prefrontal cortex is highly active during visual and spatial problem solving. It is known as the executive decision-making area of the brain, which includes planning, organizing, and controlling behaviours.

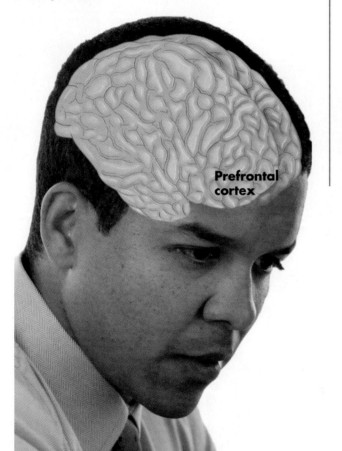

Prefrontal cortex

they cannot recall the practice sessions (Reed & Squire, 1997).

The thalamus is involved in the formation of verbal memories. Part of the thalamus of a U.S. Air Force cadet known as N.A. was damaged in a fencing accident. Afterward, N.A. could no longer form verbal memories, but he could form visual memories (Squire, 2004). (One might measure visual memory by showing people pictures, allowing time to pass, and then asking them to point out those they have been shown.)

The encoding, storage, and retrieval of information thus involve biological activity. As we learn, new synapses are developed, and changes occur at existing synapses. Parts of the brain are also involved in the formation of memories. In the next chapter, we see how people manipulate information they have stored to adapt to the environment or create new environments.

Thinking,
Intelligence,
and
Language

Learning Outcomes

LO1 Define thinking and the various concepts involved in thinking

LO2 Identify the concept of intelligence and the techniques used to measure intelligence

LO3 Describe the controversy surrounding intelligence testing

LO4 Describe how language develops

"Intelligence may be the most controversial topic in psychology."

What form of life is so adaptive that it can survive in desert temperatures of 50°C or Arctic climes of –40°C? What form of life can run, walk, climb, swim, live underwater for months on end, and fly to the moon and back? We won't keep you in suspense any longer. We are that form of life. Yet our unclad bodies do not allow us to adapt to these extremes of temperature. Brute strength does not allow us to live underwater or travel to the moon. Rather, it is our cognitive processes that allow us to adapt to these conditions and surpass our physical limitations.

In this chapter we explore thinking, intelligence, and language. Thinking enables us to pose problems and solve them, and to make judgments and decisions. Intelligence may be the most controversial topic in psychology. Psychologists do not agree on exactly what intelligence is or exactly how people develop intelligence. By and large, however, psychologists view intelligence as the underlying ability to understand the world and cope with its challenges. Humans use language not only in communicating, but also in thinking. Humans attach words and sentences to the objects and concepts they think about, taking them into abstract realms.

DID YOU KNOW?

- Only humans can use insight to solve problems.
- You can make your children smarter by taking them shopping.
- "Street smarts" are a sign of intelligence.
- Young children say things like "Daddy goed away" and "Mommy sitted down" because they understand rules of grammar.
- Canada is a bilingual country, but less than 10 percent of the English-speaking population is fluent in French.

LO1 Thinking

The Greek philosopher Aristotle pointed out that people differ from lower organisms in their capacity for rational thinking. *What is thinking?* Thinking means paying attention to information, representing it mentally, reasoning about it, and making judgments and decisions about it. Thinking refers to conscious, planned attempts to make sense of and change the world. By contrast, mental processes such as dreaming and daydreaming do not represent thinking; they may be unplanned and proceed more or less on their own.

We begin with concepts, which provide many of the building blocks for thinking.

thinking
paying attention to information, mentally representing it, reasoning about it, and making decisions about it

concept
a mental category that is used to class together objects, relations, events, abstractions, or qualities that have common properties

Concepts

Concepts are mental categories used to group together objects, relations, events, abstractions, or qualities that have common properties. Concepts are crucial to cognition. Concepts can represent objects, events, and activities—and visions of things that never were or cannot be measured, such as Middle-earth in *The Lord of the Rings* or Pandora in *Avatar*.

Labels for objects depend on experience with them and on one's cultural setting (Sloman et al., 2002). For example, squares, circles, and triangles are not all that common in nature, and some peoples, such as the Himba of northern Namibia, have no concepts of them (Roberson et al., 2002). But these shapes are concepts that are basic to geometry. Much thinking has to do with categorizing new concepts and manipulating relationships among concepts, as in problems in geometry.

We tend to organize concepts in *hierarchies*. For example, newspapers, college and university textbooks, and catalogues can be combined into higher-order categories such as *printed matter* or *printed devices that store information*. If you add hard drives and DVDs, you can create a still higher category—*objects that store information*. Now consider a question that requires categorical thinking: How are a newspaper and a DVD alike? Answers to such questions entail supplying the category that includes both objects. In this case, we can say that both objects store information. Their functions are alike, even if their technology differs.

Prototypes are good examples. They best match the key features of categories. Which animal seems more birdlike to you: a robin or an ostrich? Why?

Which better fits the prototype of a fish: a sea horse or a tuna? Why?

Many simple prototypes, such as *dog* and *red*, are taught by means of examples, or **exemplars**. Research suggests that it is more efficient for most of us to learn what *fruits* and *vegetables* are from experience with exemplars of each, rather than by working from definitions of them (Smits et al., 2002). We point to a dog and tell a child "dog" or "This is a dog." Dogs are *positive instances* of the dog concept. *Negative instances*—things that are *not* dogs—are then shown to the child while we say, "This is *not* a dog." Negative instances of one concept may be positive instances of another. So, in teaching a child, we may be more likely to say, "This is not a dog—it's a cat" than simply, "This is not a dog."

Children may at first include horses and other four-legged animals within the dog concept until the differences between dogs and horses are pointed out. In language development, such overinclusion of instances in a category (reference to horses as dogs) is labelled *overextension*. Children's prototypes become refined after children are shown positive and negative instances and given explanations. Abstract concepts such as *bachelor* or *square root* tend to be formed through explanations that involve more basic concepts.

Problem Solving

Problem solving is an important aspect of thinking. Here's a problem for you to solve. What are the next two letters in this series?

OTTFFSSE_ _?

How did you try to find the answer? Did you search your personal memory banks and ask yourself what O can stand for, then T, and so on? Did you try to think of some phrase the letters might represent? Perhaps the first letters of the stars in a constellation? (If you don't resort to a search engine answer and do not arrive at the answer on your own, we'll discuss it within a few pages.)

Circles, squares, and triangles are found only rarely in nature and not among the Himba of northern Namibia. It is not surprising, then, that they have no words for these concepts.

Understanding the Problem

Successful understanding of a problem generally requires three features:

1 *The parts or elements of our mental representation of the problem relate to one another in a meaningful way.* If we are trying to solve a problem in geometry, our mental triangles, like actual triangles, should have angles that total 180 degrees.

2 *The elements of our mental representation of the problem correspond to the elements of the problem in the outer world.* If we are assessing a patient in the emergency room of a hospital, we want to arrive at a diagnosis of what might be wrong before we make a treatment plan. To do so, we take the patient's "vital signs," including heart rate, temperature, and blood pressure, so that our mental picture of the patient conforms to what is going on in his or her body.

3 *We have a storehouse of background knowledge that we can apply to the problem.* We have the necessary experience or course work to solve the problem.

The Use of Algorithms

An **algorithm** is a specific procedure for solving a type of problem. An algorithm invariably leads to the solution—if it is used properly, that is. Mathematical formulas like the Pythagorean theorem are examples of algorithms. They yield correct answers to problems *as long as the right formula is used*. Finding the right formula to solve a problem may require scanning one's memory for all formulas that contain variables that represent one or more of the elements in the problem. The Pythagorean theorem concerns right triangles. Therefore, it is appropriate to consider using this formula for problems concerning right triangles, but not others.

If you are going to be meeting someone for the first time and want to make a good impression, you consider the nature of the encounter (for example, a job interview or a "blind date") and then consider how to dress and behave for the encounter. If it's a job interview, the algorithm may be to dress neatly, be well-groomed, and not to wear too much cologne or perfume. If it's a date, you may ditch the suit but hike up the cologne or perfume a notch. In either case, smile and make eye contact—it's all part of the formula.

Anagrams are scrambled words. *Korc* is an anagram for *rock* or *cork*. The task in anagram problems is to try to reorganize jumbles or groups of letters into words. Some anagram problems require us to use every letter from the pool of letters; others allow us to use only some of the letters. How many words can you make from the pool of letters *DWARG*? If you were to use the **systematic random search** algorithm, you would list every possible letter combination, using from one to all five letters. You could use a dictionary or a spell-checking program to see whether each result is, in fact, a word. The method might take a while, but it would work.

The Use of Heuristic Devices

Is it best to use a tried-and-true formula to solve a problem? Sometimes people use shortcuts to "jump to conclusions"—and these are often correct conclusions. The shortcuts are called **heuristics**, or heuristic devices—rules of thumb that help us simplify and solve problems. Heuristics are often based on strategies that worked in the past (Klaczynski, 2001).

In contrast to algorithms, heuristics do not guarantee a correct solution. But when they work, they permit more rapid solutions. A heuristic device for solving the anagram problem would be to look for familiar letter combinations and then check the remaining letters for words that include these combinations. In *DWARG*, for example, we find some familiar combinations: *dr* and *gr*. We may then quickly find *draw*, *drag*, and *grad*. The drawback to this method is that we might miss some words.

One type of heuristic device is the **means–end analysis**. In using this heuristic device, we assess the difference between our current situation and our goals and do what we can to reduce this difference. Let's say that you are out in your car and have gotten lost. One heuristic device based on analysis of what you need to do to get to where you want to go might be to ask for directions. This approach requires no "sense of direction." An algorithm might be more complicated and require some scientific knowledge. For example, if you know your destination is west of your current location, you might try driving toward the setting sun.

The Use of Analogies

An *analogy* is a partial similarity among things that are different in other ways. The analogy heuristic applies the solution of an earlier problem to the solution of a new one. We use the analogy heuristic whenever we try to solve a new problem by referring to a previous problem (Halpern et al., 1990). Now take a look at the Try It! box on page 146.

algorithm
a systematic procedure for solving a problem that works invariably when it is correctly applied

systematic random search
an algorithm for solving problems in which each possible solution is tested according to a particular set of rules

heuristics
rules of thumb that help us simplify and solve problems

means–end analysis
a heuristic device in which we try to solve a problem by evaluating the difference between the current situation and the goal

You use the analogy heuristic regularly. For example, when you begin a new term with a new instructor, you probably consider who the instructor reminds you of. Then, perhaps, you recall the things that helped you get along with the analogous instructor and try them on the new one. We tend to look for things that helped us in the past in similar situations. When we considered OTTFFSSENT, we used the first letters of the numbers 1 through 10. In the Try It! box, looking at the numbers 8, 5, 4, 9, 1, 7, 6, 3, 2, and 0, we can again think of their first letters when they are spelled out. It happens that they are in alphabetical order (eight, five, four, and so on). Did you figure it out?

Try It!

Let us see whether you can use the analogy heuristic to your advantage in the following number series problem. Scan the following series of numbers and find the rule that governs their order:

8, 5, 4, 9, 1, 7, 6, 3, 2, 0

Can you figure out the series?

Factors That Affect Problem Solving

The way you approach a problem is central to how effective you are at solving it. Other factors also influence your effectiveness. *What factors make it easier or harder to solve problems?* Three such factors reside within you: (1) your level of expertise, (2) whether you fall prey to a mental set, and (3) whether you develop insight into the problem.

Expertise To appreciate the role of expertise in problem solving, unscramble the following anagrams, taken from Novick and Coté (1992). In each case use all of the letters to form an actual English word:

DNSUO
RCWDO
IASYD

How long did it take you to unscramble each anagram ("sound," "crowd," and "daisy")? Would a person whose native language is English—that is, an "expert"—unscramble each anagram more efficiently

than a bilingual person who spoke another language in the home? Why or why not?

Experts solve problems more efficiently and rapidly than novices do. Generally speaking, people who are experts at solving a certain kind of problem share the following characteristics:

- They know the particular area well.
- They have a good memory for the elements in the problems.
- They form mental images or representations that facilitate problem solving (Szala, 2002).
- They relate the problem to similar problems (Gorodetsky & Klavir, 2003).
- They are more goal-directed and have efficient methods for problem solving (Gorodetsky & Klavir, 2003).

These factors are interrelated. Art historians, for example, acquire a database that permits them to understand the intricacies of paintings. As a result, their memory for details of paintings mushrooms.

Novick and Coté (1992) found that the solutions to the anagram problems seemed to "pop out" in under two seconds among experts. The experts apparently used more efficient methods than the novices. Experts seemed to use *parallel processing*. That is, they dealt simultaneously with two or more elements of the problems. In the case of DNSUO, for example, they may have played with the order of the vowels (*UO* or *OU*) at the same time that they tested which consonant (D, N, or S) was likely to precede them, arriving quickly at *sou* and *sound*. Novices were more likely to engage in *serial processing*—that is, to handle one element of the problem at a time.

Mental Sets The tendency to respond to a new problem with the same approach that helped solve similar problems is termed a **mental set**. Mental sets usually make our work easier, but they can mislead us when the similarity between problems is illusory.

Insight To gain insight into the role of **insight** in problem solving, consider the following problem, posed by Metcalfe (1986):

A stranger approached a museum curator and offered him an ancient bronze coin. The coin had an authentic appearance and was marked with the date 544 BCE. The curator had happily made acquisitions from suspicious sources before, but this time he promptly called the police and had the stranger arrested. Why?

We're not going to give you the answer to this problem just yet. But here's a guarantee. When you arrive at the solution, it will hit you all at once. You'll think "Of course!" It will seem as though the pieces of information in the problem have suddenly been reorganized so that the solution leaps out—in a flash.

FIGURE 7.1

Insight Problems

Water lilies

Problem: Water lilies growing in a pond double in area every 24 hours. On the first day of spring, only one lily pad is on the surface of the pond. Sixty days later, the pond is entirely covered. On what day is the pond half-covered?

Twenty dollars

Problem: Jessica and Blair both have the same amount of money. How much must Jessica give Blair so that Blair has $20 more than Jessica?

How many pets?

Problem: How many pets do you have if all of them are birds except two, all of them are cats except two, and all of them are dogs except two?

Between 2 and 3

Problem: What one mathematical symbol can you place between 2 and 3 that results in a number greater than 2 and less than 3?

One word

Problem: Rearrange the letters NEWDOOR to make one word.

Solutions to these problems are listed on page 166.

From COON/MILTERER/BROWN/MALIK/MCKENZIE. *Psychology: A Journey*, 3E. © 2010 Nelson Education Ltd. Reproduced by permission. www.cengage.com/permissions.

Figure 7.1 presents some additional problems that can be solved using insight. See how many of them you can answer. The answers can be found at the end of the chapter.

Bismarck, one of psychologist N.R.F. Maier's rats, provided evidence of insight in his species (Maier & Schneirla, 1935). Bismarck had been trained to climb a ladder to a tabletop where food was placed. On one occasion, Maier used a mesh barrier to prevent the rat from reaching his goal. But, as shown in Figure 7.2, a second ladder was provided and was visible to the animal. At first Bismarck sniffed and scratched and tried to find a path through the mesh. Then he spent some time washing his face, an activity that may signal frustration in rats. Suddenly, he jumped into the air, turned, ran down the familiar ladder and around to the new ladder, ran up the new ladder, and claimed his just desserts. Did Bismarck suddenly perceive the relationships between the elements of the problem so that the solution occurred by insight? He seems to have had what Gestalt psychologists have termed an "Aha! experience."

incubation
in problem solving, a hypothetical process that sometimes occurs when we stand back from a frustrating problem for a while and the solution "suddenly" appears

functional fixedness
tendency to view an object in terms of its name or familiar usage

Incubation An incubator warms chicken eggs so that they will hatch. Incubation in problem solving refers to standing back from the problem for a while as some process within may continue to work on it. Later, the answer may come to us in a flash of insight. Standing back from the problem may help by distancing us from unprofitable but persistent mental sets (Both et al., 2004; Segal, 2004).

Functional Fixedness Functional fixedness may hinder problem solving. For example, first ask yourself what a pair of pliers is. Is it a tool for

FIGURE 7.2

Bismarck Uses a Cognitive Map to Claim His Just Desserts

Bismarck has learned to reach dinner by climbing ladder *A*. But now the food goal (*F*) is blocked by a wire mesh barrier *B*. Bismarck washes his face for a while, but then, in an apparent flash of insight, he runs back down ladder *A* and up new ladder *N* to reach the goal.

grasping, a paperweight, or a weapon?

A pair of pliers could function as any of these, but your tendency to think of it as a grasping tool is fostered by your experience with it. You have probably used pliers only for grasping things. Functional fixedness is the tendency to think of an object in terms of its name or its familiar function. It can be similar to a mental set in that it makes it difficult to use familiar objects to solve problems in novel ways.

Judgment and Decision Making

How do people make judgments and decisions? You might like to think that people are so rational that they carefully weigh the pros and cons when they make judgments or decisions. Or you might think that they insist on finding and examining all the relevant information. Actually, people make most of their decisions on the basis of limited information. They take shortcuts. They use heuristic devices—rules of thumb—in judgments and decision making just as they do in problem solving (Gilovich et al., 2002). For example, they may let a financial advisor select stocks for them rather than research the companies themselves. Or they may see a doctor recommended by a friend rather than look at the doctor's credentials. In this section we consider various factors in judgment and decision making.

Heuristics in Decision Making

Let us begin by asking you to imagine that you flip a coin six times. In the following three possible outcomes, H stands for heads and T for tails. Circle the most likely sequence:

H	H	H	H	H	H
H	H	H	T	T	T
T	H	H	T	H	T

Did you select T H H T H T as the most likely sequence of events? Most people do. Why? There are two reasons. First, people recognize that the

sequence of six heads in a row is unlikely. (The probability of achieving it is $1/2 \times 1/2 \times 1/2 \times 1/2 \times 1/2 \times 1/2$, or $1/64$.) Three heads and three tails are more likely than six heads (or six tails). Second, people recognize that the sequence of heads and tails ought to appear random. T H H T H T has a random look to it, whereas H H H T T T does not.

People tend to select T H H T H T because of the **representativeness heuristic**. According to this decision-making heuristic, people make judgments about events (samples) according to the populations of events that they appear to represent (Kahneman & Frederick, 2002; Shepperd & Koch, 2005). In this case, the sample of events is six coin tosses. The "population" is an infinite number of random coin tosses. But guess what? *Each* sequence is equally likely (or unlikely). If the question had been whether six heads or three heads and three tails had been more likely, the correct answer would have been three and three.

If the question had been whether heads and tails would be more likely to be consecutive or in random order, the correct answer would have been random order. But each of the three sequences is a *specific* sequence. What is the probability of attaining the *specific* sequence T H H T H T? The probability that the first coin toss will result in a tail is $1/2$. The probability that the second will result in a head is $1/2$, and so on. Thus, the probability of attaining the exact sequence T H H T H T is identical to that of achieving any other specific sequence: $1/2 \times 1/2 \times 1/2 \times 1/2 \times 1/2 \times 1/2 = 1/64$. (Try this out on a friend.)

Another heuristic device used in decision making is the **availability heuristic**. According to this heuristic, our estimates of frequency or probability are based on how easy it is to find examples of relevant events. Let me ask you whether there are more art majors or sociology majors at your school. Unless you are familiar with the enrollment statistics, you will probably answer on the basis of the numbers of art majors and sociology majors that you know.

The **anchoring and adjustment heuristic** suggests that there can be a good deal of inertia in our judgments. In forming opinions or making estimates, we have an initial view, or presumption. This is the anchor. As we receive additional information, we make adjustments, sometimes grudgingly. That is, if you grow up believing that one religion or one political party is the "right" one, that belief serves as a cognitive anchor. When inconsistencies show up in your religion or political party, you may adjust your views of them, but perhaps not very willingly.

The Framing Effect

What is the framing effect? The **framing effect** refers to the way in which wording, or the context in which

Try It!

Anchoring and Adjustment Heuristics

Write each of the following multiplication problems on a separate piece of paper:

A. $8 \times 7 \times 6 \times 5 \times 4 \times 3 \times 2 \times 1$

B. $1 \times 2 \times 3 \times 4 \times 5 \times 6 \times 7 \times 8$

Show problem A to a few friends. Give them each five seconds to estimate the answer. Show problem B to some other friends and give them five seconds to estimate the answer.

The answers to the multiplication problems are the same because the order of quantities being multiplied does not change the outcome. When Tversky and Kahneman (1982) showed these problems to high school students, the average estimate given by students who were shown version A was significantly higher than that given by students who were shown version B. Students who saw 8 in the first position offered an average estimate of 2250. Students who saw 1 in the first position gave an average estimate of 512. That is, the estimate was larger when 8 served as the anchor. By the way, what is the correct answer to the multiplication problems? Can you use the anchoring and adjustment heuristic to explain why both groups were so far off?

information is presented, affects decision making (Gonzalez et al., 2005; Tetlock & McGraw, 2005). Political groups, like advertisers, are aware of the *framing effect* and choose their words accordingly. For example, proponents of legalized abortion refer to themselves as "pro-choice" and opponents refer to themselves as "pro-life." Each group frames itself in a positive way ("pro" something) and refers to a popular value (freedom or life).

Overconfidence

Whether our decisions are correct or incorrect, most of us tend to be overconfident about them. We also tend to view our situations with 20–20 hindsight. When we are proven wrong, we frequently find a way to show that we "knew it all along." We also become overconfident that we would have known the actual outcome if we had had access to the information that became available after the event.

> Whereas thinking involves the understanding and manipulating of information, intelligence is considered to be the underlying ability to understand the world and cope with its challenges.

For example, if we had known that a key player would pull a hamstring muscle, we would have predicted a different outcome for the football game. If we had known that it would be blustery on Election Day, we would have predicted a smaller voter turnout and a different outcome. *Why do people tend to be convinced that they are right, even when they are dead wrong?* There are several reasons for overconfidence, even when our judgments are wrong:

- We tend to be unaware of how flimsy our assumptions may be.
- We tend to focus on examples that confirm our judgments and ignore those that do not.
- Because our working memories have limited space, we tend to forget information that runs counter to our judgments.
- We work to bring about the events we believe in, so they sometimes become self-fulfilling prophecies.

intelligence
a complex and controversial concept; according to David Wechsler (1975), the "capacity ... to understand the world [and] resourcefulness to cope with its challenges"

LO2 Intelligence

The concept of intelligence is closely related to thinking. Whereas thinking involves the understanding and manipulating of information, **intelligence** is considered to be the underlying ability to understand the world and cope with its challenges. Intelligence is seen as making thinking possible. Although these concepts overlap, psychologists tend to be concerned with *how* we think, but laypeople and psychologists are often concerned with *how much* intelligence we have. At an early age, we gain impressions of how intelligent or bright we are compared to other people.

Intelligence allows people to learn from experience and adapt to the environment (Neisser et al., 1996). As we see in architecture and space travel, intelligence also permits people to create environments. Although intelligence, like thinking, cannot be directly seen or touched, psychologists tie the concept to achievements such as school performance and occupational status (Pind et al., 2003; Wagner, 1997).

Theories of Intelligence

Although psychologists have engaged in thousands of studies on intelligence, they do not quite agree on what it is. Psychologists have therefore developed theories to help them understand and define intelligence.

g
Spearman's symbol for general intelligence, which he believed underlay more specific abilities

s
Spearman's symbol for *specific* factors, or *s factors*, which he believed accounted for individual abilities

primary mental abilities
according to Thurstone, the basic abilities that make up intelligence; examples include word fluency and numerical ability

Factor Theories

Many investigators have viewed intelligence as consisting of one or more factors. Factor theories argue that intelligence is made up of a number of mental abilities, ranging from one kind of ability to hundreds.

In 1904, British psychologist Charles Spearman suggested that the behaviours we consider intelligent have a common underlying factor that he labelled g, for "general intelligence" or broad reasoning and problem-solving abilities. Spearman supported his view by noting that people who excel in one area (such as vocabulary) are also likely to excel in others (such as math). But he also noted that even the most capable people are relatively superior in some areas—such as music or business or poetry. For this reason, he suggested that specific, or s, factors account for specific abilities.

Contemporary psychologists continue to use the term *g* in research, speaking, for example, of the extent to which they believe a particular kind of test, such as the SATs, measure *g* (Gignac & Vernon, 2003; Rushton et al., 2003).

The American psychologist Louis Thurstone (1938) analyzed tests of specific abilities and concluded that Spearman had oversimplified intelligence. Thurstone's data suggested the presence of nine specific factors, which he labelled **primary mental abilities** (see Table 7.1). Thurstone's primary mental abilities con-

TABLE 7.1

Primary Mental Abilities, According to Thurstone

Ability	Definition
Visual and spatial abilities	Visualizing forms and spatial relationships
Perceptual speed	Grasping perceptual details rapidly, perceiving similarities and differences between stimuli
Numerical ability	Computing numbers
Verbal meaning	Knowing the meanings of words
Memory	Recalling information (e.g., words and sentences)
Word fluency	Thinking of words quickly (e.g., rhyming and doing crossword puzzles)
Deductive reasoning	Deriving examples from general rules
Inductive reasoning	Inferring general rules from examples

tain the types of items measured on the most widely used intelligence tests today. The question remains as to whether his primary mental abilities are distinct or whether they are different ways of assessing *g*.

In 1967, J.P. Guilford proposed that the *structure of intellect* was three dimensions: mental operations, contents, and products. The first dimension, *mental operations*, includes thinking, memory, and evaluation. The second dimension, *contents*, refers to what we are thinking about or evaluating. For example, are we thinking about, or remembering, or evaluating a sound, smell, behaviour, language, and so forth? The last dimension, *products*, is the end result of our mental activity or the outcome.

The Theory of Multiple Intelligences

Thurstone wrote about various factors or components of intelligence. Howard Gardner (1983/1993), instead, proposes that there are a number of intelligences, not just one. *What is meant by multiple intelligences?* Gardner refers to each kind of intelligence in his theory as "an intelligence" because they can differ so much. Two of these "intelligences" are familiar ones: language ability and logical–mathematical ability. Gardner also refers, however, to bodily–kinesthetic talents (of the sort shown by dancers and athletes), musical talent, spatial–relations skills, and two kinds of personal intelligence: awareness of one's own inner feelings and sensitivity to other people's feelings. Gardner (2001) has recently added "naturalist intelligence" and "existential intelligence." Naturalist intelligence refers to the ability to look at natural events, such as kinds of animals and plants, or the stars above, and to develop insights into their nature and the laws that govern their behaviour. Existential intelligence means dealing with the larger philosophical issues of life. According to Gardner, one can compose symphonies or advance mathematical theory yet be average in, say, language and personal skills. Figure 7.3 illustrates Gardner's eight frames of mind.

Critics of Gardner's view agree that people function more intelligently in some aspects of life than in others. They also agree that many people have special talents, such as bodily–kinesthetic talents, even if their overall intelligence is average. But these critics question whether such talents are best thought of as "intelligences" (Neisser et al., 1996). Language skills, reasoning ability, and ability to solve math problems seem to be more closely related than musical or gymnastic talent to what most people mean by intelligence.

The Triarchic Theory of Intelligence

Psychologist Robert Sternberg (2000; Sternberg et al., 2003) has constructed a three-pronged, or triarchic, theory of intelligence that resembles a view proposed by the Greek philosopher Aristotle (Tigner & Tigner, 2000). *What is Sternberg's triarchic model of intelligence?* These types of intelligence are analytical, creative, and practical (see Figure 7.4).

Analytical intelligence is similar to Aristotle's "theoretical intelligence" and can be defined as academic ability. It enables us to solve problems and acquire new knowledge. It is the type of intelligence measured by standard intelligence tests. Problem-solving skills include encoding information, combining and comparing bits of information, and generating a solution. Consider the following analogy problem:

> *Day* is to *month* as *minute* is to
>
> (a) week, (b) hour,
> (c) second, (d) year?

To solve the analogy, we must first correctly *encode* the elements—*day, month,* and *minute*—by identifying them and comparing them to other information. We can first encode *day* and *minute* as units of time,

FIGURE 7.3

Gardner's Eight Frames of Mind

and then try to combine *day* and *month* in a meaningful manner. When we try to see the connection

FIGURE 7.4

Sternberg's Theory of Intelligence

According to Robert Sternberg, there are three types of intelligence: analytical (academic ability), creative, and practical ("street smarts"). Psychologists discuss the relationships between intelligence and creativity, but within Sternberg's model, creativity is a type of intellectual functioning.

Analytical intelligence
(Academic ability)
Abilities to solve problems,
compare and contrast, judge,
evaluate, and criticize

Creative intelligence
(Creativity and insight)
Abilities to invent, discover,
suppose, or theorize

Practical intelligence
("Street smarts")
Abilities to adapt to the demands
of one's environment, apply
knowledge in practical situations

CHAPTER 7 Thinking, Intelligence, and Language **151**

or relationship between *day* and *month*, we see that a month is broken down into days. So, the basic "units" of a month are days (or a month is made up of days). So, next we need to determine whether a week, hour, second, or year is made up of minutes. The answer is (b) hour. An hour is made up of minutes.

Creative intelligence is similar to Aristotle's "productive intelligence" and is defined by the abilities to cope with novel situations and generate many possible solutions to problems.

It is creative to quickly relate novel situations to familiar situations (that is, to perceive similarities and differences). Psychologists who consider creativity to be separate from analytical intelligence or academic ability note that there is only a moderate relationship between academic ability and creativity (Simonton, 2000). To Sternberg, however, creativity *is* a form of intelligence.

Aristotle and Sternberg both speak of practical intelligence ("street smarts"). Practical intelligence enables people to deal with other people, including difficult people, and to meet the demands of their environment. For example, keeping a job by adapting one's behaviour to the employer's requirements is adaptive. But if the employer is making unreasonable demands, finding a more suitable job is also adaptive. Street smarts appear to help people get by in the real world, especially with other people, but are not particularly predictive of academic success.

The Measurement of Intelligence

Although psychologists disagree about the nature of intelligence, laypeople and educators are concerned with "how much" intelligence people have, because the issue affects educational and occupational choices. In this section we consider two of the most widely used intelligence tests.

The Stanford–Binet Intelligence Scale

Many of the concepts of psychology have their origins in common sense. The commonsense notion that academic achievement depends on children's intelligence led Alfred Binet and Theodore Simon to invent measures of intelligence.

What is the Stanford–Binet Intelligence Scale? Early in the 20th century, the French public school system was looking for a test that could identify children who were unlikely to benefit from regular classroom instruction. If these children were identified, they could be given special attention. The first version of that test, the Binet–Simon scale, came into use in 1905. Since that time it has undergone extensive revision and refinement. The current version is the Stanford–Binet Intelligence Scale (SBIS).

Binet assumed that intelligence increases with age, so older children should get more items right than younger children. Binet therefore included a series of age-graded questions, as in Table 7.2, arranged in order of difficulty.

The Binet–Simon scale yielded a score called a **mental age (MA)**. The MA shows the intellectual level at which a child is functioning. For example, a child with an MA of six is functioning intellectually like the average six-year-old. In taking the test children earned "months" of credit for each correct answer. Their MA was determined by adding up the years and months of credit they attained.

Louis Terman adapted the Binet–Simon scale for use with American children at Stanford University. The first version of the resultant Stanford–Binet Intelligence Scale was published in 1916. The SBIS included more items than the original test and was used with children aged two to 16. The SBIS also yielded an **intelligence quotient (IQ)** rather than an MA. As a result, American educators developed interest in learning the IQs of their pupils. The SBIS is used today with children from the age of two upward and with adults.

The IQ reflects the relationship between a child's mental age and his or her actual or chronological age (CA). Use of this ratio reflects the fact that the same MA score has different implications for children of different ages. That is, an MA of eight is an above-average score for a six-year-old but below average for a ten-year-old. In 1912 the German psychologist Wilhelm Stern suggested the IQ as a way to deal with this problem. Stern computed IQ using the formula

$$IQ = \frac{\text{Mental age (MA)}}{\text{Chronological age (CA)}} \times 100$$

According to this formula, a child with an MA of six and a CA of six would have an IQ of 100. Children who can handle intellectual problems as well as older children do have IQs above 100. For example, an eight-year-old who does as well on

TABLE 7.2

Items Similar to Those on the Stanford–Binet Intelligence Scale

Level (Years)	Item
2	1. Children show knowledge of basic vocabulary words by identifying parts of a doll, such as the mouth, ears, and hair.
	2. Children show counting and spatial skills along with visual–motor coordination by building a tower of four blocks to match a model.
4	1. Children show word fluency and categorical thinking by filling in the missing words when they are asked questions such as:
	"Father is a man; mother is a ___?"
	"Hamburgers are hot; ice cream is ___?"
	2. Children show comprehension by answering correctly when they are asked questions such as:
	"Why do people have automobiles?"
	"Why do people have medicine?"
9	1. Children can point out verbal absurdities, as in this question: "In an old cemetery, scientists unearthed a skull which they think was that of George Washington when he was only five years of age. What is silly about that?"
	2. Children display fluency with words, as shown by answering these questions:
	"Can you tell me a number that rhymes with snore?"
	"Can you tell me a colour that rhymes with glue?"
Adult	1. Adults show knowledge of the meanings of words and conceptual thinking by correctly explaining the differences between word pairs like "sickness and misery," "house and home," and "integrity and prestige."
	2. Adults show spatial skills by correctly answering questions like: "If a car turned to the right to head north, in what direction was it heading before it turned?"

Mike Kemp/Rubberball/Jupiterimages

the SBIS as the average ten-year-old would attain an IQ of 125. Children who do not answer as many items correctly as other children of the same age attain MAs lower than their CAs. Thus, their IQ scores are below 100.

IQ scores on the SBIS today are derived by comparing their results to those of other people of the same age. People who answer more items correctly than the average for people of the same age attain IQ scores above 100. People who answer fewer items correctly than the average for their age attain scores below 100. Therefore, two children can answer exactly the same items on an intelligence test correctly, yet one can be above average in IQ. This is because the ages of the children may differ. The more intelligent child would be the younger of the two.

The Wechsler Scales

In contrast to the SBIS, David Wechsler developed a series of scales for use with children and adults.

What is different about the Wechsler scales of intelligence? The Wechsler scales group test questions into a number of separate subtests (see Figure 7.5 on page 154). Each subtest measures a different intellectual task. For this reason, the test shows how well a person does on one type of task (such as defining words) as compared with another (such as using blocks to construct geometric designs). In this way, the Wechsler scales highlight children's relative strengths and weaknesses, as well as measure overall intellectual functioning.

Wechsler described some of his scales as measuring *verbal* tasks and others as assessing *performance* tasks. In general, verbal subtests require knowledge of verbal concepts, whereas performance subtests require familiarity with spatial–relations concepts. Wechsler's scales permit the computation of verbal and performance IQs. College and university students who are not technically oriented often attain higher verbal than performance IQs. Less-well-educated people often obtain higher

FIGURE 7.5

Items Similar to Those on the Wechsler Adult Intelligence Scale

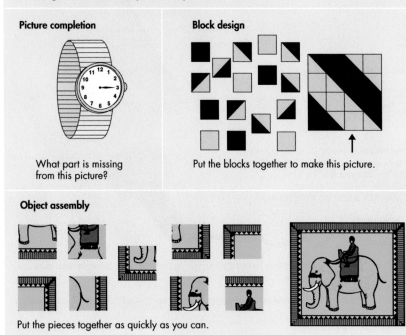

Figure 7.6, IQ scores cluster around the average. Only 4 percent of the population have IQ scores of above 130 or below 70.

Group Tests

The SBIS and Wechsler scales are administered to one person at a time. This one-to-one ratio is optimal because it allows the examiner to observe the test taker closely. Examiners are alerted to factors that impair performance, such as language difficulties, illness, or a noisy or poorly lit room. But large institutions with few trained examiners, such as the public schools and armed forces, require tests that can be administered simultaneously to large groups.

Group tests for children were first developed during World War I. Today, several group tests are widely used, such as the Canadian Cognitive Abilities Test, the California Test of Mental Maturity, and the Otis-Lennon Mental Ability Test. At first these tests were

performance than verbal IQs.

Wechsler also introduced the concept of the *deviation IQ*. Instead of dividing mental age by chronological age to compute an IQ, he based IQ scores on how a person's answers compared with those attained by people in the same age group. The average test result at any age level is defined as an IQ score of 100. Wechsler distributed IQ scores so that the middle 50 percent were defined as the "broad average range" of 90 to 110. As you can see in

FIGURE 7.6

Approximate Distribution of IQ Scores

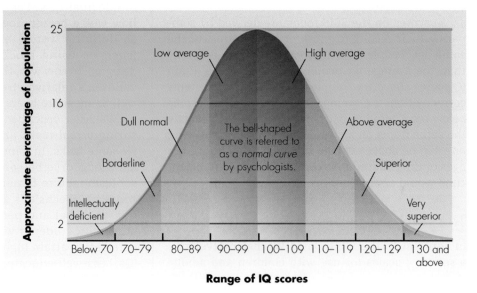

hailed as remarkable instruments because they helped school administrators place children. As the years passed, however, group tests came under attack because many administrators relied on them exclusively and did not seek other sources of information about children's abilities.

At their best, intelligence tests provide just one source of information about individual children. Numbers alone, and especially IQ scores, cannot adequately define children's special abilities and talents.

Differences in Intellectual Functioning

What factors influence our IQ score?

Gender Differences

It was once widely believed that males were more intelligent than females because of their greater knowledge of world affairs and their skills in science and industry. But these differences did not reflect differences in cognitive ability. Rather, they reflected exclusion of females from world affairs, science, and industry. Moreover, intelligence tests do not show overall gender differences in cognitive abilities (Halpern & LaMay, 2000).

Do males and females differ in intellectual functioning? Reviews of the research suggest that girls are somewhat superior to boys in verbal abilities, such as vocabulary, ability to generate sentences and words that are similar in meaning to other words, spelling, knowledge of foreign languages, and pronunciation (Halpern, 2003). Girls seem to acquire language somewhat faster than boys do. Males seem to do somewhat better at manipulating visual images in working memory. Males as a group excel in visual–spatial abilities of the sort used in math, science, and reading maps (Collaer & Nelson, 2002; Halpern & LaMay, 2000). Studies find that males generally obtain higher scores on math tests than females

do (Halpern & LaMay, 2000; Leahey & Guo, 2001). But note that the reported gender differences are *group* differences.

There is greater variation in these skills between individuals *within* the groups than between males and females (Halpern, 2003). That is, there may be a greater difference in, say, verbal skills between two women than between the typical woman and the typical man. Millions of females outdistance the "average" male in math and spatial abilities. Men have produced their verbally adept Shakespeares. Moreover, Hyde and Plant (1995) assert that in most cases, gender differences in cognitive skills are small. Differences in verbal, math, and visual–spatial abilities also appear to be narrowing as more females pursue course work in fields that had been typically populated by males. In addition, a recent study conducted by Ian Spence and colleagues at the University of Toronto (2009) found that women could perform both basic and complex spatial tasks as well as men, once they had participated in training tasks to develop their basic spatial abilities.

While scholars sit around and debate gender differences in intellectual functioning, women are voting on the issue by flooding fields once populated almost exclusively by men (Cox & Alm, 2005). Figure 7.7 shows that women are tossing these

FIGURE 7.7

Women Flood Professions Once Populated Almost Exclusively by Men

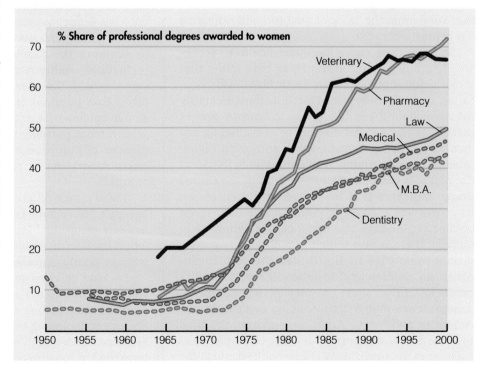

stereotypes out the window by entering the sciences and professional fields ranging from business to law to medicine in increasing numbers.

Socioeconomic and Ethnic Differences

Over the past 25 years there has been much controversy about the relationship between race and intelligence. There is evidence that intelligence—or, more precisely, intelligence test scores— differs between ethnic groups. Specifically, European North Americans and Asian North Americans tend to score higher than other ethnic groups (Neisser et al., 1996). But why would people from different races have different IQ scores? On one side of this IQ debate stands individuals like Arthur Jensen (Jensen, 1985), Canadian researcher J. Philippe Rushton (Rushton 1991; 1992; 1997), and Richard Herrntein and Charles Murray (1994), who maintain that IQ differences are solely due to genetic factors—meaning that some racial groups are just genetically or biologically more intelligent than other racial groups and that will never change. Based on measurements of head and brain size, Rushton reports that Asians are the most intelligent, followed by whites, and then blacks. On the other side of this debate are researchers like Michael Peters (1995a, 1995b) and Andrew Winston (1996, 2003, 2004), both from the University of Guelph, who question the validity of these findings and maintain that differences in IQ are due to testing biases that favour certain races over others and various environmental factors, such as poverty and education. Winston further condemns the work of Rushton and others as dangerous and racist.

So, what does cause the difference in IQ scores among ethnic groups? Researchers have found that socioeconomic status, cultural attitudes toward education, and culturally biased test questions are partly responsible for these differences. In Canada, over 15 percent of the population may be classified as low income (Statistics Canada, 2006), with even higher rates of poverty among visible minorities (National Council of Welfare, 2006). Research from the United States indicates that lower-class children obtain IQ scores some 10 to 15 points lower than those obtained by middle- and upper-class children. As in Canada, there is also a high rate of poverty among visible minorities in the United States. African-American children tend to obtain IQ scores some 15 points lower than those obtained by their European-American age-mates (Neisser et al., 1996). Hispanic-American and Native-American children also tend to score below the norms for European Americans (Neisser et al., 1996). Many studies of IQ confuse the factors of social class and ethnicity because disproportionate numbers of African Americans, Hispanic Americans, and Native Americans are found among the lower socioeconomic classes (Neisser et al., 1996). When we limit our observations to particular ethnic groups, we still find an effect for social class. That is, middle-class European Americans outscore poorer European Americans. Middle-class African Americans, Hispanic Americans, and Native Americans outscore poorer members of their own ethnic groups.

There may also be intellectual differences between Asians and Caucasians. Asian North Americans, for example, frequently outscore European North Americans on the math portion of the Scholastic Aptitude Test. Students in China (Taiwan) and Japan also outscore European North Americans on achievement tests in math and science (Stevenson et al., 1986). In the United States, moreover, people of Asian Indian, Korean, Japanese, Filipino, and Chinese descent are more likely than European Americans, African Americans, and Hispanic Americans to graduate from high school and complete college (Xie & Goyette, 2003; Yeh & Chang, 2004). They are also highly overrepresented in competitive colleges and universities.

Most psychologists believe that such ethnic differences reflect cultural attitudes toward education rather than inborn racial differences (Neisser et al., 1996). That is, Asian children may be more motivated to work in school (Fuligni & Witkow, 2004; Xie & Goyette, 2003). Research shows that Chinese and Japanese students and their mothers tend to attribute academic successes to hard work (Randel et al., 2000). European North Americans are more likely to attribute their children's academic successes to "natural" ability (Basic Behavioral Science Task Force, 1996b). Steinberg and his colleagues (1996) claim that parental encouragement and supervision in combination with peer support for academic achievement partially explain the superior performances of European North Americans and Asian North Americans as compared with other ethnic groups.

These ethnic differences lead us to ask: *Do intelligence tests contain cultural biases against ethnic minority groups and immigrants? Are the tests valid when used with ethnic minority groups or people who are poorly educated?*

Because children reared in poor socioeconomic conditions may be at a cultural disadvantage in intelligence testing (Helms, 1992; Kwate, 2001), many psychologists, including Raymond B. Cattell (1949) and Florence Goodenough (Goodenough & Harris, 1950), have tried to construct culture-free intelligence tests.

Cattell's Culture-Fair Intelligence Test evaluates reasoning through the child's ability to understand and use the rules that govern a progression of geometric designs (see Figure 7.8). Goodenough's Draw-A-Person test is based on the premise that children from all cultural backgrounds have had the opportunity to observe people and note the relationships between the parts and the whole. Her instructions simply require children to draw a picture of a man or woman.

Ironically, European-American children outperform African-American children on "culture-free" tests (Rushton et al., 2003), perhaps because they are more likely than disadvantaged children to have played with blocks (practice relevant to the Cattell test) and to have sketched animals, people, and things (practice relevant to the Goodenough test). Nor do culture-free tests predict academic success as well as other intelligence tests.

LO3 Nature and Nurture in Intelligence

If different ethnic groups tend to score differently on intelligence tests, psychologists—like educators and other people involved in public life—want to know why. As discussed earlier, this is a highly controversial debate. However, most researchers agree that intelligence is the result of complex interactions between nature (genetic influences) and nurture (environmental influences).

Genetic Influences on Intelligence

What are the genetic influences on intelligence? Research on genetic influences has employed kinship studies, twin studies, and adoptee studies (Neisser

et al., 1996). Let us consider each of these to see whether heredity affects intellectual functioning.

We can examine the IQ scores of closely and distantly related people who have been reared together or apart. If heredity is involved in human intelligence, closely related people ought to have more similar IQs than distantly related or unrelated people, even when they are reared separately (Petrill & Deater-Deckard, 2004).

Figure 7.9 (page 158) is a composite of the results of more than 100 studies of IQ and heredity in human beings (Bouchard et al., 1990). The IQ scores of identical (monozygotic, or MZ) twins are more alike than scores for any other pairs, even when the twins have been reared apart. There are moderate correlations between the IQ scores of fraternal (dizygotic, or DZ) twins, between those of siblings, and between those of parents and their children. Correlations between the scores of children and their foster parents and between those of cousins are weak.

The results of large-scale twin studies are consistent with the data in Figure 7.9. A classic study of 500 pairs of MZ and DZ twins in Louisville, Kentucky (Wilson, 1983), found that the correlations in intelligence between MZ twins were about the same as that for MZ twins. The correlations in intelligence between DZ twin pairs was the same as that between other siblings. The *MacArthur Longitudinal Twin Study* examined the intellectual abilities of 200 14-month-old pairs of twins (Plomin et al., 1993). The study found that MZ twins were more similar than DZ twins in spatial memory, ability to categorize things, and word comprehension.

In sum, studies generally suggest that the **heritability** of intelligence is between 40 percent and 60 percent (Neisser et al., 1996). In other words, about half of the difference between your IQ score and the IQ scores of other people can be explained by heredity.

Note, too, that genetic pairs (such as MZ twins) who were reared together show higher correlations in their IQ scores than similar genetic pairs (such as other MZ twins) who were reared apart. This finding holds for DZ twins, siblings, parents and their children, and unrelated people. Being reared together

heritability
the degree to which the variations in a trait from one person to another can be attributed to, or explained by, genetic factors

FIGURE 7.8

Sample Items from Cattell's Culture-Fair Intelligence Test

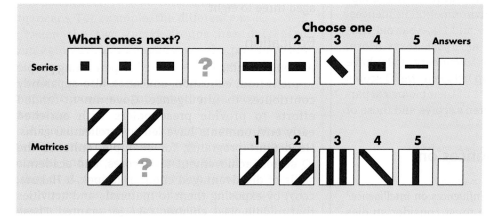

creativity
the ability to generate novel and useful solutions to problems

convergent thinking
a thought process that narrows in on the single best solution to a problem

divergent thinking
a thought process that attempts to generate multiple solutions to problems

In addition, researchers have shown that a person's emotional intelligence is not related to their IQ score (i.e., Lam & Kirby, 2002; van der Zee, Thijs, & Schakel, 2002).

There are thus many views of intelligence—what intelligence is and how many kinds of intelligence there may be. We do not yet have the final word on the nature of intelligence, but we would like to share David Wechsler's definition. Wechsler originated the most widely used series of intelligence tests, and he defined intelligence as the "capacity of an individual to understand the world [and the] resourcefulness to cope with its challenges" (1975, p. 139).

Creativity and Intelligence

Think of artists, musicians, poets, scientists who innovate research methods, and other creative individuals. *What is creativity? How is it connected to intelligence?*

Like the concept of intelligence, the concept of creativity has been difficult to define. One issue is whether creativity is distinct from intelligence, or is, as Sternberg suggests, a type of intelligence. For example, we would not ask the question, "Do creative people tend to be intelligent?" unless we saw creativity as distinct from intelligence. If you consider creativity to be an aspect of intelligence, then the two concepts—intelligence and creativity—overlap. But if you think of intelligence as more closely related to academic ability, it is not always true that a highly intelligent person is creative or that a creative person is highly intelligent. Research findings suggest that the relationship between intelligence test scores and standard measures of creativity is only moderate (Simonton, 2000; Sternberg & Williams, 1997).

Within his triarchic theory, Sternberg defines **creativity** as the ability to do things that are novel and useful (Sternberg, 2001). Other psychologists note that creative people can solve problems to which there are no pre-existing solutions and no tried and true formulas (Simonton, 2000). According to Sternberg and Lubart (1995, 1996), creative people take chances. They refuse to accept limitations. They appreciate art and music. They use common materials to make unique things. They challenge social norms and take unpopular stands. They challenge ideas that other people accept at face value.

Many psychologists see creativity as the ability to make unusual, sometimes remote, associations to the elements of a problem to generate new combinations. An essential aspect of a creative response is the leap from the elements of the problem to the novel solution.

Creative problem solving demands divergent rather than convergent thinking. In **convergent thinking**, thought is limited to present facts; the problem solver narrows his or her thinking to find the best solution. (You use convergent thinking to arrive at the right answer to a multiple-choice question.) In **divergent thinking**, the problem solver associates freely to the elements of the problem, allowing "leads" to run a nearly limitless course. (You may use divergent thinking when you are trying to generate ideas to answer an essay question on a test.)

Problem solving can involve both kinds of thinking. At first divergent thinking helps generate

One chimp, Kanzi, picked up language from observing another chimp being trained and has the grammatical abilities of a two-and-a-half-year-old child.

© Michael Nichols/National Geographic Image Collection

many possible solutions. Convergent thinking is then used to select likely solutions and reject others.

Intelligence test questions usually require analytical, convergent thinking to focus in on the one right answer. Tests of creativity determine how flexible a person's thinking is (Simonton, 2000). Here is an item from a test used by Getzels and Jackson (1962) to measure associative ability, a factor in creativity: "Write as many meanings as you can for each of the following words: (a) duck; (b) sack; (c) pitch; (d) fair." Those who write several meanings for each word, rather than only one, are rated as potentially more creative.

LO4 Language

Communication by Nonhumans

In recent years the exclusive human claim to language has been brought into question by studies of communication with various animal species. The African Grey parrot, like many other parrots, can mimic human speech, but it is also suspected of being intelligent enough to understand some of the words it imitates. It has long been suspected that spontaneous language development occurs among many species of dolphins and whales, but we lack solid scientific evidence. Monkeys signal the peril of nearby predators with characteristic hoots. But none of these sounds contains *symbols*.

A language is a system of symbols along with rules that are used to manipulate the symbols. Symbols such as words stand for or represent other objects, events, or ideas. Because chimpanzees and gorillas have been taught to communicate by making signs with their hands, the question as to whether or not they are actually using language in the way that humans do is much more complex.

Chimpanzees are our closest genetic relatives, sharing an estimated 98.42 percent of their genetic code with humans (Zimmer, 2002–2003). MRI studies with chimpanzees and gorillas show that most of them, like humans, show enlargement in the left hemisphere of the cerebral cortex, in part of Broca's area (Cantalupo & Hopkins, 2001; see Figure 7.11). The differences that remain between humans and chimps are at least in part associated with capabilities such as fine control of the mouth and larynx that are not found in apes (Enard et al., 2002). The genetic codes of chimps and humans are apparently similar enough to give chimps some ability to use language, but different enough to prevent chimps from speaking.

Do Apes Really Use Language?

Although apes do not speak, they have been taught to use American Sign Language and other symbol systems. For example, a chimpanzee named Washoe, who was a pioneer in the effort to teach apes to use language, was using 181 signs by the age of 32. Loulis, a baby chimp adopted by Washoe, gained the ability to use signs just by observing Washoe and some other chimps who had been trained in sign language (Fouts, 1997). Other chimps have used plastic symbols or pressed keys on a computer keyboard to communicate.

Sue Savage-Rumbaugh and her colleagues (1993; Shanker et al., 1999) believe that pygmy chimpanzees can understand some of the semantic subtleties of language. She claims that one chimp, Kanzi, picked up language from observing another chimp being trained and has the grammatical abilities of a two-and-a-half-year-old child. Kanzi also understands several words spoken by humans. Kanzi held a toy snake to a toy dog's mouth when asked to make the dog bite the snake.

Critics of the view that apes can learn to produce language, such as Herbert Terrace (1979) and

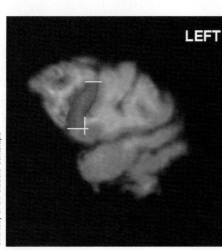

Courtesy of Dr. Claudio Cantalupo

FIGURE 7.11

MRI Results of the Left and Right Hemispheres of the Cerebral Cortexes of a Great Ape

In their MRI study of the brains of 25 chimpanzees and two gorillas, Cantalupo and Hopkins found that the great majority, 20, showed larger areas similar to Broca's area in the left hemisphere. So do most humans. Six apes showed larger areas in the right hemisphere. Only one showed no difference. It would thus appear that chimpanzees and gorillas have some rudimentary language structures in their brains, even if they are not "wired" for speech.

language
the communication of information by means of symbols arranged according to rules of grammar

semanticity
meaning; the quality of language in which words are used as symbols for objects, events, or ideas

infinite creativity
the capacity to combine words into original sentences

displacement
the quality of language that permits one to communicate information about objects and events in another time and place

Steven Pinker (1994a), note the following:

- Apes can string together signs in a given sequence to earn rewards, but animals lower on the evolutionary ladder, such as pigeons, can also peck buttons in a certain sequence to obtain a reward.

- It takes apes longer to learn new signs than it takes children to learn new words.

- Apes are unreliable in their sequencing of signs, suggesting that by and large they do not comprehend rules of grammar.

- People observing apes signing may be subject to *observer bias*—that is, they may be seeing what they want to see.

Scientists will continue to debate how well chimpanzees and gorillas understand and produce language, but there is little doubt that they have learned to use symbols to communicate (Savage-Rumbaugh & Fields, 2000).

What Is Language?

As you can see from the discussion of apes and language, the way in which one defines language is no small matter. *Just how do we define language?* If we define language simply as a system of communication, many animals have language, including the birds and the bees.

Through particular chirps and shrieks, birds may communicate that they have taken possession of a tree or bush. The waggle dances of bees inform other bees of the location of a food source or a predator. None of these are instinctive communication patterns, or what we mean by language.

In language, sounds or signs are symbols for objects and actions. There is apparently no doubt that apes have learned to use symbols to communicate. But is the use of symbols to communicate an adequate definition of language? Many language experts require one more piece. They define **language** as the communication of thoughts and feelings by means of symbols *that are arranged according to rules of grammar*. Instinctive waggle dances and shrieks have no symbols and no grammar. By these

rigorous rules, only humans use language. Whether apes can handle rules of grammar is under debate.

Language makes it possible for one person to communicate knowledge to another and for one generation to communicate to another. It creates a vehicle for recording experiences. It allows us to put ourselves in the shoes of other people, to learn more than we could learn from direct experience. Language also provides many units of thinking.

True language is distinguished from the communication systems of lower animals by properties such as semanticity, infinite creativity, and displacement (Hoff, 2005):

- *Semanticity:* The sounds (or signs) of a language have meaning. Words serve as symbols for actions, objects, relational concepts (*over, in, more,* and so on), and other ideas. The communications systems of the birds and the bees lack semanticity.
- *Infinite creativity:* The capacity to create rather than imitate sentences.
- *Displacement:* The capacity to communicate information about events and objects in another time or place. Language makes it possible to transmit knowledge from one person to another and from one generation to another, furthering human adaptation.

Language and Cognition

The relationships between language and thinking are complex and not always obvious. For example, can you think *without* using language? Would you be able to solve problems without using words or sentences?

Kevin Arnold/Brand X Pictures/Jupiterimages

Jean Piaget (Inhelder & Piaget, 1958) believed that language reflects knowledge of the world but that much knowledge can be acquired without language. For example, it is possible to understand the concepts of roundness or redness even when we do not know or use the words *round* or *red*.

Language and Culture

Different languages have different words for the same concepts, and concepts do not necessarily overlap. Concepts expressed in our own language (such as *square* and *triangle*) may not exist in the language of another culture—and vice versa. Is it possible for English speakers to share the thoughts experienced by people who speak other languages? The answer is probably yes in many or most cases, but in some cases, no. In any event, the question brings us to the linguistic-relativity hypothesis.

The Linguistic-Relativity Hypothesis

The **linguistic-relativity hypothesis** was proposed by Benjamin Whorf (1956). Whorf believed that language structures the way we perceive the world. That is, the categories and relationships we use to understand the world are derived from our language. Therefore, speakers of various languages conceptualize the world in different ways.

The Inuit have many words for snow. The words differ according to whether the snow is hard-packed, falling, melting, and so on. In English, in contrast, we have fewer words to choose from and must choose descriptive adjectives to describe snow. Are English speakers limited in their ability to think about skiing conditions? Probably not. English-speaking skiers who are concerned about different skiing conditions have developed a comprehensive vocabulary about snow, including the terms *powder, slush, ice, hard-packed*, and *corn snow*, that allows them to communicate and think about snow. When a need to expand a language's vocabulary arises, the speakers of that language apparently have little trouble meeting the need.

In English, we have hundreds of words to describe colours. Shona-speaking people use only three words for colours, and Bassa speakers use only two words for colours, corresponding to light and dark. Nevertheless, a study of 100 languages spoken in nonindustrialized societies finds overlaps for white, black, red, green, yellow, and blue (Regier et al., 2005). Moreover, people who use only a few words to distinguish among colours seem to perceive the same colour variations as people with more words. For example, the Dani of New Guinea have just two words for colours: one that refers to yellows and reds and one that refers to greens and blues. Yet performance on matching and memory tasks shows that the Dani can discriminate the many colours of the spectrum.

Most cognitive scientists no longer accept the linguistic-relativity hypothesis (Pinker, 1990). For one thing, adults use images and abstract logical propositions, as well as words, as units of thought. Infants, moreover, display considerable intelligence before they have learned to speak. Another criticism is that a language's vocabulary suggests the range of concepts that the speakers of the language have traditionally found important, not their cognitive limits. For example, people who were magically lifted from the 19th century and placed inside an airplane probably would not think they were flying inside a bird or a large insect, even if their language lacked a word for airplane.

> **linguistic-relativity hypothesis**
> the view that language structures the way in which we view the world
>
> **phonemes**
> the smallest units of sounds in spoken language
>
> **morphemes**
> the smallest units of meaning in spoken language
>
> **syntax**
> the arrangement and organization of words to form meaningful sentences; rules to create grammatical sentences
>
> **semantics**
> the meanings associated with a morpheme or sentence
>
> **pragmatics**
> the ways in which we use language to convey social meanings of spoken language

What Makes Up a Language?

All languages are made up of **phonemes**, which are the smallest units of sound in spoken language. Each language uses a unique and very small set of phonemes. In English we use about 45 phonemes. No two languages use exactly the same set of phonemes. We put phonemes together to form meaningful utterances. These smallest units of meaning are called **morphemes**. We use **syntax** to organize and arrange words to form meaningful sentences and phrases. But how do we determine what words, or sentences mean? We study these meanings using **semantics**. When using semantics, we can either examine the superficial or surface structure of morphemes, words, or phrases, which will give us the literal meaning, or we can examine the deeper or underlying meaning of a morpheme or sentence. Finally, we use **pragmatics**, such as intonation, to determine the social meaning of spoken language. That is, we use pragmatics to determine what someone is *really* trying to tell us, when they say, "You look lovely today."

Language Development: The Two-Year Explosion

How does language develop? Languages around the world develop in a specific sequence of steps, beginning with the *prelinguistic* vocalizations of crying, cooing, and babbling. These sounds are not symbols. That is, they do not represent objects or events. Therefore, they are prelinguistic, not linguistic.

Prelinguistic Vocalizations

As parents are well aware, newborn children have one inborn, highly effective form of verbal expression: crying—and more crying. But crying does not represent language; it is a prelinguistic event. During the second month, babies begin *cooing,* another form of prelinguistic expression that appears to be linked to feelings of pleasure. By the fifth or sixth month, children begin to *babble.* Children babble sounds that occur in many languages, including the throaty German *ch,* the clicks of certain African languages, and rolling *r*'s. Babies' babbling frequently combines consonants and vowels, as in "ba," "ga," and, sometimes, the much-valued "dada." "Dada" at first is purely coincidental (sorry, dads), despite the family's delight over its appearance.

Babbling, like crying and cooing, is inborn and prelinguistic. Deaf children babble, and children from cultures whose languages sound very different all seem to babble the same sounds (Hoff, 2005). But within a few months, children single out the sounds used in the home. By the age of nine or ten months they are repeating the sounds regularly, and foreign sounds are dropping out. In fact, early experience in acquiring the phonemes native to one's own language can make it difficult to pronounce and even discriminate the phonemes used in other languages later in life (Iverson et al., 2003).

Children tend to utter their first word at about one year of age, but many parents miss it, often because it is not pronounced clearly or because pronunciation varies from one usage to the next (Nelson et al., 1993). The growth of vocabulary is slow at first. It may take children three to four months to achieve a ten-word vocabulary after they have spoken their first word. By about 18 months, children are producing a couple of dozen words.

Development of Grammar

The first linguistic utterances of children around the globe are single words that can express complex meanings. These initial utterances of children are called **holophrases**. For example, *mama* may be used by the child to signify meanings as varied as "There goes Mama," "Come here, Mama," and "You are my Mama." Similarly, *cat* can signify "There is a cat," "That stuffed animal looks just like my cat," or "I want you to give me my cat right now!" Most children show their parents what they intend by augmenting their holophrases with gestures and intonations. That is, they act delighted when parents do as requested and howl when they do not.

Toward the end of the second year, children begin to speak two-word sentences. These sentences are termed *telegraphic speech* because they resemble telegrams. Telegrams cut out the "unnecessary" words. "Home Tuesday" might stand for "I expect to be home on Tuesday." Two-word utterances seem to appear at about the same time in the development of all languages (Slobin, 1983). Two-word utterances are brief but grammatically correct. The child says, "Sit chair" to tell a parent to sit in a chair, not "Chair sit." The child says, "My shoe," not "Shoe my," to show possession. "Mommy go" means Mommy is leaving. "Go Mommy" expresses the wish for Mommy to go away.

There are different kinds of two-word utterances. Some, for example, contain nouns or pronouns and verbs ("Daddy sit"). Others contain verbs and objects ("Hit ball"). The sequence of emergence of the various kinds of two-word utterances is also apparently the same in all languages—languages diverse as English, Luo (an African tongue), German, Russian, and Turkish (Slobin, 1983). The invariance of this sequence has implications for theories of language development, as we will see.

Overregularization

Overregularization is an important development for understanding the roles of nature and nurture in language development. In English, we add *d* or *ed* to make the past tense of regular verbs and *s* or *z* sounds to make regular nouns plural. Thus, *walk* becomes *walked,* and *look* becomes *looked. Cat* becomes *cats,* and *doggy* becomes *doggies.* There are also irregular verbs and nouns. For example, *see* becomes *saw, sit* becomes *sat,* and *go* becomes *went. Sheep* remains *sheep* (plural) and *child* becomes *children.*

At first children learn irregular verbs and nouns by imitating older people. Two-year-olds tend to form them correctly—at first! Then they become aware of the grammatical rules for forming the past tense and plurals. As a result, they tend to make charming errors (Pinker, 1997). A three- to five-year-old, for example, may be more likely to say "I seed it" than "I saw it," and more likely to say "Mommy sitted down" than "Mommy sat down." They are likely to talk about the "gooses" and "sheeps" they "seed" on the farm and about all the "childs" they ran into at the playground. This tendency to regularize the irregular is what is meant by overregularization.

Should parents be concerned about overregularization? Not at all. Overregularization reflects knowledge of grammar, not faulty language development. In another year or two, *mouses* will be boringly transformed into *mice,* and Mommy will no longer have *sitted* down. Parents might as well enjoy overregularization while they can.

Other Developments

By the age of six, children's vocabularies have expanded to 10 000 words, give or take a few thousand. By seven to nine, most children realize that words can have more than one meaning, and they are entertained by riddles and jokes that require some sophistication with language.

Between the elementary school and high school years, language grows more complex, and children rapidly add on to their vocabularies. Vocabulary, in fact, can grow for a lifetime, especially in one's fields of specialization and interest.

Nature and Nurture in Language Development

Billions of children have acquired the languages spoken by their parents and passed them down, with minor changes, from generation to generation. Language development, like many other areas of development, apparently reflects the interactions between nature and nurture. *What are the roles of nature and nurture in language development?*

Learning Theory and Language Development

Learning theorists see language as developing according to laws of learning (Hoff, 2005). They usually refer to the concepts of imitation and reinforcement. From a social-cognitive perspective, parents serve as *models.* Children learn language, at least in part, through observation and imitation. Many words, especially nouns and verbs (including irregular verbs), are apparently learned by imitation.

At first children accurately repeat the irregular verb forms they observe. This repetition can probably be explained by modelling, but modelling does not explain all the events involved in learning. Children later begin to overregularize irregular verb forms *because of* knowledge of rules of grammar, and not imitation. Nor does imitative learning explain how children come to utter phrases and sentences they have *not* observed. Parents, for example, are unlikely to model utterances such as "Bye-bye sock" and "All gone Daddy," but children say them.

Learning theory cannot account for the unchanging sequence of language development and the spurts in children's language acquisition. Even the types of two-word utterances emerge in a consistent pattern in diverse cultures. Although timing differs from one child to another, the types of questions used, passive versus active sentences, and so on, all emerge in the same order.

The Nativist Approach to Language Development

The nativist theory of language development holds that the innate factors—which make up children's nature—cause children to attend to and acquire language in certain ways. From this perspective,

psycholinguistic theory
the view that language learning involves an interaction between environmental factors and an inborn tendency to acquire language

language acquisition device (LAD)
in psycholinguistic theory, neural "prewiring" that facilitates the child's learning of grammar

children bring neurological "prewiring" to language learning (Newport, 1998; Pinker, 1994a, 1999).

According to **psycholinguistic theory**, language acquisition involves the interaction of environmental influences—such as exposure to parental speech and reinforcement—and the inborn tendency to acquire language. Noam Chomsky (1980, 1991) refers to the inborn tendency as a **language acquisition device (LAD)**. Evidence for an LAD is found in the universality of human language abilities and in the specific sequence of language development (Baker, 2001).

The LAD prepares the nervous system to learn grammar. On the surface, languages differ a great deal. However, the LAD serves children all over the world because languages share what Chomsky refers to as a "universal grammar"—an underlying set of rules for turning ideas into sentences (Pinker, 1994a).

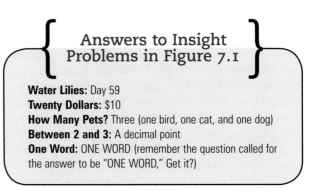

Answers to Insight Problems in Figure 7.1

Water Lilies: Day 59
Twenty Dollars: $10
How Many Pets? Three (one bird, one cat, and one dog)
Between 2 and 3: A decimal point
One Word: ONE WORD (remember the question called for the answer to be "ONE WORD," Get it?)

{ Bilingualism in Canada }

Canada has two official languages: English and French. Can you speak, write, and understand both of these languages? Are you bilingual? If you are, then you are in the minority. Despite being a bilingual country since 1967, the vast majority of Canadians are not bilingual. The Canadian Council on Learning (2008) reports that while 42 percent of Francophones speak English, only 9 percent of Anglophones report that they speak French.

While becoming bilingual requires an investment in time, and sometimes finances, individuals who are bilingual reap many cognitive, social, and occupational benefits. For example, bilingual adults experience less age-related cognitive decline compared to monolingual adults (Bialystok, Craik, Klein & Viswanathan, 2004). In addition, employment rates and salaries are higher among bilingual individuals than monolingual individuals (Canadian Council on Learning, 2008).

Why are so few Canadians bilingual, given the benefits? First, despite the fact that most Canadian schools teach English or French as a second language, students in these core language programs are not learning the necessary language skills to be bilingual. The rates of bilingualism among students in French immersion were only slightly better. In addition, because a second language is not used as often as a first language or mother tongue, the attained language skills quickly fade over time.

The Canadian government has recognized the need for more intensive language training and has developed the "Roadmap for Canada's Linguistic Duality" (2008–2013), which will focus on education, immigration, health, and arts and culture (Canadian Council on Learning, 2008).

Here's an outline of Canada's bilingual history:

• 1867: The *British North America Act* (now the *Constitution Act*) states that both languages must be used in all government documents.

• 1927: Postage stamps become bilingual.
• 1936: Bank notes become bilingual.
• 1963–1970: The Royal Commission on Bilingualism and Biculturalism is established and produces its reports.
• 1969: The first *Official Languages Act* is adopted by Parliament. This *act* recognizes English and French as the official languages of all federal institutions in Canada. It grants equality of status of French and English not only in Parliament and before courts, but also throughout the federal administration.
• 1970: Creation of the Official Languages in Education Program.
• 1974: The *Consumer Packaging and Labelling Act* comes into force, along with regulations respecting bilingual labelling of consumer products.
• 1982: The *Constitution Act*, 1982, including the *Canadian Charter of Rights and Freedoms*, guarantees respecting the status and use of the official languages of Canada in federal institutions. In addition, the provinces and territories must offer primary and secondary schooling to their official-language minorities in their mother tongue, where the numbers justify (English in Quebec, French elsewhere). In 1990, the Supreme Court of Canada also established that the *Constitution Act* would give official-language minorities the right to manage their own schools.
• 1988: The new Official Languages Act is adopted by Parliament. It repeats and qualifies the obligations under the 1982 *Charter of Rights and Freedoms* regarding the use of the two official languages in the provision of government services and throughout government institutions.
• 2003: The federal government announces its Action Plan for Official Languages (2003/04–2007/08), which aims to provide a "new momentum for Canada's linguistic duality" through increased interdepartmental coordination and new investments in education, community development, and the public service.

Source: Canadian Heritage, 2010.

86% of Canadian students surveyed prefer the 4LTR Press text and website combination to a traditional text.

GET ONLINE

The easy-to-navigate website for **PSYCH** offers guidance on key topics in **psychology** in a variety of engaging formats. You have the opportunity to refine and check your understanding via interactive quizzes and flashcards. Power visuals and games provide inspiration for your own further exploration. And, in order to make **PSYCH** an even better learning tool, we invite you to speak up about your experience with **PSYCH** by completing a survey form and sending us your comments.

Get online and discover the following resources:

- Flashcards
- Interactive quizzing
- Multimedia
- Build a Summary activities

"I think this book is awesome for students of all ages. It is a much simpler way to study."

—Yasmine Al-Hashimi, Fanshawe College

Visit **www.icanpsych.com** to find the resources you need today!

Development

Learning Outcomes

LO1 Explain the stages of prenatal development and the major influences on prenatal growth

LO2 Explain physical development over the life span

LO3 Explain cognitive and moral development over the life span

LO4 Explain social development over the life span

LO5 Understand stages of death and dying

> ## **❝**Developmental milestones are much more than just developments. They are also markings of our celebrations of life.**❞**

S.M.: I sometimes wonder why it is that my brother (who is younger than I) is 1.8 metres (six feet) tall and I am not. Or why it is that my brother and I act so differently from one another as adults. Just recently, I have wondered why my good friend's parents, who just turned 60, both opted for buying each other tattoos as birthday presents. It wouldn't seem natural if we weren't trying to understand why we look the way we do, or why we behave the way we do (or don't).

Developmental psychologists are interested in studying our development over the life span for several reasons. Understanding early influences and developmental sequences helps psychologists understand adults. Psychologists are also interested in the effects of genetic factors, early interactions with parents and siblings, and the school and community on traits such as aggressiveness and intelligence.

Developmental psychologists seek to learn the causes of developmental abnormalities. For example, should pregnant women abstain from smoking and drinking? (Yes.) Some developmental psychologists focus on adult development. For example, what factors are important for maintaining healthy relationships? What conflicts and or changes can we expect as we develop through our 30s, 40s, and 50s? What about development as an older adult? The information acquired by developmental psychologists can help us understand how our physical, social, and cognitive development unfolds and explain factors that are required for normal growth. Perhaps knowing how we develop can also help us make decisions about how we rear our children and lead our own lives.

DID YOU KNOW?

- Within nine months, the zygote develops from a nearly microscopic cell to a newborn child about 50 centimetres long. Its weight increases a billion-fold!

- Your heart started beating when you were only half a centimetre long and weighed a few grams.

- For adolescents, risk taking and feeling invulnerable is part of their cognitive development.

- Memory functioning in late adulthood does not necessarily decline; vocabulary and general knowledge are maintained into advanced old age.

Chapter 2 introduced you to the term *heredity*—the biological structures and processes that make up one's nature. There, you were introduced to terms such as *genes*, and *chromosomes*—basic structures that create our traits as individuals. You may wish to refer back to Chapter 2 to refresh your memory on these biological terms.

Let us now turn to prenatal development—the changes that occur between conception and birth.

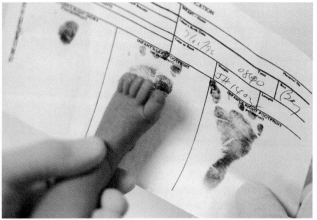

Comstock/Jupiterimages

zygote
a fertilized ovum (egg cell) that travels to the uterus and attaches to the uterine wall

germinal stage
the first stage of prenatal development (lasts approximately two weeks), during which the dividing mass of cells becomes implanted in the uterine wall

embryonic stage
the second stage of prenatal development (three to eight weeks), during which the major body structures and organs develop

fetal stage
the third stage of prenatal development (nine weeks to birth), during which further growth of the body and organ systems continue—especially the heart and lungs in the final three months—to allow the fetus to thrive outside the womb

LO1 Prenatal Development

The most dramatic gains in height and weight occur during prenatal development. *What developments occur from conception through birth?*

Conception begins with the fertilization of the sperm cell and ovum—called the zygote—which forms a single cell.

The zygote divides repeatedly as it proceeds on its three- to four-day travel to the uterus. The ball-like mass of multiplying cells wanders about the uterus for another three to four days before beginning to implant in the uterine wall. Implantation takes another week or so as the clusters of cells divide to form the structures for growing the fetus. This first period from conception to implantation is called the **germinal stage**.

The **embryonic stage** lasts from implantation until about the eighth week of development. During this second stage, the major body structures and organ systems develop. As you can see from Figure 8.1, the growth of the head precedes that of other parts of the body (called *cephalocaudal* development). Growth of the organs—heart, lungs, and so on—also precedes the growth of the extremities (called *proximodistal* development). By the end of the second month (eight weeks), the head has become rounded and the facial features distinct—all in an embryo that is about 2.5 centimetres long and weighs about 4 grams.

When do the sex organs grow? By about the seventh week, the genetic code (XY for male; or XX for female) begins to assert itself, causing the sex organs to differentiate. If a Y sex chromosome is present, testes form and begin to produce *androgens* (male sex hormones), which further masculinize the sex organs. In the absence of these hormones, the embryo develops sex organs typical of a female (the ovaries), regardless of its genetic code. The **fetal stage** lasts from the beginning of the third month (nine weeks) until birth. By the end of the third month, the major organ systems and the fingers and toes have formed. By the end of the sixth month (24 weeks), the fetus moves its limbs and turns its body quite regularly. Mothers often can see and feel these "kicks" and turns. The fetus opens and shuts its eyes, sucks its thumb, alternates between periods of being awake and sleeping, and responds to light.

During the three months prior to birth (24–38 weeks), the organ systems of the fetus continue to mature. The heart and lungs become increasingly capable of sustaining independent life. The fetus gains about 2 kilograms and doubles in length.

How is the developing fetus protected? As the fetus develops, it is

> **The heart will continue to beat without rest every minute of every day for most of a century, perhaps longer.**

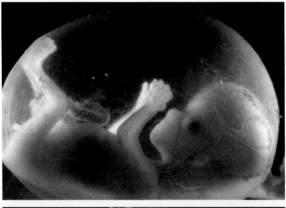

FIGURE 8.1

A Human Fetus at 14 Weeks

By the end of the first trimester, formation of all the major organ systems is complete. Fingers and toes are fully formed, and the sex of the fetus can be determined visually.

Edelmann/Science Photo Library

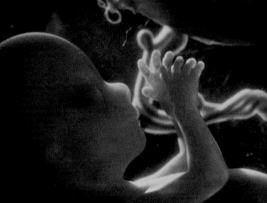

A Human Fetus at 4 Months

At this midway point between conception and birth, the fetus is covered with fine, downy hair, called *lanugo*.

Edelmann/Science Photo Library

suspended within a protective *amniotic sac* in the mother's uterus. The sac is surrounded by a clear membrane and contains amniotic fluid. The fluid is a sort of natural air bag, which allows the fetus to move around without injury. It also helps maintain an even temperature inside the womb and helps with the development of the fetus's lungs.

From this point until birth, the developing fetus exchanges nutrients and wastes with the mother through the **placenta**, which is connected by the *umbilical cord*. The placenta is connected to the mother by blood vessels in the uterine wall.

Influences on Prenatal Development

As we have learned, prenatal development is a time of rapid physical growth. This growth may sometimes be interrupted by negative environmental influences. The effects of these negative influences, called **teratogens**, can harm the developing fetus. *What are the effects of teratogens?* The effects of teratogens depend on the initiation, frequency, and intensity of use. Teratogens are most harmful during *critical periods* in prenatal development. Figure 8.2 shows that developing body systems and organs are more vulnerable to teratogens at different stages of prenatal development. For example, alcohol consumption during pregnancy can lead to a child born with fetal alcohol spectrum disorder (FASD). FASD is associated with slowed growth of the physical body and heart damage, likely caused by interruptions to growth of the heart and body structures during the embryonic stage.

In the following sections of this chapter, we will explore the major developmental milestones that affect different stages of our development physically, cognitively, morally, and socially.

LO2 Physical Development over the Life Span

As a parent, I (S.M.) have experienced such wonderment with how quickly my children have grown. It seems like yesterday that I was encouraging my youngest child as he tried to get up and chase his older brothers. Now, I am wondering where time has gone as I see him keep up with them while having a (loud and obnoxious) game of soccer in the field!

placenta
a membrane that permits the exchange of nutrients and waste products between the mother and her developing child but does not allow the maternal and fetal bloodstreams to mix

teratogen
a harmful (or toxic) agent, such as a disease, a drug, a chemical, or radiation that has the potential to cause birth defects or abnormalities to the developing fetus

Physical Development in Infancy and Childhood

During infancy—the first two years of childhood—dramatic gains in weight and height continue. Infants usually double their birth weight in about five months and triple it by their first birthday (Kuczmarski et al., 2000). Their height increases by about 25 centimetres in the first year. Children grow another 10 to 15 centimetres during the second year and gain some 2 to 3 kilograms. After that, they grow about 5 to 8 centimetres a year until they reach the adolescent growth spurt. Weight gains also remain fairly consistent at about 2 to 3 kilograms per year until the spurt. Other aspects of physical development in infancy and childhood include motor and perceptual development.

FIGURE 8.2

Critical Periods of Prenatal Development

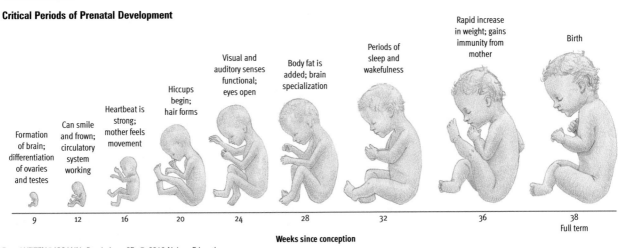

From WEITEN/MCCANN. *Psychology*, 2E. © 2010 Nelson Education Ltd. Reproduced with permission. www.cengage.com/permissions.

reflex
a simple unlearned, automatic response to a stimulus; essential to an infant's survival

Motor Development: Infant Reflexes

Soon after you were born, a doctor or nurse probably pressed his or her fingers against the palms of your hands. Although you would have had no idea what to do in response, most likely you grasped the fingers firmly—so firmly that you could have been lifted from your cradle!

Grasping at birth is an example of the importance of nature in human development. It is one of an infant's rich set of **reflexes**—simple, unlearned, automatic responses elicited by specific

Elyse Lewin/Brand X Pictures/Jupiterimages

environmental stimuli. Infants turn their head toward stimuli that stroke their cheek, chin, or corner of the mouth, and they suck objects that touch their lips. These are the *rooting* and *sucking* reflexes that signal "time to eat."

Infants use the withdrawal reflex to avoid painful stimuli. In the startle, or Moro, reflex, they draw up their legs and arch their backs in response to sudden noises, bumps, or loss of support while being held. They grasp objects that press against the palms of their hands (the grasp, or palmar, reflex), and they fan their toes when the soles of their feet are stimulated (the Babinski reflex). Pediatricians test these reflexes to assess babies' neural functioning. Infants also breathe, sneeze, cough, yawn, blink, defecate, and urinate reflexively.

Motor Development: Getting Around

The motor development in childhood focuses on the progression from simple skills like lifting the head to more complex skills like walking. Motor development provides some of the most fascinating changes in infants, in part because so much seems to happen so quickly—and so much of it during the first year. Maturation and experience both play key roles in motor development (Muir, 2000; Pryce et al., 2001; Roncesvalles et al., 2001). Figure 8.3 shows the progression of motor development of infants. The

---

FIGURE 8.3

The Progression of Motor Development

Most children develop motor skills as a result of maturation of the central nervous system and progress as shown below. Parents often try to capture these milestones and celebrate each with pride and excitement.

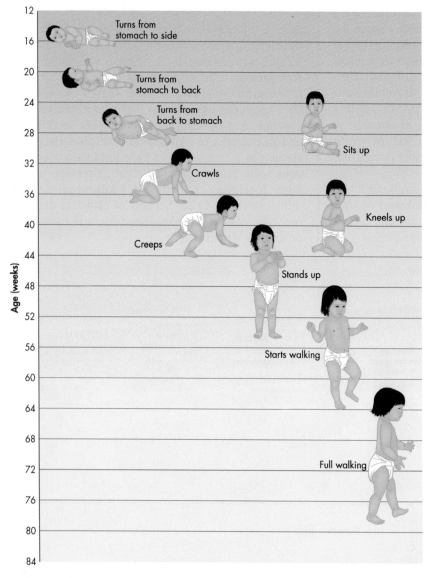

Age (weeks)

Turns from stomach to side
Turns from stomach to back
Turns from back to stomach
Crawls
Creeps
Sits up
Kneels up
Stands up
Starts walking
Full walking

ages at which infants first succeed at these skills vary, but the sequence generally remains the same.

The role of maturation in physical development (for example, gains in height and weight, and later, the effects of puberty) and motor development is evident. For example, children may have a certain genetic potential for body size and growth rates. But environmental factors are also important. For example, some children do not reach their genetic potential unless environmental factors such as nutrition, relatively clean air, and so on, are available.

Perceptual Development: The Senses

Newborns perceive their world reasonably well soon after birth. In fact, all five senses are present at birth (although not fully developed). Within a couple of days, infants can follow, or "track," a moving light with their eyes (Kellman & von Hofsten, 1992). By three months, they can discriminate most colours (Banks & Shannon, 1993; Teller, 1998). Newborns are nearsighted, but by about four months, they can focus on distant objects about as well as adults do.

Infants prefer their own mother's face over that of an unfamiliar face (Field et al., 1984) and spend more time looking at a human face than other stimuli. In classic research by Robert Fantz (1961), two-month-old infants preferred visual stimuli that

Sound perception in the womb has demonstrated that infants who are read to by mother 'experience' this learning through sucking patterns.

Michael Newman/PhotoEdit Inc.

resembled the human face to newsprint, a bull's eye, and featureless red, white, and yellow disks (Fantz, 1961).

Newborns hear well. They reflexively turn their heads toward unusual sounds (and also toward their mother's voice). This finding, along with findings about visual tracking, suggests that infants are preprogrammed to survey their environments. Speaking or singing softly in a low-pitched tone soothes infants. This is why lullabies help infants fall asleep.

Infants, of course, have had months of "experience" in the uterus. For at least two or three months before birth, they have been able to hear. Because they are predominantly exposed to sounds produced by their mother, learning may contribute to newborn preferences (DeCasper & Spence, 1986).

DeCasper and Spence (1986) had pregnant mothers read Dr. Suess's *The Cat in the Hat* to their fetuses twice a day for the last 6.5 weeks of their pregnancy. A few weeks after birth, they found that infants adjusted their sucking and preferred to hear recordings of their mother reading the *The Cat in the Hat* over a story they had never heard before, *The King, the Mice, and the Cheese*.

Physical Development in Adolescence

Perhaps no other period of life is as exciting—and as bewildering—as adolescence. **Adolescence** is bounded by puberty and the assumption of adult responsibilities. Except for infancy, more changes occur during adolescence than during any other time. Like childhood, adolescence entails physical, cognitive, social, and emotional changes.

What physical developments occur during adolescence? One of the most noticeable physical developments of adolescence is a growth spurt that lasts two to three years and ends the gradual changes in height and weight that characterize most of childhood. Within this short span of years, adolescents grow some 20 to 30 centimetres. Most boys wind up taller and heavier than most girls.

In boys, the weight of muscle mass increases considerably. The width of the shoulders and circumference of the chest also increase. Adolescents may eat enormous quantities of food to fuel their growth spurt.

Puberty: More Than "Just a Phase"?

Puberty—often referred to as the onset of adolescence—is the period during which the body becomes sexually mature. Puberty begins with the

adolescence
the period of life bounded by puberty and the assumption of adult responsibilities

puberty
the period of physical development during which sexual reproduction first becomes possible

appearance of **secondary sex characteristics** such as body hair, deepening of the voice in males, and rounding of the breasts and hips in females. In boys, pituitary hormones stimulate the testes to increase the output of testosterone, which in turn causes enlargement of the penis and testes and the appearance of body hair. By the early teens, erections become common, and boys may ejaculate. Ejaculatory ability usually precedes the presence of mature sperm by at least a year. Ejaculation thus is not evidence of reproductive capacity.

In girls, a critical body weight of approximately 45 kilograms is thought to trigger a cascade of hormonal secretions in the brain that cause the ovaries to secrete higher levels of the female sex hormone, estrogen (Frisch, 1997). Estrogen stimulates the growth of breast tissue and tissue in the hips and buttocks. The pelvis widens, rounding the hips. Small amounts of androgens produced by the adrenal glands, along with estrogen, spur the growth of pubic and underarm hair. Estrogen and androgens also stoke the development of female sex organs. Estrogen production becomes cyclical during puberty and regulates the menstrual cycle. The beginning of menstruation, or **menarche**, usually occurs between 11 and 14. Girls cannot become pregnant until they ovulate, however, and ovulation may begin two years after menarche.

Physical Development in Adulthood

The most obvious aspects of development during adulthood are physical. *What physical developments occur during adulthood?* Let us consider the physical developments that take place in young, or early, adulthood, which covers the ages between 20 and 40; middle adulthood, which spans the ages of 40 to 65; and late adulthood, which begins at 65.

Young Adulthood

Most young adults are at their height of sensory sharpness, strength, reaction time, and cardiovascular fitness. On the other hand, women gymnasts find themselves lacking a competitive edge in their 20s because they are accumulating (normal) body fat and losing suppleness and flexibility. Other athletes, such as football, baseball, and basketball players, are more likely to experience a decline in their 30s. Most athletes retire by age 40. Sexually speaking, most people in early adulthood become readily aroused. They tend to attain and maintain erections as desired and to lubricate readily.

Middle Adulthood

In our middle years, we are unlikely to possess the strength, coordination, and stamina that we had during our 20s and 30s. The decline is most obvious in professional sports, where peak performance is at a premium.

The years between 40 and 60 are reasonably stable. There is gradual physical decline, but it is minor and likely to be of concern only if a person competes with young adults—or with idealized memories of oneself. There are exceptions. The 20-year-old couch potato occasionally becomes the 50-year-old marathoner. By any reasonable standard, people in middle adulthood can maintain excellent cardiorespiratory condition. Because the physical decline in middle adulthood is gradual, people who begin to exercise and eat more nutritious diets (e.g., decrease intake of animal fats and increase intake of fruits and vegetables) may find themselves looking and feeling better than they did in young adulthood.

For women, **menopause**—the cessation of menstruation—is usually considered to be the single most important change of life that occurs during middle adulthood. Menopause usually occurs during the late 40s or early 50s. Menopause is the final phase of the *climacteric*, which is caused by a decline in secretion of female sex hormones. Ovulation comes to an end, and there is some loss of breast tissue and of elasticity of the skin. Loss of bone density can lead to **osteoporosis** (brittle bones). During the climacteric, many women experience hot flashes, loss of sleep, and some anxiety and depression. Women's experiences during and following the climacteric reflect the intensity of their physical symptoms—which vary considerably—and the extent to which their self-concept was wrapped up with their reproductive capacity (Dennerstein, 2003; Hvas et al., 2004). Recently, Health Canada approved several hormone replacement therapies (HRTs) to relieve the physical symptoms of menopause, such as severe hot flashes and vaginal dryness, as well as reduce the risk of osteoporosis. See the box entitled "Hormone Replacement Therapies," which outlines some of the risks of HRTs.

Late Adulthood

Various changes—some of them troublesome—do occur during the later years (see Figure 8.4). Changes in calcium metabolism increase the brittleness of the bones and heighten the risk of breaks due to falls. The skin becomes less elastic and subject to wrinkles

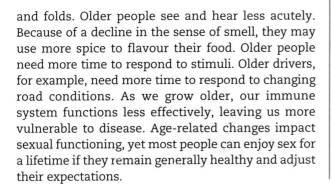

FIGURE 8.4

Physical Changes in Adulthood

Go to www.icanpsych.com to access an interactive version of this figure.

Hair and nails
Hair often turns grey and thins out. Men may go bald. Fingernails can thicken.

Brain
The brain shrinks, but it is not known if that affects mental functions.

The senses
The sensitivity of hearing, sight, taste, and smell can all decline with age.

Skin
Wrinkles occur as the skin thins and the underlying fat shrinks, and age spots often appear.

Glands and hormones
Levels of many hormones drop, or the body becomes less responsive to them.

Immune system
The body becomes less able to resist some pathogens.

Lungs
It doesn't just *seem* harder to climb those stairs— lung capacity drops.

Heart and blood vessels
Cardiovascular problems become more common.

Muscles
Strength usually peaks in the 20s, then declines.

Kidneys and urinary tract
The kidneys become less efficient. The bladder can't hold as much, so urination is more frequent.

Digestive system
Digestion slows down as the secretion of digestive enzymes decreases.

Reproductive system
Women go through menopause, and testosterone levels drop for men.

Bones and joints
Wear and tear can lead to arthritic joints, and osteoporosis is common, especially in women.

and folds. Older people see and hear less acutely. Because of a decline in the sense of smell, they may use more spice to flavour their food. Older people need more time to respond to stimuli. Older drivers, for example, need more time to respond to changing road conditions. As we grow older, our immune system functions less effectively, leaving us more vulnerable to disease. Age-related changes impact sexual functioning, yet most people can enjoy sex for a lifetime if they remain generally healthy and adjust their expectations.

Following the results of a 15-year study in the United States by the Women's Health Initiative, Health Canada presented a report informing postmenopausal women about the risks of the use of HRTs. Health Canada warns that HRTs are not scientifically found to prevent heart disease, colon cancer, Alzheimer's disease, or breast cancer, and they may even increase risk of heart disease, stroke, and dementia. More research is necessary, and Health Canada recommends that women considering the use of HRT ensure they are aware of the risks before beginning any drug treatment (Health Canada, 2006).

LO3 Cognitive and Moral Development over the Life Span

Let us now explore the ways in which children mentally represent and think about the world. As we might expect, cognitive functioning develops over many years. Researchers agree that both maturation and experience are important for cognitive growth. Young children have ideas about the world that differ considerably from those of adults. Many of these ideas are charming but illogical— at least to adults. One of the most influential developmentalists, Jean Piaget, studied the origins of knowledge by experimenting with children. He believed that children constantly want to make sense of their experiences and as a result, construct their understanding of the world.

Cognitive Theory

What are the basic principles of Piaget's theory? According to Piaget, children's interaction with the world helps them to develop **schemas**, mental structures that organize experiences through classification and organization of information. These mental representations help us to understand and make sense of our world. Schemas are built as children learn about new events, objects, and situations around them. For example, if a child were to see an adult woman walking into the playroom at day care, he or she might call her "teacher" based on the child's knowledge of having a female teacher at day care. Piaget believed that children form schemas in two interacting ways: *assimilation and accommodation.*

Assimilation is incorporating a new experience into an existing schema. Infants, for example, usually

schema
a mental structure that organizes our experiences of the world through classification and organization of information

assimilation
the inclusion of a new event (or experience) into an existing schema

accommodation
the modification of an existing schema or creation of a new schema so that information inconsistent with existing schemas can be integrated or understood

sensorimotor stage
the first of Piaget's stages of cognitive development, characterized by coordination of sensory information and motor activity through exploration of the environment, and the representation of mental thought demonstrated by object permanence

try to place new objects in their mouth to suck, feel, or explore. Piaget would say that the child is assimilating a new toy into the sucking schema. Consider the instance where a child has a cute little Shih Tzu for a pet (some people call this a lap dog). If he or she sees a Siamese cat and exclaims "doggie," this would be assimilation. The child has incorporated the cat into his or her existing schema for dog.

Accommodation is modifying existing schemas or creating new schemas to incorporate new experiences. Children (and adults) accommodate to objects and situations that cannot be integrated into existing schemas. For example, children who study biology learn that whales cannot be assimilated into the "fish" schema. They accommodate by constructing new schemas, such as "mammals without legs that live in the sea." The ability to accommodate to novel stimuli advances as a result of maturation and experience. Let us apply these concepts to Piaget's stages of cognitive development (refer to the box entitled "Schemata for Ball").

Piaget's Stages of Cognitive Development

What are Piaget's stages of cognitive development? Piaget hypothesized that children's cognitive processes develop in an orderly sequence. Some children may be more advanced than others, but the sequence remains the same. Piaget (1963) identified

Jean Piaget (1896–1980) earned his Ph.D. in biology. In 1920 he obtained a job at the Binet Institute in Paris, where work on intelligence tests was being conducted. Piaget became intrigued by children's *wrong* answers on verbal reasoning items; he perceived patterns in the children's "mistakes." The wrong answers reflected consistent, if illogical, cognitive processes. Piaget's observations led to his theory of cognitive development.

four major stages of cognitive development: sensorimotor, preoperational, concrete operational, and formal operational.

The Sensorimotor Stage In this first stage, the **sensorimotor stage**, an infant is capable of assimilating novel stimuli into existing reflexes (or ready-made schemas) such as the rooting and sucking reflexes. But by the time an infant reaches the age of one month, he or she already shows purposeful behaviour by repeating behaviour patterns

{ **Schemata for Ball-Playing** }

To understand Piaget's concept of schemas in organizing and understanding our world, consider the following example:

- A young boy has a schema for playing with a tennis ball—it fits easily into his hand and he can manipulate it fairly well (e.g., pick it up, throw it, or roll it on the floor).

- He then finds a similarly shaped ball, such as a baseball; he can simply *assimilate* the baseball into his pre-existing ball-playing schema, as the balls are similar in shape and size and can be manipulated in a similar manner.

- However, when the child tries to manipulate a football, which is a different shape, and finds that he must use a different manner of

holding, throwing, and catching it, he will have to *accommodate* his ball-playing schema in order to make sense of this new ball.

Piaget believes that accommodating various schemas is a (slightly) more complex mental operation (versus assimilating) that results in a child reconceptualizing his or her views on how the world works.

that are pleasurable, such as sucking his or her hand. Soon after the first few months, an infant begins to coordinate vision with grasping, to look at the object being held or touched.

An infant becomes increasingly interested in acting on the environment to make interesting results (such as the sound of a rattle) last longer or occur again. Behaviour becomes increasingly intentional and purposeful. Between four and eight months of age, an infant explores cause-and-effect relationships, such as the thump made by tossing an object or the swinging that results from kicking a hanging toy.

For most infants younger than six months, objects that cannot be seen, are "out of mind." For this reason, as you can see in Figure 8.5, a child makes no effort to search for an object that has been removed or placed behind a screen. By the age of 8 to 12 months, however, infants realize that objects removed from sight still exist and attempt to find them. In this way, they show what is known as **object permanence**, thereby making it possible to play peek-a-boo. Object permanence includes the start of make-believe play and imitation, as a child can now mentally represent objects without their presence.

FIGURE 8.5

Object Permanence

To this infant, who is in the early part of the sensorimotor stage, out of sight is truly out of mind. Once a sheet of paper is placed between the infant and the toy animal, the infant loses all interest in it. The toy is apparently not yet mentally represented.

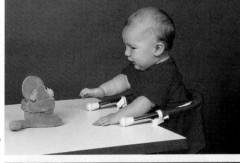

Doug Goodman/Photo Researchers, Inc.

The Preoperational Stage

Piaget's second stage, the **pre-operational stage**, is characterized by the use of words and symbols to represent objects and relationships among them. In this stage of cognitive development, preschool children's thoughts remain restricted and guided by perception—children may use the same words as adults, but this does not mean their views of the world are the same.

Preoperational children tend to think one dimensionally; they focus on one aspect of a problem or situation at a time. **Egocentrism** refers to children's inability to understand other people's perspectives. They believe that others see and understand things the same way they do.

For example, when asked, "Why does the sun shine?" a preoperational child may say, "To keep me warm." Preoperational children also show *animism* and *artificialism*. They attribute life and consciousness to physical objects like a car and a book, or they believe that environmental events like rain and thunder are human inventions. Asked why the sky is blue, a four-year-old may answer, "'Cause Mommy painted it." Examples of egocentrism, animism, and artificialism are shown in Table 8.1.

The law of **conservation** holds that basic properties of substances such as mass, weight, and volume remain the same—that is, are

object permanence
recognition that objects removed from sight still exist, as demonstrated by a child's continued exploration for the object

preoperational stage
the second of Piaget's stages, characterized by one-dimensional, perceptual thought processes (rather than logical, rapid development of language) and egocentrism

egocentrism
the assumption that others view the world the same as you do without considering that different views exist

conservation
according to Piaget, recognition that basic properties of a substance, object, or number, such as weight and mass, remain the same when superficial features change

TABLE 8.1

Examples of Preoperational Thought

Type of Thought	Sample Questions	Typical Answers
Egocentrism	Why does it get dark out?	So I can go to sleep.
	Why does the sun shine?	To keep me warm.
	Why is there snow?	For me to play in.
Animism	Why do trees have leaves?	To keep them warm.
	Why do stars twinkle?	Because they're happy and cheerful.
Artificialism	What makes it rain?	Someone emptying a watering can.
	Why is the sky blue?	Somebody painted it.
	What is the wind?	A man blowing.

concrete operational stage
Piaget's third stage, characterized by logical thought concerning tangible objects, conservation, and reversibility

decentration
simultaneous focusing on more than one dimension of a problem, so that flexible, reversible thought becomes possible

conserved—when one changes superficial properties such as their shape or arrangement.

Conservation requires the ability to think about, or *centre* on, more than one aspect of a situation at once, such as height and width. Conserving the mass, weight, or volume of a substance requires the recognition that a change in one dimension can compensate for a change in another. Refer to Figure 8.6 and the Try It! box to understand the concept of conservation.

The Concrete Operational Stage   By about age seven, the typical child is entering the stage of **concrete operations**. In this stage, which lasts until about age 12, children show the beginnings of the capacity for adult logic. However, their logical thoughts, or *operations*, generally involve tangible objects—concrete and observable—rather than abstract ideas. Concrete operational children are capable of **decentration**; that is, they can centre on two dimensions of a problem at once and can, therefore, complete conservation and reversibility tasks.

If the boy in Figure 8.6 were a few years older, he would say that the squat glass still contains the same amount of water. If asked why, he might reply, "Because you can pour it back into the other one." Such an answer also suggests awareness of the concept of *reversibility*—the recognition that many processes can be reversed or undone so that things

are restored to their previous condition. Centring simultaneously on the height and the width of the glasses, the boy recognizes that the loss in height compensates for the gain in width.

Children in this stage are less egocentric. They are able to take on the roles of others and to view the world, and themselves, from other people's perspectives. They recognize that people see things in different ways because of different situations and different sets of values.

During the concrete operational stage, children's own sets of values begin to emerge and acquire

---

FIGURE 8.6

Concept of Conservation

In this example, the preoperational child is first shown two short, squat glasses of water and agrees that they contain the same amount of water. Then, while he watches, water is poured from a squat glass into a tall, thin glass. Now the child is asked which glass contains more water. After mulling over the problem, he points to the tall glass. Why? Because when he looks at the glasses he is "overwhelmed" by the fact that the thinner glass is taller. He does not realize that the increased width of the squat glass compensates for the decreased height.

A.   B.   C.

stability. Children come to understand that feelings of love between them and their parents can endure even when someone is temporarily angry or disappointed.

The Formal Operational Stage   Piaget believed that cognitive maturity begins by the onset of adolescence—age 11 or 12 (in Western society). Piaget's fourth stage, the **formal operational stage**, is characterized by abstract logical thought and deduction from principles. Formal operations are represented by major achievements that involve classification, logical thought, and the ability to hypothesize. Central features are the ability to think about ideas as well as objects and to group and classify ideas—symbols, statements, and entire theories. In this stage, children (adolescents) can generally follow arguments from premises to conclusions and back again. They can appreciate both the external environment and the world of the imagination: They engage in hypothetical thinking and deductive reasoning.

Formal operational adolescents (and adults) think abstractly, derive rules for behaviour from general principles, and can focus, or centre, on multiple aspects of a situation at once to solve problems.

Evaluation of Piaget's Theory

A number of questions have been raised concerning the accuracy of Piaget's views. Among them are these:

• *Was Piaget's timing accurate?* Some critics argue that Piaget's methods led him to underestimate children's abilities (Bjorklund, 2000; Meltzoff & Gopnik, 1997). Other researchers using different methods have found, for example, that preschoolers are less egocentric and that children are capable of conservation at earlier ages than Piaget initially thought.

• *Does cognitive development occur in stages?* Cognitive events such as egocentrism and conservation appear to develop more continuously than Piaget thought—that is, they may not occur in stages (Bjorklund, 2000; Flavell, 2000). Although cognitive developments appear to build on previous cognitive developments, the process may be more gradual than stage-like.

• *Are developmental sequences always the same?* Here, Piaget's views have fared better. It seems there is no dispute about or variation in the sequence in which cognitive developments occur.

Lev Vygotsky's Sociocultural Theory

Lev Vygotsky (1896–1934) was a Russian psychologist whose work was banned in communist Russia. More than 70 years after his death, his work has been rediscovered. Unlike Piaget, Vygotsky was not a stage theorist. Instead, he saw the transmission of knowledge as cumulative, and focused on the ways in which children's interactions with their elders enhance their cognitive development.

What is Vygotsky's sociocultural theory? The term *sociocultural theory* has different meanings. For example, the term can refer to the roles of factors such as ethnicity and gender in behaviour and mental processes. Vygotsky's sociocultural theory focuses instead on the ways in which children's cognitive development is influenced by the cultures in which they are reared and the people who teach them.

Vygotsky's theory (1978) focuses on the transmission of information and cognitive skills from generation to generation. The transmission of skills involves teaching and learning, but Vygotsky was no behaviourist. He did not view learning as a mechanical process that can be described in terms of the conditioning of units of behaviour. Rather, he focused more generally on how the child's social interaction with adults, largely in the home, organized a child's learning experiences in such a way that the child can obtain cognitive skills—such as computation or reading skills—and use them to acquire information. Like Piaget, Vygotsky saw the child's functioning as adaptive (Piaget & Smith, 2000), and the child adapts to his or her social and cultural interactions.

What are the key concepts of Vygotsky's theory of cognitive development? Key concepts in Vygotsky's theory include the zone of proximal development and *scaffolding*. The word *proximal* means "nearby" or "close," as in the words *approximate* and *proximity*. The **zone of proximal development (ZPD)** refers to a range of tasks that a child can carry out with the help of someone who is more skilled (Haenen, 2001). The "zone" refers to the relationship between the child's abilities and what she or he can do with help from others. Adults or older children best guide the child through this zone by gearing their assistance to the child's capabilities (Flavell et al., 2002).

Within the zone we find an apprenticeship in which the child works with, and learns from, others (Meijer & Elshout, 2001). When learning with others, the child tends to internalize—or bring inward—the conversations and explanations that help him or her gain skills (Prior & Welling, 2001; Vygotsky, 1962; Yang, 2000). Children not only learn the meanings of words from teachers but also learn ways of talking to themselves about solving problems within a cultural context (DeVries, 2000). The idea of a ZPD follows

Proximal means "nearby" or "close."

formal operational stage Piaget's fourth stage, characterized by abstract logical thought and deduction from principles

zone of proximal development (ZPD) Vygotsky's term for the situation in which a child carries out tasks with the help of someone who is more skilled, frequently an adult who represents the culture in which the child develops

from Vygotsky's basic premise that cognition develops first in a social setting and gradually comes under a child's independent control.

According to Vygotsky, cognitive **scaffolding** is a key concept that explains how this shift from social to individual learning occurs. Scaffolding refers to the temporary support provided by a parent or teacher to a child who is learning to perform a task aimed at matching the amount of assistance to the learner's needs. Guidance decreases as the child becomes more skilled and self-sufficient (Clarke-Stewart & Beck, 1999; Maccoby, 1992). For example, a child's teacher may offer advice on sounding out letters and words that provide a temporary support until reading "clicks" and the child no longer needs the sound cue. Children may be offered scaffolding that enables them to use their fingers to do calculations.

Piaget's focus was largely maturational. It was assumed that maturation of the brain allowed the child to experience new levels of insights and suddenly develop new kinds of problem solving. Vygotsky focused on the social processes in the teacher–learner relationship. To Vygotsky, culture and social interaction was important for cognitive development.

Cognitive Development in Adolescence

The adolescent thinker approaches problems differently from the elementary school child. *What cognitive developments occur during adolescence?* Let us begin to answer this question by comparing the child's thought processes to that of the adolescent. The child sticks to the facts, to concrete reality. Speculating about abstract possibilities and what might be is very difficult. The adolescent, on the other hand, is able to deal with the abstract and the hypothetical.

Adolescent Egocentrism

Adolescents in the formal operational stage reason deductively. They classify objects or people and then draw conclusions about them. Adolescents can be proud of their new logical abilities, leading to a new sort of egocentrism: They demand acceptance

of their logic without recognizing the exceptions or practical problems that may be considered by adults. Consider this example: "It is wrong to hurt people. Company A hurts people" (perhaps through pollution or economic pressures). "Therefore, Company A must be severely punished or shut down." This thinking is logical. But by impatiently demanding major changes or severe penalties, one may not fully consider various practical problems such as the thousands of workers who might be laid off. Adults have often had life experiences that encourage them to see shades of grey rather than black and white.

The thought of preschoolers is characterized by egocentrism in which they cannot take another's point of view. Adolescent thought is marked by an egocentrism in which they can understand the thoughts of others but still have trouble separating things that are of concern to others and those that are of concern only to themselves (Elkind, 1967, 1985). Adolescent egocentrism gives rise to two interesting cognitive developments: the *imaginary audience* and the *personal fable*.

The concept of the **imaginary audience** refers to the belief that other people are as concerned with our thoughts and behaviour as we are. Adolescents thus see themselves as the centre of attention and assume that other people are also preoccupied with their appearance and behaviour (Milstead et al., 1993). Adolescents may feel on stage with all eyes on them. The concept of the imaginary audience may drive the intense adolescent desire for privacy. It helps explain why adolescents are so self-conscious, why they worry about every facial blemish and spend hours grooming. Self-consciousness seems to peak at about 13 and then decline. Girls tend to be more self-conscious than boys (Elkind & Bowen, 1979).

The **personal fable** is the belief that our feelings and ideas are special, even unique, and that we are invulnerable. The personal fable seems to underlie adolescent showing off and risk taking (Cohn et al., 1995).

Cognitive Development in Adulthood

What cognitive developments occur during adulthood? As in the case of physical development, people are also at the height of their cognitive powers during early adulthood. Cognitive development in adulthood has many aspects—creativity, memory functioning, and intelligence.

People can be creative for a lifetime. At the age of 80, Merce Cunningham choreographed a dance that made use of computer-generated digital images (Teachout, 2000). Hans Hofmann created some of his most vibrant paintings at 85, and Pablo Picasso was painting in his 90s. Grandma Moses did not even begin painting until she was 78 years old. Giuseppe Verdi wrote his joyous opera *Falstaff* at the age of 79.

Memory functioning, however, does decline with age. But declines in memory are not usually as large as people assume and are often reversible (Villa & Abeles, 2000). Memory tests usually measure ability to recall meaningless information. Older people show better memory functioning in areas in which they can apply their experience, especially their specialties, to new challenges. For example, who would do a better job of learning and remembering how to solve problems in chemistry—a college history major or a retired professor of chemistry?

You might choose the chemistry professor because of his or her crystallized intelligence, not his or her fluid intelligence. **Crystallized intelligence** represents one's lifetime of intellectual attainments. We are using the example of knowledge of chemistry, but crystallized intelligence is shown more generally by vocabulary and accumulated facts about world affairs. Therefore, crystallized intelligence can increase over the decades. **Fluid intelligence** is defined as mental flexibility, demonstrated by the ability to process information rapidly, as in learning and solving problems in new areas. It is the sort of intellectual functioning that is typically measured on intelligence tests, especially with problems that have time limits.

Young adults obtain the highest intelligence test scores (Schaie et al., 2004). Yet people tend to retain verbal skills, as demonstrated by vocabulary and general knowledge, into advanced old age. The performance of older people on tasks that require speed and visual–spatial skills, such as piecing puzzles together, tends to decline (Schaie et al., 2004; Zimprich & Martin, 2002).

imaginary audience
an aspect of adolescent egocentrism; the belief that other people are as concerned with our thoughts and behaviours as we are

personal fable
an aspect of adolescent egocentrism; the belief that our feelings and ideas are special and unique and that we are invulnerable

crystallized intelligence
one's lifetime of intellectual achievement, as shown largely through vocabulary and knowledge of world affairs

fluid intelligence
mental flexibility as shown in learning rapidly to solve new kinds of problems

{ Rising Tide: Impact of Dementia on Canadian Society }

The Alzheimer Society of Canada released a comprehensive report in January 2010 that presented the health and economic impacts of dementia. Here are some of the highlights from the report:

- In 2010 alone, more than 103 000 Canadians would develop dementia. This is equivalent to one person every five minutes. By 2038, this will become one person every two minutes, or more than 257 000 people per year.

- If nothing changes, the number of people living with Alzheimer's disease or a related dementia is expected to more than double, reaching 1.1 million Canadians within 25 years.

- Dementia costs Canadians $15 billion a year, and this figure is expected to grow more than ten times—to $153 billion—by 2038.

- Several critical factors in reducing the impact of dementia have been identified. These include encouraging physical activity, promoting risk-reduction strategies in delaying the onset of dementia, supporting family caregivers who are struggling to provide care, and providing a "system navigator" to help families find the right services at the right time.

Rising Tide: The Impact of Dementia on Canadian Society, Alzheimer Society of Canada, 2010. www.alzheimer.ca.

Alzheimer's disease
a progressive disease of the brain, characterized by loss of memory, language, problem solving, and other cognitive functions; most common form of dementia

dementia
a syndrome that affects cognitive functioning, causing social, language, physical, and emotional impairments

preconventional level
according to Kohlberg, a period during which moral judgments are based largely on expectation of rewards or punishments

conventional level
according to Kohlberg, a period during which moral judgments largely reflect social conventions; a "law and order" approach to morality

postconventional level
according to Kohlberg, a period during which moral judgments are derived from moral principles and people look to themselves to set moral standards

One of the most severe assaults on intellectual functioning, especially among older adults, is **Alzheimer's disease**, a progressive disease of the brain that disrupts memory and thinking skills. In Canada, Alzheimer's disease is the most common form of **dementia**, affecting about 1 percent of people at age 65 and older (Alzheimer Society, 2010). Furthermore, 72 percent of those suffering from Alzheimer's disease are women (Alzheimer Society, 2010).

Moral Development

Let us now turn to another aspect of cognitive development—the ways in which children and adults arrive at judgments as to what is right and what is wrong.

How do children reason about right and wrong? Cognitive–developmental theorist Lawrence Kohlberg (1981) used the following tale in his research on children's moral reasoning:

In Europe a woman was near death from a special kind of cancer. There was one drug that the doctors thought might save her. It was a form of radium that a druggist in the same town had recently discovered. The drug was expensive to make, but the druggist was charging ten times what the drug cost him to make. He paid $200 for the radium and charged $2000 for a small dose of the drug. The sick woman's husband, Heinz, went to everyone he knew to borrow the money, but he could get together only about $1000, which was half of what it cost. He told the druggist that his wife was dying and asked him to sell it cheaper or let him pay later. But the druggist said: "No, I discovered the drug, and I'm going to make money from it." So Heinz got desperate and broke into the man's store to steal the drug for his wife (Kohlberg, 1969).

Heinz is caught in a moral dilemma. In such dilemmas, a legal or social rule (in this case, the law forbidding stealing) is pitted against a strong human need (his desire to save his wife). Children and adults arrive at yes or no answers for different reasons. According to Kohlberg, the reasons can be classified according to the level of moral development they reflect.

As a stage theorist, Kohlberg argues that the stages of moral reasoning follow a specific sequence. Children progress at different rates, and not all children (or adults) reach the highest stage. But the sequence is always the same: Children must go through stage 1 before they enter stage 2, and so on. According to Kohlberg, there are three levels of moral development—the preconventional level, the conventional level, and the postconventional level—and two stages within each level (see Table 8.2).

TABLE 8.2

Kohlberg's Theory of Moral Development

The Preconventional Level	The preconventional level applies to most children through about the age of nine. Children at this level base their moral judgments on the consequences of behaviour. For example, stage 1 is oriented toward obedience and punishment. Good behaviour is obedient and allows one to avoid punishment. However, a child in stage 1 can decide whether Heinz should or should not steal the drug.
	In stage 2, good behaviour allows people to satisfy their needs and those of others. (Heinz's wife needs the drug; therefore, stealing it—the only way of obtaining it—is not wrong.)
The Conventional Level	In the conventional level of moral reasoning, right and wrong are judged by conformity to conventional (familial, religious, societal) standards of right and wrong. According to the stage 3 "good-boy orientation," moral behaviour is that which meets the needs and expectations of others. Moral behaviour is what is "normal"—what the majority does. (Heinz should steal the drug because that is what a "good husband" would do. It is "natural" or "normal" to try to help one's wife. Or, Heinz should not steal the drug because "good people do not steal.")
	In stage 4, moral judgments are based on rules that maintain the social order. Showing respect for authority and doing one's duty are valued highly. (Heinz must steal the drug; it would be his fault if he let his wife die. He would pay the druggist later, when he had the money.) Many people do not mature beyond the conventional level.
The Postconventional Level	Postconventional moral reasoning is more complex. In stages 5 and 6, individuals recognize the value of laws and their needs to maintain social order. At the same time, they focus on dilemmas in which individual needs are pitted against the need to maintain the social order and on personal conscience. (Heinz realizes that under "normal" circumstances—where every party in the dilemma is being fair and equitable—stealing is not necessary and would not be considered. But since this is not the case in Heinz's mind, it becomes terribly difficult for him to decide to break the law, although he may do so.)

When it comes to the dilemma of Heinz, Kohlberg believed that people could justify Heinz's stealing of the drug or his decision not to steal it by the reasoning of any level or stage of moral development. In other words, Kohlberg was not as interested in the eventual "yes" or "no" as he was in *how a person reasoned* to arrive at "yes" or "no."

Evaluation of Kohlberg's Theory

As Kohlberg's theory predicts, evidence supports the view that the moral judgments of children develop in an upward sequence (Boom et al., 2007). Formal-operational thinking is apparently necessary, and education is likely to play a role (Boom et al., 2007; Patenaude et al., 2003) in whether an adolescent (or adult) achieves postconventional thought.

Kohlberg believed that the stages of moral development were universal, but he may have underestimated the influence of social, cultural, and educational institutions (Dawson, 2002). Parents are also important. Using reason in discipline and discussing the feelings of others advances moral reasoning (Dawson, 2002).

Are There Gender Differences in Moral Development?

A number of studies using Heinz's dilemma have found that boys show higher levels of moral reasoning than girls. But Carol Gilligan (1982; Gilligan et al., 1989) argues that this gender difference reflects different patterns of socialization for boys and girls—not differences in morality. Gilligan considers 11-year-old Jake. Jake weighs the scales of justice like a math problem. He shows that life is worth more than property and concludes that it is Heinz's duty to steal the drug (stage 4 reasoning). Gilligan also points to 11-year-old Amy. Amy vacillates. Amy says that stealing the drug and letting Heinz's wife die are both wrong. So Amy looks for alternatives, such as getting a loan, because it wouldn't help Heinz's wife if he went to jail.

Gilligan finds Amy's reasoning to be as sophisticated as Jake's, yet Amy would be rated as having a lower level of moral development in Kohlberg's scheme. Gilligan argues that girls are socialized to focus on the needs of others and forgo simple judgments of right and wrong. Amy is therefore more likely to show stage 3 reasoning, which focuses in part on empathy—or caring for others. Jake has been socialized to make judgments based on logic. He wants to derive clear-cut conclusions from premises.

We could argue endlessly about which form of moral reasoning—Jake's or Amy's—is "higher." Instead, let us note a review of the research that shows only slight tendencies for boys to favour Jake's "justice" approach and girls to favour Amy's "caring" approach (Jaffee & Hyde, 2000). Thus, the justice orientation does not "belong" to boys and the care orientation does not "belong" to girls.

ego conflict
Erikson's term for the unique, contradictory developmental tasks associated with each stage of psychosocial development, during which individuals must resolve a conflict prior to progressing successfully through later psychosocial stages throughout the life span

LO4 Social Development and Social Relationships

Social relationships are crucial to us throughout our life. When we are infants, our very survival depends on them. Later in life, they contribute to our feelings of happiness and satisfaction. Developmental psychologists are very interested in our social (and emotional) development and study how our social relationships grow and change over our life span. In this section we discuss Erikson's theory of psychosocial development, and introduce influential research on infant attachment, parenting styles, and adolescent perspectives that shape our social development.

Erik Erikson's Stages of Psychosocial Development

Erik Erikson, like Piaget and Kohlberg, developed a stage theory of development. His theory focuses on key social aspects that influence our development, each defined by a social challenge—or ego conflict— that must be resolved in order to maintain a healthy development. *What are Erikson's stages of psychosocial development?* Erikson proposed eight psychosocial stages that we progress through during our life span. In the first stage, trust versus mistrust, we depend on our primary caregivers (usually our parents) and come to expect that our environments will—or will not—meet our needs. During early childhood and the preschool years, we begin to explore the environment more actively and try new things. At this time, our relationships with our parents and friends can encourage us to develop *autonomy* (self-direction) and *initiative*, or feelings of *shame* and *guilt*. During the elementary school years, friends and teachers take on more importance, encouraging us to become *industrious* or to develop feelings of *inferiority*. During adolescence, our relationships with our peers become more important as we struggle to define ourselves, to seek an *identity* or fail to know where we belong—*role confusion*. At the same time, the beginning of the establishment of *intimate* and loving relationships may develop with another person as we learn about ourselves. During adulthood, our social relationships may deepen as we strive for a better world for our children and promote *generativity* versus *stagnation*. As we continue to age, we may look back on our lives with *integrity* and satisfaction or we may have *despair* about regrets and mistakes we have made. Table 8.3 describes Erikson's eight psychosocial stages of development.

Infant Attachment

John Bowlby (1969) was recognized as the first attachment theorist. His ideas about the importance of the bond of attachment between an infant and his or her mother led to the pioneering work of Mary Ainsworth (1913–1999), who empirically studied Bowlby's attachment theory. **Attachment** is defined as an emotional tie that is formed between one animal or person and another specific individual. Attachment keeps organisms together—it is vital to the survival of the infant—and it tends to endure. The behaviours that define attachment include (1) attempts to maintain contact or nearness, and (2) shows of anxiety when separated (separation anxiety). Babies and children try to maintain contact with caregivers to whom they are attached. They engage in eye contact, pull and tug at them, ask to be picked up, and may even jump in front of them in such a way that they will be "run over" if they are not picked up. *How do feelings of attachment develop? What kinds of experiences affect attachment?*

Theoretical Views of Attachment

Early in the 20th century, behaviourists argued that attachment behaviours are learned through experience. Caregivers feed

TABLE 8.3

Erikson's Psychosocial Stages of Development

	Ego Conflict	Age	Description
1	Trust vs. Mistrust	Infant	Infant depends on caregiver to provide basic necessities, such as food, comfort, and warmth. If trust is not established, the infant will not survive his or her social world.
2	Autonomy vs. Shame and Doubt	Toddler	As a child learns to be independent, encouragement and support should be provided. Failure to do so will result in the toddler feeling ashamed and not confident.
3	Initiative vs. Guilt	Preschooler	The child begins school and now must acquire new skills and learn new social routines. The risk of guilt exists if the child is not able to espouse his or her social wishes.
4	Competence vs. Inferiority	School-aged child	As the child learns new skills and masters them, he or she becomes "ready" for adult life. Failure to complete tasks or making mistakes can lead to the child feeling inferior.
5	Ego Identity vs. Role Confusion	Adolescent	Adolescents must determine who they are and what they want to do with their lives. *Identity crisis* refers to the conflict that exists in this stage where an individual struggles with being able to make a decision and plan for his or her future.
6	Intimacy vs. Isolation	Young adult	In this stage, young adults begin to share their life with a partner and make commitments toward a future. Failure to establish a meaningful relationship results in feeling isolated and lonely.
7	Generativity vs. Stagnation	Middle-aged adult	*Generativity* refers to a focus on the future of generations ahead. Becoming a parent is common in our society, and it becomes productive and important for generativity. Parents often feel like they wish to leave the world a better place for their children. *Stagnation* is feeling complacent and "stuck" in one's life, which leads to unhappiness.
8	Ego Integrity vs. Despair	Older adult	Older adults who strive to accept their lives and their accomplishments and failures feel integral and full of wisdom. Feelings of despair and sorrow about life are considered unhealthy in this stage.

FIGURE 8.7

Attachment in Infant Monkeys

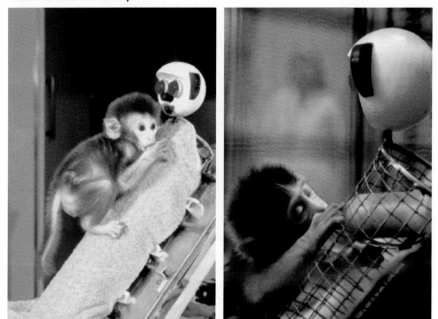

Left: © Martin Rogers/Stock Boston; right: © Martin Rogers/Woodfin Camp & Associates

Nina Leen/Time Life Pictures/Getty Images

contact comfort
a hypothesized primary drive to seek physical comfort through contact with another

ethologist
a scientist who studies the characteristic behaviour patterns of species of animals

critical period
a period of time when an instinctive response can be elicited by a particular stimulus

imprinting
a process occurring during a critical period in the development of an organism, in which that organism responds to a stimulus in a manner that will afterward be difficult to modify

their infants and tend to their other physiological needs. Thus, infants associate their caregivers with gratification of needs and learn to approach them to meet their needs. The feelings of gratification associated with the meeting of basic needs generalize into feelings of security when the caregiver is present.

Classic research by psychologist Harry F. Harlow suggests that skin contact may be more important than learning experiences. Harlow noted that infant rhesus monkeys reared without mothers or companions became attached to pieces of cloth in their cages. They maintained contact with them and showed distress when separated from them. Harlow conducted a series of experiments to find out why (Harlow, 1959).

In one study, Harlow placed infant rhesus monkeys in cages with two surrogate mothers, as shown in Figure 8.7. One "mother" was made of wire mesh from which a baby bottle was extended. The other surrogate mother was made of soft, cuddly terry cloth. The infant monkeys spent most of their time clinging to the cloth mother, even though "she" did not gratify their need for food. Harlow concluded that monkeys—and perhaps

humans—have an inborn need for **contact comfort** that is as basic as the need for food. Gratification of the need for contact comfort, rather than food, might be why infant monkeys (and humans) cling to their mothers.

Other researchers, such as **ethologist** Konrad Lorenz, argue that for many animals, attachment is an instinct—inborn. (Ethologists study the behavioural characteristics of various species of animals.) Attachment, like other instincts, is theorized to occur in the presence of a specific stimulus and during a **critical period** of life—that is, a period during which the animal is sensitive to the stimulus.

Some animals become attached to the first moving object they encounter. The formation of an attachment in this manner is therefore called **imprinting**. Lorenz (1981) became well known when pictures of his "family" of goslings were made public. How did Lorenz acquire his following? He was present when the goslings hatched and during their critical period, and he allowed them to follow him. The critical period for geese and some other animals is bounded, at the younger end, by the age at which they first walk and, at the older end, by the age at which they develop fear of strangers. The goslings followed Lorenz persistently, ran to him when frightened, honked with distress at his departure, and tried to overcome barriers between them. If you substitute crying for honking, it all sounds rather human.

The Strange Situation and Patterns of Attachment

The ways in which infants behave in strange situations are connected with their bonds of attachment with their caregivers. Given this fact, Ainsworth and her colleagues (1978) designed the *strange situation assessment* to learn how infants respond to separations and reunions with a caregiver (usually the mother) and a stranger. Using this method, Ainsworth and her colleagues identified three major types of attachment:

1 *Secure attachment.* Securely attached infants mildly protest their mother's departure, seek interaction upon reunion, and are readily comforted by her.

2 *Avoidant attachment.* Infants who show avoidant attachment are least distressed by their mother's departure. They play by themselves without fuss and ignore their mothers when they return.

3 *Resistant attachment.* Infants who show resistant attachment are the most emotional. They show severe signs of distress when their mother leaves and show ambivalence upon reunion by alternately clinging to and pushing their mother away when she returns.

A fourth type of attachment style was later added by Main and Solomon (1986) to account for infants who showed contradictory and disoriented responses upon their caregivers' departure and return.

4 *Disorganized/disoriented attachment.* Infants who show disorganized attachment exhibit contradictory or ambivalent responses that are indicative of distress upon caregivers' return. The infant may not look at the caregiver while being held or be noncompliant with returning affection.

Ainsworth and her colleagues' (1978) and later researchers' (Main & Soloman, 1986) attachment studies demonstrate that attachment is connected with the quality of care that infants receive. The parents of securely attached children are more likely to be affectionate and reliable caregivers (Isabella, 1998; Posada et al., 2002). A wealth of research literature speaks of the benefits of secure attachment. For example, secure children are happier, more sociable, and more cooperative than insecure children (Bohlin et al., 2000). At ages five and six, securely attached children are liked better by their peers and teachers, are more competent, and have fewer behaviour problems than insecurely attached children (Granot & Mayseless, 2001; Moss & St-Laurent, 2001). In this vein, we can also note that having the primary caregiver present during stressful situations, such as pediatric exams, helps children cope with these situations (Ybarra et al., 2000).

Ainsworth's research suggests that child care provided by nonmaternal caregivers (for example, day-care centres) may interfere with a child's secure attachment. This might raise your eyebrows for a moment, considering that over 50 percent of infants and toddlers between the ages of six months and five year in Canada receive nonparental child care (Statistics Canada, 2006). So, does this mean that children in nonparental care as infants and toddlers are less able to form secure attachments to their primary (or parental) caregivers? Not exactly, but some research supports lower levels of emotional difficulties and less aggression when maternal care is present for low-risk families (Cote, Geoffroy, Borge, Rutter, & Tremblay, 2008). The *National Longitudinal Survey of Children and Youth* (NLSCY) (2006) provides a comprehensive report on child-care experiences in Canada (see the box entitled "Child Care in Canada").

Parenting Styles

Many psychologists have been concerned about the relationships between parenting styles and the personality development of the child. *What types of parental behaviour are connected with variables such as self-esteem, achievement motivation,*

{ Child Care in Canada }

Here are a few highlights about child care from the *National Longitudinal Survey of Children and Youth* (2006):

- Nonparental child-care rates increased from 42 percent in 1994–1995 to 54 percent in 2002–2003.
- This increase includes children from almost all backgrounds, regardless of geographical location, household income, family structure, or parental employment status.

- During the same period, there was a decline in care by nonrelatives but an increase in care by relatives and day-care centres.
- Use of child care by relatives was more common for parents born outside of Canada; use of day-care centres was more common among lower-income households.

and independence in children? Diana Baumrind (1973) has been particularly interested in the connections between parental behaviour and the development of *instrumental competence* in their children. (Instrumental competence refers to the ability to manipulate the environment to achieve one's goals.) Baumrind has focused largely on four aspects of parental behaviour: (1) strictness; (2) demands for the child to achieve intellectual, emotional, and social maturity; (3) communication ability; and (4) warmth and involvement. She labelled the three parenting styles the *authoritative, authoritarian,* and *permissive* styles. Other researchers also speak of the *uninvolved* style. These four styles are defined in the following ways:

1 *Authoritative parents.* The parents of the most competent children rate high in all four areas of behaviour. They are strict (restrictive) and demand mature behaviour. But they temper their strictness with desire to reason with their children and with love and support (Galambos et al., 2003). They expect much, but they explain why and offer help. Baumrind labelled these parents **authoritative parents** to suggest that they know what they want but are also loving and respectful of their children.

2 *Authoritarian parents.* Authoritarian parents view obedience as a virtue for its own sake. They have strict guidelines about what is right and wrong, and they demand that their children stick to them. Both authoritative and authoritarian parents have strict standards, but authoritative parents explain their demands and are supportive, whereas authoritarian parents rely on force and communicate poorly with their children. Authoritarian parents do not respect their children's points of view, and they may be cold and rejecting. When children ask them why they should do this or that, authoritarian parents often answer, "Because I say so!"

3 *Permissive parents.* Permissive parents are generally easygoing with their children. As a result, the children do pretty much what the children want. Permissive parents are warm and supportive, but poor at communicating their wishes. Permissive parents are often more concerned with being liked by their children than with demanding expectations that may hinder the friendship between them and their children.

4 *Uninvolved parents.* Uninvolved parents tend to leave their children on their own. They make few demands and show little warmth or encouragement. Uninvolved parents are unaware of their children's feelings and emotions. They may not spend time communicating with their children daily and are often cold when spoken to.

Research evidence shows that the children of warm parents are more likely to be socially and emotionally well adjusted. They are also more likely to internalize moral standards—that is, to develop a conscience (Grusec, 2002; Rudy & Grusec, 2001).

Strictness seems to pay off, provided it is tempered with reason and warmth. Children of authoritative parents have the greatest self-reliance, self-esteem, social competence, and achievement motivation (Galambos et al., 2003; Grusec, 2002; Kim & Rohner, 2002). Children of authoritarian parents are often withdrawn or aggressive and usually do not do as well in school as children of authoritative parents (Kim & Rohner, 2002; Steinberg, 2001). Children of permissive parents seem to be less mature. They are often impulsive, moody, and aggressive. In adolescence, lack of parental monitoring is often linked to delinquency and poor academic performance. Children of uninvolved parents tend to obtain poorer grades than children whose parents make demands on them. The children of uninvolved parents also tend to be more likely to hang out with crowds who "party" a good deal and use drugs (Durbin et al., 1993). The message? Simple enough: Children profit when parents make reasonable demands, show warmth and encouragement, and spend time with them.

Social Development in Adolescence

What social developments occur during adolescence? Adolescence has been associated with social and emotional turbulence. In the 19th century, psychologist G. Stanley Hall described adolescence as a time

authoritative parents parents who are strict and warm; they demand mature behaviour but use reason and fairness rather than force in discipline

authoritarian parents parents who are rigid in their rules and who demand obedience for the sake of obedience

permissive parents parents who impose few, if any, rules and who do not supervise their children closely

uninvolved parents parents who generally leave their children to themselves and who are likely unaware of their children's feelings and emotions

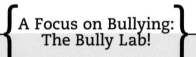
{ A Focus on Bullying: The Bully Lab! }

Dr. Wendy Craig, Ph.D., Department of Psychology at Queen's University, has co-created the research program called PREVNet (Promoting Relationships and Eliminating Violence Network). This program focuses on communicating the protective factors associated with bullying and victimization in all types of relationships (including sexual violence in adolescence and adulthood). The program is based on the education for developing healthy relationships among children, adolescents, and adults. For additional information and resources (toolkits), you can view the websites for the Bully Lab (www.bullylab.com) or PREVNet (www.prevnet.ca).

of *Sturm und Drang*—storm and stress. Current views challenge the assumption that "storm and stress" is the norm (Griffin, 2001). Many adolescents experience a rather calm and joyous period of development. We need to consider individual differences and cultural variations (Arnett, 1999).

Striving for Independence

As these biological changes take place, adolescents strive to become more independent from parents, which may lead to bickering (Smetana et al., 2003). Bickering usually concerns homework, chores, money, appearance, curfews, and dating. Disagreements about clothes and friends are common.

Adolescents and parents are often in conflict because adolescents experiment with things that can be harmful to their health. Yet—apparently because of the personal fable—adolescents may not perceive such activities to be as risky as their parents do. Cohn and his colleagues (1995) found, for example, that parents perceived drinking, smoking, failure to use seat belts, drag racing, and a number of other activities to be riskier than did their teenagers.

Some distancing from parents is beneficial (Smetana et al., 2003). After all, adolescents do have to form relationships outside the family. But greater independence does not necessarily mean that adolescents become emotionally detached from parents or fall completely under the spell of peers. Most adolescents continue to feel love, respect, and loyalty toward parents (Eberly & Montemayor, 1999). Adolescents who feel close to their parents actually show more self-reliance and independence than do those who distance themselves. They fare better in school and have fewer adjustment problems (Flouri & Buchanan, 2003). Despite conflict over issues of control, parents and adolescents tend to share social, political, religious, and economic views (Sagrestano et al., 1999). In sum, there are frequent differences between parents and adolescents on issues of personal control. However, there is apparently less of a "generation gap" on broader matters.

Ego Identity versus Role Confusion

Refer back to Table 8.3 on page 184. You will see that *ego identity versus role confusion* are important psychosocial stages of development in adolescence. **Ego identity** is a firm sense of who one is and what one stands for. It can carry one through difficult times

and lend meaning to achievements. Adolescents who do not develop ego identity may experience **role confusion**. They spread themselves too thin, running down one blind alley after another and placing themselves at the mercy of leaders who promise to give them the sense of identity they cannot find for themselves.

The creation of an adult identity is a key challenge, involving learning about one's interests and abilities and connecting them with occupations and roles in life. Identity also involves sexual, political, and religious beliefs and commitments. Will the individual be monogamous or sexually active with several people? Will he or she lean left or right along the political spectrum? What role will be played by religion?

Emerging Adulthood

Erikson's concept of role diffusion as an important conflict to resolve in adolescence has been recently studied. There is now the perspective that an extended period of transition—called emerging adulthood—is an additional developmental stage that should be recognized in contemporary society (Arnett, 2001). Changing demographics, such as delaying marriage and parenthood until the late 20s or early 30s and the increase in enrollment in post-secondary education, are now considered important and distinct transitions for young adults between the ages of 18 and 25. These changes also may address why only a small portion of adolescents reach *identity achievement* before adulthood. James Marcia (1980) identified four identity statuses in adolescent development: *identity diffusion, identity foreclosure, identity moratorium,* and *identity achievement* (see Table 8.4). These four identity statuses are formed through the presence or absence of identity crisis and a lack of or move toward life commitments. Marcia believed that adolescents move through the "orientations" as they mature.

Social Development in Adulthood

Changes in social and emotional development during adulthood are probably the most "elastic" or fluid. These changes are affected by cultural expectations and individual behaviour patterns. As a result, there is much variety. Nevertheless, many developmental theorists suggest that there are enough commonalities that we can speak of trends. One trend is that the outlook for older people has become more optimistic over the past generation—not only because of medical advances but also because the behaviour and mental processes of many older people are remaining younger than at any other time in history.

TABLE 8.4

Marcia's Four Identity Statuses

Identity diffusion	Involves no identity crisis and no sense of commitment to life goals
Identity foreclosure	Involves a sense of commitment to goals through learned values (i.e., parental, societal) without truly exploring self
Identity moratorium	Involves questioning and exploring aspects of self to try to understand identity
Identity achievement	Achievement of identity and personal commitment to life goals

There is more good news. Research evidence suggests that people tend to grow psychologically healthier as they advance from adolescence through middle adulthood. Psychologists Constance Jones and William Meredith (2000) studied information on 236 participants in California growth studies who had been followed from early adolescence for about 50 years and found that they generally became more productive and had healthier relationships as time went on. Even some people with a turbulent adolescence showed bet ter psychological health at age 62 than they had half a century earlier.

Young Adulthood

What social developments occur during young adulthood? Many theorists suggest that young adulthood is the period of life during which people tend to establish themselves as independent members of society.

At some point during the 20s, many people become fuelled by ambition. Many strive to advance in their careers. Those who seek professional careers may spend much of their 20s acquiring the skills that will enable them to succeed (Levinson et al., 1978; Levinson, 1996). It is largely during the 20s that people become generally responsible for their own support, make their own choices, and are freed from parental influences.

During young adulthood, people tend to leave their families of origin and create families of their own. Erik Erikson (1963) characterized young adulthood as the stage of **intimacy versus isolation.** Erikson saw the establishment of intimate relationships as central to young adulthood. Young adults who have evolved a firm sense of identity during adolescence are ready to "fuse" their identities with those of other people through marriage and abiding friendships. People who do not reach out to develop intimate relationships risk retreating into isolation and loneliness.

At age 30 or so, many people reassess their lives, asking themselves, "Where is my life going?" "Why am

I doing this?" (Levinson et al., 1978). It is not uncommon for them to switch careers or form new intimate relationships. The later 30s are often characterized by settling down—planting roots. They become focused on career advancement, children, and long-term mortgages.

Middle Adulthood

A number of key changes in social and emotional development occur during middle adulthood. *What social and emotional developments occur during middle adulthood?* Consider Erikson's views on the middle years.

Erikson (1963) labelled the life crisis of the middle years as **generativity versus stagnation.** *Generativity* involves doing things that we believe are worthwhile, such as rearing children or producing on the job. Generativity enhances and maintains self-esteem. Generativity also involves making the world a better place through joining church or civic groups. *Stagnation* means treading water, as in keeping the same job at the same pay for 30 years. Stagnation damages self-esteem.

According to Levinson and colleagues (1978), whose research involved case studies of 40 men, there is a *midlife transition* at about age 40 to 45. Previously, men had viewed their age in terms of the number of years that had elapsed since birth. Now they begin to think of their age in terms of the number of years they have left.

Research suggests that women may undergo a midlife transition sooner than men do (Zucker et al., 2002). Why? Much of it has to do with the winding down of the "biological clock"—that is, the abilities

intimacy versus isolation Erikson's life crisis of young adulthood, which is characterized by the task of developing abiding intimate relationships

generativity versus stagnation Erikson's term for the crisis of middle adulthood, characterized by the task of being productive and contributing to younger generations

Franklin Lloyd Wright Foundation/SODRAC

midlife crisis
a crisis experienced by many people during the midlife transition when they realize that life may be more than halfway over and they reassess their achievements in terms of their dreams

ego integrity versus despair
Erikson's term for the crisis of late adulthood, characterized by the task of maintaining one's sense of identity despite physical deterioration

to conceive and bear children. For example, once they turn 35, pregnant women are usually advised to have their fetuses routinely tested for Down syndrome and other chromosomal disorders.

In both sexes, according to Levinson, the midlife transition may trigger a **midlife crisis**. For example, a middle-level, middle-aged businessperson looking ahead to another 10 to 20 years of grinding out accounts in a corporate cubbyhole may encounter severe depression. A homemaker with two teenagers, an empty house from 8:00 AM to 4:00 PM, and a 40th birthday on the way may feel that she or he is coming apart at the seams. Both feel a sense of entrapment and loss of purpose.

Yet many Canadians find that these years present opportunities for new direction and fulfillment. Meditation practices, such as yoga, Zen, and transcendental meditation have become popular and regular practices for many middle-aged adults. Many, perhaps most, of today's active 45- to 55-year-olds can look forward to another 30 to 40 healthy years.

Late Adulthood

What social developments occur during late adulthood? Generativity does not end with middle age. Research suggests that many individuals in late adulthood continue to be creative and also to maintain a firm sense of who they are and what they stand for (Webster, 2003). The Greek philosopher Plato was so optimistic about late adulthood that he argued that one could achieve great pleasure in one's later years, engage in meaningful public service, and also achieve wisdom (McKee & Barber, 2001).

According to psychologist Erik Erikson, late adulthood is the stage of **ego integrity versus despair**. The basic chal-

lenge is to maintain the belief that life is meaningful and worthwhile as one ages and faces the inevitability of death. Erikson, like Plato, spoke of the importance of wisdom. He believed that ego integrity derives from wisdom, which can be defined as expert knowledge about the meaning of life, balancing one's own needs and those of others, and pushing toward excellence in one's behaviour and achievements (Baltes & Staudinger, 2000; Sternberg, 2000). We spend most of our lives accumulating objects and relationships, and Erikson argues that adjustment in the later years requires the ability to let go of them. Other views of late adulthood stress the importance of creating new challenges; however, biological and social realities may require older people to become more selective in their pursuits.

LO5 Stages of Death and Dying

Elisabeth Kübler-Ross (1969) wrote a book called *On Death and Dying* that discussed stages of dying after interviewing terminally ill patients during her career as a psychiatrist. She discovered a number of similarities in the ways in which dying patients coped with their illness and the emotional responses while waiting for their impending death. Table 8.5 summarizes Kübler-Ross's stages as discussed in her book—a widely accepted stage model in psychology in understanding death and dying. Kübler-Ross asserts that in addition to the terminally ill person, families and close friends also experience similar stages as they cope with the realization of death.

TABLE 8.5

Summary of Stages of Dying by Elisabeth Kübler-Ross

Stage of Death	Explanation
1. Denial and isolation	The person denies the inevitable and can't believe that what is happening is happening to him or her.
	He or she feels alone and unable to talk about the inevitable.
2. Anger	The person becomes angry that this has happened to him or her.
	He or she may display resentment and may be difficult to talk to.
3. Bargaining	The person pleads for more time with others, especially children and loved ones.
	The person promises to make changes to delay or prolong death.
4. Depression	The person begins to feel a sense of loss and defeat, and fails to continue to play his or her roles (e.g., mother, father, career).
	The person may think about impending losses following his or her death for others and feels great sadness for how others are feeling.
5. Acceptance	The person realizes the end is coming, and considers how to resolve fears and sadness.
	The person begins preparing for his or her impending death.

Learning Outcomes

LO1 Define motivation including needs, drives, and incentives

LO2 Identify the theories of motivation

LO3 Describe the biological and psychological contributions to hunger

LO4 Explain the role of sex hormones and the sexual response cycle in human sexuality

LO5 Describe achievement motivation

LO6 Identify the theoretical explanations of emotions

Motivation and Emotion

> ## "I didn't see it go in the net, I just heard everybody scream."

With the crowd chanting his name "Crosby, Crosby!" a gold medal was slipped over Sidney Crosby's head and came to rest comfortably on his chest. This was a fitting moment for the talented young hockey player from Cole Harbour, Nova Scotia, who scored the game-winning overtime goal against the American men's hockey team at the Vancouver 2010 Olympics. The moment that the puck went into the net, the Canadian men's Olympic hockey team—and most of Canada— erupted into a frenzy of emotion. Just like Paul Henderson's goal of the century against the Russians in 1972, Crosby's goal will be remembered for many years to come by young and old hockey fans alike.

The 2010 Olympics in Vancouver was a successful competition for many Canadian athletes, with the final medal count for Canada at 14 gold, 7 silver, and 5 bronze. The success of the Canadian athletes has been attributed to several things, including increased funding for training prior to the games, the location of the games in Canada, the support of Canadian fans at the events, and cash incentives of up to $20 000 for athletes who won a gold medal. For a professional hockey player like Sidney Crosby, who makes nearly $8 million a year, what possible motivation could another $20 000 be? However, for a young Canadian amateur athlete like Jon Montgomery (skeleton gold medal winner), who works as a sales consultant and automobile auctioneer, $20 000 might be nearly half a year's salary.

External motivating factors such as money are only part of each success story. Of the roughly 2600 athletes who participated in the 2010 winter games, they all have in common an internally motivated intense desire to compete and win in their sport of choice. They all sacrificed years of their lives training both their minds and their bodies in order to compete in the Olympics. In fact, internal motivations, such as a strong desire to win and a sense of obligation to one's country and supporters (often fuelled by strong emotion) can be more powerful than the strongest external motivation. Underlying each gold-medal athlete's story—from the successful professional hockey player to the amateur skater—is a mixture of strong internal motivations, supportive external motivations, and powerful underlying emotions, which combine into a record-breaking victory.

DID YOU KNOW?

- One would think that getting away from it all by going on a vacation from all sensory input for a few hours is relaxing and pleasant, but rather it is disorienting, discomforting, and boring.

- People feel hunger due to contractions ("pangs") in the stomach, but other things also strongly influence hunger, such as anxiety, stress, social expectations, and the quality of the food.

- Fashion magazines can contribute to eating disorders among women.

- Money can't buy you happiness, but having no money leads to misery.

- You may be able to fool an electronic lie detector by biting your tongue and squiggling your toes.

LO1 The Psychology of Motivation

The psychology of motivation is concerned with the *whys* of behaviour. Why do we eat? Why do some of us strive to get ahead? Why do some of us ride motorcycles at breakneck speeds? Why are some people aggressive? Why do rich professional athletes compete in events such as the Olympics that have no substantial financial rewards? In order to answer these questions, psychologists use concepts such as motives, needs, drives, and incentives. *What are motives, needs, drives, and incentives?* **Motives** are hypothetical states that activate behaviour, propelling us toward goals. We call these states hypothetical because motives are not seen and measured directly. They are inferred from behaviour. Motives may take the form of *needs, drives,* and *incentives,* which are also inferred from behaviour.

We have physiological and psychological **needs**. We must meet physiological needs to survive—for example, the needs for oxygen, food, drink, pain avoidance, proper temperature, and elimination of waste products. Some physiological needs, such as hunger and thirst, are states of physical deprivation. When we have not eaten or drunk for a while, we develop needs for food and water. The body also needs oxygen, vitamins, and so on.

Psychological needs include needs for achievement, power, self-esteem, social approval, and belonging. Psychological needs are not necessarily based on states of deprivation. A person with a need for achievement may already have a history of successful achievements. Further, since our survival is rarely dependent on psychological need fulfillment, we refer in day-to-day language to psychological needs as "wants." We are more likely to say "I *want* to hang out with you tonight" rather than "I *need* to hang out with you tonight."

People's biological makeups are similar, and we share similar physiological needs. But because we are influenced by our cultural settings, our needs may be expressed in different ways. We all need food, but some prefer a vegetarian diet whereas others prefer meat. Because learning enters into psychological needs, they can differ markedly from one person to another.

Needs give rise to **drives**. Depletion of food gives rise to the hunger drive, and depletion of liquids gives rise to the thirst drive. **Physiological drives** are the counterparts of physiological needs. When we have gone without food and water, our body may *need* these substances. However, our *experience* of the drives of hunger and thirst is psychological. Drives arouse us to action and tend to be stronger when we have been deprived longer. We are hungrier when we haven't eaten for ten hours than one hour.

Psychological needs for approval, achievement, and belonging also give rise to drives. We can have a drive to get ahead in the business world just as we have a drive to eat. Psychologists are working to learn more about the origins of these drives. We do know that we can also be driven to obtain *incentives*. An **incentive** is an object, person, or situation that can satisfy a need or is desirable for its own sake. Money, food, a sexually attractive person, social approval, and attention can all act as incentives.

LO2 Theories of Motivation

Although psychologists agree that it is important to understand why humans and lower animals do things, they do not agree about the precise nature of motivation. Let us consider various theoretical perspectives on motivation.

The Evolutionary Perspective

The evolutionary perspective notes that many animals are neurally "prewired"—that is, born with preprogrammed tendencies—to respond to certain situations in certain ways. Spiders spin webs instinctively. Bees "dance" instinctively to communicate the location of food to other bees.

These instinctive behaviours are found in particular species. They are *species-specific*. *What is meant by species-specific behaviours?* Species-specific behaviours are also called **instincts** and are inborn. They are genetically transmitted from generation to generation.

Psychologists have asked whether humans have instincts, and if so, how many. A century ago, psychologists William James (1890) and William McDougall (1908) argued that humans have instincts

Spiders spin webs instinctively.

that foster survival and social behaviour. James considered love, sympathy, and modesty to be social instincts. McDougall compiled 12 "basic" instincts, including hunger, sex, and self-assertion. Other psychologists have made longer lists, and still others deny that people have instincts. The question of whether people have instincts—and what they might be—remains unresolved.

Drive-Reductionism and Homeostasis

Sigmund Freud believed that tension motivates us to behave in ways that restore us to a resting state. His views are similar to those of the **drive-reduction theory** of learning, as set forth by psychologist Clark Hull in the 1930s. *What is drive-reduction theory?*

According to Hull, *primary drives* such as hunger, thirst, and pain trigger arousal (tension) and activate behaviour. We learn to engage in behaviours that reduce the tension. We also acquire drives—called *acquired drives*—through experience. We may acquire a drive for money because money enables us to obtain food, drink, and homes that protect us from crime and extremes of temperature. We might acquire drives for social approval and affiliation because other people, and their goodwill, help us reduce primary drives, especially as infants. In all cases, reduction of tension is the goal. Yet some people appear to acquire what could be considered excessive drives for money. They gather money long after their material needs have been met.

Primary drives like hunger are triggered when we are in a state of deprivation. Sensations of hunger motivate us to act in ways that will restore the bodily balance. This tendency to maintain a steady state is called **homeostasis**. Homeostasis works like a thermostat. When the temperature in a room drops below the set point, the furnace turns on. The furnace stays on until the set point is reached. Similarly, most animals eat until they are no longer hungry. But many people eat "recreationally"—as when they see an appealing dessert—suggesting there is more to eating than drive reduction.

The Search for Stimulation

Physical needs give rise to drives like hunger and thirst. In such cases, we are motivated to *reduce* the tension or stimulation that impinges on us. *Are all motives aimed at the reduction of tension?*

In the case of *stimulus motives*, organisms seek to *increase* stimulation. A study conducted at McGill University in Montreal during the 1950s suggests the importance of sensory stimulation and activity. Some "lucky" students were paid $20 a day (which, with inflation, would now be more like $200) for doing nothing—literally. Would you like to "work" by doing nothing for $200 a day? Don't answer too quickly. According to the results of this study, you might not like it at all. In this experiment, student volunteers were placed in quiet cubicles and blindfolded (Bexton et al., 1954). Their arms were bandaged; they could hear nothing but the dull, continuous hum of air conditioning. Many slept for a while, but after a few hours of sensory-deprived wakefulness, most felt bored and irritable. As time went on, many grew more uncomfortable, and some even reported experiencing visual and auditory hallucinations. Many students quit the experiment during the first day despite the financial incentive. Many of those who remained for a few days found it hard to concentrate on simple problems for days afterward. For many, the experiment did not provide a relaxing vacation. Instead, it produced boredom, discomfort, and disorientation.

Humans and other animals appear motivated to seek novel stimulation. Even when they have been deprived of food, rats may explore unfamiliar arms of mazes rather than head straight for the food source. Animals that have just copulated and thereby reduced their primary sex drives often show renewed interest in sex when presented with a novel sex partner. People (and nonhumans) take in more calories at buffets and smorgasbords than when fewer kinds of food are available (Raynor & Epstein, 2001). Children spend hour after hour playing video games for the pleasure of zapping virtual people or

What motivates children to spend hour after hour playing video games?

self-actualization
a state of being that includes perceptive clarity, peacefulness, simplicity, a sense of mission, sensitivity to the needs of others, being comfortable alone, a healthy sense of humour, and moments of profound emotional experience

monsters. Infants play with "busy boxes"—boxes filled with objects that honk, squeak, rattle, and buzz when manipulated in certain ways. Finding ways to control the gadgets is apparently reinforcing, even though learning is not rewarded with desserts or parental hugs.

Humanistic Theory

Humanistic psychologists such as Abraham Maslow (1908–1970) suggest that human behaviour is more than mechanical and more than aimed toward tension reduction and survival. *How does humanistic theory differ from other theories of motivation?* Maslow believed that people are also motivated by a conscious desire for personal growth. Humanists note that people tolerate pain, hunger, and many other kinds of tension to seek personal fulfillment.

Maslow believed that we are separated from other animals by our capacity for **self-actualization**, which is the highest fulfillment of being that is achievable by a person (Potkay & Allen, 1986). Maslow considered self-actualization to be as vital a need in humans as hunger. The need for self-actualization pushes people to strive to become concert pianists, chief executive officers, or best-selling authors—even when they have plenty of money to live on.

Maslow (1970) organized human needs into a hierarchy. *What is Maslow's hierarchy of needs?* Maslow's hierarchy is divided into a hierarchical arrangement of the five major categories of common human needs (see Figure 9.1). The first level includes physiological needs such as hunger and thirst. The second level includes safety needs such as shelter and an environment free of threats. At the third level we form

FIGURE 9.1

Maslow's Hierarchy of Needs

Maslow believed we progress toward higher psychological needs once basic survival needs have been met. Where do you fit in this picture?

Go to www.icanpsych.com to access an interactive version of this figure.

RubberBall/Alamy

fulfilling friendships and romantic relationships so our love and belongingness needs are met. The fourth level includes recognition and esteem, and these needs are met when our actions and work are valued by others. Finally, at the top of the pyramid is self-actualization, a place where a person lives to his or her fullest potential and is completely satisfied with his or her work and contribution to the world. A person progresses up the hierarchy once the needs of a given level are mostly met (complete satisfaction of a given level is not needed). Maslow suggested that many in our world never fully satisfy the first two needs and live an isolated life merely focused on survival. He also believed that we naturally strive to climb this hierarchy; however, if our lower needs become threatened, we will focus our attention again on them until they are satisfied. For example, if a person loses a job and is in danger of losing his or her house, the self-actualization, esteem, and relationship needs may suffer temporarily until the base physiological needs can again be met.

Critics of Maslow's theory argue that there is too much individual variation for the hierarchy of motives to apply to everyone. Some people whose physiological, safety, and love needs are met show little interest in achievement and recognition. And some artists devote themselves fully to their craft, even if they have to pass up the comforts of a warm home or end up alienating their families.

Evaluating the Theories of Motivation

Each theory of motivation may have something to offer. Drive-reduction theory may explain why we drink when thirsty, stimulus motives might explain why we go clubbing and drink alcohol, and self-actualization motives could explain why amateur athletes sacrifice their time and resources in training and competitions. Each theory might apply to certain aspects of behaviour. As the chapter progresses, we will describe research that lends support to each theory. Let us first consider the hunger drive. Hunger is based on physiological needs, and drive-reduction would appear to explain some—although not all—eating behaviour. Then we consider two powerful motives: sex and achievement.

LO3 Hunger

We need food to survive, but food means more than survival. Food is a symbol of family togetherness and caring. We associate food with the nurturance of the parent–child relationship, with visits home on holidays. Friends and relatives offer us food when we enter their homes, and saying no may be viewed as a personal rejection. Roast turkey and mashed potatoes, a Montreal smoked meat sandwich, coffee with cream and sugar, or a heaping plate of poutine—all seem to be part of sharing Canadian values of abundance and generosity. *How is the hunger drive regulated?*

Biological Influences on Hunger

In considering the bodily mechanisms that regulate hunger, let us begin at the entry point, with the mouth. After we chew and swallow a certain amount of food, we receive signals of **satiety**. We also get signals of satiety from the digestive tract, although these signals take longer to reach the brain.

To demonstrate that chewing and swallowing provide feelings of satiety, researchers conducted classic "sham feeding" experiments with dogs. They implanted a tube in the animals' throats so that any food swallowed fell out of the body. Even though no food reached the stomach, the animals stopped feeding after a while (Janowitz & Grossman, 1949). But the dogs in the study, however, resumed feeding sooner than animals whose food did reach the stomach. Let us proceed to the stomach, too, as we seek further regulatory factors in hunger.

An empty stomach leads to stomach contractions, which we call *hunger pangs*. Classic research suggested that stomach contractions are crucial to hunger. A man (A.L. Washburn) swallowed a balloon that was inflated in his stomach. His stomach contractions squeezed the balloon, so the contractions could be recorded by observers. Washburn also pressed a key when he felt hungry, and the researchers found a correspondence between his stomach contractions and his feelings of hunger (Cannon & Washburn, 1912).

Medical observations and classic research find that humans and nonhumans whose stomachs have been removed still regulate food intake

satiety
the state of being satisfied; fullness

Jupiterimages

ventromedial nucleus (VMN) a central area on the underside of the hypothalamus that appears to function as a stop-eating centre

hyperphagic characterized by excessive eating

lateral hypothalamus an area at the side of the hypothalamus that appears to function as a start-eating centre

aphagic characterized by undereating

so as to maintain a normal weight (Tsang, 1938). (Food is absorbed through their intestines.) This finding led to the discovery of other mechanisms that regulate hunger, including the hypothalamus, blood sugar level, and receptors in the liver. The amount of sugar in our blood drops when we are deprived of food. The drop is communicated to the hypothalamus, which stokes the hunger drive.

The hypothalamus has been found to be important to the hunger drive. When a researcher destroys the **ventromedial nucleus (VMN)** of a rat's hypothalamus during surgery, the rat will grope toward food as soon as its eyes open. Then it eats vast quantities of Rat Chow or whatever. The VMN seems to be able to function like a "stop-eating centre" in the rat's brain. If the VMN is electrically stimulated—that is, "switched on"—the rat stops eating until the current is turned off. When the VMN is destroyed, the rat becomes **hyperphagic** (see Figure 9.2). That is, it continues to eat until it has about doubled its normal weight. Then it will level off its eating rate and maintain the higher weight. It is as if the set point of the stop-eating centre has been raised to a higher level. There have been reported cases of people developing tumours near the base of the brain that damage the VMN and apparently lead them to overeat (Miller, 1995).

The **lateral hypothalamus** may function like a "start-eating centre" by switching on the production of hormones that signal the rat to eat (Chua, 2004).

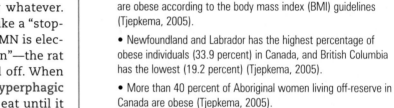

FIGURE 9.2

Hyperphagic Rats

John Sholtis, The Rockefeller University, New York, NY.
© 1995 Amgen, Inc.

If you destroy the lateral hypothalamus, the rat may stop eating altogether—that is, become **aphagic**.

Psychological Influences on Hunger

Although many areas of the body work in concert to regulate the hunger drive, this is only part of the story. In human beings, the hunger drive is more complex. Psychological as well as physiological factors play an important role. How many times have you been made hungry by the sight or aroma of food? How many times have you eaten not because you were hungry but because you were at a relative's home or hanging around a cafeteria or coffee shop? Or because you felt anxious or depressed? Or simply because you were bored?

Obesity: A Serious and Pervasive Problem

Consider some facts about obesity:

- More than 5.5 million Canadians (about one out of five adults) are obese according to the body mass index (BMI) guidelines (Tjepkema, 2005).

- Newfoundland and Labrador has the highest percentage of obese individuals (33.9 percent) in Canada, and British Columbia has the lowest (19.2 percent) (Tjepkema, 2005).

- More than 40 percent of Aboriginal women living off-reserve in Canada are obese (Tjepkema, 2005).

- In Canada, roughly 2.2 percent of total health-care costs ($4.3 billion per year) are directly attributable to obesity (Katzmarzyk & Janssen, 2004).

- Between 1985 and 2000, about 57 000 Canadians died because of health problems related to obesity (Katzmarzyk & Ardern, 2004).

- Weight control is elusive for most people; even those who have dieted "successfully" regain most of the weight they have lost (Cooper & Fairburn, 2001).

North American culture idealizes slender heroes and heroines. For those who want to "measure up" to TV and film idols, food may have replaced sex as the central source of guilt. Obese people encounter more than their fair share of health problems, including hypertension, heart disease, diabetes, gallbladder disease, osteoarthritis, sleep apnea, respiratory problems, and certain kinds of cancer (Centers for Disease Control and Prevention, 2005a). A study found that severely obese young adults (those with a BMI above 45) live shorter lives than people who are normal in weight (Fontaine et al., 2003; see Table 9.1). Why are so many people obese?

TABLE 9.1

Years of Life Lost Due to Obesity for White and Black Young Adults

	Female	Male
White	8	13
Black	5	20

Origins of Obesity

Many biological and psychological factors are involved in obesity. Overweight runs in families. Studies of monkeys (Kavanagh et al., 2007) and of human twins (Silventoinen et al., 2007) suggest there are strong roles for heredity. Efforts by overweight and obese people to maintain a slender profile may be sabotaged by an adaptive mechanism that would help preserve life in times of famine—*adaptive thermogenesis*. This mechanism causes the body to produce less energy (burn fewer calories) when someone goes on a diet (Major et al., 2007). This does not mean that overweight people will not lose weight by dieting; it means that it will take longer than expected.

Fatty tissue in the body also metabolizes (burns) food more slowly than muscle. For this reason, a person with a high fat-to-muscle ratio metabolizes food more slowly than a person of the same weight with more muscle. That is, two people of the same weight may metabolize food at different rates, depending on their distribution of muscle and fat. The average man is 40 percent muscle and 15 percent fat, whereas the average woman is 23 percent muscle and 25 percent fat. Therefore, if a typical man and woman are equal in weight, the woman has to eat less to maintain that weight.

Psychological factors, such as observational learning, stress, and emotional states also contribute to obesity. People in Canada are exposed to thousands of food commercials a year—many of them for fatty fast foods, sweetened cereals, and sugar-laden soft drinks. Situations such as family celebrations, watching TV, arguments, and tension at work can all lead to overeating or falling off a diet (Fletcher et al., 2007). Negative emotions such as depression and anxiety can trigger binge eating (Reas & Grilo, 2007).

Eating Disorders

The *eating disorders* are characterized by persistent, gross disturbances in eating patterns, from which 1.5 percent of Canadian women aged 15 to 24 suffer (Government of Canada, 2006). In this section we focus on an eating disorder in which individuals are too thin, *anorexia nervosa,* and one in which the person may be normal in weight, but certainly not in the methods used to maintain that weight—*bulimia nervosa.*

anorexia nervosa
a life-threatening eating disorder characterized by dramatic weight loss and a distorted body image

Anorexia Nervosa

Anorexia nervosa is a life-threatening eating disorder characterized by extreme fear of being too heavy, dramatic weight loss, a distorted body image, and resistance to eating enough to reach or maintain a healthful weight.

Anorexia nervosa mostly afflicts women during adolescence and young adulthood. The typical person with anorexia is a young white woman of higher socioeconomic status (McLaren, 2002). Approximately 1 percent of Canadian women will suffer from anorexia nervosa at some point of their life (Hudson, Hiripi, Pope, & Kessler, 2007).

Affluent women have greater access to fitness centres and health clubs and are more likely to subscribe to the magazines that idealize slender bodies and shop in the boutiques that cater to svelte women. They are regularly confronted with unrealistic standards of slimness that make them dissatisfied with their own figures (Neumark-Sztainer et al., 2002a).

We also find eating disorders among some men, particularly among men who are compelled by their chosen activities—for example, wrestling or dancing—to keep their weight at a certain limit (Bailey, 2003a; Goode, 2000). But women with these disorders outnumber men who have them by more than six to one (Striegel-Moore & Cachelin, 2001).

Women with anorexia nervosa can drop 25 percent or more of their weight within a year. Severe weight loss can prevent ovulation and cause general health to deteriorate. Females with anorexia are also at risk for premature development of osteoporosis (Jacoangeli et al., 2002). Given these problems, there is a 10 percent chance that someone diagnosed with anorexia nervosa will die within ten years (Sullivan, 2002).

In one common pattern, a young woman sees that she has gained some weight after reaching puberty, and she resolves that she

Brand X Pictures/Jupiterimages

bulimia nervosa
an eating disorder characterized by repeated cycles of binge eating and purging

must lose it. But even after the weight is gone, she maintains her pattern of dieting and, in many cases, exercises at a fever pitch. This pattern continues as she plunges below her "desirable" weight. People with the disorder are in denial about health problems; some point to feverish exercise routines as evidence of strength. Distortion of the body image is a major feature of the disorder (Striegel-Moore et al., 2004).

Bulimia Nervosa

Bulimia nervosa entails repeated cycles of binge eating and purging. Binge eating often follows efforts to diet (Corwin, 2000). There are various methods of purging, including vomiting, strict dieting or fasting, laxatives, and prolonged exercise. Individuals with eating disorders will not settle for less than their idealized body shape and weight. Bulimia, like anorexia, triggers hormonal imbalances: One study found that nearly half of women with bulimia nervosa have irregular menstrual cycles (Gendall et al., 2000). Bulimia nervosa, like anorexia nervosa, tends to afflict women during adolescence and young adulthood (Lewinsohn et al., 2000b).

Origins of the Eating Disorders

What are the origins of the eating disorders? Health professionals have done a great deal of research into the origins of eating disorders, but they admit that many questions about them remain unanswered (Striegel-Moore & Cachelin, 2001).

Many parents are obsessed with getting their children—especially their infants—to eat. Thus some psychologists suggest that children may use refusal to eat as a way of resisting or punishing parents. ("You have to eat something!" "I'm not hungry!") Parents in such families often have issues with eating and dieting themselves. They also "act out" against their daughters—letting them know that they consider them unattractive and that they should slim down (Baker et al., 2000; Cooper et al., 2001).

A particularly disturbing risk factor for eating disorders in adolescent women is a history of child abuse, particularly sexual abuse (Ackard et al., 2001; Leonard et al., 2003). One study found that fear of being fat and bulimia was predicted by child physical abuse. Further, women who reported multiple forms of child abuse who were revictimized as an adult showed the most eating disorder symptoms (Messman-Moore & Scheer Garrigus, 2007).

The sociocultural climate also affects eating behaviour (Williams et al., 2003). Slimness is

Tim Mosenfelder/Getty Images

Canadian musician Alanis Morissette has revealed how she struggled with both anorexia and bulimia early in her career.

idealized in the Canada. When you check out current fashion magazines and catalogues, you are looking at models who, on average, are 9 percent taller and 16 percent thinner than the typical woman—and who still manage to have ample bustlines. Miss America, the annually renewed American role model, has also been slenderizing across the years. Over the past 80 years, the winner has added only 2 percent in height but has lost over 5 kilograms in weight. In the 1920s, Miss America's weight relative to her height yielded a body mass index (BMI) of 20 to 25, which is considered normal by the World Health Organization (WHO). The WHO labels people as malnourished when their BMIs are lower than 18.5. Recent Miss Americas, however, come in with a BMI near 17 (Rubinstein & Caballero, 2000). So Miss America adds to the woes of "normal" young women.

As the cultural ideal slenderizes, women with average body weights according to the health charts feel overweight, and more-than-average women feel gargantuan (Utter et al., 2003; Williams et al., 2003).

LO4 Sexual Motivation

What triggers the sex drive? Many factors contribute to the sex drive. People vary greatly in the cues that excite them sexually and in the frequency with which they experience sexual thoughts and feelings. Sex hormones and cultural beliefs also influence sexual behaviour and the pleasure people find—or do not find—in sex. Sexual motivation may be natural, but this natural function is strongly influenced by religious and moral beliefs, cultural tradition, folklore, and superstition.

Regardless of our ethnicity, our levels of education, and cultural influences, our sex drives are connected with sex hormones. *What are the effects of sex hormones on sexual motivation?*

Hormones and Sexual Motivation

Sex hormones can be said to fuel the sex drive. Research with men who produce little testosterone—due to age or health problems—shows that their sex drive increases when they receive testosterone replacement therapy (Seidman, 2003). The most common sexual problem among women is lack of sexual desire or interest, and the sex drive in women is also connected with testosterone levels (Apperloo et al., 2003). Although men produce 10 to 20 times the testosterone produced by women, women produce androgens ("male" sex hormones) in the adrenal glands. Testosterone injections, patches, or pills can heighten the sex drive in women who do not produce enough of the hormone (Van Anders et al., 2005).

Sex hormones promote the development of male and female sex organs and regulate the menstrual cycle. They also have activating and organizing effects on sexual behaviour. **Activating effects** involve the sex drive. Female mice, rats, cats, and dogs are receptive to males only during **estrus**, when female sex hormones are plentiful. During estrus, female rats respond to males by hopping, wiggling their ears, and arching their backs with their tails to one side, thus enabling males to penetrate them. Sex hormones also have directional or **organizing effects**. That is, they predispose lower animals toward stereotypical masculine or feminine mating patterns. Sex hormones are thus likely candidates for influencing the development of sexual orientation (Lalumière et al., 2000).

Sex hormones may further "masculinise" or "feminize" the brain by creating predispositions consistent with some gender-role tendencies (Collaer & Hines, 1995; Crews, 1994). For example, male rats are generally superior to females in maze-learning ability, a task that requires spatial skills. But female rats that are exposed to androgens in the uterus (e.g., because they have several male siblings in the uterus with them) or soon after birth learn maze routes as rapidly as males (Vandenbergh, 1993).

Sexual Response

What happens to the body when people are sexually aroused? Men show more interest in sex than women do (Peplau, 2003). Women are more likely to want to combine sex with a romantic relationship (Fisher, 2000). A survey of more than 1000 undergraduates found that men reported being more interested than women in casual sex and multiple sex partners (Schmitt et al., 2001).

Although we may be more culturally attuned to focus on sex differences rather than similarities, William Masters and Virginia Johnson (1966) found that the biological responses of males and females to sexual stimulation are quite similar. Masters and Johnson use the term *sexual response cycle* to describe the changes that occur in the body as men and women become sexually aroused. They divide the **sexual response cycle** into four phases: *excitement, plateau, orgasm,* and *resolution.*

The cycle is characterized by *vasocongestion* and *myotonia.* **Vasocongestion** is the swelling of the genital tissues with blood, causing erection of the penis and swelling of the area surrounding the vaginal opening. The testes and the nipples swell as blood vessels dilate in these areas. **Myotonia** is muscle tension, which causes grimaces, spasms in the hands and feet, and the spasms of orgasm.

Erection, vaginal lubrication, and orgasm are all reflexes. That is, they occur automatically in response to adequate sexual stimulation.

Excitement Phase

Vasocongestion during the **excitement phase** can cause erection in young men within a few seconds after sexual stimulation begins. The scrotal skin thickens, becoming less baggy. The testes increase in size and become elevated.

activating effect
the arousal-producing effects of sex hormones that increase the likelihood of sexual behaviour

estrus
the periodic sexual excitement of many female mammals, as governed by levels of sex hormones

organizing effect
the directional effect of sex hormones—for example, along stereotypically masculine or feminine lines

sexual response cycle
Masters and Johnson's model of sexual response, which consists of four stages or phases

vasocongestion
engorgement of blood vessels with blood, which swells the genitals and breasts during sexual arousal

myotonia
muscle tension

excitement phase
the first phase of the sexual response cycle, which is characterized by muscle tension, increases in the heart rate, and erection in the male and vaginal lubrication in the female

clitoris
the female sex organ that is most sensitive to sexual sensation; a smooth, round knob of tissue that is situated above the urethral opening

plateau phase
the second phase of the sexual response cycle, which is characterized by increases in vasocongestion, muscle tension, heart rate, and blood pressure in preparation for orgasm

ejaculation
propulsion of seminal fluid (semen) from the penis by contraction of muscles at the base of the penis

orgasm
the height or climax of sexual excitement, involving involuntary muscle contractions, release of sexual tensions, and, usually, subjective feelings of pleasure

resolution phase
the fourth phase of the sexual response cycle, during which the body gradually returns to its pre-aroused state

refractory period
in the sexual response cycle, a period of time following orgasm during which an individual is not responsive to sexual stimulation

For women, excitement is characterized by vaginal lubrication, which may start 10 to 30 seconds after sexual stimulation begins. Vasocongestion swells the **clitoris** and flattens and spreads the vaginal lips. The inner part of the vagina expands. The breasts enlarge, and blood vessels near the surface become more prominent. The nipples may become erect in both men and women. Heart rate and blood pressure increase.

Plateau Phase

The level of sexual arousal remains somewhat stable during the **plateau phase**. Because of vasocongestion, the circumference of the head of the penis increases somewhat. The testes are elevated into position for **ejaculation** and may reach one and a half times their unaroused size.

In women, vasocongestion swells the outer part of the vagina, contracting the vaginal opening in preparation for grasping the penis. The inner part of the vagina expands further. The clitoris withdraws beneath the clitoral hood and shortens.

Breathing becomes rapid, like panting. Heart rate may increase to 100 to 160 beats per minute. Blood pressure continues to rise.

Orgasmic Phase

During **orgasm** for men, muscle contractions propel semen from the body. Sensations of pleasure tend to be related to the strength of the contractions and the amount of seminal fluid. The first three to four contractions are generally most intense and occur at 0.8-second intervals (five contractions every four

© Walter Lockwood/Workbook Stock/Getty Images

seconds). Additional contractions are slower.

An orgasm for women is manifested by 3 to 15 contractions of the pelvic muscles that surround the vaginal barrel. The contractions first occur at 0.8-second intervals. Weaker and slower contractions follow.

Blood pressure and heart rate reach a peak, with the heart beating up to 180 times per minute. Respiration may increase to 40 breaths per minute.

Resolution Phase

In the **resolution phase**, after orgasm, the body returns to its unaroused state. Erection and clitoral swelling subside. Blood pressure, heart rate, and breathing return to normal levels.

Unlike women, men enter a **refractory period** during which they cannot experience another orgasm or ejaculate. The refractory period of adolescent males may last only minutes, whereas that of men age 50 and above may last from several hours to a day. Women do not undergo a refractory period and therefore can become quickly re-aroused to the point of repeated (multiple) orgasm if they desire and receive continued sexual stimulation.

The sexual response cycle describes what happens when women and men are exposed to sexual stimulation. But what kinds of sexual experiences do people seek? How many sex partners do they have? Who are their partners? *What do we know about the sex lives of people in Canada?*

Surveys of Sexual Behaviour

The well-known Kinsey reports (Kinsey et al., 1948, 1953) interviewed 5300 males and 5940 females in the United States between 1938 and 1949. Interviewers asked about sexual experiences including masturbation, oral sex, and premarital sex. Americans were astounded to learn that most males masturbated and had had sexual intercourse prior to marriage. Moreover, significant minorities of females reported these behaviours. But Kinsey had not obtained a random sample of the population. His samples underrepresented people of colour, people in rural areas, older people, poor people, Catholics, and Jews. There is thus no way of knowing whether or not Kinsey's results accurately mirrored general

American sexual behaviour at the time. But the *relationships* Kinsey uncovered, such as the positive link between level of education and premarital sex, may be accurate enough.

A recent government-sponsored study on Canadian youth tells an interesting story about how sexually active teens are in Canada. One in five grade 9 students report having had sex at least once (38 percent of those reporting frequent sexual activity), and that number increases to two in five for grade 11 students (with 55 percent of those reporting frequent sexual activity) (Boyce et al., 2003). Consistent with data from adults (see Laumann et al., 1994), Canadian teenage boys report having a greater number of sex partners compared to teenage girls (see Table 9.2).

Even though the numbers of sexually active youth are significantly higher than ever before, the majority of Canadian high school teens are still choosing not to have sex. Reasons given for not having sex by grade 9 students include not feeling ready (29 percent and 40 percent for boys and girls, respectively), not having met the right person (23 percent and 20 percent), and wanting to be a virgin until marriage (5 percent and 11 percent). Personal religious adherence also acts as a restraint. Adolescents who reported that their religious faith was an important part of their lives showed a delayed onset of sexual activity (Burdette & Hill, 2009).

Sexual Orientation

The great majority of people have a **heterosexual** orientation; they are sexually attracted to, and interested in forming romantic relationships with, people of the other sex. Some people, however, have a **homosexual** orientation; they are attracted to and interested in forming romantic relationships with people of their own sex. Men with a homosexual orientation are referred to as *gay men*. Homosexual women are referred to as *lesbians*. *Bisexual* people are attracted to both women and men.

The *Canadian Community Health Survey*, conducted by Statistics Canada, found that 1.3 percent of men and 0.7 percent of women in Canada identify themselves as homosexual. The survey also revealed that 0.6 percent of men report a bisexual sexual orientation, whereas 0.9 percent of women do (*The Daily*, 2004). One should be aware that the percentages may be slightly higher, as on average 2 percent of survey respondents do not answer questions about sexual orientation, and same-sex sexual behaviour often is reported at higher numbers compared to sexual identity (how a person perceives himself or herself).

Theories of the origins of sexual orientation look both at nature and nurture—the biological makeup of the individual and environmental influences. Several theories bridge the two. *What do we know about the origins of gay men's and lesbians' sexual orientations?*

heterosexual referring to people who are sexually aroused by, and interested in forming romantic relationships with, people of the other sex

homosexual referring to people who are sexually aroused by, and interested in forming romantic relationships with, people of the same sex (derived from the Greek *homos*, meaning "same," not from the Latin *homo*, meaning "man")

sexual orientation the directionality of one's sexual and romantic interests; that is, whether one is sexually attracted to, and desires to form a romantic relationship with, members of the other sex or of one's own sex

TABLE 9.2

Number of Sex Partners as Found in the Canadian Youth, Sexual Health and HIV/AIDS Study

	Number of Sex Partners (%)					
	0	1	2	3	4–10	11 +
Grade 9						
Boys	77	10	4	3	5	2
Girls	81	10	4	3	3	0
Grade 11						
Boys	60	17	8	4	9	2
Girls	54	25	8	5	6	1

Boyd, W., Doherty, M., Fortin, C., & MacKinnon, D. (2003). *Canadian youth, sexual health and HIV/AIDS study: Factors influencing knowledge, attitudes and behaviours.* Council of Ministers, Canada, and authors' calculations.

CHAPTER 9 Motivation and Emotion **203**

One theory that ties the influence of nature and nurture together is the exotic becomes erotic theory of Daryl Bem (2000). Bem's theory is based on observations that many adults who report nonheterosexual sexual orientations also reported nonconforming gender-stereotypical behaviour while growing up. Bem suggests that when one starts developing sexually, one looks to people who are different from oneself, and finds these individuals arousing. Thus, it is an interaction of predisposing temperament (nature) with the environment (nurture) that ultimately influences which gender one is attracted to. Another line of research that has suggested the importance of environment is the examination of the concordance (agreement) rates of sexual orientation for adoptive children with their siblings. Adoptive siblings share zero genetic similarity to their adoptive brothers and sisters, yet an 11 percent (for gay men) and 6 percent (for lesbians) concordance rate of sexual orientation. This rate is higher than the incidence rate for the general population, suggesting some environmental factors for sexual orientation (Bailey & Pillard, 1991, Bailey & Benishay, 1993).

There is also evidence for genetic factors in sexual orientation (Dawood et al., 2000). One study suggesting a genetic factor in sexual orientation found that 21 percent of those reporting a nonheterosexual orientation had a sibling who was also gay, lesbian, or bisexual (Kendler et al., 2000c). The study also reported that about 32 percent of identical (MZ) twin pairs are concordant for a nonheterosexual sexual orientation, as compared with 13 percent for fraternal (DZ) twins (Kendler et al., 2000c).

In many species, there is little room for thinking about sex and deciding whether an individual will pursue sexual relationships with males or females. Sexual motivation comes under the governance of sex hormones (Hill et al., 2005; Holmes et al., 2005). And much sexual motivation is determined by whether the brains and sex organs of fetuses are bathed in large doses of testosterone in the uterus. In male fetuses, testosterone is normally produced by the developing testes. Yet female fetuses are exposed to testosterone when they share the uterus with many male siblings. Researchers have also injected male sex hormones into the uteruses of rodents. When they do, the sex organs of females become masculinized in appearance, and they show a tendency toward masculine-typed behaviour patterns at maturity, including mating with other females (Crews, 1994).

It has been shown, then, that sex hormones predispose nonhumans to stereotypical masculine or feminine mating patterns. Do sex hormones influence the developing human embryo and fetus as they affect rodents? We're not sure, but it is possible that the brains of some gay males were feminized in utero and that the brains of some lesbians were masculinized in utero (Collaer & Hines, 1995). Canadian researcher Tony Bogaert at Brock University in Ontario found some data that lends further support to this possibility. Bogaert discovered that the number of fraternal (but not adopted) older male siblings a man has is directly related to an increase in the likelihood that he will have a same-sex sexual orientation (2006). What this finding suggests is that a mother's uterus may change with each boy she has, and thus the prenatal environment is fundamentally different for each subsequent boy (she may transfer increasingly more antibodies that attack male-specific proteins through the placenta). However, the fraternal birth order effect on sexual orientation is not without its critics (see Bearman & Bruckner, 2002), and we will have to see if future research supports this new theory. It is also worth noting that this effect has been found only for gay men, and not for lesbians.

LO5 Achievement Motivation

Many students persist in studying despite being surrounded by distractions. Many people strive relentlessly to get ahead, to "make it," to earn large sums of money, to be an Olympic medal winner, to invent, or to accomplish the impossible. *Why do some people strive to get ahead?* Psychological research suggests that these people have *achievement motivation* (Robbins et al., 2005).

Psychologist David McClelland (1958) helped pioneer the assessment of achievement motivation through evaluation of fantasies. One method involves the Thematic Apperception Test (TAT), developed by Henry Murray. The TAT contains cards with pictures and drawings that are subject to various interpretations (see the Try It! box). Individuals are shown one or more TAT cards and asked to construct stories about the pictured theme: to indicate what led up to it, what the characters are thinking and feeling, and what is likely to happen.

McClelland (1965) used the types of answers given on the TAT to sort college students into groups—students with high achievement motivation and students with low achievement motivation. He found that 83 percent of college graduates with high achievement motivation found jobs in occupations characterized by risk, decision making, and the chance for great success, such as business management, sales, or self-employment. Most (70 percent) of the graduates who chose non-entrepreneurial positions showed low achievement motivation. People with high achievement motivation seem to prefer challenges and are willing to take moderate risks to achieve their goals.

Extrinsic versus Intrinsic Motives

At the outset of the chapter we explored possible reasons why a person may strive to win an Olympic medal. Carol Dweck (e.g., Molden & Dweck, 2000) finds that achievement motivation can be driven by performance goals, or learning goals, or both. For example, is a downhill skier motivated mainly by performance goals, such as his or her world standing and competition results? If so, it may be in part because his or her motives concern tangible rewards such as getting corporate sponsorship, international recognition, reaping approval from friends and family or his or her coach, or avoiding public criticism. Performance goals are usually met through extrinsic rewards such as praise, awards, and income. Research suggests that tangible rewards, such as money, can serve as an incentive for maintaining good grades. Growing up I (S.V.) remember the excitement of report-card day as my parents paid my siblings and me a dollar for each A and 50 cents for each B we earned. Rewards tend to have a more lasting effect, however, when students look upon incentives as signs that they are intelligent and capable (Spencer et al., 2005).

Or is it learning goals that mainly motivate athletes to do well? That is, is the athlete's central motive the enhancing of his or her knowledge and skills—his or her ability to understand and master the sport of choice? Learning goals usually lead to intrinsic rewards, such as self-satisfaction. Students

Try It!

One TAT card is similar to the image shown below. The meaning of the card is ambiguous—unclear. Is the girl sleeping, thinking about the book, wishing she were out with friends? Before you continue reading, try to tell a short story about what is happening in this picture. Describe who the person is, what she is doing, why she is doing it, and how she feels about it.

Now, after you have told your story, consider two other stories that could be told about this card:

- *Story 1:* "She's upset that she's got to read the book because she's behind in her assignments and doesn't particularly like to work. She'd much rather be out with her friends, and she may very well sneak out to do just that."

- *Story 2:* "She's thinking, 'Someday I'll be a great scholar. I'll write books like this, and everybody will be proud of me.' She reads all the time."

Which of the two stories is yours more similar to? The second story suggests the presence of more achievement motivation than the first. Classic studies find that people with high achievement motivation earn higher grades than people with comparable learning ability but lower achievement motivation. They are more likely to earn high salaries and be promoted than less motivated people with similar opportunities (Aronoff & Litevin, 1971; Orpen, 1995).

who develop learning goals often have parents with strong achievement motivation who encourage their children to think and act independently. Parents and teachers help children develop learning goals by showing warmth and praising them for their efforts to learn, exposing them to novel and stimulating experiences, and encouraging persistence (Dweck, 2002a). Children who are stimulated in this way tend to set high standards for themselves, associate their achievements with self-worth, and attribute their achievements to their own efforts rather than to chance or to the intervention of others (Dweck, 2002b; Marshall & Brown, 2004).

Olympic athletes, as well as many of us, strive to meet both performance and learning goals in the sports we participate in, our coursework, and in other areas of life. Awards, medals, and grades are important because they are connected with tangible benefits, but learning and performing for their own sake are also of value and can provide great pleasure.

LO6 Emotion

Emotions colour our lives. We are green with envy, red with anger, blue with sorrow. Positive emotions such as love and desire can fill our days with pleasure. Negative emotions such as fear, depression, and anger can fill us with dread and make each day a chore. **Just what is an emotion?**

First, emotion can be a reaction to a situation. We may experience fear as a response to a threat. Second, emotion can motivate behaviour, as anger can motivate us to act aggressively. Third, emotion can also be a goal in itself. We may behave in ways that will lead us to experience happiness or love. In these three ways emotions are intertwined with motivation. We are driven by emotions and meeting—or failing to meet—our needs can have powerful emotional results.

Emotions are defined as feeling states with physiological, cognitive, and behavioural components (Carlson & Hatfield, 1992). Strong emotions arouse the autonomic nervous system (Gomez et al., 2005; see Chapter 2). It is also the case that the greater the physiological arousal, the more intense the experienced emotion. It also appears that the type of arousal affects the emotion being experienced. Although the word *emotion* might seem to be about feeling and not about thinking, cognitions—particularly interpretations of the meanings of events—are important aspects of emotions. *Fear*, which usually occurs in response to a threat, involves cognitions that one is in danger as well as arousal of the **sympathetic nervous system** (e.g., rapid heartbeat and breathing, sweating, muscle tension). Emotions also involve behavioural tendencies. Fear is connected with behavioural tendencies to avoid or escape a situation (see Table 9.3). As a response to a social provocation, *anger* involves cognitions that the provocateur should be paid back, arousal of both the sympathetic and **parasympathetic nervous systems**, and tendencies to attack. *Depression* usually involves cognitions of helplessness and hopelessness, parasympathetic arousal, and tendencies toward inactivity—or, sometimes, self-destruction. *Happiness, grief, jealousy, disgust, embarrassment, liking*—all have cognitive, physiological, and behavioural components.

The Expression of Emotions

Happiness and sadness are found in all cultures, but **how can we tell when other people are happy or sad?** It turns out that the expression of many emotions may be universal (Ekman, 2003). Smiling is apparently a universal sign of friendliness and approval. Baring the teeth, as noted by Charles Darwin (1872) in the 19th century, may be a universal sign of anger. As the originator of the theory of evolution, Darwin believed that the universal recognition of facial expressions would have survival value. In the absence of language, facial expressions could signal the approach of enemies (or friends).

Most investigators (e.g., Ekman, 2003; Izard, 1994) concur that certain facial expressions suggest the same emotions in all people. Moreover, people in diverse cultures recognize the emotions indicated by certain facial expressions. Paul Ekman (1999) describes his classic research in which he took photographs of people exhibiting anger, disgust, fear, happiness, sadness, and surprise (see Figure 9.3). He then asked people

TABLE 9.3

Components of Emotions

Emotion	Physiological	Cognitive	Behavioural
Fear	Sympathetic arousal	Belief that one is in danger	Avoidance tendencies
Anger	Sympathetic and parasympathetic arousal	Frustration or belief that one is being mistreated	Attack tendencies
Depression	Parasympathetic arousal	Thoughts of helplessness, hopelessness, worthlessness	Inactivity, possible self-destructive tendencies

FIGURE 9.4

Theories of Emotion

Go to www.icanpsych.com to access an interactive version of this figure.

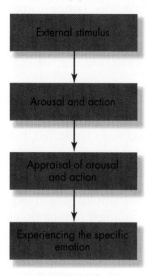

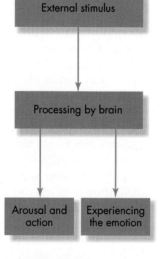

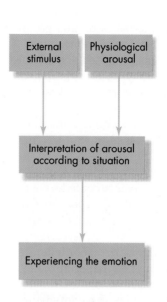

A. James–Lange

Events trigger specific arousal patterns and actions. Emotions result from our appraisal of our body responses.

B. Cannon–Bard

Events are first processed by the brain. Body patterns of arousal, action, and our emotional responses are then triggered simultaneously.

C. Cognitive appraisal

Events and arousal are appraised by the individual. The emotional response stems from the person's appraisal of the situation and his or her level of arousal.

sadness (Ekman, 1993). The theory also suggests that we may be able to change our feelings by changing our behaviour. Changing one's behaviour to change one's feelings is one aspect of behaviour therapy. When David's psychologist urges him to get out and do things, she is assuming that by changing his behaviour, David can have a positive effect on the way he feels.

Walter Cannon (1927) criticized the James–Lange assertion that each emotion has distinct physiological correlates. For example, he argued that the physiological arousal associated with fear is not as distinct from the arousal associated with anger as the theory asserts.

The Cannon–Bard Theory

Walter Cannon (1927) and Philip Bard (1934) suggested that an event might *simultaneously* trigger bodily responses (arousal and action) and the experience of an emotion. As shown in Figure 9.4 (part B), when an event is perceived (processed by the brain), the brain stimulates autonomic and muscular activity (arousal and action) *and* cognitive activity (experience of the emotion). Thus, according to the Cannon–Bard theory, emotions *accompany* bodily responses. They are not *produced by* bodily changes,

as in the James–Lange theory.

The central criticism of the Cannon–Bard theory focuses on whether bodily responses (arousal and action) and emotions are in fact stimulated simultaneously. For example, pain or the perception of danger may trigger arousal before we begin to feel distress or fear. Also, many of us have had the experience of having a "narrow escape" and becoming aroused and shaky afterward, when we have had time to consider the damage that might have occurred. What is needed is a theory that allows for an ongoing interaction of external events, physiological changes (such as autonomic arousal and muscular activity), and cognitive activities.

The Theory of Cognitive Appraisal

More recent theoretical approaches to emotion stress cognitive factors. Among those who argue that thinking comes first are Gordon Bower, Richard Lazarus, Stanley Schachter, Jerome Singer, and Robert Zajonc.

Schachter asserts that emotions are associated with similar patterns of bodily arousal that vary in strength, but that the way we label an emotion depends largely on our appraisal of the situation. Cognitive appraisal is based on many factors, including our perception of events and the ways other people respond to those events (see Figure 9.4, part C). When other people are present, we engage in social comparison to arrive at a response.

In a classic experiment, Schachter and Singer (1962) showed that arousal can be labelled quite differently, depending on the situation. The investigators told participants they wanted to determine the effects of a vitamin on vision. Half the participants received an injection of adrenaline, a hormone that stimulates the sympathetic branch of the autonomic nervous system. A control group received an injection of a placebo. Those who had been given adrenaline received one of three "cognitive manipulations." Group 1 was told nothing about possible emotional effects of the "vitamin." Group 2 was deliberately misinformed; members of this group were led to expect itching, numbness, or other irrelevant symptoms. Group 3 was informed accurately about the increased arousal they would experience. Group 4 was a control group injected with a placebo and given no information about its effects.

After receiving injections and cognitive manipulations, the participants were asked to wait in pairs while the experimental apparatus was being set up. The participants did not know that the person with whom they were waiting was a confederate of the experimenter. The confederate's purpose was to respond in a way that the participant would believe was caused by the injection.

Some participants waited with a confederate who acted happy-go-lucky. He flew paper airplanes about the room and tossed paper balls into a wastebasket. Other participants waited with a confederate who acted angry. He complained about the experiment, tore up a questionnaire, and stormed out of the room. As the confederates worked for their Oscar awards, the real participants were observed through a one-way mirror.

The people in groups 1 and 2 were likely to imitate the behaviour of the confederate. Those who were exposed to the happy-go-lucky confederate acted jovial and content. Those who were exposed to the angry confederate imitated that person's complaining, aggressive behaviour. But those in groups 3 and 4 were less influenced by the confederate's behaviour.

Schachter and Singer concluded that participants in groups 1 and 2 were in an ambiguous situation. Members of these groups felt arousal from the adrenaline injection but couldn't label it as a specific emotion. Social comparison with a confederate led them to attribute their arousal either to happiness or to anger. Members of group 3 expected arousal from the injection, but no particular emotional consequences. These participants did not imitate the confederate's display of happiness or anger because they were not in an ambiguous situation; they knew their arousal was caused by adrenaline. Members of group 4 had no arousal for which they needed an attribution, except perhaps for some arousal induced by observing the confederate. Nor did they imitate the behaviour of the confederate.

Now, happiness and anger are very different emotions. Yet Schachter and Singer suggest that the bodily differences between these two emotions are slight enough that different views of the situation can lead one person to label arousal as happiness and another person to label it as anger. The Schachter–Singer view could not be further removed from the James–Lange theory, which holds that each emotion is associated with specific and readily recognized body sensations. The truth, it happens, may lie somewhere in between.

In science, it must be possible to replicate experiments and attain identical or similar results; otherwise, a theory cannot be considered valid. The Schachter and Singer study has been replicated, but with *different* results (Ekman, 1993). For example, some studies found that participants were less likely to imitate the behaviour of the confederate and were likely to perceive unexplained arousal negatively, attributing it to nervousness or anger (Zimbardo et al., 1993).

The connections between arousal and emotions have led to the development of many kinds of lie detection, as we see in the following section.

The Polygraph: Just What Do Lie Detectors Detect?

Lying—for better or worse—is a part of life. A *New York Times* poll found that three out of five people believe that it is sometimes necessary to lie, especially to protect people's feelings (Smiley, 2000). Political leaders lie to get elected. Many people lie to get dates or initiate sexual relations—for example, about other relationships, making professions of love, or in the case of the Internet, about one's appearance or age (Suler, 2005). Canadian research even suggests that toddlers who lie will do

Image Source Black/Jupiterimages

better in life, as lying at an early age is a marker for later intelligence (Talwar & Lee, 2008). People also lie about their qualifications to get jobs, and, of course, some people lie in denying guilt for crimes. Although we are unlikely to subject political leaders and lovers to lie detector tests, such tests are frequently used in hiring and in criminal investigations.

Facial expressions often offer clues to deceit, but some people can lie with a straight face—or a smile. As Shakespeare pointed out in *Hamlet*, "One may smile, and smile, and be a villain." The use of devices to detect lies has a long, if not laudable, history:

> The Bedouins of Arabia … until quite recently required conflicting witnesses to lick a hot iron; the one whose tongue was burned was thought to be lying. The Chinese, it is said, had a similar method for detecting lying: Suspects were forced to chew rice powder and spit it out; if the powder was dry, the suspect was guilty (Kleinmuntz & Szucko, 1984, pp. 766–767).

These methods may sound primitive, even bizarre, but they are broadly consistent with modern psychological knowledge. Anxiety about being caught in a lie is linked to arousal of the sympathetic division of the autonomic nervous system. One sign of sympathetic arousal is lack of saliva, or dryness in the mouth. The emotions of fear and guilt are also linked to sympathetic arousal and, hence, to dryness in the mouth (and perhaps a burnt tongue).

How do lie detectors work? How reliable are they? Modern polygraphs monitor indicators of sympathetic arousal during an interrogation: heart rate, blood pressure, respiration rate, and electrodermal response (sweating). But questions have been raised about the validity of assessing truth or fiction by means of polygraphs (Branaman & Gallagher, 2005).

The American Polygraph Association claims that use of the polygraph is 85 percent to 95 percent accurate. Critics find polygraph testing to be less accurate and claim that it is sensitive to more than lies (Saxe & Ben-Shakhar, 1999). Tense muscles, drugs, and previous experience with polygraph tests can significantly reduce their accuracy rate. In one experiment, people were able to reduce the accu-

racy of polygraph-based judgments to about 50 percent by biting their tongue (to produce pain) or pressing their toes against the floor (to tense muscles) while being interrogated (Honts et al., 1985). You might thus give the examiner the impression that you are lying even when you are telling the truth, throwing off the test's results.

Iacono and Lykken (1997) conducted a mail survey of members of the Society for Psychophysiological Research and the General Psychology division of the American Psychological Association. Response rates were high—91 percent and 74 percent, respectively. Most respondents replied that polygraph lie detection was not theoretically sound, that claims for its validity were overstated, that people can easily learn to beat the test, and that polygraph results should not be admitted as evidence in courts of law.

It appears that no specific pattern of bodily responses pinpoints lying (*Nature* editorial, 2004). Because of validity problems, since 1987 the results of polygraph examinations are no longer admitted as evidence in Canadian courts (*R. v. Beland*, 1987), but they are still used as an investigation technique by police. The lure of technology to determine lying remains strong. Research is underway in the development of techniques that measure brain waves, heat patterns in the face, and other biological events (*Nature* editorial, 2004).

Evaluation

What can we make of all this? First of all, stronger emotions are connected with higher levels of arousal (Gomez et al., 2005), but research by Paul Ekman (1993) suggests that the patterns of arousal connected with various emotions are more specific than suggested by Schachter and Singer. They are, however, apparently less specific than suggested by James and Lange. Brain imaging suggests that different emotions, such as happiness and sadness, involve different structures within the brain (Goleman, 1995). Moreover, lack of control over our emotions and lack of understanding of what is happening to us are disturbing experiences (Zimbardo et al., 1993). Thus our cognitive appraisals of situations affect our emotional responses, even if not quite in the way envisioned by Schachter.

Keith Brofsky/Getty Images

In sum, various components of an experience—cognitive, physiological, and behavioural—contribute to our emotional responses. Our bodies may become aroused in a given situation, but as we saw in the classic research of Schachter and Singer, people also appraise those situations so that arousal alone does not appear to directly cause one emotion or another. The fact that none of the theories of emotion we have discussed applies to all people in all situations is comforting. Apparently our emotions are not quite as easily understood, manipulated, or—as in the case of the polygraph—even detected as some theorists have suggested.

Stress, Health, and Adjustment

Learning Outcomes

LO1 Define stress and identify various sources of stress

LO2 Describe the impact of stress on the body

LO3 Identify the psychological moderators of stress

LO4 Explain the relationships between psychology and health

Martin Barraud/Getty Images

"The adrenaline was rushing. It was like something from a movie. It was completely unbelievable and incredible."

CBC News Canada reported the following on September 14, 2006, following the Dawson College shooting in Montreal:

The gunman who went on a shooting rampage at a Montreal college Wednesday [September 13, 2006] apparently left an online journal with chilling comments and photos of himself brandishing a rifle. Kimveer Gill was the author of an online diary posted at the website vampirefreaks.com. One woman was shot to death and 19 people were injured, at least six of them critically, in the rampage that followed. Montreal police said the victims ranged in age from 17 to 48. Eyewitnesses say they saw a tall, Goth-looking man in a long black coat drive up near the college on Maisonneuve Street in a black Pontiac Sunfire at around 12:30 p.m. He got out of his car, opened the trunk and removed a rifle. [He] then walked toward the college's southwest entrance. Witnesses said they saw him shoot at least one person outside before entering the building. Police said the first gunshots were heard at 12:41 p.m. It was lunchtime and the school was packed when the gunman entered through the main doors and headed to the cafeteria. "He was shooting randomly," said Dawson student Michel Boyer, who witnessed the gunfire. "I'm not sure who he was shooting at, but the [cafeteria] atrium was completely cleared." Chaos ensued, said Boyer. "The adrenaline was rushing. It was like something from a movie. It was completely unbelievable and incredible." Officers with guns drawn rushed into the building, at which point witnesses reported hearing more shots fired. Montreal police confirmed that the officers exchanged gunfire with the suspect, and that the suspect was hit by at least one officer. Police said the gunman died during the shootout. Preliminary autopsy results released [the following day] showed Gill died of a self-inflicted wound, Quebec police said.

© CBC News; Reprinted by permission of The Canadian Press.

DID YOU KNOW?

- Some stress, called *eustress*, is good for us.
- Vacations can be stressful.
- Daily hassles, such as traffic jams or annoying professors, can be more stressful than major life events, such as divorce or loss of a job.
- People with Type A behaviours are more prone to stress than people with Type B behaviours, and they are less satisfied with themselves.
- Humour helps us cope with stress.
- One in four workers in Canada reports experiencing workplace stress.
- Despite warnings about the risks associated with unprotected sex, 44 percent of adults aged 20 to 24 continue to engage in unsafe sex.

It is not surprising that a traumatic event like the shooting at Dawson College was a stressful experience for those who witnessed the brutal shooting of students, professors, and staff, and for the families of those injured and killed in the early afternoon of September 13, 2006. This traumatic event has similarities to other catastrophic events, such as Hurricane Katrina in 2005 and the 2010 earthquake in Haiti.

The Canadian Press/Ryan Remiorz

stress
the physical and psychological response of the body to any demand that is made on an organism that requires it to adapt, cope, or adjust

**eustress
(YOU-stress)**
stress that is pleasant, desirable, healthful

In all of these traumatic events, *unpredictability, devastation,* and *unexpected loss* were experienced. Even years later, many who survived or witnessed such horrific events continue to be traumatized and may suffer serious stress disorders (Galea & Resnick, 2005).

This chapter will discuss issues related to health and stress. We will look at the effects of stress in our lives, both physically and psychologically, and how we cope with stress.

LO1 Stress: What It Is, Where It Comes From

What is stress? In physics, stress is defined as a pressure or force exerted on a body. Tonnes of rock pressing on the earth, one car smashing into another, a rubber band stretching—all are types of physical stress. Psychological forces, or stresses, also press, push, or pull. We may feel "crushed" by the weight of a big decision, "smashed" by adversity, or "stretched" to the point of snapping. In the case of the victims of the shooting in Montreal, Hurricane Katrina, or the Haitian earthquake, physical events had psychological as well as physical consequences. As we will see throughout the chapter, those psychological consequences of stress can also affect our health.

Psychologists define **stress** as the responses of the body to any demand made on it. This demand requires us to adapt, cope, or adjust to it. Some stress is positive and necessary to keep us alert and occupied. Stress researcher Hans Selye (1980) referred to such healthful stress as **eustress**. We may experience eustress when we begin a sought-after job or are trying to choose the colour of an iPod. But intense or prolonged stress, such as that caused by catastrophic events like the Montreal shooting, Hurricane Katrina, or social or financial problems, can affect our moods, impair our ability

to experience pleasure, and harm the body (Kiecolt-Glaser et al., 2002a, 2002b; Schneiderman et al., 2005).

Daily Hassles and Life Changes

What are daily hassles? Daily hassles are the irritating, frustrating, and annoying stresses of everyday life, which can pile up until we can no longer deal with them. Lazarus and his colleagues (1985) analyzed a scale that measures daily hassles (created by Kanner et al., 1981; called the Hassles Scale). They found that daily hassles significantly impact our psychological and physical health and can add up to more stress than major life changes. Pett and Johnson (2005) identified 11 categories of hassles most common to university students (see Table 10.1).

What are life changes? Life changes differ from daily hassles in two ways:

- Many life changes are positive, whereas all hassles are negative.
- Hassles occur regularly, whereas life changes occur at irregular intervals.

Peggy Blake and her colleagues (1984) constructed a scale of "life-change units" to measure the impact

TABLE 10.1

Most Common Hassles for University Students, by Category

Category	Most Common Hassle Reported
Time constraints	Too many things to do, too many responsibilities
Financial constraints	Not enough money for school expenses (e.g., housing)
Race/ethnicity	Being treated differently because of race/ethnicity
Gender	Not being taken seriously or being treated differently based on gender
Friendships	Being lonely, and not having close friends
Traffic	Driving to school (e.g., parking problems)
Religion	Closed-mindedness due to religious beliefs
Safety	Safety of personal belongings
Employment	Problems on the job (e.g., satisfaction and scheduling)
Physical appearance	Weight concerns
Parental expectations	Parental demands, lack of independence

Pett, M.A., and Johnson, M.J.M. (2005). Development and psychometric evaluation of the revised university student hassle scale. *Education and Psychological Measurement, 65*(6): 984–1010, copyright © 2005 by SAGE Publications. Reprinted by permission of SAGE Publications.

of life changes among college students. Surveys with students revealed that death of a spouse or parent were considered the most stressful life changes (94 and 88 life-change units, respectively). Academic failure (77 units) and graduation from college (68 units) were also considered highly stressful, even though graduation from college is a positive event—considering the alternative. Positive life changes such as an outstanding personal achievement (49 units) and going on vacation (30 units) also made the list.

Still, research on college students and stress report that the majority of stress placed on students is from daily hassles rather than major life events (Kanner et al, 1981). In fact, Ross, Niebling & Heckert (1999) found that 81 percent of college student stress is related to daily hassles, such as interpersonal and intrapersonal and academic sources of stress. Hassles, such as lack of

money and not enough time, were related to anxiety and depression for some students, and they led to lower grades (Carleton University Study, 2001).

stressor
any event that causes stress, physical and/or psychological

Hassles, Life Changes, and Health Problems

Daily hassles and life changes—especially negative life changes—can cause us to worry and affect our moods (Lavee & Ben-Ari, 2003). **Stressors** such as hassles and negative life changes also predict physical health problems such as heart disease and athletic injuries (Schneiderman et al., 2005). Similar to Renner and Mackin's (1998) College Undergraduate Stress Scale (see Table 10.2), Holmes and Rahe (1967) found

TABLE 10.2

College Life Stress Inventory

Circle the "stress rating" number for any event item that has happened to you in the last year, and then add them up. Scores of 300 or higher indicate relatively high stress and major health risks; scores between 150 and 299 indicate moderate stress and chance of health problems within the next two years; scores less than 150 indicate low stress and less chance of health problems.

Event	Stress Rating	Event	Stress Rating
Being raped	100	Talking in front of a class	72
Finding out that you are HIV-positive	100	Lack of sleep	69
Being accused of rape	98	Change in housing situation (hassles, moves)	69
Death of a close friend	97	Competing or performing in public	69
Death of a close family member	96	Getting in a physical fight	66
Contracting a sexually transmitted infection (other than AIDS)	94	Difficulties with a roommate	66
Concerns about being pregnant	91	Job changes (applying, new job, work hassles)	65
Final exams	90	Declaring a major or concerns about future plans	65
Concerns about your partner being pregnant	90	A class you hate	62
Oversleeping for an exam	89	Drinking or use of drugs	61
Flunking a class	89	Confrontations with professors	60
Having a boyfriend or girlfriend cheat on you	85	Starting a new semester	58
Ending a steady dating relationship	85	Going on a first date	57
Serious illness in a close friend or family member	85	Registration	55
Financial difficulties	84	Maintaining a steady dating relationship	55
Writing a major term paper	83	Commuting to campus or work, or both	54
Being caught cheating on a test	83	Peer pressures	53
Drunk driving	82	Being away from home for the first time	53
Sense of overload in school or work	82	Getting sick	52
Two exams in one day	80	Concerns about your appearance	52
Cheating on your boyfriend or girlfriend	77	Getting straight A's	51
Getting married	76	A difficult class that you love	48
Negative consequences of drinking or drug use	75	Making new friends; getting along with friends	47
Depression or crisis in your best friend	73	Fraternity or sorority rush	47
Difficulties with parents	73	Falling asleep in class	40
		Attending an athletic event (e.g., football game)	20

Renner, M.J., and Mackin, R.S. (1998). A life stress instrument for classroom use. *Teaching of Psychology, 25*(1): 46–48. Reprinted by permission of the publisher, Taylor & Francis Group, http://www.informaworld.com.

that people who "earned" 300 or more life-change units within a year, according to their Social Readjustment Rating Scale (SRRS), were at greater risk for major health problems. Eight of ten developed health problems, compared with only one of three people whose totals of life-change units for the year were below 150.

Stress in the Workplace

It may be a surprise to many people that stress in the workplace affects 25 percent of workers in Canada (Canadian Institute for Stress, 2005). **Workplace stress**—or job stress—refers to negative physical and emotional responses to a job, and it can lead to job dissatisfaction and an increase in absenteeism at work (Canadian Centre for Occupational Health & Safety, 2008). It is becoming a major health and safety issue, especially its connections to mood disorders such as anxiety and depression (see the box entitled "A Biological Link: Stress, Anxiety, and Depression"). As reported by the Canadian Mental Health Institute (2004), common workplace stressors include fear of job redundancy, fears about job security, increased demands for overtime, and pressure to perform. Also, poor interpersonal relationships at work and shift work are associated with increased stress (Canadian Centre for Occupational Health and Safety, 2008).

Conflicting Motives

Should you eat dessert or try to stick to your diet? Should you live on campus, which is more convenient, or should you rent an apartment, where you may have more independence?

Often, choices like these can become a source of stress because we may feel like

we are being pulled in two or more directions by opposing motives. Conflicting motives can be frustrating and stressful. Psychologists often classify these conflicts into four types: approach–approach, avoidance–avoidance, approach–avoidance, and multiple approach–avoidance.

Classic experimental research by Neal E. Miller (1944) and others suggests that the *approach–approach conflict* is the least stressful type of conflict. In approach–approach conflict, each conflicting choice is desirable. For example, you may need to decide between eating pizza or tacos, or choose between a trip to Tahiti or one to Hawaii. No matter which choice you make, it will be pleasant. Those who experience this type of conflict may waiver back and forth until they make a decision, as shown by people who put off decisions and reflect about conflicting choices (Emmons & King, 1988).

Avoidance–avoidance conflict is more stressful because you are motivated to avoid each of two negative choices. But avoiding one means approaching the other. For example, you may be fearful of visiting the dentist but also afraid that your teeth will decay if you do not make an appointment and go. Each potential outcome in an avoidance–avoidance conflict is undesirable. When an avoidance–avoidance conflict is highly stressful and no resolution is in sight, some people withdraw from the conflict by focusing on other matters or doing nothing.

In *approach–avoidance conflict,* making a choice produces pluses and minuses. For example, cheesecake may be delicious, but oh, the calories! Choices that produce mixed motives may seem more attractive from a distance but undesirable from up close (Miller, 1944). Many couples who repeatedly break up and reunite recall each other fondly when apart and swear that they could make the relationship work if they got together again. But after they do spend time together, they again wonder, "How could I ever have believed that this so-and-so would change?"

The most complex situation of conflicting motives is the *multiple approach–avoidance conflict,* in which each of several alternative courses of action has pluses and minuses. This conflict might arise on the eve of an examination, when you are faced with the choice of studying or, say, going to a movie. Each alternative has both positive and negative aspects: "Studying is boring, but if I stay home and study, I won't have to worry about failing the test. At the same time, I would love to see the movie, but I'd just be worrying about how I'll do tomorrow on the test."

Irrational Beliefs

Psychologist Albert Ellis noted that our beliefs about events, as well as the events themselves, can be stressors (Ellis, 2001, 2004a, 2004b). Consider a case in which a person is fired from a job and is anxious and depressed about it. It may seem logical that losing the job is responsible for the misery, but Ellis pointed out how the individual's beliefs about the loss compounded his or her misery (see Table 10.3).

How do irrational beliefs create or compound stress? Let us examine this situation according to Ellis's A → B → C approach: Losing the job is an *activating event* (A). The eventual outcome, or *consequence* (C), is misery. Between the activating event (A) and the consequence (C), however, lie *beliefs* (B), such as these: "This job was the most important thing in my life," "I am such a failure," "My family will starve," "I'll never find a job as good." Beliefs such as these compound misery, foster helplessness, and divert us from planning and deciding what to do next. The belief that "I am such a failure" internalizes the blame and may be an exaggeration. The belief that "My family will starve" may also be an exaggeration.

As you can see, the beliefs of the person who lost the job tend to **catastrophize** the extent of the loss and contribute to anxiety and depression—and thus raise the person's blood pressure (Dunkley et al., 2003; Melmed, 2003). By heightening the individual's emotional reaction to the loss and fostering feelings of helplessness, these beliefs also impair coping ability.

Ellis proposed that many of us carry the irrational beliefs shown in Table 10.4 (p. 222). They are our personal doorways to distress. In fact, they can give rise to problems in themselves. When problems assault us from other sources, these beliefs can magnify their effect, causing or increasing stress.

Personality Types

Some people create stress and health issues for themselves if they maintain a **Type A behaviour** pattern. *What is Type A behaviour?* Type A people tend to be highly driven, competitive, impatient, hostile, and aggressive—so much so that they have an increased risk of cardiovascular disease (Bunde & Suls, 2006). Type A personalities feel rushed and pressured. They eat, walk, and talk rapidly, find it difficult to surrender control or share power, and are preoccupied with responsibilities.

On the other hand, people who are characterized as being of **Type B behaviour** pattern relax more readily than Type A people and focus more on the quality of life. They are less ambitious and less impatient, and are laid back.

catastrophize
to interpret negative events as being disastrous; to "blow out of proportion"

Type A behaviour
behaviour characterized by a sense of time urgency, competitiveness, and hostility

Type B behaviour
behaviour characterized by a calm, patient and relaxed attitude

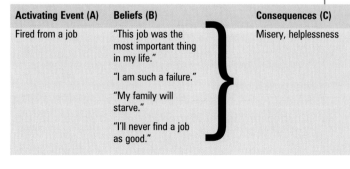

TABLE 10.3

Ellis's A → B → C Approach

Activating Event (A)	Beliefs (B)	Consequences (C)
Fired from a job	"This job was the most important thing in my life." "I am such a failure." "My family will starve." "I'll never find a job as good."	Misery, helplessness

general adaptation syndrome (GAS)
the predictable physical response to stressors that is explained in three stages: alarm, resistance, exhaustion

alarm reaction
the first stage of the GAS, which is triggered by the impact of a stressor and characterized by sympathetic activity in the body

fight-or-flight reaction
an innate adaptive response to the perception of danger

TABLE 10.4

Irrational Beliefs: Cognitive Doorways to Distress

Irrational Belief 1:	You must have sincere love and approval almost all the time from the people who are important to you.
Irrational Belief 2:	You must prove yourself to be thoroughly competent, adequate, and achieving at something important.
Irrational Belief 3:	Things must go the way you want them to go. Life is awful when you don't get your first choice in everything.
Irrational Belief 4:	Other people must treat everyone fairly and justly. When people act unfairly or unethically, they are rotten.
Irrational Belief 5:	When there is danger or fear in your world, you must be preoccupied with and upset by it.
Irrational Belief 6:	People and things should turn out better than they do. It's awful and horrible when you don't find quick solutions to life's hassles.
Irrational Belief 7:	Your emotional misery stems from external pressures that you have little or no ability to control. Unless these external pressures change, you must remain miserable.
Irrational Belief 8:	It is easier to evade life's responsibilities and problems than to face them and undertake more rewarding forms of self-discipline.
Irrational Belief 9:	Your past influenced you immensely and must therefore continue to determine your feelings and behaviour today.
Irrational Belief 10:	You can achieve happiness by inertia and inaction, or by just enjoying yourself from day to day.

Workbook Stock/Jupiterimages

LO2 Stress and the Body

Stress has very definite effects on the body that, as we will see, can lead to psychological and physical health problems. Stress researcher Hans Selye (1976) outlined a number of the bodily effects in his concept of the general adaptation syndrome (GAS).

The General Adaptation Syndrome

Hans Selye suggested that under stress the body is like a clock with an alarm that does not shut off until the clock shakes apart or its energy has been depleted. The body's response to different stressors shows certain similarities, whether the stressor is a bacterial invasion, perceived danger, or a major life change (Selye, 1976). Selye found that the physical response to a variety of stressors was so predictable that he labelled this response the **general adaptation syndrome (GAS)**. GAS occurs in three stages: an alarm reaction stage, a resistance stage, and an exhaustion stage. These changes mobilize the body for action and—like that alarm that goes on ringing—can eventually wear out the body.

The Alarm Reaction Stage

An **alarm reaction** is triggered by the perception of a stressor. This reaction mobilizes or arouses the body, biologically speaking. Early in the 20th century, physiologist Walter B. Cannon (1932) argued that this mobilization was the basis for an instinctive **fight-or-flight reaction**. The alarm reaction involves bodily changes that are initiated by the brain and regulated by the endocrine system and the sympathetic nervous system (SNS).

Stress has a domino effect on the endocrine system (Bauer et al., 2003; Melmed, 2003; see Figure 10.1). The hypothalamus secretes corticotrophin-releasing hormone (CRH). CRH causes the pituitary gland to secrete adrenocorticotrophic hormone (ACTH). ACTH then causes the adrenal cortex to secrete cortisol and other corticosteroids (steroidal hormones produced by the adrenal cortex). Corticosteroids help protect the body by combating allergic reactions (such as difficulty in breathing) and producing inflammation (Leonard, 2005). (However, corticosteroids can be harmful to the

{ **Hans Selye (1907–1982): Canadian Researcher, McGill University** }

Hans Selye, best known as the foremost stress researcher, began as a researcher at McGill University studying sex organs in rats. To his surprise, he found something odd about how they responded to hormones, thus leading to his discovery of predictable physical responses to stress. He was also the co-founder of the Canadian Institute of Stress in 1979, which offers programs, consultations, and tools on stress management for workplaces, educators, and individuals.

cardiovascular system, which is one reason that chronic stress can impair one's health and why athletes who use steroids to build the muscle mass can experience cardiovascular problems.) Inflammation increases circulation to parts of the body that are injured.

Two other hormones that play a major role in the alarm reaction are secreted by the adrenal medulla. The SNS activates the adrenal medulla, causing it to release a mixture of adrenaline and noradrenaline. This mixture arouses the body by accelerating the heart rate and causing the liver to release glucose (sugar). This provides the energy that fuels the fight-or-flight reaction, which activates the body so that it is prepared to fight or flee from a stressor.

For example, it may be aroused when you are caught in stop-and-go traffic or learn that your mortgage payments are going to increase. Once the threat is removed, the body returns to a lower state of arousal. Many of the bodily changes that occur in the alarm reaction are outlined in Table 10.5 (p. 224).

Many contemporary theorists do not believe that the fight-or-flight reaction is universal. Shelley Taylor and her colleagues (2000) report evidence that many women engage in a tend-and-befriend response to threats, rather than a fight-or-flight response. Margaret Kemeny and her colleagues (e.g., Updegraff et al., 2002) also observe that some people attempt to respond productively to stress by pulling back from the situation to better appraise it and conserve their resources while they are doing so. This response pattern to stress is described by two theories that are currently under development: cognitive adaptation theory and conservation of resources theory.

The Resistance Stage

According to Selye's theory, if the alarm reaction mobilizes the body and the stressor is not removed,

FIGURE 10.1

Stress and the Endocrine System

Stress has a domino effect on the endocrine system, leading to the release of corticosteroids and a mixture of adrenaline and noradrenaline. Corticosteroids combat allergic reactions (such as difficulty in breathing) and cause inflammation. Adrenaline and noradrenaline arouse the body to cope by accelerating the heart rate and providing energy for the fight-or-flight reaction.

Go to www.icanpsych.com to access an interactive version of this figure.

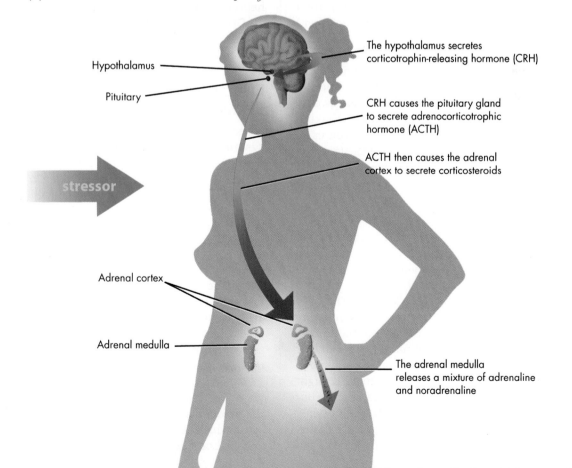

resistance stage
the second stage of the GAS, characterized by prolonged sympathetic activity in an effort to restore lost energy and repair damage; also called the *adaptation stage*

exhaustion stage
the third stage of the GAS, characterized by weakened resistance and possible deterioration of body functioning, possibly leading to disease

immune system
the system of the body that recognizes and destroys foreign agents (antigens) that invade the body

leukocytes
white blood cells, which act as a defence in the body against infectious diseases and other toxins

TABLE 10.5

Components of the Alarm Reaction*

Corticosteroids are secreted.
Adrenaline is secreted.
Noradrenaline is secreted.
Respiration rate increases.
Heart rate increases.
Blood pressure increases.
Muscles tense.
Blood shifts from internal organs to the skeletal musculature.
Digestion is inhibited.
Sugar is released from the liver.
Blood coagulability increases.

© Alex Gumerov/iStockphoto.com

*The alarm reaction is triggered by stressors. It is defined by the release of corticosteroids and adrenaline and by activity of the sympathetic branch of the autonomic nervous system.

we enter the adaptation or **resistance stage** of the GAS. Levels of endocrine and sympathetic activity are lower than in the alarm reaction but still higher than normal. (It's as if the alarm is still on, but a bit softer.) But make no mistake: The person feels tense, and the body remains under a heavy burden.

Consider how your body feels following your involvement in a minor fender-bender: Initially your body responds by becoming anxious—sweaty palms, heart rate increases, dry mouth, shaking (alarm reaction)—but after a short time, you calm down such that your heart may still beat fast, but you have adapted by not having sweaty palms or shaking (resistance).

The Exhaustion Stage

If the stressor is still not dealt with adequately, we may enter the **exhaustion stage** of the GAS. Individual capacities for resisting stress vary, but anyone will eventually become exhausted when stress continues indefinitely. The muscles become fatigued. The body is depleted of the resources required for combating stress. With exhaustion, the parasympathetic nervous system (PNS) may predominate. As a result, our heartbeat and respiration rate slow down, and many aspects of sympathetic activity are reversed. It might sound as if we would profit from the respite, but remember that we are still under stress—possibly an external threat. Continued stress in the exhaustion stage may lead to what Selye terms "diseases of

adaptation." These are connected with constriction of blood vessels and alternation of the heart rhythm, and can range from allergies to hives and coronary heart disease (CHD)—and, ultimately, death.

Discussion of the effects of stress on the immune system paves the way for understanding the links between psychological factors and physical illness.

Effects of Stress on the Immune System

Research shows that stress suppresses the **immune system**, as measured by the presence of various substances in the blood that make up the immune system (Antoni et al., 2005; Hawkley & Cacioppo, 2004). Psychological factors such as feelings of control and social support moderate these effects (Cohen et al., 2001a).

The Immune System

Given the complexity of the human body and the fast pace of scientific change, we often feel that we are dependent on trained professionals to cope with illness. Yet we actually do most of this coping by ourselves, by means of the immune system. *How does the immune system work?*

The immune system combats disease in several ways (Delves & Roitt, 2000; Leonard, 2005). One way is the production of white blood cells, known as **leukocytes**, which destroy pathogens such as bacteria, fungi, and viruses, and worn-out and cancerous body cells.

Leukocytes recognize foreign substances—or **antigens**—by their shapes. The body reacts to antigens by generating specialized proteins, or **antibodies**. Antibodies attach themselves to the antigens, deactivating them and marking them for destruction. The immune system "remembers" how to battle antigens by maintaining their antibodies in the bloodstream, often for years.[1]

Inflammation is another function of the immune system. When injury occurs, blood vessels in the area first contract (to stem bleeding) and then dilate. Dilation increases the flow of blood, cells, and natural chemicals to the damaged area, causing the redness, swelling, and warmth that characterize inflammation (Leonard, 2005). The increased blood supply also floods the region with white blood cells to destroy invading microscopic bacteria, which otherwise might use the local damaged area to enter into the body.

Stress and the Immune System

How does stress affect the immune system? One of the reasons that stress eventually exhausts us is that it stimulates the production of steroids. Steroids suppress the functioning of the immune system. When a person is stressed over a period of time, secretion of steroids decreases inflammation and interferes with the formation of antibodies. As a consequence, we become more vulnerable to infections, including the common cold (Barnard et al., 2005; Cohen et al., 2001b, 2003).

In one study, dental students showed lower immune system functioning, as measured by lower levels of antibodies in their saliva, during stressful periods of the school year than immediately following vacations (Jemmott et al., 1983). In contrast, social support buffers the effects of stress and enhances the functioning of the immune system (Cohen et al., 2001a, 2001b). In the Jemmott (1983) study, students who had many friends showed less suppression of immune system functioning than students with few friends.

antigen
a substance that stimulates the body to mount an immune system response to it

antibodies
substances formed by white blood cells that recognize and destroy antigens

inflammation
increased blood flow to an injured area of the body, resulting in redness, warmth, and an increased supply of white blood cells

{ **Are There Gender Differences in Response to Stress?** }

For a century, it has been widely believed that humans are prewired to experience what biologist Walter Cannon labelled a "fight-or-flight" reaction to stress. Cannon believed we are instinctively pumped up to fight like demons or, when advisable, to beat a hasty retreat.

Or are we? Not all of us, according to UCLA psychologist Shelley E. Taylor and her colleagues (2000). Taylor found that women under stress are more likely to tend to the kids or "interface" with family and friends than either fight or flee. The "woman's response" to stress, the "tend-and-befriend" response, involves nurturing and seeking social support rather than fighting or fleeing. When females face a threat, a disaster, or even an especially bad day at the office, they often respond by caring for their children and seeking social contact and support from others, especially other women.

This response may be prewired in female humans and in females of other mammalian species. Evolutionary psychologists suggest that the tend-and-befriend response might have become sealed in human genes because it promotes the survival of females who are tending their young. Females who choose to fight might die or be separated from their young—no evolutionary brass ring there.

Males may be more aggressive than females under stress because of the balance of hormones in their bodies. Due to such differences, women tend to outlive men. "Men are more likely than women to respond to stressful experiences by developing certain stress-related disorders, including hypertension, aggressive behaviour, or abuse of alcohol or hard drugs," Taylor added in a press release (May, 2000).

plainpicture/FirstLight.com

---

[1] A vaccination introduces a weakened form of an antigen (usually a bacteria or a virus) into the body to stimulate the production of antibodies. Antibodies can confer immunity for many years, in some cases for a lifetime.

CHAPTER 10 Stress, Health, and Adjustment **225**

primary appraisal
evaluating a potential stressor as a positive, negative or neutral event

secondary appraisal
evaluating how to cope with a stressful event by using available resources

psychological hardiness
a cluster of traits that buffer stress and are characterized by commitment, challenge, and control

locus of control
the place (locus) to which an individual attributes control over the receiving of reinforcers—either inside or outside the self

Other studies with students show that the stress of exams depresses the immune system's response to the Epstein-Barr virus, which causes fatigue and other problems (Glaser et al., 1993). Here, too, lonely students showed greater suppression of the immune system than students who had social support. All in all, however, there is only modest evidence that psychological interventions enhance the functioning of the immune system. A review of the research found that hypnosis (intended to help people relax), stress management methods, and conditioning methods were of some use, but less than reliable (Cohen, Miller, & Rabin, 2001b).

LO3 Psychological Moderators of Stress

For many people stress causes both physical and psychological symptoms. But, have you ever noticed how some things make you feel really stressed, but those same things don't seem to be stressful to others? Take a messy house, for example. It drives me (S.M.) crazy. It makes me completely stressed to have items lying all over the house. I must pick them all up first, and then I sit down before I can begin to feel relaxed (not to mention how stressed I feel that I am the one who must pick them up!). My husband, on the other hand, can calmly walk over the items, and not even notice they are there—in other words, he *doesn't* stress about these things! (You get my point, I think.) Stress depends on how we perceive a situation. Lazarus (1993) believes that we evaluate stressors (as being positive, neutral or negative) and then consider how to confront them. He believes that we engage in a **primary appraisal**—that is, we evaluate the event as a potential stressor—before we engage in any more thought about the event. If we evaluate the situation (appraise it) as a threat, or a challenge, we then engage in a **secondary appraisal** to assess how we will cope with the stressful situation by responding to it physically, emotionally, and/or behaviourally. So, as in the example of the messy house, Lazarus would say that I perceive the mess as a challenge or threat (to my sanity, for sure!), which results in my responding to the mess by picking up the items (behavioural response). My husband just does not perceive the mess as a potential threat to him, so he thinks nothing more of it.

In the next section we discuss several psychological factors that can influence, or *moderate*, the effects of stress.

Psychological Hardiness

Psychological hardiness also helps people resist stress (Kaddour, 2003; Richardson, 2002). Our understanding of hardiness is derived largely from the pioneering work of Suzanne Kobasa and her colleagues (1994). They studied business executives who seemed able to resist illness despite stress. In one phase of the research, executives completed a battery of psychological tests. Kobasa (1990) found that the psychologically hardy executives had three key characteristics. *What characteristics are connected with psychological hardiness?* The characteristics include commitment, challenge, and control:

• Kobasa found that psychologically hardy executives were high in *commitment*. They tended to involve themselves in, rather than feel alienated from, whatever they were doing or encountering. A Slovakian study found that psychologically hardy secondary school students try to actively solve problems rather than avoid them (Baumgartner, 2002).

• They were also high in *challenge*. They believed that change, rather than stability, is normal in life. They appraised change as an interesting incentive to personal growth, not as a threat to security.

• They were high in perceived *control* over their lives. A sense of control is one of the keys to psychological hardiness (Folkman & Moskowitz, 2000b; Tennen & Affleck, 2000). Hardy participants felt and behaved as though they were influential, rather than helpless, in facing the various rewards and punishments of life. Psychologically hardy people tend to have what Julian B. Rotter (1990) terms an internal locus of control.

Hardy people may be more resistant to stress because they *choose* to face it (Baumgartner, 2002; Kobasa, 1990). They also interpret stress as making life more interesting. For example, they see a conference with a supervisor as an opportunity to persuade the supervisor rather than as a risk to their position.

Sense of Humour

The idea that humour lightens the burdens of life and helps people cope with stress has merits. Consider the phrase "Laughter is the best medicine." *Is there any evidence that humour helps us cope with stress?* Research suggests that humour can moderate the effects of stress (Godfrey, 2004). In one classic study, for example, students completed a checklist of negative life events and a measure of mood disturbance (Martin & Lefcourt, 1983). The measure of mood disturbance yielded a stress score. The students also rated their sense of humour. Students were asked to try to produce humour in an experimental stressful situation, and their ability to do so was rated by the researchers. Students who had a greater sense of humour and were capable of producing humour in the stressful experimental condition were less affected by the stress than other students. In other experiments, Lefcourt (1997) found that exposing students to humorous videotapes raised the level of immunoglobin A (a measure of the functioning of the immune system) in their saliva.

How does humour help people cope with stress? Well there are a few possibilities: One is that laughter stimulates the output of endorphins, which might enhance the functioning of the immune system. Another is that the benefits of humour may be explained in terms of the positive cognitive shifts they entail and the positive emotions that accompany them.

Predictability and Control

The ability to predict a stressor or feel a sense of control over events in our lives allow us to brace ourselves for the inevitable and, in many cases, plan ways of coping with it (Folkman & Moskowitz, 2000b; Tennen & Affleck, 2000). There is also a relationship between the desire to assume control over one's situation and the usefulness of information about impending stressors. People who want information about medical procedures and what they will experience cope better with pain when they undergo those procedures (Ludwick-Rosenthal & Neufeld, 1993).

Social Support

People are social beings, and social support also seems to act as a buffer against the effects of stress (Cohen et al., 2003; Folkman & Moskowitz, 2000a). The concept of social support has many definitions:

- *Emotional concern:* listening to people's problems and expressing feelings of sympathy, caring, understanding, and reassurance.
- *Instrumental aid:* the material supports and services that facilitate adaptive behaviour. For example, relief organizations may provide foodstuffs, medicines, and temporary living quarters following a disaster.
- *Information:* guidance and advice that enhance people's ability to cope.
- *Appraisal:* feedback from others about how one is doing. This kind of support involves helping people interpret, or "make sense of," what has happened to them.
- *Socializing:* conversation, recreation, going shopping with someone. Socializing is beneficial even when it is not oriented toward solving problems.

Social support can have positive effects on our body's cardiovascular and endocrine systems (Miller, Cohen, & Richey, 2002). Stress is less likely to lead to high blood pressure or alcohol abuse in people who have social support (Linden et al., 1993). Even online social support helps people cope with the stresses of cancer and other health problems (Broom, 2005; Hoybye et al., 2005).

LO4 Psychology and Chronic Health Problems

Stress is one of the key topics in health psychology. **Health psychology** studies the relationships between psychological factors and the prevention and treatment of physical health problems. Health psychologists investigate the following:

- How psychological factors such as stress, behaviour patterns, and attitudes can lead to or aggravate illness.
- How people can cope with stress.
- How stress and pathogens (disease-causing organisms such as bacteria and viruses) interact to influence the immune system.
- How people decide whether or not to seek health care.
- How psychological interventions such as health education (e.g., concerning nutrition, smoking, and exercise) and behaviour modification can contribute to physical health.

Why do people become ill? Why do some people develop cancer? Why do others have heart attacks?

health psychology
the field of psychology that studies the relationships between psychological factors (e.g., attitudes, beliefs, situational influences, and behaviour patterns) and the prevention and treatment of physical illness

pathogen
a microscopic organism (e.g., bacterium or virus) that can cause disease

biopsychosocial having to do with the interactions of biological, psychological, and sociocultural factors

Why do still others seem to be immune to these illnesses? *What is the biopsychosocial model?* The **biopsychosocial** model recognizes that there is no single, simple answer to these questions. The likelihood of contracting an illness—be it a case of the flu or cancer—can reflect the interaction of many factors, including biological, psychological, and sociocultural factors (Schneiderman et al., 2005).

Biological factors such as pathogens, inoculations, injuries, age, gender, and a family history of disease may strike us as the most obvious causes of illness. Genetics, in particular, tempts some people to assume that there is little they can do about their health. Some cases of health problems are unavoidable for people with certain genes. However, if you have a family history of heart disease or cancer, it is *not* true that there is little or nothing you can do to prevent developing the disease. In many cases, especially with heart problems and cancer, genes create only *predispositions* toward the health problem. The life choices we make—the behaviours

Keith Brofsky/Photodisc/Getty Images

FIGURE 10.2

Leading Causes of Death in Canada

Some of the leading causes of death in Canada are shown in this figure. Many of them, including some cancers, other lung diseases, heart disease, and liver disease, are related to behavioural risk factors such as alcohol use, smoking, lack of exercise, and risky sexual behaviours.

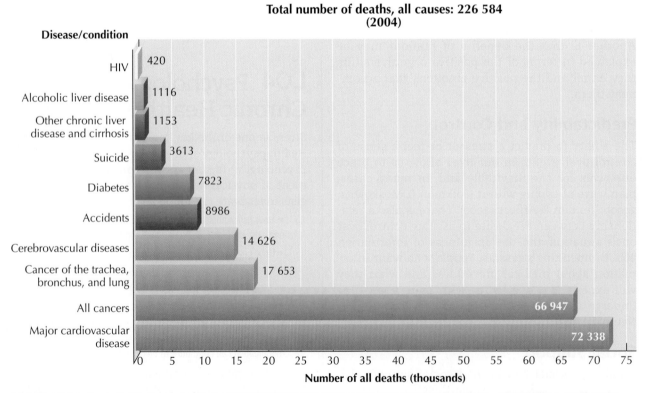

Total number of deaths, all causes: 226 584
(2004)

Adapted from Statistics Canada, *Mortality, Summary List of Causes*, 84F0209XWE2004000, 2007. http://www.statcan.gc.ca/bsolc/olc-cel/olc-cel?catno=84F0209XWE&lang=eng#formatdisp.

we select—also affect our likelihood of becoming ill (Hoover, 2000).

Biological, psychological (behaviour and personality), sociocultural factors, and stressors all play roles in health and illness. Many health problems are affected by psychological factors, such as attitudes, emotions, and behaviour (Kiecolt-Glaser et al., 2002b; Salovey et al., 2000). Figure 10.2 reveals that many of the leading causes of death in Canada are preventable, stemming from health-damaging personal habits. Stopping smoking, eating healthy, exercising, and controlling alcohol use would prevent most of these. Behavioural risk factors, such as these, increase the chances of disease and chronic illness if they are not controlled. Also, anxiety and depression can impair the functioning of the immune system, rendering us more vulnerable to physical disorders ranging from viral infections to cancer (McGuire, Kiecolt-Glaser, & Glaser, 2002; Salovey et al., 2000).

Let us now discuss the chronic health problems of heart disease, cancer, and HIV/AIDS and other sexually transmitted infections. Each involves biological, psychological, and environmental factors—including the social and technological environments. Although these are medical problems, we also explore ways in which psychologists have contributed to their prevention and treatment.

Coronary Heart Disease

Coronary heart disease (CHD) remains the leading cause of death in Canada, most often from heart attacks (Heart & Stroke Foundation, 2009). In 2006, 30 percent of all deaths were related to coronary heart disease. Both men and women are at similar risk for coronary heart disease (Statistics Canada, 2006).

What are the major risk factors for coronary heart disease? The Canadian Heart & Stroke Foundation (2009) reported that 90 percent of Canadians have at least one risk factor for heart disease or stroke. These include smoking, overconsumption of alcohol, physical inactivity, obesity (poor eating habits), high blood pressure, high blood cholesterol, and diabetes, most of which are preventable risks.

Health-promoting behaviours—such as quitting smoking, healthy eating (reducing saturated fats and getting more fruits, vegetables, and whole grains), reducing hypertension and lowering harmful serum cholesterol, and exercising regularly—may help reduce the risk of getting coronary heart disease.

Cancer

According to Statistics Canada (2006), cancer is the third leading cause of death in Canada. Lung cancer is the most common (and most preventable) for both men and women (accounting for 30 percent of all cancer deaths). Cancer is characterized by the development of abnormal, or mutant, cells that may take root anywhere in the body: in the blood, bones, digestive tract, lungs, and sex organs. If their spread is not controlled early, the cancerous cells may *metastasize*—that is, establish colonies elsewhere in the body. It appears that our bodies develop cancerous cells frequently. However, these are normally destroyed by the immune system. People whose immune system is damaged by physical or psychological factors may be more likely to develop tumours (Antoni, 2009).

> ## { Fruits and Vegetables Prevent Cancer? }
>
> Despite the fight for better food choices as part of a healthy lifestyle, recent studies may challenge the usefulness of eating fruits and vegetables in preventing cancer. For example:
>
> - Karin Michels and her colleagues (2000) followed approximately 80 000 women and 40 000 men over several years and found little connection between eating fruits and vegetables and the risk of colon and rectal cancers.
>
> - Similarly, Arthur Schatzkin and his colleagues (2000) studied about 2000 women and men who had had pre-cancerous growths removed from their colons. The participants were randomly assigned to eat low-fat diets that were high in fibre, fruits, and vegetables, and were assessed four years later. There were no differences in the incidence of new pre-cancerous growths in the colons of the two groups.

Getting regular medical checkups, stopping smoking, eating fewer saturated (and trans) fats, and exercising regularly all may help reduce the risk of developing coronary heart disease and cancer.

chlamydia
a sexually transmitted bacterial infection that is most commonly reported in young female adults

gonorrhea
a sexually transmitted bacterial infection that infects the penis, cervix, rectum, throat, and eyes; it is most commonly reported in young adults

HIV
human immunodeficiency virus; a sexually transmitted disease that attacks the immune system, typically progressing to AIDS (acquired immune deficiency syndrome) in which the body's immune system is weak and highly susceptible to infection and even death

Risk Factors

What are the major risk factors for cancer? As with many other diseases, people can inherit a disposition toward cancer. Heredity plays a role in many cancers, such as breast, colon, and prostate cancer. Other risk factors, however, are *behavioural,* such as smoking, drinking, unsafe sexual behaviours, and maintaining a poor diet; some factors are *environmental,* such as workplace hazards, sunlight, and radiation.

Prolonged psychological conditions such as depression or stress may also heighten the risk of some kinds of cancer by depressing the functioning of the immune system (Bauer et al., 2003; McGuire et al., 2002; Salovey et al., 2000).

Also consider cultural differences in health. Death rates from cancer are higher in such nations as the Netherlands, Denmark, England, the United States, and—yes—Canada, where average rates of animal fat intake are high (Bray & Atkin, 2004). Death rates from cancer are lower in such nations as Thailand, the Philippines, and Japan, where fat intake is lower and people eat more fruits and vegetables.

Researchers have also suggested possible links between stress and cancer (Salovey et al., 2000). Yehuda (2002) suggests that stress lowers levels of cortisol and impairs the ability of the immune system to destroy cancer cells.

Measures such as getting regular medical checkups to detect cancer early; stopping smoking; eating fewer saturated fats; and exercising regularly may help reduce the risk of developing cancer. Cancer is most curable when it is detected early, before it metastasizes.

HIV/AIDS and Other Sexually Transmitted Infections

Health Canada (2005b) reported that young adults aged 20 to 24 continue to be at the highest risk for sexually transmitted infections (STIs). In fact 44 percent of those aged 20 to 24 continue to engage in unsafe sex despite informative education campaigns that warn of the dangers of having unprotected sex. More frightening is that the transmission of STIs continues to rise for 15- to 24-year-olds (Public Health Agency, 2008).

Among the 25 classifications of STIs, **chlamydia** is the most common, followed by **gonorrhea** (Public Health Agency, 2006). For many who are carriers of these infections, symptoms are minor or not apparent. This is why nearly 75 percent of people who are infected with these STIs do not know (Public Health Agency, 2006).

The most feared sexually transmitted disease is **human immunodeficiency virus (HIV)**, which destroys the immune system so that it is no longer functional. Carriers of HIV can live symptom-free but typically progress into full-blown *acquired immune deficiency syndrome* (AIDS) within ten years. Progression to AIDS increases the risk for cancer or infection due to an extremely weak immune system. In Canada, 60 160 cases of HIV were reported to the Public Health Agency (PHA) of Canada between 1985 and 2005, and approximately 30 percent of those with the illness were unaware that they carried the infection (PHA, 2006). HIV is transmitted through blood, semen, or vaginal secretions during sexual intercourse, so the best protection against HIV is using a condom. Other risk-reduction strategies include refraining from injecting drugs, getting tested for HIV and other STIs, limiting your sexual partners, and knowing your partners' sexual history.

HIV/AIDS remains a social stigma in Canada and throughout the world. This stigma influences how people living with HIV/AIDS cope with the demands of their daily life. The current treatment for AIDS is drug therapy. Often antidepressants and antianxiety drugs are used for psychological treatment for patients dealing with the social issues related to the disease.

Personality:
Theory and
Measurement

Learning Outcomes

LO1 Describe the psychoanalytical perspective and how it contributed to the study of personality

LO2 Explain the trait perspective and the "Big Five" trait model

LO3 Identify the contributions of learning theory in understanding personality

LO4 Describe the humanistic perspective of personality

LO5 Describe the sociocultural perspective of personality

LO6 Describe the different kinds of tests psychologists use to measure personality

> ## **"** *The strength of a person's personality can act to draw others toward him or her, or act as a repellent?* **"**

Who is the greatest Canadian? CBC asked this question in 2004, and over 1.2 million Canadians from coast to coast voted on who they thought was the greatest. Can you guess who won the award as the greatest Canadian? If you guessed George Stroumboulopoulos, you are more correct than you realize.

"Hold on a second," you might be saying, "Tommy Douglas won the 'Greatest Canadian' contest, did he not?" Well, yes, technically people voted for Tommy Douglas, the founder of Canadian medicare, but there was a glaring problem with the contest. Each "Greatest Canadian" had an advocate who presented for him or her. For example, Terry Fox was presented by actor Sook-Yin Lee, Pierre Elliott Trudeau was presented by writer Rex Murphy, Don Cherry was presented by wrestler Bret "The Hitman" Hart, and Tommy Douglas was presented by MuchMusic heartthrob George Stroumboulopoulos (whose name is just so much fun to say). As Canadians watched the short video essays on each of the candidates for greatest Canadian, it was impossible to separate the impact of the personality of the presenter from the facts about the candidate's life. Thus, when people voted, they were probably voting for the effectiveness and attractiveness of the presenter as much as they were voting for the actual candidate. Tommy Douglas no doubt played an important role in Canadian politics, but the popularity of George Stroumboulopoulos, especially with Canadian youth, and the strength of George's personality, may have ultimately won the contest for Tommy Douglas.

DID YOU KNOW?

- Psychologists once thought that biting one's fingernails or smoking cigarettes was a sign of conflict experienced during early childhood (and some still do).

- Bloodletting and vomiting were once recommended as ways of coping with depression (Maher & Maher, 1994).

- About 2500 years ago, a Greek physician devised a way of looking at personality that—with a little "tweaking"—remains in use today.

- Most research suggests that there are five basic personality traits. The interactions of these traits from low to high give us our unique personalities.

- The most well-adjusted immigrants are those who retain the language and customs of their country of origin, as well as learn the language and customs of the new host country.

- Psychologists have strong methods to determine whether a person has told the truth on a personality test, but nothing is foolproof.

- Just as you have seen in some movies, there is a psychological test made up of inkblots, and test-takers are asked to say what the blots look like to them. If the test-taker sees the wrong things, this may indicate psychosis.

How is it that a personality can have such an impact? Personality, or one's reasonably stable way of thinking, feeling, and behaving, is one of the ways we make our unique contributions to the world. The strength of a person's personality can act to draw others toward him or her, or act as a repellent, depending on the personality of the observer.

Canada, although not a very populous country, has produced many individuals with eccentric, charismatic, and abrasive personalities. This list of Canadian personalities would include names such as William Shatner, Mike Myers, Rick Mercer, Kim Cattrall, David Suzuki, Howie Mandel, Michael J. Fox, Jim Carrey, Avril Lavigne, Celine Dion, John Candy, Robert Munsch, James Cameron, Neil Young, Don Cherry, Pierre Elliott Trudeau, Kiefer Sutherland, Dave Foley, and many, many more.

What makes these Canadians the unique people that they are? As you will soon learn, psychologists study personality from many different perspectives. Some think of personality as consisting of the person's most striking traits, as in "This person has an outgoing personality" or "That person has an agreeable personality." But many psychological theorists look deeper, trying to find the origins of a person's personality. Those schooled in the Freudian tradition look at personality as consisting of underlying mental structures that jockey for supremacy outside the range of our ordinary awareness. Other theorists focus on how personality is shaped by learning. And to the humanistic theorists, personality is not something people *have* but rather something they *create*, to give meaning and direction to their lives. Then, too, sociocultural theorists remind us that we must always consider the influences of culture, race, and ethnicity on personality.

Before we examine these different theoretical views, let us define our subject matter. Psychologists define **personality** as the reasonably stable patterns of emotions, motives, and behaviour that distinguish one person from another.

LO1 The Psychoanalytic Perspective

Where do we get the idea that there is something like an unconscious mind that can exert control over our behaviour? One source is psychoanalytic theory.

There are several **psychoanalytic theories** of personality, each of which owes its origin to Sigmund Freud. Each teaches that personality is characterized by conflict. At first the conflict is external: Drives like sex, aggression, and the need for superiority come into conflict with laws, social rules, and moral codes. But at some point, laws and social rules are brought inward—that is, *internalized*. The conflict is then between opposing *inner* forces.

At any given moment our behaviour, our thoughts, and our emotions represent the outcome of these inner contests. *What is Freud's psychoanalytic theory?*

Sigmund Freud's Theory of Psychosexual Development

Sigmund Freud (1856–1939) was a mass of contradictions. Some have lauded him as one of the greatest thinkers of the 20th century. Others have criticized him as overrated. He preached liberal views on sexuality but was himself a model of sexual restraint. He invented a popular form of psychotherapy but experienced lifelong psychologically related problems such as migraine headaches, fainting under stress, hatred of the telephone, and an addiction to cigars. He smoked 20 cigars a day and could not break the habit even after he developed cancer of the jaw.

Freud was trained as a physician. Early in his practice, he was surprised to find that some people apparently experienced loss of feeling in a hand or paralysis of the legs even though they had no medical disorder. These odd symptoms often disappeared once the person recalled and discussed stressful events and feelings of guilt or anxiety that seemed to be related to the symptoms. Although these events and feelings lay hidden beneath the surface of awareness, they could influence behaviour.

Tommy Douglas

FIGURE 11.1

The Human Iceberg According to Freud

According to psychoanalytic theory, only the tip of human personality rises above the surface of the mind into conscious awareness. Material in the preconscious can become conscious if we direct our attention to it. Unconscious material tends to remain shrouded in mystery.

Go to www.icanpsych.com to access an interactive version of this figure.

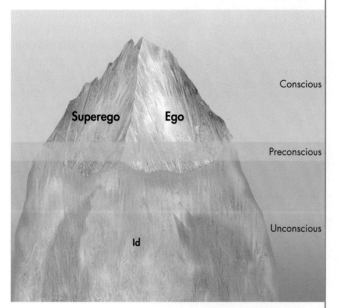

From this sort of clinical evidence, Freud concluded that the mind is like an iceberg. Only the tip of an iceberg rises above the surface of the water; the great mass of it lies hidden in the deep (see Figure 11.1). Freud came to believe that people, similarly, are aware of only a small part of the ideas and impulses that dwell within their minds. He thought that a larger portion of the mind—one that contained our deepest images, thoughts, fears, and urges—lies beneath the surface of awareness, where little light illumines them.

Freud labelled the region that pokes into the light of awareness the *conscious* part of the mind. He called the regions below the surface the *preconscious* and the *unconscious*. The preconscious mind contains ideas that are out of awareness but can be made conscious by focusing on them. The unconscious mind contains primitive instincts such as sex and aggression. Some

Sigmund Freud

unconscious urges cannot be experienced consciously because mental images and words cannot portray them in all their colour and fury. Other unconscious urges may be kept below the surface by repression because they would create anxiety. *Repression* is defined as the automatic ejection of anxiety-evoking ideas from awareness. People forget many ugly experiences, and some research evidence suggests that people *might* repress them (Furnham et al., 2003; Myers & Brewin, 1994). Other investigators allow that forgetting and distortion of memory occurs, but view the concept of repression as nothing but a myth (Kihlstrom, 2002).

In the unconscious mind, primitive drives seek expression, while learned values try to keep them in check. The conflict can arouse emotional outbursts and psychological problems. To explore the unconscious mind, Freud used a form of mental detective work called *psychoanalysis*. In psychoanalysis, people are encouraged to talk about anything that pops into their mind while they remain comfortable and relaxed.

The Structure of Personality

Freud spoke of mental or *psychic structures* to describe the clashing forces of personality. Psychic structures cannot be seen or measured directly, but their presence is suggested by behaviour, expressed thoughts, and emotions. Freud believed there are three psychic structures: the id, the ego, and the superego.

The **id** is present at birth. It represents biological drives and is unconscious. Freud described the id as "the pleasure principle" and "a chaos, a cauldron of seething excitations" (1927/1964, p. 73). The conscious mind might find it inconsistent to love and hate the same person, but such conflicting emotions can dwell side by side in the id. In the id, one can hate one's mother for failing to gratify immediately all of one's needs, while also loving her. The id seeks instant gratification without consideration for law, social custom, or other people.

id
the psychic structure, present at birth, that represents physiological drives and is fully unconscious

Imagno/Getty Images

The **ego** begins to develop during the first year of life, largely because a child's demands for gratification cannot all be met immediately. The ego stands for reason and good sense, for rational ways of coping with frustration. It curbs the appetites of the id and seeks ways to find gratification yet avoid social disapproval. The id informs you that you are hungry, but the ego decides to microwave popcorn. The ego takes into account what is practical along with what is urged by the id. The ego also provides the conscious sense of self.

Although most of the ego is conscious, some of its business is carried out unconsciously. For example, the ego also acts as a censor that screens the impulses of the id. When the ego senses that improper impulses are rising into awareness, it may use psychological defences to prevent them from surfacing. Repression is one such psychological defence, or *defence mechanism*.

The **superego** develops as the child incorporates the moral standards and values of parents and other members of the community. The child does so through **identification**, by trying to become like these people. The superego holds up shining models of an ideal self and monitors the intentions of the ego, handing out judgments of right and wrong. It floods the ego with feelings of guilt and shame when the verdict is negative.

Freud believed that a healthy personality has found ways to gratify most of the id's demands without seriously offending the superego. It is like those cartoons of a person with an angel on one shoulder (the superego) and the devil on the other shoulder (the id) and the person in the middle (the ego) trying to negotiate between the two. Most of the id's demands are contained or repressed. If the ego is not a good problem solver, or if the superego is too stern, the ego will have a hard time of it. Can you relate the conflict of strong desires compelling you to act in a way that is contrary to what you think you should do? Many people report feeling this mental struggle, and if Freud's theory had stopped here, most people would have little difficulty accepting it. However, the second part of Freudian theory stretched people's sensibilities (both during his time and still today).

Nanka (Kucherenko Olena)/Shutterstock.com

Stages of Psychosexual Development

Freud stirred controversy by arguing that sexual impulses are a central factor in personality development, even among children. Freud believed that sexual feelings are closely linked to children's basic ways of relating to the world, such as nursing and moving their bowels.

Freud believed that a major instinct, *eros,* aims to preserve and perpetuate life. Eros is fuelled by psychological, or psychic, energy, which Freud labelled *libido.* Libidinal energy involves sexual impulses, so Freud considered it to be *psychosexual.* As the child develops, this energy is expressed through sexual feelings in different parts of the body, or *erogenous zones.* To Freud, human development involves the transfer of libidinal energy from one erogenous zone to another. He hypothesized five periods of **psychosexual development**: oral, anal, phallic, latency, and genital.

During the first year of life a child experiences much of her or his world through the mouth. If it fits, into the mouth it goes. This is the **oral stage**.

Freud argued that oral activities such as sucking and biting give the child sexual gratification as well as nourishment.

Freud believed that children encounter conflict during each stage of psychosexual development. During the oral stage, conflict centres on the nature and extent of oral gratification. Early weaning (cessation of breastfeeding) can lead to frustration. Excessive gratification, on the other hand, can lead infants to expect that they will routinely get anything they want. Insufficient or excessive gratification in any stage could lead to *fixation* in that stage and to the development of traits that are characteristic of the stage. Oral traits include dependency, gullibility, and excessive optimism or pessimism (depending on the child's experiences with gratification).

Freud theorized that adults with an *oral fixation* could experience exaggerated desires for "oral activities," such as smoking, overeating, alcohol abuse, and nail biting. Like the infant whose survival depends on the mercy of an adult, adults with oral fixations may desire clinging, dependent relationships.

The anal stage begins in the second year. During the **anal stage**, gratification is attained through contraction and relaxation of the muscles that control elimination of waste products. Elimination, which is reflexive during most of the first year, comes under voluntary muscular control, even if such control is not reliable at first. During the anal stage, children learn to delay the gratification that comes from eliminating whenever they feel the urge. The general issue of self-control may bring conflict between parent and child. *Anal fixations* may stem from this conflict and lead to either of two sets of traits in adulthood. *Anal-retentive* traits involve excessive use of self-control: perfectionism, a strong need for order, and exaggerated neatness and cleanliness. *Anal-expulsive* traits, on the other hand, "let it all hang out": carelessness, messiness, even sadism.

Children enter the **phallic stage** during the third year. The major erogenous zone is the penis in boys and the clitoris in girls. Parent–child conflict is likely to develop over masturbation, to which parents may respond with threats or punishment. During this stage children may develop strong sexual attachments to the parent of the other sex and begin to view the parent of the same sex as a rival for the other parent's affections. Thus boys may want to marry their mothers, and girls may want to marry their fathers.

Children have difficulty dealing with feelings of lust and jealousy. These feelings, therefore, remain unconscious, but their influence is felt through fantasies about marriage with the parent of the other sex and hostility toward the parent of the same sex. In boys, this conflict is labelled the **Oedipus complex**, after the legendary Greek king who unwittingly killed his father and married his mother. Similar feelings in girls give rise to the **Electra complex**. According to Greek legend, Electra was the daughter of the king Agamemnon. She longed for him after his death and sought revenge against his slayers—her mother and her mother's lover.

The Oedipus and Electra complexes are resolved by about the ages of five or six. Children repress their hostilities toward the parent of the same sex and begin to identify with her or him. In psychoanalytic theory, identification is the key to gender-typing: It leads children to play the gender roles of the parent of the same sex and to internalize his or her values.

Sexual feelings toward the parent of the other sex are repressed for several years. When the feelings re-emerge during adolescence, they are displaced, or transferred, to socially appropriate members of the other sex.

Freud believed that by the age of five or six, children have been in conflict with their

anal stage
the second stage of psychosexual development, when gratification is attained through anal activities

phallic stage
the third stage of psychosexual development, characterized by a shift of libido to the phallic region (from the Greek *phallos*, referring to an image of the penis; however, Freud used the term *phallic* to refer both to boys and girls)

Oedipus complex
a conflict of the phallic stage in which the boy wishes to possess his mother sexually and perceives his father as a rival in love

Electra complex
a conflict of the phallic stage in which the girl longs for her father and resents her mother

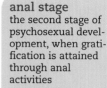

PhotoLink/Getty Images

latency
a phase of psychosexual development characterized by repression of sexual impulses

genital stage
the mature stage of psychosexual development, characterized by preferred expression of libido through intercourse with an adult of the other gender

analytical psychology
Jung's psychoanalytic theory, which emphasizes the collective unconscious and archetypes

collective unconscious
Jung's hypothesized store of vague memories that represent the history of humankind

parents over sexual feelings for several years. The pressures of the Oedipus and Electra complexes cause them to repress all sexual urges. In so doing, they enter a period of **latency**, during which their sexual feelings remain unconscious, they prefer playmates of their own sex, and they focus on schoolwork.

Freud believed that we enter the final stage of psychosexual development, the **genital stage**, at puberty. Adolescent males again experience sexual urges toward their mother, and adolescent females experience such urges toward their father. But the *incest taboo* causes them to repress these impulses and displace them onto other adults or adolescents of the other sex. Boys might seek girls "just like the girl that married dear old Dad." Girls might be attracted to boys who resemble their fathers.

People in the genital stage prefer to find sexual gratification through intercourse with a member of the other sex. In Freud's view, oral or anal stimulation, masturbation, and sexual activity with people of the same sex all represent *pre-genital* fixations and immature forms of sexual conduct.

Other Psychoanalytic Theorists

Freud had several intellectual heirs. Their theories, like his, include conflict and defence mechanisms. In other respects, they differ considerably. *Who are some other psychoanalytic theorists? What are their views on personality?*

Carl Jung

Carl Jung (1875–1961) was a Swiss psychiatrist who had been a member of Freud's inner circle. He fell into disfavour with Freud when he developed his own psychoanalytic theory—**analytical psychology**. Jung downplayed the importance of sex, which he saw as one of several important instincts.

Jung, like Freud, was intrigued by unconscious processes. He believed that we not only have a *personal* unconscious that contains repressed memories and impulses, but also a **collective unconscious** containing primitive images, or archetypes, that reflect the history of our species. Examples of archetypes are the all-powerful God, the young hero, the fertile and nurturing mother, the wise old man, the hostile brother—even fairy godmothers, wicked witches, and themes of rebirth or resurrection. Archetypes themselves remain unconscious, but Jung believed they affect our thoughts and feelings and cause us to respond to cultural themes in the media.

Alfred Adler

Alfred Adler (1870–1937), another follower of Freud, also felt that Freud had placed too much emphasis on sex. Adler believed that people are basically

---

{ ## Why Do We Need to Have Sports Heroes? }

What have psychologists learned about the appeal of celebrities, and especially sports celebrities? Many people form deep and enduring bonds of attachment with athletes and sports teams. Once they identify with a team, their self-esteem rises and falls with the team's wins and losses (Wann et al., 2000). Wins lead to a surge of testosterone in males (Bernhardt et al., 1998), which is connected with aggressiveness and self-confidence. Wins increase the optimism of both males and females.

Psychoanalytic theory suggests that children identify with parents and other "big" people in their lives because big people seem to hold the keys to the resources they need for sustenance and stimulation or excitement. Athletes and entertainers—the rich and famous—have their fan clubs, filled with people who tie their own lights to the brilliant suns of their stars.

Teams and sports heroes provide both entertainment and the kind of gutsy competition that evolutionary psychologists

believe whispers to us from our genes, pushing us toward aggression and dominance. If we can't do it on our own, we can do it *through* someone else. In some kind of psychological sense, we can *be* someone who is more effective at climbing the heap of humankind into the sun.

Richard Lautens/GetStock.com

motivated by an **inferiority complex**. In some people, feelings of inferiority may be based on physical problems and the need to compensate for them. Adler believed, however, that all of us encounter some feelings of inferiority because of our small size as children, and that these feelings give rise to a drive for superiority. As a child, Adler was crippled by rickets and suffered from pneumonia, and it may be that his theory developed in part from his own striving to overcome bouts of illness.

Adler believed that self-awareness plays a major role in the formation of personality. He spoke of a **creative self**, a self-aware aspect of personality that strives to overcome obstacles and develop the person's potential. Because each person's potential is unique, Adler's views have been termed **individual psychology**.

Karen Horney

Karen Horney (1885–1952) was criticized by the New York Psychoanalytic Institute because she took issue with the way in which psychoanalytic theory portrayed women. Early in the 20th century, psychoanalytic theory taught that a woman's place was in the home. Women who sought to compete with men in the business world were assumed to be suffering from unconscious *penis envy*. Psychoanalytic theory taught that little girls feel inferior to boys when they learn that boys have a penis and they do not. But Horney argued that little girls do *not* feel inferior to boys and that these views were founded on Western cultural prejudice, not scientific evidence.

Karen Horney

Science Source/Photo Researchers, Inc.

Horney agreed with Freud that childhood experiences are important in psychological development. Like other neoanalysts, however, she asserted that unconscious sexual and aggressive impulses are less important than social relationships. She also believed that genuine and consistent love can alleviate the effects of a traumatic childhood.

Erik Erikson

Like many other modern psychoanalysts, Erik Erikson (1902–1994) believed that Freud had placed undue emphasis on sex. Like Horney, he believed that social relationships are more important than sex. Erikson also believed that to a large extent we are the conscious architects of our own personalities.

Erikson, like Freud, is known for devising a comprehensive theory of personality development. But whereas Freud proposed stages of psycho*sexual* development, Erikson proposed stages of psycho*social* development. The first stage of **psychosocial development** is labelled the stage of trust versus mistrust because two outcomes are possible: (1) a warm, loving relationship with the mother and others during infancy might lead to a sense of basic trust in people and the world; or (2) a cold, ungratifying relationship with the mother and others might generate a general sense of mistrust. For Erikson, the goal of adolescence is the attainment of **ego identity**, not genital sexuality. The focus is on who we see ourselves as being and what we stand for, not on sexual interests.

Erik Erikson

Ted Streshinsky/Time & Life Pictures/Getty Images

Evaluation of the Psychoanalytic Perspective

Psychoanalysis has tremendous appeal. It is rich in concepts and seems to explain many human traits.

inferiority complex
feelings of inferiority hypothesized by Adler to serve as a central motivating force

creative self
according to Adler, the self-aware aspect of personality that strives to achieve its full potential

individual psychology
Adler's psychoanalytic theory, which emphasizes feelings of inferiority and the creative self

psychosocial development
Erikson's theory of personality and development, which emphasizes social relationships and eight stages of growth

ego identity
a firm sense of who one is and what one stands for

trait
a relatively stable aspect of personality that is inferred from behaviour and assumed to give rise to consistent behaviour

> "In most of us by the age of thirty, the character has set like plaster, and will never soften again."
> —William James

What are the strengths and weaknesses of the psychoanalytic perspective?

On the positive side, Freud fought for the idea that personality is subject to scientific analysis. He developed his theory at a time when many people viewed psychological problems as signs of possession by the devil or evil spirits. Freud argued that psychological disorders stem from psychological problems—not spirits. His views contributed to the development of compassion for people with psychological disorders and to methods of psychotherapy.

Psychoanalytic theory also focused attention on the far-reaching effects of childhood events and suggested that parents respond to the emotional needs of their children.

Freud taught us that sexual and aggressive urges are common, and that recognizing them is not the same as acting on them. As W. Bertram Wolfe put it, "Freud found sex an outcast in the outhouse, and left it in the living room an honoured guest."

Critics note that "psychic structures"—id, ego, and superego—are too vague to measure scientifically (Hergenhahn, 2009). Nor can they be used to predict behaviour. Nor have the stages of psychosexual development escaped criticism. Children begin to masturbate as early as the first year, not in the phallic stage. As parents know from discovering their children playing "doctor," the latency stage is not as sexually latent as Freud believed.

The evidence for Erikson's developmental views seems sturdier. For example, people who fail to develop ego identity in adolescence seem to have problems with intimate relationships later on.

Freud's clinical method of gathering evidence is also suspect (Hergenhahn, 2009). Therapists may subtly guide clients into producing memories and feelings they expect to find. Also, most psychoanalytic theorists restricted their evidence gathering to case studies with individuals who sought help, particularly people from the middle and upper classes. People who seek therapy differ from the general population.

Psychoanalytic theory focused on reasons that people develop certain traits. We next discuss trait theory, which is not so much concerned with the origins of traits as with their description and categorization.

LO2 The Trait Perspective

The notion of **traits** is familiar enough. If we asked you to describe yourself, you would probably do so in terms of traits such as bright, sophisticated, and witty. (That is you, is it not?) We also describe other people in terms of traits. *What are traits?*

Traits are reasonably stable elements of personality that are inferred from behaviour. If you describe a friend as "shy," it may be because you have observed anxiety or withdrawal in that person's social encounters. Traits are assumed to account for consistent behaviour in different situations. You probably expect your "shy" friend to be retiring in most social confrontations.

From Hippocrates to the Present

What is the history of the trait perspective? The trait perspective dates at least to the Greek physician Hippocrates (ca. 460–377 BCE). It

Mike Kemp/Rubberball/Jupiterimages

has generally been assumed that traits are embedded in people's bodies. Hippocrates believed they were embedded in bodily fluids. In his view, a person's personality depends on the balance of four basic fluids, or "humours," in the body. Yellow bile is associated with a choleric (quick-tempered) disposition; blood with a sanguine (warm, cheerful) one; phlegm with a phlegmatic (sluggish, calm, cool) disposition; and black bile with a melancholic (gloomy, pensive) temperament. Disease was believed to reflect an imbalance among the humours. Depression, for example, represented an excess of black bile. Although Hippocrates' theory was speculative, the terms *choleric, sanguine,* and so on remain in use.

More contemporary trait theories assume that traits are heritable and are embedded in the nervous system. These theories rely on the mathematical technique of factor analysis to determine which traits are basic to others.

Early in the 20th century, Gordon Allport and a colleague (Allport & Oddbert, 1936) catalogued some 18 000 human traits from a search through word lists like dictionaries. Some were physical traits such as *short, weak,* and *brunette.* Others were behavioural traits such as *shy* and *emotional.* This exhaustive list has served as the basis for personality research by many other psychologists. *How have psychologists reduced Allport's traits to more manageable lists?*

Hans Eysenck's Trait Theory

British psychologist Hans J. Eysenck (1916–1997) focused much of his research on the relationships between two personality traits: **introversion–extraversion** and emotional stability–instability (Eysenck & Eysenck, 1985). (Emotional *instability* is also called *neuroticism*). Carl Jung was the first to distinguish between introverts and extraverts. Eysenck added the dimension of emotional stability–instability to introversion–extraversion. He catalogued various personality traits according to where they are situated along these dimensions (see Figure 11.2). For example, an anxious person would be high in both introversion and neuroticism—that is, preoccupied with his or her own thoughts and emotionally unstable.

Eysenck acknowledged that his scheme is similar to Hippocrates'. According to Eysenck's dimensions, the choleric type would be extraverted and unstable; the sanguine type, extraverted and stable; the phlegmatic type, introverted and stable; and the melancholic type, introverted and unstable.

introversion
a trait characterized by intense imagination and the tendency to inhibit impulses

extraversion
a trait characterized by tendencies to be socially outgoing and to express feelings and impulses freely

The "Big Five": The Five-Factor Model

More recent research suggests that there may be five basic personality factors, not two. These include the two found by Eysenck—extraversion and neuroticism—along with conscientiousness, agreeableness, and openness to experience (see Table 11.1 on the next page).

Many personality theorists, especially Robert McCrae and Paul T. Costa, Jr., have developed the five-factor model. Cross-cultural research has found that these five factors appear to define the personality structure of American, German, Portuguese, Israeli, Chinese, Korean, Japanese, and Philippine people (Katigbak et al., 2002; McCrae & Costa, 1997). A study of more than 5000 German, British, Spanish, Czech, and Turkish people suggests that the factors are related to people's basic temperaments, which are considered to be largely inborn (McCrae et al., 2000). The researchers interpreted the results to suggest that our personalities tend to mature over time rather than be shaped by environmental conditions, although the expression of personality traits is certainly affected by culture.

FIGURE 11.2

Eysenck's Personality Dimensions and Hippocrates' Personality Types

Various personality traits shown in the outer ring fall within the two major dimensions of personality suggested by Hans Eysenck. The inner circle shows how Hippocrates' four major personality types—choleric, sanguine, phlegmatic, and melancholic—fit within Eysenck's dimensions.

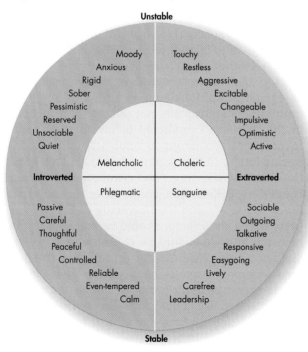

The five-factor model—also known as the "Big Five" model—is quite popular. There are hundreds of studies correlating scores on the five factors, according to a psychological test constructed by Costa and McCrae (the *NEO Five-Factor Inventory*), with various behaviour patterns, psychological disorders, and kinds of "personalities." Consider driving. Significant negative correlations have been found between the numbers of traffic accidents a person gets into and the factor of agreeableness (Cellar et al., 2000). In other words, it's safer to share the freeway with agreeable people. People who are not judgmental—who will put up with your every whim—tend to score low on conscientiousness (they don't examine you closely) and high on agreeableness (you can be yourself) (Bernardin et al., 2000). Despite the stereotype that older people, especially men, are "crotchety," assessment of 65- to 100-year-olds using the *NEO Five-Factor Inventory* suggests that people, especially men, become more agreeable as they grow older (Weiss et al., 2005). People who are anxious or depressed tend to score higher on the trait of neuroticism (Bienvenu et al., 2005). Introverts are more likely than extraverts to fear public gatherings and public speaking (Bienvenu et al., 2005).

Evaluation of the Trait Perspectives and the Big Five

What are the strengths and weaknesses of trait theory? Trait theorists have focused much attention on the development of personality tests. They have also given rise to theories about the fit between personality and certain kinds of jobs (Holland, 1996). The qualities that suit a person for various kinds of work can be expressed in terms of abilities, personality traits, and interests. By using interviews and tests to learn about an individual's abilities and traits, testing and counselling centres can make helpful predictions about that person's chances of success and personal fulfillment in certain kinds of jobs.

One limitation of trait theory is that it has tended to be more descriptive than explanatory. It has historically focused on describing traits rather than on tracing their origins or finding out how they may be modified.

Some trait theorists also criticize the "Big Five" theory, stating that limiting personality to five factors ignores other important personality factors, ones that predict future behaviour and action better than the "Big Five." In a cross-cultural study (including participants from Canada, England, Germany, and Finland) led by Canadian researcher Sampo Paunonen at the University of Western Ontario, the researchers discovered that traits such as egoism, traditionalism, and masculinity/femininity (traits statistically not related to or included in the "Big Five") predicted behaviours like using tobacco and consuming alcohol, attending parties, buying lottery tickets, and driving fast, much better than any of the "Big Five" (Paunonen, Haddock, Forsterling, & Keinonen, 2003). Other research from Brock University and the University of Calgary suggests that a sixth factor should be included in trait research and we should be talking about the "Big Six" not the "Big Five" (Ashton & Lee, 2008). The sixth factor proposed by Michael Ashton and Kibeom Lee is called honesty-humility, and it far outperforms the traditional five factors in predicting moral behaviours and matters like ethical business decisions (see the Try It! box).

TABLE 11.1

The "Big Five": The Five-Factor Model (OCEAN)

Factor	Name	Traits
O	Openness to experience	Contrasts imagination, curiosity, and creativity with shallowness and lack of perceptiveness
C	Conscientiousness	Contrasts organization, thoroughness, and reliability with carelessness, negligence, and unreliability
E	Extraversion	Contrasts talkativeness, assertiveness, and activity with silence, passivity, and reserve
A	Agreeableness	Contrasts kindness, trust, and warmth with hostility, selfishness, and distrust
N	Neuroticism	Contrasts nervousness, moodiness, and sensitivity to negative stimuli with coping ability

Jim Scherer/StockFood Creative/Getty Images

LO3 Learning-Theory Perspectives

Trait theory focused on enduring personality characteristics that were generally presumed to be embedded in the nervous system. Learning theorists tend not to theorize in terms of traits. They focus, instead, on behaviours and presume that those behaviours are largely learned.

That which is learned is also, in principle, capable of being unlearned. As a result, learning theory and personality theory may not be a perfect fit. Nevertheless, learning theorists—both behaviourists and social-cognitive theorists—have contributed to the discussion of personality. *What does behaviourism contribute to our understanding of personality?*

Behaviourism

At Johns Hopkins University in 1924, John B. Watson sounded the battle cry of the behaviourist movement:

Give me a dozen healthy infants, well-formed, and my own specified world to bring them up in, and I'll guarantee to take any one at random and train him to become any type of specialist I might suggest—doctor, lawyer, merchant-chief and, yes, even beggar-man and thief, regardless of his talents, penchants, tendencies, abilities, vocations, and the race of his ancestors (p. 82).

This proclamation underscores the behaviourist view that personality is plastic—that situational or environmental influences, not internal, individual variables, are the key shapers of personality. In contrast to the psychoanalysts and structuralists of his day, Watson argued that unseen, undetectable mental structures must be rejected in favour of that which can be seen and measured. In the 1930s Watson's flag was carried onward by B.F. Skinner, who agreed that psychologists should avoid trying to see into the "black box" of the organism and instead emphasize the effects of reinforcements on behaviour.

The views of Watson and Skinner largely ignored the notions of personal freedom, choice, and self-direction. Most of us assume that our wants originate within us. Watson and Skinner suggested that environmental influences such as parental approval and social custom shape us into *wanting* certain things and *not wanting* others.

In his novel *Walden Two*, Skinner (1948) described a Utopian society in which people are happy and content because they are allowed to do as they please. From early childhood, however, they have been trained or conditioned to be cooperative. Because of their reinforcement histories, they *want* to behave in decent, kind, and unselfish ways. They see themselves as free because society makes no effort to force them to behave in particular ways. The American poet Robert Frost wrote, "You have freedom when you're easy in your harness." Society in Skinner's *Walden Two* made children "easy" in

social-cognitive theory
a cognitively oriented learning theory in which observational learning and person variables such as values and expectancies play major roles in individual differences

their "harnesses," but the harnesses were very real.

Some object to behaviourist notions because they play down the importance of consciousness and choice. Others argue that humans are not blindly ruled by pleasure and pain. In some circumstances people have rebelled against the so-called necessity of survival by choosing pain and hardship over pleasure, or suicide. Many people have sacrificed their own lives to save those of others; and some commit suicide as a weapon. The behaviourist "defence" might be that the apparent choice of pain or death is forced on some just as conformity to social custom is forced on others.

Social-Cognitive Theory

Social-cognitive theory was developed primarily by Canadian psychologist Albert Bandura (1986, 1999, 2002). *How does social-cognitive theory differ from the behaviourist view?* In contrast to behaviourism, which focuses on observable behaviour and the situations in which behaviour occurs, social-cognitive theory focuses on learning by observation and on the cognitive processes that underlie personal differences. Social-cognitive theorists see people as influencing their environment just as their environment affects them. Social-cognitive theorists agree with behaviourists that discussions of human nature should be tied to observable behaviour, but they assert that variables within people—*person variables*—must also be considered if we are to understand people. *Situational variables* include rewards and punishments. Person variables include knowledge and skills, ways of interpreting experience, expectancies, emotions, and self-regulatory systems and plans (Bandura & Locke, 2003; Mischel & Shoda, 1995; see Figure 11.3).

FIGURE 11.3

Situational and Personal Variables

Social-cognitive theorists believe that we must consider both situational variables and variables within the person if we are going to understand people and predict behaviour.

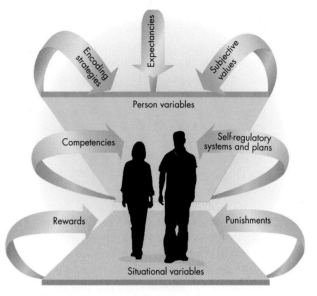

We cannot predict behaviour from situational variables alone. Whether a person will behave in a certain way also depends on the person's *expectancies* about the outcomes of that behaviour and the perceived or *subjective values* of those outcomes. There are various kinds of expectancies. Some are predictions about what will follow what. For example, people might predict other people's behaviour on the basis of body language such as "tight lips" or "shifty eyes." *Self-efficacy expectations* are beliefs that we can accomplish certain things, such as doing a back-flip into a swimming pool or solving math problems (Bandura & Locke, 2003). People with positive self-efficacy expectations tend to have high self-esteem (Sanna & Meier, 2000) and achievement motivation

Many males tie their self-esteem to prowess in sports.

(Heimpel et al., 2002). Psychotherapy often motivates people to try new things by changing their self-efficacy expectations from "I can't" to "Perhaps I can" (Bandura, 1999).

Observational Learning

Observational learning (also termed *modelling* or *cognitive learning*) is one of the foundations of Bandura's (1986) social-cognitive theory. It refers to acquiring knowledge by observing others. For operant conditioning to occur, an organism must first engage in a response, and that response must be reinforced. But observational learning occurs even when the learner does not perform the observed behaviour. Direct reinforcement is not required either. Observing others extends to reading about them or seeing what they do and what happens to them in books, and on TV, film, and the Internet.

Social-Cognitive Theory and Gender-Typing

There seems to be little question that hormonal influences and organization of the brain contribute to gender-typing. Social-cognitive theorists, however, suggest that children also learn what is considered masculine or feminine by observational learning. Research evidence shows that children's views of what is masculine and feminine are related to those of their parents (Tenenbaum & Leaper, 2002).

Parents and other adults—even other children—inform children about how they are expected to behave. They reinforce or reward children for behaviour they consider appropriate for their anatomic sex. They punish (or fail to reinforce) children for behaviour they consider inappropriate.

Girls, for example, are given dolls while they are still sleeping in cribs. They are encouraged to use the dolls to rehearse care-taking behaviours in preparation for traditional feminine adult roles. Reinforcement helps, but, according to social-cognitive theorists, not mechanically. Rather, reinforcement provides information about what behaviours people consider to be proper for girls and boys.

Gender-schema theory further emphasizes the role of cognition in gender-typing (Martin et al., 2002; Martin & Ruble, 2004). Cultures tend to polarize males and females into opposing groups because social life is organized around exclusive gender roles. For example, girls often accept the role of nurturer (playing with dolls). Unless parents or unusual events encourage them to challenge the validity of gender polarization, children attempt to construct identities that are consistent with the "proper" script.

Most children reject behaviour that deviates. Children's self-esteem becomes wrapped up in the ways in which they measure up to the gender schema. For example, many boys tie their self-esteem to prowess in sports.

Once children understand the labels *boy* and *girl,* they have a basis for blending their self-concepts with the gender schema of their culture. No external pressure is required. Children who have developed a sense of being male or being female, which usually occurs by the age of three, seek to learn what is considered appropriate for them by observing other people (Tenenbaum & Leaper, 2002).

gender-schema theory
a cognitive view of gender-typing that proposes that once girls and boys become aware of their anatomic sex, they begin to blend their self-expectations and self-esteem with the ways in which they fit the gender roles prescribed in a given culture

humanism
the view that people are capable of free choice, self-fulfillment, and ethical behaviour

Evaluation of the Learning Perspective

Psychoanalytic theorists and trait theorists propose the existence of psychological structures that cannot be seen and measured directly. Learning theorists—particularly behaviourists—have dramatized the importance of referring to publicly observable variables, or behaviours, if psychology is to be accepted as a science.

Similarly, psychoanalytic theorists and trait theorists focus on internal variables such as unconscious conflict and traits to explain and predict behaviour. Learning theorists emphasize the importance of environmental conditions, or situational variables, as determinants of behaviour. They have also elaborated on the conditions that foster learning, including automatic kinds of learning. They have shown that we can learn to do things because of reinforcements and that many behaviours are learned by observing others.

Social-cognitive theory does not account for self-awareness, and, like its intellectual forebear, behaviourism, it may not pay enough attention to genetic variation in explaining individual differences in behaviour.

LO4 The Humanistic Perspective

Humanists dwell on the meaning of life. Self-awareness is the hub of the humanistic search for meaning. *What is humanism?*

Humanism puts people and self-awareness at the centre of consideration and argues that they

self-actualization
in humanistic theory, the innate tendency to strive to realize one's fullest potential of perceptive clarity, peacefulness, simplicity, a sense of mission, sensitivity to the needs of others, being comfortable alone, a healthy sense of humour, and moments of profound emotional experience

are capable of free choice, self-fulfillment, and ethical behaviour. It became a third force in American psychology in the 1950s and 1960s, partly in response to the predominant psychoanalytic and behavioural models. Psychoanalysis put people at the mercy of unconscious conflict, and behaviourism argued that people were shaped by the environment.

Abraham Maslow and the Challenge of Self-Actualization

Freud wrote that people are basically motivated to gratify biological drives and that their perceptions are distorted by their psychological needs. *How do humanistic psychologists differ from psychoanalytic theorists?* The humanistic psychologist Abraham Maslow—whose hierarchy of needs we described in Chapter 9—argued that people also have a conscious need for **self-actualization**, or to become all that they can be. Because people are unique, they must follow unique paths to self-actualization. People are not at the mercy of unconscious, primitive impulses. Rather, the

main threat to individual personality development is control by other people. We must each be free to get in touch with and actualize our selves. But self-actualization requires taking risks. Many people are more comfortable with the familiar. But people who adhere to the "tried and true" may find their lives slipping into monotony and mediocrity.

Carl Rogers's Self Theory

The humanistic psychologist Carl Rogers (1902–1987) wrote that people shape themselves through free choice and action. *What is the self?* Rogers defined the *self* as the centre of experience. Your self is your ongoing sense of who and what you are, your sense of how and why you react to the environment and how you choose to act on the environment. Your choices are made on the basis of your values, and your values are also part of your self. *What is self theory?* Rogers's self theory focuses on the nature of the self and the conditions that allow the self to develop freely. Two of his major concerns are the self-concept and self-esteem.

The Self-Concept and Frames of Reference

Our self-concepts consist of our impressions of ourselves and our evaluations of our adequacy. It may be

---

{ Virtuous Traits: Positive Psychology and Trait Theory }

Trait theory has applications within positive psychology, a field that studies character strengths and virtues, such as those in the table below—how they come into being and how they are related to life satisfaction. Christopher Peterson and Martin E.P. Seligman (2004) summarized many of the research findings in their book *Character Strengths and Virtues: A Handbook and Classification* (the *CSV*). The handbook lists six major virtuous traits found in 40 different countries as different as Azerbaijan and Venezuela, along with the United States and other

developed nations. These virtues were widely recognized and valued, despite cultural and religious differences (Park et al., 2005).

The *CSV* was partly developed as a counterpoint to the *DSM*, which is the *Diagnostic and Statistical Manual of Mental Disorders* published by the American Psychiatric Association (2000). Whereas the *DSM* is a catalogue of (nearly) everything that can go wrong with people, the *CSV* is a catalogue of things that go right. Fortunately, there are many of them.

Virtue	Corresponding Character Strengths
Wisdom and knowledge	Creativity, curiosity, open-mindedness, love of learning, perspective (ability to provide other people with sound advice)
Courage	Authenticity (speaking one's mind), bravery, persistence, zest
Humanity	Kindness, love, social intelligence (see emotional intelligence, discussed in Chapter 7)
Justice	Fairness, leadership, teamwork
Temperance	Forgiveness, modesty, prudence, self-regulation
Transcendence	Appreciation of beauty and excellence, gratitude (when appropriate), hope, humour, religiousness (having a belief system about the meaning of life)

Source: Peterson & Seligman, 2004.

---

helpful to think of us as rating ourselves according to various scales or dimensions such as good–bad, intelligent–unintelligent, strong–weak, and tall–short.

Rogers believed that we all have unique ways of looking at ourselves and the world—that is, unique frames of reference. It may be that we each use a different set of dimensions in defining ourselves and that we judge ourselves according to different sets of values. To one person, achievement–failure may be the most important dimension. To another person, the most important dimension may be tolerance–intolerance. A third person may not even think in these terms.

Self-Esteem and Positive Regard

Rogers assumed that we all develop a need for self-regard, or self-esteem. At first, self-esteem reflects the esteem in which others hold us. Parents help children develop self-esteem when they show them **unconditional positive regard**—that is, when they accept them as having intrinsic merit regardless of their behaviour at the moment. But when parents show children **conditional positive regard**—that is, when they accept them only when they behave in a desired manner—children may develop **conditions of worth**. Therefore, children may come to think that they have merit only if they behave as their parents wish them to behave.

Because each individual has a unique potential, children who develop conditions of worth must be somewhat disappointed in themselves. They cannot fully live up to the wishes of others and be true to themselves. This does not mean that the expression of the self inevitably leads to conflict. Rogers believed that we hurt others or act in antisocial ways only when we are frustrated in our efforts to develop our potential. When parents and others are loving and tolerant of our differentness, we, too, are loving—even if our preferences, abilities, and values differ from those of our parents.

Children in some families, however, learn that it is bad to have ideas of their own, especially about sexual, political, or religious matters. When they perceive their caregivers' disapproval, they may come to see themselves as rebels and label their feelings as selfish, wrong, or evil. If they wish to retain a consistent self-concept and self-esteem, they may have to deny their feelings or disown parts of themselves. In this way their self-concept becomes distorted. According to Rogers, anxiety often stems from recognition that people have feelings and desires that are inconsistent with their distorted self-concept. Because anxiety is unpleasant, people may deny the existence of their genuine feelings and desires.

Rogers believed that the path to self-actualization requires getting in touch with our genuine feelings, accepting them, and acting on them. This is the goal of Rogers's method of psychotherapy, *client-centred therapy*. Rogers also believed that we have mental images of what we are capable of becoming. These are termed *self-ideals*. We are motivated to reduce the difference between our self-concepts and our self-ideals.

unconditional positive regard a persistent expression of esteem for the value of a person, but not necessarily an unqualified acceptance of all of the person's behaviours

conditional positive regard judgment of another person's value on the basis of the acceptability of that person's behaviours

conditions of worth standards by which the value of a person is judged

Evaluation of the Humanistic Perspective

What are the strengths and weaknesses of humanistic theory? The humanistic perspective has tremendous appeal for college and university students because of its focus on the importance of personal experience. We tend to treasure our conscious experiences (our "selves"). For most nonhumans, to live is to move, to process food, to exchange oxygen and carbon dioxide, and to reproduce. But for humans, an essential aspect of life is conscious experience—the sense of oneself as progressing through space and time.

Ironically, the primary strength of the humanistic approach—its focus on conscious experience—is also its main weakness. Conscious experience is private and subjective. Therefore, the validity of formulating theories in terms of consciousness has been questioned.

Humanistic theories, like learning theories, have little to say about the development of traits and personality types. They assume that we are all unique, but they do not predict the sorts of traits, abilities, and interests we will develop.

"You are unique, and if that is not fulfilled, then something has been lost."
—Martha Graham

LO5 The Sociocultural Perspective

Why is the sociocultural perspective important to the understanding of personality? Undoubtedly, Canada is a multicultural society. According to Statistics

sociocultural perspective
the view that focuses on the roles of ethnicity, gender, culture, and socioeconomic status in personality formation, behaviour, and mental processes

Sven Hope/Shutterstock.com

Canada, every major people group from every continent has a representative population living in Canada (Statistics Canada, 2009a). More than 16 percent of Canada's population belongs to a visible minority group, including Chinese, Black, Filipino, Latin American, Arab, Korean, and Japanese (Statistics Canada, 2009b). In this multicultural society, personality cannot be understood without reference to the **sociocultural perspective**. According to a national poll, 71 percent of people in the country agreed that "they were proud to be Canadian" (Geddes, 2006). The same poll found 38 percent of Canadians citing multiculturalism and 25 percent citing bilingualism as important aspects of a Canadian identity (Geddes, 2006). Forty-four percent of Canadians say that their religion is an important part of their life (Clark & Schellenberg, 2006). However, it seems that the most unifying force in Canada, more so than multiculturalism, bilingualism and religion, is hockey. With four out of every five Canadians who tuned in to the men's final hockey game of the 2010 Winter Olympics, hockey is clearly an important part of many Canadians' identities. *Maclean's* writer John Geddes writes about the importance of hockey in Canadian life and identity:

> On our $5 bill, in a spot where another country might offer an old Latin motto, there's a bilingual quotation from Roch Carrier's short story "The Hockey Sweater." When Michael Ignatieff wrote an essay about Canada's two solitudes, back before he entered politics, his epiphany about the language divide occurred—where else?—in a Trois-Rivières, Que., hockey arena. Not to be outdone, Prime Minister Stephen Harper burnishes his image by letting it be known that he toils during spare moments over some sort of history of the game (Geddes, 2010).
>
> Reprinted by permission of *Maclean's*.

With such a large percentage of Canadians who originate from so many diverse areas of the globe, we encounter a rich mixture of cultural values, customs, and

Hill Street Studio/Blend/GetStock.com

expectations. Let's explore how contrasting cultural values may coincide within an individual to produce what many Canadians experience. Meet Hannah: she's the daughter of Korean parents who immigrated to Canada five years before she was born. Growing up in a Toronto suburb, she learns about Korean culture and norms from parents. Information about Canadian culture is supplied by friends, television, and the public school system. Hannah's traits include exceptional academic ability and musical talent, which were at least partly determined by her heredity. She is consciously striving to become a great violinist. Hannah, now a teenager, is strongly influenced by her peers—she is completely at home with blue jeans and French fries. She is also a daughter in an Asian immigrant group that often views education as the key to success in our culture (Leppel, 2002). Belonging to this ethnic group had probably contributed to her ambition. But being a Korean Canadian has not prevented her from becoming an outspoken teenager. Her outspoken behaviour has struck her parents as brazen and inappropriate on several occasions. Her parents often lament that she thinks of herself first, and her family second.

Let us consider how sociocultural factors can affect one's sense of self, but first, take a look at the Try It! box.

Try It!

Complete the following statements with different aspects of how you would describe yourself to a new friend:

I am _____

I am _____

I am _____

I am _____

I am _____

I am _____

Now, take a moment and look over how you completed these statements. Did you include information about your personality characteristics (e.g., kind, humorous, quiet), or your abilities (e.g., an athlete, a guitar player), or your occupation (e.g., a student)? If so, you are like many Canadians who understand themselves in an individualistic way. However, if you are like others who see themselves from a collectivistic viewpoint, your statements might include details such as your family name, your relationships (e.g., a sister, a brother, a friend), or group memberships (e.g., a Christian, a Canadian). Perhaps you have statements that include both a collectivist and individualistic perspective. If so, you are reflecting the multiculturalism and diversity of perspectives that is Canada.

Individualism versus Collectivism: Who Am I (in This Cultural Setting)?

One could say that Hannah's mother's complaint was that Hannah saw herself as an individual and a musician to a greater extent than as a family member and a Korean girl. *What is meant by individualism and collectivism?* Cross-cultural research reveals that people in Canada, the United States, and many northern European nations tend to be more individualistic. **Individualists** tend to define themselves in terms of their personal identities and to give priority to their personal goals (Triandis, 2005). When asked to complete the statement "I am…," they are likely to respond in terms of their personality traits ("I am outgoing," "I am artistic") or their occupations ("I am a nurse," "I am a systems analyst") (Triandis & Suh, 2005). In contrast, many people from cultures in Africa, Asia, and Central and South America tend to be collectivistic. **Collectivists** tend to define themselves in terms of the groups to which they belong and to give priority to the group's goals (Bandura, 2003; Triandis, 2005). They feel complete in terms of their relationships with others (see Figure 11.4). They are more likely than individualists to conform to group norms and judgments. When asked to complete the statement "I am…," collectivists are more likely to respond in terms of their families, gender, or nation ("I am a father," "I am a Buddhist," "I am Japanese") (Triandis, 2005).

The seeds of individualism and collectivism are found in the culture in which a person grows up. The capitalist system fosters individualism to some degree. It assumes that individuals are entitled to amass personal fortunes and that the process of doing so creates jobs and wealth for large numbers of

individualist a person who defines herself or himself in terms of personal traits and gives priority to her or his own goals

collectivist a person who defines herself or himself in terms of relationships to other people and groups and gives priority to group goals

---

FIGURE 11.4

The Self in Relation to Others from the Individualist and Collectivist Perspectives

To an individualist, the self is separate from other people (part A). To a collectivist, the self is complete only in terms of relationships to other people (part B). (Based on Markus & Kitayama, 1991).

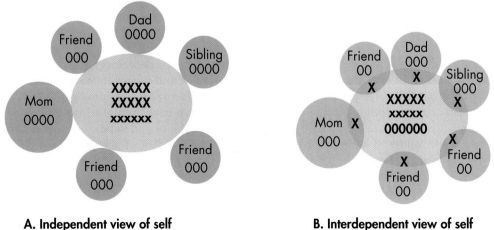

A. Independent view of self

B. Interdependent view of self

acculturation
the process of adaptation in which immigrants and native groups identify with a new, dominant culture by learning about that culture and making behavioural and attitudinal changes

validity
in psychological testing, the degree to which a test measures what it is supposed to measure

people. The individualist perspective is found in the self-reliant heroes and antiheroes of Western literature and mass media—from Homer's Odysseus to James Bond. The traditional writings of the East have exalted people who resist personal temptations to do their duty and promote the welfare of the group.

Another issue from the sociocultural perspective is acculturation. Just how much acculturation is good for you? *How does acculturation affect the psychological well-being of immigrants and their families?*

Acculturation, Adjustment, and Self-Esteem

Should Muslim women who immigrate to Canada remove their niqab or hijab when working in the public sector, as is being suggested by some in Quebec (CBC News, 2009, May 14)? Should Sikh Mounties remove their turbans when they are on duty (the right for Sikh Mounties to keep their turbans on was won in 1990; CBC Digital Archives, n.d.)? Should South Asian children be acquainted with the movies, music, and art of South Asia, or those of Canada and the United States? Should all immigrants be required to learn either English or French? Such activities are examples of **acculturation**, the process by which immigrants become acclimated to the customs and behaviour patterns of their new host culture.

Canadian researcher John Berry has shown that self-esteem is connected with patterns of acculturation among immigrants (Berry et al., 2006; Phinney, 2005). Those patterns take various forms. Some immigrants are completely assimilated by the dominant culture. They lose the language and customs of their country of origin and identify with the dominant culture in the new host country. Others maintain almost complete separation. They retain the language and customs of their country of origin and never acclimate to those of the new country. Most of the research suggests that the most adaptive pattern of acculturation is for the newcomer to become bicultural. They remain fluent in the language of their country of origin but also become conversant in the language of their new country. They blend the customs and values of both cultures. They can switch "mental gears"; they apply the values of one culture under some circumstances and apply the values of the other culture under others. Perhaps they relate to other people in one way at work or in school, and in another way at home or in the neighbourhood.

Research evidence suggests that people who do not surrender their traditional backgrounds have relatively higher self-esteem than those who do (Kim et al., 2003; Phinney & Devich-Navarro, 1997). Usborne and Taylor (2010) studied several groups, including Anglophone Quebecers, Francophone Québécois, Chinese North Americans, and Aboriginal Canadians. They found that those who had a strong understanding of his or her culture had higher levels of self-esteem, a clearer knowledge of him- or herself, and reported a more positive well-being. Berry and his colleagues have discovered that integrating both one's traditional background with the dominant culture is associated with the most beneficial outcomes for immigrant, sojourner (short-term relocation), refugee, and native populations in Canada (as cited in Sam & Berry, 2006).

Evaluation of the Sociocultural Perspective

The sociocultural perspective provides valuable insights into the roles of ethnicity, gender, culture, and socioeconomic status in personality formation. It enhances our sensitivity to cultural differences and expectations and allows us to appreciate the richness of human behaviour and mental processes.

LO6 Measurement of Personality

Physicians have an easy time of it measuring heart rate and blood pressure. Psychologists, biologists, and neuroscientists find it easier to measure electricity in the brain or substances in the blood than to measure psychological concepts such as intelligence, depression, extraversion, or emotional stability. It may take time, money, and expertise to develop and operate the proper instruments, but once you have them, the measurements tend to be accurate enough.

In Chapter 7 we saw that many critics argue that "intelligence tests" measure many things other than intelligence, including motivation and familiarity with white middle-class culture. In Chapter 9 we saw that "lie detectors" measure four physiological variables and detect much more than lies. The reliability and validity of intelligence tests and lie detectors have been brought into question. So too have the reliability and validity of personality tests.

The **validity** of a test is the extent to which it measures what it is supposed to measure. We usually assess the validity of personality tests by comparing test results to external criteria or standards. For example, a test of hyperactivity might be compared with teachers' reports about whether or not children

Laurence Gough/Shutterstock.com

in their classes are hyperactive. The **reliability** of a test is the stability of one's test results from one testing to another. We usually determine the reliability of tests by comparing test results on different occasions or at different ages. A reliable IQ test should provide scores during childhood that remain reasonably similar in adolescence and adulthood. Test **standardization** is a process that checks out the scores, validity, and reliability of a test with people of various ages and from various groups. We cannot assess the intellectual functioning of an individual without relating it to other people in the same age group. Such information is made available when tests are professionally developed and scored.

Behaviour-rating scales assess behaviour in settings such as classrooms or mental hospitals. With behaviour-rating scales, trained observers usually check off each occurrence of a specific behaviour within a certain time frame—say, 15 minutes. Standardized objective and projective tests, however, are used more frequently, and we focus on them in this section.

How are personality measures used? Measures of personality are used to make important decisions, such as whether a person is suited for a certain type of work, a particular class in school, or a drug to reduce agitation. As part of their admissions process, graduate schools often ask professors to rate prospective students on scales that assess traits such as intelligence, emotional stability, and cooperation. Students may take tests to measure their *aptitudes* and interests to gain insight into whether they are suited for certain occupations. It is assumed that students who share the aptitudes and interests of people who function well in certain positions are also likely to function well in those positions.

Let us consider the two most widely used types of personality tests: objective tests and projective tests.

Objective Tests

What are objective personality tests? **Objective tests** present respondents with a standardized group of test items in the form of a questionnaire. Respondents are limited to a specific range of answers. One test might ask respondents to indicate whether items are true or false for them. Another might ask respondents to select the preferred activity from groups of three.

Some tests have a *forced-choice format*, in which respondents are asked to indicate which of two or more statements is more true for them or which of several activities they prefer. The respondents are not usually given the option of answering "none of the above." Forced-choice formats are frequently used in interest inventories, which help predict whether the person would function well in a certain occupation. They are typically the only means of responding to online assessments because the test-taker is usually required to "click" the chosen answer. The following item is similar to those found in occupational interest inventories:

I would rather

a. be a forest ranger.
b. work in a busy office.
c. play a musical instrument.

The *Minnesota Multiphasic Personality Inventory* (MMPI) contains hundreds of items presented in a true–false format. The MMPI is designed to be used by clinical and counselling psychologists to help diagnose psychological disorders. Accurate measurement of an individual's problems should point to appropriate treatment. The MMPI is the most widely used psychological test in clinical work and is widely used in psychological research.

The MMPI is usually scored for the four *validity scales* and ten *clinical scales* described in Table 11.2 on the next page. The validity scales suggest whether answers actually represent the person's thoughts, emotions, and behaviours.

The validity scales in Table 11.2 assess different **response sets**, or biases, in answering the questions. People with high Lie (L) scores, for example, are probably attempting to present themselves as excessively moral and well-behaved individuals (faking good). People with high Frequency (F)

reliability
in psychological testing, the consistency or stability of test scores from one testing to another

standardization
in psychological testing, the process by which one obtains and organizes test scores from various population groups, so that the results of a person completing a test can be compared to those of others of his or her sex, in his or her age group, and so on

objective tests
tests whose items must be answered in a specified, limited manner; tests whose items have concrete answers that are considered correct

response set
a tendency to answer test items according to a bias—for example, to make oneself seem perfect or bizarre

projective test
a psychological test that presents ambiguous stimuli onto which the test-taker projects his or her own personality in making a response

scores may be trying to seem bizarre or are answering haphazardly (faking bad). Those with high Correction (K) scores are probably in denial or trying to hide something (faking that nothing is wrong). Many personality measures have some kind of validity scale. The clinical scales of the MMPI assess the problems shown in Table 11.2, as well as stereotypical masculine or feminine interests and introversion.

The MMPI scales were constructed and validated *empirically*—that is, on the basis of actual clinical data rather than psychological theory. A test-item bank of several hundred items was derived from questions that are often asked in clinical interviews.

Here are some examples of the kinds of items that were used:

My father was a good man	T	F
I am very seldom troubled by headaches.	T	F
My hands and feet are usually warm enough.	T	F
I have never done anything dangerous for the thrill of it.	T	F
I work under a great deal of tension.	T	F

The items were administered to people with previously identified symptoms, such as depressive or schizophrenic symptoms. Items that successfully set these people apart were included.

Projective Tests

How do projective tests differ from objective tests? In **projective tests** there are no clear, specified answers.

TABLE 11.2

Minnesota Multiphasic Personality Inventory (MMPI) Scales

Scale	Abbreviation	Possible Interpretations
Validity scales		
Question	?	Corresponds to number of items left unanswered
Lie	L	Lies or is highly conventional
Frequency	F	Exaggerates complaints or answers items haphazardly; may have bizarre ideas
Correction	K	Denies problems
Clinical scales		
Hypochondriasis	Hs	Has bodily concerns and complaints
Depression	D	Is depressed; has feelings of guilt and helplessness
Hysteria	Hy	Reacts to stress by developing physical symptoms; lacks insight
Psychopathic deviate	Pd	Is immoral, in conflict with the law; has stormy relationships
Masculinity/femininity	Mf	High scores suggest interests and behaviour considered stereotypical of the other gender
Paranoia	Pa	Is suspicious and resentful, highly cynical about human nature
Psychasthenia	Pt	Is anxious, worried, high-strung
Schizophrenia	Sc	Is confused, disorganized, disoriented; has bizarre ideas
Hypomania	Ma	Is energetic, restless, active, easily bored
Social introversion	Si	Is introverted, timid, shy; lacks self-confidence

Stockbyte/Getty Images

People are shown ambiguous stimuli such as inkblots or ambiguous drawings and asked to say what they look like or to tell stories about them. There is no one correct response. It is assumed that people *project* their own personalities into their responses. The meanings they attribute to these stimuli are assumed to reflect their personalities as well as the drawings or blots themselves.

The Rorschach Inkblot Test

There are a number of psychological tests made up of inkblots, and test-takers are asked to say what the blots look like to them. (If you want to try one, see

Try It!

Of all the inkblot tests, the Rorschach is the most widely used projective personality test. What does this inkblot look like to you? What could it be? Although there is no single "correct" response to the inkblot shown, some responses are not in keeping with the features of the blots and reveal to the examiner that the test-taker is projecting his or her personality onto the test stimuli. The shape of the inkblot might commonly suggest a bat, a butterfly, or a moth. A test-taker who makes unusual or uncommon responses to the features of the blot may be revealing personality problems.

the Try It! box.) The best-known example of these is the Rorschach inkblot test, named after its originator, Hermann Rorschach.

People are handed the inkblots, one by one, and are asked what they look like or what they could be. A response that reflects the shape of the blot is considered a sign of adequate *reality testing*. A response that richly integrates several features of the blot is considered a sign of high intellectual functioning. Supporters of the Rorschach believe that it provides insight into a person's intelligence, interests, cultural background, personality traits, psychological disorders, and many other variables. Critics argue that there is little empirical evidence to support the test's validity (Garb et al., 2005).

Although the Internet has offered many benefits, the freedom of information it provides has also led to challenges for some psychological measurement tools. For example, The Rorschach inkblot test is only valid if the test-taker is encountering the ten inkblot slides for the first time. However, the ten slides have been published online in several locations (including Wikipedia), along with common responses to the images. Due to the public release of the slides, the test's already questionable validity has taken a further hit.

The Thematic Apperception Test

The Thematic Apperception Test (TAT) was developed in the 1930s by Henry Murray and Christiana Morgan. It consists of drawings, like the one shown in the Try It! box on page 205 in Chapter 9, that are open to various interpretations. Individuals are given the cards one at a time and asked to make up stories about them.

The TAT is widely used in research on motivation and in clinical practice. The assumption is that we are likely to project our own needs into our responses to ambiguous situations, even if we are unaware of them or reluctant to talk about them. The TAT is also widely used to assess attitudes toward other people, especially parents and intimate partners.

Psychological Disorders

Learning Outcomes

LO1 Define psychological disorders and describe their prevalence

LO2 Describe the symptoms, types, and possible origins of schizophrenia

LO3 Describe the symptoms and possible origins of mood disorders

LO4 Describe the symptoms and possible origins of six types of anxiety disorders

LO5 Describe the symptoms and possible origins of somatoform disorders

LO6 Describe the symptoms and possible origins of dissociative disorders

LO7 Describe the symptoms and possible origins of personality disorders

"Each year I would withdraw and get depressed as soon as the leaves were off the trees."

Heather groaned as she peeked out from under her duvet at her loudly buzzing alarm clock. It read 8:30 but the room was still dark. "Why is it still so dark in here?" thought Heather as she looked toward the window. She hated getting out of bed when it was still dark outside, and in December at 8:30 a.m. the sun had just started peeking up over the horizon. She felt a degree of anxiety thinking about getting up on this cold morning and trudging through the deep snow. "I'll probably just be late again for class anyway," she despondently mused as she reached over, turned off the alarm clock, and pulled the covers up over her head. "A few more hours are all I need," she tiredly thought as she drifted back off to sleep.

Heather suffers from **seasonal affective disorder (SAD)**. It is a mood disorder that affects an estimated 1 million other Canadians every year. Every winter Heather slips into a state of depression that affects her ability to cope with her studies and maintain her relationships. She eats a lot more, puts on weight, and seems to constantly crave sugary and starchy foods in great quantities. She feels frequently tired and devoid of energy, and no matter how early she gets to bed, she wakes up tired and groggy. When she does get to class, she is irritable and easily distracted. All of these difficulties have led her to feel anxious when considering going out, and she has begun to avoid social situations. Each winter, Heather shuffles around, as if in a fog, trying to make it until March, when suddenly it is as if a switch is flipped, and Heather has increased energy, less fatigue, more balanced eating habits.

SAD is estimated to affect 3 percent of the Canadian population, with a further 15 percent (5 million) afflicted with a milder version of the disorder (Canadian Mental Health Association, 2010). It generally appears after the age of 20, and seems to affect women more than men. As researchers tried to find the cause of the disorder, some interesting facts have emerged. The latitude hypothesis suggests that the distance one is from the equator, the greater likelihood that one could suffer from SAD (Magnusson & Partonen, 2005). Data from around the world seems to support this hypothesis, and this is why so many Canadians suffer from this disorder. It is thought that reduced sunlight causes the emergence of the symptoms associated with SAD in some individuals. However, even though there are days in the winter when the sun shines for only four hours in Reykjavík, Iceland, those who live there seem to be largely immune to SAD. Perhaps there is something genetically different for those of Icelandic descent that protects them from SAD (Axelsson et al., 2002). Thus, for SAD,

DID YOU KNOW?

- People with schizophrenia may see and hear things that are not really there.
- Feeling elated is not always a good thing.
- Some people have more than one personality dwelling within them, and each one may have different allergies and eyeglass prescriptions.
- Some people can kill or maim others without any feelings of guilt.

seasonal affective disorder (SAD) depressive mood disorder that manifests during the winter months, marked with increased eating, sleeping, weight gain, and a depressed mood

psychological disorders
patterns of behaviour or mental processes that are connected with emotional distress or significant impairment in functioning

hallucination
a perception in the absence of sensory stimulation that is confused with reality

ideas of persecution
erroneous beliefs that one is being victimized or persecuted

flat affect
a severe reduction in emotional expressiveness, found among many people with schizophrenia or serious depression

and for all psychological disorders, it is ultimately the interaction of genetics and environment that determines if a person will be afflicted.

LO1 What Are Psychological Disorders?

Psychology is the study of behaviour and mental processes. **Psychological disorders** are behaviours or mental processes that are connected with distress or disability. They are not predictable responses to specific events.

Some psychological disorders are characterized by anxiety, but many people are anxious now and then without being considered disordered. It is appropriate to be anxious before an important date or on the eve of a midterm exam. When, then, are feelings like anxiety deemed to be abnormal or signs of a psychological disorder?

For one thing, anxiety may suggest a disorder when it does not fit the situation. For example, there is (usually) little or no reason to be anxious when entering an elevator or looking out of a fourth-storey window. The magnitude of the problem may also suggest disorder. Some anxiety can be expected before a job interview. However, feeling that your heart is pounding so intensely that you are about to suffer a heart attack—and then avoiding the interview—are not.

Behaviours or mental processes are suggestive of psychological disorders when they meet some combination of the following standards:

• *Is the behaviour unusual?* Heather's sleeping and eating habits that are dependent on the seasons are unusual, found among only a small minority of the population. Yet uncommon behaviour or mental processes are not necessarily abnormal in themselves. Only one person holds the record for running or swimming the fastest mile. That person is different from you and me but is not abnormal. Thus rarity or statistical deviance is not sufficient for behaviour or mental processes to be labelled abnormal. We must also consider the situation. Although many of us feel "panicked" when we realize that a term paper or report is due the next day, most of us do not have panic attacks "out of the blue." Unpredictable panic attacks are thus a psychological disorder.

• *Does the behaviour suggest faulty perception or interpretation of reality?* Hearing voices and seeing things that are not there are considered hallucinations. Ideas of persecution, such as believing that the Mafia or the police are "out to get you," are also considered signs of disorder. (Unless, of course, they *are* out to get you.)

• *Is the person's emotional response appropriate to the situation?* Irrational fears, such as intense fear of injections and depression among people with "good lives," may be considered inappropriate and thus abnormal. It is also possible to show too little emotional response compared to what would be expected by the situation. This flat affect is often found among people with schizophrenia or serious depression.

• *Is the behaviour self-defeating?* Behaviour or mental processes that cause misery rather than happiness and fulfillment may suggest psychological disorder. Chronic drinking impairs one's health and may therefore be deemed abnormal. Fear of needles is more likely to be considered abnormal if it prevents one from receiving necessary medical treatment. Heather's behaviour every winter was causing damage to her relationships and negatively impacting her grades, thus it is considered self-defeating.

• *Is the behaviour dangerous?* Behaviour or mental processes that are hazardous to the self or others may be considered suggestive of psychological disorders. People who threaten or attempt suicide may be considered abnormal, as may people who threaten or attack others. But aggressive behaviour in athletics—within certain limits, as in contact sports—is not considered disordered.

• *Is the behaviour socially unacceptable?* We must consider the cultural context of a behaviour pattern in judging whether or not it is normal.

Classifying Psychological Disorders

Classification is at the heart of science. Without classifying psychological disorders, investigators would not be able to communicate with each other and scientific progress would come to a halt. The most widely used classification scheme for psychological disorders is the *Diagnostic and Statistical Manual of Mental Disorders (DSM)* of the American Psychiatric Association (2000). *How are psychological disorders classified?*

The current edition of the *DSM* is the *DSM-IV-TR* (fourth edition, text revision), and it provides information about a person's overall functioning as well as a diagnosis. People may receive diagnoses for clinical syndromes or personality disorders, or for both. It also includes information about people's medical conditions, psychosocial problems, and a global assessment of functioning. Medical conditions include physical disorders or problems that may affect people's response to psychotherapy or drug treatment. Psychosocial and environmental problems include difficulties that may affect the diagnosis, treatment, or outcome of a psychological disorder. The global assessment of functioning allows the clinician to compare the client's current level of functioning with her or his highest previous level of functioning to help set goals for restoring functioning.

Although the *DSM* is widely used, researchers have some concerns about it. Two of them concern the *reliability* and *validity* of the diagnostic standards. The *DSM* might be considered *reliable* if different interviewers would make the same diagnosis when they evaluate the same people. In the case of Heather, the *DSM* might be considered reliable if various evaluators who were using the manual arrived at the same diagnosis—seasonal affective disorder. The *DSM* might be considered *valid* if the diagnoses described in the manual cor-

respond to clusters of behaviours observed in the real world. Referring once more to Heather, the *DSM* might be considered valid if the diagnosis of SAD, described in the manual, fits Heather's actual behaviour. A specific type of validity, called **predictive validity**, means that if a diagnosis is valid, we should be able to predict what will happen to the person over time (that is, the *course* of the disorder) and what type of treatment may be of help.

> **predictive validity** in this usage, the extent to which a diagnosis permits one to predict the course of a disorder and the type of treatment that may be of help

Classification is at the heart of science.

Prevalence of Psychological Disorders

At first glance, psychological disorders might seem to affect only a few of us. Relatively few people are admitted to psychiatric hospitals. Most people will never seek the help of a psychologist or psychiatrist. And the insanity plea—although well publicized—is a rarity in the criminal justice system. Many of us have "eccentric" relatives or friends, but most of them are not considered to be literally "crazy." Nonetheless, psychological disorders affect us all in one way or another.

About half of us will meet the criteria for a *DSM-IV-TR* disorder at some time or another in our lives, with the disorder possibly beginning in childhood or adolescence (Kessler et al., 2005a). Slightly more than one-quarter of us will experience a psychological disorder in any given year (Kessler et al., 2005c; see Table 12.1). But if we include the problems of family members, friends, and co-workers, add in the number of those who foot the bill in terms of health insurance and taxes, and factor in increased product costs due to lost productivity, perhaps everyone is affected.

Let us now consider the various kinds of psychological disorders found in the *DSM-IV-TR* that affect adults. We begin with schizophrenia.

LO2 Schizophrenia

Let's listen in on part of an interview with Etta:

Etta: Well …, ah …, Jesus was giving me all these cracks, window cracks, and screen crack sounds telling me that they was going to break into the house. So I put the camera stereo in the room where they jiggled the window off to come through the window. And the camera stereo, the security guards picked that up, the message by putting that camera in that room.

Interviewer: Were you in danger?

Etta: Well, if anyone gets into the house they said I'd get shot.

Interviewer: Who said?

TABLE 12.1

Past-Year Prevalences of Common Psychological Disorders

	Anxiety Disorders	Mood Disorders	Substance Use Disorders
Men	3.6%	3.8%	4.4%
Women	5.8%	5.9%	1.6%

Note: The data in this table are based on a nationally representative sample of 36 984 Canadian residents aged 15 and above. Respondents could report symptoms of more than one type of disorder. For example, anxiety and mood disorders are often "comorbid"—that is, go together. Anxiety and mood disorders are discussed in this chapter. Substance use disorders include abuse of, or dependence on, alcohol or other drugs, as described in Chapter 4.

Adapted from Statistics Canada, *Canadian Community Health Survey - Mental Health and Well-being* (Highlights section), 82-617-XIE2003001, 2004. http://www.statcan.gc.ca/bsolc/olc-cel/olc-cel?catno=82-617-X&lang=eng.

delusions
false, persistent beliefs that are unsubstantiated by sensory or objective evidence

affect (AFF-ekt)
feeling or emotional response, particularly as suggested by facial expression and body language

schizophrenia
a psychotic disorder characterized by loss of control of thought processes and inappropriate emotional responses

stupor
a condition in which the senses, thought, and movement are dulled

Etta: That's The Eagle.

Interviewer: Can you say a little something about The Eagle?

Etta: The Eagle works through General Motors. It has something to do with my General Motors cheque I get every month.

Interviewer: And you get that cheque because it's part of your husband's work with GM?

Etta: Yes.

Interviewer: Say something about the relationship between GM and The Eagle.

Etta: Well …, ah …, when you do the 25 of the clock it means that you leave the house after one to mail letters so that they can check on you what how you're mailing the mail and they know when you're at that time.

Interviewer: And who's "they"?

Etta: That's The Eagle.

If you have the feeling that Etta is not making sense, you are quite correct. Normally our thoughts are rather tightly knit, having a beginning, a middle, and an end. Etta's thoughts—the way things are associated with one another—have come loose. She jumps from Jesus to cracks in the window to her "camera stereo" to "The Eagle" to General Motors to 25 o'clock (which does not exist) and the mail.

Etta also sees herself as being under attack. "They" are trying to break into the house. There's some kind of plot afoot having to do with The Eagle and General Motors. "They" are checking on her. Etta has false beliefs, or **delusions**, that she is being observed and persecuted. Yet for someone who believes she is being persecuted, Etta doesn't appear to be all that upset. Her **affect**—that is, her emotional response—is "flat" and inappropriate to the situation.

When interviewers listened to Etta's incoherent story about Jesus and cracks in the window and her "camera stereo," they suspected that she could be diagnosed with schizophrenia. *What is schizophrenia?* **Schizophrenia** is a severe psychological disorder that touches every aspect of a person's life. It is characterized by disturbances in thought and language, perception and attention, motor activity, and mood, and by social withdrawal and

absorption in daydreams or fantasy (Heinrichs, 2005).

Schizophrenia has been referred to as the worst disorder affecting people. It afflicts nearly 1 percent of the population worldwide. Its onset occurs relatively early in life, and it tends to endure.

People with schizophrenia have problems in memory, attention, and communication. Their thinking and communication ability becomes unravelled (Kerns & Berenbaum, 2002). Unless we allow our thoughts to wander, our thinking is normally tightly knit. We start at a certain point, and thoughts are logically connected. But people with schizophrenia often think illogically. As with Etta, their speech may be jumbled. They may combine parts of words into new words or make meaningless rhymes. They may jump from topic to topic, conveying little useful information. They usually do not recognize that their thoughts and behaviour are abnormal.

Many people with schizophrenia, like Etta, have delusions—for example, delusions of grandeur, persecution, or reference. In the case of delusions of grandeur, a person may believe that he is a famous historical figure such as Jesus, or a person on a special mission. He may have grand, illogical plans for saving the world. Delusions tend to be unshakable even in the face of evidence that they are not true. People with delusions of persecution, like Etta, may believe that they are sought by the Mafia, police, or some other group. A woman with delusions of reference said that news stories contained coded information about her. A man with such delusions complained that neighbours had "bugged" his walls with "radios." Other people with schizophrenia have had delusions that they have committed unpardonable sins, that they were rotting away from disease, or that they or the world did not exist.

People with schizophrenia may see or hear things that are not really there. Their perceptions often include hallucinations—imagery in the absence of external stimulation that the person cannot distinguish from reality. Other people who experience hallucinations may see colours or even obscene words spelled out in midair. Auditory hallucinations are most common.

In individuals with schizophrenia, motor activity may become wild or so slowed that the person is said to be in a **stupor**—that is, a condition in which the senses, thought, and movement are inhibited. There may be strange gestures and grimaces. The person's emotional responses may be flat or blunted, or inappropriate—as in giggling upon hearing bad news. People with schizophrenia tend to withdraw from social contacts, and become wrapped up in their own thoughts and fantasies.

In the film *A Beautiful Mind,* Russell Crowe plays the brilliant mathematician John Nash, who could be diagnosed as schizophrenic because of the hallucinations and delusions of persecution he experienced.

Positive versus Negative Symptoms

Many investigators find it useful to distinguish between positive and negative symptoms of schizophrenia. *What are the positive and negative symptoms of schizophrenia?* The **positive symptoms** are the excessive and sometimes bizarre symptoms, including hallucinations, delusions, and looseness of associations. The **negative symptoms** are the deficiencies we find among people with schizophrenia, such as lack of emotional expression and motivation, loss of pleasure in activities, social withdrawal, and poverty of speech. Etta showed an abundance of positive symptoms, including delusions, along with negative symptoms, such as flat affect. The distinction is useful not only in terms of description, but also in terms of development of the disorder and likely outcome. For example, people with mainly positive symptoms are more likely to experience an abrupt onset of the disorder and tend to preserve their intellectual abilities. The positive symptoms also respond more favourably to antipsychotic medication (Roth et al., 2004; Walker et al., 2004). People with mainly negative symptoms tend to experience a more gradual development of the disorder and severe intellectual impairments in attention, memory, and so on. The negative symptoms also respond more poorly to antipsychotic drugs.

It may be that positive and negative symptoms represent different but related biological processes. Positive symptoms may involve deficiency in the brain mechanisms that normally inhibit excessive or bizarre behaviours. They may reflect a disturbance in regulation of dopamine in the brain, because drugs that regulate dopamine levels generally reduce bizarre behaviour. Negative symptoms may reflect structural damage to the brain. Even so, positive and negative symptoms can coexist in the same person. Thus, these groups of symptoms have descriptive value but do not appear to represent distinct types of schizophrenia. *What types of schizophrenia are there?*

All types of schizophrenia involve a thought disorder. There are, however, various "types" with different emphases on positive and negative symptoms, including paranoid, disorganized, and catatonic schizophrenia.

Paranoid Schizophrenia

People with **paranoid schizophrenia,** such as Etta, have systematized delusions and, frequently, related auditory hallucinations. They usually have delusions of grandeur and persecution, but they may also have delusions of jealousy, in which they believe that a spouse or lover has been unfaithful. They may show agitation, confusion, and fear, and may experience vivid hallucinations that are consistent with their delusions. People with paranoid schizophrenia often construct complex or systematized delusions involving themes of wrongdoing or persecution. John Nash, whose life was depicted in the movie *A Beautiful Mind,* believed that the government was recruiting him to decipher coded messages by Cold War enemies.

positive symptoms the excessive and sometimes bizarre symptoms of schizophrenia, including hallucinations, delusions, and loose associations

negative symptoms the deficiencies among people with schizophrenia, such as flat affect, lack of motivation, loss of pleasure, and social withdrawal

paranoid schizophrenia a type of schizophrenia characterized primarily by delusions—commonly of persecution—and vivid hallucinations

Disorganized Schizophrenia

People with **disorganized schizophrenia** show incoherence, loosening of associations, disorganized behaviour, disorganized delusions, fragmentary delusions or hallucinations, and flat or highly inappropriate emotional responses. Extreme social impairment is common. People with this type of schizophrenia may also exhibit silliness and giddiness of mood, giggling, and nonsensical speech. They may neglect their appearance and personal hygiene and lose control of their bladder and bowels.

Catatonic Schizophrenia

People with **catatonic schizophrenia** show a striking impairment in their motor activity. It is characterized by a slowing of activity into a stupor that may suddenly change into an agitated phase. Catatonic people may maintain unusual and even difficult postures for hours, even as their limbs grow swollen or stiff. A striking feature of this condition is **waxy flexibility**, in which the person maintains positions into which he or she has been manipulated by others. Catatonic individuals may also show **mutism**, but afterward they usually report that they heard what others were saying at the time.

Schizophrenia is thus characterized by extremely unusual behaviour. *What is known about the origins of schizophrenia?*

Explaining Schizophrenia

Biological, psychological, and sociocultural factors may all contribute to schizophrenia.

{ The Mental Disorder Plea }

In 1997, 40-year-old Jeffrey Arenburg calmly approached broadcaster Brian Smith in the parking lot outside of the CJOH radio station in Ottawa, and fatally shot him. Two years later, Arenburg was found not criminally responsible in the death of Smith. During the trial, lawyers revealed that Arenburg believed that the radio station Smith worked for was broadcasting messages into his head. Expert witnesses testified that he should be diagnosed with paranoid schizophrenia. Arenburg was found not criminally responsible of murder and committed to a psychiatric institution in Penetanguishene. He was unconditionally released nine years later, on November 20, 2006 (CBC News, 2006).

In pleading not criminally responsible due to mental disorder, lawyers refer to section 16(1) of the Canadian Criminal Code that states "No person is criminally responsible for an act committed or an omission made while suffering from a mental disorder that rendered the person incapable of appreciating the nature and quality of the act or omission or of knowing that it was wrong" (Criminal Code, 1985, c.46 s.16(1)). Determining guilt in the Canadian justice system is built on two primary factors: the accused must have been responsible for his or her actions and the accused must have a "guilty mind," in that the person is aware that his or her actions are wrong. The mental disorder defence suggests that the accused was not fully aware that his or her actions were wrong, and thus not capable of being found guilty of many crimes, including murder.

Some would like to ban the mental disorder defence because they equate it with people's "getting away with murder." But there may not be all that much cause for concern. The mental disorder defence is raised in only about 1 percent of cases (Silver, 1994). Moreover, people found to be not criminally responsible by reason of mental disorder are institutionalized for indefinite terms—supposedly until they are no longer a danger to themselves or the public.

Sun Media

Jeffrey Arenburg shot radio broadcaster Brian Smith because he believed the radio station was broadcasting voices into his head. He was found not criminally responsible by reason of mental disorder, and held in a forensic hospital facility for nine years.

Biological Perspectives

Schizophrenia appears to be a brain disorder (Heinrichs, 2005). Many studies have been done to determine how the brains of schizophrenic people may differ from those of others. Studies have focused on the amount of grey matter in the brain, the size of ventricles (hollow spaces), activity levels in the brain, and brain chemistry.

One avenue of brain research connects the major deficits we find in schizophrenia—problems in attention, working memory, abstract thinking, and language—with dysfunction in the prefrontal cortex of the brain (Heinrichs, 2005). Brain imaging has shown that some but not all people with schizophrenia have less grey matter than other people (Heinrichs, 2005; Kasai et al., 2003; Thompson et al., 2001; see Figure 12.1). Many have smaller brains and, in particular, a smaller prefrontal region of the cortex (Heinrichs, 2005; Selemon et al., 2003). They also tend to have larger ventricles in the brain than other people (Keller et al., 2003). Brain scans suggest that people with schizophrenia also tend to have a lower level of activity in the frontal region of the

Catatonic Schizophrenia
People with catatonic schizophrenia show striking motor impairment and may hold unusual positions for hours.

Grunmitus Studio/Photo Researchers, Inc.

brain (Lahti, et al., 2001; Meyer-Lindenberg et al., 2001). Still other research connects the lower activity levels with a loss in synapses in the region (Glantz & Lewis, 2000; Selemon et al., 2003; Wolkin et al., 2003).

What might account for differences in brain structure and functioning? Heredity, complications during pregnancy and birth, and birth during winter are all risk factors for schizophrenia. Schizophrenia, like many other psychological disorders, runs in families (Conklin & Iacono, 2002; Hwu et al., 2003). People with schizophrenia make up about 1 percent of the population. Yet children with one parent who has been diagnosed with schizophrenia have about a 10 percent chance of being diagnosed with schizophrenia themselves. Children with two such parents have about a 35 percent to 40 percent chance of being so diagnosed (Gottesman, 1991; Straube & Oades, 1992). Twin studies also find about a 45 percent matching rate for the diagnosis among pairs of identical (MZ) twins, whose genetic codes are the same, compared with a 17 percent rate among pairs of fraternal (DZ) twins, who share half their genetic code (Plomin & Crabbe, 2000). Moreover, adoptee studies find that the biological parent typically places the child at greater risk for schizophrenia than the adoptive parent—even though the child has been reared by the adoptive parent (Gottesman, 1991). Sharing genes with

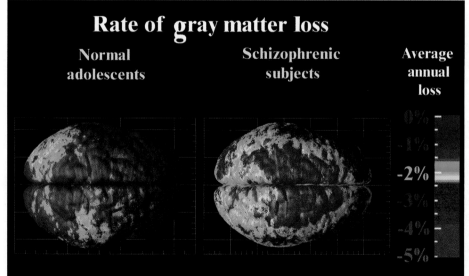

Rate of gray matter loss

Normal adolescents	Schizophrenic subjects	Average annual loss

FIGURE 12.1

Average Rates of Loss of Grey Matter among Normal Adolescents and Adolescents Diagnosed with Schizophrenia

High-resolution MRI scans show rates of grey matter loss in normal 13- to 18-year-olds and among adolescents of the same age diagnosed with schizophrenia. Maps of brain changes reveal profound, progressive loss in schizophrenia (right). Loss also occurs in normal adolescents (left), but at a slower rate.

Source: Thompson P.M., Vidal C., Giedd J.N., Gochman P., Blumenthal J., Nicolson R., Toga A.W., Rapoport J.L. 2001. Mapping adolescent brain change reveals dynamic wave of accelerated gray matter loss in very early-onset schizophrenia. *Proceedings of the National Academy of Sciences,* September 25. Copyright 2001 National Academy of Sciences, USA.

relatives who have schizophrenia apparently places a person at risk of developing the disorder. Many studies have been carried out to try to isolate the gene or genes involved in schizophrenia. Some studies find locations for multiple genes on several chromosomes.

Many people with schizophrenia have undergone complications during pregnancy and birth (Heinrichs, 2005). For example, the mothers of many people with schizophrenia had the flu during the sixth or seventh month of pregnancy (Brown & Susser, 2002). An interaction between biology and the sociocultural setting is found in the link between poor maternal nutrition and schizophrenia (Hulshoff et al., 2000; Pol et al., 2000). Complications during childbirth, especially prolonged labour, seem to be connected with the larger ventricles we find among people with schizophrenia (McNeil et al., 2000). People with schizophrenia are also somewhat more likely to have been born during winter than would be predicted by chance (Pol et al., 2000; Suvisaari et al., 2002). Alcohol abuse may also lead to differences in brain structures among people with schizophrenia (E.V. Sullivan et al., 2000). On the other hand, research evidence is mixed about whether viral infections in childhood are connected with schizophrenia (Suvisaari et al., 2003). But taken together, these risk factors suggest that schizophrenia involves faulty development of the central nervous system.

Problems in the nervous system may involve brain chemistry as well as brain structures, and research along these lines has led to the dopamine theory of schizophrenia. According to the dopamine theory, people with schizophrenia overuse dopamine (use more of it than other people do) although they may not produce more of it (Gijsman et al., 2002; Tsai & Coyle, 2002). Why? Research suggests that people with schizophrenia have increased concentrations of dopamine at the synapses in the brain and also larger numbers of dopamine receptors (Butcher, 2000)—a sort of "double hit" of neural transmission that may be connected with the confusion that characterizes schizophrenia.

Psychological Perspectives

Most learning theorists have explained schizophrenia in terms of conditioning and the social setting. They have suggested that people engage in schizophrenic behaviour when it is more likely to be reinforced than normal behaviour. This may occur when a person is reared in a socially unrewarding or punitive situation. Inner fantasies then become more reinforcing than social realities. Patients in a psychiatric hospital may learn what is "expected" by observing others. Hospital staff may reinforce schizophrenic behaviour by paying more attention to patients who behave bizarrely. This view is consistent with folklore that the child who disrupts the class attracts more attention from the teacher than the "good" child. Family discord and stress also appear to contribute to schizophrenia.

Sociocultural Perspectives

Many investigators have considered whether and how social and cultural factors such as poverty, discrimination, and overcrowding contribute to schizophrenia—especially among people with a genetic vulnerability. Classic research in New Haven, Connecticut, showed that the rate of schizophrenia was twice as high in the lowest socioeconomic class as in the next-higher class on the socioeconomic ladder (Hollingshead & Redlich, 1958). Poor-quality housing may contribute to schizophrenia (Mueser & McGurk, 2004). Some sociocultural theorists therefore suggest that "treatment" of schizophrenia requires alleviation of poverty and other social ills.

Critics of this view suggest that low socioeconomic status may be a result, rather than a cause, of schizophrenia. People with schizophrenia may drift toward low social status because they lack the social skills and cognitive abilities to function at higher social-class levels. Thus, they may wind up in poor neighbourhoods or among the homeless in disproportionately high numbers.

Evidence for the hypothesis that people with schizophrenia drift downward in socioeconomic status is mixed. Many people with schizophrenia do drift downward occupationally in comparison with their fathers' occupations. Many others, however, were reared in families in which the father came from the lowest socioeconomic class. Because poverty may play a role in the development of schizophrenia, many researchers are interested in the possible interactions between biological and psychosocial factors (Buckley et al., 2000; Sawa & Snyder, 2002).

Quality of parenting is also connected with the development of schizophrenia (Buckley et al., 2000), but critics note that many people who are reared in socially punitive settings are apparently immune to the extinction of socially appropriate behaviour. Other people develop schizophrenic behaviour without having had opportunities to observe other people with schizophrenia.

The Biopsychosocial Perspective

Because biological, psychological, and sociocultural factors are implicated in schizophrenia, most

FIGURE 12.2

The Biopsychosocial Model of Schizophrenia

According to the biopsychosocial model of schizophrenia, people with a genetic vulnerability to the disorder experience increased risk for schizophrenia when they encounter problems such as viral infections, birth complications, stress, and poor parenting. People without the genetic vulnerability would not develop schizophrenia despite psychological and social/sociocultural problems.

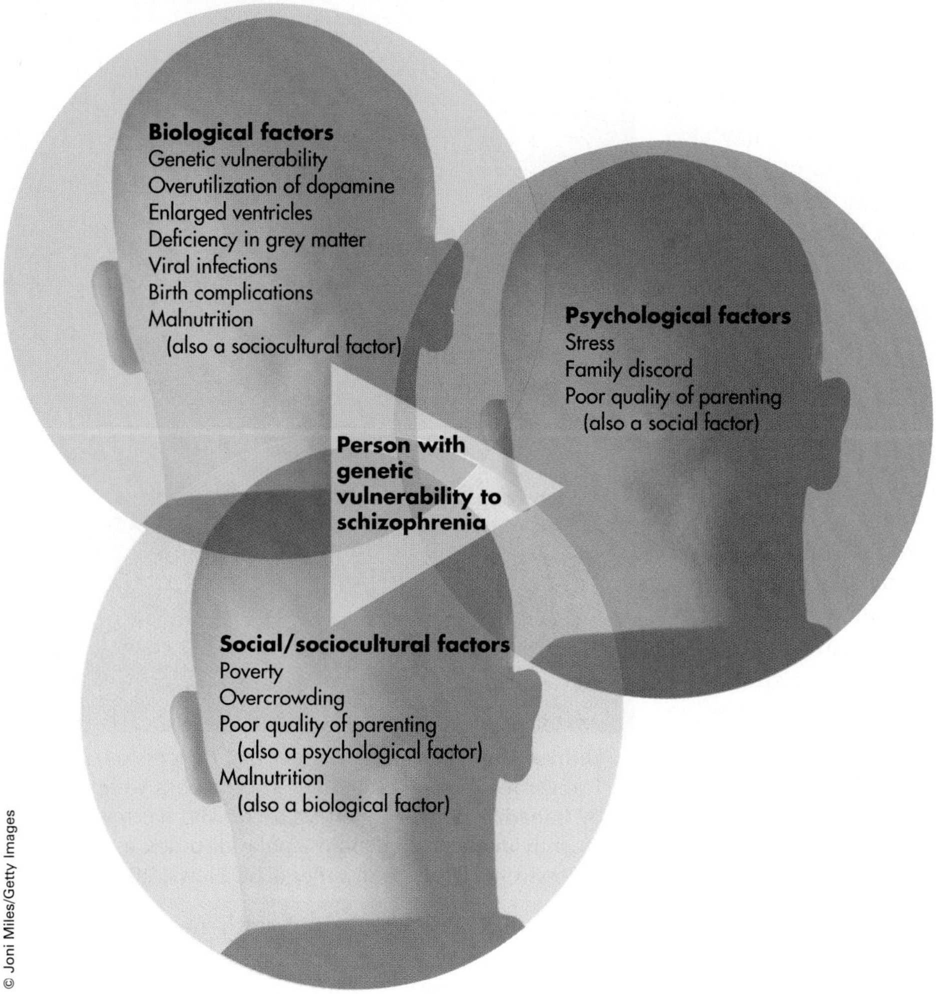

Biological factors
Genetic vulnerability
Overutilization of dopamine
Enlarged ventricles
Deficiency in grey matter
Viral infections
Birth complications
Malnutrition
    (also a sociocultural factor)

Person with genetic vulnerability to schizophrenia

Psychological factors
Stress
Family discord
Poor quality of parenting
    (also a social factor)

Social/sociocultural factors
Poverty
Overcrowding
Poor quality of parenting
    (also a psychological factor)
Malnutrition
    (also a biological factor)

© Joni Miles/Getty Images

major depressive disorder (MDD)
a serious to severe depressive disorder in which the person may show loss of appetite, psychomotor retardation, and impaired reality testing

psychomotor retardation
slowness in motor activity and (apparently) in thought

an important test, if you have lost money in a business venture, or if your closest friend becomes ill, it is understandable and fitting for you to be sad about it. It would be odd, in fact, if you were *not* affected by adversity.

What kinds of mood disorders are there? We already encountered seasonal affective disorder in the introduction to this chapter. In this section we discuss two more common mood disorders: major depression and bipolar disorder.

Major Depression

People with run-of-the-mill depression may feel sad, blue, or "down in the dumps." They may complain of lack of energy, loss of self-esteem, difficulty concentrating, loss of interest in activities and other people (Nezlek et al., 2000), pessimism, crying, and thoughts of suicide.

These feelings are more intense in people with **major depressive disorder (MDD)**. According to a nationally representative sample of 36 984 adults in Canada, MDD affects 3.7 percent of men and about 5.9 percent of women within any given year. For those 15 to 24 years of age, the percentages are slightly higher, with 4.5 percent of men and 8.3 percent of women reporting a MDD. Canadians in Alberta report the highest percentage of MDDs at 5.6 percent, and those living in Prince Edward Island rank the lowest with 2.6 percent (Statistics Canada, 2002). About half of those with MDD experience severe symptoms such as poor appetite, serious weight loss, and agitation or **psychomotor retardation**. They may be unable to

investigators today favour the biopsychosocial model. According to this model, genetic factors create a predisposition toward or vulnerability to schizophrenia (see Figure 12.2). Genetic vulnerability to the disorder interacts with other factors, such as complications of pregnancy and birth, stress, quality of parenting, and social conditions to give rise to the disorder (Buckley et al., 2000; Sawa & Snyder, 2002).

LO3 Mood Disorders

Mood disorders are characterized by disturbance in expressed emotions. The disruption generally involves sadness or elation. Most instances of sadness are normal, or "run-of-the-mill." If you have failed

bipolar disorder
a disorder in which the mood alternates between two extreme poles (elation and depression); also referred to as *manic–depressive disorder*

manic
elated, showing excessive excitement

rapid flight of ideas
rapid speech and topic changes, characteristic of manic behaviour

neuroticism
a personality trait characterized largely by persistent anxiety

learned helplessness
a model for the acquisition of depressive behaviour, based on findings that organisms in aversive situations learn to show inactivity when their actions go unreinforced

concentrate and make decisions. They may say that they "don't care" anymore and in some cases attempt suicide. A minority may display faulty perception of reality—so-called psychotic behaviours. These include delusions of unworthiness, guilt for imagined wrongdoings, even the notion that one is rotting from disease. There may also be delusions, as of the devil administering deserved punishment, or hallucinations, as of strange bodily sensations.

Bipolar Disorder

People with **bipolar disorder**, formerly known as *manic–depressive disorder,* have mood swings from ecstatic elation to deep depression. The cycles seem to be unrelated to external events. The **manic** person may also be argumentative. He or she may show poor judgment, destroying property, making huge contributions to charity, or giving away expensive possessions. People often find manic individuals abrasive and avoid them. They are often oversexed and too restless to sit still or sleep restfully. They often speak rapidly (showing "pressured speech") and jump from topic to topic (showing **rapid flight of ideas**). It can be hard to get a word in edgewise.

Depression is the other side of the coin. People with bipolar depression often sleep more than usual and are lethargic. People with major (or unipolar) depression are more likely to have insomnia and agitation. Those with bipolar depression also exhibit social withdrawal and irritability. Some people with bipolar disorder attempt suicide when the mood shifts from the elated phase toward depression (Jamison, 2000). They will do almost anything to escape the depths of depression that lie ahead.

Explaining Mood Disorders

What is known about the origins of mood disorders?

Biological Perspectives

Researchers are searching for biological factors in mood disorders. Depression, for example, is often associated with the trait of **neuroticism**, which is heritable (Chioqueta & Stiles, 2005; Khan et al., 2005).

Did you enjoy having *The Paper Bag Princess* or *Love You Forever* read to you as a child? These books were written by Canadian author Robert Munsch, who has revealed recently that he suffers from bipolar disorder, as well as obsessive-compulsive disorder (CBC News, 2010).

Anxiety is also connected with neuroticism, and mood and anxiety disorders are frequently found in the same person (Khan et al., 2005). Genetic factors appear to be involved in major depression and bipolar disorder, as suggested by twin and adoption studies (Evans et al., 2005; Farmer et al., 2005).

Psychological Perspectives

Many learning theorists suggest that depressed people behave as though they cannot obtain reinforcement. For example, they appear to be inactive and apathetic. Many people with depressive disorders have an *external locus of control.* That is, they do not believe they can control events so as to achieve reinforcements (Tong, 2001; Weinmann et al., 2001).

Research conducted by learning theorists has also found links between depression and **learned helplessness**. In classic research, psychologist Martin

Seligman taught dogs that they were helpless to escape an electric shock. The dogs were prevented from leaving a cage in which they received repeated shocks. Later, a barrier to a safe compartment was removed, offering the animals a way out. When they were shocked again, however, the dogs made no effort to escape. They had apparently learned that they were helpless. Seligman's dogs were also, in a sense, reinforced for doing nothing. That is, the shock *eventually* stopped when the dogs were showing helpless behaviour—inactivity and withdrawal. "Reinforcement" might have increased the likelihood of repeating the "successful behaviour"—that is, doing nothing—in a similar situation. This helpless behaviour resembles that of people who are depressed.

Other cognitive factors contribute to depression. For example, perfectionists set themselves up for depression by making irrational demands on themselves. They are likely to fall short of their (unrealistic) expectations and to feel depressed as a result (Flett & Hewitt, 2002).

Cognitive psychologists also note that people who ruminate about feelings of depression are more likely to prolong the feelings (Spasojevic & Alloy, 2001). Women are more likely than men to ruminate about feelings of depression (Nolen-Hoeksema, 2001). Men are more likely than women to fight negative feelings by distracting themselves or turning to alcohol (Nolen-Hoeksema, 2001). They thus expose themselves and their families to further problems.

Still other cognitions involve the ways in which people explain their failures and shortcomings to themselves (Hankin et al., 2005). Seligman (1996) suggests that when things go wrong we may think of the causes of failure as *internal* or *external*, *stable* or *unstable*, and *global* or *specific*. These various **attribution styles** can be illustrated using the example of having a date that does not work out. An internal attribu-

tion involves self-blame, as in "I really screwed it up." An external attribution places the blame elsewhere (as in "Some couples just don't take to each other," or, "She was the wrong person for me"). A stable attribution ("It's my personality") suggests a problem that cannot be changed. An unstable attribution ("It was because I had a head cold") suggests a temporary condition. A global attribution of failure ("I have no idea what to do when I'm with other people") suggests that the problem is quite large. A specific attribution ("I have problems making small talk at the beginning of a relationship") chops the problem down to a manageable size. Research has shown that people who are depressed are more likely to attribute the causes of their failures to *internal*, *stable*, and *global* factors— factors that they are relatively powerless to change (Riso et al., 2003).

Let's add one remarkable note about attribution styles and the mind–body connection. Shelley Taylor and her colleagues (2000a) found that self-blame for negative events is connected with poorer functioning of the immune system. Too much self-blame, in other words, is not only depressing; it may also be able to make us physically ill.

The Biopsychosocial Perspective

Relationships between mood disorders and biological factors are complex and under intense study. Even if people are biologically predisposed toward depression, self-efficacy expectations and attitudes—particularly attitudes about whether one can change things for the better—may also play a role.

Although the mood disorders are connected with processes within the individual, many kinds of situations are also connected

> **attribution style** the tendency to attribute one's behaviour to internal or external factors, stable or unstable factors, and so on

An internal attribution involves self-blame, as in "I really screwed it up." An external attribution places the blame elsewhere.

Brand X Pictures/Jupiterimages

with depression. For example, depression may be a reaction to loss or stress (Cowen, 2002). Sources of chronic strain such as marital discord, physical discomfort, incompetence, and failure or pressure at work all contribute to depression. We tend to be more depressed by things we bring on ourselves, such as academic problems, financial problems, unwanted pregnancy, conflict with the law, arguments, and fights. Some people recover from depression less readily than others, however. People who remain depressed have lower self-esteem, are less likely to be able to solve social problems, and have less social support.

Suicide

Why do people commit suicide? The most common reason for suicide is to escape feelings of depression, hopelessness, and helplessness. We may think many of these people have "so much to live for." Apparently, they disagree. So do the thousands of others who take their own lives each year.

In any given year, about 3.7 percent of Canadian men and women consider suicide (Statistics Canada, 2002). About 3700 Canadians follow through with those thoughts and commit suicide each year, with men being three times more likely than women to commit suicide (Statistics Canada, 2005). Suicide is the second-leading cause of death among Canadian adolescents (Cheung & Dewa, 2006).

Risk Factors in Suicide

Who is most at risk of attempting or committing suicide? Most suicides are linked to feelings of depression and hopelessness (Beautrais, 2003). Jill Rathus and her colleagues (Miller et al., 2000) found that suicidal adolescents experience four areas of psychological problems: (1) confusion about the self, (2) impulsiveness, (3) emotional instability, and (4) interpersonal problems. Some suicidal teenagers, like suicidal adults, are highly achieving, rigid perfectionists who have set impossibly high expectations for themselves (Miller et al., 2000). Many people throw themselves into feelings of depression and hopelessness by comparing themselves negatively with others, even when the comparisons are inappropriate (Barber, 2001). For example, some people criticize themselves for being hired at a lower salary than others were, even though the financial climate of a company has changed.

Suicide attempts are more common following stressful life events, especially "exit events" (Beautrais, 2003). Exit events entail loss of social support, as in the death of a parent or friend, divorce, or a family member's leaving home. These exit events

---

{ **Women and Depression** }

Women are nearly twice as likely to be diagnosed with depression as men (Keyes & Goodman, 2006). This sex difference begins to emerge during adolescence, at about the age of 13. In any given year, about 5.9 percent of women and 3.7 percent of men in Canada are diagnosed with depression. It was once assumed that depression was most likely to accompany menopause in women, because women could no longer carry out their "natural" function of childbearing. However, women are more likely to encounter depression during the childbearing years (Deecher et al., 2008; Keyes & Goodman, 2006; Statistics Canada, 2002).

Many people assume that biological sex differences largely explain why women are more likely to become depressed (Deecher et al., 2008). Low levels of estrogen are widely seen as the culprit. Estrogen levels plummet prior to menstruation, and the deficit may trigger psychological changes. How often do we hear degrading remarks such as "It must be that time of the month" when a woman expresses feelings of anger or irritation? Some theorists suggest that women may also have a "cognitive vulnerability" to depression, connected with greater tendencies than men to ruminate about stresses and other negative events (Hankin & Abramson, 2001).

Some of the sex difference may also reflect the greater stresses placed on women, which tend to be maximized when they are working a triple shift—one in the workforce and the others meeting the demands of homemaking, childrearing, and aging parents (Plaisier et al., 2008; Rathus, 2009–2010). Women are more likely to experience physical and sexual abuse, poverty, single parenthood, and sexism. Single mothers, in particular, have lower socioeconomic status than men, and depression and other psychological disorders are more common among poor people (Nicholson et al., 2008). A part of treatment for depressed women, then, is to modify the demands on women. The pain may lie in the individual, but the cause often lies in society.

Ghislain and Marie David de Lossy/Getty Images

result in what Shneidman (2001) refers to as psychological pain, or "psychache." Other contributors to suicidal behaviour among adolescents include concerns over sexuality, grades in school, problems at home, and substance abuse (Cuellar & Curry, 2007). It is not always a stressful event itself that precipitates suicide but can also be the individual's anxiety or fear of being "found out" about something, such as failing a course or getting arrested (Marttunen, 1998).

There is a tendency for suicide to run in families (Miller et al., 2007). Many suicide attempters have family members with serious psychological problems, and about 25 percent have family members who have taken their lives (Segal & Roy, 2001; Sorenson & Rutter, 1991). The causal connections are unclear, however. Do people who attempt suicide inherit disorders that can lead to suicide? Does the family environment subject family members to feelings of hopelessness? Does the suicide of a family member give a person the idea of committing suicide, or create the impression that he or she is destined to commit suicide? These possibilities and others—such as poor problem-solving ability—form a complex web of contributors.

> More teenagers and young adults die from suicide than from cancer, heart disease, AIDS, birth defects, stroke, pneumonia, influenza, and chronic lung disease combined.

Sociocultural Factors in Suicide

Suicide is connected not only with feelings of depression and stressful events, but also with age, educational status, ethnicity, and gender.

Consider some facts about suicide:

• Suicide is the second-leading cause of death among Canadian young people (Cheung & Dewa, 2006). More teenagers and young adults die from suicide than from cancer, heart disease, AIDS, birth defects, stroke, pneumonia, influenza, and chronic lung disease combined (Statistics Canada, 2003).

• Suicide is more common among college students than among people of the same age who do not attend college.

• The tragedy of teenage suicide often makes them the focus of media attention, and thus we sometimes incorrectly assume that teens have the highest rates of suicide compared to people of other ages. The relation between age, gender, and suicide in Canada is a complex one. Figure 12.3 reveals that the likelihood of suicide for men rises steadily to peak at 47 years of age, then declines until age 67, and then rises again

FIGURE 12.3

Yearly Average Suicide Rate by Age and Gender in Canada (2000–2005)

Source: Adapted from Statistics Canada, 2006, CANSIM, table 102-0551 and Catalogue no. 84F0209X.

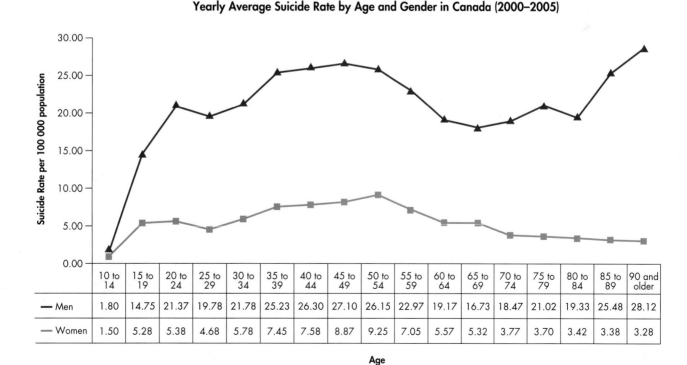

Yearly Average Suicide Rate by Age and Gender in Canada (2000–2005)

	10 to 14	15 to 19	20 to 24	25 to 29	30 to 34	35 to 39	40 to 44	45 to 49	50 to 54	55 to 59	60 to 64	65 to 69	70 to 74	75 to 79	80 to 84	85 to 89	90 and older
— Men	1.80	14.75	21.37	19.78	21.78	25.23	26.30	27.10	26.15	22.97	19.17	16.73	18.47	21.02	19.33	25.48	28.12
— Women	1.50	5.28	5.38	4.68	5.78	7.45	7.58	8.87	9.25	7.05	5.57	5.32	3.77	3.70	3.42	3.38	3.28

Age

Adapted from Statistics Canada, 2006, CANSIM, table 102-0551 and Catalogue no. 84F0209X.

specific phobia
persistent fear of
a specific object or
situation

to its highest rate at 90 years of age. For women, the highest suicide rates occur at around 52 years of age, before slowly declining again as they get older (Statistics Canada, 2006). The suicide rate among older people who are single is twice that of older people who are married (National Center for Injury Prevention and Control, 2005).

Rates of suicide and suicide attempts also vary among different ethnic groups and according to gender. For Aboriginal peoples in Canada, suicide and self-injury was the leading cause of death among youth, accounting for 38 percent of deaths (Royal Commission on Aboriginal Peoples, 1995). The suicide rate on average for Aboriginal peoples is about three times as high as that of the Canadian general population. But it is not one's minority status alone that suggests an increased risk of suicide. Interestingly, men who immigrate to Canada are at a reduced risk of suicide. The average suicide rate for Canadian men of all ages in 2003 was 21.6 per 100 000, whereas for men who had immigrated to Canada the average suicide rate was significantly lower at 12.9 per 100 000. The suicide rates for immigrant women (4.9) are not statistically different when compared to the rates for Canadian-born women (5.3) (Malenfant, 2004).

About three times as many women as men attempt suicide, but three or four times as many men "succeed," in part because men are likely to choose more deadly methods (National Center for Injury Prevention and Control, 2005). Men are more likely to shoot or hang themselves; women more often use drugs, such as overdoses of tranquilizers or sleeping pills, or poisons. Women often do not take enough of these chemicals. It also takes a while for the chemicals to work, giving others the opportunity to find the person and intervene.

Myths about Suicide

Some believe that those who fail at suicide attempts are only seeking attention. But many people who commit suicide have made prior attempts (Jackson & Nuttall, 2001; Waters, 2000). Contrary to widespread belief, discussing suicide with a person who is depressed does not prompt the person to attempt suicide (National Center for Injury Prevention and Control, 2005). Extracting a promise not to commit suicide before calling or visiting a helping professional seems to prevent some suicides.

Some believe that only "insane" people (meaning people who are out of touch with reality) would take their own lives. However, suicidal thinking is not necessarily a sign of bizarre thinking. Instead, people may consider suicide when they think they

have run out of options (Nock & Kazdin, 2002; Townsend et al., 2001).

LO4 Anxiety Disorders

Anxiety has psychological and physical symptoms. Psychological symptoms include worrying, fear of the worst things happening, fear of losing control, nervousness, and inability to relax. Physical symptoms reflect arousal of the sympathetic branch of the autonomic nervous system. They include trembling, sweating, a pounding or racing heart, elevated blood pressure (a flushed face), and faintness. Anxiety is an appropriate response to a real threat. It can be abnormal, however, when it is excessive or when it comes out of nowhere—that is, when events do not seem to warrant it. *What kinds of anxiety disorders are there?*

There are different kinds of anxiety disorders, but all of them are characterized by excessive or unwarranted anxiety. The anxiety disorders include phobias, panic disorder, generalized anxiety, obsessive–compulsive disorder, and stress disorders.

Phobias

Phobias include specific phobias, social phobia, and agoraphobia. They can be detrimental to one's quality of life. **Specific phobias** are irrational fears of

George Doyle/Getty Images

specific objects or situations, such as spiders, snakes, or heights. One specific phobia is fear of elevators. Some people will not enter elevators despite the hardships they incur as a result (such as walking up ten flights of steps). Yes, the cable *could* break. The ventilation *could* fail. One *could* be stuck in midair waiting for repairs. But these problems are uncommon, and it affects one's quality of life to walk up and down several flights of stairs to elude them. Similarly, some people with a specific phobia for hypodermic needles will not have injections, even to treat serious illness. Injections can be painful, but most people who do not have a phobia for needles would gladly suffer a painful pinch if it would help them fight a serious illness. Other specific phobias include **claustrophobia** (fear of tight or enclosed places), **acrophobia** (fear of heights), and fear of mice, snakes, and other creepy crawlies. **Social phobias** are persistent fears of scrutiny by others or of doing something that will be humiliating or embarrassing. Fear of public speaking is a common social phobia.

Agoraphobia is also widespread among adults, with 1.1 percent of Canadian women and 0.4 percent of Canadian men suffering from it (in total that's over half a million Canadians; Statistics Canada, 2002). Agoraphobia is derived from the Greek words meaning "fear of the marketplace," or fear of being out in open, busy areas. Persons with agoraphobia fear being in places from which it might be difficult to escape or in which help might not be available if they get upset. In practice, people who receive this diagnosis often refuse to venture out of their homes, especially by themselves. They find it difficult to hold a job or to maintain an ordinary social life.

Panic Disorder

Panic disorder is an abrupt attack of acute anxiety that is not triggered by a specific object or situation. People with panic disorder have strong physical symptoms such as shortness of breath, heavy sweating, tremors, and pounding of the heart. They are particularly aware of cardiac sensations. It is not unusual for them to think they are having a heart attack. People with the disorder may also experience choking sensations; nausea; numbness or tingling; flushes or chills; and fear of going crazy or losing control. Panic attacks may last minutes or hours. Afterward, the person usually feels drained.

Many people panic now and then. The diagnosis of panic disorder is reserved for those who undergo a series of attacks or live in fear of attacks.

Panic attacks seem to come from nowhere. Thus, some people who have had them stay home for fear of having an attack in public. They are diagnosed as having panic disorder with agoraphobia.

Generalized Anxiety Disorder

The central feature of **generalized anxiety disorder** is persistent anxiety. As with panic disorder, the anxiety cannot be attributed to a phobic object, situation, or activity. Rather, it seems to be free-floating. The core of the disorder appears to be pervasive worrying about numerous problems. Features of the disorder include motor tension (shakiness, inability to relax, furrowed brow, fidgeting); autonomic overarousal (sweating, dry mouth, racing heart, light-headedness, frequent urinating, diarrhea); and excessive vigilance, as shown by irritability, insomnia, and a tendency to be easily distracted.

Obsessive–Compulsive Disorder

Obsessions are recurrent, anxiety-provoking thoughts or images that seem irrational and beyond control. They are so compelling and recurrent that they disrupt daily life. They may include doubts about whether one has locked the doors and shut the windows, or images such as one mother's repeated fantasy that her children had been run over on the way home from school. One woman became obsessed with the idea that she had contaminated her hands with Sani-Flush and that the chemicals were spreading

claustrophobia
fear of tight, small places

acrophobia
fear of high places

social phobia
an irrational, excessive fear of public scrutiny

agoraphobia
fear of open, crowded places

panic disorder
the recurrent experiencing of attacks of extreme anxiety in the absence of external stimuli that usually elicit anxiety

generalized anxiety disorder
feelings of dread and foreboding and sympathetic arousal of at least six months' duration

obsession
a recurring thought or image that seems beyond control

compulsion
an irresistible urge to repeat an act or engage in ritualistic behaviour such as hand washing

post-traumatic stress disorder (PTSD)
a disorder that follows a distressing event outside the range of normal human experience and that is characterized by features such as intense fear, avoidance of stimuli associated with the event, and reliving of the event

to everything she touched. A 16-year-old boy complained that he was distracted by "numbers in my head" when he was about to study or take a test. The more he tried to ignore them, the louder they became. A key component of an obsession is that the person suffering from them realizes that they are irrational. Thus, the person who is convinced her hands are covered in disease, filth, and germs is diagnosed as delusional if she believes this is a normal belief, and is diagnosed as obsessive if she believes these are irrational thoughts, yet cannot seem to think otherwise.

125   10,789

3.14159265...

21 21 21!

Compulsions are thoughts or behaviours that tend to reduce the anxiety connected with obsessions. They are seemingly irresistible urges to engage in specific acts, often repeatedly, such as elaborate washing after using the bathroom or repeatedly checking that one has locked the door or turned off the gas burners before leaving home. The impulse is recurrent and forceful, interfering with daily life.

Stress Disorders

Sharia, now 65 years old, still dreams of a man assaulting her in the night at the residential school where she was staying in Manitoba. Darla, who lives in Toronto, dreams that she is trapped in a World Trade Center tower in New York City when it is hit by an airplane. About one in six Canadian soldiers who return from Afghanistan have nightmares and flashbacks about buddies being killed by snipers or explosive devices (Marin, 2001). These all-too-real nightmarish events have caused many bad dreams. Such dreams are part of the experience of post-traumatic stress disorder.

Post-traumatic stress disorder (PTSD) is characterized by a rapid heart rate and feelings of anxiety and helplessness that are caused by a traumatic experience. Such experiences may include a natural or human-made disaster, a threat or assault, or witnessing a death. PTSD may occur months or years after the event. It frequently occurs among firefighters, combat veterans, and people whose homes and communities have been swept away by natural disasters or who have been victims of accidents or violence (DeAngelis, 2008).

The traumatic event is revisited in the form of intrusive memories, recurrent dreams, and flashbacks—the sudden feeling that the event is recurring. People with PTSD typically try to avoid thoughts and activities connected to the traumatic event. They may find it more difficult to enjoy life and have sleep problems, irritable outbursts, difficulty concentrating, extreme vigilance, and an intensified "startle" response (Griffin, 2008). The attacks of September 11, 2001, took their toll on sleep. According to a poll taken by the National Sleep Foundation (2001) two months afterward, nearly half of Americans had difficulty falling asleep, as compared with about one-quarter of Americans before the attacks (see Figure 12.4). The Canadian Mental Health Association claims that one out of every ten Canadians is affected by PTSD (2010).

Canadian comedian Howie Mandel suffers from obsessive-compulsive disorder. He has intense obsessions and complex compulsions to cope with the crippling thoughts.

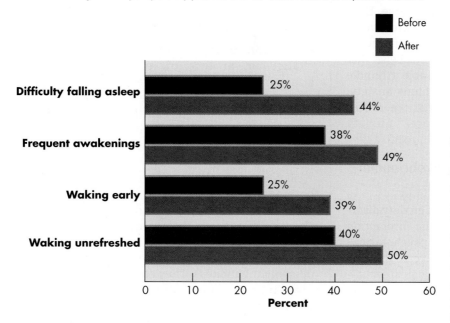

FIGURE 12.4

Sleep Problems among Americans Before and After September 11, 2001

Insomnia is one of the symptoms of stress disorders. A poll by the National Sleep Foundation found that Americans had a greater frequency of sleep problems after the terrorist attacks of September 11, 2001.

acute stress disorder
a disorder, like PTSD, that is characterized by feelings of anxiety and helplessness and caused by a traumatic event; acute stress disorder occurs within a month of the event and lasts from two days to four weeks

Acute stress disorder, like PTSD, is characterized by feelings of anxiety and helplessness that are caused by a traumatic event. PTSD, however, can occur six months or more after the traumatic event and tends to persist. Acute stress disorder occurs within a month of the event and lasts from two days to four weeks. Women who have been raped, for example, experience acute distress that tends to peak in severity a few weeks after the assault. Yet the same women often go on to experience PTSD (Koss et al., 2002).

Explaining Anxiety Disorders

What is known about the origins of anxiety disorders?

Biological Perspectives

Biological factors play a role in anxiety disorders. Genetic factors are implicated in most psychological disorders, including anxiety disorders (Low et al., 2008). Anxiety disorders tend to run in families. Twin studies find a higher rate of match for anxiety disorders among identical twins than among fraternal twins (Kendler et al., 2001). Studies of adoptees who are anxious similarly show that the biological parent places the child at risk for anxiety and related traits.

Perhaps a predisposition toward anxiety—in the form of a highly reactive autonomic nervous system—can be inherited. What might make a nervous system "highly reactive"?

In the case of panic disorder, faulty regulation of levels of serotonin and norepinephrine may be involved. Other anxiety disorders may involve the neurotransmitter glutamate, and receptor sites in the brain may not be sensitive enough to gamma-aminobutyric acid (GABA), a neurotransmitter that may counteract glutamate (Kalin, 2003). The benzodiazepines, a class of drugs that reduce anxiety, may work by increasing the sensitivity of receptor sites to GABA.

Psychological and Social Perspectives

Some learning theorists—particularly behaviourists—consider phobias to be conditioned fears that were acquired in early childhood. Therefore, their origins are beyond memory. Avoidance of feared stimuli is reinforced by the reduction of anxiety.

Other learning theorists—social-cognitive theorists—dwell on the social aspects of developing phobias (Basic Behavioral Science Task Force, 1996b). If parents squirm, grimace, and shudder at the sight of mice, blood, or dirt on the kitchen floor, children might assume that these stimuli are awful and imitate their parents' behaviour.

Cognitive theorists note that people's appraisals of the magnitude of threats help determine whether they are traumatic and can lead to PTSD (Folkman & Moskowitz, 2000a; Koss et al., 2002). People with panic attacks tend to overreact to physical sensations. Obsessions and compulsions may serve to divert attention from more frightening issues, such as "What am I going to do with my life?" When anxieties are acquired at a young age, we may later interpret them as enduring traits and label ourselves as "people who fear _____" (you fill it in). We then live up to the labels. We also entertain thoughts that heighten and perpetuate anxiety such as "I've got to get out of here," or "My heart is going to leap out of my chest." Such ideas intensify physical features of anxiety, disrupt planning, make stimuli seem worse than they are, motivate avoidance, and lower self-efficacy expectations. The belief that we will not be able to handle a threat heightens anxiety. The belief that we are in control reduces anxiety (Bandura et al., 1985).

The Biopsychosocial Perspective

Many cases of anxiety disorders reflect the interaction of biological, psychological, and social factors. In panic disorder, biological imbalances may initially trigger attacks. However, subsequent fear of attacks—and of the bodily cues that signal their onset—may heighten discomfort and give one the idea that nothing can be done about them (Craske & Zucker, 2001). Moreover, panic attacks are likely to occur in social situations, especially in crowds. Feelings of helplessness increase fear. People with panic disorder can be helped by methods that reduce physical discomfort—including regular breathing—and show them that there are ways to cope with attacks (Craske & Zucker, 2001). They are also sometimes taken into social settings, such as crowded streets or stores, by psychologists who offer them social support and show them that they can tolerate such situations.

LO5 Somatoform Disorders

People with **somatoform disorders** complain of physical problems such as paralysis, pain, or a persistent belief that they have a serious disease. But health professionals can find no evidence of a physical abnormality. *What kinds of somatoform disorders are there?* In this section we discuss three somatoform disorders: conversion disorder, hypochondriasis, and body dysmorphic disorder.

Conversion Disorder

Conversion disorder is characterized by a major change in, or loss of, physical functioning, although there are no medical findings to explain the loss of functioning. The behaviours are not intentionally produced. That is, the person is not faking. Conversion disorder is so named because it appears to "convert" a source of stress into a physical difficulty.

If you lost the ability to see at night, or if your legs became paralyzed, you would understandably show concern. But some people with conversion disorder show indifference to their symptoms, a remarkable feature referred to as **la belle indifférence**.

During World War II, some bomber pilots developed night blindness. They could not carry out their night-time missions, although no damage to the optic nerves was found. In rare cases, women with large families have been reported to become paralyzed in the legs, again with no medical findings. More recently, a Cambodian woman who had witnessed atrocities during the Khmer Rouge genocide became blind as a result.

Hypochondriasis

Another more common type of somatoform disorder is **hypochondriasis** (also called *hypochondria*). People with this disorder insist that they are suffering from a serious physical illness, even though no medical evidence of illness can be found. They become preoccupied with minor physical sensations and continue to believe that they are ill despite the reassurance of physicians that they are healthy. They may run from doctor to doctor, seeking the one who will find the causes of the sensations. Fear of illness may disrupt their work or home life.

Body Dysmorphic Disorder

People with **body dysmorphic disorder** are preoccupied with a fantasized or exaggerated physical defect in their appearance. They may spend hours examining themselves in the mirror and go to extreme lengths to correct the "problem," including cosmetic surgery. Others remove all mirrors from their homes so as not to be

© Jenny Swanson/iStockphoto.com

reminded of the "flaw." People with the disorder may assume that others see them as deformed. They may compulsively groom themselves or pay close attention to styling every strand of hair.

Explaining Somatoform Disorders

What is known about the origins of somatoform disorders? The somatoform disorders offer a fascinating study in the biopsychosocial perspective. Psychologically speaking, the somatoform disorders have much to do with what one focuses on—actual social and financial problems, for example, or one's body. Some investigators consider conversion disorder to be a form of self-hypnosis (Roelofs et al., 2002), and they note that there is research evidence that people with conversion disorder are highly susceptible to being hypnotized. The idea here would be that people with conversion disorder focus on an imaginary physical problem to the point where they exclude conflicting information.

In the case of hypochondriasis, people may misinterpret run-of-the-mill physical sensations—or symptoms—as signifying deadly illness. There is research evidence that people who develop hypochondriasis are particularly sensitive to bodily sensations and tend to ruminate about them (Lecci & Cohen, 2002). Moreover, enacting the role of a sick person has the "benefits" of relieving one of ordinary responsibilities and concerns. For example, how can one focus on work or family life when one believes he or she is rotting away with disease?

Certainly the social value of personal attractiveness can contribute to dissatisfaction with one's body. But people with body dysmorphic disorder may focus irrationally on an exaggerated blemish or other minor feature, suggestive of perfectionistic and ruminative tendencies.

Biologically speaking, tendencies toward perfectionism and rumination, which are found among many people with somatoform disorders, are thought to be at least partly heritable. Squeamishness about one's body may be too much of a good thing from the evolutionary perspective. That is, concern about bodily harm will presumably encourage one to avoid danger and provide advantages in survival and reproduction. But too much concern may lead to useless preoccupations.

LO6 Dissociative Disorders

During one long fall semester, the Ohio State University campus lived in terror. Four college women were kidnapped, forced to take out cash from ATMs, and raped. A mysterious phone call led to the arrest of a 23-year-old drifter—let's call him "William"—who had been dismissed from the U.S. Navy.

William was not the boy next door.

Psychologists and psychiatrists who interviewed William concluded that ten personalities—eight male and two female—dwelled in him (Keyes, 1995). His personality had been "fractured" by an abusive childhood. His several personalities displayed distinct facial expressions, speech patterns, and memories. They performed differently on psychological tests.

Arthur, the most rational personality, spoke with a British accent. Danny and Christopher were quiet adolescents. Christine was a three-year-old girl. Tommy, a 16-year-old, had enlisted in the Navy. Allen was 18 and smoked. Adelena, a 19-year-old lesbian personality, had committed the rapes. Who had placed the mysterious phone call? Probably David, aged nine, an anxious child.

The defence claimed that William's behaviour was caused by *dissociative identity disorder*. Of the identities or personalities dwelling within him, some were aware of the others. Some believed they were unique. As a child, Billy, the core identity, had learned to sleep to avoid his father's abuse. A psychiatrist asserted that Billy had also been "asleep," or in a "psychological coma," during the abductions. Billy should therefore be found not guilty by reason of insanity.

William was found not guilty. He was committed to a psychiatric institution and released six years later.

Dissociative identity disorder is one of the **dissociative disorders**. In dissociative disorders, there is a splitting of psychological processes such as thoughts, emotions, identity, memory, or consciousness—the processes that make the person feel whole. *What kinds of dissociative disorders are there?* The dissociative disorders include dissociative amnesia, dissociative fugue, and William's disorder: dissociative identity disorder (formerly termed *multiple personality disorder*).

Dissociative Amnesia

In **dissociative amnesia**, the person is suddenly unable to recall important personal information (that is, explicit episodic memories). The loss of memory cannot be attributed to biological problems such as a blow to the head or excessive drinking.

dissociative disorders disorders in which there are sudden, temporary changes in consciousness or self-identity

dissociative amnesia a dissociative disorder marked by loss of memory or self-identity; skills and general knowledge are usually retained

It is thus a psychological disorder and not an organic one. In the most common example, the person cannot recall events for a number of hours after a stressful incident, as in warfare or in the case of an uninjured survivor of an accident. In generalized amnesia, people forget their entire lives. Amnesia may last for hours or years.

Dissociative Fugue

In **dissociative** fugue, the person abruptly leaves his or her home or place of work and travels to another place, having lost all memory of his or her past life. While at the new location, the person either does not think about the past or reports a past filled with invented memories. The new personality is often more outgoing and less inhibited than the "real" identity. Following recovery, the events that occurred during the fugue are not recalled.

Dissociative Identity Disorder

In **dissociative identity disorder** (formerly termed **multiple personality disorder**), two or more identities or personalities, each with distinct traits and memories, "occupy" the same person. Each identity may or may not be aware of the others or of events experienced by the others.

The different personalities might have different eyeglass prescriptions (Braun, 1988). Braun reports cases in which assorted identities showed different allergic responses. In one person, an identity named Timmy was not sensitive to orange juice. But when another identity drank orange juice, he would break out with hives. Hives would also erupt if another identity emerged while the juice was being digested. If Timmy reappeared when the allergic reaction was present, the itching of the hives would cease and the blisters would start to subside. In other cases reported by Braun, different identities within a person might show various responses to the same medicine. Or one identity might exhibit colour blindness while others have normal colour vision.

Explaining Dissociative Disorders

The dissociative disorders are some of the odder psychological disorders. *What is known about the origins of dissociative disorders?* Biopsychosocial factors may well be involved in dissociative disorders. According to learning and cognitive psychologists, people with dissociative disorders may have learned *not to think* about bad memories or disturbing impulses in an effort to avoid feelings of anxiety, guilt, and shame. Dissociative disorders may help people keep disturbing ideas out of mind.

John Lund/Blend Images/Jupiterimages

What might such memories contain? The answer is painful interpersonal—or social—information. Research suggests that many cases of dissociative disorders involve memories of sexual or physical abuse during childhood, usually by a relative or caretaker (Martinez-Taboas & Bernal, 2000; Migdow, 2003).

On a biological level, research with abused children and adolescents suggests that the trauma-related dissociation observed in dissociative disorders may have a neurological basis (Diseth, 2005). Child abuse may lead to some permanent neurochemical and structural abnormalities in parts of the brain involved in cognition and memory. Although it seems that the nature of the trauma in such cases is interpersonal, it need not necessarily be sexual in nature. In any event, one might expect resultant impairments in the recall of personal information.

LO7 Personality Disorders

Personality disorders, like personality traits, are characterized by enduring patterns of behaviour. Personality disorders, however, are inflexible and maladaptive. They impair personal or social functioning and are a source of distress to the individual or to other people. *What kinds of personality disorders are there?* There are a number of personality disorders, including paranoid, schizotypal, schizoid, borderline, antisocial, and avoidant personality disorders.

Paranoid Personality Disorder

The defining trait of the paranoid personality disorder is a tendency to interpret other people's behaviour as threatening or demeaning. People with the disorder do not show the grossly disorganized thinking of paranoid schizophrenia. They are mistrustful of others, however, and their relation-

ships suffer for it. They may be suspicious of co-workers and supervisors, but they can generally hold a job.

Schizotypal and Schizoid Personality Disorders

Schizotypal personality disorder is characterized by peculiarities of thought, perception, or behaviour, such as excessive fantasy and suspiciousness, feelings of being unreal, or odd usage of words. The bizarre behaviours that characterize schizophrenia are absent, so this disorder is schizotypal, not schizophrenic.

The schizoid personality is defined by indifference to relationships and flat emotional response. People with this disorder are "loners." They do not develop warm, tender feelings for others. They have few friends and rarely maintain long-term relationships. Some people with schizoid personality disorder do very well on the job, provided that continuous social interaction is not required. They do not have hallucinations or delusions. The paranoid, schizotypal, and schizoid personality disorders are quite uncommon, with lower than 1 percent combined prevalence in the Canadian population (Weissman, 1993).

Borderline Personality Disorder

Roughly 1.5 percent of women and 0.5 percent of men in the general population (Widiger & Weissman, 1991) have a borderline personality disorder and show instability in their relationships, self-image, and mood, and lack of control over impulses. They tend to be uncertain of their values, goals, loyalties, careers, choices of friends, and sometimes even their sexual orientations. Instability in self-image or identity may leave them with feelings of emptiness and boredom. Many cannot tolerate being alone and make desperate attempts to avoid feelings

personality disorders enduring patterns of maladaptive behaviour that are sources of distress to the individual or others

paranoid personality disorder a personality disorder characterized by persistent suspiciousness, but not involving the disorganization of paranoid schizophrenia

schizotypal personality disorder a personality disorder characterized by oddities of thought and behaviour, but not involving bizarre psychotic behaviours

schizoid personality disorder a personality disorder characterized by social withdrawal

borderline personality disorder a personality disorder characterized by instability in relationships, self-image, and mood, and lack of impulse control

© Ed Hidden/iStockphoto.com

antisocial personality disorder the diagnosis given a person who is in frequent conflict with society, yet who is undeterred by punishment and experiences little or no guilt and anxiety

of abandonment. They may be clinging and demanding in social relationships, but clinging often pushes away the people on whom they depend. They alternate between extremes of adulation in their relationships (when their needs are met) and loathing (when they feel scorned). They tend to view other people as all good or all bad, shifting abruptly from one extreme to the other. As a result, they may flit from partner to partner in brief and stormy relationships. People whom they had idealized are treated with contempt when they feel the other person has failed them.

Instability of moods is a central characteristic of borderline personality disorder. Moods run the gamut from anger and irritability to depression and anxiety, with each lasting from a few hours to a few days. People with the disorder have difficulty controlling anger and are prone to fights or smashing things. They often act on impulse, such as eloping with someone they have just met. This impulsive and unpredictable behaviour is often self-destructive and linked to a risk of suicidal attempts and gestures. It may involve spending sprees, gambling, drug abuse, engaging in unsafe sexual activity, reckless driving, binge eating, or shoplifting. People with the disorder may also engage in self-mutilation, such as scratching their wrists or burning cigarettes on their arms. Self-mutilation is sometimes a means of manipulating others, particularly in times of stress. Frequent self-mutilation is also associated with suicide attempts.

Antisocial Personality Disorder

People with **antisocial personality disorder** often show a superficial charm and are at least average in intelligence. They fail to learn to improve their behaviour from punishment, and they do not form

Characteristics of People Diagnosed with Antisocial Personality Disorder

Key Characteristics
History of delinquency and truancy
Persistent violation of the rights of others
Impulsiveness
Poor self-control
Lack of remorse for misdeeds
Lack of empathy
Deceitfulness and manipulativeness
Irresponsibility
Glibness; superficial charm
Exaggerated sense of self-worth

Other Common Characteristics
Lack of loyalty or of formation of enduring relationships
Failure to maintain good job performance over the years
Failure to develop or adhere to a life plan
Sexual promiscuity
Substance abuse
Inability to tolerate boredom
Low tolerance for frustration
Irritability

Sources: Levenston et al., 2000; Romero et al., 2001.

Paul Irish/GetStock.com

Paul Bernardo, serial killer and rapist from Toronto, displayed a pattern of behaviour that clearly fits the criteria for antisocial personality disorder.

meaningful bonds with other people. Although they are often heavily punished by their parents and rejected by peers, they continue in their impulsive, careless styles of life. Table 12.2 lists the characteristics of people with antisocial personality disorder. While women are more likely than men to have anxiety and depressive disorders, men are more likely than women to have antisocial personality disorder. There is about a 2 to 3 percent prevalence rate of antisocial personality disorder among the Canadian population (Weissman, 1993).

Avoidant Personality Disorder

People with **avoidant personality disorder** are generally unwilling to enter a relationship without some assurance of acceptance because they fear rejection and criticism. As a result, they may have few close relationships outside their immediate families. Unlike people with schizoid personality disorder, however, they have some interest in, and feelings of warmth toward, other people.

Explaining Personality Disorders

What is known about the origins of personality disorders? Numerous biological, psychological, and sociocultural factors have been implicated in the personality disorders.

Biological Factors

Genetic factors are apparently involved in some personality disorders (Rutter & Silberg, 2002). Personality traits are to some degree heritable (Plomin, 2000), and many personality disorders seem to be extreme variations of normal personality traits. An analysis of 51 twin and adoption studies estimated that genetic factors were the greatest influences on antisocial behaviour (Rhee & Waldman, 2002). Referring to the five-factor model of personality, people with schizoid personalities tend to be highly introverted (Ross et al., 2002; Widiger & Costa, 1994). People with avoidant personalities tend to be both introverted and emotionally unstable (Ross et al., 2002; Widiger & Costa, 1994).

Perhaps the genetics of antisocial personality involve the prefrontal cortex of the brain, a part of the brain connected with emotional responses. There is some evidence that people with antisocial personality, as a group, have less grey matter (associative neurons) in the prefrontal cortex of the brain than other people do (Damasio, 2000; Yang et al., 2005). The lesser amount of grey matter could lessen the level of arousal of the nervous system. As a result, it could be more difficult to condition fear responses (Blair & James, 2003). People with the disorder would then be unlikely to show guilt for their misdeeds and would seem to be unafraid of punishment. But a biological factor such as a lower-than-normal level of arousal might not in itself cause the development of an antisocial personality (Rutter & Silberg, 2002). Perhaps a person must also be reared under conditions that do not foster the self-concept of a law-abiding citizen.

avoidant personality disorder a personality disorder in which the person is unwilling to enter relationships without assurance of acceptance because of fears of rejection and criticism

Psychological Factors

Learning theorists suggest that childhood experiences can contribute to maladaptive ways of relating to others in adulthood—that is, can lead to personality disorders. Cognitive psychologists find that antisocial adolescents encode social information in ways that bolster their misdeeds. For example, they tend to interpret other people's behaviour as threatening, even when it is not (Crick & Dodge, 1994). Aggressive individuals often find it difficult to solve social problems in useful ways (McMurran et al., 2002). Cognitive therapists have encouraged some antisocial male adolescents to view social provocations as problems to be solved rather than as threats to their "manhood," with some favourable initial results (Lochman & Dodge, 1994).

Sociocultural Factors

The label of borderline personality has been applied to people as diverse as Marilyn Monroe and Lawrence of Arabia. Some theorists believe we live in fragmented and alienating times that tend to create problems in forming a stable identity and stable relationships. "Living on the edge," or border, can be seen as a metaphor for an unstable society.

Although the causes of many psychological disorders remain in dispute, various methods of therapy have been devised to deal with them. Those methods are the focus of Chapter 13.

Methods
of Therapy

Learning Outcomes

LO 1 Define psychotherapy and describe the history of treatment

LO 2 Describe traditional psychoanalysis and short-term psychodynamic therapies

LO 3 Define humanistic therapy and contrast its two main approaches

LO 4 Define behaviour therapy and identify various behavioural approaches to therapy

LO 5 Define cognitive therapy and describe Beck's approach and REBT

LO 6 Identify advantages, disadvantages, and types of group therapy

LO 7 Explain whether psychotherapy works and who benefits from it

LO 8 Describe methods of biological therapy and their benefits and side effects

ZenShui/Alix Minde/Getty Images

> # "*Had she broken her leg, her treatment would have followed a fairly standard course.*"

Jasmine, a 19-year-old college student, has been crying almost without let-up for several days. She feels that her life is falling apart. Her college aspirations lie in shambles. She believes she has brought shame upon her family. Thoughts of suicide have crossed her mind. She can barely drag herself out of bed in the morning. She is avoiding friends. She can pinpoint some sources of stress in her life: a couple of less-than-shining grades, an argument with a boyfriend, friction with roommates. Still, her misery seemed to descend on her from nowhere.

Jasmine is depressed—she feels so down that family and friends have finally prevailed upon her to seek professional help. Had she broken her leg, her treatment would have followed a fairly standard course. Yet treatment of psychological problems and disorders like depression is sometimes approached from different perspectives. Depending on whom Jasmine sees, she may be

- lying on a couch, talking about anything that pops into awareness, and exploring the possible meaning of her recurrent dreams;

- sitting face to face with a warm, gentle therapist who expresses faith in Jasmine's ability to manage her problems;

- listening to a frank, straightforward therapist assert that Jasmine's problems stem from self-defeating attitudes and perfectionistic beliefs;

- taking medication; or

- participating in some combination of these approaches.

These methods, although very different, all represent methods of therapy. In this chapter we explore various methods of psychotherapy and biological therapy. *What is psychotherapy?*

LO1 What Is Psychotherapy?

There are many kinds of psychotherapy, but they all have certain common characteristics.

Psychotherapy is a systematic interaction between a therapist and a client that applies psychological principles

DID YOU KNOW?

- In the 19th century, vacationers in Toronto, Ontario, would sometimes visit the Queen Street insane asylum as part of their holiday itinerary.

- Some psychotherapists let their clients take the lead in psychotherapy.

- Some psychotherapists tell their clients exactly what to do.

- Lying in a reclining chair and fantasizing can be an effective way of confronting fears.

- Smoking cigarettes can be an effective method for helping people stop smoking cigarettes.

- There is growing scientific evidence that psychotherapy helps people with psychological disorders.

- The originator of a surgical technique to reduce violence learned that it was not always successful when one of his patients shot him.

psychotherapy
a systematic interaction between a therapist and a client that brings psychological principles to bear on influencing the client's thoughts, feelings, or behaviour to help the client overcome abnormal behaviour or adjust to problems in living

to affect the client's thoughts, feelings, or behaviour in an effort to help the client overcome psychological disorders, adjust to problems in living, or develop as an individual.

Quite a mouthful? True. But note the essentials:

- *Systematic interaction.* Psychotherapy is a systematic interaction between a client and a therapist. The therapist's theoretical point of view interacts with the client's to determine how the therapist and client relate to each other.

- *Psychological principles.* Psychotherapy is based on psychological theory and research in areas such as personality, learning, motivation, and emotion.

- *Thoughts, feelings, and behaviour.* Psychotherapy influences clients' thoughts, feelings, and behaviour. It can be aimed at any or all of these aspects of human psychology.

- *Psychological disorders, adjustment problems, and personal growth.* Psychotherapy is often used with people who have psychological disorders. Other people seek help in adjusting to problems such as shyness, weight problems, or loss of a life partner. Still other clients want to learn more about themselves and to reach their full potential as individuals, parents, or creative artists.

The History of Therapies

Historically speaking, "treatments" of psychological disorders often reflected the assumption that people who behaved in strange ways were possessed by demons. *How, then, have people with psychological problems and disorders been treated throughout the ages?* Because of this belief, treatment tended to involve cruel practices such as exorcism and execution. Some people who could not meet the demands of everyday life were tossed into prisons. Others begged in the streets, stole food, or became prostitutes. A few found their way to monasteries or other retreats that offered a kind word and some support. Generally speaking, they died early.

Asylums

Asylums originated in European monasteries. They were the first institutions meant primarily for people with psychological disorders. But their function was warehousing, not treatment. Their inmate populations mushroomed until the stresses created by noise, overcrowding, and disease aggravated the problems they were meant to ease. Inmates were frequently chained and beaten.

The word *bedlam* (which means wild uproar) derives from St. Mary's of *Bethlehem*, the London asylum that opened its gates in 1547. Here unfortunate people with psychological disorders were chained, whipped, and allowed to lie in their own waste.

Humanitarian reform movements began in the 18th century. In Paris, the physician Philippe Pinel unchained the patients at La Salpêtrière. Rather than run amok, as had been feared, most patients profited from kindness and freedom. Many eventually re-entered society. Later movements to reform institutions were led by William Tuke in England and

The Unchaining of the Patients at La Salpêtrière
Philippe Pinel sparked the humanitarian reform movement by unchaining the patients at this asylum in Paris.

NEL

Dorothea Dix in the United States. Even with these reform movements, asylums played a central role in Canadian health care until the end of the 19th century. As part of standard operations at many Ontario asylums (found in Toronto, Hamilton, and London), they were open to public viewing from noon until 3:00 p.m. every day, and tens of thousands of tourists passed through their halls throughout the 19th century (Miron, 2006).

Mental and General Hospitals

In Canada mental hospitals gradually replaced asylums. In contrast to the asylum, the mental hospital's function is treatment, not warehousing. However, a focus on large provincially run mental hospitals was short-lived, and currently 90 percent of hospitalizations for mental illness occur in general hospitals. Data indicates that provincially run psychiatric hospitals are utilized for individuals with more serious psychological disorders, and individuals in psychiatric facilities remain hospitalized for longer periods of time (an average of 100 days versus 16 days in general hospitals) (Canadian Institute for Health Information, 2008).

The Community Mental Health Movement

Since the 1970s, efforts have been made to maintain people with serious psychological disorders in their communities. Community mental health centres attempt to maintain new patients as outpatients and to serve patients who have been released from mental hospitals. Today most people with chronic psychological disorders live in the community, not the hospital. Social critics note that many people who

Large mental hospitals, such as Weyburn Mental Hospital in Saskatchewan (demolished in 2009), which had a 3000-patient capacity, are now becoming a thing of the past.

had resided in hospitals for decades were suddenly discharged to "home" communities that seemed foreign and forbidding to them. To combat this problem, halfway houses were formed as a way for people to transition from various institutions (e.g., psychiatric hospitals, prisons, and youth detention facilities) into the community. Without these houses to ease patients back into society, many patients eventually join the ranks of the homeless or are quickly readmitted into the hospital (Coursey, Ward-Alexander, & Katz, 1990).

Another goal of community mental health centres is education. Through programs that educate community members regarding mental health issues and the resources available to them (e.g., crisis intervention programs such as suicide hotlines, books and DVDs about mental health issues, group workshops and weekend courses), the goal is to combat mental health issues before they become a major problem (Tausig, Michello, & Subedi, 2004). These centres have been largely successful in providing care through the use of paraprofessionals. These individuals are often ex-patients or ex-addicts who now work under the supervision of a professional. Part of the success of these programs may be due to the approachability of the paraprofessionals (Everly, 2002). The Canadian Mental Health Association's website (www.cmha.ca) provides the contact information for the local community health centre in your area.

LO2 Psychoanalytic Therapies

Psychoanalytic therapies are based on the thinking of Sigmund Freud, the founder of psychoanalytic theory. These therapies assume that psychological problems reflect early childhood experiences and internal conflicts. According to Freud, these conflicts involve the shifting of psychic energy among the id, ego, and superego. These shifts of psychic energy determine our behaviour. When primitive urges threaten to break through from the id or when the superego floods us with excessive guilt, defences are established and distress is created. Freud's therapy method—psychoanalysis—aims to bulwark the ego against the torrents of energy released by the id and the superego. With impulses and feelings of guilt and shame placed under greater control, clients are freer to develop adaptive behaviour. *How, then, do psychoanalysts conduct a traditional Freudian psychoanalysis?*

Traditional Psychoanalysis

Imagine your therapist asking you to lie on a couch in a slightly darkened room. She or he would sit behind

psychoanalysis
Freud's method of psychotherapy (also the name of Freud's theory of personality)

catharsis
release of emotional tension, as after a traumatic experience, that has the effect of restoring one's psychological well-being

free association
in psychoanalysis, the uncensored uttering of all thoughts that come to mind

resistance
the tendency to block the free expression of impulses and primitive ideas—a reflection of the defence mechanism of repression

transference
responding to one person (such as a spouse or the psychoanalyst) in a way that is similar to the way one responded to another person (such as a parent) in childhood

you and encourage you to talk about anything that comes to mind, no matter how trivial, no matter how personal. To avoid interfering with your self-exploration, she or he might say little or nothing for session after session. That would be par for the course. A traditional psychoanalysis can extend for months, even years.

Psychoanalysis is the clinical method devised by Sigmund Freud. It aims to provide *insight* into the conflicts that are presumed to lie at the roots of a person's problems. Insight means many things, including knowledge of the experiences that lead to conflicts and maladaptive behaviour, recognition of unconscious feelings and conflicts, and conscious evaluation of one's thoughts, feelings, and behaviour.

Psychoanalysis also aims to help the client express feelings and urges that have been repressed (for a

A View of Freud's Consulting Room
Freud would sit in a chair by the head of the couch while a client free-associated. The basic rule of free association is that no thought is censored. Freud did not believe that free association was really "free"; he assumed that significant feelings would rise to the surface and demand expression.

review of psychoanalytic personality theory, check back to LO1 in Chapter 11). By so doing, Freud believed that the client spilled forth the psychic energy that had been repressed by conflicts and guilt. He called this spilling forth catharsis. Catharsis would provide relief by alleviating some of the forces assaulting the ego. Freud also sought to replace impulsive and defensive behaviour with coping behaviour. In this way, for example, a man with a phobia for knives might discover that he had been repressing the urge to harm someone who had taken advantage of him. He might also find ways to confront the person verbally.

Early in his career as a therapist, Freud found that hypnosis allowed his clients to focus on repressed conflicts and talk about them. He also found, however, that some clients denied the accuracy of this material once they were out of the trance. Others found the memories to be brought out into the open prematurely and painfully. Freud therefore turned to free association, a more gradual method of breaking through the walls of defence that block a client's insight into unconscious processes. In free association, the client is made comfortable—for example, by lying on a couch—and asked to talk about any topic that comes to mind. No thought is to be censored—that is the basic rule. Psychoanalysts ask their clients to wander "freely" from topic to topic, but they do not believe that the process occurring *within* the client is fully free. Repressed impulses clamour for release.

The ego persists in trying to repress unacceptable impulses and threatening conflicts. As a result, clients might show resistance to recalling and discussing threatening ideas. The therapist observes the dynamic struggle between the compulsion to talk about disturbing ideas and resistance. Through discreet comments and questions, the analyst hopes to encourage the client to discuss his or her problems. Talking helps the client gain insight into his or her true wishes and explore ways of fulfilling them.

Transference

Freud believed that clients not only responded to him as an individual but also in ways that reflected their attitudes and feelings toward other people in their lives. He labelled this process transference. For example, a young woman client might respond to him as a father figure and displace her feelings toward her father onto Freud, perhaps seeking affection and wisdom.

Analyzing and working through transference has been considered a key aspect of psychoanalysis.

> Analyzing and working through transference has been considered a key aspect of psychoanalysis.

Freud believed that clients re-enact their childhood conflicts with their parents when they are in therapy.

Dream Analysis

Freud often asked clients to jot down their dreams upon waking so they could discuss them in therapy. Freud considered dreams the "royal road to the unconscious." He believed that the content of dreams is determined by unconscious processes as well as by the events of the day. Unconscious impulses were expressed in dreams as wish fulfillment.

Short-Term Dynamic Therapies

How do modern psychoanalytic approaches differ from traditional psychoanalysis? Although some psychoanalysts still adhere to Freud's techniques, shorter-term dynamic therapies have been devised. Modern psychodynamic therapy is briefer and less intense and makes treatment available to clients who do not have the time or money to make therapy part of their lifestyle. One out of four Canadian psychologists register psychodynamic therapy as their therapy of specialization (Ronson, Cohen, & Hunsley, 2010). These modern psychodynamic therapists continue to focus on revealing unconscious material and breaking through psychological defences. Nevertheless, they differ from traditional psychoanalysis in several ways (Prochaska & Norcross, 2007). One is that the client and therapist usually sit face to face (i.e., the client does not lie on a couch). The therapist may rective. That is, modern therapists often suggest helpful behaviour instead of focusing on insight alone. Finally, there is more focus on the ego as the "executive" of personality and less emphasis on the id.

Interpersonal Psychotherapy

One contemporary dynamic therapy, interpersonal psychotherapy (IPT), focuses on clients' current relationships rather than their childhoods and usually lasts no longer than 9 to 12 months. Developers of IPT view problems such as anxiety and depression as often occurring within social relationships. They therefore focus on clients' relationships and also try to directly alleviate feelings of anxiety and depression (de Mello et al., 2005; Kirschenbaum & Jourdan, 2005).

LO3 Humanistic Therapies

Psychoanalytic therapies focus on internal conflicts and unconscious processes. Humanistic therapies focus on the quality of the client's subjective, conscious experience (see LO4 in Chapter 11 for a review of humanistic personality theory). Traditional psychoanalysis focuses on early childhood experiences. Humanistic therapies are more likely to focus on what clients are experiencing here and now. Thirty-one percent of Canadian psychologists report humanistic therapy as their therapy of specialization (Ronson et al., 2010).

Client-Centred Therapy

What is Carl Rogers's method of client-centred therapy? Rogers believed that we are free to make choices and control our destinies, despite the burdens of the past. He also believed that we have natural tendencies toward health, growth, and fulfillment. Psychological problems arise from roadblocks placed in the path of self-actualization—that is, what Rogers believed was an inborn tendency to strive to realize one's fullest potential. If, when we are young, other

wish fulfillment
a primitive method used by the id to attempt to gratify basic instincts

psychodynamic therapy
therapy based on the principles of psychoanalysis, but less time-consuming as the therapist takes a more directive role

interpersonal psychotherapy (IPT)
a short-term dynamic therapy that focuses on clients' relationships and direct alleviation of negative emotions such as anxiety and depression

Carl Rogers believed that our psychological well-being is connected with our freedom to develop our unique frames of reference and potentials. Do you think you can separate your "real self" from your sociocultural experiences and religious training?

people approve of us only when we are doing what they want us to do, we may learn to disown the parts of ourselves to which they object. We may learn to be seen but not heard—not even by ourselves. As a result, we may experience stress and discomfort and the feeling that we—or the world—are not real.

Client-centred therapy aims to provide insight into the parts of us that we have disowned so that we can feel whole. It creates a warm, therapeutic atmosphere that encourages self-exploration and self-expression. The therapist's acceptance of the client is thought to foster self-acceptance and self-esteem. Self-acceptance frees the client to make choices that develop his or her unique potential.

Client-centred therapy is nondirective. An effective client-centered therapist has several qualities:

1 *Unconditional positive regard:* respect for clients as human beings with unique values and goals.

2 *Empathy:* recognition of the client's experiences and feelings. Therapists view the world through the client's *frame of reference* by setting aside their own values and listening closely.

3 *Genuineness:* Openness and honesty in responding to the client. Client-centred therapists must be able to tolerate

By showing the qualities of unconditional positive regard, empathic understanding, and genuineness, client-centred therapists create an atmosphere in which clients can explore their feelings.

David Buffington/Photographer's Choice/Getty Images

*The Psychotherapy of Carl Rogers: Cases and Commentary by Brink, Debora. Copyright 1996 by GUILFORD PUBLICATIONS, INC. Reproduced with permission of GUILFORD PUBLICATIONS, INC. in the format Textbook via Copyright Clearance Center.

differentness because they believe that every client is different in important ways.

The following excerpt* from a therapy session shows how Carl Rogers uses empathetic understanding and paraphrases a client's (Jill's) feelings. His goal is to help her recognize feelings that she has partially disowned:

Jill: I'm having a lot of problems dealing with my daughter. She's 20 years old; she's in college; I'm having a lot of trouble letting her go…. And I have a lot of guilt feelings about her; I have a real need to hang on to her.

C.R.: A need to hang on so you can kind of make up for the things you feel guilty about. Is that part of it?

Jill: There's a lot of that…. Also, she's been a real friend to me, and filled my life…. And it's very hard … a lot of empty places now that she's not with me.

C.R.: The old vacuum, sort of, when she's not there.

Jill: Yes. Yes. I also would like to be the kind of mother that could be strong and say, you know, "Go and have a good life," and this is really hard for me, to do that.

C.R.: It's very hard to give up something that's been so precious in your life, but also something that I guess has caused you pain when you mentioned guilt.

Jill: Yeah. And I'm aware that I have some anger toward her that I don't always get what I want. I have needs that are not met. And, uh, I don't feel I have a right to those needs. You know … she's a daughter; she's not my mother. Though sometimes I feel as if I'd like her to mother me … it's very difficult for me to ask for that and have a right to it.

C.R.: So, it may be unreasonable, but still, when she doesn't meet your needs, it makes you mad.

Jill: Yeah I get very angry, very angry with her.

C.R.: (*Pauses*) You're also feeling a little tension at this point, I guess.

Jill: Yeah. Yeah. A lot of conflict…. (C.R.: M-hm.) A lot of pain.

C.R.: A lot of pain. Can you say anything more about what that's about? (Farber et al., 1996, pp. 74–75)

Client-centred therapy is practised widely in college and university counselling centres, not just to help students experiencing, say, anxieties or depression but also to help them make decisions. Many students have not yet made career choices, or wonder whether they should become involved with particular people or in sexual activity. Client-centred therapists do not tell clients what to do. Instead, they help clients arrive at their own decisions.

Gestalt Therapy

Gestalt therapy was originated by Fritz Perls (1893–1970). *What is Fritz Perls's method of Gestalt therapy?* Like client-centred therapy, Gestalt therapy assumes that people disown parts of themselves that might meet with social disapproval or rejection. People also don social masks, pretending to be things that they are not. Therapy aims to help individuals integrate conflicting parts of their personality. Perls used the term *Gestalt* to signify this.

Although Perls's ideas about conflicting personality elements owe much to psychoanalytic theory, his form of therapy, unlike psychoanalysis, focuses on the here and now. Exercises heighten clients' awareness of their current feelings and behaviour. One way a Gestalt therapist might do this is by making the client aware of a particular mannerism, or action. For example, a client may nervously wring her hands when talking about a problem, and the therapist might then ask the client to wring her hands exaggeratedly and explain why she behaves in this way when she is nervous. Another example of a Gestalt therapy exercise is the "empty chair" technique. A client is asked to imagine that a person he is in conflict with is sitting in an empty chair. The client then speaks to the imagined person, revisiting the event that caused the emotional pain. Then the client would sit in the empty chair and respond to his questions and accusations, pretending to be the other person. These exercises are designed to heighten the experience of one's emotions and behaviours in the present moment, with the goal of integrating them.

Perls also believed, along with Rogers, that people are free to make choices and to direct their personal growth. But the charismatic and forceful Perls was unlike the gentle and accepting Rogers in temperament (Prochaska & Norcross, 2007). Thus, unlike client-centred therapy, Gestalt therapy is directive. The therapist leads the client through planned experiences.

LO4 Behaviour Therapy

Psychoanalytic and humanistic forms of therapy tend to focus on what people think and feel. Behaviour therapists tend to focus on what people *do*. *What is behaviour therapy?* Behaviour therapy—also called *behaviour modification*—applies principles of learning to directly promote desired behavioural changes. Behaviour therapists rely heavily on principles of conditioning and observational learning. They help clients discontinue self-defeating behaviour patterns such as overeating, smoking, and phobic avoidance of harmless stimuli. They help clients acquire adaptive behaviour patterns such as the social skills required to start social relationships or say no to insistent salespeople.

Behaviour therapists may help clients gain "insight" into maladaptive behaviours such as feelings of anxiety by helping the person become aware of the circumstances in which the behaviours occur. They do not help unearth the childhood origins of problems and the symbolic meanings of maladaptive behaviours as psychoanalysts do. Behaviour therapists, like other therapists, may also build warm, therapeutic relationships with clients, but they see the effectiveness of behaviour therapy as deriving from specific, learning-based procedures (Rachman, 2000). They insist that their methods be established by experimentation and that results be assessed in terms of measurable behaviour. In this section we consider some frequently used behaviour-therapy techniques. The fear-reduction and aversive conditioning procedures are both based on the principles of classical conditioning (see Chapter 5).

Fear-Reduction Methods

Many people seek therapy because of fears and phobias (see Chapter 12, p. 268) that interfere with their functioning. This is one of the areas in which behaviour therapy has made great inroads. *What are some behaviour-therapy methods for reducing fears?* These include systematic desensitization, virtual therapy, and modelling.

Systematic Desensitization

Adam has a phobia about receiving injections. His behaviour therapist treats him as he reclines in a comfortable padded chair. In a state of deep muscle relaxation, Adam observes slides projected on a screen. A slide of a nurse holding a needle has just been shown three times, 30 seconds at a time. Each time Adam

Gestalt therapy
Fritz Perls's form of psychotherapy, which attempts to integrate conflicting parts of the personality through directive methods designed to help clients perceive their whole selves

behaviour therapy
systematic application of the principles of learning to the direct modification of a client's problem behaviours

Kelly Redinger/DesignPics/GetStock.com

systematic desensitization
Wolpe's method for reducing fears by associating a hierarchy of images of fear-evoking stimuli with deep muscle relaxation

hierarchy
an arrangement of stimuli according to the amount of fear they evoke

modelling
a behaviour-therapy technique in which a client observes and imitates a person who approaches and copes with feared objects or situations

has shown no anxiety. So now a slightly more discomforting slide is shown: one of the nurse aiming the needle toward someone's bare arm. After 15 seconds, our armchair adventurer notices twinges of discomfort and raises a finger as a signal (speaking might disturb his relaxation). The projector operator turns off the light, and Adam spends two minutes imagining his "safe scene"—lying on a beach beneath the tropical sun. Then the slide is shown again. This time Adam views it for 30 seconds before feeling anxiety.

Adam is undergoing **systematic desensitization**, a method for reducing phobic responses originated by psychiatrist Joseph Wolpe (1915–1997). Systematic desensitization is a gradual process in which the client learns to handle increasingly disturbing stimuli while anxiety to each one is being counterconditioned. About 10 to 20 stimuli such as slides are arranged in a sequence, or **hierarchy**, according to their "fear factor"—their capacity to trigger anxiety. In imagination or by being shown photos, the client travels gradually up through this hierarchy, approaching the target behaviour. In Adam's case, the target behaviour was the ability to receive an injection without undue anxiety. If you recall what you learned about classical conditioning in Chapter 5, the conditioned stimulus no longer evokes the automatic fear response; extinction of the conditioned response has occurred.

Virtual Therapy

Virtual therapy may use more elaborate equipment than slides, but the principle is desensitization. New York Fire Chief Stephen King was in the north tower at the World Trade Center on September 11, 2001, which was hit first by the airplanes. The experience led him to retire from the department, avoid bridges and tunnels, and stay out of Manhattan (Lake, 2005). "Where I was and what I saw that day—the many people that jumped, the magnitude of it—was just overwhelming."

But virtual therapy has helped King face the past—and his future. Using the technology we find in video games, programs mimic traumatic settings and events—public speaking in an auditorium, flying in an airplane, spiders, or, in King's case, images of the World Trade Center. "The idea

Image of 9/11, copyright Hunter Hoffman, www.vrpain.com

FIGURE 13.1

A Program Containing Images of the World Trade Center Intended to Help People with Posttraumatic Stress Disorder

Virtual therapy clients are exposed to virtual stimuli that represent their source of anxiety and stress to help them gradually confront their fears.

behind the treatment," explains Dr. JoAnn Difede (Lake, 2005), "is to systematically expose the patient to aspects of their experience in a graded fashion so they can confront their fear of the trauma" (see Figure 13.1). Psychologist Albert Rizzo has developed scenes from classrooms and parties to help people overcome social anxieties. "To help people deal with their problems, you must get them exposed to what they fear most," Rizzo (Lubell, 2004) notes.

The Virtually Better treatment centre has developed scenes of a bridge and a glass elevator to desensitize patients to fear of heights, a virtual airplane cabin for people who fear flying, and a virtual thunderstorm to help people lessen fear of tempestuous weather. The U.S. Army has asked Virtually Better to use its 3D imaging software to create programs that will help soldiers returning from Iraq and Afghanistan. Virtually Better is also working on programs to help treat addictions. Psychologists are studying whether virtual exposure to alcohol, drugs, and cigarettes can evoke cravings that patients can learn to resist. Virtually Better's contributions include scenes of a virtual crack house and a virtual bar.

Psychologist Hunter Hoffman (2004) describes a virtual environment, *SpiderWorld,* that helps people with spider phobias overcome their aversion by gradually approaching virtual spiders and reaching out to touch them. A toy spider and a device that tracks the patient's hand movements provide tactile sensations akin to touching a real spider (see Figure 13.2). This virtual-reality therapy is also based on classical conditioning theory (see Chapter 5), with the extinction of the conditioned fear response.

Modelling

Modelling relies on observational learning. In this method clients observe, and then imitate, people who approach and cope with the objects or situations that the clients fear. Bandura and his colleagues (1969) found that modelling worked as well as systematic

Dr. Hunter Hoffman of the University of Washington Uses Virtual Therapy to Treat "Miss Muffet"

Miss Muffet is the name playfully given by Hoffman to a woman with a phobia for spiders. She is wearing virtual-reality headgear and sees the scene displayed on the monitor, which shows a large and hairy—but virtual—tarantula.

Photo by Stephen Dagadakis, copyright Hunter Hoffman, www.vrpain.com

desensitization—and more rapidly—in reducing fear of snakes. Like systematic desensitization, modelling is likely to increase self-efficacy expectations in coping with feared stimuli.

Aversive Conditioning

Many people also seek behaviour therapy because they want to break bad habits, such as smoking, excessive drinking, nail biting, and the like. One behaviour-therapy approach to helping people do so is **aversive conditioning**. Aversive conditioning is also based on the theories of classical conditioning. *How do behaviour therapists use aversive conditioning to help people break bad habits?* Aversive conditioning is a controversial procedure in which painful or aversive stimuli are paired with unwanted impulses, such as desire for a cigarette or desire to engage in antisocial behaviour, in an effort to make the impulse less appealing. For example, to help people control alcohol intake, tastes of different alcoholic beverages can be paired with drug-induced nausea and vomiting or with electric shock. The conditioned stimulus (taste of alcohol) then becomes associated with the reflexive response of nausea rather than pleasure (see Chapter 5).

Aversive conditioning has been used with problems as diverse as cigarette smoking, sexual abuse, and retarded children's self-injurious behaviour. **Rapid smoking** is an aversive conditioning method designed to help smokers quit. In this method, the would-be quitter inhales every six seconds. In another method the hose of a hair dryer is hooked up to a chamber containing several lit cigarettes. Smoke is blown into the quitter's face as he or she also smokes a cigarette. A third method uses branching

pipes so that the smoker draws in smoke from several cigarettes at the same time. In these methods, overexposure makes once-desirable cigarette smoke aversive. The quitter becomes motivated to avoid, rather than seek, cigarettes. Interest in aversive conditioning for quitting smoking has waned, however, because of side effects such as raising blood pressure and the availability of nicotine-replacement techniques.

Operant Conditioning Procedures

We tend to repeat behaviour that is reinforced. Behaviour that is not reinforced tends to become extinct. Behaviour therapists have used these principles of operant conditioning (see Chapter 5) with psychotic patients as well as with clients with milder problems. *How do behaviour therapists apply principles of operant conditioning in behaviour modification?*

The staff at one mental hospital was at a loss about how to encourage withdrawn schizophrenic patients to eat regularly. Ayllon and Haughton (1962) observed that staff members were making the problem worse by coaxing patients into the dining room and even feeding them. Staff attention apparently reinforced the patients' lack of cooperation. Some rules were changed. Patients who did not arrive at the dining hall within 30 minutes after serving were locked out. Staff could not interact with patients at mealtime. With uncooperative behaviour no longer reinforced, patients quickly changed their eating habits. Then patients were required to pay one penny to enter the dining hall. Pennies were earned by interacting with other patients and showing other socially appropriate behaviours. These target behaviours also became more frequent.

eye-movement desensitization and reprocessing (EMDR) a method of treating stress disorders by having clients visually follow a rapidly oscillating finger while they think of the traumatic events connected with the disorders

token economy a controlled environment in which people are reinforced for desired behaviours with tokens (such as poker chips) that may be exchanged for privileges

successive approximations in operant conditioning, a series of behaviours that gradually become more similar to a target behaviour

Health professionals are concerned about whether people who are, or have been, dependent on alcohol can exercise control over their drinking. One study showed that rewards for remaining abstinent from alcohol can exert a powerful effect (Petry et al., 2000). In the study, one group of alcohol-dependent veterans was given a standard treatment while another group received the treatment *plus* the chance to win prizes for remaining alcohol-free, as measured by a Breathalyzer test. By the end of the eight-week treatment period, 84 percent of the veterans who could win prizes remained in the program, as compared with 22 percent of the standard treatment group. The prizes had an average value of $200, far less than what alcohol-related absenteeism from work and other responsibilities can cost.

The Token Economy

Many psychiatric wards and hospitals use **token economies** in which patients need tokens such as poker chips to purchase TV viewing time, extra visits to the canteen, or a private room (Comaty et al., 2001). The tokens are dispensed as reinforcers for productive activities such as making beds, brushing teeth, and socializing. Token economies have not eliminated all symptoms of schizophrenia but have increased patients' activity and cooperation. Tokens have also been used to modify the behaviour of children with conduct disorders.

Successive Approximations

The operant conditioning method of **successive approximations** is often used to help clients build good habits. For example: You want to study three hours each evening but can concentrate for only half an hour. Rather than attempting to increase your study time all at once, you could do so gradually by adding, say, five minutes each evening. After every hour or so of studying, you could reinforce yourself with five minutes of playing a game on your phone, or people-watching in a busy section of the library. As long as you find the reward pleasant, this method should help you reach your goal.

{ Eye-Movement Desensitization and Reprocessing }

Helping professionals are often inspired to develop therapy methods based on their personal experiences. Such was the case with Francine Shapiro. As she paints it, Shapiro (1989) had troubling thoughts on her mind when she strolled into a park one day. But as her eyes darted about, taking in the scene, she found her troubled thoughts disappearing. Thus she developed a therapy method called **eye-movement desensitization and reprocessing (EMDR)**, which has joined the arsenal of therapeutic weapons against stress disorders. In this method, the client is asked to imagine a traumatic scene while the therapist moves a finger rapidly back and forth before his or her eyes for about 20 to 30 seconds. The client follows the finger while keeping the troubling scene in mind. Evidence from a number of studies suggests that EMDR helps decrease the anxiety associated with traumatic events.

Devilly (2002) allows that EMDR is often effective, but his review finds other exposure therapies to be more effective. Research even challenges the idea that eye movements are a necessary part of therapy (May, 2005; Devilly, 2002). Skeptics have tried EMDR—or a cousin of it—using finger tapping rather than finger wagging, or instructing clients to keep their eyes straight ahead, and the results have remained the same. Clients receiving EMDR may profit from a "therapeutic alliance" with the helping professional and from expectations of success. Moreover, the client is to some degree being exposed to the trauma that haunts him or her, and under circumstances in which the client believes he or she will be able to manage the trauma.

Conclusion? Exposure helps people cope with trauma. Eye movements may not be needed.

Biofeedback Training

Through **biofeedback training (BFT)**, therapists help clients become more aware of, and gain control over, various bodily functions. Therapists attach clients to devices that measure bodily functions such as heart rate. "Bleeps" or other electronic signals are used to indicate (and thereby reinforce) changes in the desired direction—for example, a slower heart rate (knowledge of results is a powerful reinforcer). One device, the electromyograph (EMG), monitors muscle tension. It has been used to increase control over muscle tension in the forehead and elsewhere, thereby alleviating anxiety, stress, and headaches (Nestoriuc et al., 2008).

BFT also helps clients voluntarily regulate functions once thought to be beyond conscious control, such as heart rate and blood pressure. Hypertensive clients use a blood pressure cuff and electronic signals to gain control over their blood pressure. The electroencephalograph (EEG) monitors brain waves and can be used to teach people how to produce alpha waves, which are associated with relaxation. Some people have overcome insomnia by learning to produce the kinds of brain waves associated with sleep.

Social Skills Training

In social skills training, behaviour therapists decrease social anxiety and build social skills through operant-conditioning procedures that employ **self-monitoring**, coaching, modelling, role-playing, **behaviour rehearsal**, and **feedback**. Social skills training has been used to help formerly hospitalized mental patients maintain jobs and apartments in the community.

For example, a worker can rehearse politely asking a supervisor for assistance or asking a landlord to fix the plumbing in an apartment. Social skills training is effective in groups. Group members can role-play important people—such as parents, spouses, or potential dates—in the lives of other members.

LO5 Cognitive Therapies

What thoughts do you have when things go wrong at school or on the job? Do you tell yourself that you're facing a problem that needs a solution? That you've

---

{ Modern Technology and Therapy }

The therapies we have been investigating so far have all assumed a face-to-face interaction between therapist and client. However, modern technologies have moved the counselling office into cyberspace, across the telephone lines, and even across the airwaves.

How different are these modern methods of therapy compared with traditional methods? In online counselling, information may be communicated conveniently between two people, but much of the meaning behind the words may be lost. It is estimated that most of the meaning behind a person's words is conveyed through the tone of voice, the speed of speech, where emphasis is placed in a sentence, and the person's body posture while speaking. All of this is lost through text-only Internet communication. Further, there are security concerns for information shared on the Internet, as well as questions regarding the qualifications of many of those offering online counselling (Robson & Robson, 2000). With voice-over-Internet and telephone counselling, like face-to-face counselling, one has the benefit of immediate responses during conversations, and much of the meaning carried by tone of voice is retained, but the visual and gestural cues of conversation are still missing. Further, there has been no evidence as to the effectiveness of telephone therapy compared to face-to-face therapy (Haas, Benedict, & Kobos, 1996). Some therapists have identified some unique benefits of Internet and telephone therapy especially for those in isolated locations (Lester, 2006; Shepard, 1987). There is cautious hope for both Internet and telephone counselling, and calls for legitimization and careful review of the methods and benefits have been made (Bloom 1998).

Sometimes counsellors make their way onto the airwaves and host radio therapy talk shows. One must remain skeptical of the motives of the therapist in this type of venue, as how much help can be given in a three-minute conversation that has no element of privacy whatsoever? It is safer to assume that these shows are more about entertainment than they are about helping those in need.

---

successfully solved problems before and will be able to create a solution this time? Or do you think, "Oh no! This is awful! It's going to get worse, and I'm going to flunk (or get fired)!" If you go the "This is awful" route, you are probably heightening your discomfort and impairing your coping ability. Cognitive therapy focuses directly on your thoughts and encourages ideas that will help you solve problems rather than blow them out of proportion and magnify your discomfort.

What is cognitive therapy? Cognitive therapy focuses on changing the beliefs, attitudes, and automatic types of thinking that create and compound people's problems. Cognitive therapists, like psychoanalytic and humanistic therapists, aim to foster self-insight, but they mainly aim to help make people more aware of their *current cognitions.* Cognitive therapists also aim to directly change maladaptive thoughts in an effort to reduce negative feelings and help clients solve problems.

Many behaviour therapists incorporate cognitive procedures in their methods. For example, techniques such as systematic desensitization, covert sensitization, and covert reinforcement ask clients to focus on visual imagery. Behavioural methods for treating bulimia nervosa focus on clients' irrational attitudes toward their weight and body shape as well as foster good eating habits. Let us look at the approaches and methods of the cognitive therapists Aaron Beck and Albert Ellis.

Aaron Beck's Cognitive Therapy

Psychiatrist Aaron Beck began his professional life as a psychoanalyst. He became impatient, however, with analysis's lengthy methods and reluctance to offer specific advice. In his own life he had successfully defeated his fear of blood by assisting in surgical operations and argued himself out of irrational fear of driving through tunnels. Similarly, his methods of cognitive therapy focus on arguing clients out of beliefs that are making them miserable and exposing them to situations they avoid because of irrational fear (Berk et al., 2004; Warman et al., 2005). *What is Aaron Beck's method of cognitive therapy?* Beck encourages clients to become their own personal scientists and challenge feelings and beliefs that make no sense.

Beck encourages clients to see the irrationality of their ways of thinking. For example, depressed people tend to minimize their accomplishments and to assume that the worst will happen. Minimizing accomplishments and expecting the worst are (usually) distortions of reality that lead to feelings of depression. Cognitive distortions can be fleeting and automatic, difficult to detect. Beck's methods help clients become aware of such distortions and challenge them.

Beck notes a number of "cognitive errors" that contribute to clients' miseries:

1 Clients may *selectively perceive* the world as a harmful place and ignore evidence to the contrary. An example of this is Alice, who only remembers the person who cut in front of her in line at the store, but forgets the pleasant conversations she had with the other shoppers while she was out.

2 Clients may *overgeneralize* on the basis of a few examples. For example, they may perceive themselves as worthless because they were laid off at work or as unattractive because they were refused a date.

3 Clients may *magnify,* or blow out of proportion, the importance of negative events. They may catastrophize failing a test by assuming they will flunk out of college or catastrophize losing a job by believing that they will never find another one and that serious harm will befall their family as a result.

4 Clients may engage in *absolutist thinking,* or looking at the world in black and white rather than in shades of grey. In doing so, a rejection on a date takes on the meaning of a lifetime of loneliness; an uncomfortable illness takes on life-threatening proportions.

Becoming aware of cognitive errors and modifying catastrophizing thoughts helps us cope with stress. Internal, stable, and global attributions of failure lead to depression and feelings of helplessness. Cognitive therapists also alert clients to cognitive errors or irrational thoughts so that the clients can change their attitudes and pave the way for more effective overt behaviour.

Aaron Beck (left) and Albert Ellis (right)

Rational Emotive Behaviour Therapy

What is Albert Ellis's method of rational emotive behaviour therapy (REBT)? In rational emotive behaviour therapy (REBT), Albert Ellis (1913–2007) pointed out that our beliefs *about* events shape our responses to them. Moreover, many of us harbour a number of irrational beliefs that can give rise to problems or magnify their impact. Two of the most important ones are the belief that we must have the love and approval of people who are important to us and the belief that we must prove ourselves to be thoroughly competent, adequate, and achieving.

Albert Ellis, like Aaron Beck, began his career as a psychoanalyst. And, also like Beck, he became disturbed by the passive role of the analyst and by the slow rate of obtaining results—if they were obtained at all. Ellis's REBT methods are active and directive. He did not sit back like the traditional psychoanalyst and occasionally offer an interpretation. Instead, he urged clients to seek out their irrational beliefs, which can be unconscious, though not as deeply buried as Freud believed. Nevertheless, they can be hard to pinpoint without some direction. Ellis's therapy is based on investigating how *activating* experiences paired with irrational *beliefs* lead to negative *consequences* (A-B-C). Ellis's goal in therapy was to show clients how those beliefs lead to misery and challenged clients to change them. A sample therapy session might appear something like this:

Jane: I'm really upset; my friend doesn't call me anymore. I think she hates me.

Ellis: Would it be the end of the world if she did hate you?

J: Well … no, but I'd be really sad.

E: Would the sadness be such a terrible thing, or just a temporary inconvenience?

J: I guess just a temporary inconvenience, but I don't like being sad.

E: What you have described to me is: Action (my friend doesn't call), Belief (I need everyone to like me), Consequence (I'm sad). We can change the consequence if we change your irrational belief. What other belief is a more realistic one?

J: Hmm.... Well, it is unreasonable to think that I should get along with everyone; perhaps we're just not that compatible. Or maybe she's going through some tough times and needs space.

E: Good, each of those more reasonable beliefs would lead to more adaptable consequences, either trying to find new

more compatible friends, or being comfortable giving your friend space.

When Ellis saw clients behaving according to irrational beliefs, he refuted the beliefs by asking, "Where is it written that you must … ?" or "What evidence do you have that … ?" According to Ellis, we need less misery and less blaming in our lives, and more action.

Toward a Cognitive-Behavioural Therapy

Many theorists consider cognitive therapy to be a collection of techniques that are a part of behaviour therapy. Aaron Beck himself appears to be comfortable referring to his approach as *cognitive* in one article and *cognitive-behavioural* in another (Berk et al., 2004; Warman & Beck, 2003). We may be headed toward an integration of the two approaches that will be termed **cognitive-behavioural therapy (CBT)**.

Ellis straddled behavioural and cognitive therapies. He originally dubbed his method of therapy *rational-emotive therapy,* because his focus was on the cognitive—irrational beliefs and how to change them. However, Ellis also always promoted behavioural changes to cement cognitive changes. In keeping with his broad philosophy, he recently changed the name of rational-emotive therapy to rational emotive *behaviour* therapy (Ellis, 1995).

There are many different types of cognitive behavioural therapies, but there are two common factors found in most. First is the focus on the here and now. The client and therapist assess what the problem is at the outset, and develop a goal that they will work toward. Consistently throughout the therapeutic relationship, both the client and therapist will monitor and evaluate to ensure that progress toward the goal is being made. Second, the client will learn how to challenge his or her beliefs in the therapy sessions, and "homework" will be given where the client tries to monitor his or her thinking and modify his or her behaviour during the week between sessions. Often this is in the form of a journal that monitors thoughts and actions, or by implementing behavioural experiments (Grazebrook & Garland, 2005). These time-limited, problem-focused, therapy sessions have become very popular and would likely be used by the counselling department of your college or university. Four out of five Canadian psychologists report cognitive-behavioural therapy as their therapy of specialization (Ronson et al., 2010).

rational emotive behaviour therapy (REBT) Albert Ellis's form of therapy that encourages clients to challenge and correct irrational expectations and maladaptive behaviours

cognitive-behaviour therapy (CBT) an approach to therapy that uses cognitive and behavioural techniques that have been validated by research

LO6 Group Therapies

When a psychotherapist has several clients with similar problems—anxiety, depression, adjustment to divorce, lack of social skills—it often makes sense to treat them in a group rather than in individual sessions. The methods and characteristics of the group reflect the needs of the members and the theoretical orientation of the leader. In group psychoanalysis, clients might interpret one another's dreams. In a client-centred group, they might provide an accepting atmosphere for self-exploration. Members of behaviour therapy groups might be jointly desensitized to anxiety-evoking stimuli or might practise social skills together. *What are the advantages and disadvantages of group therapy?*

Group therapy has the following advantages:

1 It is economical. It allows the therapist to work with several clients at once.

2 Compared with one-to-one therapy, group therapy provides more information and life experience for clients to draw upon.

3 Appropriate behaviour receives group support. Clients usually appreciate an outpouring of peer approval.

4 When we run into troubles, it is easy to imagine that we are different from other people or inferior to them. Affiliating with people with similar problems is reassuring.

5 Group members who show improvement provide hope for other members.

6 Many individuals seek therapy because of problems in relating to other people. People who seek therapy for other reasons also may be socially inhibited. Members of groups have the opportunity to practise social skills in a relatively nonthreatening atmosphere. In a group consisting of men and women of different ages, group members can role-play one another's employers, employees, spouses, parents, children, and friends. Members can role-play asking one another out on dates, saying no (or yes), and so on.

But group therapy is not for everyone. Some clients fare better with individual treatment. Many prefer not to disclose their problems to a group. They may be overly shy or want individual attention. It is the responsibility of the therapist to insist that group disclosures be kept confidential, to establish a supportive atmosphere, and to ensure that group members obtain the attention they need.

Many types of therapy can be conducted either individually or in groups. Couple therapy and family therapy are conducted only with groups.

Couple Therapy

Couple therapy helps couples enhance their relationship by improving their communication skills and helping them manage conflict (Prochaska & Norcross, 2007). There are often power imbalances in relationships, and couple therapy helps individuals find "full membership" in the couple. Correcting power imbalances increases happiness and can decrease the incidence of domestic violence. Ironically, in situations of domestic violence, the partner with *less* power in the relationship is usually the violent one. Violence sometimes appears to be a way of compensating for inability to share power in other aspects of the relationship (Rathus & Sanderson, 1999).

Today the main approach to couple therapy is cognitive behavioural (Rathus & Sanderson, 1999). It teaches couples communications skills (such as how to listen and how to express feelings), ways of handling feelings like depression and anger, and ways of solving problems.

Family Therapy

What is family therapy? Family therapy is a form of group therapy in which one or more families constitute the group. Family therapy may be undertaken from various theoretical viewpoints. One is the systems approach, in which family interaction is studied and modified to enhance the growth of individual family members and of the family unit as a whole (Prochaska & Norcross, 2007). Twenty-one percent of Canadian psychologists register family systems therapy as their therapy of specialization (Ronson et al., 2010).

Family members with low self-esteem often cannot tolerate different attitudes and behaviours in other family members. Faulty communication within the family also creates problems. In addition, it is not uncommon for the family to present an "identified patient"—that is, the family member who has *the* problem and is *causing* all the trouble. Yet family therapists usually assume that the identified patient is a scapegoat for other problems within and among family members. It is a sort of myth: Change the bad

Barry Rosenthal/UpperCut Images/Getty Images

apple—or identified patient—and the barrel—or family—will be functional once more. The family therapist—often a specialist in this field—attempts to teach the family to communicate more effectively and encourage growth and autonomy in each family member.

LO7 Does Psychotherapy Work?

We have discussed several types of psychotherapies. Some focus on gaining insight into why a problem occurs; others focus on taking action to improve for the future. Some work best when one-on-one with a therapist; others work only in a group setting (see Table 13.1 for a comparison of psychotherapies). This leads to the natural question: Which therapy works the best?

In 1952, the British psychologist Hans Eysenck published a review of psychotherapy research—"The Effects of Psychotherapy"—that sent shock waves through the psychotherapy community. On the basis of his review of the research, Eysenck concluded that the rate of improvement among people in psychotherapy was no greater than the rate of "spontaneous remission"—that is, the rate of improvement that would be shown by people with psychological disorders who received no treatment at all. Eysenck was not addressing people with schizophrenia, who typically profit from biological forms of therapy, but he argued that whether or not people with problems such as anxiety and depression received therapy, two out of three reported substantial improvement within two years.

That was half a century ago. There is now quite a bit of research evidence—with many studies employing a sophisticated statistical averaging method called **meta-analysis**—that show that psychotherapy is effective (Luborsky et al., 2002; Shadish et al., 2000). *What, then, has research shown about the effectiveness of psychotherapy?*

In their classic early use of meta-analysis, Mary Lee Smith and Gene Glass (1977) analyzed the results of dozens of outcome studies of various types of therapies. They concluded that people who obtained psychoanalytic therapy showed greater well-being, on the average, than 70 percent to 75 percent of those who did not obtain treatment. Similarly, nearly 75 percent of the clients who obtained client-centred therapy were better off than people who did not obtain treatment. Psychoanalytic and client-centred therapies appear to be most effective with well-educated, verbal, strongly motivated clients who report problems with anxiety,

meta-analysis
a method for combining and averaging the results of individual research studies

> It is a sort of myth: Change the bad apple—or identified patient—and the barrel—or family—will be functional once more.

TABLE 13.1

Types of Psychotherapy

	Insight or Action?	Individual or Group	Therapy's Strength
Psychoanalysis	Insight	Individual	Searching honestly
Psychodynamic	Insight	Individual	Productive use of conflict
Client-centred	Insight	Both	Acceptance, empathy
Gestalt	Insight	Both	Focus on immediate awareness
Behavioural	Action	Both	Observable changes in behaviour
Cognitive	Action	Individual	Constructive guidance
REBT	Action	Individual	Clarity of thinking and goals
Family	Both	Group	Shared responsibility of problems

Source: From COON/MILTERER/BROWN/MALIK/MCKENZIE. *Psychology: A Journey*, 3E. © 2010 Nelson Education Ltd. Reproduced by permission. www.cengage.com/permissions.

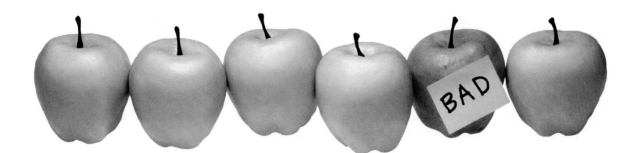

depression (of light to moderate proportions), and interpersonal relationships. Neither form of therapy appears to be effective with people with psychotic disorders such as major depression, bipolar disorder, and schizophrenia. Smith and Glass (1977) found that people who obtained Gestalt therapy showed greater well-being than about 60 percent of those who did not obtain treatment. The effectiveness of psychoanalysis and client-centred therapy thus was reasonably comparable. Gestalt therapy fell behind.

Smith and Glass (1977) did not include cognitive therapies in their meta-analysis because at the time of their study many cognitive approaches were relatively new. Because behaviour therapists also incorporate many cognitive techniques, it can be difficult to sort out which aspects—cognitive or otherwise—of behavioural treatments are most effective. Many meta-analyses of cognitive-behavioural therapy have been conducted since the early work of Smith and Glass, however. Their results are encouraging (e.g., DeRubeis et al., 2005; Hollon et al., 2005). A meta-analysis of 90 studies by William R. Shadish and his colleagues (2000) concurred that psychotherapy is generally effective. Generally speaking, the more therapy the better; that is, people who have more psychotherapy tend to fare better than people who have less of it. Therapy also appears to be more effective when the outcome measures reflect the treatment (e.g., when the effects of treatment aimed at fear-reduction are measured in terms of people's ability to approach fear-inducing objects and situations).

Studies of cognitive therapy have shown that modifying irrational beliefs of the type described by Albert Ellis helps people with problems such as anxiety and depression (Engels et al., 1993; Haaga & Davison, 1993). Modifying self-defeating beliefs of the sort outlined by Aaron Beck also frequently alleviates anxiety and depression (Butler & Beck, 2001). Cognitive therapy has also helped people with personality disorders (Beck et al., 2001; Trull et al., 2003).

Behavioural therapy techniques, such as applied behaviour analysis (see Chapter 5, p. 117), have shown great success with autistic children. Autistic children who start intensive applied behavioural treatment at an early age show significant increases in IQ and adaptive functioning, and decreases in social problems

> It is not enough to ask which type of therapy is most effective. We must ask which type is most effective for a particular problem and a particular patient.

(Eikeseth, Smith, Jahr, & Eldevik, 2007). Combining behavioural and cognitive therapies has provided strategies for treating anxiety disorders, social skills deficits, and problems in self-control. These therapies—which are often integrated as cognitive-behavioural therapy (CBT)—have also provided empirically supported methods for helping couples and families in distress (Baucom et al., 1998), and for modifying behaviours related to health problems such as headaches, smoking, chronic pain, and bulimia nervosa (Agras et al., 2000). Cognitive-behavioural therapists have also innovated treatments for sexual dysfunctions for which there had been no effective treatments.

Cognitive-behavioural therapy has been used to help anorexic and bulimic individuals challenge their perfectionism and their attitudes toward their bodies. It has also been used to systematically reinforce appropriate eating behaviour. Studies that compare the effectiveness of CBT and antidepressants find them to be comparably effective, with CBT sometimes showing a slight advantage (e.g., De Maat et al., 2006). Drugs, after all, do not directly "attack" people's perfectionist attitudes and their distorted body images. They ease the presence of negative feelings and may help individuals enlist their own psychological resources, but pills do not offer advice or even a sympathetic ear.

The combination of cognitive therapy or CBT and drug therapy has helped many people with schizophrenia modify their delusional beliefs and behave in more socially acceptable ways (Turkington et al., 2004; Warman et al., 2005). But psychological therapy alone is apparently inadequate to treat the quirks of thought exhibited in people with severe psychotic disorders.

Thus, it is not enough to ask which type of therapy is most effective. We must ask which type is most effective for a particular problem and a particular patient. What are its advantages? Its limitations? Clients may successfully use systematic desensitization or virtual therapy to overcome stage fright, but if they also want to know *why* they have stage fright, behaviour therapy alone will not provide the answer. But, then again, insight-oriented forms of therapy might also not be able to provide the answer.

All in all, despite Hans Eysenck's skepticism noted at the beginning of the section, research suggests that psychotherapy appears to be effective more often than not. But, we might wonder, does psychotherapy help because of **specific factors** and treatment methods or because a client is receiving the support of an educated and trained helping professional?

So-called **nonspecific factors** in therapy, such as the formation of the client–therapist "alliance," are connected with better therapeutic results (Scaturo, 2005). However, specific techniques—such as specific cognitive and behavioural methods—appear to be much more effective than the therapist–client relationship in bringing about helpful changes (Stevens et al., 2000).

Psychotherapy and Race/Ethnicity

Multiculturalism raises other issues concerning the effectiveness of psychotherapy. Most of the "prescriptions" for psychotherapy discussed in this chapter were originated by white men. Let us note that people from different racial or ethnic backgrounds often have unique concerns, such as the following:

- a belief there is a stigma associated with therapy
- unawareness that therapy can help with certain problems
- lack of information about the availability of professional services, or inability to pay for them
- distrust of professionals, particularly white professionals and (for women) male professionals
- language barriers
- reluctance to open up about personal matters to strangers—especially strangers who are not members of one's own ethnic group
- cultural inclinations toward other approaches to problem solving, such as religious approaches and psychic healers
- negative experiences with professionals and authority figures

Clinicians need to be sensitive to the cultural heritage, language, and values of the people they see in therapy (Canadian Psychological Association, 2001). Canadian psychologists seem to be successful at welcoming visible-minority Canadians into therapy, as research shows that 14 percent of clients are from visible minorities, which is just below the 16.2 percent of Canadians who are members of visible minorities (Ronson et al., 2010; Statistics Canada, 2006). Let us now consider some of the issues involved in conducting psychotherapy with specific minority groups, notably, Asian Canadians, Aboriginal Canadians, and Black Canadians.

Asian Canadians

Canadians of Asian descent (9.5 percent of Canadians; Statistics Canada 2006) tend to stigmatize people with psychological disorders. As a result, they may deny problems and refuse to seek help for them (Chen & Davenport, 2005). Asian Canadians, especially recent immigrants, also may not understand or believe in Western approaches to psychotherapy. For example,

> Clinicians need to be sensitive to the cultural heritage, language, and values of the people they see in therapy.

Western psychotherapy typically encourages people to express their feelings openly. This mode of behaviour may conflict with the Asian tradition of restraint in public. Many Asians prefer to receive concrete advice rather than Western-style encouragement to develop their own solutions (Chen & Davenport, 2005).

nonspecific factors those factors in psychotherapy that are common to many approaches, such as the "therapeutic alliance" with the client

Because of a cultural tendency to deny painful thoughts, many Asians experience and express psychological problems as physical symptoms (Chen & Davenport, 2005). Rather than thinking of themselves as being anxious, they may focus on physical features of anxiety such as a pounding heart and heavy sweating. Rather than thinking of themselves as depressed, they may focus on fatigue and low energy levels.

Aboriginal Canadians

The 2006 census registered 3.75 percent of Canadians as Aboriginal (Statistics Canada, 2006). Many psychological disorders experienced by our Native population involve the disruption of their traditional culture caused by European colonization (Walle, 2004). Aboriginal Canadians have also been denied full access to key institutions in Western culture. Loss of cultural identity and social disorganization have set the stage for problems such as alcoholism, substance abuse, and depression (Walle, 2004). If psychologists are to help Aboriginal Canadians cope with psychological disorders, they need to do so in a way that is sensitive to their culture, customs,

Alvis Uptis/Brand X Pictures/Jupiterimages

and values. Efforts to prevent such disorders should focus on strengthening Aboriginal cultural identity, pride, and cohesion.

Black Canadians

Approximately 2.5 percent of Canadians identify themselves as Black (Statistics Canada, 2006). In addition to addressing the psychological problems of Black clients, therapists often need to help them cope with the effects of prejudice and discrimination. Some Blacks develop low self-esteem because they internalize negative stereotypes (Boyd-Franklin, 2001).

Blacks are sometimes reluctant to seek psychological help because of cultural assumptions that people should manage their own problems and because of mistrust of the therapy process. They tend to assume that people are supposed to solve their own problems. Signs of emotional weakness such as tension, anxiety, and depression are stigmatized (Ivey & Brooks-Harris, 2005).

Some Blacks are also suspicious of their therapists—especially when the therapist is white. They may withhold personal information because of society's history of racial discrimination.

Individualism versus Collectivism

Therapists need to be aware of potential conflicts between the traditional values of collectivism in the family and the typical Western belief in independence and self-reliance (see Chapter 11) (Anger-Díaz et al., 2004). The following measures may help bridge the gaps between psychotherapists and Aboriginal Canadians, immigrants, and Canadian visible minorities who value collectivism over individualism:

- Interacting with clients in the language requested by them or, if this is not possible, referring them to professionals who can do so.

- Using methods that are consistent with the client's values and levels of acculturation, as suggested by fluency in English and level of education.

- Developing therapy methods that incorporate clients' cultural values (Cervantes & Parham, 2005). For example, a study by McCormick (1996) found that Aboriginals in British Columbia found counselling effective only if it was based in a Native cultural tradition, if it included traditional values of respect and noninterference, and if it included the input of tribal elders.

LO8 Biological Therapies

The kinds of therapy we have discussed are psychological in nature—forms of *psychotherapy*. Psychotherapies apply *psychological* principles to treatment, principles based on psychological knowledge of matters such as learning and motivation. People with psychological disorders are also often treated with biological therapies. Biological therapies apply what is known of people's *biological* structures and processes to the amelioration of psychological disorders. For example, they may work by altering events in the nervous system, as by changing the action of neurotransmitters. In this section, we discuss three biological, or medical, approaches to treating people with psychological disorders: drug therapy, electroconvulsive therapy, and psychosurgery. *What kinds of drug therapy are available for psychological disorders?*

Drug Therapy

In the 1950s Fats Domino popularized the song "My Blue Heaven." Fats was singing about the sky and happiness. Today "blue heavens" is one of the street names for the 10-milligram dose of the antianxiety drug Valium. Clinicians prescribe Valium and other drugs for people with various psychological disorders. Table 13.2 gives an overview of the most frequently prescribed psychiatric drugs.

Antianxiety Drugs

Most antianxiety drugs, such as Valium, belong to the chemical class known as *benzodiazepines*. Antianxiety drugs are usually prescribed for outpatients who complain of generalized anxiety or panic attacks, although many people also use them as sleeping pills. Valium and other antianxiety drugs depress the activity of the central nervous system (CNS). The CNS, in turn, decreases sympathetic activity, reducing the heart rate, respiration rate, and nervousness and tension.

TABLE 13.2

Commonly Prescribed Psychiatric Drugs

Class	Examples (Trade Names)	Effects
Minor tranquilizers (antianxiety drugs)	Ativan, Halcion, Librium, Restoril, Valium, Xanax	Reduce anxiety, tension, fear
Antidepressants	Anafranil, Elavil, Nardil, Norpramin, Parnate, Paxil, Prozac, Tofranil, Zoloft	Counteract depression
Antipsychotics (major tranquilizers)	Clozaril, Haldol, Mellaril, Navane, Risperdal, Thorazine	Reduce agitation, delusions, hallucinations, thought disorders

Source: From COON/MILTERER/BROWN/MALIK/MCKENZIE. *Psychology: A Journey*, 3E. © 2010 Nelson Education Ltd. Reproduced by permission. www.cengage.com/permissions.

Many people come to tolerate antianxiety drugs very quickly. When tolerance occurs, dosages must be increased for the drug to remain effective.

Sedation (feelings of being tired or drowsy) is the most common side effect of antianxiety drugs. Problems associated with withdrawal from these drugs include **rebound anxiety**. That is, some people who have been using these drugs regularly report that their anxiety becomes worse than before once they discontinue them. Antianxiety drugs can induce physical dependence, as evidenced by withdrawal symptoms such as tremors, sweating, insomnia, and rapid heartbeat.

Antipsychotic Drugs

People with schizophrenia are often given antipsychotic drugs (also called *major tranquilizers*). In most cases these drugs reduce agitation, delusions, and hallucinations. Many antipsychotic drugs, including phenothiazines (e.g., Thorazine) and clozapine (Clozaril) are thought to act by blocking dopamine receptors in the brain. Research along these lines supports the theory that schizophrenia is connected with overactivity of the neurotransmitter dopamine.

Antidepressants

People with major depression often take so-called **antidepressant** drugs. These drugs are also helpful for some people with eating disorders, panic disorder, obsessive–compulsive disorder, and social phobia. Problems in the regulation of noradrenaline and serotonin may be involved in eating and panic disorders as well as in depression. Antidepressants are believed to work by increasing levels of these neurotransmitters, which can affect both depression and the appetite. As noted in our discussion on the effectiveness of psychotherapy, however, cognitive therapy addresses irrational attitudes concerning weight and body shape, fosters normal eating habits, and helps people resist the urges to binge and purge, often making therapy more effective than drugs for people with bulimia. But when cognitive therapy does not help people with bulimia nervosa, drug therapy may do so.

There are various antidepressants. Each increases the concentration of noradrenaline or serotonin in the brain. **Selective serotonin-reuptake inhibitors (SSRIs)** such as Prozac and Zoloft block the reuptake of serotonin by presynaptic neurons. As a result, serotonin remains in the synaptic cleft longer, influencing receiving neurons.

Antidepressant drugs must usually build up to a therapeutic level over several weeks. Because overdoses can be lethal, some people stay in a hospital during the build-up to prevent suicide attempts. There are also side effects, some of which are temporary, such as nausea, agitation, and weight gain.

Lithium

The ancient Greeks and Romans were among the first to use the metal lithium as a psychoactive drug. They prescribed mineral water—which contains lithium—for people with bipolar disorder. They had no inkling as to why this treatment sometimes helped. A salt of the metal lithium (lithium carbonate), in tablet form, flattens out cycles of manic behaviour and depression in most people. It is not known exactly how lithium works, although it affects the functioning of neurotransmitters.

People with bipolar disorder may have to use lithium indefinitely, as a person with diabetes must use insulin to control the illness. Lithium also has been shown to have side effects such as hand tremors, memory impairment, and excessive thirst and urination. Memory impairment is reported as the main reason why people discontinue lithium.

Does Drug Therapy Work?

There are thus a number of drugs available to treat psychological disorders. There is little question that drug therapy has helped many people with severe psychological disorders. For example, antipsychotic drugs largely account for the reduced need for the use of

rebound anxiety anxiety that can occur when one discontinues use of a tranquilizer

antidepressant acting to relieve depression

selective serotonin-reuptake inhibitors (SSRIs) antidepressant drugs that work by blocking the reuptake of serotonin by presynaptic neurons

PhotoLink/Getty Images

restraint and supervision (e.g., padded cells, straitjackets, hospitalization, and so on) with people diagnosed with schizophrenia. Antipsychotic drugs have allowed hundreds of thousands of former mental hospital residents to lead largely normal lives in the community, hold jobs, and maintain family lives. Most of the problems related to these drugs concern their side effects.

But many comparisons of psychotherapy (in the form of cognitive therapy) and drug therapy for depression suggest that cognitive therapy is as effective as, or more effective than, antidepressants (DeRubeis et al., 2005; De Maat et al., 2006). Cognitive therapy appears to provide coping skills that reduce the risk of recurrence of depression once treatment ends (Hollon et al., 2005).

Many psychologists and psychiatrists are comfortable with the short-term use of antianxiety drugs in helping clients manage periods of unusual anxiety or tension. Many people, however, use antianxiety drugs routinely to dull the arousal stemming from anxiety-producing lifestyles or interpersonal problems. Rather than make the often painful decisions required to confront their problems and change their lives, they prefer to take a pill.

One study found that both tranquilizers and CBT (stress management training plus imagined exposure to the fearful stimuli) helped phobic people get through a dental session. However, 70 percent of those who received CBT continued to go for dental treatment, as compared with only 20 percent of those who took the tranquilizer (Thom et al., 2000). CBT apparently taught people in the study coping skills, whereas the tranquilizers afforded only temporary relief.

In sum, drug therapy is effective for some disorders that do not respond to psychotherapy alone. Yet common sense and research evidence suggest that psychotherapy is preferable for problems such as anxiety and mild depression. No chemical can show a person how to change an idea or solve an interpersonal problem.

Light Therapy

It has been hypothesized that part of the cause of seasonal affective disorder (SAD; depression felt during winter months, see Chapter 12, p. 255) may be linked to the amount of melatonin (a hormone linked to sleep) one produces during the prolonged winter

jochem wijnands/GetStock.com

night. In support of this hypothesis is the finding that light therapy—daily exposure to large artificial bright lights during the winter months—has been effective in treating the depressive symptoms of many who suffer from SAD (Howland, 2009). A common treatment schedule for people who suffer from SAD during the winter months is to sit in front of a large natural light source while they eat breakfast and start their day. For some patients, light therapy works faster than antidepressant drug medication, and for others it works well in combination with drug therapies (Howland, 2009).

Electroconvulsive Therapy

What is electroconvulsive therapy? Electroconvulsive therapy (ECT) is a biological form of therapy for psychological disorders that was introduced by the Italian psychiatrist Ugo Cerletti in 1939. Cerletti had noted that some slaughterhouses used electric shock to render animals unconscious. The shocks also produced convulsions. Along with other European researchers of the period, Cerletti erroneously believed that convulsions were incompatible with schizophrenia and other major psychological disorders.

ECT was originally used for a variety of psychological disorders. Because of the advent of antipsychotic drugs, however, it is now used mainly for people with major depression who do not respond to antidepressants and for severe bipolar disorder.

People typically obtain one ECT treatment three times a week for up to ten sessions. Electrodes are attached to the temples and an electrical current strong enough to produce a convulsion is induced. The shock causes unconsciousness, so the patient does not recall it. Nevertheless, patients are given a sedative so that they are asleep during the treatment and muscle relaxants so the convulsions are mild.

ECT is controversial for many reasons, such as the fact that many professionals are distressed by

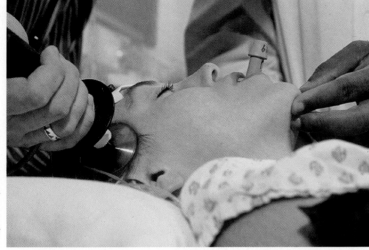

Electroconvulsive Therapy

In ECT, electrodes are placed on each side of the patient's head and a current is passed between them, inducing a seizure. ECT is used mainly in cases of major depression when antidepressant drugs and psychotherapy are not sufficient.

the thought of passing an electric shock through a patient's head and producing convulsions. There are also side effects, including memory problems. Recent research shows that passing the current only through the right hemisphere of the brain leads to less memory loss, with only a slight decrease in overall ECT effectiveness (Sackeim et al., 2000).

Psychosurgery

Psychosurgery is more controversial than ECT. *What is psychosurgery? How is it used to treat psychological disorders?* The best-known modern technique, prefrontal lobotomy, has been used with people with severe disorders. In this method, a pick-like instrument severs the nerve pathways that link the prefrontal lobes of the brain to the thalamus. It is intended to sever thought from emotion and enable severely disturbed patients to regain control.

The method was pioneered by the Portuguese neurologist Antonio Egas Moniz and was brought to North America in the 1930s. The theoretical rationale for the operation was vague and misguided and Moniz's reports of success were exaggerated. Nevertheless, by 1950 prefrontal lobotomies had been performed on thousands of people in an effort to reduce violence and agitation. Anecdotal evidence of the method's unreliable outcomes is found in an ironic footnote to history: One of Dr. Moniz's patients returned to shoot him.

Prefrontal lobotomy also has side effects, including hyperactivity and distractibility, impaired learning ability, overeating, apathy and withdrawal, epileptic-type seizures, reduced creativity, and, now and then, death. Because of these side effects, and because of the advent of antipsychotic drugs, this method has been discontinued in Canada.

> **psychosurgery**
> surgery intended to promote psychological changes or to relieve disordered behaviour
>
> **prefrontal lobotomy**
> the severing or destruction of a section of the frontal lobe of the brain

{ Seeking Help }

Should I seek help? You have probably gone to a doctor when you experienced a certain level of physical discomfort. If you feel psychologically unwell (e.g., have anxiety or depression) at a comparable level of discomfort, you might consider seeking help. You should also monitor your behaviour: If your grades are slipping, you miss days at work or classes, or your friendships are suffering, these can be indicators that you may require assistance. Listen to your friends and family; if people start suggesting that you should get help, they might be right. Finally, if you have persistent thoughts about hurting yourself or others, seek help immediately (Coon et al., 2010).

Where do I go for help? If you have a family doctor that you know and trust, this is often a good first step. Another good resource is the counselling centre at your college or university. Such centres are often equipped to provide same-day crisis counselling and longer-term therapy as well. These two options are usually free of charge (that is, they are included in your provincial health-care plan and school fees). Community mental health centres are great locations to find group therapy sessions and education regarding the resources available in your community (go to www.cmha.ca). If you can afford the average fee of $125 an hour (sometimes on a sliding scale), the Yellow Pages can also be a useful resource for finding counsellors near you. A quick visit to the Canadian Psychological Association (www.cpa.ca) or Canadian Counselling Association (www.ccacc.ca) will assist in ensuring your chosen therapist is qualified. Finally, if you need help but want to remain anonymous, the Kids Help Phone (1-800-668-6868) is for those aged 20 and under (and if you are older than 20, they will be able to help direct your call to your city or provincial crisis hotline).

Learning Outcomes

LO1 Define social psychology

LO2 Define attitude and discuss factors that shape it

LO3 Define social perception and describe the factors that contribute to it

LO4 Explain why people obey authority figures and conform to social norms

LO5 Describe how and why people behave differently as group members than as individuals

Social Psychology

The Canadian Press/Michael Hudson

> ## "People can be goaded by social influences into doing things that are not necessarily consistent with their personalities."

James picked up a large steel trash can and hurled it through the storefront window. Glass exploded in all directions with the violence of the assault, and a loud emergency siren started blaring from the store's intercom. James cheered from behind the bandana that covered his nose and mouth, and jumped through the now-open window, heading into the back of the store. His way was lit by the dim light of the exit signs and the flickering glow of a burning police car in the street. James grabbed four boxes of basketball shoes before turning and running back toward the storefront. Others were streaming in through the open window now, also grabbing whatever they could get their hands on. James jumped back into the street, and heard a sharp clank of metal as something hit the pavement nearby. His eyes started to sting as the smoke from the tear-gas canister billowed out and drifted his way. James looked down the street and saw a phalanx of black-clad riot police advancing toward him and the thousands of other Montreal citizens.

On the evening of April 21, 2008, thousands of rioting individuals vandalized and looted ten stores, threw bottles and bricks at police officers, and damaged 16 police cars, with five of those being set ablaze. The damage to the police cars alone was estimated at $500 000 (CBC News, 2008). What was the event that triggered this behaviour? This was not a food-shortage riot or a civil rights demonstration gone wrong. This riot was the result of the jubilant celebrations of hockey fans. The Montreal Canadiens had just won game seven of the first round of the Stanley Cup playoffs, and they were now advancing to the next round.

DID YOU KNOW?

- People sometimes act in accord with their consciences, but often we are left wondering why we acted the way we did. It is more common that our consciences change to match our behaviour.

- We appreciate things more when we have to work for them.

- Beauty is in the eye of the beholder, but there are also some distinct facial characteristics that indicate beauty.

- Although you may have heard that "opposites attract," it is much more likely for "birds of a feather to flock together."

- We tend to hold others responsible for their misdeeds but to see ourselves as victims of circumstances when we misbehave.

- The pressure to obey is very strong. In the right situation most people will torture, and perhaps even kill, an innocent person if they are ordered to do so.

- Seeing is not always believing—especially when the group sees things differently.

situationist perspective
the view that social influence can goad people into doing things that are inconsistent with their usual behaviour

social psychology
the field of psychology that studies the nature and causes of people's thoughts and behaviour in social situations

attitude
an enduring mental representation of a person, place, or thing that evokes an emotional response and related behaviour

Is James a violent and aggressive individual? If we focus only on James himself as the cause of his behaviour that night, we are left with no other possible conclusion. However, could it also be that was he caught up in something that strongly influenced his behaviour? Social psychologist Philip Zimbardo (2004) argues that we must look to the situationist perspective to understand all behaviour, from donating to a charity, to riots, to suicide terrorism. The **situationist perspective** studies the ways in which people can be goaded by social influences into doing things that are not necessarily consistent with their personalities. In particular, Zimbardo (2004) has investigated the relative ease with which "ordinary" men and women can be incited to behave in evil ways. So what really was the root cause of this 2008 Montreal riot? There are probably several situational factors that are largely to blame. This chapter will explore what social psychologists have discovered about how the situation you find yourself in might compel your behaviour more than you realize, for good or for evil.

LO1 What Is Social Psychology?

The situationist perspective is part of the field of **social psychology**. *What is social psychology?* Social psychology studies the nature and causes of behaviour and mental processes in social situations. The social psychological topics we discuss in this chapter include attitudes, social perception, social influence, and group behaviour. As we explore each of these, we will ask what they might offer to those of us who have difficulty imagining why people would be celebrating a victory of a favourite team one moment, and then throw a brick through a storefront window the next.

LO2 Attitudes

How do you feel about abortion, stem cell research, and same-sex marriage? These are hot-button topics because people have strong attitudes toward them. They each give rise to cognitive evaluations (such as approval or disapproval), feelings (such as liking, disliking, or something stronger), and behavioural tendencies (such as approach or avoidance). Although we asked you how you "feel," attitudes are not just feelings or emotions. Many psychologists view thinking—or judgment—as more basic. Feelings and behaviour follow. *What are attitudes?* **Attitudes** are behavioural and cognitive tendencies that are

{ Suicide Bombers: Evil? Ordinary? }

On June 2, 2006, counterterrorist action in the Greater Toronto Area led to the arrest of 18 alleged Islamic terrorists. According to testimony from the trials, the accused, who were linked to international terrorist groups, were planning on collecting assault weapons (AK-47s and M-16s), storming Parliament in Ottawa in order to "cut off some heads," and detonating truck bombs at the Toronto Stock Exchange, the Toronto CSIS building, and a military base (CBC news, 2010). Why did these 18 men plan to commit these horrific events that would certainly have led to the death of many? Was it a matter of personality and personal choice? Was it a web of situational factors? Were they evil? Social psychologists who have studied the nature of evil find that many, perhaps most, perpetrators of evil are "ordinary people" (Baumeister, 1996; Berkowitz, 2004b). How can this be true? As you'll read later in this chapter, when we seek to "profile" someone, we might be making a fundamental attribution error—that is, we attribute too much of other people's behaviour to internal factors such as attitude (Gilovich & Eibach, 2001; Reeder, 2001). Indeed, in 2003, the Consortium of Social Science Associations (COSSA) testified to the U.S. Congress that they had to conclude there was no common personality profile of a terrorist.

Zakaria Amara was one of the ringleaders of the plot to set off three massive bombs in Toronto and was sentenced to life in prison on January 18, 2010.

Toronto Star/GetStock.com

expressed by evaluating particular people, places, or things with favour or disfavour.

Attitudes are largely learned, and they affect behaviour. They can foster love or hate. They can give rise to helping behaviour or to mass destruction. They can lead to social conflict or to the resolution of conflicts. Attitudes can change, but not easily. Most people do not change their religion or political affiliation without serious reflection or coercion.

The A–B Problem

Is our behaviour consistent with our attitudes—that is, with our beliefs and feelings? *Do people do as they think? (For example, do people really vote their consciences?)* When we are free to do as we wish, the answer is often yes. But, as indicated by the term A–B problem, there are exceptions. For example, research reveals that attitudes toward health-related behaviours such as excessive drinking, smoking, and drunken driving do not necessarily predict these behaviours (Stacy et al., 1994).

Several factors affect the likelihood that we can predict behaviour from attitudes:

1 *Specificity.* We can better predict specific behaviour from specific attitudes than from global attitudes. For example, we can better predict religious group attendance by knowing people's attitudes toward religious group attendance than by knowing whether they are religious people.

2 *Strength of attitudes.* Strong attitudes are more likely to determine behaviour than weak attitudes (Huskinson & Haddock, 2004; Petty et al., 1997). A person who believes that Canada's destiny depends on the Green Party taking control of the House of Commons is more likely to vote in the next election than a person who likes what the Green Party stands for but does not believe that elections make much difference.

3 *Vested interest.* People are more likely to act on their attitudes when they have a vested interest in the outcome. People are more likely to vote for (or against) unionization of their workplace when they believe that their job security depends on it (Lehman & Crano, 2002).

4 *Accessibility.* People are more likely to behave in accord with their attitudes when they are accessible—that is, when they are brought to mind (Kallgren et al., 2000; Petty et al., 1997). This is why politicians attempt to "get out the vote" by means of media blitzes just prior to an election. It does little good to have supporters who forget them on Election Day. Attitudes with a strong emotional impact are more accessible, which is one reason that politicians strive to get their supporters "worked up" over issues.

Attitude Formation

Where do attitudes come from? As with our behaviours and emotions, our attitudes are partially influenced by our genes. Identical twins raised in separate families share a correlation of 0.34 to 0.53 on a variety of social attitudes (Bouchard et al., 1990). However, these genetic influences are quite general; the specifics of your attitudes are often learned. Thus, you might have been born with a sweet-tooth, but your preference for Pepsi or Coca-Cola was influenced by advertising and what your parents brought home. The specific details of your attitudes are learned and derived from cognitive processes.

> **A–B problem**
> the issue of how well we can predict behaviour on the basis of attitudes

Conditioning may play a role in attitude formation (Walther et al., 2005). Laboratory experiments have shown that attitudes toward national groups can be influenced by associating them with positive words (such as *gift* or *happy*) or negative words (such as *ugly* or *failure*) (De Houwer et al., 2001). Parents often reward children for saying and doing things that agree with their own attitudes. As we witnessed in the 2010 Winter Olympics in Vancouver, patriotism is encouraged by showing children approval when they cheer for a Canadian athlete, sing the national anthem, or wave the flag.

Attitudes formed through direct experience may be stronger and easier to recall, but we also acquire attitudes by observing, listening to, or reading the works of other people. The approval or disapproval of peers leads adolescents to prefer short or long hair, baggy jeans, or preppy sweaters. How do the things you read in newspapers or hear on the radio influence your attitudes?

Cognitive Appraisal

Nevertheless, attitude formation is not fully mechanical. People are also motivated to understand the

Politicians participate in media blitzes just prior to an election so that they will be "accessible" to their voters on Election Day.

environment so that they can make predictions and exercise some control over it (Bizer et al., 2004; Wood, 2000). People also sometimes form or change attitudes on the basis of new information (Dovidio et al., 2004; Petty et al., 1999; Walther et al., 2005). For example, we may believe that a car is more reliable than we had previously thought if a survey by *Consumer Reports* finds that it has an excellent repair record. Even so, initial attitudes act as cognitive anchors (Wegener et al., 2001; Wood, 2000). We often judge new ideas in terms of how much they deviate from our existing attitudes. Accepting larger deviations requires more information processing—in other words, more intellectual work (Petty et al., 1999; Tormala & Petty, 2004). For this reason, perhaps, great deviations—such as changes from liberal to conservative attitudes, or vice versa—are apt to be resisted.

Changing Attitudes through Persuasion

Will Rogers's comment below sounds on the mark, but he was probably wrong. It does little good to have a wonderful product if it remains a secret. *Can you really change people's attitudes and behaviour?*

The **elaboration likelihood model** describes the ways in which people respond to persuasive messages (Crano, 2000; Salovey & Wegener, 2003). Consider two routes to persuading others to change attitudes. The first, or central, route inspires thoughtful consideration of arguments and evidence. The second, or peripheral, route associates objects with positive or negative cues. When politicians avow, "This bill is supported by liberals (or conservatives)," they are seeking predictable, knee-jerk reactions (peripheral route) rather than careful consideration of a bill's merits. Other cues are rewards (such as a smile or a hug), punishments (such as parental disapproval), and such factors as the trustworthiness and attractiveness of the communicator.

Advertisements, which are a form of persuasive communication, also rely on central and peripheral routes. Some ads focus on the quality of the product (central route) such as ads for Special K cereal that highlight its nutritional benefits and provide

> "Let advertisers spend the same amount of money improving their product that they do on advertising and they wouldn't have to advertise it."
> —Will Rogers

information about the quality of the product. So, too, did the "Pepsi Challenge" taste-test ads, which claimed that Pepsi tastes better than Coca-Cola. Others advertisements attempt to associate the product with appealing emotions and images (peripheral route). Peripheral route ads are ones that show famous athletes or celebrities enjoying a product or any beer commercial that shows a crazy party. These peripheral route commercials actually offer no information about the product itself.

In this section we look at one central factor in persuasion—the nature of the message—and three peripheral factors: the messenger, the context of the message, and the audience.

The Persuasive Message

How do we respond when TV commercials are repeated until we have memorized the dimples on the actors' faces? Research suggests that familiarity breeds content, not contempt (Zajonc, 2001; Zizak & Reber, 2004). It appears that repeated exposure to people and things as diverse as the following enhances their appeal (called the mere-exposure effect):

- political candidates (who are seen in repeated TV commercials)
- photos of people of minority groups
- photos of college or university students
- abstract art
- classical music

When trying to persuade someone, is it helpful or self-defeating to alert them to the arguments presented by the opposition? In two-sided arguments, the communicator recounts the arguments of the opposition in an effort to refute them. In research concerning a mock trial, college undergraduates were presented with two-sided arguments—those of the prosecution and those of the defendant (McKenzie et al., 2002). When one argument was weak, the college "jurors" expressed more confidence in their decision than when they did not hear the other side at all. Theologians and politicians sometimes forewarn their followers about the arguments of the opposition and then refute each one. Forewarning creates a kind of psychological immunity to them (Jacks & Devine, 2000).

It would be nice to think that people are too sophisticated to be persuaded by emotional factors in attitude formation, but they usually aren't (DeSteno et al., 2004). Consider the **fear appeal**: Women who are warned of the dire risk they run if they fail to be screened for breast cancer are more likely to obtain mammograms than women who are informed of the *benefits* of mammography (Ruiter et al., 2001). Interestingly, although suntanning has been shown to increase the likelihood of skin cancer, warnings against suntanning were shown to be more effective when students were warned of risks to their *appearance* (e.g., premature aging, wrinkling, and scarring of the skin) than when the warning dealt with the risk

to their health. That is, students informed of tanning's cosmetic effects were more likely to say they would protect themselves from the sun than were students informed about the risk of cancer. Fear appeals are most effective when the audience believes that the risks are serious— as in causing wrinkles!—and that the audience members can change their behaviour to avert the risks—as in preventing cancer or wrinkling. Scaring people without explaining how to avoid the risk just leads people to ignore the message; it ends up being just too scary to think about.

Audiences also tend to believe arguments that appear to run counter to the vested interests of the communicator (Lehman & Crano, 2002). If the president of Ford or General Motors said that Toyotas and Hondas were superior, you can bet that we would prick up our ears.

Try It!

One of the strongest social conventions is reciprocity. When someone does something nice for you, you probably feel a strong need to return the favour. This social convention can also be used to persuade people to change their attitudes and behaviour. In a technique called "door-in-the-face," first a large request is made—one that is anticipated to be denied (e.g., you are asked to donate $500 to send a kid to camp this summer). Then, a second more reasonable request is made, and it is more likely to be agreed to (e.g., you are asked to buy a $5 chocolate bar with the proceeds going to the camp). This technique often works because the person feels bad saying "no" to the first request. The asker then offers a concession; he or she says, "No problem, how about this less costly option?" The perception is that the concession needs to be reciprocated, and thus people feel strong pressure to agree to the second request.

So, try it! Next time you want to ask someone for something that they might refuse, first ask for something larger. Then when they refuse, be polite and then ask for your original desire. You may just get what you want!

"Hey dad, can you lend me $4000 to buy a car?"
"No, I can't afford that!"
"Ok, no problem, how about if I just borrow the car for the weekend?"
"Sure, here are the keys."

The Persuasive Communicator

Would you go to a doctor who admitted he or she was behind the times? Would you buy a used car from a person who had been convicted of larceny? Research shows that persuasive communicators are characterized by expertise, trustworthiness, attractiveness, or similarity to their audiences (Petty et al., 1997). Because of the adoration of their fans, sports superstars such as Wayne Gretzky are the most valuable endorsers.

People find it painful when they are confronted with information that counters their own views (Foerster et al., 2000). Therefore, they often show **selective avoidance** and **selective exposure** (Lavine et al., 2005). That is, they tend to watch news channels that endorse their own views and switch channels when the news coverage counters their own attitudes. They also seek communicators who share their views.

The Context of the Message

You are too shrewd to let someone persuade you by buttering you up, but perhaps someone you know would be influenced by a sip of wine, a bite of cheese, and a sincere compliment. Aspects of the immediate environment, such as music, increase

Photo Alto/Ale Ventura/Getty Images

the likelihood of persuasion. When we are in a good mood, we apparently are less likely to evaluate the situation carefully (Petty et al., 1997).

It is also counterproductive to call your friends foolish when they differ with you—even though their ideas are bound to be "foolish" if they do not agree with yours. Agreement and praise are more effective ways to encourage others to embrace your views.

The Persuaded Audience

Why can some people say no to salespeople? Why do others enrich the lives of every door-to-door salesperson? It may be that people with high self-esteem and low social anxiety are more likely to resist social pressure (Ellickson et al., 2001).

A classic study by Schwartz and Gottman (1976) describes the cognitive nature of the social anxiety that can make it difficult to refuse requests. They found that people who comply with unreasonable requests are more apt to report thoughts such as:

- "I was worried about what the other person would think of me if I refused."
- "It is better to help others than to be self-centred."
- "The other person might be hurt or insulted if I refused."

People who refuse unreasonable requests reported thoughts like these:

- "It doesn't matter what the other person thinks of me."
- "I am perfectly free to say no."
- "This request is unreasonable."

Changing Attitudes and Behaviour by Means of Cognitive-Dissonance

What is cognitive-dissonance theory? According to **cognitive-dissonance theory**, people are thinking creatures who seek consistency in their behaviours and their attitudes—that is, their views of the world. People must apparently mentally represent the world

accurately to predict and control events. Consistency in beliefs, attitudes, and behaviour helps make the world seem like a predictable place. Therefore, if we find ourselves in the uncomfortable spot where two cherished ideas conflict, we are motivated to reduce the discrepancy.

In the first and still one of the best-known studies on cognitive-dissonance, one group of participants received $1 (worth about $10 today) for telling someone else that a boring task was interesting (Festinger & Carlsmith, 1959). Members of a second group received $20 (worth about $200 today) to describe the chore positively. Both groups were paid to engage in **attitude-discrepant behaviour**—that is, behaviour that ran counter to what they actually thought. After presenting their fake enthusiasm for the boring task, the participants were asked to rate their own liking for it. Ironically, those who were paid *less* rated the task as actually more interesting than their better-paid colleagues reported.

Leonard McLane/Photodisc/Getty Images

Try It!

Ever been hit with a low-ball? If so, someone used cognitive-dissonance against you to get you to pay more than you initially agreed to for something. Next time you want to sell something, you might want to try using this technique to get a little extra money. Here's how it works. Let's say you are selling an old textbook (other than this one, of course!). Someone emails you about your ad in Kijiji and you agree that you'll sell the book to him or her for $30. When the buyer shows up to pick it up, say that you miscalculated and you can only let it go for $40. Often buyers will grudgingly fork over the extra money because of the cognitive-dissonance they would experience if they walked away. They want to keep their behaviour (actually buying the book) consistent with their attitude (stating that they need and want the book). If they walk away they are left with conflicting thoughts like these: "I drove across town, I need the textbook, and I walked away and I still don't have it!" Of course, most people find this sales technique a little shady (and it is). If they already have read this chapter, they'll know what you're trying to do, and you may end up with $0. Buyer and seller beware!

Learning theorists (see Chapter 5) might predict a different outcome—the more we are reinforced for doing something (given more money, for example), the more we should like it (not find the task quite as boring, that is). But that is not what happened here. Cognitive-dissonance theorists rightly predicted that because the ideas (cognitions) of (a) "I was paid very little" and (b) "I told someone that this assignment was interesting" are dissonant, people will tend to engage in **effort justification**. The discomfort of cognitive-dissonance motivates people to explain their behaviour to themselves in such a way that unpleasant undertakings seem worth it. Participants who were paid only $1 may have justified their lie by convincing themselves that they may not have been lying in the first place.

Prejudice and Discrimination

Prejudice is an attitude toward a group that leads people to evaluate members of that group negatively—even though they have never met them. On a cognitive level, prejudice is linked to expectations that members of the target group will behave poorly, say, in the workplace, or engage in criminal behaviour or terrorism. On an emotional level, prejudice is associated with negative feelings such as fear, dislike, or hatred (No, 2004).

In behavioural terms, prejudice is connected with avoidance, aggression, and discrimination—with possible outcomes such as the genocide of millions of people. Discrimination takes many other forms as well, including bullying, preference in hiring, segregated housing, and voting restrictions.

Stereotypes

When you read the story at the beginning of the chapter, what race did you picture James to be as he threw the trash can through the storefront window? What beliefs do you have about French and English Canadians? How are people from Alberta different from those from Newfoundland? The content of your answers to these questions illustrate the concept of **stereotypes**— beliefs about the attributes of individuals who belong to a group. Stereotypes can lead people to view and behave toward members of those groups in a biased fashion.

> By and large, we assume that "good things come in pretty packages."

Some stereotypes are positive rather than negative, such as the cultural stereotypes about physically attractive people. By and large, we assume that "good things come in pretty packages." Attractive children and adults are judged and treated more positively than their unattractive peers (Langlois et al., 2000). We expect attractive people to be poised, sociable, popular, intelligent, mentally healthy, fulfilled, persuasive, and successful in their jobs.

Sources of Prejudice

The sources of prejudice are many and varied:

1 *Dissimilarity.* We are apt to like people who share our attitudes. In forming impressions of others, we are influenced by attitudinal similarity and dissimilarity (Duckitt et al., 2002). People of different religions and races often have different backgrounds, however, giving rise to dissimilar attitudes. Even when people of different races share important values, they may assume that they do not.

2 *Competition for resources.* When two groups are in competition for limited resources it often leads to prejudice and discrimination between members of the groups (Sherif et al., 1988). Examples of this can be witnessed in the land-claim disputes between various Aboriginal peoples in Canada and the Canadian government. A recent example (and at time of printing still largely unresolved) is the Grand River land dispute in Caledonia, Ontario.

effort justification
in cognitive-dissonance theory, the tendency to seek justification (acceptable reasons) for strenuous efforts

stereotypes
beliefs about the attributes of individuals who belong to a group

© MGM/Courtesy Everett Collection/Canadian Press

The Canadian Press/Shaney Komulainen

3 *Social learning.* Children acquire some attitudes from other people, especially their parents. Children tend to imitate their parents, and parents reinforce their children for doing so (Duckitt et al., 2002). In this way prejudices can be transmitted from generation to generation.

4 *Information processing.* Prejudices act as cognitive filters through which we interpret information from our social world. If we associate "foreign" with "bad" then we are more likely to notice, interpret, and recall negative things when we interact with those we see as "foreign" (Crisp & Nicel, 2004).

5 *Social categorization.* We also tend to divide our social world into "us" and "them." People usually view those who belong to their own groups—the "in-group"—more favourably than those who do not—the "out-group" (Förster et al., 2004; Smith & Weber, 2005). Separation from the out-group makes it easier to maintain our stereotypes.

Interpersonal Attraction

Attitudes of liking and loving can lead to important, lasting relationships. They are the flip side of the coin of prejudice—positive attitudes that are associated with interpersonal **attraction** rather than avoidance. *What factors contribute to attraction in our culture?* Among the factors contributing to attraction are physical appearance, similarity, and reciprocity (Smith & Weber, 2005).

Physical Appearance

Physical appearance is a key factor in attraction and in the consideration of romantic partners (Langlois et al., 2000). What determines physical allure? Are our standards subjective—that is, "in the eye of the beholder"? Or is there general agreement on what is appealing?

Many standards for beauty appear to be cross-cultural (Langlois et al., 2000; Little & Perrett, 2002). For example, a study of people in England and Japan found that both British and Japanese men consider women with large eyes, high cheekbones, and narrow jaws to be most attractive (Perrett, May, & Yoshikawa, 1994). *What is more beautiful—a distinct face or an average face?* Researchers who morph multiple faces into one suggest that it is averageness that is strongly related to attractiveness (Rubenstein, Langlois, & Roggman, 2002). This occurs largely because when multiple faces are morphed into one, overall facial asymmetry (e.g., having one eye slightly lower than the other, or a lop-sided nose) is reduced (see Figure 14.1). However, this is only part of the story, as other research challenges this "average is attractive" suggestion. In their research, Perrett and his colleagues (1994) used computer enhance-

ment to exaggerate the differences between a composite face made from 60 women and a composite face made from 15 very attractive women. The final exaggerated image (that was far from average) had higher cheekbones and a narrower

FIGURE 14.1

What Features Contribute to Facial Attractiveness?

Facial features such as large eyes, high cheekbones, and fuller lips contribute to perceptions of attractiveness of women. Features seen as attractive in men include a prominent chin, square jawbones, high cheekbones, and relatively large, dark eyebrows. Male and female faces high in symmetry are also seen as more attractive. These attractive facial features can be seen in the Canadian actors Rachel McAdams and Ryan Reynolds, who consistently receive high ratings of attractiveness.

Frazer Harrison/Getty Images

Mike Coppola/Getty Images

jaw than the overall average, but it received the highest ratings of attractiveness. Similar results were found for the image of a Japanese woman. Works of art suggest that the ancient Greeks and Egyptians favoured similar facial features. These and other findings suggest an objective standard of physical beauty.

Gender Differences in Selection of a Partner

Physical appearance may be a major factor in the selection of a romantic partner, but cross-cultural studies on mate selection find that women tend to place greater emphasis on traits such as professional status, consideration, dependability, kindness, and fondness for children. Men tend to place relatively greater emphasis on physical allure, cooking ability, and even thrift (Buss, 1994).

Susan Sprecher and her colleagues (1994) surveyed more than 13 000 young adults, attempting to represent the ethnic diversity we find in North America. They found that women were more willing than men to marry someone who was not good-looking, but less willing to marry someone who did not hold a steady job (see Figure 14.2).

Why do males tend to place relatively more emphasis than females on physical appearance in mate selection? Why do females tend to place relatively more emphasis on personal factors such as financial status and reliability? Evolutionary psychologists believe that evolutionary forces favour the survival of women who desire status in their mates and men who emphasize physical allure because these preferences provide reproductive advantages. According to the "parental investment model," a woman's appeal is more strongly connected with her age and health, both of which

are markers of reproductive capacity. The value of men as reproducers, however, is more intertwined with factors that contribute to a stable environment for child rearing—such as social standing and reliability (Schmitt, 2003).

The Attraction–Similarity Hypothesis

The *attraction–similarity hypothesis* holds that people tend to develop romantic relationships with people who are similar to themselves in physical attractiveness and other traits (Morry & Gaines, 2005). Researchers have found that people who are involved in committed relationships are most likely to be similar to their partners in their attitudes and cultural attributes (Amodio & Showers, 2005).

Our partners tend to be like us in race and ethnicity, age, level of education, and religion. Consider some findings of the *National Health and Social Life Survey* (Michael et al., 1994):

- The dating partners of nearly 94 percent of single white men are white women.

FIGURE 14.2

Gender Differences in Preferences for Mates

The study by Sprecher and her colleagues find that women are more likely than men to be willing to marry someone who is older, makes more money, is better educated, but not good-looking. Men, on the other hand, are less willing to marry someone who is not good-looking. Men are also more willing to have partners who are younger, earn less, and are less well-educated. How would you interpret these findings?

How willing would you be to marry someone who . . .

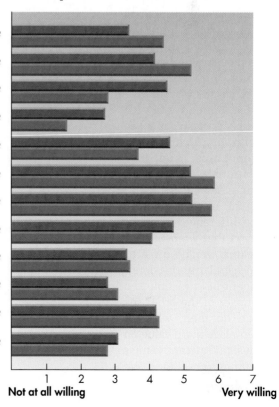

was not "good looking"?
was older than you by 5 or more years?
was younger than you by 5 or more years?
was not likely to hold a steady job?
would earn much less than you?
would earn much more than you?
had more education than you?
had less education than you?
had been married before?
already had children?
was of a different religion?
was of a different race?

Men
Women

1 2 3 4 5 6 7
Not at all willing   Very willing

triangular model of love
Sternberg's view that love involves combinations of three components: intimacy, passion, and commitment

intimacy
close acquaintance and familiarity; a characteristic of a relationship in which partners share their inmost feelings

passion
strong romantic and sexual feelings

commitment
the decision to maintain a relationship

- The dating partners of nearly 82 percent of Black men are Black women.
- Nearly 8 percent of Black men are partnered with white women. Fewer than 5 percent are partnered with Latino women.
- About 83 percent of the women and men in the study chose partners within five years of their own age and of the same or a similar religion.
- Of all the women in the study, not one with a graduate college degree had a partner who had not finished high school.

Similarity in Attitudes

We are more likely to be attracted to people who agree with our views and tastes than to people who disagree with them (Singh et al., 2007).

Why do the great majority of us have partners from our own backgrounds? One reason is *proximity*, or nearness. Although mobility has increased in Western societies in recent decades, we still tend to live among people who are reasonably similar to us in background. Another is that we are drawn to people who are similar to us in their attitudes. People similar in background are more likely to be similar in their attitudes. Similarity in attitudes and tastes is a key contributor to attraction, friendships, and love relationships (Morry & Gaines, 2005).

Let us also note a sex difference. Evidence shows that women place greater weight on attitude similarity as a determinant of attraction to a stranger of the other sex than do men, whereas men place more value on physical attractiveness (Laumann et al., 1994). We also tend to assume that people we find attractive

share our attitudes (Morry, 2005). Although similarity may be important in determining initial attraction, compatibility appears to be a stronger predictor of maintaining an intimate relationship (Amodio & Showers, 2005).

Love

Just what is love? Love is a strong positive emotion. We had a look at love between children and parents in Chapter 8. Here we will focus on that most dramatic, heated, passionate love we label *romantic love*.

There are a number of theories about romantic love. One theory is Robert Sternberg's (1988) **triangular model of love**. This love triangle does not refer to two men wooing the same woman. It refers to Sternberg's view that love involves three components: intimacy, passion, and commitment (see Figure 14.3).

Intimacy refers to a couple's closeness, to their mutual concern and sharing of feelings and resources. **Passion** means romance and sexual feelings. **Commitment** is the decision to maintain a relationship. Passion is most crucial in short-term

FIGURE 14.3

The Triangular Model of Love

According to this model, love has three components: intimacy, passion, and commitment. The ideal of consummate love consists of a balance of all three components.

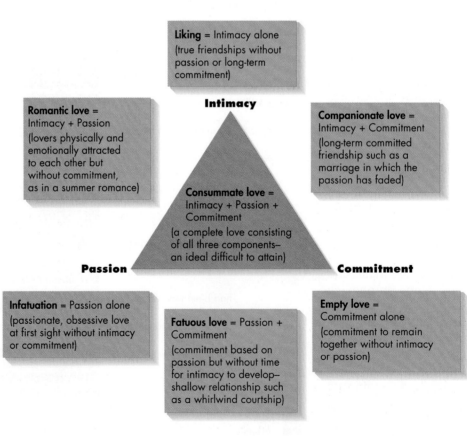

Liking = Intimacy alone (true friendships without passion or long-term commitment)

Intimacy

Romantic love = Intimacy + Passion (lovers physically and emotionally attracted to each other but without commitment, as in a summer romance)

Companionate love = Intimacy + Commitment (long-term committed friendship such as a marriage in which the passion has faded)

Consummate love = Intimacy + Passion + Commitment (a complete love consisting of all three components— an ideal difficult to attain)

Passion

Commitment

Infatuation = Passion alone (passionate, obsessive love at first sight without intimacy or commitment)

Fatuous love = Passion + Commitment (commitment based on passion but without time for intimacy to develop— shallow relationship such as a whirlwind courtship)

Empty love = Commitment alone (commitment to remain together without intimacy or passion)

Source: From *The Psychology of Love* by R.J. Sternberg. Copyright © 1988 Yale University Press. Reprinted by permission of the publisher.

relationships. Intimacy and commitment are more important in enduring relationships. The ideal form of love—**consummate love**—combines all three. Consummate love is made up of romantic love (intimacy and passion) plus commitment.

Romantic love, in Sternberg's scheme, is characterized by passion and intimacy. Passion involves fascination (preoccupation with the loved one); sexual craving; and the desire for exclusiveness (a special relationship with the loved one). Intimacy involves caring—championing the interests of the loved one, even if it entails sacrificing one's own. People are cognitively biased toward evaluating their partners positively (Loving & Agnew, 2001). That is, we idealize those we love.

LO3 Social Perception

An important area of social psychology concerns the ways in which we perceive other people—for example, the importance of the first impressions they make on us. Next we explore some factors that contribute to **social perception**: the primacy and recency effects, attribution theory, and body language.

Primacy and Recency Effects

Why do you wear a suit to a job interview? Why do defence lawyers make sure that their clients dress neatly and get their hair cut before they are seen by the jury? *Do first impressions really matter?* Apparently first impressions do matter—a great deal.

What are the primacy and recency effects? Whether we are talking about the business or social worlds, or even the relationship between a therapist and a client, first impressions are important (Bidell et al., 2002). First impressions are an example of the **primacy effect**.

Participants in a classic experiment on the primacy effect each read the same story about "Jim" (Luchins, 1957). The story consisted of two paragraphs. One paragraph portrayed Jim as friendly and the other paragraph portrayed Jim as unfriendly. All participants in the study read these two paragraphs, but the order they appeared changed for half of them. Seventy-eight percent of those who read the two-paragraph story in the "friendly–unfriendly" order labelled Jim as friendly. When they read the same paragraphs in the "unfriendly–friendly" order, only 18 percent rated Jim as friendly.

How can we encourage people to pay more attention to impressions occurring after the first encounter? In the research just mentioned, this was accomplished by allowing time to elapse between the presentations of the two paragraphs. In this way, fading memories allowed more recent information to take precedence. This is known as the **recency effect**. Luchins (1957) also found a second way to counter first impressions: He simply asked participants to avoid making snap judgments and to weigh all the evidence.

Attribution Theory

What is attribution theory? Why do we assume that other people intend the mischief that they do? An **attribution** is an assumption about why people do things. When you assume that James threw the trash can through the window because he is "aggressive," you are making an attribution. This section focuses on *attribution theory,* or the processes by which people draw conclusions about the factors that influence one another's behaviour. Attribution theory is important because attributions lead us to perceive others either as purposeful actors or as victims of circumstances.

Dispositional and Situational Attributions

Social psychologists describe two types of attributions. **Dispositional attributions** ascribe a person's behaviour to internal factors such as personality traits and free will. **Situational attributions** attribute a person's actions to external factors such as social influence or socialization. If you judge that James threw the trash can through the window because his friends were cheering him on and the presence of hundreds of others he saw looting and vandalizing made it appear more normal at the time, you are making a situational attribution.

The Actor–Observer Effect

We tend to blame the causes of behaviour on whatever the focus of our attention is on when we make the judgment. So when we watch someone do something we blame that person for his or her actions, because our focus is on him or her. But when it comes

consummate love
the ideal form of love within Sternberg's model, which combines passion, intimacy, and commitment

romantic love
an intense, positive emotion that involves sexual attraction, feelings of caring, and the belief that one is in love

social perception
a subfield of social psychology that studies the ways in which we form and modify impressions of others

primacy effect
the tendency to evaluate others in terms of first impressions

recency effect
the tendency to evaluate others in terms of the most recent impression

attribution
a judgment concerning why people behave in a certain way

dispositional attribution
an assumption that a person's behaviour is determined by internal causes such as personal attitudes or goals

situational attribution
an assumption that a person's behaviour is determined by external circumstances such as the social pressure found in a situation

to our own actions, unless we are in front of a mirror, our attention is often on the situation we are in. So we judge ourselves to be victims of circumstances (Baron et al., 2006; Stewart, 2005). The tendency to make attributions based on where our attention is (e.g., dispositional factors for others and situational factors for ourselves) is called the **actor–observer effect**.

Parents and teenagers often argue about the teen's choice of friends or partners. When they do, the parents tend to infer traits from behaviour and to see the teens as stubborn and resistant. The teenagers also infer traits from behaviour. Thus they may see their parents as bossy and controlling. Parents and teens alike attribute the others' behaviour to internal causes. That is, both make dispositional attributions about other people's behaviour.

How do the parents and teenagers perceive themselves? The parents probably see themselves

as being forced into combat by their children's foolishness. If they become insistent, it is in response to the teens' stubbornness. The teenagers probably see themselves as responding to peer pressures. Both parents and children make situational attributions for their own behaviour.

The Fundamental Attribution Error

In cultures that view the self as independent, such as ours, people tend to attribute other people's behaviour primarily to internal factors such as personality, attitudes, and free will (Gilovich & Eibach, 2001; Reeder, 2001). This bias is known as the **fundamental attribution error**. If a teenager gets into trouble with the law, individualistic societies are more likely to blame the teenager than the social environment in which the teenager lives.

One reason for the fundamental attribution error is that we tend to infer traits from behaviour. But in collectivist cultures that stress interdependence, such as Asian cultures, people are more likely to attribute other people's behaviour to that person's social roles and obligations (Basic Behavioral Science Task Force, 1996c). For example, Japanese people might be more likely to attribute a businessperson's extreme competitiveness to the "culture of business" rather than to his or her personality. Another reason we make the fundamental attribution error is the previously mentioned actor–observer effect.

The Self-Serving Bias

There is also a **self-serving bias** in the attribution process. We are likely to ascribe our successes to internal, dispositional factors but our failures to external, situational influences (Smith & Weber, 2005). A study with 27 college wrestlers found that they tended to attribute their wins to stable and internal conditions such as their abilities, but their losses to unstable and external conditions such as an error by a referee (De Michele et al., 1998). Sports fans fall into the same trap. They tend to attribute their team's victories to internal conditions and their losses to external conditions (Wann & Shrader, 2000).

Another interesting attribution bias is a gender difference in attributions for friendly behaviour. Men are more likely than women to interpret a woman's smile or friendliness toward a man as flirting (Abbey, 1987).

Flying Colours Ltd./Getty Images

The Actor–Observer Effect
Who is at fault here? People tend to make dispositional attributions for other people's behaviour, but they tend to see their own behaviour as motivated by situational factors. Thus people are aware of the external forces acting on themselves when they behave, but tend to attribute other people's behaviour to choice and will.

Body Language

Body language is important in social perception. *What is body language?* Body language is nonverbal language; it refers to the meanings we infer from the ways in which people carry themselves and the gestures they make. The way people carry themselves provides cues to how they feel and are likely to behave. When people are emotionally "uptight" they may also be rigid and straight-backed. People who are relaxed are more likely to "hang loose." Factors such as eye contact, posture, and the distance between two people provide cues to their moods and their feelings toward one another. When people face us and lean toward us, we may assume that they like us or are interested in what we are saying.

Touching

Women are more likely than men to touch other people when they are interacting with them (Stier & Hall, 1984). In one "touching" experiment, Kleinke (1977) showed that appeals for help can be more effective when the distressed person makes physical contact with people who are asked for aid. A woman obtained more coins for phone calls when she touched the arm of the person she was asking for money. In another experiment, waitresses obtained higher tips when they touched patrons on the hand or the shoulder while making change (Crusco & Wetzel, 1984).

Gazing and Staring

When other people "look us squarely in the eye," we may assume that they are being assertive or open with us. Avoidance of eye contact may suggest deception or depression. Gazing is interpreted as a sign of liking or friendliness (Kleinke, 1986). In one study, men and women were asked to gaze into each other's eyes for two minutes (Kellerman et al., 1989). After doing so, they reported having passionate feelings toward one another.

A gaze is not the same thing as a persis-tent hard stare. A hard stare is interpreted as a provocation or a sign of anger. Adolescent males sometimes engage in staring contests as an asser-tion of dominance. The male who blinks or looks away first loses the contest. In a classic series of field experiments, Phoebe Ellsworth and her colleagues (1972) subjected drivers stopped at red lights to hard stares by riders of motor scooters. When the light changed, people who were stared at crossed the intersection more rapidly than people who were not. (Figure 14.4 shows the results of a similar study in 1978 by Greenbaum and Rosenfeld.) People who are stared at have higher levels of physi-ological arousal compared to people who are not (Strom & Buck, 1979).

LO4 Social Influence

Other people and groups can exert enormous pres-sure on us to behave according to their norms. **Social influence** is the area of social psychology that studies the ways in which people alter the thoughts, feelings, and behaviour of others. Let us describe a

> **social influence**
> the area of social psychology that studies the ways in which people influ-ence the thoughts, feelings, and behav-iour of others

FIGURE 14.4

Diagram of an Experiment in Hard Staring and Avoidance

A 1978 study by Greenbaum and Rosenfeld found that the confederate of the experimenter stared at some drivers and not at others. Recipients of the stares drove across the intersection more rapidly once the light turned green. Why?

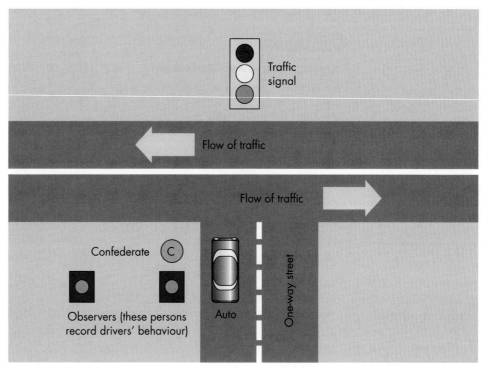

couple of classic experiments that demonstrate how people influence others to engage in destructive obedience or conform to social norms.

Obedience to Authority

Throughout history soldiers have followed orders—even when it comes to slaughtering innocent civilians. The Turkish slaughter of Armenians, the Nazi slaughter of Jews, the mutual slaughter of Hutus and Tutsis in Rwanda—these are all examples of the tragedies that can arise from simply following orders. We may say we are horrified by such crimes, and we cannot imagine why people engage in them. But how many of us would refuse to follow orders issued by authority figures? *Why will so many people commit crimes against humanity if they are ordered to do so? (Why don't they refuse?)*

The Milgram Studies

Yale University psychologist Stanley Milgram also wondered how many people would resist immoral requests made by authority figures. To find out, he undertook a series of classic experiments at the university that have become known as the Milgram studies on obedience.

In an early phase of his work, Milgram (1963) placed ads in local newspapers for people who would be willing to participate in studies on learning and memory. He enlisted 40 people ranging in age from 20 to 50—teachers, engineers, labourers, salespeople, people who had not completed elementary school, and people with graduate degrees.

Let's suppose that you have answered the ad. You show up at the university in exchange for a reasonable fee ($4.50, which in the early 1960s might easily fill your gas tank) and to satisfy your own curiosity. You might be impressed. After all, Yale is a venerable institution that dominates the city. You are no less impressed by the elegant labs, where you meet a distinguished behavioural scientist dressed in a white coat and another person who has responded to

the ad. The scientist explains that the purpose of the experiment is to study the *effects of punishment on learning.* The experiment requires a "teacher" and a "learner." By chance, you are appointed the teacher and the other recruit the learner.

You, the scientist, and the learner enter a laboratory room containing a threatening chair with dangling straps. The scientist straps the learner in. The learner expresses some concern, but this is, after all, for the sake of science. And this is Yale isn't it? What could happen to a person at Yale?

You follow the scientist to an adjacent room, from which you are to do your "teaching." This teaching promises to have an impact. You are to punish the learner's errors by pressing levers marked from 15 to 450 volts on a fearsome-looking console. Labels describe 28 of the 30 levers as running the gamut from "Slight Shock" to "Danger: Severe Shock." The last two levers are simply labelled "XXX." Just in case you have no idea what electric shock feels like, the scientist gives you a sample 45-volt shock. It stings. You pity the person who might receive more.

Your learner is expected to learn pairs of words, which are to be read from a list. After hearing the list once, the learner is to produce the word that pairs with the stimulus word from a list of four alternatives. This is done by pressing a switch that lights one of four panels in your room. If it is the correct panel, you proceed to the next stimulus word. If not, you are to deliver an electric shock. With each error, you are to increase the voltage of the shock (see Figure 14.5).

You probably have some misgivings. Electrodes have been strapped to the learner's wrists, and the scientist has applied electrode paste "to avoid

FIGURE 14.5

The Experimental Setup in the Milgram Studies

When the "learner" makes an error, the experimenter prods the "teacher" to deliver a painful electric shock.

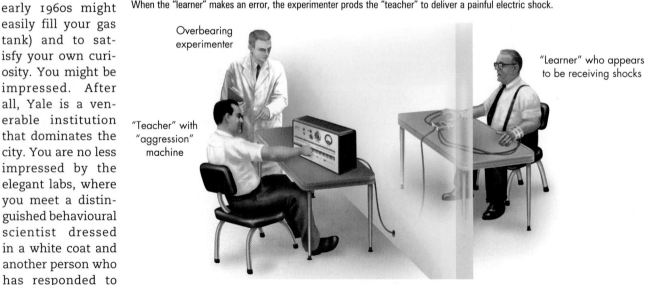

Overbearing experimenter

"Teacher" with "aggression" machine

"Learner" who appears to be receiving shocks

blisters and burns." You have also been told that the shocks will cause "no permanent tissue damage," although they might be painful. Still, the learner is going along. And after all, this is Yale.

The learner answers some items correctly and then makes some errors. With mild concern you press the levers up through 45 volts. You've tolerated that much yourself. Then a few more mistakes are made. You press the 60-volt lever, then 75. The learner makes another mistake. You pause and look at the scientist, who is reassuring: "Although the shocks may be painful, there is no permanent tissue damage, so please go on." The learner makes more errors, and soon you are up to a shock of 300 volts. But now the learner is pounding on the other side of the wall! Your chest tightens, and you begin to perspire. "Damn science and the $4.50!" you think. You hesitate and the scientist says, "The experiment requires that you continue." After the delivery of the next stimulus word, the learner chooses no answer at all. What are you to do? "Wait for 5 to 10 seconds," the scientist instructs, "and then treat no answer as a wrong answer." But after the next shock the pounding on the wall resumes! Now your heart is racing, and you are convinced you are causing extreme pain and discomfort. Is it possible that no lasting damage is being done? Is the experiment that important, after all? What to do? You hesitate again, and the scientist says, "It is absolutely essential that you continue." His voice is very convincing. "You have no other choice," he says, "you *must* go on." You can barely think straight, and for some unaccountable reason you feel laughter rising in your throat. Your finger shakes above the lever. *What are you to do?*

Milgram had foreseen that some "teachers" in his experiment would hesitate. He had therefore conceived standardized statements that his assistants would use when subjects balked—for example: "Although the shocks may be painful, there is no permanent tissue damage, so please go on." "The experiment requires that you continue." "It is absolutely essential that you continue." "You have no other choice, you *must* go on."

To repeat: If you are a teacher in the Milgram study, what do you do? Milgram (1963, 1974) found out what most people in his sample would do. The sample was a cross-section of the male population of New Haven, Connecticut. Of the 40 men in this phase of his research, only five refused to go beyond the 300-volt level, the level at which the learner first pounded the wall. Nine other "teachers" defied the scientist within the 300 to 450 volt range. But 65 percent of the subjects complied with the scientist throughout the series, believing they were delivering 450-volt, XXX-rated shocks.

Were these subjects unfeeling? Not at all. Milgram was impressed by their signs of stress. They trembled, they stuttered, they bit their lips. They groaned, they sweated, they dug their fingernails into their flesh. Some had fits of laughter, although laughter was inappropriate. One salesperson's laughter was so convulsive that he could not continue with the experiment.

Milgram's initial research on obedience was limited to a sample of New Haven men.

Could he generalize his findings to other men or to women? Would college students, who are considered to be independent thinkers, show more defiance? A replication of Milgram's study with a sample of Yale men yielded similar results. What about women, who are supposedly less aggressive than men? In subsequent research, women, too, administered shocks to the learners. All this took place in a Western nation that values independence and free will.

On Deception and Truth

We have said that the "teachers" in the Milgram studies *believed* that they were shocking other people when they pressed the levers on the console. They weren't. The only real shock in this experiment was the 45-volt sample given to the teachers. Its purpose was to make the procedure believable.

The learners in the experiment were actually confederates of the experimenter. They had not answered the newspaper ads but were in on the truth from the start. The "teachers" were the only real participants. They were led to believe they had been chosen at random for the teacher role, but the choice was rigged so that newspaper recruits would always become teachers.

Milgram debriefed his subjects after the experiment was complete. He explained the purpose and methods of his research in detail. He emphasized the fact that they had not actually harmed anyone. But of course the subjects did believe that they were hurting other people as the experiment was being carried out. As you can imagine, the ethics of the Milgram studies have been debated by psychologists for decades. College and university review committees would most likely prevent them from being conducted today.

Why Did People in the Milgram Studies Obey the Experimenters?

Many people obey the commands of others even when they are required to perform immoral tasks. But *why*? Why did Germans "just follow orders" during the Holocaust? Why did "teachers" obey the

foot-in-the-door technique a method for inducing compliance in which a small request is followed by a larger request

experimenter in Milgram's study? We do not have all the answers, but we can offer a number of hypotheses:

1 *Socialization.* Despite the expressed Western ideal of independence, we are socialized from early childhood to obey authority figures such as parents and teachers (Blass, 1999).

2 *Lack of social comparison.* In Milgram's experimental settings, experimenters displayed command of the situation, but the participants did not have the opportunity to compare their ideas and feelings with those of other people in the same situation. This can also lead to increased obedience if others around us are obeying questionable orders.

3 *Perception of legitimate authority.* An experimenter at Yale might have appeared to be a highly legitimate authority figure—as might a government official or a high-ranking officer in the military (Blass & Schmitt, 2001). Yet further research showed that the university setting contributed to compliance but was not fully responsible for it. The percentage of individuals who complied with the experimenter's demands dropped from 65 percent to 48 percent when Milgram (1974) replicated the study in a dingy storefront in a nearby town. At first glance, this finding might seem encouraging. But the main point of the Milgram studies is that most people are willing to engage in morally reprehensible acts at the behest of a legitimate-looking authority figure. Hitler and his henchmen were authority figures in Nazi Germany. "Science" and Yale University legitimized the authority of the experimenters in the Milgram studies.

4 *Foot-in-the-door.* The foot-in-the-door technique might have contributed to the obedience of the teachers. Once they had begun to deliver shocks to learners, they might have conceptualized themselves as people who help researchers and found it progressively more difficult to extricate themselves from the situation (Rodafinos et al., 2005). If a person has agreed to participate and begins acting in a particular way, he or she will feel pressure to remain consistent with the commitment and prior behaviours.

5 *Inaccessibility of values.* Most people believe that it is wrong to harm innocent people. But strong emotions interfere with clear thinking. As the teachers in the Milgram experiments became more aroused, their values might thus have become less "accessible."

6 *Buffers.* Several buffers decreased the effect of the learners' pain on the teachers. For example, the "learners" were in another room. When they were in the same room with the teachers, the teachers' compliance rate dropped from 65 percent to 40 percent. Moreover, when the teacher held the learner's hand on the shock plate, the compliance rate dropped to 30 percent.

Conformity

We are said to *conform* when we change our behaviour to adhere to *social norms*. Explicit social norms are often made into rules and laws such as those that require us to whisper in libraries and to slow down when driving past a school. There are also unspoken or implicit social norms, such as those that cause us to face the front in an elevator or to be "fashionably late" for social gatherings. Can you think of some instances in which you have conformed to social pressure?

The tendency to conform to social norms is often good. Many norms have evolved because they promote comfort and survival. Group pressure can also promote maladaptive behaviour, as when people engage in risky behaviour because "everyone is doing it." *Why do so many people tend to follow the crowd?* To answer this question, let us look at a classic experiment on conformity conducted by Solomon Asch in the early 1950s.

The Asch Study

Can you believe what you see with your own eyes? Seeing is believing, isn't it? Not if you were a participant in Asch's (1952) study.

Let's say you entered a laboratory room with seven other participants, supposedly taking part in an experiment on visual discrimination. At the front of the room stood a man who was holding cards with lines drawn on them.

The eight of you were seated in a series. You were given the seventh seat, a minor fact at the time. The man explained the task. There was a single line on the card on the left. Three lines were drawn on the card at the right (see Figure 14.6). One line on the right card was the same length as the line on the left card. You and the other subjects were to call out, one at a time, which of the three

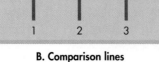

A. Standard line

B. Comparison lines

FIGURE 14.6

Cards Used in the Asch Study on Conformity

Which line on card B—1, 2, or 3—is the same length as the line on card A? Line 2, right? But would you say "2" if you were a member of a group and six people answering ahead of you all said "3"? Are you sure?

lines—1, 2, or 3—was the same length as the one on the card on the left. Simple.

The subjects to your right spoke out in order: "3," "3," "3," "3," "3," "3." Now it was your turn. Line 3 was clearly the same length as the line on the first card, so you said "3." The fellow after you then chimed in: "3." That's all there was to it. Then two other cards were set up at the front of the room. This time line 2 was clearly the same length as the line on the first card. The answers were "2," "2," "2," "2," "2," "2." Again it was your turn. You said "2," and perhaps your mind began to wander. Your stomach was gurgling a bit. The fellow after you said "2." Another pair of cards was held up. Line 3 was clearly the correct answer. The six people on your right spoke in turn: "1," "1 …" Wait a second! "…1," "1." You forgot about dinner and studied the lines briefly. No, line 1 was too short by about a centimetre. But the next two subjects said "1" and suddenly it was your turn. Your hands had become sweaty, and there was a lump in your throat. You wanted to say "3," but was it right? There was really no time, and you had already paused noticeably. You said "1," and so did the last fellow.

Now your attention was riveted on the task. Much of the time you agreed with the other seven judges, but sometimes you did not. And for some reason beyond your understanding, they were in perfect agreement even when they were wrong—assuming you could trust your eyes. The experiment was becoming an uncomfortable experience, and you began to doubt your judgment.

The discomfort in the Asch study was caused by the pressure to conform. Actually, the other seven recruits were confederates of the experimenter. They prearranged a number of incorrect responses. The sole purpose of the study was to see whether you would conform to the erroneous group judgments.

How many people in Asch's study caved in? How many went along with the crowd rather than give what they thought to be the right answer? *Seventy-five percent, or three out of four agreed with the majority's wrong answer at least once.*

Factors That Influence Conformity

Several factors increase the tendency to conform, including belonging to a collectivist rather than an individualistic society, the desire to be liked by other members of the group (but valuing being right over being liked decreases the tendency to conform), low self-esteem, social shyness, and lack of familiarity with the task (Phalet & Schoenpflug, 2001; Santee & Maslach, 1982). Other factors in conformity include group size and social support. The likelihood of conformity, even to incorrect group judgments, increases rapidly as group size grows to five members, then rises more slowly as the group grows to about eight members. At about that point the maximum chance of conformity is reached. Yet finding one other person who supports your minority opinion is apparently enough to encourage you to stick to your guns (Morris et al., 1977).

social facilitation
the process by which a person's performance is increased when other members of a group engage in similar behaviour

LO5 Group Behaviour

To be human is to belong to groups. Groups have much to offer us. They help us satisfy our needs for affection, attention, and belonging. They empower us to do things we could not manage by ourselves. But groups can also pressure us into doing things we might not do if we were acting alone, such as taking great risks or attacking other people.

This section considers ways in which people behave differently as group members than they would as individuals. We begin with social facilitation.

Social Facilitation

When you are given a group assignment, do you work harder or less hard than you would alone? Why? One effect of groups on individual behaviour is **social facilitation**. Runners and bicycle riders tend to move faster when they are members of a group. Research

Julian Finney/Getty Images

CHAPTER 14 Social Psychology **317**

suggests that the presence of other people increases our levels of arousal, or motivation (Platania & Moran, 2001; Thomas et al., 2002). At high levels of arousal, our performance of simple tasks is facilitated. Our performance of complex responses may be impaired, however. For this reason, a well-rehearsed speech may be delivered masterfully before a larger audience, while an impromptu speech may be hampered by a large audience.

Social facilitation may be influenced by **evaluation apprehension** as well as arousal—that is, by concern that they are evaluating us (Platania & Moran, 2001; Thomas et al., 2002). When giving a speech, we may "lose our thread" if we are distracted by the audience and focus too much on its apparent reaction. If we believe that we have begun to flounder, evaluation apprehension may skyrocket. As a result, our performance may falter even more.

The presence of others can also impair performance—not when we are acting *before* a group

+ = −

"Smart people working collectively can be dumber than the sum of their brains."
—Schwartz & Wald, 2003

but when we are anonymous members *of* a group (Guerin, 1999). Workers, for example, may "goof off" or engage in *social loafing* when they believe they will not be found out and held accountable. Under these group conditions there is no evaluation apprehension, but rather there may be **diffusion of responsibility** in groups. Each person may feel less obligation to help because others are present, especially if the others are perceived as being capable of doing the job (Hart et al., 2001). Group members may also reduce their efforts if an apparently capable member makes no contribution but "rides free" on the efforts of others.

Group Decision Making

Organizations use groups such as committees or juries to make decisions in the belief that group decisions are more accurate than individual decisions (Gigone & Hastie, 1997). *How do groups make decisions?* Social psychologists have discovered a number of "rules," or **social decision schemes**, that govern much of group decision making (Stasser, 1999). Here are some examples:

1 *The majority-wins scheme.* In this commonly used scheme, the group arrives at the decision that was initially supported by the majority. This scheme appears to guide decision making most often when there is no single objectively correct decision. An example is a decision about which car models to build when their popularity has not been tested in the court of public opinion.

2 *The truth-wins scheme.* In this scheme, as more information is provided and opinions are discussed, the group comes to recognize that one approach is objectively correct. For example, a group deciding whether to use SAT scores in admitting students to college would profit from information about whether the scores do predict college success.

3 *The two-thirds majority scheme.* Juries tend to convict defendants when two-thirds of the jury initially favours conviction.

4 *The first-shift rule.* In this scheme, the group tends to adopt the decision that reflects the first shift in opinion expressed by any group member. If a jury is deadlocked, the members may eventually follow the lead of the first juror to switch his position.

© Royalty-Free/Corbis

Polarization and the "Risky Shift"

Are group decisions more risky or more conservative than those of the individual members of the group? We might think that a group decision would be more conservative than an individual decision. After all, shouldn't there be an effort to compromise, to "split the difference"? We might also expect that a few mature individuals would be able to balance the opinions of daredevils.

Groups do not always appear to work as we might expect, however. Consider the *polarization* effect. As an individual, you might recommend that your company risk an investment of $500 000 to develop or market a new product. Other company executives, polled individually, might risk similar amounts. If you were gathered together to make a group decision, however, you would probably recommend either an amount well above this figure or nothing at all (Kamalanabhan et al., 2000). This group effect is called *polarization,* or the taking of an extreme position. If you had to gamble on which way the decision would go, however, you would do better to place your money on movement toward the higher sum—that is, to bet on a *risky shift.* Why?

One possibility is that one member of the group may reveal information of which the others were not aware. This information may clearly point in one direction or the other. With doubts removed, the group moves decisively in the appropriate direction. It is also possible that social facilitation occurs in the group setting and that the resulting greater motivation prompts more extreme decisions.

Why, however, do groups tend to take *greater* risks than those their members would take as individuals? One answer is diffusion of responsibility (Kamalanabhan et al., 2000). If the venture flops, the blame will not be placed on you alone.

groupthink
a process in which group members are influenced by cohesiveness and a dynamic leader to ignore external realities as they make decisions

Groupthink

Groupthink, a concept originated by Irving Janis (1982), is a problem that sometimes arises in group decision making. *What is groupthink?* In **groupthink,** group members tend to be more influenced by group cohesiveness and a dynamic leader than by the realities of the situation (Turner et al., 2007). Group problem solving may degenerate into groupthink when a group senses an external threat (Underhill, 2008). Groupthink is usually fuelled by a dynamic group leader. The threat heightens the cohesiveness of the group and is a source of stress. Under stress, group members tend not to consider all their options carefully and frequently make flawed decisions.

Groupthink has been connected with fiascos such as the Bay of Pigs invasion of Cuba, the escalation of the Vietnam War, the Watergate scandal, and NASA's decision to launch the *Challenger* and *Columbia* space shuttles despite engineers' warnings about the dangers created by cold weather and falling foam (Brownstein, 2003; Schwartz & Wald, 2003). Janis (1982) and other researchers (Pratkanis, 2007) note several characteristics of groupthink that contribute to flawed group decisions:

1 *Feelings of invulnerability.* Each decision-making group might have believed that it was beyond the reach of critics or the law.

2 *The group's belief in its rightness.* These groups apparently believed in the rightness of what they were doing.

3 *Discrediting of information contrary to the group's decision.* The government group involved in the Iran-Contra affair knowingly broke the law. Its members apparently discredited the law by (a) deciding that it was inconsistent with the best interests of the United States, and (b) enlisting private citizens to do the dirty work so that the government was not directly involved.

4 *Pressures on group members to conform.* Striving for unanimity overrides the quest for realism, and authority can trump expertise.

5 *Stereotyping of members of the out-group.* Members of the group that broke the law in the Iran-Contra affair reportedly stereotyped people who would oppose them as "communist sympathizers" and "knee-jerk liberals."

{ **Strength in Numbers? Maybe Not.** }

In their classic experiment, Darley and Latané (1968) had male subjects perform meaningless tasks in cubicles. Then, while they were working they heard a (convincing) recording of a person apparently having an epileptic seizure. When the men thought that four other persons were immediately available, only 31 percent tried to help the victim. When they thought that no one else was available, however, 85 percent of them tried to help.

As in other areas of group behaviour, it seems that diffusion of responsibility inhibits helping behaviour in groups or crowds. When we are in a group, we are often willing to let someone else do it. When we are the only one around, we are more willing to help others.

© Digital Vision/Photolibrary

deindividuation
the process by which group members may discontinue self-evaluation and adopt group norms and attitudes

social role
a group position that is accompanied by norms for behaviour

altruism
unselfish concern for the welfare of others

Groupthink can be averted if group leaders encourage members to remain skeptical about options and to feel free to ask probing questions and disagree with one another.

Mob Behaviour and Deindividuation

Have you ever done something as a member of a group that you would not have done as an individual? What was it? What motivated you? How do you feel about it?

The Frenchman Gustave Le Bon (1895/1960) branded mobs and crowds as irrational, resembling a "beast with many heads." Mob actions such as hockey riots sometimes seem to operate on a psychology of their own. *How is it that mild-mannered people, such as James whom we read about at the outset of the chapter, commit mayhem when they are part of a mob?*

Deindividuation

When people act as individuals, fear of consequences and self-evaluation tend to prevent them from engaging in antisocial behaviour. But in a mob, they may experience **deindividuation**, a state of reduced self-awareness and lowered concern for social evaluation. Many factors lead to deindividuation, including anonymity, diffusion of responsibility, arousal due to noise and crowding, and a focus on emerging group norms rather than on one's own values (Baron et al., 2006). Under these circumstances, crowd members behave more aggressively than they would as individuals. Thus James, as he threw the trash can through the storefront window, probably was not as aware of his actions compared to if he was alone on the street at night. He experienced a diffusion of responsibility in relation to his behaviour that resulted from being one in a crowd.

Social Roles

Groups can also influence behaviour by the **social roles** that people assume in a group. For example, you are assigned to do group work and the roles in the group include leader, note-taker, researcher, and presenter. Your actions and responsibilities in the group will predominantly be influenced by the role you assume. Philip Zimbardo and two of his graduate students (Haney, Banks, & Zimbardo, 1973) demonstrated the power of social roles by randomly assigning college-age men to act as prisoners or guards in a mock prison. Those who assumed the role of guard quickly became abusive and sadistic, and those acting as prisoners became anxious, withdrawn, and depressed. The study was originally planned for two weeks, but it had to be cancelled after six days because the power of the social roles influenced the guards to act in dehumanizing ways toward the prisoners.

Altruism and the Bystander Effect

Altruism—selfless concern for the welfare of others—is connected with some heroic behaviour. Humans have sacrificed themselves to ensure the survival of their children or of comrades in battle. So how, one might ask, could the death of 49-year-old Esmin Green, in the emergency room of Kings County Hospital in New York, have happened? Surveillance footage shows Green rolling off her chair and landing facedown on the floor while two others in the room did not react (CNN.com, 2008). As she lay there convulsing on the floor, no one, including hospital staff, came to her aid. Nearly 30 minutes after she had stopped convulsing, a hospital employee came and nudged her with his foot.

Why did this happen? Is it easier to turn a blind eye to people who are in distress? Some groups claimed that there is a culture of abuse and neglect associated with institutions like the Kings County Hospital, which specializes in psychiatric illnesses. Are we a callous bunch who would rather watch than help when others are in trouble?

The Helper

Why do people come to the aid of others, or ignore them? It turns out that many factors are involved in helping behaviour:

1 Observers are more likely to help when they are in a good mood (Baron et al., 2006). Perhaps good moods impart a sense of personal power—the feeling that we can handle the situation.

2 People who are empathic are more likely to help people in need (Darley and Pittman, 2003). Women are more likely than men to be empathic and thus more likely to help people in need (Trobst et al., 1994).

3 Bystanders may not help unless they believe that an emergency exists (Baron et al., 2006).

4 Observers must assume the responsibility to act (Baron et al., 2006). Perhaps the witnesses to Green collapsing thought it was the hospital staff's responsibility to act, and thus did nothing. *Diffusion of responsibility* may inhibit helping behaviour in crowds.

5 Observers must know what to do. Observers who are not sure that they can take charge of the situation may stay on the sidelines for fear of making a social blunder or of getting hurt themselves.

6 Observers are more likely to help people they know (Rutkowski et al., 1983). Evolutionary psychologists suggest that altruism is selfish from an evolutionary point of view when it helps close relatives or others who are similar to us to survive (Bruene & Ribbert, 2002). It helps us perpetuate a genetic code similar to our own.

7 Observers are more likely to help people who are similar to themselves. Being able to identify with the person in need promotes helping behaviour (Cialdini et al., 1997).

Ordinary People in Extraordinary Times

But let us not end this chapter and this book on a negative note. Let us think, instead, about the altruism of the firefighters, police officers, and ordinary people who came to the aid of the victims of the suicide terrorism of September 11, 2001. Let us remember the generosity of the residents of Gander, Newfoundland, on that fateful day. This small Canadian town found nearly 7000 stranded travellers on their doorstep when the U.S. airspace was closed suddenly on September 11, 2001. Residents of Gander and the surrounding towns responded by opening their homes to strangers, providing food, clothes, showers, and beds to the stranded travellers. They converted all halls and schools into temporary shelters and provided free meals and laundry facilities. Tour operators also made free "excursion trips" for those stranded and many were able to see the beautiful Gander wilderness and lakes. Stores stayed open longer hours, and many refused to charge those who were stranded. The lives of the stranded passengers were so affected by the hospitality of the residents of Gander that when one organized a scholarship fund for Gander high school students who were headed to college, many donated generously (MSNBC, 2010). Ordinary people in extraordinary times often give much and ask little in return.

References

A

Abbey, A. (1987). Misperceptions of friendly behavior as sexual interest. *Psychology of Women Quarterly, 11,* 173–194.

Ackard, D.M., Neumark-Sztainer, D., Hannan, P.J., French, S., & Story, M. (2001). Binge and purge behavior among adolescents: Associations with sexual and physical abuse in a nationally representative sample: The Commonwealth Fund survey. *Child Abuse & Neglect, 25*(6), 771–785.

Agras, W.S., Walsh, T., Fairburn, C.G., Wilson, G.T., & Kraemer, H.C. (2000). A multicenter comparison of cognitive-behavioral therapy and interpersonal psychotherapy for bulimia nervosa.

Ainsworth, M.D.S., Blehar, M.C., Waters, E., & Wall, S. (1978). *Patterns of attachment: A psychological study of the strange situation.* Hillsdale, NJ: Erlbaum.

Alexander, C.N., et al. (1996). Trial of stress reduction for hypertension in older African Americans: II. Sex and risk subgroup analysis. *Hypertension, 28,* 228–237.

Allport, G.W., & Oddbert, H.S. (1936). Trait names: A psycholexical study. *Psychological Monographs, 47,* 1–36. Altman, L.K. (2005, May 16). Studies find disparity in U.S. cancer care. *The New York Times online.*

Alzheimer's Society of Canada (2010). Key facts about Alzheimer's disease and dementia. Retrieved on August 16, 2010, from http://www.alzheimer.ca/english/disease/stats-intro.htm.

American Psychiatric Association. (2000). Diagnostic and statistical manual of mental disorders (4th ed., text revision). Washington, DC: Author.

Amodio, D.M., & Showers, C.J. (2005). "Similarity breeds liking" revisited: The moderating role of commitment. *Journal of Social and Personal Relationships, 22*(6), 817–836.

Anderson, C.A. (2004). An update on the effects of violent video games. *Journal of Adolescence, 27,* 113–122.

Anderson, C.A., & Dill, K.E. (2000). Video games and aggressive thoughts, feelings, and behavior in the laboratory and in life. *Journal of Personality and Social Psychology, 78*(4), 772–790.

Anderson, C.A., Berkowitz, L., Donnerstein, E., Huesmann, R.L., Johnson, J., Linz, D., Malamuth, N., & Wartella, E. (2003). The influence of media violence on youth. *Psychological Science in the Public Interest, 4,* 81–110.

Anderson, C.A., et al. (2004). Violent video games: Specific effects of violent content on aggressive thoughts and behavior. *Advances in Experimental Social Psychology, 36,* 199–249.

Anderson, C., & Horne, J.A. (2004). Presleep relaxed 7–8 Hz EEG from left frontal region: Marker of localised neuropsychological performance? *Physiology & Behavior, 81*(4), 657–664.

Anderson, C.A., Carnagey, N.L., & Eubanks, J. (2003). Exposure to violent media: The effects of songs with violent lyrics on aggressive thoughts and feelings. *Journal of Personality and Social Psychology, 84,* 960–971.

Andreou, G., et al. (2002). Handedness, asthma, and allergic disorders: Is there an association? *Psychology, Health & Medicine, 7*(1), 53–60.

Anger-Diáz, B., Schlanger, K., Rincon, C., & Abbey, A. (1987). Misperceptions of friendly behavior as sexual interest. *Psychology of Women Quarterly, 11,* 173–194.

Antoni, M.H. (2009). Stress management effects on biobehavioral processes in breast cancer. *Brain, Behavior, and Immunity, 23*(Suppl. 2), S26.

Antoni, M.H., et al. (2005). Increases in a marker of immune system reconstitution are predated by decreases in 24-h urinary cortisol output and depressed mood during a 10-week stress management intervention in symptomatic HIV-infected men. *Journal of Psychosomatic Research, 58*(1), 3–13.

Apperloo, M.J.A., Van Der Stege, J.G., Hoek, A., & Weijmar Schultz, W.C.M. (2003). In the mood for sex: The value of androgens. *Journal of Sex & Marital Therapy, 29*(2), 87–102.

Arendt, J. (2000). Melatonin, circadian rhythms, and sleep. *The New England Journal of Medicine online, 343*(15).

Arnett, J.J. (1999). Adolescent storm and stress, reconsidered. *American Psychologist, 54*(5), 317–326.

Arnett, J.J. (2001). Conceptions of the transition to adulthood: Perspectives from adolescence to midlife. *Journal of Adult Development, 8,* 133–143.

Aronoff, J., & Litevin, G.H. (1971). Achievement motivation training and executive advancement. *Journal of Applied Behavioral Science, 7*(2), 215–229. *Psychological Bulletin, 131*(3), 410–411.

Asch, S.E. (1952). *Social psychology.* Englewood Cliffs, NJ: Prentice-Hall.

Aserinsky, E., & Kleitman, N. (1955). Two types of ocular motility occurring in sleep. *Journal of Applied Physiology, 8,* 1–10.

Ashton, M.C., & Lee, K. (2008). The prediction of Honesty-Humility-related criteria by the HEXACO and Five-Factor Models of personality. *Journal of Research in Personality, 42,* 1216–1228.

Atkins, M.S., et al. (2002). Suspensions and detention in an urban, low-income school: Punishment or reward? *Journal of Abnormal Child Psychology, 30*(4), 361–371.

Atkinson, R.C., & Shiffrin, R.M. (1968). Human memory: A proposed system and its control processes. In K. Spence (Ed.), *The psychology of learning and motivation* (Vol. 2). New York: Academic Press.

Axelsson, J., Stefansson, J.G., Magnusson, A., Sigvaldason, H., Karlsson, M.M. (2002). Seasonal affective disorders: Relevance of Icelandic and Icelandic Canadian evidence to etiologic hypotheses. *Canadian Journal of Psychiatry, 47,* 153–158.

Ayllon, T., & Haughton, E. (1962). Control of the behavior of schizophrenic patients by food. *Journal of the Experimental Analysis of Behavior, 5,* 343–352.

B

Baddeley, A. (1982). *Your memory: A user's guide.* New York: Macmillan.

Bahrick, H.P., Bahrick, P.O., & Wittlinger, R.P. (1975). Fifty years of memory for names and faces. *Journal of Experimental Psychology: General, 104,* 54–75.

Bailey, J.M. (2003a). Personal communication.

Bailey, J.M., & Pillard, R.C. (1991). A genetic study of male sexual orientation. *Archives of general psychiatry, 48,* 1089–1096.

Baily, J.M. & Benishay, D.S. (1993). Familial aggregation of female sexual orientation. *American Journal of Psychiatry, 150,* 272–277.

Baker, C.W., Whisman, M.A., & Brownell, K.D. (2000). Studying intergenerational transmission of eating attitudes and behaviors: Methodological and conceptual questions. *Health Psychology, 19*(4), 376–381.

Baker, L.A., DeFries, J.C., & Fulker, D.W. (1983). Longitudinal stability of cognitive ability in the Colorado adoption project. *Child Development, 54,* 290–297.

Baker, M.C. (2001). *The atoms of language: The mind's hidden rules of grammar.* New York: Basic Books.

Baldo, J.V., Delis, D.C., Wilkins, D.P., & Shimamura, A.P. (2004). Is it bigger than a breadbox? Performance of patients with prefrontal lesions on a new executive function test. *Archives of Clinical Neuropsychology, 19*(3), 407–419.

Baltes, P.B., & Staudinger, U.M. (2000). Wisdom: A meta-heuristic (pragmatic) to orchestrate mind and virtue toward excellence. *American Psychologist, 55,* 122–136.

Bandura, A. (1986). *Social foundations of thought and action: A social-cognitive theory.* Englewood Cliffs, NJ: Prentice-Hall.

Bandura, A. (1999). Social cognitive theory: An agentic perspective. *Asian Journal of Social Psychology, 2*(1), 21–41.

Bandura, A. (2002). Social cognitive theory in cultural context. *Applied Psychology: An International Review, 51*(2), 269–290.

Bandura, A. (2003). Observational learning. In J.H. Byrne (ed.), *Encyclopedia of learning and memory* (2nd ed., pp. 482–484). New York: Macmillan.

Bandura, A., & Locke, E.A. (2003). Negative self-efficacy and goal effects revisited. *Journal of Applied Psychology, 88*(1), 87–99.

Bandura, A., Blanchard, E.B., & Ritter, B. (1969). The relative efficacy of desensitization and modeling approaches for inducing behavioral, affective, and cognitive changes. *Journal of Personality and Social Psychology, 13,* 173–199. 274–281.

Bandura, A., Pastorelli, C., Barbaranelli, C., & Caprara, G.V. (1999). Self-efficacy pathways to childhood depression. *Journal of Personality & Social Psychology, 76*(2), 258–269.

Bandura, A., Ross, S.A., & Ross, D. (1963). Imitation of film-mediated aggressive models. *Journal of Abnormal and Social Psychology, 66,* 3–11.

Bandura, A., Taylor, C.B., Williams, S.L., Medford, I.N., & Barchas, J.D. (1985). Catecholamine secretion as a function of perceived coping self-efficacy. *Journal of Consulting and Clinical Psychology, 53,* 406–414.

Banks, M.S., & Shannon, E. (1993). Spatial and chromatic visual efficiency in human neonates. In C.E. Granrud (Ed.), *Visual perception and cognition in infancy.* Hillsdale, NJ: Erlbaum.

Barber, J.G. (2001). Relative misery and youth suicide. *Australian & New Zealand Journal of Psychiatry, 35*(1), 49–57.

Barber, T.X. (2000). A deeper understanding of hypnosis: Its secrets, its nature, its essence. *American Journal of Clinical Hypnosis, 42*(3–4), 208–272.

Bard, P. (1934). The neurohumoral basis of emotional reactions. In C.A. Murchison (Ed.), *Handbook of general experimental psychology.* Worcester, MA: Clark University Press.

Barnard, C.J., Collins, S.A., Daisley, J.N., & Behnke, J.M. (2005). Maze performance and immunity costs in mice. *Behaviour, 142*(2), 241–263.

Baron, R.A., Byrne, D., & Branscombe, N.R. (2006). *Social psychology* (11th ed.). Boston: Allyn & Bacon.

Bartels, M., Rietveld, M.J.H., Van Baal, G.C.M., & Boomsma, D.I. (2002). Genetic and environmental influences on the development of intelligence. *Behavior Genetics, 32*(4), 237–249.

Bartholow, B.D., & Anderson, C.A. (2002). Effects of violent video games on aggressive behavior: Potential sex differences. *Journal of Experimental Social Psychology, 38,* 283–290.

Bartoshuk, L.M. (2000). Psychophysical advances aid the study of genetic variation in taste. *Appetite, 34*(1), 105.

Basic Behavioral Science Task Force of the National Advisory Mental Health Council. (1996b). Basic behavioral science research for mental health: Perception, attention, learning and memory. *American Psychologist, 51,*133–142.

Basic Behavioral Science Task Force of the National Advisory Mental Health Council. (1996c). Basic behavioral science research for mental health: Sociocultural and environmental practices. *American Psychologist, 51,* 722–731.

Bassetti, C., Vella, S., Donati, F., Wielepp, P., & Weder, B. (2000). SPECT during sleepwalking. *Lancet, 356,* 484–485.

Battaglia, F.P., Sutherland, G.R., & McNaughton, B.L. (2004). Local sensory cues and place cell directionality: Additional evidence of prospective coding in the hippocampus. *Journal of Neuroscience, 24*(19), 4541–4550.

Baucom, D.H., Shoham, V., Mueser, K.T., Daiuto, A.D., & Stickle, T.R. (1998). Empirically supported couple and family interventions for marital distress and adult mental health problems. *Journal of Consulting and Clinical Psychology, 66,* 53–88.

Bauer, M.E., et al. (2003). Altered glucocorticoid immunoregulation in treatment resistant depression. *Psychoneuroendocrinology, 28*(1), 49–65.

Baumeister, R.F. (1996). *Evil: Inside human cruelty and violence.* New York: W.H. Freeman /Times Books/ Henry Holt & Co.

Baumgartner, F. (2002). The effect of hardiness in the choice of coping strategies in stressful situations. *Studia Psychologica, 44*(1), 69–75.

Baumrind, D. (1973). The development of instrumental competence through socialization. In A. Pick (Ed.), *Minnesota symposia on child psychology, 7* (pp. 3–46). Minneapolis: University of Minnesota Press.

Bearman, P. & Bruckner, H. (2002). Opposite-sex twins and adolescent same-sex attraction. *American Journal of Sociology, 107,* 1179–1205.

Beautrais, A.L. (2003). Suicide and serious suicide attempts in youth: A multiple-group comparison study. *American Journal of Psychiatry, 160,* 1093–1099.

Beck, A.T., et al. (2001). Dysfunctional beliefs discriminate personality disorders. *Behaviour Research & Therapy, 39*(10), 1213–1225.

Bekoff, M. (2002). *Minding animals: Awareness, emotions, and heart.* New York: Oxford University Press.

Belsky, J., Weinraub, M., Owen, M., & Kelly, J. (2001, April). Quantity of child care and problem behavior. In J. Belsky (Chair), *Early childcare and children's development prior to school entry.* Symposium conducted at the 2001 Biennial Meetings of the Society for Research in Child Development, Minneapolis, MN.

Bem, D.J. (2000). Exotic becomes erotic: Interpreting the biological correlates of sexual orientation. *Archives of Sexual Behavior, 29,* 531–548.

Bem, D.J., & Honorton, C. (1994). Does Psi exist? Replicable evidence for an anomalous process of information transfer. *Psychological Bulletin, 115,* 4–18.

Benson, H. (1975). *The relaxation response.* New York: Morrow.

Berk, M.S., Henriques, G.R., Warman, D.M., Brown, G.K., & Beck, A.T. (2004). A cognitive therapy intervention for suicide attempters: An overview. *Cognitive and Behavioral Practice. 11*(3), 265–277.

Berkowitz, L. (2004b). Two views of evil: Evil is not only banal. *PsycCRITIQUES.*

Bernardin, H.J., Cooke, D.K., & Villanova, P. (2000). Conscientiousness and agreeableness as predictors of rating leniency. *Journal of Applied Psychology, 85*(2), 232–236.

Bernhardt, P.C., Dabbs, J.M., Jr., Fielden, J.A., & Lutter, C.D. (1998). Testosterone changes during vicarious experiences of winning and losing among fans at sporting events. *Physiology & Behavior, 65*(1), 59–62.

Berry, J.W., Phinney, J.S., Sam, D.L., & Vedder, P. (Eds.) (2006). *Immigrant youth in cultural transition.* Mahwah, NJ: Erlbaum.

Better Sleep Council of Canada. (2009). Retrieved on May 8, 2010 from http://www.bettersleep.ca.

Bexton, W.H., Heron, W., & Scott, T.H. (1954). Effects of decreased variation in the sensory environment. *Canadian Journal of Psychology, 8,* 70–76.

Bialystok, E., Craik, F.I.M., Klein, R., & Viswanathan, M. (2004). Bilingualism, aging, and cognitive control: Evidence from the Simon task. *Psychology and Aging, 19,* 290–303.

Bibby, R. (1990). *Mosaic Madness.* Toronto: Stoddart.

Bidell, M.P., Turner, J.A., & Casas, J.M. (2002). First impressions count: Ethnic/racial and lesbian/gay/bisexual content of professional psychology application materials. *Professional Psychology: Research & Practice, 33*(1), 97–103.

Bienvenu, O.J., et al. (2005). Anxiety and depressive disorders and the five-factor model of personality: A higher- and lower-order personality trait investigation in a community sample. *Depression & Anxiety, 20*(2), 92–97.

Bilkey, D.K. (2004). Neuroscience: In the place space. *Science, 305,* 1245–1246.

Birch, C.D., Stewart, S.H., & Brown, C.G. (2007). Exploring differential patterns of situational risk for binge eating and heavy drinking. *Addictive Behaviors, 32*(3), 433.

Bishop, G.D., et al. (2003). Job demands, decisional control, and cardiovascular responses. *Journal of Occupational Health Psychology, 8*(2), 146–156.

Bizer, G.Y., et al. (2004). The impact of personality on cognitive, behavioral, and affective political processes: The effects of need to evaluate. *Journal of Personality, 72*(5), 995–1027.

Bjorklund, D.F. (2000). *Children's thinking* (3rd ed.). Pacific Grove, CA: Brooks/Cole.

Blagrove, M., Farmer, L., & Williams, E. (2004). The relationship of nightmare frequency and nightmare distress to well-being. *Journal of Sleep Research, 13*(2), 129–136.

Blair, R., & James, R. (2003). Neurobiological basis of psychopathy. *British Journal of Psychiatry, 182*, 5–7.

Blake, P., Frye, R., & Pejsach, M. (1984). Self-assessment and behavior change manual. New York: Random House. p. 218

Blass, T. (1999). The Milgram paradigm after 35 years: Some things we now know about obedience to authority. *Journal of Applied Social Psychology, 29*(5), 955–978.

Blass, T., & Schmitt, C. (2001). The nature of perceived authority in the Milgram paradigm: Two replications. *Current Psychology: Developmental, Learning, Personality, Social, 20*(2), 115–121.

Bloom, J.W. (1998). The ethical practice of Web Counselling. *British Journal of Guidance & Counselling, 26*, 53–59.

Bogaert, A.F. (2006). Biological versus nonbiological older brothers and sexual orientation in men. *Proceedings of the National Academy of Sciences (PNAS), 103*, 10771–10774.

Bogen, J.E. (1969). The other side of the brain II: An appositional mind. *Bulletin of the Los Angeles Neurological Society, 34*, 135–162.

Bogen, J.E. (1998). My developing understanding of Roger Wolcott Sperry's philosophy. *Neuropsychologia, 36*(10), 1089–1096.

Bogen, J.E. (2000). Split-brain basics: Relevance for the concept of one's other mind. *Journal of the American Academy of Psychoanalysis, 28*(2), 341–369.

Bohlin, G., Hagekull, B., & Rydell, A. (2000). Attachment and social functioning: A longitudinal study from infancy to middle childhood. *Social Development, 9*(1), 24–39.

Bonin, M.F., McCreary, D.R., & Sadava, S.W. (2000). Problem drinking behavior in two community-based samples of adults: Influence of gender, coping, loneliness, and depression. *Psychology of Addictive Behaviors, 14*(2), 151–161.

Bonn-Miller, M.O., Zvolensky, M.J., & Bernstein, A. (2007). Marijuana use motives: Concurrent relations to frequency of past 30-day use and anxiety sensitivity among young adult marijuana smokers. *Addictive Behaviors, 32*(1) 49–62.

Boom, J., Wouters, H., & Keller, M. (2007). A cross cultural validation of stage development. A Rasch re-analysis of longitudinal socio-moral reasoning data. *Cognitive Development, 22*(2), 213–229.

Both, L., Needham, D., & Wood, E. (2004). Examining tasks that facilitate the experience of incubation while problem-solving. *Alberta Journal of Educational Research, 50*(1), 57–67.

Bouchard, T., Jr., & Loehlin, J. (2001). Genes, evolution, and personality. *Behavior Genetics, 31*(3), 243–273.

Bouchard, T.J., Jr., Lykken, D., McGue, M., Segal, N.L., & Tellegen, A. (1990). Sources of human psychological differences: The Minnesota study of twins reared apart. *Science, 250*, 223–228.

Bowlby, J. (1969). Attachment and loss: Volume 1: Attachment. *The International Psycho-Analytical Library, 79*, 1–401. London: The Hogarth Press and the Institute of Psychoanalysis.

Boyatzis, R.E. (1974). The effect of alcohol consumption on the aggressive behavior of men. *Quarterly Journal of Studies on Alcohol, 35*(3), 929–972.

Boyce, W., Doherty, M., Fortin, C., & MacKinnon, D. (2003). *Canadian youth, sexual health and HIV/AIDS study: Factors influencing knowledge, attitudes and behaviours.* Council of Ministers of Education, Canada.

Boyd-Franklin, N. (2001). Using the multisystems model with an African American family: Crossracial therapy and supervision. In S.H. McDaniel, et al. (Eds.), *Casebook for integrating family therapy: An ecosystemic approach* (pp. 395–400). Washington, DC: American Psychological Association.

Bradley, R.H., et al. (1989). Home environment and cognitive development in the first 3 years of life. *Developmental Psychology, 25*, 217–235.

Branaman, T.F., & Gallagher, S.N. (2005). Polygraph testing in sex offender treatment: A review of limitations. *American Journal of Forensic Psychology, 23*(1), 45–64.

Brand, J. (2000). Cited in McFarling, U.L. (2000, August 27). Sniffing out genes' role in our senses of taste and smell. *The Los Angeles Times online.*

Braun, B.G. (1988). *Treatment of multiple personality disorder.* Washington, DC: American Psychiatric Press.

Bray, F., & Atkin, W. (2004). International cancer patterns in men: Geographical and temporal variations in cancer risk and the role of gender. *Journal of Men's Health & Gender, 1*(1), 38–46.

Brigman, S., & Cherry, K.E. (2002). Age and skilled performance: Contributions of working memory and processing speed. *Brain & Cognition, 50*(2), 242–256.

Brody, J.E. (2000, April 25). Memories of things that never were. *The New York Times,* p. F8.

Brody, J.E. (2008, May 20). Trying to break nicotine's grip. *The New York Times online.*

Brook, J.S., Zheng, L., Whiteman, M., & Brook, D.W. (2001). Aggression in toddlers: Associations with parenting and marital relations. *Journal of Genetic Psychology, 162*(2), 228–241.

Broom, A. (2005). The eMale: Prostate cancer, masculinity and online support as a challenge to medical expertise. *Journal of Sociology, 41*(1), 87–104.

Brown, A.S., & Susser, E.S. (2002). In utero infection and adult schizophrenia. *Mental Retardation & Developmental Disabilities Research Reviews, 8*(1), 51–57.

Brown, R., & McNeill, D. (1966). The tip-of-the tongue phenomenon. *Journal of Verbal Learning and Verbal Behavior, 5,* 325–337.

Brownstein, A.L. (2003). Biased predecision processing. *Psychological Bulletin, 129*(4), 545–568.

Bruene, M., & Ribbert, H. (2002). Grundsaetzliches zur Konzeption einer evolutionaeren Psychiatrie. *Schweizer Archiv für Neurologie und Psychiatrie, 153*(1), 4–11.

Buchanan, R.W., Pearlson, G., & Tamminga, C.A. (2004). Prefrontal cortex, structural analysis: Segmenting the prefrontal cortex. *American Journal of Psychiatry, 161*(11), 1978.

Buckley, P.F., Buchanan, R.W., Tamminga, C.A., & Schulz, S.C. (2000). Schizophrenia research. *Schizophrenia Bulletin, 26*(2), 411–419.

Buckner, R.L., Wheeler, M.E., & Sheridan, M.A. (2001). Encoding processes during retrieval tasks. *Journal of Cognitive Neuroscience, 13*(3), 406–415.

Budney, A.J., Vandrey, R.G., Hughes, J.R., Moore, B.A., & Bahrenburg, B. (2007). Oral delta-9-tetrahydrocannabinol suppresses cannabis withdrawal symptoms. *Drug and Alcohol Dependence, 86*(1), 22–29.

Bull, N.J., Hunter, M., & Finlay, D.C. (2003). Cue gradient and cue density interact in the detection and recognition of objects defined by motion, contrast, or texture. *Perception, 32*(1), 29–39.

Bunde, J., & Suls, J. (2006). A quantitative analysis of the relationship between the cook-medley hostility scale and traditional coronary artery disease risk factors. *Health Psychology, 25,* 493–500.

Burdette, A.M. & Hill, T. (2009). Religious involvement and transitions into adolescent sexual activities. *Sociology of Religion, 70,* 28–48.

Buss, D.M. (1994). *The evolution of desire.* New York: Basic Books.

Buss, D.M. (2000). The evolution of happiness. *American Psychologist, 55,* 15–23.

Butcher, J. (2000). Dopamine hypothesis gains further support. *The Lancet, 356,* 139–146.

Butler, A.C., & Beck, J.S. (2001). Cognitive therapy outcomes. A review of meta-analyses. *Tidsskrift for Norsk Psykologforening, 38*(8), 698–706.

C

Cacioppo, J.T., Martzke, J.S., Petty, R.E., & Tassinary, L.G. (1988). Specific forms of facial EMG response index emotions during an interview.

Caffray, C.M., & Schneider, S.L. (2000). Why do they do it? Affective motivators in adolescents' decisions to participate in risk behaviours. *Cognition & Emotion, 14*(4), 543–576.

Canadian Association of the Deaf (2007, May 26). *Statistics on Deaf Canadians.* Retrieved March 1, 2010, from http://www.cad.ca/en/issues/statistics_on_deaf_canadians.asp.

Canadian Broadcasting Corporation (2007, February 27). *The CBC Digital Archives Website.* Retrieved February 9, 2010, from http://archives.cbc.ca/science_technology/unexplained/clips/4366/.

Canadian Cancer Society (2009). Lung cancer statistics. Retrieved on May 20, 2010, from http://www.cancer.ca/Canadawide/About%20cancer/Cancer%20statistics/Stats%20at%20a%20glance /Lung%20cancer.aspx?sc_lang=en.

Canadian Centre for Occupational Health & Safety (2008). Workplace stress—General. Retrieved on August 11, 2010, from http://www.ccohs.ca/oshanswers/psychosocial/stress.html.

Canadian Council on Animal Care (2008). Guidelines for use of Animals in Research and Teaching. Retrieved on August 17, 2010, from http://www.ccac.ca/en/CCAC_Main.htm.

Canadian Council on Learning (2008). *Lessons in Learning. The Advantages of Bilingualism in Canada.* Retrieved August 17, 2010, from http://www.ccl-cca.ca/pdfs/LessonsInLearning/Oct-16-08-The-advantages-of-bilingualism.pdf.

Canadian Heritage. History of Bilingualism in Canada. Retrieved August 17, 2010, from http://canadianheritage.gc.ca/pgm/lo-ol/bllng/hist-eng.cfm.

Canadian Institute for Health Information (2008). *Hospital mental health services in Canada, 2005–2006.* Ottawa: CIHI.

Canadian Institute for Stress (2005). Stress and wellness consultant. Retrieved on August 11, 2010, from http://www.stresscanada.org/csw.html.

Canadian Lung Association. (2008). *Facts about Smoking.* Retrieved on May 6, 2010 from http://www.lung.ca/protect-protegez/tobacco-tabagisme/facts-faits/index_e.php.

Canadian Mental Health Association (2010). *Post Traumatic Stress Disorder.* Retrieved on June 29, 2010, from: http://www.cmha.ca/bins/content_page.asp?cid=3-94-97.

Canadian Mental Health Association (2010). *Seasonal Affective Disorder.* Retrieved on June 17, 2010, from: http://www.cmha.ca/bins/content_page.asp?cid=3-86-93.

Canadian Mental Health Institute. (2004). *Stress.* Retrieved on August 16, 2010 from http://www.cmha.ca/bins/content_page.asp?cid=2-28-30&lang=1.

Canadian Psychological Association (2000). Canadian Code of ethics for psychologists (3rd ed.). Retrieved on August 17, 2010, from http://www.cpa.ca/cpasite/userfiles/Documents/Canadian%20Code%20of%20Ethics%20for%20Psycho.pdf.

Canadian Psychological Association (2001). *Guidelines for Non-Discriminatory Practice.* Retrieved July 6, 2010, from http://www.cpa.ca/cpasite/userfiles/Documents/publications/NonDiscPractrev%20cpa.pdf.

Canadian Sleep Society. (2009). Retrieved May 15, 2010, from http://www.ccs.to.

Canalis, R.F., & Lambert, P.R. (2000). *The ear: Comprehensive otology.* Philadelphia: Lippincott Williams & Wilkins.

Cannon, W.B. (1927). The James-Lange theory of emotions: A critical examination and an alternative theory. *American Journal of Psychology, 39,* 106–124.

Cannon, W.B. (1932). *The wisdom of the body.* New York: Norton.

Cannon, W.B., & Washburn, A. (1912). An explanation of hunger. *American Journal of Physiology, 29,* 441–454.

Cantalupo, C., & Hopkins, W.D. (2001). Asymmetric Broca's area in great apes: A region of the ape brain is uncannily similar to one linked with speech in humans. *Nature, 414*(6863), 505.

Carleton University Study. (2001). Student Stress Study 2000–2001. Retrieved on July 16, 2010, from http://www.carleton.ca/diversity/studentstress.htm.

Carlson, J.G., & Hatfield, E. (1992). *Psychology of emotion.* Fort Worth: Harcourt Brace Jovanovich.

Carmichael, L., Hogan, H.P., & Walter, A.A. (1932). An experimental study of the effect of language on the reproduction of visually perceived form. *Journal of Experimental Psychology, 15,* 73–86.

Cartwright, R.D. (2004). The role of sleep in changing our minds: A psychologist's discussion of papers on memory reactivation and consolidation in sleep. *Learning and Memory, 11,* 660–663.

Cattell, R.B. (1949). *The culture-free intelligence test.* Champaign, IL: Institute for Personality and Ability Testing.

CBC Digital Archives. (n.d.). Sikh Mounties permitted to wear turbans. Retrieved May 21, 2010, from http://archives.cbc.ca/on_this_day/03/15/.

CBC News. (2005, April 10). Canadians deeply split on same-sex marriage, poll suggests. *CBC.CA News.* Retrieved May 24, 2006, from http://www.cbc.ca.

CBC News. (2005, June 29). Same-sex marriage law passes 158–133. *CBC.CA News.* Retrieved May 24, 2006, from http://www.cbc.ca.

CBC News. (2006, November 22). Widow shocked by unconditional release of husband's killer. Retrieved on June 21, 2010, from http://www.cbc.ca/news/story/2006/11/22/arenburg.html.

CBC News. (2008, April 22). Police cars burned, stores looted in Montreal hockey riot. Retrieved May 27, 2010, from http://www.cbc.ca/canada/montreal/story/2008/04/22/mtl-habs.html.

CBC News. (2009, May 14). Quebec opposition wants hijab policy for public service. Retrieved May 21, 2010, from http://www.cbc.ca/canada/montreal/story/2009/05/14/quebec-hijab-publicservants.html.

CBC News. (2010, January 18). "Toronto 18" mastermind gets life sentence. Retrieved May 27, 2010, from http://www.cbc.ca/canada/story/2010/01/18/toronto-18-sentence.html.

CBC News. (2010, May 17). Robert Munsch speaks of addiction battle. Retrieved on June 23, 2010, from: http://www.cbc.ca/arts/books/story/2010/05/17/munsch-addiction.html.

CBC News. (2010, June 18). Toronto 18 details emerge as jury sequestered: What the jury didn't get to hear about Fahim Ahmad. Retrieved June 21, 2010, from http://www.cbc.ca/canada/story/2010/06/18/toronto-18-jury.html.

Cellar, D.F., Nelson, Z.C., & Yorke, C.M. (2000). The five-factor model and driving behavior: Personality and involvement in vehicular accidents. *Psychological Reports, 86*(2), 454–456.

Centers for Disease Control and Prevention. (2005a, April 21). Overweight and obesity: Health consequences. http://www.cdc.gov/nccdphp/dnpa/obesity/consequences.htm.

Centre for Addiction and Mental Health. (2009). Retrieved on May 15, 2010, from http://www.camh.net/About_Addiction_Mental_Health/Mental_Health_Information/index.html.

Cervantes, J.M., & Parham, T.A. (2005). Toward a meaningful spirituality for people of color: Lessons for the counseling practitioner. *Cultural Diversity & Ethnic Minority Psychology, 11*(1), 69–81.

Chafee, M.V., & Goldman-Rakic, P.S. (2000). Inactivation of parietal and prefrontal cortex reveals interdependence of neural activity during memory-guided saccades. *Journal of Neurophysiology, 83*(3), 1550–1566.

Chen, C., et al. (2004). Association analysis of dopamine D2-like receptor genes and methamphetamine abuse. *Psychiatric Genetics, 14*(4), 223–226.

Chen, S.W., & Davenport, D.S. (2005). Cognitive behavioral therapy with Chinese American clients: Cautions and modifications. *Psychotherapy: Theory, Research, Practice, Training, 42*(1), 101–110.

Cheng, H., & Furnham, A. (2001). Attributional style and personality as predictors of happiness and mental health. *Journal of Happiness Studies, 2*(3), 307–327.

Cheung, A.H., & Dewa, C.S. (2006). Canadian community health survey: Major depressive disorder and suicidality in adolescents. *Healthcare Policy, 2*(2), 76–89.

Chioqueta, A.P., & Stiles, T.C. (2005). Personality traits and the development of depression, hopelessness, and suicide ideation. *Personality & Individual Differences, 38*(6), 1283–1291.

Chomsky, N. (1980). Rules and representations. *Behavioral and Brain Sciences, 3,* 1–16.

Chomsky, N. (1991). Linguistics and cognitive science. In A. Kasher (Ed.), *The Chomskyan turn.* Cambridge, MA: Blackwell.

Chu, L., Ma, E.S.K., Lam, K.K.Y., Chan, M.F., & Lee, D.H.S. (2005). Increased alpha 7 nicotinic acetylcholine receptor protein levels in Alzheimer's disease patients. *Dementia & Geriatric Cognitive Disorders, 19*(2–3), 106–112.

Chua, S.C., Jr. (2004). Molecular and cellular correlates of the developmental acquisition of mechanisms modulating ingestive behavior. *Physiology & Behavior, 82*(1), 145–147.

Cialdini, R.B., et al. (1997). Reinterpreting the empathy-altruism relationship: When one into one equals one-ness. *Journal of Personality & Social Psychology, 73*(3), 481–494.

Clark, W. & Schellenberg, G. (2006). Who's religious? *Statistics Canada, No. 11-008.*

Clarke-Stewart, K.A., & Beck, R.J. (1999). Maternal scaffolding and children's narrative retelling of a movie story. *Early Childhood Research Quarterly, 14*(3), 409–434.

Clénet, F., Hascoët, M., Fillion, G., Galons, H., & Bourin, M. (2005). Role of GABA-ergic and serotonergic systems in the anxiolytic-like mechanism of action of a 5-HT-moduline antagonist in the mouse elevated plus maze. *Behavioural Brain Research, 158*(2), 339–348.

CNN.com. (2008, July 1). Tape shows woman dying on waiting room floor. Retrieved June 15, 2010, from http://www.cnn.com/2008/US/07/01/waiting.room.death/index.html.

Cohen, S., Doyle, W.J., Turner, R., Alper, C.M., & Skoner, D.P. (2003). Sociability and susceptibility to the common cold. *Psychological Science, 14*(5), 389–395.

Cohen, S., Gottlieb, B.H., & Underwood, L.G. (2001a). Social relationships and health: Challenges for measurement and intervention. *Advances in Mind-Body Medicine, 17*(2), 129–141.

Cohen, S., Miller, G.E., & Rabin, B.S. (2001b). Psychological stress and antibody response to immunization: A critical review of the human literature. *Psychosomatic Medicine, 63*(1), 7–18.

Cohn, L.D., Macfarlane, S., Yanez, C., & Imai, W.K. (1995). Risk-perception: Differences between adolescents and adults. *Health Psychology, 14,* 217–222.

Cole, J.O., & Chiarello, R.J. (1990). The benzodiazepines as drugs of abuse. *Journal of Psychiatric Research, 24,* 135–144.

Collaer, M.L., & Hines, M. (1995). Human behavioral sex differences: A role for gonadal hormones during early development? *Psychological Bulletin, 118,* 55–107.

Collaer, M.L., & Nelson, J.D. (2002). Large visuospatial sex difference in line judgment: Possible role of attentional factors. *Brain & Cognition, 49*(1), 1–12.

College of Family Physicians of Canada. (2007). Insomnia: How to get a good night sleep. Retrieved on August 14, 2010, from http://www.cfpc.ca/English/cfpc/programs/patient%20education/insomnia/default.asp.

Colvin, M.K., Funnell, M.G., & Gazzaniga, M.S. (2005). Numerical processing in the two hemispheres: Studies of a split-brain patient. *Brain & Cognition, 57*(1), 43–52.

Comaty, J.E., Stasio, M., & Advokat, C. (2001). Analysis of outcome variables of a token economy system in a state psychiatric hospital: A program evaluation. *Research in Developmental Disabilities, 22*(3), 233–253.

Conklin, H.M., & Iacono, W.G. (2002). Schizophrenia: A neurodevelopmental perspective. *Current Directions in Psychological Science, 11*(1), 33–37.

Conrad, P.J., Peterson, J.B., & Pihl, R.O. (2001). Reliability and validity of alcohol-induced heart rate increase as a measure of sensitivity to the stimulant properties of alcohol. *Psychopharmacology, 157*(1), 20–30.

Constantinidis, C., Franowicz, M.N., & Goldman- Rakic, P.S. (2001). Coding specificity in cortical microcircuits: A multiple-electrode analysis of primate prefontal cortex. *Journal of Neuroscience, 21*(10), 3646–3655.

Coon, D., Mitterer, J.O., Brown, P., Malik, R., McKenzie, S. (2010). *Psychology: A journey* (3rd Canadian ed.). Toronto, ON: Nelson.

Cooper, M., Galbraith, M., & Drinkwater, J. (2001). Assumptions and beliefs in adolescents with anorexia nervosa and their mothers. *Eating Disorders: The Journal of Treatment & Prevention, 9*(3), 217–223.

Cooper, Z., & Fairburn, C.G. (2001). A new cognitive behavioural approach to the treatment of obesity. *Behaviour Research & Therapy, 39*(5), 499–511.

Corballis, P.M., Funnell, M.G., & Gazzaniga, M.S. (2002). Hemispheric asymmetries for simple visual judgments in the split brain. *Neuropsychologia, 40*(4), 401–410.

Corwin, R.L. (2000). Biological and behavioral consequences of food restriction. *Appetite, 34*(1), 112.

Cory, G.A. (2002). MacLean's evolutionary neuroscience, the CSN model and Hamilton's rule: Some developmental, clinical, and social policy implications. *Brain & Mind, 3*(1), 151–181.

Cote, S., Geoffroy, M-C., Borge, A., Rutter, M., & Tremblay, R.E. (2008). Nonmaternal care in infancy and emotional/behavioural difficulties at 4 years old: Moderation by family risk characteristics. *Developmental Psychology, 44,* 155–168.

Coursey, R.D., Ward-Alexander, L., & Katz, B. (1990). Cost-effectiveness of providing insurance benefits for posthospital psychiatric halfway house stays. *American Psychologist, 45,* 1118–1126.

Cowen, P.J. (2002). Cortisol, serotonin and depression: All stressed out? *British Journal of Psychiatry, 180*(2), 99–100.

Cox, W.M., & Alm, R. (2005, February 25). Scientists are made, not born. *The New York Times online.*

Craik, F.I.M., & Lockhart, R.S. (1972). Levels of processing. *Journal of Verbal Learning and Verbal Behavior, 11,* 671–684.

Crano, W.D. (2000) Milestones in the psychological analysis of social influence. *Group Dynamics, 4*(1), 68–80.

Craske, M.G., & Zucker, B.G. (2001). Consideration of the APA practice guideline for the treatment of patients with panic disorder: Strengths and limitations for behavior therapy. *Behavior Therapy, 32*(2), 259–281.

Crews, D. (1994). Animal sexuality. *Scientific American, 270*(1), 108–114.

Crick, N.R., & Dodge, K.A. (1994). A review and reformulation of social information-processing mechanisms in children's social adjustment. *Psychological Bulletin, 115,* 74–101.

Criminal Code R.S.C. 1985, c.46 s.16(1).

Crisp, R.J., & Nicel, J.K. (2004). Disconfirming intergroup evaluations: Asymmetric effects for ingroups and out-groups. *Journal of Social Psychology, 144*(3), 247–271.

Crusco, A.H., & Wetzel, C.G. (1984). The Midas touch: The effects of interpersonal touch on restaurant tip-ping. *Personality and Social Psychology Bulletin, 10,* 512–517.

Cuellar, J.C., & Curry, T.R. (2007). The prevalence and comorbidity between delinquency, drug abuse, suicide attempts, physical and sexual abuse, and self-mutilation among delinquent Hispanic females. *Hispanic Journal of Behavioral Sciences, 29*(1), 68–82.

Cummins, R.A., & Nistico, H. (2002). Maintaining life satis-faction: The role of positive cognitive bias. *Journal of Happiness Studies, 3*(1), 37–69.

Cumsille, P.E., Sayer, A.G., & Graham, J.W. (2000). Perceived exposure to peer and adult drinking as predictors of growth in positive alcohol expectancies during adolescence. *Journal of Consulting and Clinical Psychology, 68*(3), 531–536.

Czeiler, C.A., Buxton, O., & Khalsa, S. (2005). The human circadian timing system and sleep-wake regulation. In M.H. Kryger, T. Roth, & W.C. Dement (eds.), *Principles and practice of sleep medicine.* Philadelphia: Elsevier Saunders.

D

The Daily. (June 15, 2004). *Canadian community health survey.* Retrieved May 6, 2010, from http://www .statcan.gc.ca/daily-quotidien/040615/dq040615b-eng .htm.

Dalkvist, J. (2001). The ganzfeld method: Its current status. *European Journal of Parapsychology, 16,* 19–22.

Damasio, A.R. (2000). A neural basis for sociopathy. *Archives of General Psychiatry online, 57*(2).

Darley, J.M., & Latané, B. (1968). Bystander intervention in emergencies: Diffusion of responsibility. *Journal of Personality and Social Psychology, 8,* 377–383.

Darley, J.M., & Pittman, T.S. (2003). The psychology of com-pensatory and retributive justice. *Personality and Social Psychology Review, 7,* 324–336.

Darwin, C.A. (1871). *The descent of man, and selection in relation to sex.* London: J. Murray.

Darwin, C.A. (1872). *The expression of the emotions in man and animals.* London: J. Murray.

Davis, C., Strachan, S., & Berkson, M. (2004). Sensitivity to reward: Implications for overeating and overweight. *Appetite, 42*(2), 131–138.

Davis, S. (2000). Testosterone and sexual desire in women. *Journal of Sex Education & Therapy, 25*(1), 25–32.

Dawood, K., Pillard, R.C., Horvath, C., Revelle, W., & Bailey, J.M. (2000). Familial aspects of male homosexuality. *Archives of Sexual Behavior, 29*(2), 155–163.

Dawson, T.L. (2002). New tools, new insights: Kohlberg's moral judgement stages revisited. *International Journal of Behavioral Development, 26*(2), 154–166.

De Houwer, J., Thomas, S., & Baeyens, F. (2001). Associative learning of likes and dislikes: A review of 25 years of research on human evaluative conditioning. *Psychological Bulletin, 127*(6), 853–869.

De Koninck, J. (1997). Sleep, the common denominator for psy-chological adaptation, *Canadian Psychology, 38,* 191–195.

De Maat, S., Dekker, J., Schoevers, R., & De Jonghe, F. (2006). Relative efficacy of psychotherapy and phar-macotherapy in the treatment of depression: A meta-analysis. *Psychotherapy Research, 16*(5), 562–572.

de Mello, M.F., et al. (2005). A systematic review of research findings on the efficacy of interpersonal therapy for depressive disorders. *European Archives of Psychiatry & Clinical Neuroscience, 255*(2), 75–82.

De Michele, P.E., Gansneder, B., & Solomon, G.B. (1998). Success and failure attributions of wrestlers: Further evidence of the self-serving bias. *Journal of Sport Behavior, 21*(3), 242–255.

DeAngelis, T. (2008). PTSD treatments grow in evidence, effectiveness. *Monitor on Psychology, 39*(1).

DeCasper, A.J., & Spence, M.J. (1986). Prenatal maternal speech influences newborns' perception of speech sounds. *Infant Behavior and Development, 9,* 133–150.

Deecher, D., Andree, T.H., Sloan, D., & Schechter, L.E. (2008). From menarche to menopause: Exploring the underlying biology of depression in women experiencing hormonal changes. *Psychoneuroendocrinology, 33*(1), 3–17.

Delgado, J.M.R. (1969). *Physical control of the mind.* New York: Harper & Row.

Delves, P.J., & Roitt, I.M. (2000). Advances in immunology: The immune system. *The New England Journal of Medicine online, 343*(1).

Dennerstein, L.L. (2003). The sexual impact of menopause. In S.B. Levine, et al. (Eds.), *Handbook of clinical sexuality for mental health professionals* (pp. 187–198). New York: Brunner-Routledge.

DeRubeis, R.J., et al. (2005). Cognitive therapy vs. medica-tions in the treatment of moderate to severe depres-sion. *Archives of General Psychiatry, 62*(4), 409–416.

DeSteno, D., Petty, R.E., Rucker, D.D., Wegener, D.T., & Braverman, J. (2004). Discrete emotions and persuasion: The role of emotion induced expectancies. *Journal of Personality & Social Psychology, 86*(1), 43–56.

Devilly, G.J. (2002). Eye movement desensitization and reprocessing: A chronology of its development and scientific standing. *Scientific Review of Mental Health Practice, 1*(2), 113–138.

DeVries, R. (2000). Vygotsky, Piaget, and education: A reciprocal assimilation of theories and educational practices. *New Ideas in Psychology, 18*(2–3), 187–213.

Diener, E., Napa Scollon, C.K., Oishi, S., Dzokoto, V., Suh, E.M. (2000). Positivity and the construction of life satisfaction judgments: Global happiness is not the sum of its parts. *Journal of Happiness Studies, 1*(2), 159–176.

Dierker, L.C., et al. (2001). Association between psychiatric disorders and the progression of tobacco use behaviors. *Journal of the American Academy of Child & Adolescent Psychiatry, 40*(10), 1159–1167.

Dietrich, A. (2004). Neurocognitive mechanisms underlying the experience of flow. *Consciousness & Cognition: An International Journal, 13*(4), 746–761.

DiLalla, D.L., Carey, G., Gottesman, I.I., & Bouchard, T.J., Jr. (1996). Heritability of MMPI personality indicators of psychopathology in twins reared apart. *Journal of Abnormal Psychology, 105,* 491–499.

Diseth, T.H. (2005). Dissociation in children and adolescents as reaction to trauma—An overview of conceptual issues and neurobiological factors. *Nordic Journal of Psychiatry, 59*(2), 79–91.

Dogil, G., et al. (2002). The speaking brain: A tutorial introduction to fMRI experiments in the production of speech, prosody and syntax. *Journal of Neurolinguistics, 15*(1), 59–90.

Domhoff, G.W. (2001). A new neurocognitive theory of dreams. *Dreaming: Journal of the Association for the Study of Dreams, 11*(1), 13–33.

Domhoff, G.W. (2003). *The scientific study of dreams: Neural networks, cognitive development, and content analysis.* Washington, DC: American Psychological Association.

Donohue, K F., Curtin, J.J., Patrick, C.J., & Lang, A.R. (2007). Intoxication level and emotional response. *Emotion, 7*(1), 103–112.

Dovidio, J.F., et al. (2004). Perspective and prejudice: Antecedents and mediating mechanisms. *Personality & Social Psychology Bulletin, 30*(12), 1537–1549.

Duckitt, J., Wagner, C., Du Plessis, I., & Birum, I. (2002). The psychological bases of ideology and prejudice: Testing a dual process model. *Journal of Personality and Social Psychology, 83,* 75–93.

Duffy, V.B., Peterson, J.M., & Bartoshuk, L.M. (2004). Associations between taste genetics, oral sensation and alcohol intake. *Physiology & Behavior, 82*(2–3), 435–445.

Dunkley, D.M., Zuroff, D.C., & Blankstein, K.R. (2003). Self-critical perfectionism and daily affect: Dispositional and situational influences on stress and coping. *Journal of Personality & Social Psychology, 84*(1), 234–252.

Durbin, D.L., Darling, N., Steinberg, L., & Brown, B.B. (1993). Parenting style and peer group membership among European American adolescents. *Journal of Research on Adolescence, 3*(1), 87–100.

Dweck, C.S. (2002a). Messages that motivate: How praise molds students' beliefs, motivation, and performance (in surprising ways). In J. Aronson, (Ed.), *Improving academic achievement: Impact of psychological factors on education* (pp. 37–60). San Diego: Academic Press.

Dweck, C.S. (2002b). The development of ability conceptions. In A. Wigfield & J.S. Eccles (Eds.), *Development of achievement motivation* (pp. 57–88). San Diego: Academic Press.

d'Ydewalle, G., Luwel, K., & Brunfaut, E. (1999). The importance of on-going concurrent activities as a function of age in time- and event-based prospective memory. *European Journal of Cognitive Psychology, 11*(2), 219–237.

E

Eagle, M. (2000). Repression, part I of II. *Psychoanalytic Review, 87*(1), 1–38.

Ebbinghaus, H. (1913). *Memory: A contribution to experimental psychology.* (H.A. Roger & C.E. Bussenius, Trans.). New York: Columbia University Press. (Original work published 1885).

Eberly, M.B., & Montemayor, R. (1999). Adolescent affection and helpfulness toward parents: A 2–year follow-up. *Journal of Early Adolescence, 19*(2), 226–248.

Egawa, T., et al. (2002). Impairment of spatial memory in kaolin-induced hydrocephalic rats is associated with changes in the hippocampal cholinergic and noradrenergic contents. *Behavioural Brain Research, 129*(1–2), 31–39.

Egerton, A., Allison, C., Brett, R.R., & Pratt, J.A. (2006). Cannabinoids and prefrontal cortical function: Insights from preclinical studies. *Neuroscience & Biobehavioral Reviews, 30*(5), 680–695.

Eichenbaum, H., & Fortin, N. (2003). Episodic memory and the hippocampus: It's about time. *Current Directions in Psychological Science, 12*(2), 53–57.

Eikeseth, S., Smith, T., Jahr, E., & Eldevik, S. (2007). Outcome for children with Autism who began intensive behavioral treatment between ages 4 and 7: A comparison controlled study. *Behaviour Modification, 31,* 264–278.

Ekman, P. (1993). Facial expression and emotion. *American Psychologist, 48,* 384–392.

Ekman, P. (1999). Facial expressions. In T. Dalgleish & M.J. Power (Eds.), *Handbook of cognition and emotion* (pp. 301–320). New York: John Wiley & Sons.

Ekman, P. (2003). Cited in Foreman, J. (2003, August 5). A conversation with: Paul Ekman: The 43 facial muscles that reveal even the most fleeting emotions. *The New York Times online.*

Ekman, P., et al. (1987). Universals and cultural differences in the judgments of facial expressions of emotion. *Journal of Personality and Social Psychology, 53,* 712–717.

Elkind, D. (1967). Egocentrism in adolescence. *Child Development, 38,* 1025–1034.

Elkind, D. (1985). Egocentrism redux. *Developmental Review, 5,* 218–226.

Elkind, D., & Bowen, R. (1979). Imaginary audience behavior in children and adolescents. *Developmental Psychology, 15*(1), 38–44.

Ellickson, P.L., Tucker, J.S., Klein, D.J., & McGuigan, K.A. (2001). Prospective risk factors for alcohol misuse in late adolescence. *Journal of Studies on Alcohol, 62*(6), 773–782.

Ellis, A. (1995). Changing rational emotive therapy (RET) to rational emotive behavior therapy (REBT). *Journal of Rational-Emotive & Cognitive-Behavior Therapy, 13,* 85–89.

Ellis, A. (2001). *Overcoming destructive beliefs, feelings, and behaviours: New directions for Rational Emotive Behaviour Therapy.* Amherst, NY: Prometheus Books.

Ellis, A. (2004a). How my theory and practice of psychotherapy has influenced and changed other psychotherapies. *Journal of Rational-Emotive & Cognitive Behavior Therapy, 22*(2), 79–83.

Ellis, A. (2004b). Why rational emotive behavior therapy is the most comprehensive and effective form of behavior therapy. *Journal of Rational-Emotive & Cognitive Behavior Therapy, 22*(2), 85–92.

Ellsworth, P.C., Carlsmith, J.M., & Henson, A. (1972). The stare as a stimulus to flight in human subjects. *Journal of Personality and Social Psychology, 21,* 302–311.

Emmons, R.A., & King, L.A. (1988). Conflict among personal strivings: Immediate and long-term implications for psychological and physical well-being. *Journal of Personality & Social Psychology, 54*(6), 1040–1048.

Enard, W., et al. (2002). Molecular evolution of FOXP2, a gene involved in speech and language. *Nature, 418*(6900), 869–872.

Engels, G.I., Garnefski, N., & Diekstra, R.F.W. (1993). Efficacy of rational-emotive therapy. *Journal of Consulting and Clinical Psychology, 61,* 1083–1090.

Erikson, E.H. (1963). *Childhood and society.* New York: W.W. Norton.

Eron, L.D. (1982). Parent–child interaction, television violence, and aggression of children. *American Psychologist, 37,* 197–211.

Eslinger, P.J., Flaherty-Craig, C.V., & Benton, A.L. (2004). Developmental outcomes after early prefrontal cortex damage. *Brain & Cognition, 55*(1), 84–403.

Evans, L., et al. (2005). Familiality of temperament in bipolar disorder: Support for a genetic spectrum. *Journal of Affective Disorders, 85*(1–2), 153–168.

Everly, G.S. (2002). Thoughts on peer (para-professional) support in the provision of mental health services. *International Journal of Emergency Mental Health, 4,* 89–92.

Eysenck, H.J., & Eysenck, M.W. (1985). *Personality and individual differences.* New York: Plenum.

F

Fantz, R.L. (1961). The origin of form perception. *Scientific American, 204*(5), 66–72.

Farber, B.A., Brink, D.C., & Raskin, P.M. (1996). *The psychotherapy of Carl Rogers: Cases and commentary* (pp. 74–75). New York: Guilford Press.

Farmer A., Elkin A., & McGuffin P. (2007). The genetics of bipolar affective disorder. *Current Opinion in Psychiatry, 20,* 8–12.

Farmer, A., Eley, T.C., & McGuffin, P. (2005). Current strategies for investigating the genetic and environmental risk factors for affective disorders. *British Journal of Psychiatry, 186*(3), 179–181.

Feeney, B.C. (2004). A secure base: Responsive support of goal strivings and exploration in adult intimate relationships. *Journal of Personality & Social Psychology, 87*(5), 631–648.

Festinger, L., & Carlsmith, J.M. (1959). Cognitive consequences of forced compliance. *Journal of Abnormal and Social Psychology, 58,* 203–210.

Field, T., Gewirtz, J., Cohen, D., Garcia, R., Greenberg, R., & Collins, K. (1984). Leave-Takings and reunions of infants, toddlers, preschoolers, and their parents. *Child Development, 55,* 628–635.

Fields, R.D. (2005, February). Making memories stick. *Scientific American,* 75–81.

Fifer, W.P., & Moon, C. (2003). Prenatal development. In A. Slater & G. Bremner (Eds.), *An introduction to developmental psychology* (pp. 95–114). Malden, MA: Blackwell Publishers.

Finkenauer, C., et al. (1998). Flashbulb memories and the underlying mechanisms of their formation: Toward an emotional-integrative model. *Memory & Cognition, 26*(3), 516–531.

Fisher, H.E. (2000). Brains do it: Lust, attraction and attachment. *Cerebrum, 2,* 23–42.

Flavell, J.H. (2000). Development of children's knowledge about the mental world. *International Journal of Behavioral Development, 24*(1), 15–23.

Fletcher, B., Pine, K.J., Woodbridge, Z., & Nash, A. (2007). How visual images of chocolate affect the craving and guilt of female dieters. *Appetite, 48*(2), 211–217.

Flett, G.L., Madorsky, D., Hewitt, P.L., & Heisel, M.J. (2002). Perfectionism cognitions, rumination, and psychological distress. *Journal of Rational-Emotive & Cognitive Behavior Therapy, 20*(1), 33–47.

Flouri, E., & Buchanan, A. (2003). The role of father involvement and mother involvement in adolescents' psychological well-being. *British Journal of Social Work, 33*(3), 399–406.

Flynn, J.R. (2003). Movies about intelligence: The limitations of g. *Current Directions in Psychological Science, 12,* 95–99.

Foerster, J., Higgins, E.T., & Strack, F. (2000). When stereotype disconfirmation is a personal threat: How prejudice and prevention focus moderate incongruency effects. *Social Cognition, 18*(2), 178–197.

Folkman, S., & Moskowitz, T. (2000). Positive affect and the other side of coping. *American Psychologist, 55*(6), 647–654.

Fontaine, K.R., Redden, D.T., Wang, C., Westfall, A.O., & Allison, D.B. (2003). Years of life lost due to obesity. *Journal of the American Medical Association, 289*(2), 187–193.

Förster, J., Higgins, E.T., & Werth, L. (2004). How threat from stereotype disconfirmation triggers self-defense. *Social Cognition, 22*(1), 54–74.

Fortin, S., Godbout, L., & Braun, C.M.J. (2002). Strategic sequence planning and prospective memory impairments in frontally lesioned head trauma patients performing activities of daily living. *Brain & Cognition, 48*(2–3), 361–365.

Foulkes, D. (1996). Dream research: 1953–1993. *Sleep, 19,* 609–624.

Fouts, R.S. (1997). *Next of kin: What chimpanzees have taught me about who we are.* New York: Morrow.

Francis, L.J., Katz, Y.J., Yablon, Y., & Robbins, M. (2004). Religiosity, personality, and happiness: A study among Israeli male undergraduates. *Journal of Happiness Studies, 5(4),* 315–333.

Freedman, J.A. (2002). *Media violence and its effect on aggression: Assessing the scientific evidence.* Toronto: University of Toronto Press.

Freud, S. (1927). A religious experience. In *Standard edition of the complete psychological works of Sigmund Freud* (Vol. 21). London: Hogarth Press, 1964.

Frisch, R. (1997). Cited in Angier, N. (1997). Chemical tied to fat control could help trigger puberty. *The New York Times,* pp. C1, C3.

Fritsch, G., & Hitzig, E. (1960). On the electrical excitability of the cerebrum. In G. von Bonin (Ed.), *Some papers on the cerebral cortex.* Springfield, IL: Charles C. Thomas. (Original work published 1870).

Fromme, K., et al. (2004). Biological and behavioral markers of alcohol sensitivity. *Alcoholism: Clinical & Experimental Research, 28*(2), 247–256.

Fuertes, A., et al. (2002). Factores asociados a las conductas sexuales de reigso en la adolencia. *Infancia y Aprendizaje, 25*(3), 347–361.

Fuligni, A.J., & Witkow, M. (2004). The postsecondary educational progress of youth from immigrant families. *Journal of Research on Adolescence, 14*(2), 159–183.

Furnham, A., Petrides, K.V., Sisterson, G., & Baluch, B. (2003). Repressive coping style and positive self-presentation. *British Journal of Health Psychology, 8*(2), 223–249.

G

Gais, S., & Born, J. (2004). Declarative memory consolidation: Mechanisms acting during human sleep. *Learning & Memory, 11*(6), 679–685.

Galambos, N.L., Barker, E.T., & Almeida, D.M. (2003). Parents do matter: Trajectories of change in externalizing and internalizing problems in early adolescence. *Child Development, 74*(2), 578–594.

Galea, S., & Resnick, H. (2005). Post-traumatic stress disorder in the general population after mass terrorist incidents: Considerations about the nature of exposure. *CNS Spectrum, 10*(2), 107–115.

Garb, H.N., Wood, J.M., Lilienfeld, S.O., & Nezworski, M.T. (2005). Roots of the Rorschach controversy. *Clinical Psychology Review, 25*(1), 97–118.

Garcia, J., & Koelling, R.A. (1966). Relation of cue to consequences in avoidance learning. *Psychonomic Science, 4,* 123–124.

Garcia, J., Brett, L.P., & Rusiniak, K.W. (1989). Limits of Darwinian conditioning. In S.B. Klein & R.R. Mowrer (Eds.), *Contemporary learning theories: Instrumental conditioning theory and the impact of biological constraints on learning.* Hillsdale, NJ: Erlbaum.

Gardner, H. (1983/1993). *Frames of mind.* New York: Basic Books.

Gardner, H. (2001, April 5). Multiple intelligence. *The New York Times,* p. A20.

Gay, P. (1999). Psychoanalyst: Sigmund Freud. *Time, 153,* 66. This article summarizes the work of Sigmund Freud and the contributions he made to psychology and the world.

Geddes, J. (2006, January 23). Canadian nationalism in decline, says poll. In *The Canadian encyclopedia: Maclean's Magazine.* Retrieved May 21, 2010, from http://www.encyclopediecanadienne.ca.

Geddes, J. (2010, May 18). Outsiders don't get us and hockey. *Macleans.ca.* Retrieved May 21, 2010, from http://www2.macleans.ca/2010/05/18/outsiders-don't-get-us-and-hockey/.

Geers, A., Spehar, B., & Sedey, A. (2002). Use of speech by children from total communication programs who wear cochlear implants. *American Journal of Speech-Language Pathology, 11*(1), 50–58.

Gegenfurtner, K.R., & Kiper, D.C. (2003). Color vision. *Annual Review of Neuroscience, 26,* 181–206.

Gendall, K.A., Bulik, C.M., Joyce, P.R., McIntosh, V.V., & Carter, F.A. (2000). Menstrual cycle irregularity in bulimia nervosa: Associated factors and changes with treatment. *Journal of Psychosomatic Research, 49*(6), 409–415.

Gentry, M.V., et al. (2000). Nicotine patches improve mood and response speed in a lexical decision task. *Addictive Behaviors, 25*(4), 549–557.

Gershoff, E.T. (2002). Corporal punishment by parents and associated child behaviors and experiences: A meta-analytic and theoretical review. *Psychological Bulletin, 128*(4), 539–579.

Geschwind, N., & Galaburda, A.M. (1987). *Cerebral lateralization: Biological mechanisms, associations, and pathology.* Cambridge, MA: Harvard University Press.

Getzels, J.W., & Jackson, P.W. (1962). *Creativity and intelligence.* New York: Wiley.

Gignac, G., & Vernon, P.A. (2003). Digit symbol rotation: A more g-loaded version of the traditional digit symbol sub-test. *Intelligence, 31*(1), 1–8.

Gigone, D., & Hastie, R. (1997). Proper analysis of the accuracy of group judgments. *Psychological Bulletin, 121,* 149–167.

Gijsman, H.J., et al. (2002). A dose-finding study on the effects of branch chain amino acids on surrogate markers of brain dopamine function. *Psychopharmacology, 160*(2), 192–197.

Gilligan, C. (1982). *In a different voice.* Cambridge, MA: Harvard University Press.

Gilligan, C., Ward, J.V., & Taylor, J.M. (1989). *Mapping the moral domain: A contribution of women's thinking to psychological theory and education.* Cambridge, MA: Harvard University Press.

Gilovich, T., & Eibach, R. (2001). The fundamental attribution error where it really counts. *Psychological Inquiry, 12*(1), 23–26.

Gilovich, T., et al. (Eds.). (2002). *Heuristics and biases: The psychology of intuitive judgment* (pp. 348–366). New York: Cambridge University Press.

Glantz, L.A., & Lewis, D.A. (2000). Decreased dendritic spine density on prefrontal cortical pyramidal neurons in schizophrenia. *Archives of General Psychiatry, 57*(1), 65–73.

Glaser, R., et al. (1993). Stress and the memory Tcell response to the Epstein-Barr virus. *Health Psychology, 12,* 435–442.

Godfrey, J.R. (2004). Toward optimal health: The experts discuss therapeutic humor. *Journal of Women's Health, 13*(5), 474–479.

Goldman-Rakic, P.S. (1995). Cited in Goleman, D. (1995, May 2). Biologists find site of working memory. *The New York Times,* pp. C1, C9.

Goldman-Rakic, P.S., et al. (2000b). Memory. In M.S. Gazzaniga (Ed.), *The new cognitive neurosciences* (2nd ed., pp. 733–840). Cambridge, MA: MIT Press.

Goldman-Rakic, P.S., Muly, E.C., III, & Williams, G.V. (2000a). D-sub-1 receptors in prefrontal cells and circuits. *Brain Research Reviews, 31*(2–3), 295–301.

Goldstein, E.B. (2004). *Sensation and perception, media edition.* (6th ed.). Belmont, CA: Wadsworth Publishing Company.

Goleman, D.J. (1995). *Emotional intelligence.* New York: Bantam Books.

Gomez, P., Zimmermann, P., Guttormsen-Schär, S., & Danuser, B. (2005). Respiratory responses associated with affective processing of film stimuli. *Biological Psychology, 68*(3), 223–235.

Gonzalez, C., Dana, J., Koshino, H., & Just, M. (2005). The framing effect and risky decisions: Examining cognitive functions with fMRI. *Journal of Economic Psychology, 26*(1), 1–20.

Goodale, M.A. & Humphrey, G.K. (1998). The objects of action and perception. *Cognition, 67,* 179–205.

Goodall, J. (2000). *Africa in my blood: An autobiography in letters.* Boston: Houghton Mifflin.

Goode, E. (2000, June 25). Thinner: The male battle with anorexia. *The New York Times,* p. MH8.

Goodenough, F.L., & Harris, D.B. (1950). Studies in the psychology of children's drawings: II 1928–1949. *Psychological Bulletin, 47,* 369–433.

Goodwin, P.J., et al. (2001). The effect of group psychosocial support on survival in metastatic breast cancer. *New England Journal of Medicine, 345*(24), 1719–1726.

Gorodetsky, M., & Klavir, R. (2003). What can we learn from how gifted/average pupils describe their processes of problem solving? *Learning & Instruction, 13*(3), 305–325.

Gottesman, I.I. (1991). *Schizophrenia genesis.* New York: Freeman.

Gould, S.J. (2002). *The structure of evolutionary theory.* Cambridge, MA: Belknap Press/Harvard University Press.

Government of Canada. (2006). *The human face of mental illness in Canada 2006.* No. HP5-19/2006E.

Grady, C.L., McIntosh, A.R., Rajah, M.N., Beig, S., & Craik, F.I.M. (1999). The effects of age on the neural correlates of episodic encoding. *Cerebral Cortex, 9*(8), 805–814.

Granot, D., & Mayseless, O. (2001). Attachment security and adjustment to school in middle childhood. *International Journal of Behavioral Development, 25*(6), 530–541.

Grazebrook, K., & Garland, A. (2005, July). *What are cognitive and/or behavioural psychotherapies?* Retrieved July 6, 2010, from http://www.babcp.com/silo/files/what-is-cbt.pdf.

Greenbaum, P. & Rosenfeld, H.M. (1978). Patterns of avoidance in response to interpersonal staring and proximity: Effects of bystanders on drivers at a traffic intersection. *Journal of Personality and Social Psychology, 36,* 575–587.

Griffin, C. (2001). Imagining new narratives of youth. *Childhood: A Global Journal of Child Research, 8*(2), 147–166.

Griffin, K.W., Botvin, G.J., Nichols, T.R., & Scheier, L.M. (2004). Low perceived chances for success in life and binge drinking among inner-city minority youth. *Journal of Adolescent Health, 34*(6), 501–507.

Griffin, M.G. (2008). A prospective assessment of auditory startle alterations in rape and physical assault survivors. *Journal of Traumatic Stress, 21*(1), 91–99.

Griggs, R.A., & Ransdell, S.E. (1987), Misconceptions tests or misconceived tests? *Teaching of Psychology*, 14, 210–214.

Grusec, J.E. (2002). Parenting socialization and children's acquisition of values. In M.H. Bornstein (Ed.), *Handbook of parenting: Vol. 5: Practical issues in parenting* (2nd ed., pp. 143–167).

Guerin, B. (1999). Social behaviors as determined by different arrangements of social consequences: Social loafing, social facilitation, deindividuation, and a modified social loafing. *Psychological Record, 49*(4), 565–578.

Guilford, J.P. (1967). *The nature of human intelligence.* New York: McGraw-Hill.

Gupta, V.B., Nwosa, N.M., Nadel, T.A., & Inamdar, S. (2001). Externalizing behaviors and television viewing in children of low-income minority parents. *Clinical Pediatrics, 40*(6), 337–341.

H

Haaga, D.A.F., & Davison, G.C. (1993). An appraisal of rational-emotive therapy. *Journal of Consulting and Clinical Psychology, 61,* 215–220.

Haas, L.J., Benedict, J.G., & Kobos, J.C. (1996). Psychotherapy by telephone: Risks and benefits for psychologists and consumers. *Professional Psychology: Research & Practice, 27,* 154–160.

Habib, M., & Robichon, F. (2003). Structural correlates of brain asymmetry: Studies in left-handed and dyslexic individuals. In K. Hugdahl & R.J. Davidson (Eds.), *The asymmetrical brain* (pp. 681–716). Cambridge, MA: MIT Press.

Haenen, J. (2001). Outlining the teaching–learning process: Piotr Gal'perin's contribution. *Learning & Instruction, 11*(2), 157–170.

Haffenden, A.M., Schiff, K.C., & Goodale, M.A. (2001). The dissociation between perception and action in the Ebbinghaus illusion: Nonillusory effects of pictorial cues on grasp. *Current Biology, 11,* 177–181.

Halpern, D.F. (2003). Sex differences in cognitive abilities. *Applied Cognitive Psychology, 17*(3), 375–376.

Halpern, D.F., & LaMay, M.L. (2000). The smarter sex: A critical review of sex differences in intelligence. *Educational Psychology Review, 12*(2), 229–246.

Halpern, D.F., Hansen, C., & Riefer, D. (1990). Analogies as an aid to understanding and memory. *Journal of Educational Psychology, 82,* 298–305.

Han, W., Leventhal, T., & Linver, M.R. (2004). The Home Observation for Measurement of the Environment (HOME) in middle childhood: A study of three large-scale data sets. *Parenting: Science & Practice, 4*(2–3), 189–210.

Haney, C., Banks, C., & Zimbardo, P. (1973). Interpersonal dynamics in a simulated prison. *International Journal of Criminology & Penology, 1*(1), 69–97.

Hankin, B.L., & Abramson, L.Y. (2001). Development of gender differences in depression: An elaborated cognitive vulnerability-transactional stress theory. *Psychological Bulletin, 127*(6), 773–796.

Hankin, B.L., Fraley, R.C., & Abela, J.R.Z. (2005). Daily depression and cognitions about cognitive style and the prediction of depressive symptoms in a prospective daily diary study. *Journal of Personality and Social Psychology, 88*(4), 673–685.

Hansell, N.K., et al. (2001). Genetic influence on ERP slow wave measures of working memory. *Behavior Genetics, 31*(6), 603–614.

Haridakis, P.M. (2002). Viewer characteristics, exposure to television violence, and aggression. *Media Psychology, 4*(4), 323–352.

Harlow, H.F. (1959). Love in infant monkeys. *Scientific American, 200,* 68–86.

Harlow, J.M. (1868). Recovery from the passage of an iron bar through the head. *Publication of the Massachusetts Medical Society, 2,* 327.

Hart, J.W., Bridgett, D., & Karau, S. (2001). Coworker ability and effort as determinants of individual effort on a collective task. *Group Dynamics, 5*(3), 181–190.

Hawkley, L., & Cacioppo, J. (2004). Stress and the aging immune system. *Brain, Behavior & Immunity, 18*(2), 114–119.

Health Canada. (2005a). *Frequently asked questions—medical marihuana.* Retrieved on May 6, 2010 from http://www.hc-sc.gc.ca/dhp-mps/marihuana/about-apropos/faq-eng.php#a3.

Health Canada. (2005b). *Sexually Transmitted Infections (STIs).* Retrieved on August 15, 2010 from http://www.hc-sc.gc.ca/hc-ps/dc-ma/sti-its-eng.php.

Health Canada. (2006). *Benefits and risks of hormone replacement therapy (estrogen with or without progestin).* Retrieved on August 8, 2010, from http://www.hc-sc.gc.ca/hl-vs/iyh-vsv/med/estrogen-eng.php.

Health Canada. (June, 2009). *Canadian Alcohol & Drug Use Monitoring Survey of 2008.* Retrieved on May 15, 2010, from http://www.hc-sc.gc.ca/hc-ps/drugs-drogues/stat/_2008/summary-sommaire-eng.php.

Heart and Stroke Foundation of Canada. (2009). *Statistics.* Retrieved August 16, 2010, from http://www .heartandstroke.com/site/c.ikIQLcMWJtE/b.3483991/ k.34A8/Statistics.htm#heartdisease.

Heidenreich, T., & Michalak, J. (2003). Mindfulness as a treatment principle in behavior therapy. *Verhaltenstherapie, 13*(4), 264–274.

Heimpel, S.A., Wood, J.V., Marshall, M.A., & Brown, J.D. (2002). Do people with low self-esteem really want to feel better? Self-esteem differences in motivation to repair negative moods. *Journal of Personality & Social Psychology, 82*(1), 128–147.

Heinrichs, R.W. (2005). The primacy of cognition in schizophrenia. *American Psychologist, 60*(3), 229–242.

Heinz, A. (2004). Reward and dependence—A psychological and neurobiological analysis of reward mechanisms and of their role in dependence (European University Studies, Vol. 685). *Addiction, 99*(11), 1482.

Helms, J.E. (1992). Why is there no study of cultural equivalence of standardized cognitive ability testing? *American Psychologist, 47,* 1083–1101.

Hergenhahn, B.R. (2005). An introduction to the history of psychology (5th ed.). Belmont, CA: Thomson Wadsworth.

Hergenhahn, B.R. (2009). *History of psychology* (6th ed.). Belmont, CA: Wadsworth Publishing Company.

Herrntein, R. & Murray, C. (1994). *The bell curve: Intelligence and class structure in American life.* New York: Free Press.

Hertz-Pannier, L., et al. (2002). Late plasticity for language in a child's non-dominant hemisphere: A pre- and post-surgery fMRI study. *Brain, 125*(2), 361–372.

Hill, W.L., Ballard, S., Coyer, M.J., & Rowley, T. (2005). The interaction of testosterone and breeding phase on the reproductive behavior and use of space of male zebra finches. *Hormones & Behavior, 47*(4), 452–458.

Hingson, R., et al. (2002). A call to action: Changing the culture of drinking at U.S. colleges. National Institutes of Health: National Institute of Alcohol Abuse and Alcoholism. Washington, DC.

Hobson, J.A. & McCarley, R.W. (1977). The brain as a dream state generator: An activation-synthesis hypothesis of the dream process, *American Journal of Psychiatry, 134,* 1335–1348.

Hoff, E. (2005). *Language development* (3rd ed.). Belmont, CA: Wadsworth Publishing Company.

Hoffman, H. (2004, August). Virtual-reality therapy. *Scientific American.*

Hohwy, J., & Frith, C. (2004). Can neuroscience explain consciousness? *Journal of Consciousness Studies, 11*(7–8), 180–198.

Holland, J.L. (1996). Exploring careers with a typology. *American Psychologist, 51,* 397–406.

Hollingshead, A.B., & Redlich, F.C. (1958). *Social class and mental illness.* New York: Wiley.

Hollon, S.D., et al. (2005). Prevention of relapse following cognitive therapy vs. medications in moderate to severe depression. *Archives of General Psychiatry, 62*(4), 417–422.

Holmes, M.M., Putz, O., Crews, D., & Wade, J. (2005). Normally occurring intersexuality and testosterone induced plasticity in the copulatory system of adult leopard geckos. *Hormones & Behavior, 47*(4), 439–445.

Holmes, T.H., & Rahe, R.H. (1967). The social readjustment rating scale. *Journal of Psychosomatic Research, 11,* 213–218.

Honorton, C. (1985). Meta-analysis of psi Ganzfeld research. *Journal of Parapsychology, 49,* 51–91.

Honorton, C., et al. (1990). Psi communication in the Ganzfeld. *Journal of Parapsychology, 54,* 99–139.

Honts, C.R., Hodes, R.L., & Raskin, D.C. (1985). Effects of physical countermeasures on the physiological detection of deception. *Journal of Applied Psychology, 70*(1), 177–187.

Hoover, R.N. (2000). Cancer: Nature, nurture, or both. *New England Journal of Medicine, 343,* 135–136.

Horn, J.M. (1983). The Texas adoption project. *Child Development, 54,* 268–275.

Hornstein, E.P., Verweij, J., & Schnapf, J.L. (2004). Electrical coupling between red and green cones in primate retina. *Nature Neuroscience, 7*(7), 745–750.

Horowitz, T.S., Cade, B.E., Wolfe, J.M., & Czeisler, C.A. (2003). Searching night and day: A dissociation of effects of circadian phase and time awake on visual selective attention and vigilance. *Psychological Science, 14*(6), 549–557.

Howland, R.H. (2009). Somatic therapies for seasonal affective disorder. *Journal of Psychosocial Nursing and Mental Health Services, 47,* 17–20.

Hoybye, M.T., Johansen, C., & Tjornhoj-Thomsen, T. (2005). Online interaction. Effects of storytelling in an Internet breast cancer support group. *Psycho-Oncology, 14*(3), 211–220.

Hubel, D.H. & Wiesel T. (1977). Ferrier lecture: Functional architecture of Macaque monkey visual cortex. *Proceedings of the Royal Society of London. Series B. Biological Sciences, 198,* 1–59.

Hudson, J.I., Hiripi, E., Pope, H.G., & Kessler, R.C. (2007). The prevalence and correlates of eating disorders in the National Comorbidity Survey Replication. *Biological Psychiatry, 61*(3), 348–358.

Huesmann, L.R., Moise-Titus, J., Podolski, C., & Eron, L.D. (2003). Longitudinal relations between children's exposure to TV violence and their aggressive and violent behavior in young adulthood: 1977–1992. *Developmental Psychology, 39*(2), 201–221.

Hulshoff, P., et al. (2000). Prenatal exposure to famine and brain morphology in schizophrenia. *American Journal of Psychiatry, 157*(7), 1170–1172.

Human Genome Sequencing Consortium. (2004, October 29). Cited in "Number of genes in human genome lower than previously estimated." News Office,

Massachusetts Institute of Technology. http://web.mit .edu/newsoffice/2004/humangenome.html.

Huskinson, T.L.H., & Haddock, G. (2004). Individual differences in attitude structure: Variance in the chronic reliance on affective and cognitive information. *Journal of Experimental Social Psychology, 40*(1), 82–90.

Hvas, L., Reventlow, S., & Malterud, K. (2004). Women's needs and wants when seeing the GP in relation to menopausal issues. *Scandinavian Journal of Primary Health Care, 22*(2), 118–121.

Hwu, H., Liu, C., Fann, C.S., Ou-Yang, W., & Lee, S.F. (2003). Linkage of schizophrenia with chromosome 1q loci in Taiwanese families. *Molecular Psychiatry, 8*(4), 445–452.

Hyde, J.S., & Plant, E.A. (1995). Magnitude of psychological gender differences. *American Psychologist, 50,* 159–161.

I

Iacono, W.G., & Lykken, D.T. (1997). The validity of the lie detector: Two surveys of scientific opinion. *Journal of Applied Psychology, 82*(3), 426–433.

Inhelder, B., & Piaget, J. (1958). *The growth of logical thinking from childhood to adolescence.* Chicago: University of Chicago Press.

Insel, T.R. (2000). Toward a neurobiology of attachment. *Review of General Psychology, 4*(2), 176–185.

Isabella, R.A. (1998). Origins of attachment: The role of context, duration, frequency of observation, and infant age in measuring maternal behavior. *Journal of Social & Personal Relationships, 15*(4), 538–554.

Isarida, T., & Isarida, T. (1999). Effects of contextual changes between class and intermission on episodic memory. *Japanese Journal of Psychology, 69*(6), 478–485.

Iverson, P., et al. (2003). A perceptual interference account of acquisition difficulties for non-native phonemes. *Cognition, 87*(1), B47–B57.

Ivey, A.E., & Brooks-Harris, J.E. (2005). Integrative psychotherapy with culturally diverse clients. In J.C. Norcross & M.R. Goldfried (Eds.), *Handbook of psychotherapy integration* (2nd ed., pp. 321–339). London: Oxford University Press.

Izard, C.E. (1984). Emotion-cognition relationships and human development. In C.E. Izard, J.

Izard, C.E. (1994). Basic emotions, relations among emotions, and emotion-cognition relations. *Psychological Bulletin, 115,* 561–565.

J

Jacks, J.Z., & Devine, P.G. (2000). Attitude importance, forewarning of message content, and resistance to persuasion. *Basic & Applied Social Psychology, 22*(1), 19–29.

Jackson, H., & Nuttall, R.L. (2001). Risk for preadolescent suicidal behavior: An ecological model. *Child & Adolescent Social Work Journal, 18*(3), 189–203.

Jacoangeli, F., et al. (2002). Osteoporosis and anorexia nervosa: Relative role of endocrine alterations and malnutrition. *Eating & Weight Disorders, 7*(3), 190–195.

Jaffee, S., & Hyde, J.S. (2000). Gender differences in moral orientation. *Psychological Bulletin, 126*(5), 703–726.

James, L.E., & Burke, D.M. (2000). Phonological priming effects on word retrieval and tip-of-the-tongue experiences in young and older adults. *Journal of Experimental Psychology—Learning, Memory, and Cognition, 26*(6), 1378–1391.

James, W. (1890). *The principles of psychology.* New York: Henry Holt.

Jamison, K.R. (2000). Suicide and bipolar disorder. *Journal of Clinical Psychiatry, 61*(Suppl. 9), 47–51.

Janis, I.L. (1982). *Groupthink* (2nd ed.). Boston: Houghton Mifflin.

Janowitz, H.D., & Grossman, M.I. (1949). Effects of variations in nutritive density on intake of food in dogs and cats. *American Journal of Physiology, 158,* 184–193, 1400–1402.

Janowsky, J.S., Chavez, B., & Orwoll, E. (2000). Sex steroids modify working memory. *Journal of Cognitive Neuroscience, 12,* 407–414.

Jemmott, J.B., et al. (1983). Academic stress, power motivation, and decrease in secretion rate of salivary secretory immunoglobin A. *Lancet, 1,* 1400–1402.

Jensen, A.R. (1985). The nature of the black-white difference on various psychometric tests: Spearman's hypothesis. *Behavioral and Brain Sciences, 8,* 192–263.

Jensen, M.P., et al. (2005). Hypnotic analgesia for chronic pain in persons with disabilities: A case series. *International Journal of Clinical & Experimental Hypnosis, 53*(2), 198–228.

Johnson, M.P., Duffy, J.F., Dijk, D-J,. Rhonda, J.M., Dyal, C.M., & Czeiler, C.A. (1992). Short-term memory, alertness and performance: A reappraisal of their relationship to body temperature, *Journal of Sleep Research, 1,* 24–29.

Johnson, W., & Krueger, R.F. (2006). How money buys happiness: Genetic and environmental processes linking finances and life satisfaction. *Journal of Personality and Social Psychology, 90*(4) 680–691.

Jones, C.J., & Meredith, W. (2000). Developmental paths of psychological health from early adolescence to later adulthood. *Psychology and Aging, 15*(2), 351–360.

Jonsdottir, I.H., Hellstrand, K., Thoren, P., & Hoffman, P. (2000). Enhancement of natural immunity seen after voluntary exercise in rats. Role of central opioid receptors. *Life Sciences, 66*(13), 1231–1239.

K

Kaddour, J. (2003). Psychological endurance (hardiness): Definitional, nomological, and critical aspects. *European Review of Applied Psychology, 53*(3–4), 227–237.

Kahneman, D., & Frederick, S. (2002). Representativeness revisited: Attribute substitution in intuitive judgment. In T. Gilovich, et al. (Eds.), *Heuristics and biases: The* psychology of intuitive judgment (pp. 49–81). New York: Cambridge University Press.

Kalin, N.H. (2003). Nonhuman primate studies of fear, anxiety, and temperament and the role of benzodiazepine receptors and GABA systems. Journal of Clinical Psychiatry, 64(Suppl. 3), 41–44.

Kallgren, C.A., Reno, R.R., & Cialdini, R.B. (2000). A focus theory of normative conduct: When norms do and do not affect behavior. Personality & Social Psychology Bulletin, 26(8), 1002–1012.

Kamalanabhan, T.J., Sunder, D., & Vasanthi, M. (2000). An evaluation of the Choice Dilemma Questionnaire as a measure of risk-taking propensity. Social Behavior & Personality, 28(2), 149–156.

Kandel, E.R. (2001). The molecular biology of memory storage: A dialogue between genes and synapses. Science, 294, 1030–1038.

Kanner, A., Coyne, J., Schaefer, C., & Lazarus, R. (1981). Comparison of two modes of stress measurement: Daily hassles and uplifts versus major life events. Journal of Behavioral Medicine, 4, 1–39.

Kapur, S. (2003). Psychosis as a state of aberrant salience: A framework linking biology, phenomenology, and pharmacology in schizophrenia. American Journal of Psychiatry, 160(1), 13–23.

Karon, B.P., & Widener, A. (1998). Repressed memories: The real story. Professional Psychology: Research & Practice, 29(5), 482–487.

Kasai, K., et al. (2003). Progressive decrease of left Heschl gyrus and planum temporale gray matter volume in first-episode schizophrenia: A longitudinal magnetic resonance imaging study. Archives of General Psychiatry, 60(8), 766–775.

Kataria, S. (2004). A clinical guide to pediatric sleep: Diagnosis and management of sleep problems. Journal of Developmental & Behavioral Pediatrics, 25(2), 132–133.

Katigbak, M.S., Church, A.T., Guanzon-Lapena, M.A., Carlota, A.J., & del Pilar, G.H. (2002). Are indigenous personality dimensions culture specific? Philippine inventories and the five-factor model. Journal of Personality & Social Psychology, 82(1), 89–101.

Katzmarzyk, P.T., & Ardern, C.I. (2004). Overweight and obesity mortality trends in Canada 1985–2000. Canadian Journal of Public Health, 95, 16–20.

Katzmarzyk, P.T., & Janssen, I. (2004). The economic costs associated with physical inactivity and obesity in Canada: An update. Canadian Journal of Applied Physiology, 29, 90–115.

Kavanagh, K., et al. (2007). Characterization and heritability of obesity and associated risk factors in vervet monkeys. Obesity, 15(7), 1666–1674.

Keller, A., et al. (2003). Progressive loss of cerebellar volume in childhood-onset schizophrenia. American Journal of Psychiatry, 160, 128–133.

Keller, S., Maddock, J.E., Laforge, R.G., Velicer, W.F., & Basler, H-D. (2007). Binge drinking and health behavior in medical students. Addictive Behaviors, 32(3), 505–515.

Kellerman, J., Lewis, J., & Laird, J.D. (1989). Looking and loving: The effects of mutual gaze on feelings of romantic love. Journal of Research in Personality, 23, 145–161.

Kellman, P.J., & von Hofsten, C. (1992). The world of the moving infant. In C. Rovee-Collier & L.P. Lipsitt (Eds.), Advances in Infancy Research (Vol. 7). Norwood, NJ: Ablex.

Kendler, K.S., et al. (2000a). Illicit psychoactive substance use, heavy use, abuse, and dependence in a U.S. population-based sample of male twins. Archives of General Psychiatry, 57, 261–269.

Kendler, K.S., Myers, J., Prescott, C.A., & Neale, M.C. (2001). The genetic epidemiology of irrational fears and phobias in men. Archives of General Psychiatry, 58(3), 257–265.

Kendler, K.S., Thornton, L.M., Gilman, S.E., & Kessler, R.C. (2000c). Sexual orientation in a U.S. national sample of twin and nontwin sibling pairs. American Journal of Psychiatry, 157, 1843–1846.

Kennedy, C.H. (2002). Effects of REM sleep deprivation on a multiple schedule of appetitive reinforcement. Behavioural Brain Research, 128(2), 205–214.

Kerns, J.G., & Berenbaum, H. (2002). Cognitive impairments associated with formal thought disorder in people with schizophrenia. Journal of Abnormal Psychology, 111(2), 211–224.

Kessler, R.C., Chiu, W.T., Demler, O., & Walters, E.E. (2005c). Prevalence, severity, and comorbidity of 12-month DSM–IV disorders in the National Comorbidity Survey Replication. Archives of General Psychiatry, 62(6), 617–627.

Kessler, R.C., et al. (2005a) Lifetime prevalence and age-of-onset distributions of DSM–IV disorders in the National Comorbidity Survey Replication. Archives of General Psychiatry, 62(6), 593–602.

Keyes, C.L.M., & Goodman, S.H. (Eds.). (2006). Women and depression: A handbook for the social, behavioral, and biomedical sciences. New York: Cambridge University Press.

Keyes, C.L.M., & Haidt, J. (2003). Flourishing: Positive psychology and the life well-lived. Washington, DC: American Psychological Association.

Keyes, D. (1995). The minds of Billy Milligan. New York: Bantam Books.

Khan, A.A., Jacobson, K.C., Gardner, C.O., Prescott, C.A., & Kendler, K.S. (2005). Personality and comorbidity of common psychiatric disorders. British Journal of Psychiatry, 186(3), 190–196.

Kiecolt-Glaser, J.K., Marucha, P.T., Atkinson, C., & Glaser, R. (2001). Hypnosis as a modulator of cellular immune dysregulation during acute stress. Journal of Consulting & Clinical Psychology, 69(4), 674–682.

Kiecolt-Glaser, J.K., McGuire, L., Robles, T.F., & Glaser, R. (2002a). Psychoneuroimmunology and psychosomatic medicine: Back to the future. *Psychosomatic Medicine, 64*(1), 15–28.

Kiecolt-Glaser, J.K., McGuire, L., Robles, T.F., & Glaser, R. (2002b). Emotions, morbidity, and mortality: New perspectives from psychoneuroimmunology. *Annual Review of Psychology, 53*(1), 83–107.

Kihlstrom, J.F. (2002). No need for repression. *Trends in Cognitive Sciences, 6*(12), 502.

Kilshaw, D., & Annett, M. (1983). Right- and left-hand skill: Effects of age, sex, and hand preferences showing superior in left-handers. *British Journal of Psychology, 74,* 253–268.

Kim, B.S.K., Brenner, B.R., Liang, C.T.H., & Asay, P.A. (2003). A qualitative study of adaptation experiences of 1.5-generation Asian Americans. *Cultural Diversity & Ethnic Minority Psychology, 9*(2), 156–170.

Kim, K., & Rohner, R.P. (2002). Parental warmth, control, and involvement in schooling: Predicting academic achievement among Korean American adolescents. *Journal of Cross-Cultural Psychology, 33*(2), 127–140.

Kinsey, A.C., Pomeroy, W.B., & Martin, C.E. (1948). *Sexual behavior in the human male.* Philadelphia: W.B. Saunders.

Kinsey, A.C., Pomeroy, W.B., Martin, C.E., & Gebhard, P.H. (1953). *Sexual behavior in the human female.* Philadelphia: W.B. Saunders.

Kirsch, I. (2000). The response set theory of hypnosis. *American Journal of Clinical Hypnosis, 42*(3–4), 274–292.

Kirschenbaum, H., & Jourdan, A. (2005). The current status of Carl Rogers and the person-centered approach. *Psychotherapy: Theory, Research, Practice, Training, 42*(1), 37–51.

Klaczynski, P.A. (2001). Framing effects on adolescent task representations, analytic and heuristic processing and decision making. Implications for the normative/descriptive gap. *Journal of Applied Developmental Psychology, 22*(3), 289–309.

Kleinke, C.L. (1977). Compliance to requests made by gazing and touching experimenters in field settings. *Journal of Experimental Social Psychology, 13,* 218–223.

Kleinke, C.L. (1986). Gaze and eye contact. *Psychological Review, 100,* 78–100.

Kleinmuntz, B., & Szucko, J.J. (1984). Lie detection in ancient and modern times. *American Psychologist, 39,* 766–776.

Klüver, H., & Bucy, P.C. (1939). Preliminary analysis of functions of the temporal lobes in monkeys. *Archive of Neurological Psychiatry, 42,* 979–1000.

Knafo, A., Iervolino, A.C., & Plomin, R. (2005). Masculine girls and feminine boys: Genetic and environmental contributions to atypical gender development in early childhood. *Journal of Personality & Social Psychology, 88*(2), 400–412.

Kobasa, S.C.O. (1990). Stress-resistant personality. In R.E. Ornstein & C. Swencionis (Eds.), *The healing brain* (pp. 219–230). New York: Guilford Press.

Kobasa, S.C.O., Maddi, S.R., Puccetti, M.C., & Zola, M.A. (1994). Effectiveness of hardiness, exercise, and social support as resources against illness. In A. Steptoe & J. Wardle (Eds.), *Psychosocial processes and health* (pp. 247–260).

Kohlberg, L. (1969). *Stages in the development of moral thought and action.* New York: Holt, Rinehart and Winston.

Kohlberg, L. (1981). *The philosophy of moral development.* San Francisco: Harper & Row.

Kolb, B., Gibb, R., & Robinson, T.E. (2003). Brain plasticity and behaviour. *Current Directions in Psychological Science, 12,* 1–5.

Kooijman, C.M., et al. (2000). Phantom pain and phantom sensations in upper limb amputees: An epidemiological study. *Pain, 87*(1), 33–41.

Kopelman, M.D. (2002). Disorders of memory. *Brain, 125*(10), 2152–2190.

Koss, M.P., Figueredo, A.J., & Prince, R.J. (2002). Cognitive mediation of rape's mental, physical and social health impact: Tests of four models in cross-sectional data. *Journal of Consulting & Clinical Psychology, 70*(4), 926–941.

Krcmar, M., & Cooke, M.C. (2001). Children's moral reasoning and their perceptions of television violence. *Journal of Communication, 51*(2), 300–316.

Kroger, J.K., et al. (2002). Recruitment of anterior dorsolateral prefrontal cortex in human reasoning: A parametric study of relational complexity. *Cerebral Cortex, 12*(5), 477–485.

Kübler-Ross, E. (1969). On death and dying. New York: Macmillan.

Kuczmarski, R.J., et al. (2000, December 4). CDC Growth charts: United States. Advance data from vital and health statistics, no. 314. Hyattsville, MD: National Center for Health Statistics.

Kumar, V.M. (2004). Body temperature and sleep: Are they controlled by the same mechanism? *Sleep and Biological Rhythms, 2,* 103–125.

Kwate, N.O.A. (2001). Intelligence or misorientation? Eurocentrism in the WICS-III. *Journal of Black Psychology, 27*(2), 221–238. Washington, DC: American Psychological Association.

L

Lahti, A.C., et al. (2001). Abnormal patterns of regional cerebral blood flow in schizophrenia with primary negative symptoms during an effortful auditory recognition task. *American Journal of Psychiatry, 158,* 1797–1808.

Lake, M. (2005, May 2). Virtual reality heals 9/11 wounds. http://www.cnn.com/2005/TECH/04/29/spark.virtual/index.html.

Lalumére, M.L., Blanchard, R., & Zucker, K.J. (2000). Sexual orientation and handedness in men and women: A meta-analysis. *Psychological Bulletin, 126*(4), 575–592.

Lam, L. & Kirby, S. (2002). Is emotional intelligence an advantage? An exploration of the impact of emotional and general intelligence on individual performance. *Journal of Social Psychology, 142,* 133–143.

Lang, A.R., Goeckner, D.J., Adesso, V.J., & Marlatt, G.A. (1975). Effects of alcohol on aggression in male social drinkers. *Journal of Abnormal Psychology, 84,* 508–518.

Lang, E.V., et al. (2000). Adjunctive non-pharmacological analgesia for invasive medical procedures: a randomised trial. *The Lancet, 355,* 1486–1490.

Langlois, J.H., et al. (2000). Maxims or myths of beauty? A meta-analytic and theoretical review. *Psychological Bulletin, 126*(3), 390–423.

Lanier, S.A., Hayes, J.E., & Duffy, V.B. (2005). Sweet and bitter tastes of alcoholic beverages mediate alcohol intake in of-age undergraduates. *Physiology & Behavior, 83*(5), 821–831.

Larkin, M. (2000). Can lost hearing be restored? *The Lancet, 356,* 741–748.

Lashley, K.S. (1950). In search of the engram. In *Symposium of the Society for Experimental Biology* (Vol. 4). New York: Cambridge University Press.

Laumann, E.O., Gagnon, J.H., Michael, R.T., & Michaels, S. (1994). *The social organization of sexuality.* Chicago: University of Chicago Press.

Lavee, Y., & Ben-Ari, A. (2003). Daily stress and uplifts during times of political tension: Jews and Arabs in Israel. *American Journal of Orthopsychiatry, 73*(1), 65–73.

Lavine, H., Lodge, M., & Freitas, K. (2005). Threat, authoritarianism, and selective exposure to information. *Political Psychology, 26*(2), 219–244.

Lazar, S.W., et al. (2000). Functional brain mapping of the relaxation response and meditation. *Neuroreport: For Rapid Communication of Neuroscience Research, 11*(7), 1581–1585.

Lazarus, R. (1993). From psychological stress to the emotions: A history of changing outlooks. *Annual Review of Psychology, 44,* 1–22.

Lazarus, R.S., DeLongis, A., Folkman, S., & Gruen, R. (1985). Stress and adaptational outcomes. *American Psychologist, 40,* 770–779.

Leahey, E., & Guo, G. (2001). Gender differences in mathematical trajectories. *Social Forces, 80*(2), 713–732.

Le Bon, G. (1960). *The crowd.* New York: Viking. (Original work published 1895).

Lecci, L., & Cohen, D.J. (2002). Perceptual consequences of an illness-concern induction and its relation to hypochondriacal tendencies. *Health Psychology, 21*(2), 147–156.

LeDoux, J.E. (1998). Fear and the brain: Where have we been, and where are we going? *Biological Psychiatry, 44*(12), 1229–1238.

Lefcourt, H.M. (1997). Cited in Clay, R.A. (1997). Researchers harness the power of humor. *APA Monitor, 28*(9), 1, 18.

LeFevre, J-A., Skwarchuk, S-L., Smith-Chant, B.L., Fast, L., Kamawar, D., & Bisanz, J. (2009). Home numeracy experiences and children's math performance in the early school years. *Canadian Journal of Behavioural Science, 41,* 55–66.

Lehman, B.J., & Crano, W.D. (2002). The pervasive effects of vested interest on attitude-criterion consistency in political judgment. *Journal of Experimental Social Psychology, 38*(2), 101–112.

Lensvelt-Mulders, G., & Hettema, J. (2001). Genetic analysis of autonomic reactivity to psychologically stressful situations. *Biological Psychology, 58*(1), 25–40.

Leonard, B.E. (2005). Mind over matter: Regulation of peripheral inflammation by the CNS. *Human Psychopharmacology: Clinical & Experimental, 20*(1), 71–72.

Leonard, S., Steiger, H., & Kao, A. (2003). Childhood and adulthood abuse in bulimic and nonbulimic women: Prevalences and psychological correlates. *International Journal of Eating Disorders, 33*(4), 397–405.

Leonardo, E.D., & Hen, R. (2006). Genetics of affective and anxiety disorders. *Annual Review of Psychology, 57,* 117–137.

Leppel, K. (2002). Similarities and differences in the college persistence of men and women. *Review of Higher Education: Journal of the Association for the Study of Higher Education, 25*(4), 433–450.

Lester, D. (2006). E-therapy: Caveats from experiences with telephone therapy. *Psychological Reports, 99,* 894–896.

Levin, R., & Fireman, G. (2002). Nightmare prevalence, nightmare distress, and self-reported psychological disturbance. *Sleep: Journal of Sleep & Sleep Disorders Research, 25*(2), 205–212.

Levinson, D.J. (1996). *The seasons of a woman's life.* New York: Knopf.

Levinson, D.J., Darrow, C.N., Klein, E.B., Levinson, M.H., & McKee, B. (1978). *The seasons of a man's life.* New York: Knopf.

Lewinsohn, P.M., Striegel-Moore, R.H., & Seeley, J.R. (2000). Epidemiology and natural course of eating disorders in young women from adolescence to young adulthood. *Journal of the American Academy of Child Adolescent Psychiatry, 39,* 1284–1292.

Lewinsohn, P.M., Brown, R.A., Seeley, J.R., & Ramsey, S.E. (2000a). Psychological correlates of cigarette smoking abstinence, experimentation, persistence, and frequency during adolescence. *Nicotine & Tobacco Research, 2*(2), 121–131.

Li, W., & DeVries, S.H. (2004). Separate blue and green cone networks in the mammalian retina.

Lidow, M.S., et al. (2001). Antipsychotic treatment induces alterations in dendrite- and spine-associated proteins in dopamine-rich areas of the primate cerebral cortex. *Biological Psychiatry, 49*(1), 1–12.

Lieber, C.S. (1990). Cited in Barroom biology: How alcohol goes to a woman's head (January 14). *The New York Times,* p. E24.

Linden, W., Chambers, L., Maurice, J., & Lenz, J.W. (1993). Sex differences in social support, self-deception, hostility, and ambulatory cardiovascular activity. *Health Psychology, 12,* 376–380.

Little, A.C., & Perrett, D.I. (2002). Putting beauty back in the eye of the beholder. *Psychologist, 15*(1), 28–32.

Lochman, J.E., & Dodge, K.A. (1994). Social-cognitive processes of severely violent, moderately aggressive, and nonaggressive boys. *Journal of Consulting and Clinical Psychology, 62,* 366–374.

Loftus, E.F. (1983). Silence is not golden. *American Psychologist, 38,* 564–572.

Loftus, E.F. (1993). Make-believe memories. *American Psychologist, 58(11),* 867–873.

Loftus, E.F. (2001). Imagining the past. *Psychologist, 14*(11), 584–587.

Loftus, E.F. (2004). Memories of things unseen. *Current Directions in Psychological Science, 13*(4), 145–147.

Loftus, E.F., & Palmer, J.C. (1974). Reconstruction of automobile destruction: An example of interaction between language and memory. *Journal of Verbal Learning and Verbal Behavior, 13,* 585–589.

Loftus, G.R. (1983). The continuing persistence of the icon. *Behavioral and Brain Sciences, 6,* 28.

Loop, M.S., Shows, J.F., Mangel, S.C., & Kuyk, T.K. (2003). Colour thresholds in dichromats and normals. *Vision Research, 43*(9), 983–992.

Lorenz, K.Z. (1981). *The foundations of ethology.* New York: Springer-Verlag.

Louie, K., & Wilson, M.A. (2001). Temporally structured replay of awake hippocampal ensemble activity during rapid eye movement sleep. *Neuron, 29*(1), 145–156.

Loving, T.J., & Agnew, C.R. (2001). Socially desirable responding in close relationships: A dualcomponent approach and measure. *Journal of Social & Personal Relationships, 18*(4), 551–573.

Low, N.C.P., Cui, L., & Merikangas, K.R. (2008). Specificity of familial transmission of anxiety and comorbid disorders. *Journal of Psychiatric Research, 42*(7), 596–604.

Lu, L. (2001). Understanding happiness: A look into the Chinese folk psychology. *Journal of Happiness Studies, 2*(4), 407–432.

Lubell, S. (2004, Feb. 19). On the therapist's couch, a jolt of virtual reality. *The New York Times.* Retrieved on Jan. 26, 2011 from http://www.nytimes.com/2004/02/19/technology/on-the-therapist-s-couch-a-jolt-of-virtual-reality.html?pagewanted=all&src=pm

Luborsky, L., et al. (2002). The dodo bird verdict is alive and well—mostly. *Clinical Psychology: Science & Practice, 9*(1), 2–12.

Luchins, A.S. (1957). Primacy-recency in impression formation. In C.I. Hovland (Ed.), *The order of presentation in persuasion.* New Haven, CT: Yale University Press.

Ludwick-Rosenthal, R., & Neufeld, R.W.J. (1993). Preparation for undergoing an invasive medical procedure. *Journal of Consulting and Clinical Psychology, 61,* 156–164.

Lykken, D.T., & Csikszentmihalyi, M. (2001). Happiness— stuck with what you've got? *Psychologist, 14*(9), 470–472.

Lykken, D.T., McGue, M., Tellegen, A., & Bouchard, T.J., Jr. (1992). Emergenesis: Genetic traits that may not run in families. *American Psychologist, 47,* 1565–1577.

Lynn, S.J., Shindler, K., & Meyer, E. (2003). Hypnotic suggestibility, psychopathology, and treatment outcome. *Sleep & Hypnosis, 5*(1), 2–10.

M

Maccoby, E.E. (1992). The role of parents in the socialization of children: An historical overview. *Developmental Psychology, 28,* 1006–1017.

Mackert, B., et al. (2003). The eloquence of silent cortex: Analysis of afferent input to deafferented cortex in arm amputees. *Neuroreport: For Rapid Communication of Neuroscience Research, 14*(3), 409–412.

Magnusson, A., & Partonen, T. (2005). The diagnosis, symptomatology, and epidemiology of Seasonal Affective Disorder. *CNS Spectrums, 10,* 625–634.

Maguire, E.A., Gadian, D.G., Johnsrude, I.S., Good, C.D., Ashburner, J., Frackowiak, R.S.J., & Frith, C.D. (2000) Navigation-related structural change in the hippocampi of taxi drivers. *Proceedings of the National Academy of Sciences, 97,* 4398–4403.

Maher, B.A., & Maher, W.B. (1994). Personality and psychopathology. *Journal of Abnormal Psychology, 103,* 72–77.

Mahmud, A., & Feely, F. (2003). Effect of smoking on arterial stiffness and pulse pressure amplification. *Hypertension, 41,* 183–187.

Maier, N.R.F., & Schneirla, T.C. (1935). *Principles of animal psychology.* New York: McGraw-Hill.

Main, M., & Soloman, J. (1986). Discovery of a disorganized/disoriented attachment. In T.B. Brazelton & M.W. Yogan (Eds.), *Affective development in infancy* (pp. 95–124). Norwood, NJ: Albex.

Major, G.C., etal. (2007). Clinical significance of adaptive thermo-genesis. *International Journal of Obesity, 31*(2), 204–212.

Malenfant, E.C. (March 2004). Suicide in Canada's immigrant population. *Health Reports, 15(2),* Statistics

Canada, catalogue 82-003. Retrieved June 24, 2010, from: http://www.statcan.gc.ca/studies-etudes/82-003/archive/2004/6807-eng.pdf.

Marcia, J.E. (1980). Identity in adolescence. In J. Adelson (Ed.), *Handbook of adolescent psychology.* New York: Wiley.

Marin, A. (2001). *Special report: Systemic treatment of CF members with PTSD.* Report to the Minister of National Defence. Retrieved June 29, 2010, from http://www.ombudsman.forces.gc.ca/rep-rap/sr-rs/pts-ssp/doc/pts-ssp-eng.pdf.

Markon, K.E., Krueger, R.F., Bouchard, T.J., Jr., & Gottesman, I.I. (2002). Normal and abnormal personality traits: Evidence for genetic and environmental relationships in the Minnesota Study of Twins Reared Apart. *Journal of Personality, 70*(5), 661–693.

Markus, H., & Kitayama, S. (1991). Culture and the self. *Psychological Review, 98*(2), 224–253.

Marsh, R.L., Hicks, J.L., & Cook, G.I. (2005). On the relationship between effort toward an ongoing task and cue detection in event-based prospective memory. *Journal of Experimental Psychology: Learning, Memory & Cognition, 31*(1), 68–75.

Marshall, M.A., & Brown, J.D. (2004). Expectations and realizations: The role of expectancies in achievement settings. *Motivation & Emotion, 28*(4), 347–361.

Martin, C.L., Ruble, D.N., & Szkrybalo J. (2002). Cognitive theories of early gender development. *Psychological Bulletin, 128*, 903–933.

Martin, C.L., & Ruble, D. (2004). Children's search for gender cues: Cognitive perspectives on gender development. *Current Directions in Psychological Science, 13*(2), 67–70.

Martin, R.A., & Lefcourt, H.M. (1983). Humor, stressors, and moods. *Journal of Personality and Social Psychology, 45*, 1313–1324.

Martinez-Taboas, A., & Bernal, G. (2000). Dissociation, psychopathology, and abusive experiences in a nonclinical Latino university student group. *Cultural Diversity & Ethnic Minority Psychology, 6*(1), 32–41.

Marttunen, M.J., et al. (1998). Completed suicide among adolescents with no diagnosable psychiatric disorder. *Adolescence, 33*(131), 669–681.

Maslow, A.H. (1970). *Motivation and personality* (2nd ed.). New York: Harper & Row.

Masters, M. (2010, June 14). University of Waterloo football program suspended after positive drug tests. *National Post*, Retrieved August 16, 2010, from http://sports.nationalpost.com/2010/06/14/university-of-waterloo-football-team-suspended-after-positive-drug-tests/.

Masters, W.H., & Johnson, V.E. (1966). *Human sexual response.* Boston: Little, Brown.

May, R. (2005). How do we know what works? *Journal of College Student Psychotherapy, 19*(3), 69–73.

McAndrew, F.T. (2002). New evolutionary perspectives on altruism: Multilevel-selection and costly-signaling theories. *Current Directions in Psychological Science, 11*(2), 79–82.

McClelland, D.C. (1958). Methods of measuring human motivation. In John W. Atkinson (ed.), *Motives in fantasy, action and society*. Princeton, NJ: D. Van Nostrand, pp. 12–13.

McClelland, D.C. (1965). Achievement motivation can be developed. *Harvard Business Review, 43*, 68.

McConkey, K., & Sheehan, P.W. (1995). Hypnosis, Memory & Behavior. New York: Guildford Press.

McCormick, R. (1996). Culturally appropriate means and ends of counselling as described by the First Nations of British Columbia. *International Journal for the Advancement of Counseling, 18*, 163–172.

McCourt, K., et al. (1999). Authoritarianism revisited: Genetic and environmental influences examined in twins reared apart and together. *Personality & Individual Differences, 27*(5), 985–1014.

McCrae, R.R., & Costa, P.T., Jr. (1997). Personality trait structure as a human universal. *American Psychologist, 52*, 509–516.

McCrae, R.R., et al. (2000). Nature over nurture: Temperament, personality, and life span development. *Journal of Personality & Social Psychology, 78*(1), 173–186.

McDougall, W. (1904). The sensations excited by a single momentary stimulation of the eye. *British Journal of Psychology, 1*, 78–113.

McDougall, W. (1908). *An introduction to social psychology.* London: Methuen.

McGahan, L. (2001). Behavioural interventions for preschool children with autism. Ottawa: Canadian Coordinating Office for Health Technology Assessment (CCOHTA). Technology report, No. 18.

McGue, M., Pickens, R.W., & Svikis, D.S. (1992). Sex and age effects on the inheritance of alcohol problems: A twin study. *Journal of Abnormal Psychology, 101*, 3–17.

McGuire, L., Kiecolt-Glaser, J.K., & Glaser, R. (2002). Depressive symptoms and lymphocyte proliferation in older adults. *Journal of Abnormal Psychology, 111*(1), 192–197.

McKee, P., & Barber, C.E. (2001). Plato's theory of aging. *Journal of Aging & Identity, 6*(2), 93–104.

McKenzie, C.R.M., Lee, S.M., & Chen, K.K. (2002). When negative evidence increases confidence: Changes in belief after hearing two sides of a dispute. *Journal of Behavioral Decision Making, 15*(1), 1–18.

McLaren, L. (2002). Cited in Wealthy women most troubled by poor body image. (2002, February 11). Reuters online.

McMurran, M., Blair, M., & Egan, V. (2002). An investigation of the correlations between aggression, impulsiveness, social problem-solving, and alcohol use. *Aggressive Behavior, 28,* 439–445.

McNeil, T.F., Cantor-Graae, E., & Weinberger, D.R. (2000). Relationship of obstetric complications and differences in size of brain structures in monozygotic twin pairs discordant for schizophrenia. *American Journal of Psychiatry, 157,* 203–212.

Meijer, J., & Elshout, J.J. (2001). The predictive and discriminant validity of the zone of proximal development. *British Journal of Educational Psychology, 71*(1), 93–113.

Melmed, R.N. (2003). Mind, body, and medicine: An integrative text. *American Journal of Psychiatry, 160*(3), 605–606.

Meltzoff, A.N., & Gopnik, A. (1997). *Words, thoughts, and theories.* Cambridge, MA: MIT Press.

Melzack, R. (1999, August). From the gate to the neuromatrix. *Pain* (Suppl. 6), S121–S126.

Messman-Moore, T.L. & Garrigus, A.S. (2007) The association of child abuse and eating disorder symptomatology: The importance of multiple forms of abuse and revictimization. *Journal of Aggression, Maltreatment and Trauma, 14,* 51–72.

Metcalfe, J. (1986). Premonitions of insight predict impending error. *Journal of Experimental Psychology: Learning, Memory, and Cognition, 12,* 623–634.

Meyer-Lindenberg, A., et al. (2001). Evidence for abnormal cortical functional connectivity during working memory in schizophrenia. *American Journal of Psychiatry, 158,* 1809–1817.

Michael, R.T., Gagnon, J.H., Laumann, E.O., & Kolata, G. (1994). *Sex in America: A definitive survey.* Boston: Little, Brown.

Michels, K.B., et al. (2000). Prospective study of fruit and vegetable consumption and incidence of colon and rectal cancers. *Journal of the National Cancer Institute, 92*(21), 1740–1752.

Migdow, J. (2003). The problem with pleasure. *Journal of Trauma & Dissociation, 4*(1), 5–25.

Milgram, S. (1963). Behavioral study of obedience. *Journal of Abnormal and Social Psychology, 67,* 371–378.

Milgram, S. (1974). *Obedience to authority.* New York: Harper & Row.

Miller, A.L., Rathus, J.H., & Linehan, M.M. (2007). *Dialectical behavior therapy with suicidal adolescents.* New York: Guilford Press.

Miller, A.L., Wyman, S.E., Huppert, J.D., Glassman, S.L., & Rathus, J.H. (2000). Analysis of behavioral skills utilized by suicidal adolescents receiving dialectical behavior therapy. *Cognitive & Behavioral Practice, 7*(2), 183–187.

Miller, G.A. (1956). The magical number seven, plus or minus two: Some limits on our capacity for processing information. *Psychological Review, 63,* 81–97.

Miller, G., Cohen, S., & Richey, A. (2002). Chronic psychological stress and the regulation of pro-inflammatory cytokines: A glucocorticoid-resistance model, *Health Psychology, 21,* 531–541.

Miller, N.E. (1944). Experimental studies of conflict behavior. In J. McV. Hunt (ed.), *Personality and behavior disorders* (pp. 431–465). New York: Ronald Press.

Miller, N.E. (1969). Learning of visceral and glandular responses. *Science, 163,* 434–445.

Miller, N.E. (1995). Clinical-experimental interactions in the development of neuroscience. *American Psychologist, 50,* 901–911.

Milne, R.D., Syngeniotis, A., Jackson, G., & Corballis, M.C. (2002). Mixed lateralization of phonological assembly in developmental dyslexia. *Neurocase, 8*(3), 205–209.

Milner, B.R. (1966). Amnesia following operation on temporal lobes. In C.W.M. Whitty & O.L. Zangwill (eds.), *Amnesia* (pp. 109–133). London: Butterworths.

Milstead, M., Lapsley, D., & Hale, C. (1993, March). *A new look at imaginary audience and personal fable.* Paper presented at the meeting of the Society for Research in Child Development, New Orleans, LA.

Milton, J., & Wiseman, R. (1999). Does psi exist? Lack of replication of an anomalous process of information transfer. *Psychological Bulletin, 125*(4), 387–391.

Miron, J. (2006). "Open to the public": Touring Ontario asylums in the nineteenth century. In David Wright and James E. Moran (eds.), *Mental Health and Canadian Society: Historical Perspective.* McGill-Queen's University Press.

Mischel, W., & Shoda, Y. (1995). A cognitive-affective system theory of personality. *Psychological Review, 102,* 246–268.

Mitchell, A.L. (2006). Medical consequences of cocaine. *Journal of Addictions Nursing, 17*(4), 249.

Molden, D.C., & Dweck, C.S. (2000). Meaning and motivation. In C. Sansone & J.M. Harackiewicz (Eds.), *Intrinsic and extrinsic motivation: The search for optimal motivation and performance* (pp. 131–159). San Diego: Academic Press.

Molfese, V.J., DiLalla, L.F., & Bunce, D. (1997). Prediction of the intelligence test scores of 3- to 8-year-old children by home environment, socioeconomic status, and biomedical risks. *Merrill-Palmer Quarterly, 43*(2), 219–234.

Molfese, V.J., Modglin, A., & Molfese, D.L. (2003). The role of environment in the development of reading skills: A longitudinal study of preschool and school-age measures. *Journal of Learning Disabilities, 36*(1), 59–67.

Morris, W.N., Miller, R.S., & Spangenberg, S. (1977). The effects of dissenter position and task difficulty on conformity and response conflict. *Journal of Personality, 45,* 251–256.

Morry, M.M. (2005). Relationship satisfaction as a predictor of similarity ratings: A test of the attraction-similarity hypothesis. *Journal of Social and Personal Relationships, 22*(4), 561–584.

Morry, M.M., & Gaines, S.O. (2005). Relationship satisfaction as a predictor of similarity ratings: A test of the attraction-similarity hypothesis. *Journal of Social and Personal Relationships, 22,* 561–584.

Moruzzi, G. & Magoun, H.W. (1949). Brain stem reticular formation and activation of the EEG. *Electroencephalograph Clinical Neurophysiology, 1,* 455–473.

Moss, D.P. (2002). Cited in Clay, R.A. (2002). A renaissance for humanistic psychology. *Monitor on Psychology, 33*(8), 42–43.

Moss, E., & St-Laurent, D. (2001). Attachment at school age and academic performance. *Developmental Psychology, 37*(6), 863–874.

Moyà-Solà, S., Köhler, M., Alba, D.M., Casanovas-Vilar, I., & Galindo, J. (2004). Pierolapithecus catalaunicus, a new middle Miocene great ape from Spain. *Science, 19,* 1339–1344.

MSNBC. (2010, March 12). Gander's enduring bond with the U.S. over 9/11. Retrieved June 15, 2010, from http://www.msnbc.msn.com/id/35841619/ns/msnbc_tv.

Mueser, K.T., & McGurk, S.R. (2004). Schizophrenia. *Lancet, 363*(9426), 2063–2072.

Muir, G.D. (2000). Early ontogeny of locomotor behaviour: A comparison between altricial and precocial animals. *Brain Research Bulletin, 53*(5), 719–726.

Myers, L.B., & Brewin, C.R. (1994). Recall of early experience and the repressive coping style. *Journal of Abnormal Psychology, 103,* 288–292.

N

Nader, K., Schafe, G.E., & Le Doux, J.E. (2000). Fear memories require protein synthesis in the amygdala for reconsolidation after retrieval. *Nature, 406*(6797), 722–726.

Nagtegaal, J.E., et al. (2000). Effects of melatonin on the quality of life in patients with delayed sleep phase syndrome. *Journal of Psychosomatic Research, 48*(1), 45–50.

Naimi, T.S., et al. (2003b). Definitions of binge drinking. *Journal of the American Medical Association, 289*(13), 1636.

National Center for Injury Prevention and Control. (2005, June 19). Suicide: Fact sheet. http://www.cdc.gov/ncipc/fact-sheets /suifacts.htm.

National Council of Welfare (2006). *Community: Poverty Profile.* Retrieved August 17, 2010, from http://ncw.gc.ca/c.4mm.5n.3ty@-eng.jsp?cmid=3.

National Longitudinal Survey of Children and Youth. (2006). *Child Care in Canada: Children and Youth Research Paper Series,* Statistics Canada. Retrieved December 3, 2010, from http://www.statcan.gc.ca/pub/89-599-m/89-599-m2006003-eng.pdf.

National Sleep Foundation. (2001, November 19). Events of 9–11 took their toll on Americans' sleep, particularly for women, according to new National Sleep Foundation poll. http://www.sleepfoundation.org/whatsnew/crisis_poll.html.

National Sleep Foundation (2008). *2005 Sleep in America Poll.* Washington, DC: National Sleep Foundation. http://www.sleepfoundation.org.

Nature editorial. (2004). *True lies. Nature, 428*(6984), 679.

Neisser, U. (1993). Cited in Goleman, D.J. (1993, April 6). Studying the secrets of childhood memory. *The New York Times,* pp. C1, C11.

Neisser, U. (1997a). Never a dull moment. *American Psychologist, 52,* 79–81.

Neisser, U. (1997b). Cited in Sleek, S. (1997). Can "emotional intelligence" be taught in today's schools? *APA Monitor, 28*(6), 25.

Neisser, U., Boodoo, G., Bouchard, T.J., Boykin, A., Bordy, N., Ceci, S., et al. (1996). Intelligences: Knowns and unknowns. *American Psychologist, 51,* 77–101.

Nelson, K., Hampson, J., & Shaw, L.K. (1993). Nouns in early lexicons: Evidence, explanations, and implications. *Journal of Child Language, 20,* 228.

Nestoriuc, Y., Rief, W., & Martin, A. (2008). Meta-analysis of biofeedback for tension-type headache: Efficacy, specificity, and treatment moderators. *Journal of Consulting and Clinical Psychology, 76*(3), 379–396.

Neumark-Sztainer, D., et al. (2002a). Ethnic/racial differences in weight-related concerns and behaviors among adolescent girls and boys: Findings from P roject EAT. *Journal of Psychosomatic Research, 53*(5), 963–974.

Neveus, T., Cnattingius, S., Olsson, U., & Hetta, J. (2002). Sleep habits and sleep problems among a community sample of schoolchildren. *Journal of the American Academy of Child & Adolescent Psychiatry, 41*(7), 828.

Newport, E.L. (1998). Cited in Azar, B. (1998). Acquiring sign language may be more innate than learned. *APA Monitor, 29*(4), 12.

Nezlek, J.B., Hampton, C.P., & Shean, G.D. (2000). Clinical depression and day-to-day social interaction in a community sample. *Journal of Abnormal Psychology, 109*(1), 11–19.

Nicholson, A. (2008). Socio-economic status over the life-course and depressive symptoms in men and women in *Eastern Europe. Journal of Affective Disorders, 105*(1–3), 125–136.

Nisbett, R.E. (2007, December 9). All brains are the same color. *The New York Times on the Web.* Retrieved online from http://www.nytimes.com/2007/12/09/opinion/09nisbett.html.

No, S. (2004). From prejudice to intergroup emotions: Differentiated reactions to social groups. *Asian Journal of Social Psychology, 7*(1), 119–122.

Nock, M.K., & Kazdin, A.E. (2002). Examination of affective, cognitive, and behavioral factors and suicide-related outcomes in children and young adolescents. *Journal of Community Psychology, 31*(1), 48–58.

Nolen-Hoeksema, S. (2001). Gender differences in depression. *Current Directions in Psychological Science, 10*(5), 173–176.

Novick, L.R., & Coté, N. (1992). The nature of expertise in anagram solution. In *Proceedings of the Fourteenth Annual Conference of the Cognitive Science Society.* Hillsdale, NJ: Erlbaum.

Nurnberger, J.I., Jr., et al. (2004). A family study of alcohol dependence: Coaggregation of multiple disorders in relatives of alcohol-dependent probands. *Archives of General Psychiatry, 61*(12), 1246–1256.

Nyberg, L., et al. (2000). Large scale neurocognitive networks underlying episodic memory. *Journal of Cognitive Neuroscience, 12*(1), 163–173.

O

O'Dell, C.D., & Hoyert, M.D. (2002). Active and passive touch: A research methodology project. *Teaching of Psychology, 29*(4), 292–294.

Ogawa, K., Nittono, H., & Hori, T. (2002). Brain potential associated with the onset and offset of rapid eye movement (REM) during REM sleep. *Psychiatry & Clinical Neurosciences, 56*(3), 259–260.

Ohayon, M.M., Guilleminault, C., & Priest, R.G. (1999). Night terrors, sleepwalking, and confusional arousals in the general population: Their frequency and relationship to other sleep and mental disorders. *Journal of Clinical Psychiatry, 60*(4), 268–276.

Ohno, H., Urushihara, R., Sei, H., & Morita, Y. (2002). REM sleep deprivation suppresses acquisition of classical eye-blink conditioning. *Sleep: Journal of Sleep Research & Sleep Medicine, 25*(8), 877–881.

Oktedalen, O., Solberg, E.E., Haugen, A.H., & Opstad, P.K. (2001). The influence of physical and mental training on plasma beta-endorphin level and pain perception after intensive physical exercise. *Stress & Health: Journal of the International Society for the Investigation of Stress, 17*(2), 121–127.

Olanow, W.M. (2000, July). Clinical and pathological perspective on Parkinsonism. Paper presented to the World Alzheimer Congress 2000, Washington, DC.

Olds, J. (1969). The central nervous system and the reinforcement of behavior. *American Psychologist, 24,* 114–132.

Olds, J., & Milner, P. (1954). Positive reinforcement produced by electrical stimulation of the septal area and other regions of the rat brain. *Journal of Comparative and Physiological Psychology, 47,* 419–427.

Ontario Addiction Treatment Centre (2009). Retrieved on May 20, 2010, from http://www.oatc.ca.

Orpen, C. (1995). The Multifactorial Achievement Scale as a predictor of salary growth and motivation among middle-managers. *Social Behavior & Personality, 23*(2), 159–162.

Ostatníková, D., et al. (2002). Biological aspects of intellectual giftedness. *Studia Psychologica, 44*(1), 3–13.

Otani, H., et al. (2005). Remembering a nuclear accident in Japan: Did it trigger flashbulb memories? *Memory, 13*(1), 6–20.

P

Park, N., Peterson, C., & Seligman, M.E.P. (2005). *Character strengths in forty nations and fifty states.* Unpublished manuscript, University of Rhode Island.

Parke, R.D. (1977). Punishment: Effects, side effects, and alternative strategies. In H. Hom & P. Robinson (Eds.), *Psychological processes in early education* (pp. 71–99). New York: Academic Press.

Parker, A. (2001). The ganzfeld: Suggested improvements of an apparently successful method for psi research. *European Journal of Parapsychology, 16,* 23–29.

Parr, L.A., Winslow, J.T., Hopkins, W.D., & de Waal, F.B.M. (2000). Recognizing facial cues: Individual discrimination by chimpanzees (*Pan troglodytes*) and Rhesus monkeys (*Macaca mulatta*).

Patenaude, J., Niyonsenga, T., & Fafard, D. (2003). Changes in students' moral development during medical school: A cohort study. *Canadian Medical Association Journal, 168*(7), 840–844.

Patterson, D.R. (2004). Treating pain with hypnosis. *Current Directions in Psychological Science, 13*(6), 252–255.

Patterson, G.R., Dishion, T.J., & Yoerger, K. (2000). Adolescent growth in new forms of problem behavior: Macro- and micro-peer dynamics.

Paunonen, S.V., Haddock, G., Forsterling, F., & Keinonen M. (2003). Broad versus narrow personality measures and the prediction of behaviour across cultures. *European Journal of Personality, 17,* 413–433.

Pavlov, I. (1927). *Conditioned reflexes.* London: Oxford University Press.

Penfield, W. (1969). Consciousness, memory, and man's conditioned reflexes. In K.H. Pribram (Ed.), *On the biology of learning.* New York: Harcourt Brace Jovanovich.

Peplau, L.A. (2003). Human sexuality: How do men and women differ? *Current Directions in Psychological Science, 12*(2), 37–40.

Perrett, D.I., May, K.A., & Yoshikawa, S. (1994). Facial shape and judgments of female attractiveness. *Nature, 368,* 239–242.

Peters, M. (1995a). Does brain size matter? A reply to Ruston and Ankney.

Peters, M. (1995b). Race differences in brain size. Things are not as clear as they seem to be. *American Psychologist, 50,* 947–948.

Peterson, C. & Seligman, M.E.P. (2004). *Character strengths and virtues: A handbook and classification.* Oxford: Oxford University Press.

Peterson, C. (2002). Children's long-term memory for autobiographical events. *Developmental Review, 22*(3), 370–402.

Peterson, L.R., & Peterson, M.J. (1959). Shortterm retention of individual verb items. *Journal of Experimental Psychology, 58,* 193–198.

Petrill, S.A., & Deater-Deckard, K. (2004). The heritability of general cognitive ability: A within family adoption design. *Intelligence, 32*(4), 403–409.

Petrill, S.A., Pike, A., Price, T., & Plomin, R. (2004). Chaos in the home and socioeconomic status are associated with cognitive development in early childhood: Environmental mediators identified in a genetic design. *Intelligence, 32*(5), 445–460.

Petry, N.M., Martin, B., Cooney, J.L., & Kranzler, H.R. "(2000). Give them prizes and they will come: Contingency management for treatment of alcohol dependence. *Journal of Consulting and Clinical Psychology, 68,* 250–257.

Pett, M.A., & Johnson, M.J.M. (2005). Development and psychometric evaluation of the revised University student hassle scale. *Education and Psychological Measurement, 65(6),* 984–1010.

Petty, R.E., Fleming, M.A., & White, P.H. (1999). Stigmatized sources and persuasion: Prejudice as a determinant of argument scrutiny. *Journal of Personality & Social Psychology, 76*(1), 19–34.

Petty, R.E., Wegener, D.T., & Fabrigar, L.R. (1997). Attitudes and attitude change. *Annual Review of Psychology, 48,* 609–647.

Phalet, K., & Schoenpflug, U. (2001). Intergenerational transmission of collectivism and achievement values in two acculturation contexts: The case of Turkish families in Germany and Turkish and Moroccan families in the Netherlands. *Journal of Cross-Cultural Psychology, 32*(2), 186–201.

Phillips, L.M., Norris, S.P., & Anderson, J. (2008). Unlocking the door: Is parents' reading to children the key to early literacy development? *Canadian Psychology, 49,* 82–88.

Phinney, J.S. (2005). Ethnic identity in late modern times. *Identity, 5*(2), 187–194.

Phinney, J.S., & Devich-Navarro, M. (1997). Variations in bicultural identification among African American and Mexican American adolescents. *Journal of Research on Adolescence, 7*(1), 3–32.

Piaget, J. (1963). *The origins of intelligence in children.* New York: W.W. Norton.

Piaget, J., & Smith, L. (Trans.). (2000). Commentary on Vygotsky's criticisms of language and thought of the child and judgment and reasoning in the child. *New Ideas in Psychology, 18*(2–3), 241–259.

Pihl, R.O., Peterson, J.B., & Finn, P. (1990). Inherited predisposition to alcoholism. *Journal of Abnormal Psychology, 99,* 291–301.

Pind, J., Gunnarsdottir, E.K., & Johannesson, H.S. (2003). Raven's Standard Progressive Matrices: New school

age norms and a study of the test's validity. *Personality and Individual Differences, 34*(3), 375–386.

Pinker, S. (1990). Language acquisition. In D.N. Osherson & H. Lasnik (Eds.), *An invitation to cognitive science: Language* (Vol. 1). Cambridge, MA: MIT Press, a Bradford Book.

Pinker, S. (1994). *The language instinct.* New York: William Morrow.

Pinker, S. (1997). Words and rules in the human brain. *Nature, 387*(6633), 547–548.

Pinker, S. (1999). Out of the minds of babes. *Science, 283*(5398), 40–41.

Pinnell, C.M., & Covino, N.A. (2000). Empirical findings on the use of hypnosis in medicine: A critical review. *International Journal of Clinical & Experimental Hypnosis, 48*(2), 170–194.

Plaisier, I., et al. (2008). Work and family roles and the association with depressive and anxiety disorders: Differences between men and women. *Journal of Affective Disorders, 105*(1–3), 63–72.

Platania, J., & Moran, G.P. (2001). Social facilitation as a function of mere presence of others. *Journal of Social Psychology, 141*(2), 190–197.

Plomin, R. (2000). Behavioural genetics in the 21st century. *International Journal of Behavioral Development, 24*(1), 30–34.

Plomin, R. (Ed.). (2002). *Behavioral genetics in the postgenomic era.* Washington, DC: American Psychological Association.

Plomin, R., & Crabbe, J. (2000). DNA. *Psychological Bulletin, 126*(6), 806–828.

Plomin, R., Emde, R., Braungart, J.M., & Campos. (1993). Genetic change and continuity from fourteen to twenty months: The MacArthur Longitudinal Twin Study. *Child Development, 64*(5), 1354–1376.

Pol, H.E.H., et al. (2000). Prenatal exposure to famine and brain morphology in schizophrenia. *American Journal of Psychiatry, 157,* 1170–1172.

Posada, G., et al. (2002). Maternal caregiving and infant security in two cultures. *Developmental Psychology, 38*(1), 67–78.

Potkay, C.R., & Allen, B.P. (1986). *Personality: Theory, research and application.* Pacific Grove, CA: Brooks/Cole.

Power, T.G., Stewart, C.D., Hughes, S.O., & Arbona, C. (2005). Predicting patterns of adolescent alcohol use: A longitudinal study. *Journal of Studies on Alcohol, 66*(1), 74–81.

Pratkanis, A.R. (Ed.). (2007). *The science of social influence: Advances and future progress.* New York: Psychology Press.

Prior, S.M., & Welling, K.A. (2001). "Read in your head": A Vygotskian analysis of the transition from oral to silent reading. *Reading Psychology, 22*(1), 1–15.

Prochaska, J.O., & Norcross, J.C. (2007). *Systems of psychotherapy* (6th ed.). Belmont, CA: Wadsworth.

Pryce, C.R., Bettschen, D., Bahr, N.I., & Feldon, J. (2001). Comparison of the effects of infant handling, isolation, and nonhandling on acoustic startle, prepulse inhibition, locomotion, and HPA activity in the adult rat. *Behavioral Neuroscience, 115*(1), 71–83.

Public Health Agency of Canada (2006). *HIV/AIDS in Canada.* Surveillance Report to December 31, 2005. Retrieved on August 15, 2010, from http://www.phac-aspc.gc.ca/publicat/aids-sida/haic-vsac1205/index-eng.php.

Public Health Agency of Canada (2008). *STI—Sexually Transmitted Infections.* Retrieved on August 15, 2010, from http://www.phac-aspc.gc.ca/publicat/std-mts/index-eng.php.

Pulley, B. (1998, June 16). Those seductive snake eyes: Tales of growing up gambling. *The New York Times,* A1, A28.

Putnam, R.D. (2000) *Bowling alone: The collapse and revival of American community.* New York: Simon & Schuster.

R

R. v. Beland (1987). [1987] 2 S.C.R. 398.

Rachman, S. (2000). Joseph Wolpe (1915–1997): Obituary. *American Psychologist, 55*(4), 431–432.

Radel, M., et al. (2005). Haplotype-based localization of an alcohol dependence gene to the 5q34 y-amino-butyric acid type A gene cluster. *Archives of General Psychiatry, 62*(1), 47–55.

Rainville, P., et al. (2002). Hypnosis modulates activity in brain structures involved in the regulation of consciousness. *Journal of Cognitive Neuroscience, 14*(6), 887–901.

Ramachandran, V.S., & Rogers-Ramachandran, D. (1996). Synaesthesia in phantom limbs induced with mirrors. *Proceedings. Biological Sciences, 263,* 377–386.

Ramel, W., Goldin, P.R. Carmona, P.E., & McQuaid, J.R. (2004). The effects of mindfulness meditation on cognitive processes and affect in patients with past depression. *Cognitive Therapy & Research, 28*(4), 433–455.

Randel, B., Stevenson, H.W., & Witruk, E. (2000). Attitudes, beliefs, and mathematics achievement of German and Japanese high school students. *International Journal of Behavioral Development, 24*(2), 190–198.

Rath, N. (2002). The power to feel fear and the one to feel happiness are the same. *Journal of Happiness Studies, 3*(1), 1–21.

Rathus, J.H., & Sanderson, W.C. (1999). *Marital distress: Cognitive behavioral interventions for couples.* Northvale, NJ: Jason Aronson.

Rathus, S.A. (2008–2009). *HDEV.* Mason, OH: 4LTR Press/Cengage Learning.

Raynor, H.A., & Epstein, L.H. (2001). Dietary variety, energy regulation, and obesity. *Psychological Bulletin, 127*(3), 325–341.

Reas, D.L., & Grilo, C.M. (2007). Timing and sequence of the onset of overweight, dieting, and binge eating in overweight patients with binge eating disorder. International *Journal of Eating Disorders, 40*(2), 165–170.

Reed, J.M., & Squire, L.R. (1997). Impaired recognition memory in patients with lesions limited to the hippocampal formation. *Behavioral Neuroscience, 111*(4), 667–675.

Reeder, G.D. (2001). On perceiving multiple causes and inferring multiple internal attributes. *Psychological Inquiry, 12*(1), 34–36.

Reese, C.M., & Cherry, K.E. (2002). The effects of age, ability, and memory monitoring on prospective memory task performance. *Aging, Neuropsychology & Cognition, 9*(2), 98–113.

Regier, T., Kay, P., & Cook, R.S. (2005). Focal colors are universal after all. *Proceedings of the National Academy of Sciences, 102*(23), 8386–8391.

Renner, M.J., & Mackin, R.S. (1998). A life stress instrument for classroom use. *Teaching of Psychology, 25*(1), 47.

Rescorla, R.A. (1967). Inhibition of delay in Pavlovian fear conditioning. *Journal of Comparative & Physiological Psychology, 64*(1), 114–120.

Rescorla, R.A. (1999). Partial reinforcement reduces the associative change produced by nonreinforcement.

Rezvani, A.H., & Levin, E.D. (2001). Cognitive effects of nicotine. *Biological Psychiatry, 49*(3), 258–267.

Rhee, S.H., & Waldman, I.D. (2002). Genetic and environmental influences on antisocial behavior: A meta-analysis of twin and adoption studies. *Psychological Bulletin, 128*(3), 490–529.

Ribeiro, S., & Nicolelis, M.A.L. (2004). Reverberation, storage, and postsynaptic propagation of memories during sleep. *Learning & Memory, 11*(6), 686–696.

Richardson, G.E. (2002). The metatheory of resilience and resiliency. *Journal of Clinical Psychology, 58*(3), 307–321.

Rickard, T.C., et al. (2000). The calculating brain: An fMRI study. *Neuropsychologia, 38*(3), 325–335.

Riley & Kendler, 2005. Riley, B., & Kendler, K.S. (2005). Genetics of schizophrenia: Linkage and association studies. In K.S. Kendler, & L.J. Eaves (Eds.), *Psychiatric genetics* (pp. 95–140). *Review of psychiatry series, 24*(1). Washington, DC: American Psychiatric Publishing, Inc.

Riso, L.P., et al. (2003). Cognitive aspects of chronic depression. *Journal of Abnormal Psychology, 112*(1), 72–80.

Robbins, S.B., Le, H., & Lauver, K. (2005). Promoting successful college outcomes for all students.

Roberson, D., Davidoff, J., & Shapiro, L. (2002). Squaring the circle: The cultural relativity of good shape. *Journal of Cognition & Culture, 2*(1), 29–51.

Roberts, D.F. Foehr, U.G., & Rideout, V. (2005). *Generation M: Medical in the lives of 8–18 year olds.* Kaiser Family Foundation March 2005. Retrieved August 7, 2010, from http://www.kff.org/entmedia/7251.cfm.

Robins, R.W., Gosling, S.D., & Craik, K.H. (1999). An empirical analysis of trends in psychology. *American Psychologist, 54*(2), 117–128.

Robson, D, & Robson, M. (2000). Ethical issues in internet counselling. *Counselling Psychology Quarterly, 13,* 249–257.

Rodafinos, A., Vucevic, A., & Sideridis, G.D. (2005). The effectiveness of compliance techniques: Foot in the door versus door in the face. *Journal of Social Psychology,* 145(2), 237–239.

Roelofs, K., et al. (2002). Hypnotic susceptibility in patients with conversion disorder. *Journal of Abnormal Psychology, 111*(2), 390–395.

Rogers, C. (1951). *Client-centered therapy: Its current practice, implications and theory.* London: Constable.

Rolling Stone. (April 29, 2010). Retrieved on September 14, 2010 from http://www.rollingstone.com/movies/news/the-tao-of-robert-downey-jr-the-new-issue-of-rolling-stone-20100429.

Romero, E., Luengo, M.A., & Sobral, J. (2001). Personality and antisocial behaviour: Study of temperamental dimensions. *Personality & Individual Differences, 31*(3), 329–348.

Roncesvalles, M.N.C., Woollacott, M.H., & Jensen, J.L. (2001). Development of lower extremity kinetics for balance control in infants and young children. *Journal of Motor Behavior, 33*(2), 180–192.

Ronson, A., Cohen, K.R., & Hunsley, J. (2010, June 4). *What does psychological practice look like across Canada?* Interim report presented at the meeting of the Canadian Psychological Association, Winnipeg, MA.

Rosenbaum, D.E. (2000). On left-handedness, its causes and costs. *The New York Times On the Web.* Retrieved online from http://partners.nytimes.com/library/national/science/health/051600hth-genetics-lefthanded.html.

Roser, M., & Gazzaniga, M.S. (2004). Automatic brains—Interpretive minds. *Current Directions in Psychological Science, 13*(2), 56–59.

Ross, S.E., Niebling, B.C., & Heckert, T.M. (1999). Sources of stress among college students. *College Student Journal, 33,* 312.

Ross, S.R., Lutz, C.J., & Bailley, S.E. (2002). Positive and negative symptoms of schizotypy and the Five-Factor Model: A domain and facet level analysis. *Journal of Personality Assessment, 79*(1), 53–72.

Roth, B.L., Hanizavareh, S., & Blum, A. (2004). Serotonin receptors represent highly favorable molecular targets for cognitive enhancement in schizophrenia and other disorders. *Psychopharmacology, 174*(1), 17–24.

Rotter, J. (1990). Internal versus external control of reinforcement. *American Psychologist, 45,* 489–493.

Rovee-Collier, C. (1999). The development of infant memory. *Current Directions in Psychological Science, 8*(3), 80–85.

Royal Commission on Aboriginal Peoples (1995). *Choosing life: Special report on suicide among Aboriginal people.* Ottawa: Minister of Supply and Services Canada.

Rubenstein, A.J., Langlois, J.H., & Roggman, L.A. (2002). What makes faces attractive and why: The role of averageness in defining facial beauty. In G. Rhodes & L.A. Zebrowitz (Eds.), *Facial attractiveness: Evolutionary, cognitive, and social perspectives. Advances in visual cognition, vol. 1* (pp. 1–22). Westport, CT: Ablex Publishing.

Rubinstein, S., & Caballero, B. (2000). Is Miss America an undernourished role model? *Journal of the American Medical Association online, 283*(12).

Rude, S.S., Hertel, P.T., Jarrold, W., Covich, J., & Hedlund, S. (1999). Depression-related impairments in prospective memory. *Cognition & Emotion, 13*(3), 267–276.

Rudy, D., & Grusec, J.E. (2001). Correlates of authoritarian parenting in individualist and collectivist cultures and implications for understanding the transmission of values. *Journal of Cross-Cultural Psychology, 32*(2), 202–212.

Ruff, S., et al. (2003). Neural substrates of impaired categorical perception of phonemes in adult dyslexics: An fMRI study. *Brain & Cognition, 53*(2) 331–334.

Ruiter, R.A.C., Abraham, C., & Kok, G. (2001). Scary warnings and rational precautions: A review of the psychology of fear appeals. *Psychology & Health, 16*(6), 613–630.

Rushton, J.P. (1991). Mongoloid-caucasoid differences in brain size from military samples. *Intelligence, 15,* 351–359.

Rushton, J.P. (1992). Contributions to the history of psychology: XC evolutionary biology and heritable traits (with reference to oriental-white-black differences). *Psychological Reports, 71,* 811–821.

Rushton, J.P. (1997). Cranial size and IQ in Asian Americans from birth to age seven. *Intelligence, 25,* 7–20.

Rushton, J.P., Skuy, M., & Fridjhon, P. (2003). Performance on Raven's Advanced Progressive Matrices by African, East Indian, and White engineering students in South Africa. *Intelligence, 31*(2), 123–137.

Rutkowski, G.K., Gruder, C.L., & Romer, D. (1983). Group cohesiveness, social norms, and bystander intervention. *Journal of Personality and Social Psychology, 44,* 545–552.

Rutter, M., & Silberg, J. (2002). Gene-environment interplay in relation to emotional and behavioral disturbance. *Annual Review of Psychology, 53*(1), 463–490.

S

Sackeim, H.A., Prudic, J. Devanand, D.P., Nobler, M.S., Lisanby, S.H., Peyser, S., Fitzsimons, L., Moody, B.J., & Clark, J. (2000) *A prospective, randomized, double-blind comparison of bilateral and right unilateral electroconvulsive therapy at different stimulus intensities, 57,* 425–534.

Safdar, S., Friedlmeier, W., Matsumoto, D., Yoo, S.H., Kwantes, C.T., Kakai, H., & Shigemasu, E. (2009). Variations of emotional display rules within and across cultures: A comparison between Canada, USA, and Japan. *Canadian Journal of Behavioural Science, 41,* 1–10.

Sagrestano, L.M., McCormick, S.H., Paikoff, R.L., & Holmbeck, G.N. (1999). Pubertal development and parent–child conflict in low-income, urban, African American adolescents. *Journal of Research on Adolescence, 9*(1), 85–107.

Salmon, P., et al. (2004). Mindfulness meditation in clinical practice. *Cognitive & Behavioral Practice, 11*(4), 434–446.

Salovey, P., & Wegener, D.T. (2003). Communicating about health: Message framing, persuasion and health behavior. In J. Suls & K.A. Wallston (Eds.), *Social psychological foundations of health and illness* (pp. 54–81). Malden, MA: Blackwell Publishers.

Salovey, P., Rothman, A.J., Detweiler, J.B., & Steward, W. (2000). Emotional states and physical health. *American Psychologist, 55,* 110–121.

Salovey, P., Stroud, L.R., Woolery, A., & Epel, E.S. (2002). Perceived emotional intelligence, stress reactivity, and symptom reports: Further explorations using the trait meta-mood scale.

Sam, D.L., & Berry, J.W. (2006). *The Cambridge handbook of acculturation psychology.* Cambridge, UK: Cambridge University Press.

Sanna, L.J., & Meier, S. (2000). Looking for clouds in a silver lining: Self-esteem, mental simulations, and temporal confidence changes. *Journal of Research in Personality, 34*(2), 236–251.

Santee, R.T., & Maslach, C. (1982). To agree or not to agree: Personal dissent amid social pressure to conform. *Journal of Personality and Social Psychology, 42*(4), 690–700.

Sarbin, T.R., & Coe, W.C. (1972). *Hypnosis.* New York: Holt, Rinehart and Winston.

Saunders, K.W. (2003). Regulating youth access to violent video games: Three responses to First Amendment concerns. http://www.law.msu.edu/lawrev/ 2003–1/2–Saunders.pdf.

Savage, C.R., et al. (2001). Prefrontal regions supporting spontaneous and directed application of verbal learning strategies. Evidence from PET. *Brain, 124*(1), 219–231.

Savage-Rumbaugh, E.S., & Fields, W.M. (2000). Linguistic, cultural and cognitive capacities of bonobos (Pan paniscus). *Culture & Psychology, 6*(2), 131–153.

Savage-Rumbaugh, E.S., et al. (1993). Monographs of the Society for Research in Child Development, *58*(3–4), v–221.

Sawa, A., & Snyder, S.H. (2002, April 26). Schizophrenia: Diverse approaches to a complex disease. *Science,* pp. 692–695.

Saxe, L., & Ben-Shakhar, G. (1999). Admissibility of polygraph tests: The application of scientific standards post-Daubert. *Psychology, Public Policy & Law, 5*(1), 203–223.

Scarr, S., & Weinberg, R.A. (1976). IQ test performance of Black children adopted by White families.

Scaturo, D.J. (2005). *A three-phase learning-based integrative model of psychotherapy: Therapeutic alliance, technical interventions, and relearning.* Washington, DC: American Psychological Association.

Schachter, S., & Singer, J.E. (1962). Cognitive, social, and physiological determinants of emotional state. *Psychological Review, 69,* 379–399.

Schacter, D.L. (1992). Understanding implicit memory: A cognitive neuroscience approach.

Schacter, D.L. (1999). The seven sins of memory: Insights from psychology and cognitive neuroscience. *American Psychologist, 54*(3), 182–203.

Schacter, D.L., Cooper, L.A., & Treadwell, J. (1993). Preserved priming of novel objects across size transformation in amnesic patients. *Psychological Science, 4*(5), 331–335.

Schacter, D.L., Dobbins, I.G., & Schnyer, D.M. (2004). Specificity of priming: A cognitive neuroscience perspective. *Nature Reviews Neuroscience, 5*(11), 853–862.

Schaie, K.W., Willis, S.L., & Caskie, G.I.L. (2004). The Seattle longitudinal study: Relationship between personality and cognition. *Aging, Neuropsychology & Cognition, 11*(2–3), 304–324.

Schatzkin, A., Lanza, E., Corle, D., Lance, P., Iber, F., Caan, B., et al. (2000). Lack of effect of a low-fat, high-fiber diet on the recurrence of colorectal adenomas. *New England Journal of Medicine, 342,* 1149–1155.

Schmitt, D.P. (2003). Universal sex differences in the desire for sexual variety: Tests from 52 nations, 6 continents, and 13 islands. *Journal of Personality and Social Psychology, 85*(1), 85–104.

Schmitt, D.P., Shackelford, T.K., Duntley, J., Tooke, W., & Buss, D.M. (2001). The desire for sexual variety as a key to understanding basic human mating strategies. *Personal Relationships, 8*(4), 425–455.

Schneider, K.J., Bugental, J.F.T., & Pierson, J.F. (Eds). (2003). The handbook of humanistic psychology: Leading edges in theory, research, and practice. *Psychotherapy Research, 13*(1), 119–121.

Schneider, R.H., et al. (1995). A randomized controlled trial of stress reduction for hypertension in older African Americans. *Hypertension, 26,* 820.

Schneiderman, N., Ironson, G., & Siegel, S.D. (2005). Stress and health: Psychological, behavioral, and biological determinants. *Annual Review of Clinical Psychology, 1*(1), 607–628

Schultz, D.P., & Schultz, S.E. (2008). *A history of modern psychology* (9th ed.). Belmont, CA: Cengage.

Schupf, N. (2000, July). Epidemiology of dementia in Down syndrome. Paper presented to the World Alzheimer Congress 2000, Washington, DC.

Schwartz, J.R.L. (2004). Pharmacologic management of daytime sleepiness. *Journal of Clinical Psychiatry, 65*(Suppl. 16), 46–49.

Schwartz, J., & Wald, M.L. (2003, March 9). NASA's curse? "Groupthink" is 30 years old, and still going strong. *The New York Times online.*

Schwartz, R.M., & Gottman, J.M. (1976). Toward a task analysis of assertive behavior. *Journal of Consulting and Clinical Psychology, 44,* 910–920.

Segal, E. (2004). Incubation in insight problem solving. *Creativity Research Journal, 16*(1), 141–148.

Segal, N.L., & Roy, A. (2001). Suicidal attempts and ideation in twins whose co-twins' deaths were non-suicides: Replication and elaboration. *Personality & Individual Differences, 31*(3), 445–452.

Segal, P. (director). (2004). *50 first dates* [motion picture]. United States: Columbia Pictures Corporation.

Seidman, S.M. (2003). The aging male: Androgens, erectile dysfunction, and depression. *Journal of Clinical Psychiatry, 64*(Suppl. 10), 31–37.

Selemon, L.D., Mrzljak, J., Kleinman, J.E., Herman, M.M., & Goldman-Rakic, P.S. (2003). Regional specificity in the neuropathologic substrates of schizophrenia: A morphometric analysis of Broca's area 44 and area 9. *Archives of General Psychiatry, 60*(1), 69–77.

Seligman, M.E.P. (1996, August). Predicting and preventing depression. Master lecture presented to the meeting of the American Psychological Association, Toronto.

Selye, H. (1976). *The stress of life* (Rev. ed.). New York: McGraw-Hill. Kutash, et al. (Eds.), *Handbook on stress and anxiety.* San Francisco: Jossey-Bass.

Selye, H. (1980). The stress concept today. In I.L. *Sex & Marital Therapy, 31*(3), 173–185.

SES Research. (2007). *Canadian Pain Survey.* Retrieved March 1, 2010, from http://www.painexplained.ca/gestion/20071102PainSurvey.pdf .

Shadish, W.R., Matt, G.E., Navarro, A.M., & Phillips, G. (2000). The effects of psychological therapies under clinically representative conditions: A meta-analysis. *Psychological Bulletin, 126*(4), 512–529.

Shanker, S.G., Savage-Rumbaugh, E.S., & Taylor, T.J. (1999). Kanzi: A new beginning. *Animal Learning & Behavior, 27*(1), 24–25.

Shapiro, F. (1989). Efficacy of the eye movement desensitization procedure in the treatment of traumatic memories. *Journal of Traumatic Stress, 2,* 199–223.

Shapley, R., & Hawken, M. (2002). Neural mechanisms for color perception in the primary visual cortex. *Current Opinion in Neurobiology, 12*(4), 426–432.

Shen, R-Y, Choong, K-C, & Thompson, A.C. (2007). Long-term reduction in ventral tegmental area dopamine neuron population activity following repeated stimulant or ethanol treatment. *Biological Psychiatry, 61*(1), 93–100.

Shenal, B.V., & Harrison, D.W. (2003). Investigation of the laterality of hostility, cardiovascular regulation, and auditory recognition. *International Journal of Neuroscience, 113*(2), 205–222.

Shenefelt, P.D. (2003). Hypnosis-facilitated relaxation using self-guided imagery during dermatologic procedures. *American Journal of Clinical Hypnosis, 45*(3), 225–232.

Shepard, P. (1987). Telephone therapy: An alternative to isolation. *Clinical Social Work Journal, 15,* 56–65.

Shepperd, J.A., & Koch, E.J. (2005). Pitfalls in teaching judgment heuristics. *Teaching of Psychology, 32*(1), 43–46.

Sherif, M., Harvey, O.J., White, B.J., Hood, W.R., & Sherif, C.W. (1988). *The Robbers Cave experiment: Intergroup conflict and cooperation.* Middletown, CT: Wesleyan University Press.

Shields, M. (2002). Shift work and health. *Health Reports, 13*(4), 11–31. Statistics Canada, catalogue 82–003.

Shimamura, A.P. (2002). Memory retrieval and executive control processes. In D.T. Stuss & R.T. Knight (Eds.), *Principles of frontal lobe function* (pp. 210–220). London: Oxford University Press.

Shneidman, E.S. (2001). *Comprehending suicide.* Washington, DC: American Psychological Association.

Siegel, J.M. (2002). The REM sleep–memory consolidation hypothesis. *Science, 294*(5544), 1058–1063.

Silventoinen, K., et al. (2007). Genetic and environmental factors in relative weight from birth to age 18: The Swedish young male twins study. *International Journal of Obesity, 31*(4), 615–621.

Silver, E. (1994). Cited in DeAngelis, T. (1994). Experts see little impact from insanity plea ruling. *APA Monitor, 25*(6), 28.

Simonton, D.K. (2000). Creativity: Cognitive, personal, developmental, and social aspects. *American Psychologist, 55,* 151–158.

Singareddy, R.K., & Balon, R. (2002). Sleep in posttraumatic stress disorder. *Annals of Clinical Psychiatry, 14*(3), 183–190.

Singer, J.A. (2009, January 10). Goodbye "H.M." H.M. taught us about identity, not just memory. *Psychology Today Blogs: Life Scripts*. Retrieved from http://www.psychologytoday.com/blog/life-scripts/200901/goodbye-hm.

Singh, R., Yeo, S.E-L., Lin, P.K.F., & Tan, L. (2007). Multiple mediators of the attitude similarity-attraction relationship: Dominance of inferred attraction and subtlety of affect. *Basic and Applied Social Psychology, 29*(1), 61–74.

Skinner, B.F. (1948). *Walden Two.* New York: Macmillan.

Slobin, D.I. (1983). Crosslinguistic evidence for basic child grammar. Paper presented to the biennial meeting of the Society for Research in Child Development, Detroit.

Sloman, S.A., Harrison, M.C., & Malt, B.C. (2002). Recent exposure affects artifact naming. *Memory & Cognition, 30*(5), 687–695.

Smetana, J.G., Daddis, C., & Chuang, S.S. (2003). "Clean your room!" A longitudinal investigation of adolescent–parent conflict and conflict resolution in middle-class African American families. *Journal of Adolescent Research, 18*(6), 631–650.

Smiley, J. (2000, May 7). The good life. *The New York Times magazine,* pp. 58–59.

Smith, M.L., & Glass, G.V. (1977). Meta-analysis of psychotherapy outcome studies. *American Psychologist, 32,* 752–760.

Smith, R.A., & Weber, A.L. (2005). Applying social psychology in everyday life. In F.W. Schneider, et al. (Eds.), *Applied social psychology: Understanding and addressing social and practical problems* (pp. 75–99). Thousand Oaks, CA: Sage Publications.

Smits, T., Storms, G., Rosseel, Y., & De Boeck, P. (2002). Fruits and vegetables categorized: An application of the generalized context model. *Psychonomic Bulletin & Review, 9*(4), 836–844.

Song, V. (2009, March 25). True happiness: The most contented place in Canada is Saint John, N.B. *The Winnipeg Sun*. Retrieved May 11, 2010, from http://www.winnipegsun.com/news/canada/2009/03/25/8882371.html#email.

Sorenson, S.B., & Rutter, C.M. (1991). Transgenerational patterns of suicide attempt. *Journal of Consulting and Clinical Psychology, 59,* 861–866.

Soussignan, R. (2002). Duchenne smile, emotional experience, and autonomic reactivity: A test of the facial feedback hypotheses. *Emotion, 2*(1), 52–74.

Spanos, N. (1991). A sociocognitive approach to hypnosis. In S.J. Lynn & J.W Rhue (eds.), *Theories of hypnosis: Current models and perspectives.* New York: Guilford Press.

Spasojevic, J., & Alloy, L.B. (2001). Rumination as a common mechanism relating depressive risk factors to depression. *Emotion, 1*(1), 25–37.

Spence, I., Yu, J.J., Feng, J. & Marshman, J. (2009). Women match men when learning a spatial Skill. *Journal of Experimental Psychology: Learning, Memory, and Cognition, 35,* 1097–1103.

Spencer, M.B., Noll, E., & Cassidy, E. (2005). Monetary incentives in support of academic achievement: Results of a randomized field trial involving high-achieving, low-resource, ethnically diverse urban adolescents. *Evaluation Review, 29*(3), 199–222.

Sperling, G. (1960). The information available in brief visual presentations. *Psychological Monographs, 74,* 1–29.

Sperry, R.W. (1982). Some effects of disconnecting the cerebral hemispheres. *Science, 217*(4566), 1223–1226.

Spiers, H.J., Maguire, E.A., & Burgess, N. (2001). Hippocampal amnesia. *Neurocase, 7*(5), 357–382.

Sprecher, S., Sullivan, Q., & Hatfield, E. (1994). Mate selection preferences. *Journal of Personality and Social Psychology, 66*(6), 1074–1080.

Squire, L.R. (2004). Memory systems of the brain: A brief history and current perspective. *Neurobiology of Learning & Memory, 82*(3), 171–177.

Stacy, A.W., Bentler, P.M., & Flay, B.R. (1994). Attitudes and health behavior in diverse populations. *Health Psychology, 13,* 73–85.

Stasser, G. (1999). A primer of social decision scheme theory: Models of group influence, competitive model-testing, and prospective modeling. *Organizational Behavior & Human Decision Processes, 80*(1), 3–20.

Statistics Canada. (2003). Canadian community health survey: Mental health and well-being. Catalogue no. 82-617-XIE. Retrieved on June 21, 2010, from http://www.statcan.gc.ca/pub/82-617-x/index-eng.htm.

Statistics Canada. (2005). Mortality, summary list of causes. Catalogue no. 84F0209X. Retrieved on June 23, 2010, from http://www.statcan.gc.ca/pub/84f0209x/84f0209x2005000-eng.pdf.

Statistics Canada. (2006). *Canada's ethnocultural mosaic, 2006 census.* Catalogue no. 97-562-X. Retrieved July 6, 2010, from http://www12.statcan.ca/census-recensement/2006/as-sa/97-562/pdf/97-562-XIE2006001.pdf.

Statistics Canada. (2006). Retrieved August 17, 2010, from http://www12.statcan.gc.ca/census-recensement/2006/dp-pd/92-596/P2-2.cfm?Lang=eng&T=PR&LINE_ID=1405&TOPIC_ID=1400.

Statistics Canada. (2009a). Population by selected ethnic origins, by province and territory (2006 Census). Retrieved May 21, 2008, from http://www40.statcan.ca/l01/cst01/demo26a-eng.htm.

Statistics Canada. (2009b). Visible minority population, by age group (2006 Census). Retrieved May 21, 2008, from http://www40.statcan.ca/l01/cst01/demo50a-eng.htm.

Stein, D.G., Brailowsky, S., & Will, B. (1995). *Brain repair.* New York: Oxford University Press.

Steinberg, L. (1996). *Beyond the classroom.* New York: Simon & Schuster.

Steinberg, L. (2001). We know some things: Parent–adolescent relationships in retrospect and prospect. *Journal of Research on Adolescence, 11*(1), 1–19.

Sternberg, R.J. (1988). Triangulating love. In R.J. Sternberg & M.J. Barnes (Eds.), *The psychology of love.* New Haven, CT: Yale University Press.

Sternberg, R.J. (2000). Wisdom as a form of giftedness. *Gifted Child Quarterly, 44*(4), 252–260.

Sternberg, R.J. (2001). What is the common thread of creativity? *American Psychologist, 56*(4), 360–362.

Sternberg, R.J., & Lubart, T.I. (1995). *Defying the crowd: cultivating creativity in a culture of conformity.* New York: Free Press.

Sternberg, R.J., & Lubart, T.I. (1996). Investing in creativity. *American Psychologist, 51,* 677–688.

Sternberg, R.J., & Williams, W.M. (1997). Does the Graduate Record Examination predict meaningful success in the graduate training of psychologists?

Sternberg, R.J., Lautrey, J., & Lubart, T.I. (2003). *Models of intelligence: International perspectives.*

Stevens, S.E., Hynan, M.T., & Allen, M. (2000). A meta-analysis of common factor and specific treatment effects across the outcome domains of the phase model of psychotherapy. *Clinical Psychology: Science and Practice, 7,* 273–290.

Stevenson, H.W., Lee, S.Y., & Stigler, J.W. (1986). Mathematics achievement of Chinese, Japanese, and American children. *Science, 231,* 693–699.

Stewart, A.E. (2005). Attributions of responsibility for motor vehicle crashes. *Accident Analysis & Prevention. 37*(4), 681–688.

Stickgold, R., Hobson, J.A., Fosse, R., & Fosse, M. (2001). Sleep, learning, and dreams: Off-line memory reprocessing. *Science, 294*(5544), 1052–1057.

Stier, D.S., & Hall, J.A. (1984). Gender differences in touch. *Journal of Personality and Social Psychology, 47,* 440–459.

Stipek, D., & Hakuta, K. (2007). Strategies to ensure that no child starts from behind. In Aber, J.L., et al. (Eds.). *Child development and social policy: Knowledge for action, APA Decade of Behavior volumes* (pp. 129–145). Washington, DC: American Psychological Association.

Straube, E.R., & Oades, R.D. (1992). *Schizophrenia.* San Diego: Academic Press.

Striegel-Moore, R.H., & Cachelin, F.M. (2001). Etiology of eating disorders in women. *Counseling Psychologist, 29*(5), 635–661.

Striegel-Moore, R.H., et al. (2004). Changes in weight and body image over time in women with eating disorders. *International Journal of Eating Disorders, 36*(3), 315–327.

Stroele, A., et al. (2002). GABA-sub(A) receptormodulating neuroactive steroid composition in patients with panic disorder before and during paroxetine treatment. *American Journal of Psychiatry, 159*(1), 145–147.

Strom, J.C., & Buck, R.W. (1979). Staring and participants' sex. *Personality and Social Psychology Bulletin, 5,* 114–117.

Stutzer, A. (2004). The role of income aspirations in individual happiness. *Journal of Economic Behavior & Organization, 54*(1), 89–109.

Sufka, K.J., & Price, D.D. (2002). Gate control theory reconsidered. *Brain & Mind, 3*(2), 277–290.

Suler, J. (2005, March 29). Psychological qualities of cyberspace. http://www.rider.edu/suler/psycyber/netself.html.

Sullivan, E.V., Rosenbloom, M.J., Lim, K.O., & Pfefferbaum, A. (2000). Longitudinal changes in cognition, gait, and balance in abstinent and relapsed alcoholic men: Relationships to changes in brain structure. *Neuropsychology, 14,* 178–188.

Sullivan, P. (2002). Course and outcome of anorexia nervosa and bulimia nervosa. In Fairburn, C.G. & Brownell, K.D. (Eds.). *Eating Disorders and Obesity* (pp. 226–232). New York, New York: Guilford.

Suttle, C.M., Banks, M.S., & Graf, E.W. (2002). FPL and sweep VEP to tritan stimuli in young human infants. *Vision Research, 42*(26), 2879–2891.

Suvisaari, J., Mautemps, N., Haukka, J., Hovi, T., & Lönnqvist, J. (2003). Childhood central nervous system viral infections and adult schizophrenia. *The American Journal of Psychiatry, 160,* 1183–1185.

Swendsen, J.D., et al. (2000). Mood and alcohol consumption: An experience sampling test of the self-medication hypothesis. *Journal of Abnormal Psychology, 109*(2), 198–204.

Swerdlow, N.R., et al. (2003). Prestimulus modification of the startle reflex: Relationship to personality and psychological markers of dopamine function. *Biological Psychology, 62*(1), 17–26.

Swinyard, W.R., Kau, A., & Phua, H. (2001). Happiness, materialism, and religious experience in the U.S. and Singapore. *Journal of Happiness Studies, 2*(1), 13–32.

Szala, M. (2002). Two-level pattern recognition in a class of knowledge-based systems. *Knowledge-Based Systems, 15*(1–2), 95–101.

T

Takahashi, T., et al. (2002). Melatonin alleviates jet lag symptoms caused by an 11-hour eastward flight. *Psychiatry & Clinical Neurosciences, 56*(3), 301–302.

Talwar, V. & Lee, K. (2008). Social and cognitive correlates of children's lying behavior. *Child Development, 79,* 866–881.

Tausig, M., Michello, J., & Subedi, S. (2004). *A sociology of mental illness (2nd ed.).* Englewood Cliffs, NJ: Prentice Hall.

Taylor, D.J., & McFatter, R.M. (2003). Cognitive performance after sleep deprivation: Does personality make a difference? *Personality & Individual Differences, 34*(7), 1179–1193.

Taylor, S.E. (2000). Cited in Goode, E. (2000, May 19). Response to stress found that's particularly female. *The New York Times,* p. A20.

Taylor, S.E., et al. (2000b). Biobehavioral responses to stress in females: Tend-and-befriend, not fight-or-flight. *Psychological Review, 107*(3), 411–429.

Teachout, T. (2000, April 2). For more artists, a fine old age. *The New York Times online.*

Teller, D.Y. (1998). Spatial and temporal aspects of infant color vision. *Vision Research, 38*(21), 3275–3282.

Tenenbaum, H.R., & Leaper, C. (2002). Are parents' gender schemas related to their children's gender-related cognitions? A meta-analysis. *Developmental Psychology, 38*(4), 615–630.

Tennen, H., & Affleck, G. (2000). The perception of personal control: Sufficiently important to warrant careful scrutiny. *Personality & Social Psychology Bulletin, 26*(2), 152–156.

Terrace, H.S. (1979, November). How Nim Chimpsy changed my mind. *Psychology Today,* pp. 65–76.

Tetlock, P.E., & McGraw, A.P. (2005). Theoretically framing relational framing. *Journal of Consumer Psychology, 15*(1), 35–37.

Thom, A., Sartory, G., & Johren, P. (2000). Comparison between one-session psychological treatment and benzodiazepine in dental phobia. *Journal of Consulting and Clinical Psychology, 68*(3), 378–387.

Thomas, S.L., Skitka, L.J., Christen, S., & Jurgena, M. (2002). Social facilitation and impression formation. *Basic & Applied Social Psychology, 24,* 67–70.

Thompson, P.M., et al. (2001). Mapping adolescent brain change reveals dynamic wave of accelerated gray matter loss in very early-onset schizophrenia.

Thurstone, L.L. (1938). Primary mental abilities. *Psychometric Monographs, 1.*

Tigner, R.B., & Tigner, S.S. (2000). Triarchic theories of intelligence: Aristotle and Sternberg. *History of Psychology, 3*(2), 168–176.

Tjepkema, M. (2005) Adult obesity in Canada: Measured height and weight. *Statistics Canada 82-620-MWE2005001.*

Tolman, E.C., & Honzik, C.H. (1930). Introduction and removal of reward, and maze performance in rats. *University of California Publications in Psychology, 4,* 257–275.

Tong, H. (2001). Loneliness, depression, anxiety, and the locus of control. *Chinese Journal of Clinical Psychology, 9*(3), 196–197.

Tormala, Z.L., & Petty, R.E. (2004). Source credibility and attitude certainty: A metacognitive analysis of resistance to persuasion. *Journal of Consumer Psychology, 14*(4), 427–442.

Townsend, E., et al. (2001). The efficacy of problem-solving treatments after deliberate self-harm. Meta-analysis of randomizes controlled trials with respect to depression, hopelessness and improvement in problems. *Psychological Medicine, 31*(6), 979–988.

Triandis, H.C. (2005). Issues in individualism and collectivism research. In R.M. Sorrentino, et al. (Eds.), *Cultural and social behavior: The Ontario Symposium, 10* (pp. 207–225). Mahwah, NJ: Erlbaum.

Triandis, H.C., & Suh, E.M. (2002). Cultural influences on personality. *Annual Review of Psychology, 53*(1), 133–160.

Trobst, K.K., Collins, R.L., & Embree, J.M. (1994). The role of emotion in social support provision. *Journal of Social and Personal Relationships, 11,* 45–62.

Trull, T.J., Stepp, S.D., & Durrett, C.A. (2003). Research on borderline personality disorder: An update. *Current Opinion in Psychiatry, 16*(1), 77–82.

Tsai, G., & Coyle, J.T. (2002). Glutamatergic mechanisms in schizophrenia. *Annual Review of Pharmacology & Toxicology, 42,* 165–179.

Tsang, Y.C. (1938). Hunger motivation in gastrectomized rats. *Journal of Comparative Psychology, 26,* 1–17.

Tsou, M., & Liu, J. (2001). Happiness and domain satisfaction in Taiwan. *Journal of Happiness Studies, 2*(3), 269–288.

Tulving, E. (1985). How many memory systems are there? *American Psychologist, 40,* 385–398.

Turk, D.C., & Okifuji, A. (2002). Psychological factors in chronic pain: Evolution and revolution. *Journal of Consulting and Clinical Psychology, 70*(3), 678–690.

Turkington, D., Dudley, R., Warman, D.M., & Beck, A.T. (2004). Cognitive-behavioral therapy for schizophrenia: A review. *Journal of Psychiatric Practice, 10*(1), 5–16.

Turner, M.E., Pratkanis, A.R., & Struckman, C.K. (2007). Groupthink as social identity maintenance. In A.R. Pratkanis (Ed.), *The science of social influence: Advances and future progress.* (pp. 223–246). New York: Psychology Press.

Tversky, A., & Kahneman, D. (1982). Judgment under uncertainty. In D. Kahneman, P. Slovic, & A. Tversky (Eds.), *Judgment under uncertainty: Heuristics and biases.* New York: Cambridge University Press.

U

Ulett, G.A., & Wedding, D. (2003). Electrical stimulation, endorphins, and the practice of clinical psychology. *Journal of Clinical Psychology in Medical Settings, 10*(2), 129–131.

Underhill, J.B. (2008). The politics of crisis management: Public leadership under pressure and Lessons on leadership by terror: Finding Shaka Zulu in the attic. *Political Psychology, 29*(1), 139–143.

Updegraff, J.A., Taylor, S.E., Kemeny, M.E., & Wyatt, G.E. (2002). Positive and negative effects of HIV infection in women with low socioeconomic resources. *Personality & Social Psychology Bulletin, 28*(3), 382–394.

Usborne, E. & Taylor, D.M. (2010). The role of cultural identity clarity for self-concept clarity, self-esteem, and subjective well-being. *Personality and Social Psychology Bulletin, 36,* 883–897.

Utter, J., Neumark-Sztainer, D., Wall, M., & Story, M. (2003). Reading magazine articles about dieting and associated weight control behaviors among adolescents. *Journal of Adolescent Health, 32*(1), 78–82.

Uzakov, S., Frey, J.U., & Korz, V. (2005). Reinforcement of rat hippocampal LTP by holeboard training. *Learning & Memory, 12,* 165–171.

V

Van Anders, S.M., Chernick, A.B., Chernick, B.A., Hampson, E., & Fisher, W.A. (2005). Preliminary clinical experience with androgen administration for pre- and post-menopausal women with hypoactive sexual desire. *Journal of Sex & Marital Therapy, 31*(3), 173–185.

van der Zee, K., Thijs, M., Schakel, L. (2002). The relationship of emotional intelligence with academic intelligence and the Big Five. *European Journal of Personality,16,* 103–125.

Vandenbergh, J.G. (1993). Cited in Angier, N. (1993, August 24). Female gerbil born with males is found to be begetter of sons. *The New York Times,* p. C4.

Veenstra-Vanderweele, J., & Cook, E.H. (2003). Genetics of childhood disorders: XLVI. Autism, part 5: Genetics of autism. *Journal of the American Academy of Child and Adolescent Psychiatry, 42*(1), 116–118.

Veenvliet, S.G., & Paunonen, S.V. (2008, June). *Attractive average faces and unattractive average faces.* Research presented at the 69th Annual Convention of the Canadian Psychological Association, Halifax, Canada.

Vernon, D., et al. (2003). The effect of training distinct neuro-feedback protocols on aspects of cognitive performance. *International Journal of Psychophysiology, 47*(1), 75–85.

Vernon, P.A., Petrides, K.V., Bratko, D., & Schermer, J.A., (2010). A behavioral genetic study of trait emotional intelligence. *Emotion, 8,* 635–642.

Villa, K.K., & Abeles, N. (2000). Broad spectrum intervention and the remediation of prospective memory declines in the able elderly. *Aging & Mental Health, 4*(1), 21–29.

von Békésy, G. (1957). The ear. *Scientific American, 197,* 66–78.

Vygotsky, L. (1978). *Mind in society: The development of higher psychological processes.* Cambridge, MA: Harvard University Press.

Vygotsky, L.S. (1962). *Thought and language.* Cambridge, MA: MIT Press.

W

Wagner, R.K. (1997). Intelligence, training, and employment. *American Psychologist, 52*(10), 1059–1069.

Walker, E., Kestler, L., Bollini, A., & Hochman, K.M. (2004). Schizophrenia: Etiology and course. *Annual Review of Psychology, 55,* 401–430.

Walle, A.H. (2004). Native Americans and alcoholism therapy: The example of Handsome Lake as a tool of recovery. *Journal of Ethnicity in Substance Abuse, 3*(2), 55–79.

Walther, E., Nagengast, B., & Trasselli, C. (2005). Evaluative conditioning in social psychology: Facts and speculations. *Cognition & Emotion, 19*(2), 175–196.

Wang, C. (2002). Emotional intelligence, general self-efficacy, and coping style of juvenile delinquents.

Wang, Q. (2003). Infantile amnesia reconsidered: A cross-cultural analysis. *Memory, 11*(1), 65–80.

Wann, D.L., & Schrader, M.P. (2000). Controllability and stability in the self-serving attributions of sport spectators. *Journal of Social Psychology, 140*(2), 160–168.

Wann, D.L., Royalty, J., & Roberts, A. (2000). The self-presentation of sports fans: Investigating the importance of team identification and self-esteem. *Journal of Sport Behavior, 23*(2), 198–206.

Warman, D.M., & Beck, A.T. (2003). Cognitive behavioral therapy for schizophrenia: An overview of treatment. *Cognitive & Behavioral Practice, 10*(3), 248–254.

Warman, D.M., & Cohen, R. (2000). Stability of aggressive behaviors and children's peer relationships. *Aggressive Behavior, 26*(4), 277–290.

Warman, D.M., Grant, P., Sullivan, K., Caroff, S., & Beck, A.T. (2005). Individual and group cognitive-behavioral therapy for psychotic disorders: A pilot investigation. *Journal of Psychiatric Practice, 11*(1), 27–34.

Waters, M. (2000). Psychologists spotlight growing concern of higher suicide rates among adolescents. *Monitor on Psychology, 31*(6), 41.

Watson, J.B. (1913). Psychology as the behaviorist views it. *Psychological Review, 20,* 158–177.

Webster, J.D. (2003). An exploratory analysis of a self-assessed wisdom scale. *Journal of Adult Development, 10*(1), 13–22.

Wechsler, D. (1975). Intelligence defined and undefined. *American Psychologist, 30,* 135–139.

Wegener, D.T., Petty, R.E., Detweiler-Bedell, B.T., & Jarvis, W.B.G. (2001). Implications of attitude change theories for numerical anchoring: Anchor plausibility and the limits of anchor effectiveness. *Journal of Experimental Social Psychology, 37*(1), 62–69.

Weinmann, M., Bader, J., Endrass, J., & Hell, D. (2001). Sind Kompetenz- und Kontrollueberzeugungen depressionsabhaengig? Eine Verlaufsuntersuchung. *Zeitschrift fuer Klinische Psychologie und Psychotherapie,* 30(3), 153–158.

Weiss, A., et al. (2005). Cross-sectional age differences in personality among Medicare patients aged 65 to 100. *Psychology and Aging, 20*(1), 182–185.

Weissman, M.M. (1993). The epidemiology of personality disorders: A 1990 update. *Journal of Personality Disorders, 7,* 44–62.

West, R., & Craik, F.I.M. (1999). Age-related decline in prospective memory: The roles of cue accessibility and cue sensitivity. *Psychology & Aging, 14*(2), 264–272.

Wetzler, S.E., & Sweeney, J.A. (1986). Childhood amnesia. In D.C. Rubin (Ed.), *Autobiographical memory.* New York: Cambridge University Press.

Wheeler, M.A., & McMillan, C.T. (2001). Focal retrograde amnesia and the episodic-semantic distinction. *Cognitive, Affective & Behavioral Neuroscience, 1*(1), 22–36.

Wheeler, M.E., & Treisman, A.M. (2002). Binding in short-term visual memory. *Journal of Experimental Psychology: General, 131*(1), 48–64.

Whorf, B. (1956). *Language, thought, and reality.* New York: Wiley.

Widiger, T.A. & Weissman, M.M. (1991). Epidemiology of borderline personality disorder. *Hosp Community Psychiatry, 42,* 1015–1021.

Widiger, T.A., & Costa, P.T., Jr. (1994). Personality and personality disorders. *Journal of Abnormal Psychology, 103,* 78–91.

Wilkinson, D., & Abraham, C. (2004). Constructing an integrated model of the antecedents of adolescent smoking. *British Journal of Health Psychology, 9*(3), 315–333.

Williams, M.S., Thomsen, S.R., & McCoy, J.K. (2003). Looking for an accurate mirror: A model for the relationship between media use and anorexia. *Eating Behaviors, 4*(2), 127–134.

Wilson, K.D., & Farah, M.J. (2003). When does the visual system use viewpoint-invariant representations during recognition? *Cognitive Brain Research, 16*(3), 399–415.

Wilson, R.S. (1983). The Louisville twin study: Developmental synchronies in behavior. *Child Development, 54,* 298–316.

Winocur, G., et al. (2000). Cognitive rehabilitation in clinical neuropsychology. *Brain & Cognition, 42*(1), 120–123. *American Journal of Psychiatry, 160,* 572–574.

Winston, A.S. (1996). The context of correctness: A comment of Ruston. *Journal of Social Distress and Homelessness, 5,* 231–250.

Winston, A.S. (2003). The Funding of Scientific Racism: Wickliffe Draper and the Pioneer Fund (review). *Journal of the History of Medicine and Allied Sciences, 58,* 91–392.

Winston, A.S. (2004). *Defining difference: Race and racism in the history of psychology.* Washington, DC: American Psychological Association.

Wolkin, A., et al. (2003). Inferior frontal white matter anisotropy and negative symptoms of schizophrenia: A diffusion tensor imaging study.

Wood, W. (2000). Attitude change: Persuasion and social influence. *Annual Review of Psychology, 51,* 539–570.

Wood, W., Wong, F.Y., & Chachere, J.G. (1991). Effects of media violence on viewers' aggression in unconstrained social interaction. *Psychological Bulletin, 109,* 371–383.

X

Xie, Y., & Goyette, K. (2003). Social mobility and the educational choices of Asian Americans. *Social Science Research, 32*(3), 467–498.

Y

Yang, Y., et al. (2005). Volume reduction in prefrontal gray matter in unsuccessful criminal psychopaths. *Biological Psychiatry, 57*(10), 1103–1108.

Yatham, L.N., et al. (2000). Brain serotonin 2 receptors in major depression: A positron emission tomography study. *Archives of General Psychiatry, 57,* 850–858.

Ybarra, G.J., Passman, R.H., & Eisenberg, C.S.L. (2000). The presence of security blankets or mothers (or both) affects distress during pediatric examinations. *Journal of Consulting and Clinical Psychology, 68,* 322–330.

Yeh, C., & Chang, T. (2004). Understanding the multidimensionality and heterogeneity of the Asian American experience. *PsycCRITIQUES.*

Yehuda, R. (2002). Posttraumatic stress disorder. *New England Journal of Medicine, 346,* 109–114.

Yumino, D., & Bradley, T.D. (2007). Editorial. *American Journal of Respiratory and Critical Care Medicine, 176,* 634–635.

Z

Zajonc, R.B. (2001). Mere exposure: A gateway to the subliminal. *Current Directions in Psychological Science, 10*(6), 224–228.

Zimbardo, P.G. (2004). A situationist perspective on the psychology of evil: Understanding how good people are transformed into perpetrators.

Zimbardo, P.G., LaBerge, S., & Butler, L.D. (1993). Psychophysiological consequences of unexplained arousal. *Journal of Abnormal Psychology, 102,* 466–473.

Zimmer, C. (2002–2003). Searching for your inner chimp. *Natural History, 112*(December, 2002–January, 2003).

Zimprich, D., & Martin, M. (2002). Can longitudinal changes in processing speed explain longitudinal age changes in fluid intelligence? *Psychology & Aging, 17*(4), 690–695.

Zizak, D.M., & Reber, A.S. (2004). Implicit preferences: The role(s) of familiarity in the structural mere exposure effect. *Consciousness & Cognition: An International Journal, 13*(2), 336–362.

Zucker, A.N., Ostrove, J.M., & Stewart, A.J. (2002). College-educated women's personality development in adulthood: Perceptions and age differences. *Psychology & Aging, 17*(2), 236–244.

Name Index

Subject Index

self-serving, 312

social desirability, 15–16

volunteer, 14

"Big Five" model of personality, 241–242, *242, 243*

bilingualism in Canada, *166*

binocular cues, **66**

biofeedback training (BFT), 115–116, **289**

biological perspective, 10

biological therapies, 296–299, *296*

biopsychosocial model, **228**

on mood disorders, 265–266

on schizophrenia, 262–263, *263*

bipolar cells, **58**

bipolar disorder, **264,** 297

bisexual people, 203–204

Black Canadians, 296

blind, 17–18, **18**

blind spot, **59,** *59*

body dysmorphic disorder, **272,** 272–273

body language, 313, *313*

body mass index (BMI), 200

borderline personality disorder, **275,** 275–276

bottom-up processing, **64,** *64*

brain

brain-imaging techniques, 34–35, *36*

cerebral cortex, 39–41, *39, 41*

electroencephalographs, 34, *35*

feature detectors in, 56

hemispheres, 41–43, *42*

injuries to, 33–34, *33*

language and, 41, *41,* 161, *161*

memory and, *38,* 138, 139–141, *140, 141*

personality disorders and, 277

plasticity of, 43

schizophrenia and, 261, *261*

size of, 24

structures of, 35–39, *37, 38, 39*

brain waves, sleep and, 82–83, *83*

breathing strips, *87*

brightness constancy, **67,** *67*

Broca's aphasia, **41,** *41*

bulimia nervosa, **200**

bullying, 187

bystander effect, 320–321

C

Canadian Code of Ethics for Psychologists, 20, *21*

Canadian Council on Animal Care (CCAC), 21

Canadian identity, 248

cancer, 229–230

Cannon–Bard theory of emotion, 211, *211*

carbon monoxide, 96

case studies, **15**

catastrophize, **221**

catatonic schizophrenia, **260**

catharsis, **282**

CBT (cognitive-behavioural therapy), **291,** 294, 298

central nervous system **30,** *31, 32–33, 32, 33*

cerebellum, **36,** *37*

cerebral cortex, **39,** 39–41, *39, 41*

cerebrum, *37,* **39**

Character Strengths and Virtues (CSV), 246

child abuse, dissociative disorders and, 275

child care, *186*

childhood

autism in, 294

child care in Canada, *186*

cognitive development in, 175–179, *177, 178*

language development in, 163–165

moral development in, 182–183, *182*

perceptual development in, 173

physical development in, 171–172, *172*

psychosexual development in, 236–238

psychosocial development in, 183–184, *184*

self-esteem in, 247

childhood amnesia, 137–138

chlamydia, **230**

chromosomes, **48,** 48–49, *48*

chunking, **130**

circadian rhythms, **82**

clairvoyance, 76–77

classical conditioning, 102–108, **103**

counterconditioning, 108–109

extinction and spontaneous recovery, 106–107, *106*

generalization and discrimination, 107

higher-order conditioning, 107

Little Albert study, 107–108

Pavlov and, 103

stimuli and responses in, 103–104, *104*

taste aversion, 104–105

claustrophobia, **269**

client-centred therapy, 247, 283–284, **284,** *293,* 293–294

clinical psychologists, 5

clitoris, **202**

closure, *62,* **63**

Clozaril, 297

cocaine, 29, 95–96, *96, 98*

coca leaves, 95

cochlea, **70,** *71*

cochlear implants, 72

cocktail party effect, 80

cognitive, **11**

cognitive appraisal theory, *211,* 211–212

cognitive-behavioural therapy (CBT), **291,** 294, 298

cognitive development

in adolescence, 180–181

in adulthood, 181–182

moral development, 182–183, *182*

Piaget's cognitive theory, 175–179, *177, 178*

Vygotsky's sociocultural theory, 179–180

cognitive-dissonance theory, **306,** 306–307

cognitive errors, 290

cognitive maps, **117,** *147*

cognitive perspective, 11

cognitive psychologists, 5

cognitive therapies, 289–291, **290,** *293*

collective unconscious, **238**

collectivism, 249–250, *249,* 296

collectivists, **249**

college students

alcohol use by, 92–93

stress in, 219, *219*

suicide by, 267

colour blindness, 62, *62*

colour constancy, **66**

colour vision, 60–62, *60, 61, 62*

colour wheel, *60*

commitment, **310,** 310–311, *310*

common fate, **64**

community mental health movement, 281

complementary colours, **60,** *61*

compulsion, **270**

computerized axial tomography (CAT or CT scan), **35,** *36*

concepts, **143,** 143–144, 163

concrete operational stage, **178,** 178–179

conditional positive regard, **247**

conditioned response (CR), **104**

conditioned stimulus (CS), **104**

conditioning. *See* classical conditioning; operant conditioning

conditions of worth, **247**

conductive deafness, 72

cones, **59,** 62

conflicting motives, stress and, 220–221

conformity, 316–317, *316*

consciousness, **80.** *See also* drugs; sleep

as awareness, 80

drugs and, 91–98

Freud on, 235, *235*

hypnosis and, 88–90, *90*

meditation and, 90–91

preconscious, unconscious, and, 80–81

sleep and, 81–88

conservation, **177,** 177–178, *178*

consummate love, **311**

contact comfort, **185**

context, 8–9, *9,* 305–306

context-dependent memory, **136**

contingency theory, **118**

continuity, **64**

continuous reinforcement, **113**

control groups, **17,** *17*

conventional level, **182,** *182*

convergence, **66**

convergent thinking, **160,** 160–161

conversion disorder, **272**

cooing, 164

cornea, **58**

coronary heart disease (CHD), 229

corpus callosum, **37,** *39*

correlational research, 19–20, *19*

correlation coefficient, **19,** *19*

correlations, **14**

corticotrophin-releasing hormone (CRH), 222, *223*

counselling psychologists, 5

counterconditioning, **108**

couple therapy, 292

crack cocaine, 95

creative self, **239**

creativity, 152, **160,** 160–162, 181

cretinism, 44

critical period, **185**

critical thinking, 12–13

crystallized intelligence, **181**

CSV (Character Strengths and Virtues), 246

CT scan (computerized axial tomography), **35,** *36*

culture. *See also* ethnicity/race; sociocultural perspective

acculturation, 250

individualism *vs.* collectivism, 296

intelligence tests and, 156–157, *157*

language and, 163

psychotherapy and, 295–296

curare, 28

Chapter in Review

LO1 psychology
the science that studies behaviour and mental processes

theory
a formulation of relationships underlying observed events

LO2 pure research
research conducted without concern for immediate applications; purely for research's sake

applied research
research conducted in an effort to find solutions to particular problems

LO3 introspection
deliberate looking into one's own cognitive processes to examine one's thoughts and feelings

structuralism
the school of psy[chology that states the] mind consists of [sen]sations, feelings, [...] to form experienc[e]

functionalism
the school of psychology that emphasizes the uses or functions of the mind rather than the elements of experience

behaviourism
the school of psychology that defines psychology as the study of observable behaviour and studies relationships between stimuli and responses

reinforcement
a stimulus that follows a response and increases the frequency of the response

Gestalt psychology
the school of psychology that emphasizes the tendency to organize perceptions into wholes and to integrate separate stimuli into meaningful patterns

psychoanalysis
the school of [psychology that stresses the] importance o[f...] flicts as deter[...]

LO4 co[...]
[...] ha[...]
cesses such [...]
memory, intel[...]
problem solv[...]

social-cogn[...]
a school of p[...]
tradition that [...]
the explanati[...]
formerly term[...]

sociocultur[...]
the view that [...]
gender, cultu[...]
behaviour an[...]

LO1 Define psychology and its goals.
Psychology is the scientific study of behaviour and mental processes. Topics of interest to psychologists include the nervous system, sensation and perception, learning and memory, intelligence, language, thought, growth and development, personality, stress and health, psychological dis[orders, methods of treatment], disorders, and the behaviour of people in social settings such as g[roups]. [...] goals of the psychologist, like other scientists, is to *describe, expl[ain...]* events he or she studies—in this case, behaviour and mental proc[esses].

LO2 Describe the various fields and subfields of psychology.
Psychologists are found in a number of different specialties:

Clinical psychologists help people with psychological disorders adjust to the demands of life.

Counselling psychologists typically see clients with adjustment problems but not serious psychological disorders.

School & Educational psychologists help school systems identify and assist students who have problems that interfere with learning. *They* research theoretical issues related to learning, measurement, and child development.

Developmental psychologists study the changes—physical, cognitive, social, and personality—that occur throughout the life span.

Personality psychologists identify and measure human traits and determine influences on human thought processes, feelings, and behaviour.

Social psychologists are concerned with the nature and causes of individuals' thoughts, feelings, and behaviour in social situations.

Environmental psychologists study the ways in which people and the environment influence one another.

Experimental psychologists specialize in basic processes such as the nervous system, sensation and perception, learning and memory, thought, motivation, and emotion.

Cognitive psychologists study our thought processes involved in behaviour.

Industrial/Organizational psychologists focus on the relationships between people and work.

Health psychologists examine the ways in which behaviour and attitudes are related to physical health.

Sport psychologists help people improve their performance in sports.

Forensic psychologists apply principles of psychology to the criminal justice system.

LO3 Describe the origins of psychology and identify those who made significant contributions to the field.
An ancient contributor to the modern field of psychology, Aristotle argued that human behaviour, like the movements of the stars and the seas, is subject to rules and laws. Today, as then, the subject matter of the study of human behaviour includes the study of personality, sensation and perception, thought, intelligence, needs and motives, feelings and emotion, and memory. The following is a list of the historic schools of psychology and the major proponent(s) of each: *Structuralism:* Wilhelm Wundt; *Functionalism:* William James; *Behaviourism:* John B. Watson and B.F. Skinner; *Gestalt Psychology:* Max Wertheimer, Kurt Koffka, and Wolfgang Köhler; and *Psychoanalysis:* Sigmund Freud, Carl Jung, Alfred Adler, Karen Horney, and Erik Erikson.

LO4 Identify theoretical perspectives of modern psychologists toward behaviour and mental processes.
There are several influential perspectives in contemporary psychology: evolutionary and biological, cognitive, humanistic–existential, psychodynamic, learning, and sociocultural.

- *Evolutionary psychologists* focus on the evolution of behaviour and mental processes.

- *Biological psychologists* focus on how the systems in the brain and our body interact with our behaviour and mental processes.

- Psychologists [...] [cogniti]ve and men[tally represent...] [...decision] making, and language.

Chapter in Review

LO1 psychology
the science that studies behaviour and mental processes

theory
a formulation of relationships underlying observed events

LO2 pure research
research conducted without concern for immediate applications; purely for research's sake

applied research
research conducted in an effort to find solutions to particular problems

LO3 introspection
deliberate looking into one's own cognitive processes to examine one's thoughts and feelings

structuralism
the school of psychology that argues that the mind consists of three basic elements—sensations, feelings, and images—that combine to form experience

functionalism
the school of psychology that emphasizes the uses or functions of the mind rather than the elements of experience

behaviourism
the school of psychology that defines psychology as the study of observable behaviour and studies relationships between stimuli and responses

reinforcement
a stimulus that follows a response and increases the frequency of the response

Gestalt psychology
the school of psychology that emphasizes the tendency to organize perceptions into wholes and to integrate separate stimuli into meaningful patterns

psychoanalysis
the school of psychology that emphasizes the importance of unconscious motives and conflicts as determinants of human behaviour

LO4 cognitive
having to do with mental processes such as sensation and perception, memory, intelligence, language, thought, and problem solving

social-cognitive theory
a school of psychology in the behaviourist tradition that includes cognitive factors in the explanation and prediction of behaviour; formerly termed *social learning theory*

sociocultural perspective
the view that focuses on the roles of ethnicity, gender, culture, and socioeconomic status in behaviour and mental processes

---

LO1 Define psychology and its goals.
Psychology is the scientific study of behaviour and mental processes. Topics of interest to psychologists include the nervous system, sensation and perception, learning and memory, intelligence, language, thought, growth and development, personality, stress and health, psychological disorders, ways of treating those disorders, and the behaviour of people in social settings such as groups and organizations. The goals of the psychologist, like other scientists, is to *describe, explain, predict, and control* the events he or she studies—in this case, behaviour and mental processes.

LO2 Describe the various fields and subfields of psychology.
Psychologists are found in a number of different specialties:

Clinical psychologists help people with psychological disorders adjust to the demands of life.

Counselling psychologists typically see clients with adjustment problems but not serious psychological disorders.

School & Educational psychologists help school systems identify and assist students who have problems that interfere with learning. *They* research theoretical issues related to learning, measurement, and child development.

Developmental psychologists study the changes—physical, cognitive, social, and personality—that occur throughout the life span.

Personality psychologists identify and measure human traits and determine influences on human thought processes, feelings, and behaviour.

Social psychologists are concerned with the nature and causes of individuals' thoughts, feelings, and behaviour in social situations.

Environmental psychologists study the ways in which people and the environment influence one another.

Experimental psychologists specialize in basic processes such as the nervous system, sensation and perception, learning and memory, thought, motivation, and emotion.

Cognitive psychologists study our thought processes involved in behaviour.

Industrial/Organizational psychologists focus on the relationships between people and work.

Health psychologists examine the ways in which behaviour and attitudes are related to physical health.

Sport psychologists help people improve their performance in sports.

Forensic psychologists apply principles of psychology to the criminal justice system.

LO3 Describe the origins of psychology and identify those who made significant contributions to the field.
An ancient contributor to the modern field of psychology, Aristotle argued that human behaviour, like the movements of the stars and the seas, is subject to rules and laws. Today, as then, the subject matter of the study of human behaviour includes the study of personality, sensation and perception, thought, intelligence, needs and motives, feelings and emotion, and memory. The following is a list of the historic schools of psychology and the major proponent(s) of each: *Structuralism:* Wilhelm Wundt; *Functionalism:* William James; *Behaviourism:* John B. Watson and B.F. Skinner; *Gestalt Psychology:* Max Wertheimer, Kurt Koffka, and Wolfgang Köhler; and *Psychoanalysis:* Sigmund Freud, Carl Jung, Alfred Adler, Karen Horney, and Erik Erikson.

LO4 Identify theoretical perspectives of modern psychologists toward behaviour and mental processes.
There are several influential perspectives in contemporary psychology: evolutionary and biological, cognitive, humanistic–existential, psychodynamic, learning, and sociocultural.

- *Evolutionary psychologists* focus on the evolution of behaviour and mental processes.

- *Biological psychologists* focus on how the systems in the brain and our body interact with our behaviour and mental processes.

- Psychologists with a *cognitive perspective* investigate the ways in which we perceive and mentally represent the world by learning, memory, planning, problem solving, decision making, and language.

LO5

hypothesis
in psychology, a specific statement about behaviour or mental processes that is tested through research

correlation
an association or relationship among variables, as we might find between height and weight or between study habits and school grades

selection factor
a source of bias that may occur in research findings when subjects are allowed to choose for themselves a certain treatment in a scientific study

sample
part of a population

population
a complete group of organisms or events

random sample
a sample drawn so that each member of a population has an equal chance of being selected to participate

stratified sample
a sample drawn so that identified subgroups in the population are represented proportionately in the sample

volunteer bias
a source of bias or error in research reflecting the prospect that people who offer to participate in research studies differ systematically from people who do not

case study
a carefully drawn biography that may be obtained through interviews, questionnaires, and psychological tests

survey
a method of scientific investigation in which a large sample of people answer questions about their attitudes or behaviour

naturalistic observation
a scientific method in which organisms are observed in their natural environments

experiment
a scientific method that seeks to confirm cause-and-effect relationships by introducing independent variables and observing their effects on dependent variables

independent variable
a condition in a scientific study that is manipulated so that its effects may be observed

dependent variable
a measure of an assumed effect of an independent variable

experimental groups
in experiments, groups whose members obtain the treatment

control groups
in experiments, groups whose members do not obtain the treatment, while other conditions are held constant

placebo
a bogus treatment that has the appearance of being genuine

blind
in experimental terminology, unaware of whether or not one has received a treatment

---

- *The humanistic–existential perspective* is cognitive in flavour, yet emphasizes more the role of subjective (personal) experience. towards self-actualization

- Neoanalysts with a *psychodynamic perspective* focus less on the unconscious—as was done in Freud's day—and more on conscious choice and self-direction.

- The first of two learning perspectives, *behaviourists* emphasize environmental influences and the learning of habits through repetition and reinforcement. *Social-cognitive theorists,* in contrast, suggest that people can modify and create their environments, and engage in intentional learning by observing others.

- A psychologist with a *sociocultural perspective* studies the influences of ethnicity, gender, culture, and socioeconomic status on behaviour and mental processes.

LO5 Describe modern approaches to research and practice—critical thinking, the scientific method, and ethical considerations. Psychologists, like

other scientists, must use careful means to observe and measure behaviour and the factors that influence behaviour. Psychologists use evidence and critical thinking—the process of thoughtfully analyzing and probing the questions, statements, and arguments of others. The scientific method is a systematic way of organizing and expanding scientific knowledge. Daily experiences, common beliefs, and scientific observations all contribute to the development of theories. Psychological theories explain observations and lead to hypotheses about behaviour and mental processes. Observations can then confirm the theory or lead to its refinement or abandonment. Many factors—such as the nature of the research sample—must be considered in interpreting the accuracy of the results of scientific research. Psychologists must also adhere to a number of ethical standards that are intended to promote individual dignity, human welfare, and scientific integrity. The standards are also intended to ensure that psychologists do not engage in harmful research methods or treatments.

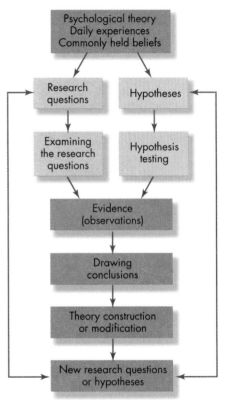

Descriptive methods of research reflect our observations about behaviour through controlled measures. Psychologists use case studies, naturalistic observation, and survey research to understand behaviour.

---

double-blind study
a study in which neither the subjects nor the observers know who has received the treatment

correlation coefficient
a number between +1.00 and −1.00 that expresses the strength and direction (positive or negative) of the relationship between two variables

informed consent
a participant's agreement to participate in research after receiving information about the purposes of the study and the nature of the treatment

debriefing
providing participants with an explanation of their role in an experiment and explaining the purposes and methods of the research following completion of the study

Chapter in Review

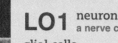

LO1 neuron
a nerve cell

glial cells
cells that nourish and insulate neurons, direct their growth, and remove waste products from the nervous system

dendrites
root-like structures, attached to the cell body of a neuron, that receive impulses from other neurons

axon
a long, thin part of a neuron that transmits impulses to other neurons from branching structures called *terminal buttons*

myelin
a fatty substance that encases and insulates axons, facilitating transmission of neural impulses

sensory neurons
neurons that transmit messages from sensory receptors to the spinal cord and brain (also called *afferent neurons*).

interneurons
neurons that connect sensory and motor neurons

motor neurons
neurons that transmit messages from the brain or spinal cord to muscles and glands (also called *efferent neurons*).

neural impulse
the electrochemical discharge of a nerve cell, or neuron

polarize
to ready a neuron for firing by creating an internal negative charge in relation to the body fluid outside the cell membrane

resting potential
the electrical potential across the neural membrane when it is not responding to other neurons

depolarize
to reduce the resting potential of a cell membrane from about 70 millivolts toward zero

action potential
the electrical impulse that provides the basis for the conduction of a neural impulse along an axon of a neuron

all-or-none principle
the fact that a neuron fires an impulse of the same strength whenever its action potential is triggered

refractory period
a phase following firing during which a neuron is less sensitive to messages from other neurons and will not fire

synapse
a junction between the axon terminals of one neuron and the dendrites or cell body of another neuron

neurotransmitters
chemical substances involved in the transmission of neural impulses from one neuron to another

receptor site
a location on a dendrite of a receiving neuron tailored to receive a neurotransmitter

LO1 Describe the nervous system, including neurons, neural impulses, and neurotransmitters.
The nervous system regulates the body and is involved in thought processes, emotional responses, heartbeat, and motor activity. The central nervous system contains the brain and the spinal cord. The somatic system transmits sensory information about skeletal muscles, skin, and joints and controls skeletal muscular activity. The autonomic system regulates glands and activities like digestion. Neurons transmit information through electrochemical neural impulses. Their dendrites receive messages and their axons conduct messages, transmitting them to other cells via neurotransmitters.

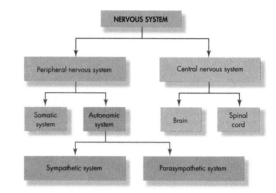

The Anatomy of a Neuron. "Messages" enter neurons through dendrites, are transmitted along the trunk-like axon, and then are sent from axon terminal buttons to muscles, glands, and other neurons. Axon terminal buttons contain sacs of chemicals called *neurotransmitters*. Neurotransmitters are released into the synaptic cleft, where many of them bind to receptor sites on the dendrites of the receiving neuron.

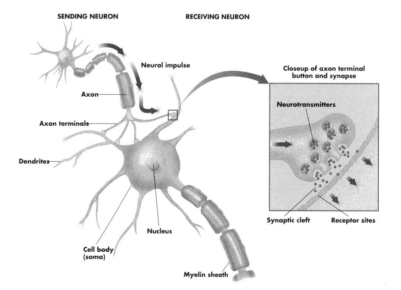

reuptake
reabsorption of the released neurotransmitter by the releasing neuron

acetylcholine (ACh)
a neurotransmitter that controls muscle contractions

hippocampus
a part of the limbic system of the brain that is involved in memory formation

dopamine
a neurotransmitter that is involved in Parkinson's disease and that appears to play a role in schizophrenia

norepinephrine
a neurotransmitter whose action is similar to that of the hormone epinephrine and that may play a role in depression

serotonin
a neurotransmitter, deficiencies of which have been linked to affective disorders, anxiety, and insomnia

gamma-aminobutyric acid (GABA)
an inhibitory neurotransmitter that apparently helps calm anxiety

endorphins
neurotransmitters that are composed of amino acids and that are functionally similar to morphine

nerve
a bundle of axons from many neurons

central nervous system
the brain and spinal cord

peripheral nervous system
the part of the nervous system consisting of the somatic nervous system and the autonomic nervous system

somatic nervous system
the division of the peripheral nervous system that connects the central nervous system with sensory receptors, skeletal muscles, and the surface of the body

autonomic nervous system (ANS)
the division of the peripheral nervous system that regulates glands and activities such as heartbeat, respiration, digestion, and dilation of the pupils

sympathetic
the branch of the ANS that is most active during emotional responses, such as fear and anxiety, that spend the body's reserves of energy

parasympathetic
the branch of the ANS that is most active during processes (such as digestion) that restore the body's reserves of energy

spinal cord
a column of nerves within the spine that transmits messages from sensory receptors to the brain and from the brain to muscles and glands throughout the body

spinal reflex
a simple, unlearned response to a stimulus that may involve only two neurons

grey matter
in the spinal cord, the greyish neurons and neural segments that are involved in spinal reflexes

white matter
in the spinal cord, axon bundles that carry messages from and to the brain

The Parasympathetic and Sympathetic Branches of the Autonomic Nervous System (ANS). The parasympathetic branch of the ANS generally acts to replenish stores of energy in the body. The sympathetic branch is most active during activities that expend energy. The two branches of the ANS frequently have antagonistic effects on the organs they service.

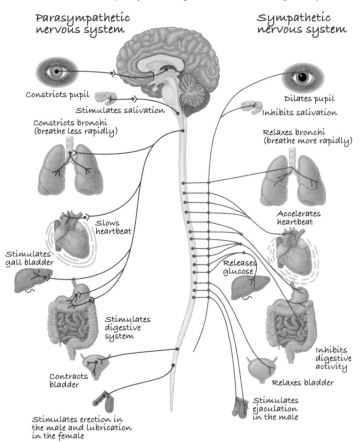

LO2 List the structures of the brain and their functions.
The hindbrain includes the medulla, the pons, and the cerebellum. The reticular activating system begins in the hindbrain and continues into the forebrain. Important structures of the forebrain include the thalamus, which serves as a relay station for sensory stimulation; the hypothalamus, which regulates body temperature and influences motivation and emotion; the limbic system, which is involved in memory, emotion, and motivation; and the cerebrum, which handles thinking and language. The outer fringe of the cerebrum is the cerebral cortex, which is divided into four lobes: frontal, parietal, temporal, and occipital.

The Parts of the Human Brain
The view of the brain, split top to bottom, shows some of the most important structures. The "valleys" in the cerebrum are called fissures.

Corpus callosum
Thick bundle of axons that serves as a bridge between the two cerebral hemispheres

Cerebrum
Centre of thinking and language; prefrontal area contains "executive centre" of brain

Thalamus
Relay station for sensory information

Hypothalamus
Secretes hormones that stimulate secretion of hormones by the pituitary gland; involved in basic drives such as hunger, sex, and aggression

Pituitary gland
Secretes hormones that regulate many body functions, including secretion of hormones from other glands; sometimes referred to as the "master gland"

Cerebellum
Essential to balance and coordination

Reticular activating system
Involved in regulation of sleep and waking; stimulation of RAS increases arousal

Pons
Involved in regulation of movement, sleep and arousal, respiration

Medulla
Involved in regulation of heart rate, blood pressure, respiration, circulation

Chapter in Review

2

LO2 electroencephalograph (EEG)
a method of detecting brain waves by means of measuring the current between electrodes placed on the scalp

computerized axial tomography (CAT or CT scan)
a method of brain imaging that passes a narrow X-ray beam through the head and measures structures that reflect the rays from various angles, enabling a computer to generate a three-dimensional image

positron emission tomography (PET scan)
a method of brain imaging that injects a radioactive tracer into the bloodstream and assesses activity of parts of the brain according to the amount of glucose they metabolize

magnetic resonance imaging (MRI)
a method of brain imaging that places a person in a magnetic field and uses radio waves to cause the brain to emit signals that reveal shifts in the flow of blood which, in turn, indicate brain activity

functional MRI (fMRI)
a form of MRI that enables researchers to observe the brain "while it works" by taking repeated scans

medulla
an oblong area of the hindbrain involved in regulation of heartbeat and respiration

pons
a structure of the hindbrain involved in respiration, sleep, and arousal

cerebellum
a part of the hindbrain involved in muscle coordination and balance

reticular activating system (RAS)
a part of the brain involved in attentiveness, sleep, and arousal

thalamus
an area near the centre of the brain involved in the relay of sensory information to the cortex and in the functions of sleep and attentiveness

hypothalamus
a bundle of nuclei below the thalamus involved in body temperature, motivation, and emotion

limbic system
a group of structures involved in memory, motivation, and emotion that forms a fringe along the inner edge of the cerebrum

hippocampus
part of brain associated with long-term memory and mental mapping

amygdala
a part of the limbic system that apparently facilitates stereotypical aggressive responses

cerebrum
the large mass of the forebrain, which consists of two hemispheres

The geography of the cerebral cortex. The cortex has four lobes: frontal, parietal, temporal, and occipital. The visual area of the cortex is in the occipital lobe. The hearing or auditory cortex lies in the temporal lobe. The motor and somatosensory areas—shown below—face each other across the central fissure. Note that the face and the hands are "super-sized" in the motor and somatosensory areas. Why do you think this is so?

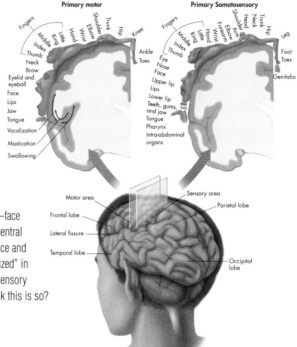

LO3 Explain the role of the endocrine system and list the endocrine glands.
The glands of the endocrine system secrete hormones regulating development and activity. The pituitary gland secretes growth hormone, prolactin, and oxytocin. The thyroid regulates metabolism. The adrenal cortex produces steroids. The adrenal medulla secretes epinephrine, which increases the metabolic rate and stimulates general emotional arousal. The sex hormones are responsible for sexual differentiation and regulate the menstrual cycle in females.

cerebral cortex
the wrinkled surface area (grey matter) of the cerebrum

corpus callosum
a thick fibre bundle that connects the hemispheres of the cortex

somatosensory cortex
the section of cortex in which sensory stimulation is projected. It lies just behind the central fissure in the parietal lobe

motor cortex
the section of cortex that lies in the frontal lobe, just across the central fissure from the sensory cortex; neural impulses in the motor cortex are linked to muscular responses throughout the body

aphasia
a disruption in the ability to understand or produce language

Wernicke's aphasia
a language disorder characterized by difficulty comprehending the meaning of spoken language

Broca's aphasia
a language disorder characterized by slow, laborious speech

epilepsy
temporary disturbances of brain functions that involve sudden neural discharges

plasticity
the brain's ability to adapt and change

LO4
Describe evolutionary psychology and the connections between heredity, behaviour, and mental processes. Evolutionary psychology studies the way natural selection influences mental processes and behaviour. Evolutionary psychologists suggest that behaviour evolves as it is transmitted from generation to generation. Evolutionarily advantageous behaviours like aggression, strategic mate selection, and familial altruism are often influenced by heredity.

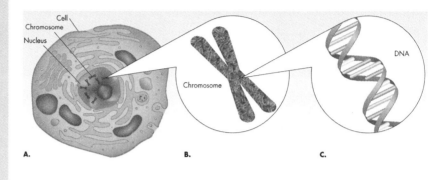

Cells, Chromosomes, and DNA

A. The nuclei of cells contain chromosomes. **B.** Chromosomes are made up of DNA. **C.** Segments of DNA are made up of genes. The genetic code—that is the order of the chemicals A, G, T, and C—determines your species and all those traits that can be inherited, from the colour of your eyes to predispositions toward many psychological traits and abilities, including sociability and musical talent.

LO3
gland
an organ that secretes one or more chemical substances such as hormones, saliva, or milk

endocrine system
the body's system of ductless glands that secrete hormones and release them directly into the bloodstream

hormone
a substance secreted by an endocrine gland that regulates various body functions

pituitary gland
the gland that secretes growth hormone, prolactin, antidiuretic hormone, and other hormones

LO4
natural selection
a core concept of the theory of evolution that holds that adaptive genetic variations among members of a species enable individuals with those variations to survive and reproduce

mutation
a sudden variation in an inheritable characteristic, as distinguished from a variation that results from generations of gradual selection

evolutionary psychology
the branch of psychology that studies the ways in which adaptation and natural selection are connected with mental processes and behaviour

species
a category of biological classification consisting of related organisms that are capable of interbreeding; *homo sapiens*—humans—make up one species

instinct
a stereotyped pattern of behaviour that is triggered by a particular stimulus and nearly identical among members of a species, even when they are reared in isolation

heredity
the transmission of traits from parent to offspring by means of genes

genetics
the area of biology that focuses on heredity

gene
a basic unit of heredity, which is found at a specific point on a chromosome

chromosome
a microscopic rod-shaped body in the cell nucleus carrying genes that transmit hereditary traits from generation to generation; humans normally have 46 chromosomes

DNA
acronym for *deoxyribonucleic acid*, the substance that forms the basic material of chromosomes. It takes the form of a double helix and contains the genetic code

polygenic
referring to traits that are influenced by combinations of genes.

genotype
one's genetic makeup, based on the sequencing of the nucleotides we term A, C, G, and T

phenotype
one's actual development and appearance, as based on one's genotype and environmental influences

nature
the inborn, innate character of an organism

nurture
the sum total of the environmental factors that affect an organism from conception onward

sex chromosomes
the 23rd pair of chromosomes, whose genetic material determines the sex of the individual

Down syndrome
a condition caused by an extra chromosome on the 21st pair and characterized by mental deficiency, a broad face, and slanting eyes

monozygotic (MZ) twins
twins that develop from a single fertilized ovum that divides in two early in prenatal development; MZ twins thus share the same genetic code; also called *identical twins*

dizygotic (DZ) twins
twins that develop from two fertilized ova and who are thus as closely related as brothers and sisters in general; also called *fraternal twins*

Chapter in Review

LO1 sensation
the stimulation of sensory receptors and the transmission of sensory information to the central nervous system

perception
the process by which sensations are organized into an inner representation of the world

absolute threshold
the minimal amount of energy that can produce a sensation

pitch
the highness or lowness of a sound, as determined by the frequency of the sound waves

difference threshold
the minimal difference in intensity required between two sources of energy so that they will be perceived as being different

Weber's constant
the fraction of the intensity by which a source of physical energy must be increased or decreased so that a difference in intensity will be perceived

just noticeable difference (jnd)
the minimal amount by which a source of energy must be increased or decreased so that a difference in intensity will be perceived

signal-detection theory
the view that the perception of sensory stimuli involves the interaction of physical, biological, and psychological factors

feature detectors
neurons in the sensory cortex that fire in response to specific features of sensory information such as lines or edges of objects

sensory adaptation
the processes by which organisms become more sensitive to stimuli that are low in magnitude and less sensitive to stimuli that are constant or ongoing in magnitude

sensitization
the type of sensory adaptation in which we become more sensitive to stimuli that are low in magnitude; also called *positive adaptation*

desensitization
the type of sensory adaptation in which we become less sensitive to constant stimuli; also called *negative adaptation*

LO2 hue
the colour of light, as determined by its wavelength

cornea
transparent tissue forming the outer surface of the eyeball

iris
a muscular membrane whose dilation regulates the amount of light that enters the eye

pupil
the black-looking opening in the centre of the iris, through which light enters the eye

LO1 Define and differentiate between sensation and perception. Stimulation of the senses is an automatic process. It results from sources of energy, like light and sound, or from the presence of chemicals, as in smell and taste. Perception is an active process. Perception may begin with sensation, but it also reflects our experiences and expectations as it makes sense of sensory stimuli.

LO2 Identify the parts of the eye; explain the properties of light and the theories of colour vision. It is visible light that triggers visual sensations. Yet visible light is just one small part of a spectrum of electromagnetic energy that surrounds us. All forms of electromagnetic energy move in waves, and different kinds of electromagnetic energy have signature wavelengths.
In both the eye and a camera, light enters through a narrow opening and is projected onto a sensitive surface. In the eye, the photosensitive surface is called the retina, and information concerning the changing images on the retina is transmitted to the brain.

LO3 Describe how visual perception is organized. Visual perception is the process by which we organize or make sense of the sensory impressions caused by the light that strikes our eyes. The attempt to identify the rules that govern these processes resulted in what are referred to as the laws of perceptual organization: *figure-ground perception,* and the laws of *proximity, similarity, continuity,* and *common fate.*

LO4 Identify the parts of the ear; describe the sense of hearing. Sound, or auditory stimulation, travels through the air like waves. A single cycle of compression and expansion is one wave of sound, which can occur many times in a second. The ear has three parts: the outer ear, middle ear, and inner ear. The outer ear funnels sound to the eardrum. Inside the eardrum, vibrations transmit sound to the inner ear. Vibrations in the cochlea transmit the sound to the auditory nerve.

LO5 Describe the chemical senses. In smell and taste, we sample molecules of substances. An odour is a sample of molecules of a substance in the air. Odours trigger firing of receptor neurons in the olfactory membrane high in each nostril. Taste is sensed through taste cells—receptor neurons located on taste buds.

LO6 Explain the properties of the skin senses and theoretical explanations for pain. The skin senses include touch, pressure, warmth, cold, and pain. Pain results when neurons called nociceptors in the skin are stimulated. The pain message to the brain is initiated by the release of chemicals such as prostaglandins, bradykinin, and P.

LO7 Describe the kinesthetic and vestibular senses. Kinesthesis and the vestibular sense alert us to our movements and body position without relying on vision. In kinesthesis, sensory information is fed back to the brain from sensory organs in the joints, tendons, and muscles. The vestibular sense makes use of sensory organs located in the semicircular canals and elsewhere in the ears to monitor the body's motion and position in relation to gravity.

LO8 Explain why psychologists are skeptical about extrasensory perception. One method for studying telepathy is the ganzfeld procedure. However, when Milton and Wiseman weighed the results of 30 ganzfeld ESP studies from seven laboratories, they found no evidence that subjects in these studies scored above chance levels on the ESP task. It has also been difficult to replicate experiments in ESP. A million dollar prize has remained unclaimed since 1964 for anyone demonstrating any ESP ability in controlled conditions.

lens
a transparent body behind the iris that focuses an image on the retina

retina
the area of the inner surface of the eye that contains rods and cones

photoreceptors
sensory neurons that respond to light

bipolar cells
neurons that conduct neural impulses from rods and cones to ganglion cells

ganglion cells
neurons whose axons form the optic nerve

optic nerve
the nerve that transmits sensory information from the eye to the brain

rods
rod-shaped photoreceptors that are sensitive only to the intensity of light

cones
cone-shaped photoreceptors that transmit sensations of colour

fovea
an area near the centre of the retina that is dense with cones and where vision is consequently most acute

blind spot
the area of the retina where axons from ganglion cells meet to form the optic nerve

visual acuity
sharpness of vision

presbyopia
a condition characterized by brittleness of the lens

dark adaptation
the process of adjusting to conditions of lower lighting by increasing the sensitivity of rods and cones

complementary
descriptive of colours of the spectrum that when combined produce white or nearly white light

afterimage
the lingering visual impression made by a stimulus that has been removed

trichromatic theory
the theory that colour vision is made possible by three types of cones, some of which respond to red light, some to green, and some to blue

opponent-process theory
the theory that colour vision is made possible by three types of cones, some of which respond to red or green light, some to blue or yellow, and some to the intensity of light

trichromat
a person with normal colour vision

monochromat
a person who is sensitive to black and white only and hence colourblind

dichromat
a person who is sensitive to black–white and either red–green or blue–yellow and hence partially colourblind

LO3 closure
the tendency to perceive a broken figure as being complete or whole

proximity
nearness; the perceptual tendency to group together objects that are near one another

similarity
the perceptual tendency to group together objects that are similar in appearance

continuity
the tendency to perceive a series of points or lines as having unity

common fate
the tendency to perceive elements that move together as belonging together

top-down processing
the use of contextual information or knowledge of a pattern in order to organize parts of the pattern

bottom-up processing
the organization of the parts of a pattern to recognize, or form an image of, the pattern they compose

illusions
sensations that give rise to misperceptions

stroboscopic motion
a visual illusion in which the perception of motion is generated by a series of stationary images that are presented in rapid succession

monocular cues
stimuli suggestive of depth that can be perceived with only one eye

perspective
a monocular cue for depth based on the convergence (coming together) of parallel lines as they recede into the distance

texture gradient
a monocular cue for depth based on the perception that closer objects appear to have rougher (more detailed) surfaces

motion parallax
a monocular cue for depth based on the perception that nearby objects appear to move more rapidly in relation to our own motion

binocular cues
stimuli suggestive of depth that involve simultaneous perception by both eyes

retinal disparity
a binocular cue for depth based on the difference in the image cast by an object on the retinas of the eyes as the object moves closer or farther away

convergence
a binocular cue for depth based on the inward movement of the eyes as they attempt to focus on an object that is drawing nearer

size constancy
the tendency to perceive an object as being the same size even as the size of its retinal image changes according to the object's distance

colour constancy
the tendency to perceive an object as being the same colour even though lighting conditions change its appearance

brightness constancy
the tendency to perceive an object as being just as bright even though lighting conditions change its intensity

shape constancy
the tendency to perceive an object as being the same shape although the retinal image varies in shape as it rotates

ventral stream
the visual pathway that forms the mental representation of everything we see

dorsal stream
the visual pathway that informs our muscles on how to act toward objects in our world

LO4 hertz (Hz)
a unit expressing the frequency of sound waves; 1 hertz equals one cycle per second

decibel (dB)
a unit expressing the loudness of a sound

cochlea
the inner ear; the bony tube that contains the basilar membrane and the organ of Corti

basilar membrane
a membrane that lies coiled within the cochlea

organ of Corti
the receptor for hearing that lies on the basilar membrane in the cochlea

auditory nerve
the axon bundle that transmits neural impulses from the organ of Corti to the brain

place theory
the theory that the pitch of a sound is determined by the section of the basilar membrane that vibrates in response to the sound

frequency theory
the theory that the pitch of a sound is reflected in the frequency of the neural impulses that are generated in response to the sound

LO5 flavour
a complex quality of food and other substances that is based on their odour, texture, and temperature as well as their taste

olfactory nerve
the nerve that transmits information concerning odours from olfactory receptors to the brain

taste cells
receptor cells that are sensitive to taste

taste buds
the sensory organs for taste. They contain taste cells and are mostly located on the tongue

LO7 kinesthesis
the sense that informs us about the positions and motion of parts of our bodies

vestibular sense
the sense of equilibrium that informs us about our bodies' positions relative to gravity

Chapter in Review

LO1 consciousness
an awareness of our external and internal environment at any given moment

selective attention
the focus of consciousness on a particular stimulus

direct inner awareness
knowledge of one's own thoughts, feelings, and memories

preconscious
in psychodynamic theory, descriptive of material that is not in awareness but can be brought into awareness by focusing one's attention

unconscious
in psychodynamic theory, descriptive of ideas and feelings that are not available to awareness; also: without consciousness

repression
in psychodynamic theory, the unconscious ejection of anxiety-evoking ideas, impulses, or images from awareness

suppression
the deliberate, or conscious, placing of certain ideas, impulses, or images out of awareness

nonconscious
descriptive of bodily processes such as growing hair, of which we cannot become conscious; for example, we may "recognize" that our hair is growing, but we cannot directly experience the biological process

LO2 circadian rhythm
a cycle that is connected with the 24-hour period of the earth's rotation

alpha waves
rapid low-amplitude brain waves that have been linked to feelings of relaxation

non–rapid eye movement (NREM) sleep
stages of sleep 1 through 4

rapid eye movement (REM) sleep
a stage of sleep characterized by rapid eye movements, which have been linked to dreaming

theta waves
slow brain waves produced during the hypnagogic state

delta waves
strong, slow brain waves usually emitted during stage 4 sleep

activation–synthesis model
the view that dreams reflect activation of cognitive activity by the reticular activating system and synthesis of this activity into a pattern by the cerebral cortex

LO3 insomnia
a chronic difficulty in falling asleep, staying asleep, or experiencing restful sleep

narcolepsy
a "sleep attack" in which a person falls asleep suddenly and irresistibly

LO1 **Define consciousness.** The concept of consciousness has various meanings. One meaning is *sensory awareness* of the environment. Another aspect of consciousness is *selective attention*. Selective attention means focusing one's consciousness on a particular stimulus. We are conscious of—or have *direct inner awareness* of—thoughts, images, emotions, and memories. Sigmund Freud, the founder of psychoanalysis, differentiated between the thoughts and feelings of which we are *conscious*, or aware, and those that are preconscious and unconscious. *Preconscious* material is not currently in awareness but is readily available. Still other mental events are *unconscious*, or unavailable, to awareness under most circumstances. Some bodily processes, such as the firings of neurons, are *nonconscious*. They cannot be experienced through sensory awareness or direct inner awareness. In the sense that the *self* forms intentions and guides its own behaviour, consciousness is *self*. The word conscious also refers to the *waking state* as opposed, for example, to sleep.

LO2 **Explain the stages of sleep and sleep cycles.** When we sleep, we slip from consciousness to unconsciousness. When we are conscious, our brains emit waves characterized by certain frequencies (numbers of waves per second) and amplitudes (heights—an index of strength). Brain waves are rough indicators of the activity of neurons. The strength or energy of brain waves is expressed in volts (an electrical unit). When we sleep, our brains emit waves that differ from those emitted when we are conscious.

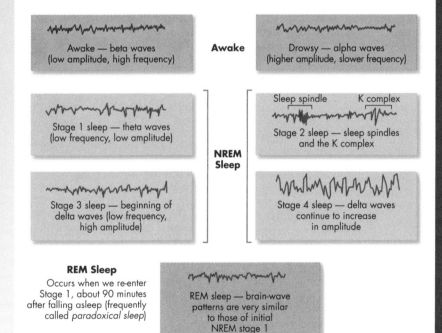

Most of our dreaming is done during REM sleep. There are several theories about why we dream what we dream: dreams as 'the residue of the day"; dreams as wish fulfillment; and the activation–synthesis model.

LO3 **Explain major sleep disorders.** Sleep disorders seriously interfere with daily functioning and include insomnia, narcolepsy, and apnea. The less-common sleep disorders—sleep terrors, bedwetting, and sleepwalking—occur during deep (stage 3 or 4) sleep and are more common in childhood.

LO4 **Explain various uses of hypnosis and forms of meditation, techniques in altering consciousness.** Hypnosis—an altered state of consciousness in which people are highly suggestible and behave as though they are in a

apnea
temporary absence or cessation of breathing

sleep terrors
frightening dreamlike experiences that occur during the deepest stage of NREM sleep; nightmares, in contrast, occur during REM sleep

LO4 hypnosis
a condition in which people are highly suggestible and behave as though they are in a trance

role theory
a social-cognitive theory that explains hypnotic events in terms of the person's expectations and ability to act (or play the "role") *as though* he or she were hypnotized

transcendental meditation (TM)
the simplified form of meditation that focuses on words or sounds to help a person achieve an altered state of consciousness; used as a method for coping with stress

mindfulness meditation (MM)
a form of meditation that provides clients with techniques they can use to focus on the present moment rather than ruminate about problems

LO5 depressant
a drug that lowers the rate of activity of the nervous system

stimulant
a drug that increases activity of the nervous system

substance abuse
persistent use of a substance even though it is causing or compounding problems in meeting the demands of life

substance dependence
loss of control over use of a substance; biologically speaking, dependence is typified by tolerance, withdrawal symptoms, or both

tolerance
habituation to a drug, with the result that increasingly higher doses of the drug are needed to achieve similar effects

withdrawal symptoms
a characteristic cluster of symptoms that results from sudden decrease in an addictive drug's level of usage

opiates
a group of narcotics derived from the opium poppy that provide a euphoric rush and depress the nervous system

narcotics
drugs used to relieve pain and induce sleep; the term is usually reserved for opiates

opioids
chemicals that act on opiate receptors but are not derived from the opium poppy

barbiturate
an addictive depressant used to relieve anxiety or induce sleep

amphetamines
stimulants derived from *alpha-methyl-beta-phenyl-ethylamine*, a colorless liquid consisting of carbon, hydrogen, and nitrogen

hydrocarbons
chemical compounds consisting of hydrogen and carbon

second-hand smoke
smoke from the tobacco products and exhalations of other people

hallucinogen
a substance that causes hallucinations

trance—is derived from the Greek word for sleep. Hypnotism can be used as an anesthetic in dentistry, childbirth, and medical procedures. Some psychologists use hypnosis to help clients reduce anxiety, overcome fears, or lessen the perception of chronic pain. One common form of meditation, transcendental meditation (TM). People practise TM by concentrating on mantras—words or sounds that are claimed to help the person achieve an altered state of consciousness. Mindfulness meditation (MM), as opposed to TM, makes no pretense of achieving spiritual goals. Instead, MM provides clients with mantra-like techniques they can use to focus on the present moment rather than ruminate about problems.

LO5 Explain how psychoactive drugs, including substance abuse, alter states of consciousness.
Substance abuse and dependence usually begin with experimental use in adolescence. People experiment with drugs for various reasons, including curiosity, conformity to peer pressure, parental use, rebelliousness, escape from boredom or pressure, and excitement or pleasure. Use of a substance may be reinforced by peers or by the drug's positive effects on mood and its reduction of anxiety, fear, and stress. Many people use drugs as a form of self-medication for anxiety and depression, even low self-esteem. For people who are physiologically dependent, avoidance of withdrawal symptoms is also reinforcing. Psychoactive drugs include depressants (alcohol, opiates, and barbiturates), stimulants (amphetamines, cocaine, and nicotine), and hallucinogens (LSD, marijuana, PHP, and mescaline).

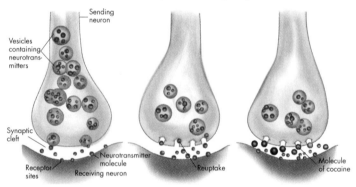

How Cocaine Produces Euphoria and Why People "Crash"

marijuana
the dried vegetable matter of the Cannabis sativa plant

LSD
lysergic acid diethylamide; a hallucinogen

flashbacks
distorted perceptions or hallucinations that occur days or weeks after LSD usage but mimic the LSD experience

mescaline
a hallucinogen derived from the mescal (peyote) cactus

phencyclidine (PCP)
a hallucinogen; its name is an abbreviation of its chemical structure

Chapter in Review

LO1 learning
a relatively permanent change in behaviour, capabilities, or knowledge that results from experience

classical conditioning
a simple form of learning in which a neutral stimulus comes to evoke the response usually evoked by another stimulus by being paired repeatedly with the other stimulus

stimulus
an environmental condition that elicits a response

unconditioned stimulus (UCS)
a stimulus that elicits a response from an organism prior to conditioning

unconditioned response (UCR)
an unlearned response to an unconditioned stimulus

orienting reflex
an unlearned response in which an organism attends to a stimulus

conditioned stimulus (CS)
a previously neutral stimulus that elicits a conditioned response because it has been paired repeatedly with a stimulus that already elicited that response

conditioned response (CR)
a learned response to a conditioned stimulus

extinction
process that occurs when stimuli lose their ability to evoke learned responses because the events that had followed the stimuli no longer occur

spontaneous recovery
the recurrence of an extinguished response as a function of the passage of time

generalization
in conditioning, the tendency for a conditioned response to be evoked by stimuli that are similar to the stimulus to which the response was conditioned

discrimination
in conditioning, the tendency for an organism to distinguish between a conditioned stimulus and similar stimuli that do not forecast an unconditioned stimulus

higher-order conditioning
a classical conditioning procedure in which a previously neutral stimulus comes to elicit the response brought forth by a *conditioned* stimulus by being paired repeatedly with that conditioned stimulus

counterconditioning
a fear-reduction technique in which pleasant stimuli are associated with fear-evoking stimuli so that the fear-evoking stimuli lose their aversive qualities

systematic desensitization
a behavioural fear-reduction technique in which a hierarchy of fear-evoking stimuli is presented while the person remains relaxed

LO1 Describe the learning process according to classical conditioning.
Classical conditioning is a simple form of associative learning that teaches animals to anticipate events. When a neutral stimulus (like a bell ringing) and one that evokes a response (like dog food) are paired together repeatedly, the conditioned neutral stimulus will begin to trigger a response (like salivation) on its own.

KIND OF LEARNING: Classical conditioning
Major theorists: Ivan Pavlov (known for basic research with dogs); John B. Watson (known as the originator of behaviourism)

WHAT IS LEARNED
Association of events; anticipations, signs, expectations; automatic responses to new stimuli

HOW IT IS LEARNED
A neutral stimulus is repeatedly paired with a stimulus (an unconditioned stimulus, or UCS) that elicits a response (an unconditioned response, or UCR) until the neutral stimulus produces a response (conditioned response, or CR) that anticipates and prepares for the unconditioned stimulus. At this point, the neutral stimulus has become a conditioned stimulus (CS).

LO2 Describe the learning process according to operant conditioning.
Under operant conditioning, animals learn to engage in behaviour because of the way it is reinforced. Positive reinforcement encourages the learner to repeat a behaviour more frequently. Negative reinforcement encourages the learner to repeat a behaviour in order to remove an aversive stimulus.

KIND OF LEARNING: Operant conditioning
Major theorist: B.F. Skinner

WHAT IS LEARNED
Behaviour that operates on, or affects, the environment to produce consequences

HOW IT IS LEARNED
A response is rewarded or reinforced so that it occurs with greater frequency in similar situations.

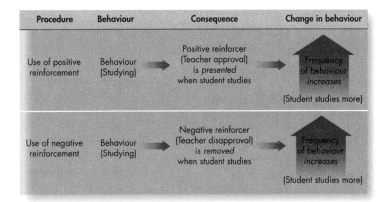

Procedure	Behaviour	Consequence	Change in behaviour
Use of positive reinforcement	Behaviour (Studying)	Positive reinforcer (Teacher approval) is *presented* when student studies	Frequency of behaviour *increases* (Student studies more)
Use of negative reinforcement	Behaviour (Studying)	Negative reinforcer (Teacher disapproval) is *removed* when student studies	Frequency of behaviour *increases* (Student studies more)

LO2 reinforce
to follow a response with a stimulus that increases the frequency of the response

operant behaviour
involuntary responses that are reinforced

operant conditioning
a simple form of learning in which an organism learns to engage in certain behaviour because it is reinforced

reinforcer
any stimulus that increases the frequency of a behaviour

positive reinforcer
a reinforcer that when *presented* increases the frequency of an operant behaviour

negative reinforcer
a reinforcer that when *removed* increases the frequency of an operant behaviour

primary reinforcer
an unlearned reinforcer

secondary reinforcer
a stimulus that gains reinforcement value through association with established reinforcers; also termed *conditioned reinforcer*

punishment
an unpleasant stimulus that suppresses the behaviour it follows

discriminative stimulus
in operant conditioning, a stimulus that indicates whether reinforcement or punishment will follow

continuous reinforcement
a schedule of reinforcement in which every correct response is reinforced

partial reinforcement
one of several reinforcement schedules in which not every correct response is reinforced

fixed-interval schedule
a schedule in which a fixed amount of time must elapse between the previous and subsequent times that reinforcement is available

variable-interval schedule
a schedule in which a variable amount of time must elapse between the previous and subsequent times that reinforcement is available

fixed-ratio schedule
a schedule in which reinforcement is provided after a fixed number of correct responses

variable-ratio schedule
a schedule in which reinforcement is provided after a variable number of correct responses

shaping
a procedure for teaching complex behaviours that at first reinforces approximations of the target behaviour

successive approximations
behaviours that are progressively closer to a target behaviour

LO3 cognitive map
a mental representation of surroundings

pervasive developmental disorders (PDD)
a diagnostic category of the DSM-IV, usually diagnosed in childhood, involving mental disability, learning disorders, and social and communication impairments

LO3 Describe cognitive factors in learning.
Learning is often more complex than association and reinforcement; it involves searching for information, weighing evidence, and making decisions. Cognitive psychologists study mental structures, schemas, templates, and information processing to prove that learning can occur without conditioning. Latent learning—like a cognitive map of a maze—may not be revealed without motivation. Contingency theory suggests that learning occurs when a conditioned stimulus provides information about the unconditioned stimulus. Finally, observational learning makes it possible to acquire skills and knowledge by watching others rather than through direct experience.

KIND OF LEARNING:
Observational learning
Major theorists: Albert Bandura; Julian Rotter; Walter Mischel

WHAT IS LEARNED
Expectations (if–then relationships), knowledge, and skills

HOW IT IS LEARNED
A person observes the behaviour of another person (live or through media such as films, television, or books) and its effects

We learn by observing parents, peers, teachers, and media. By observing the consequences of others' actions, we can decide whether or not we will engage in certain behaviours. Modelling has a powerful influence on our behaviour.

autism spectrum disorder (ASD)
a neurobiological disorder resulting in developmental impairment and affecting communication, social understanding, and behaviour

latent
hidden or concealed

contingency theory
the view that learning occurs when stimuli provide information about the likelihood of the occurrence of other stimuli

observational learning
the acquisition of knowledge and skills through the observation of others (who are called *models*) rather than by means of direct experience

model
a person who engages in a response, which serves as an example that is then imitated by another person

Chapter in Review

LO1 memory
the processes by which information is encoded, stored, and retrieved

encoding
modifying information so that it can be placed in memory; the first stage of information processing

selective attention
focusing on one piece of information and ignoring other information in the background

storage
the maintenance of information over time; the second stage of information processing

maintenance rehearsal
mental repetition of information to store it in memory

elaborative rehearsal
the kind of coding in which new information is related to information that is already known as a way to store it in memory

metamemory
self-awareness of the ways in which memory functions, allowing the person to encode, store, and retrieve information effectively

retrieval
the location of stored information and its return to consciousness; the third stage of information processing

paired associates
nonsense syllables presented in pairs in tasks that measure recall

method of savings
a measure of memory in which the difference between the number of repetitions originally required to learn a list and the number of repetitions required to relearn the list after a certain amount of time has elapsed is calculated

savings
the difference between the number of repetitions originally required to learn a list and the number of repetitions required to relearn the list after a certain amount of time has elapsed

LO2 sensory memory
the type or stage of memory first encountered by a stimulus

memory trace
an assumed change in the nervous system that reflects the impression made by a stimulus

icon
a mental representation of a visual stimulus that is held briefly in sensory memory

iconic memory
the sensory register that briefly holds mental representations of visual stimuli

eidetic imagery
the maintenance of detailed visual memories over several minutes

LO1 Define memory and explain the processes of memory.
Memory is the processes by which information is encoded, stored, and retrieved.

The first stage of information processing is changing information so that we can place it in memory: encoding. When we encode information, we transform it into psychological formats that can be represented mentally. To do so, we commonly use visual, auditory, and semantic codes. The second memory process is storage. Storage means maintaining information over time. The third memory process is retrieval. The retrieval of stored information means locating it and returning it to consciousness.

LO2 Explain memory systems and differentiate between types of memories.
The Atkinson–Shiffrin model proposes that there are three stages of memory: (a) sensory memory, (b) short-term memory, and (c) long-term memory. Part A shows that sensory information impacts on the registers of sensory memory. Memory traces are held briefly in sensory memory before decaying. If we attend to the information, much of it can be transferred to short-term memory (STM). Part B: Information may be maintained in STM through maintenance rehearsal or elaborative rehearsal. Otherwise, it may decay or be displaced. Part C: Once information is transferred to long-term memory (LTM), it may be filed away indefinitely. However, if the information in LTM is organized poorly, or if we cannot find cues to retrieve it, it can be lost.

Three Stages of Memory: The Atkinson–Shiffrin Model

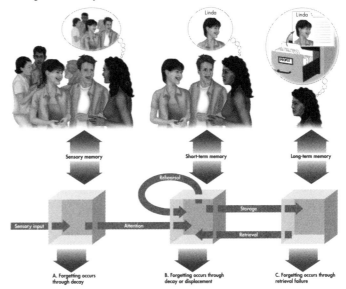

Explicit memory—also referred to as declarative memory—is memory for specific information. Two kinds of explicit memories are identified according to the type of information they hold: episodic memories are memories of the things that happen to us or take place in our presence ("I remember..."); and semantic memory refers to general knowledge ("I know..."). *Implicit memory*—also referred to as nondeclarative memory—is memory of how to perform a procedure or skill; it is the act itself, doing something, like riding a bike.

Retrospective memory is the recalling of information that has been previously learned. Explicit and implicit memories involve remembering things that were learned. *Prospective memory* refers to remembering to do things in the future.

echo
a mental representation of an auditory stimulus (sound) that is held briefly in sensory memory

echoic memory
the sensory register that briefly holds mental representations of auditory stimuli

short-term memory (STM)
the memory system that can hold information only briefly after the trace of the stimulus decays

working memory
another term for *short-term memory*

serial-position effect
the tendency to recall more accurately the first and last items in a series

chunking
encoding (organizing) a stimulus or group of stimuli as a distinct piece of information; grouping stimuli together

long-term memory (LTM)
the type or stage of memory capable of relatively permanent storage

explicit memory
memory that clearly and distinctly expresses (declares) specific information; also called declarative memory

episodic memory
memories of events experienced by a person or that take place in the person's presence

semantic memory
general knowledge and information we know about, as opposed to episodic memory

implicit memory
memory that is suggested (implied) but not plainly expressed, as illustrated in the things that people *do* but do not state clearly; also called nondeclarative memory

priming
the activation of specific associations in memory, often as a result of repetition and without making a conscious effort to access the memory

retrospective memory
memory for past events, activities, and learning experiences, as shown by explicit (episodic and semantic) and implicit memories

prospective memory
memory to perform an act in the future, as at a certain time or when a certain event occurs

schema
a way of mentally representing the world, such as a belief or an expectation, that can influence perception of persons, objects, and situations

tip-of-the-tongue (TOT) phenomenon
the feeling that information is stored in memory although it cannot be readily retrieved

context-dependent memory
information that is better retrieved in the context in which it was encoded and stored, or learned

state-dependent memory
information that is better retrieved in the physiological or emotional state in which it was encoded and stored, or learned

LO3 **encoding failure**
failure to store sensory information to STM in order to be useful for retrieval later

interference theory
the view that we may forget stored material because other learning, old or new, interferes with it

retroactive interference
the interference of new learning with the ability to retrieve material learned previously

LO3 Identify why we forget. According to interference theory, we forget material in short-term and long-term memory because newly learned material interferes with it. The two basic types of interference are retroactive interference and proactive interference. According to Sigmund Freud, we are motivated to repress painful memories and unacceptable ideas because they produce anxiety, guilt, and shame. Freud also believed that young children repress memories of aggressive impulses and perverse lusts toward their parents, which would explain why people could not recall episodes in their early childhoods (infantile amnesia). Adults also experience amnesia, although usually for biological reasons, as in the cases of anterograde and retrograde amnesia.

Ebbinghaus's Classic Curve of Forgetting

Recollection of lists of words drops precipitously during the first hour after learning. Losses of learning then becomes more gradual. Retention drops by half within the first hour. It takes a month (thirty-one days), however, for retention to be cut in half again.

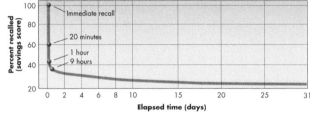

LO4 Describe the biological aspects of memory. Psychologists assume that mental processes such as the encoding, storage, and retrieval of information—that is, memory—are accompanied by changes in the brain. Much research on the biology of memory focuses today on the roles of stimulants, neurons, neurotransmitters, hormones, and structures in the brain.

One Avenue to Long-Term Potentiation (LTP)

LTP can occur via the action of neurotransmitters such as serotonin and glutamate at synapses. Structurally, LTP can also occur as shown in Parts A and B, when dendrites sprout new branches that connect with transmitting axons, increasing the amount of stimulation they receive.

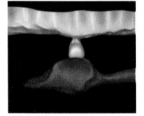

Part A

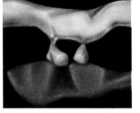

Part B

proactive interference
the interference by old learning with the ability to retrieve material learned recently

dissociative amnesia
amnesia thought to stem from psychological conflict or trauma

infantile amnesia
inability to recall events that occur prior to the age of two or three; also termed *childhood amnesia*

hippocampus
a structure in the limbic system that plays an important role in the formation of new memories

anterograde amnesia
failure to remember events that occur after physical trauma because of the effects of the trauma

retrograde amnesia
failure to remember events that occur prior to physical trauma because of the effects of the trauma

LO4 **engram**
(1) an assumed electrical circuit in the brain that corresponds to a memory trace; (2) an assumed chemical change in the brain that accompanies learning (from the Greek *en-*, meaning "in," and *gramma*, meaning "something that is written or recorded")

long-term potentiation (LTP)
enhanced efficiency in synaptic transmission that follows brief, rapid stimulation

Chapter in Review

LO1

thinking
paying attention to information, mentally representing it, reasoning about it, and making decisions about it

concept
a mental category that is used to class together objects, relations, events, abstractions, or qualities that have common properties

prototype
a concept of a category of objects or events that serves as a good example of the category

exemplar
a specific example

algorithm
a systematic procedure for solving a problem that works invariably when it is correctly applied

systematic random search
an algorithm for solving problems in which each possible solution is tested according to a particular set of rules

heuristics
rules of thumb that help us simplify and solve problems

means–end analysis
a heuristic device in which we try to solve a problem by evaluating the difference between the current situation and the goal

mental set
the tendency to respond to a new problem with an approach that was successfully used with similar problems

insight
in Gestalt psychology, a sudden perception of relationships among elements of the "perceptual field," permitting the solution of a problem

incubation
in problem solving, a hypothetical process that sometimes occurs when we stand back from a frustrating problem for a while and the solution "suddenly" appears

functional fixedness
tendency to view an object in terms of its name or familiar usage

representativeness heuristic
a decision-making heuristic in which people make judgments about samples according to the populations they appear to represent

LO1 Define thinking and the various concepts involved in thinking. Thinking entails attending to information, representing it mentally, reasoning about it, and making judgments and decisions about it; thinking means making conscious, planned attempts to make sense of our world, as well as categorizing new concepts and manipulating relationships among concepts. Three factors that affect problem solving include: level of expertise; whether you fall prey to a mental set; and whether you develop insight into the problem. Strategies used to problem-solve include heuristic devices, algorithms, and means–end analysis.

LO2 Identify the concept of intelligence and the techniques used to measure intelligence. Intelligence is broadly thought of as the underlying ability to understand the world and cope with its challenges. Intelligence allows people to: think, understand complex ideas, reason, solve problems, learn from experience, and adapt to the environment. Several theories of intelligence have been developed: factor theories suggest that intelligence is made up of a number of primary mental abilities; the theory of multiple intelligences suggests that there are a number of intelligences; and triarchic theory suggests that there are three types of intelligence.

LO3 Describe the controversy surrounding intelligence testing. The role that nature and nurture play in intellectual functioning is a controversial topic in psychology. Education contributes to intelligence. For example, Head Start programs enhance IQ scores, achievement scores, and academic skills of disadvantaged children. Adoptee studies suggest a genetic influence on intelligence. But they also suggest a role for environmental influence. All in all, studies generally suggest that the heritability of intelligence is between 40% and 60%. Intellectual functioning would appear to reflect the interaction of genetic, physical, personal, and sociocultural factors.

Approximate Distribution of IQ Scores

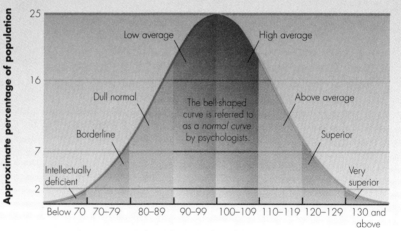

Range of IQ scores

Primary Mental Abilities, According to Thurstone

Ability	Definition
Visual and spatial abilities	Visualizing forms and spatial relationships
Perceptual speed	Grasping perceptual details rapidly, perceiving similarities and differences between stimuli
Numerical ability	Computing numbers
Verbal meaning	Knowing the meanings of words
Memory	Recalling information (e.g., words and sentences)
Word fluency	Thinking of words quickly (e.g., rhyming and doing crossword puzzles)
Deductive reasoning	Deriving examples from general rules
Inductive reasoning	Inferring general rules from examples

availability heuristic
a decision-making heuristic in which our estimates of frequency or probability of events are based on how easy it is to find examples

anchoring and adjustment heuristic
a decision-making heuristic in which a presumption or first estimate serves as a cognitive anchor; as we receive additional information, we make adjustments but tend to remain in the proximity of the anchor

framing effect
the influence of wording, or the context in which information is presented, on decision making

LO2 intelligence
a complex and controversial concept; according to David Wechsler (1975), the "capacity . . . to understand the world [and] resourcefulness to cope with its challenges"

g
Spearman's symbol for general intelligence, which he believed underlay more specific abilities

s
Spearman's symbol for *specific* factors, or *s factors*, which he believed accounted for individual abilities

primary mental abilities
according to Thurstone, the basic abilities that make up intelligence; examples include word fluency and numerical ability

mental age (MA)
the accumulated months of credit that a person earns on the Stanford–Binet Intelligence Scale

intelligence quotient (IQ)
(1) originally, a ratio obtained by dividing a child's score (or mental age) on an intelligence test by chronological age; (2) generally, a score on an intelligence test

LO3 heritability
the degree to which the variations in a trait from one person to another can be attributed to, or explained by, genetic factors

creativity
the ability to generate novel and useful solutions to problems

convergent thinking
a thought process that narrows in on the single best solution to a problem

divergent thinking
a thought process that attempts to generate multiple solutions to problems

LO4 language
the communication of information by means of symbols arranged according to rules of grammar

semanticity
meaning; the quality of language in which words are used as symbols for objects, events, or ideas

infinite creativity
the capacity to combine words into original sentences

LO4 Describe how language develops.
Language is the communication of thoughts and feelings by means of symbols that are arranged according to rules of grammar. True language is distinguished from the communication systems of lower animals by properties such as semanticity, infinite creativity, and displacement. Language development reflects the interactions between the influences of heredity (nature) and the environment (nurture). Learning theorists see language developing according to imitation and reinforcement, where parents serve as models.

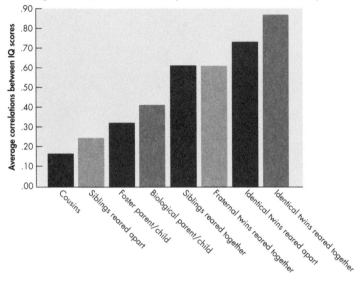

Findings of Studies of the Relationship between IQ Scores and Heredity

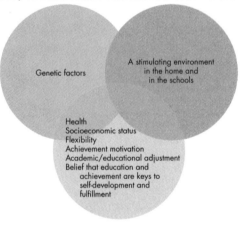

The Complex Web of Factors That Affect Intellectual Functioning

displacement
the quality of language that permits one to communicate information about objects and events in another time and place

linguistic-relativity hypothesis
the view that language structures the way in which we view the world

phonemes
the smallest units of sounds in spoken language

morphemes
the smallest units of meaning in spoken language

syntax
the arrangement and organization of words to form meaningful sentences; rules to create grammatical sentences

semantics
the meanings associated with a morpheme or sentence

pragmatics
the ways in which we use language to convey social meanings of spoken language

holophrase
a single word used to express complex meanings

overregularization
the application of regular grammatical rules for forming inflections (e.g., past tense and plurals) to irregular verbs and nouns

psycholinguistic theory
the view that language learning involves an interaction between environmental factors and an inborn tendency to acquire language

language acquisition device (LAD)
in psycholinguistic theory, neural "prewiring" that facilitates the child's learning of grammar

Chapter in Review

8

LO1 zygote
a fertilized ovum (egg cell) that travels to the uterus and attaches to the uterine wall

germinal stage
the first stage of prenatal development (lasts approximately two weeks), during which the dividing mass of cells becomes implanted in the uterine wall

embryonic stage
the second stage of prenatal development (three to eight weeks), during which the major body structures and organs develop

fetal stage
the third stage of prenatal development (nine weeks to birth), during which further growth of the body and organ systems continue—especially the heart and lungs in the final three months—to allow the fetus to thrive outside the womb

placenta
a membrane that permits the exchange of nutrients and waste products between the mother and her developing child but does not allow the maternal and fetal bloodstreams to mix

teratogen
a harmful (or toxic) agent, such as a disease, a drug, a chemical, or radiation that has the potential to cause birth defects or abnormalities to the developing fetus

LO2 reflex
a simple unlearned response to a stimulus; essential to an infant's survival

adolescence
the period of life bounded by puberty and the assumption of adult responsibilities

puberty
the period of physical development during which sexual reproduction first becomes possible

secondary sex characteristics
characteristics that distinguish the sexes, such as distribution of body hair and depth of voice, but that are not directly involved in reproduction

menarche
the beginning of menstruation

menopause
the cessation of menstruation

osteoporosis
bone disease characterized by deterioration of bone tissues and low bone mass

LO3 schema
a mental structure that organizes our experiences of the world through classification and organization of information

assimilation
the inclusion of a new event (or experience) into an existing schema

accommodation
the modification of an existing schema or creation of a new schema so that information inconsistent with existing schemas can be integrated or understood

LO1
Explain the stages of prenatal development and the major influences on prenatal growth. The fetal stage lasts from the beginning of the third month until birth. By the end of the third month, the major organ systems and the fingers and toes have formed. In the middle of the fourth month, the mother usually detects the first fetal movements. By the end of the sixth month, the fetus moves its limbs so vigorously that mothers often feel that they are being kicked. The fetus opens and shuts its eyes, sucks its thumb, alternates between periods of being awake and sleeping, and responds to light. It also turns somersaults, which can be perceived by the mother. During the three months prior to birth, the organ systems of the fetus continue to mature. The heart and lungs become increasingly capable of sustaining independent life. The fetus gains about 2.5 kilograms and doubles in length. Newborn boys average about 3.4 kilograms and newborn girls about 3.2 kilograms.

LO2
Explain physical development over the life span. Childhood begins with birth. During infancy—the first two years of childhood—dramatic gains in height and weight continue. Babies usually double their birth weight in about five months and triple it by their first birthday. Their height increases by about 25 centimetres in the first year. Children grow another 10 to 15 centimetres during the second year and gain some 2 to 3 kilograms. After that, they gain about 5 to 7 centimetres a year until they reach the adolescent growth spurt. Other aspects of physical development in childhood include reflexes and perceptual development. One of the most noticeable physical developments of adolescence is a growth spurt that lasts 2 to 3 years and ends the gradual changes in height and weight that characterize most of childhood. Within this short span of years, adolescents grow some 20 to 30 centimetres. Most boys wind up taller and heavier than most girls.

In boys, the weight of muscle mass increases considerably. The width of the shoulders and circumference of the chest also increase. Adolescents may eat enormous quantities of food to fuel their growth spurt. Most young adults are at their height of sensory sharpness, strength, reaction time, and cardiovascular fitness. On the other hand, women gymnasts find themselves lacking a competitive edge in their 20s because they are accumulating (normal) body fat and losing suppleness and flexibility. The years between 40 and 60 are reasonably stable. There is gradual physical decline, but it is minor and only likely to be of concern if a person competes with young adults—or with idealized memories of oneself. For women, menopause is usually considered to be the single most important change of life that occurs during middle adulthood. Menopause usually occurs during the late 40s or early 50s. Osteoporosis also becomes a concern for many women. For older adults, changes in calcium metabolism increase the brittleness of the bones and heighten the risk of breaks due to falls. The skin becomes less elastic and subject to wrinkles and folds. Older adults see and hear less acutely.

LO3
Explain cognitive and moral development over the life span. Piaget's theory of cognitive development, Vygotsky's sociocultural theory and Kohlberg's theory of moral development provide a look at the ways in which we develop cognitively and morally over the life span. According to Piaget, *children* undergo three stages of cognitive development: sensorimotor, preoperational, and concrete operational. The stage of formal operations is the final stage in Piaget's theory, and it represents cognitive maturity. Formal operational thought generally begins at about the beginning of adolescence. The major achievements of the stage of formal operations involve classification, logical thought, and the ability to hypothesize. Vygotzky's theory focuses on children's learning through the zone of proximity, where adults or older children best guide a child through tasks by assisting them towards their capabilities. Kohlberg's research on the levels of moral reasoning found that children progress through a series of levels: preconventional; conventional; and postconventional. He believed that postconventional moral judgments were absent until about age 16. He also believed that not many adults mature beyond the conventional level.

sensorimotor stage
the first of Piaget's stages of cognitive development, characterized by coordination of sensory information and motor activity through exploration of the environment, and the representation of mental thought demonstrated by object permanence

object permanence
recognition that objects removed from sight still exist, as demonstrated by a child's continued exploration for the object

preoperational stage
the second of Piaget's stages, characterized by one-dimensional, perceptual thought processes (rather than logical, rapid development of language) and egocentrism

egocentrism
the assumption that others view the world the same as you do without considering that different views exist

conservation
according to Piaget, recognition that basic properties of a substance, object, or number, such as weight and mass, remain the same when superficial features change

concrete operational stage
Piaget's third stage, characterized by logical thought concerning tangible objects, conservation, and reversibility

decentration
simultaneous focusing on more than one dimension of a problem, so that flexible, reversible thought becomes possible

formal operational stage
Piaget's fourth stage, characterized by abstract logical thought and deduction from principles

zone of proximal development (ZPD)
Vygotsky's term for the situation in which a child carries out tasks with the help of someone who is more skilled, frequently an adult who represents the culture in which the child develops

scaffolding
Vygotsky's term for temporary cognitive structures or methods of solving problems that help the child as he or she learns to function independently

imaginary audience
an aspect of adolescent egocentrism; the belief that other people are as concerned with our thoughts and behaviours as we are

personal fable
an aspect of adolescent egocentrism; the belief that our feelings and ideas are special and unique and that we are invulnerable

crystallized intelligence
one's lifetime of intellectual achievement, as shown largely through vocabulary and knowledge of world affairs

fluid intelligence
mental flexibility as shown in learning rapidly to solve new kinds of problems

Alzheimer's disease
a progressive disease of the brain, characterized by loss of memory, language, problem solving, and other cognitive functions; most common form of dementia

dementia
a syndrome that affects cognitive functioning, causing social, language, physical, and emotional impairments

preconventional level
according to Kohlberg, a period during which moral judgments are based largely on expectation of rewards or punishments

conventional level
according to Kohlberg, a period during which moral judgments largely reflect social conventions; a "law and order" approach to morality

---

Cognitive development in adulthood has many aspects—creativity, memory functioning, and intelligence. Changes in social and emotional development during adulthood are probably the most "elastic" or fluid.

LO4 Explain social development over the life span.
Erik Erikson's theory of psychosocial development and Ainsworth's attachment studies explore critical aspects of social and emotional development in childhood. Erickson believed that children progress through a series of psychosocial stages—called ego conflicts, in which a child must resolve a conflict in order to progress to the next stage. In childhood, Erikson indicated that children struggle with trust vs. mistrust; autonomy vs. guilt and shame; industry vs. inferiority. According to Erikson, the fifth stage-ego identity versus role confusion—occurs in adolescence. Young adulthood is characterized by the task of developing abiding intimate relationships; middle adulthood involves being productive and contributing to younger generations; the challenge for late adulthood is to maintain one's sense of identity despite physical deterioration.

LO5 Understand stages of death and dying.
Kübler-Ross identified several similarities in the ways in which dying patients coped with their terminal illness and the emotional responses while waiting for their impending death. These stages are (1) denial and isolation; (2) anger; (3) bargaining; (4) depression; and (5) acceptance.

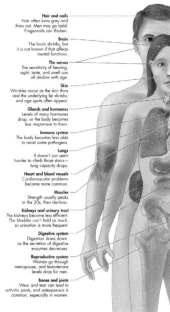

Hair and nails Hair often turns grey and thins out. Men may go bald. Fingernails can thicken.

Brain The brain shrinks, but it is not known if that affects mental functions.

The senses The sensitivity of hearing, sight, taste, and smell can all decline with age.

Skin Wrinkles occur as the skin thins and the underlying fat shrinks, and age spots often appear.

Glands and hormones Levels of many hormones drop, or the body becomes less responsive to them.

Immune system The body becomes less able to resist some pathogens.

Lungs It doesn't just seem harder to climb those stairs—lung capacity drops.

Heart and blood vessels Cardiovascular problems become more common.

Muscles Strength usually peaks in the 20s, then declines.

Kidneys and urinary tract The kidneys become less efficient. The bladder can't hold as much, so urination is more frequent.

Digestive system Digestion slows down as the secretion of digestive enzymes decreases.

Reproductive system Women go through menopause, and testosterone levels drop for men.

Bones and joints Wear and tear can lead to arthritic joints, and osteoporosis is common, especially in women.

---

postconventional level
according to Kohlberg, a period during which moral judgments are derived from moral principles and people look to themselves to set moral standards

LO4 ego conflict
Erikson's term for the unique, contradictory developmental tasks associated with each stage of psychosocial development, during which individuals must resolve a conflict prior to progressing successfully through later psychosocial stages throughout the life span

attachment
the enduring affectional tie that binds one person to another

contact comfort
a hypothesized primary drive to seek physical comfort through contact with another

ethologist
a scientist who studies the characteristic behaviour patterns of species of animals

critical period
a period of time when an instinctive response can be elicited by a particular stimulus

imprinting
a process occurring during a critical period in the development of an organism, in which that organism responds to a stimulus in a manner that will afterward be difficult to modify

authoritative parents
parents who are strict and warm; they demand mature behaviour but use reason and fairness rather than force in discipline

---

authoritarian parents
parents who are rigid in their rules and who demand obedience for the sake of obedience

permissive parents
parents who impose few, if any, rules and who do not supervise their children closely

uninvolved parents
parents who generally leave their children to themselves and who are likely unaware of their children's feelings and emotions

ego identity
Erikson's term for a firm sense of who one is and what one stands for

role confusion
Erikson's term for lack of clarity in one's life roles (due to failure to develop ego identity)

intimacy versus isolation
Erikson's life crisis of young adulthood, which is characterized by the task of developing abiding intimate relationships

generativity versus stagnation
Erikson's term for the crisis of middle adulthood, characterized by the task of being productive and contributing to younger generations

midlife crisis
a crisis experienced by many people during the midlife transition when they realize that life may be more than halfway over and they reassess their achievements in terms of their dreams

ego integrity versus despair
Erikson's term for the crisis of late adulthood, characterized by the task of maintaining one's sense of identity despite physical deterioration

Chapter in Review

LO1 motive
a hypothetical state within an organism that propels the organism toward a goal (from the Latin *movere,* meaning "to move")

need
a state of deprivation

drive
a condition of arousal in an organism that is associated with a need

physiological drives
unlearned drives with a biological basis, such as hunger, thirst, and avoidance of pain

incentive
an object, person, or situation that can satisfy a need

LO2 instinct
an inherited disposition to activate specific behaviour patterns that are designed to reach certain goals

drive-reduction theory
the view that organisms learn to engage in behaviours that have the effect of reducing drives

homeostasis
the tendency of the body to maintain a steady state

self-actualization
a state of being that includes perceptive clarity, peacefulness, simplicity, a sense of mission, sensitivity to the needs of others, being comfortable alone, a healthy sense of humour, and moments of profound emotional experience

LO3 satiety
the state of being satisfied; fullness

ventromedial nucleus (VMN)
a central area on the underside of the hypothalamus that appears to function as a stop-eating centre

hyperphagic
characterized by excessive eating

lateral hypothalamus
an area at the side of the hypothalamus that appears to function as a start-eating centre

aphagic
characterized by undereating

anorexia nervosa
a life-threatening eating disorder characterized by dramatic weight loss and a distorted body image

bulimia nervosa
an eating disorder characterized by repeated cycles of binge eating and purging

LO1 Define motivation including needs, drives, and incentives. The psychology of motivation concerns the *whys* of behaviour. Motives are hypothetical states that activate behaviour toward goals and may take the form of needs, drives, and/or incentives. *Needs* come in two types: physiological (e.g., eating, drinking, needs necessary for survival) and psychological (e.g., attachment, self-esteem, needs for achievement, power, self-esteem, etc.). Physiological and psychological needs differ in two ways: psychological needs are not necessarily based on deprivation; psychological needs may be acquired through experience. Needs give rise to *drives,* that arouse us to action. *Incentives* are objects, persons, or situations viewed as capable of satisfying a need or as desirable for their own sake.

LO2 Identify the theories of motivation. Psychologists do not agree about the precise nature of motivation. The evolutionary perspective holds that animals are naturally prewired to respond to certain stimuli in certain ways. The drive reductionism and homeostasis perspective holds that primary drives trigger arousal (tension) and activate behaviour. Organisms engage in behaviours that reduce tension and are motivated to maintain a steady state (homeostasis). Other theorists hold with the stimulus motivation perspective—that an organism is motivated to increase stimulation, not reduce a drive. A humanistic theorist, Abraham Maslow believed that people are motivated by the conscious desire for personal growth. Maslow's hierarchy of needs ranges from physiological needs such as hunger and thirst through self-actualization (the highest fulfillment of being that is achievable by a person). Critics argue that there is too much individual variation for the hierarchy of motives to apply to everyone.

Self-actualization

Esteem needs

Love and belongingness

Safety needs

Physiological needs

LO3 Describe the biological and psychological contributions to hunger. Biological mechanisms that regulate hunger include stomach pangs associated with stomach contractions, the functions of the hypothalamus, blood sugar level, and receptors in the liver. The ventromedial nucleus of the hypothalamus partially functions as the "stop-eating" centre of the brain; the lateral hypothalamus partially functions as the "start-eating" centre of the brain. Some psychological factors that influence hunger include the aroma of food, because a person feels anxious or depressed, or bored.

Problems associated with unhealthy weight are on the upswing. The origins of eating disorders aren't entirely clear. Exposure to cultural standards and role models that emphasize excessive slenderness plays a major role. Eating disorders are also more common when the family environment is negative—possibly a history of child abuse or exposure to high parental expectations. Genetic factors might not directly cause eating disorders but are likely to involve obsessionistic and perfectionistic personality traits.

LO4 Explain the role of sex hormones and the sexual response cycle in human sexuality. Sexual motivation, although natural, is also strongly influenced by religious and moral beliefs, cultural tradition, folklore, and superstition. What is considered "normal" depends on the society in which one lives. Much about the development of sexual orientation remains speculative. Sex hormones have activating effects: they affect the sex drive and promote sexual response. Sex hormones also have organizing effects: they motivate lower animals toward masculine or feminine mating patterns.

LO4 activating effect
the arousal-producing effects of sex hormones that increase the likelihood of sexual behaviour

estrus
the periodic sexual excitement of many female mammals, as governed by levels of sex hormones

organizing effect
the directional effect of sex hormones—for example, along stereotypically masculine or feminine lines

sexual response cycle
Masters and Johnson's model of sexual response, which consists of four stages or phases

vasocongestion
engorgement of blood vessels with blood, which swells the genitals and breasts during sexual arousal

myotonia
muscle tension

excitement phase
the first phase of the sexual response cycle, which is characterized by muscle tension, increases in the heart rate, and erection in the male and vaginal lubrication in the female

clitoris
the female sex organ that is most sensitive to sexual sensation; a smooth, round knob of tissue that is situated above the urethral opening

plateau phase
the second phase of the sexual response cycle, which is characterized by increases in vasocongestion, muscle tension, heart rate, and blood pressure in preparation for orgasm

ejaculation
propulsion of seminal fluid (semen) from the penis by contraction of muscles at the base of the penis

orgasm
the height or climax of sexual excitement, involving involuntary muscle contractions, release of sexual tensions, and, usually, subjective feelings of pleasure

resolution phase
the fourth phase of the sexual response cycle, during which the body gradually returns to its prearoused state

refractory period
in the sexual response cycle, a period of time following orgasm during which an individual is not responsive to sexual stimulation

heterosexual
referring to people who are sexually aroused by, and interested in forming romantic relationships with, people of the other sex

homosexual
referring to people who are sexually aroused by, and interested in forming romantic relationships with, people of the same sex (derived from the Greek *homos*, meaning "same," not from the Latin *homo*, meaning "man")

sexual orientation
the directionality of one's sexual and romantic interests; that is, whether one is sexually attracted to, and desires to form a romantic relationship with, members of the other sex or of one's own sex

LO5 Describe achievement motivation.
Henry Murray developed the Thematic Apperception Test (TAT) in an attempt to assess motivation. The TAT contains cards with pictures and drawings that are subject to various interpretations. Subjects are to construct stories about the picture.

Performance goals are usually met through extrinsic or intrinsic rewards. Examples of extrinsic rewards include praise and income, while self-satisfaction is an example of an intrinsic reward. Extrinsic, or tangible, rewards can serve as an incentive for maintaining good grades. An intrinsic goal—e.g., feeling capable and intelligent—tends to have more long-lasting effects.

LO6 Identify the theoretical explanations of emotions.
Emotions are feeling states with physiological, cognitive, and behavioural components. A physiological reaction can involve the sympathetic nervous system and result in rapid heartbeat, breathing, sweating, or muscle tension. Behavioural tendencies occur with emotions. For example, fear leads to avoidance or escape, and anger may lead to "pay-back" behaviours. Parasympathetic nervous system arousal can also occur. Joy, grief, jealousy, disgust, and so on, all have cognitive, physiological, and behavioural components.

Various perspectives hold that cognitive processes—or a combination of arousal and thoughts—may determine the emotional response (see graphic below). All three theories have aspects of correctness but none fully explain emotions.

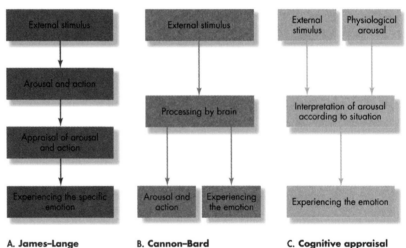

A. James–Lange   **B. Cannon–Bard**   **C. Cognitive appraisal**

LO6 emotion
a feeling state with cognitive, physiological, and behavioural components

sympathetic nervous system
the branch of the autonomic nervous system that is most active during processes that spend body energy from stored reserves, such as in a fight-or-flight reaction to a predator or when you are anxious about a big test

parasympathetic nervous system
the branch of the autonomic nervous system that is most active during processes that restore reserves of energy to the body, such as relaxing and eating

display rules
culturally learned and enforced influences on the appropriateness and intensity of public and private emotional displays

positive psychology
the field of psychology that is about personal well-being and satisfaction; joy, sensual pleasure, and happiness; and optimism and hope for the future

facial-feedback hypothesis
the view that stereotypical facial expressions can contribute to stereotypical emotions

Chapter in Review

10

LO1

stress
the physical and psychological response of the body to any demand that is made on an organism that requires it to adapt, cope, or adjust

eustress (YOU-stress)
stress that is pleasant, desirable, healthful

stressor
any event that causes stress, physical and/or psychological

workplace stress
a negative physical or emotional response to an event or factor at work, which requires an employee to adapt or adjust in order to cope

catastrophize
to interpret negative events as being disastrous; to "blow out of proportion"

Type A behaviour
behaviour characterized by a sense of time urgency, competitiveness, and hostility

Type B behaviour
behaviour characterized by a calm, patient and relaxed attitude

LO2

general adaptation syndrome (GAS)
the predictable physical response to stressors that is explained in three stages: alarm, resistance, exhaustion

alarm reaction
the first stage of the GAS, which is triggered by the impact of a stressor and characterized by sympathetic activity in the body

fight-or-flight reaction
an innate adaptive response to the perception of danger

resistance stage
the second stage of the GAS, characterized by prolonged sympathetic activity in an effort to restore lost energy and repair damage; also called the *adaptation stage*

exhaustion stage
the third stage of the GAS, characterized by weakened resistance and possible deterioration of body functioning, possibly leading to disease

immune system
the system of the body that recognizes and destroys foreign agents (antigens) that invade the body

leukocytes
white blood cells, which act as a defence in the body against infectious diseases and other toxins

antigen
a substance that stimulates the body to mount an immune system response to it

antibodies
substances formed by white blood cells that recognize and destroy antigens

LO1 Define stress and identify various sources of stress.

Psychological factors such as stress, behaviour patterns, and attitudes can lead to or aggravate illness. People can cope with stress, and in fact there is such a thing as healthful stress (eustress). Small stressors, such as daily hassles, can threaten or harm our well-being and lead to nervousness, worrying, inability to get started, feelings of sadness, and feelings of loneliness. Hassles can predict health problems such as heart disease, cancer, and athletic injuries.

Conflict is the feeling of being pulled in two or more directions by opposing motives and can be frustrating and stressful. There are four types of conflict as illustrated in the figure below: *Approach-approach conflict* (A) is the least stressful type. Each of two goals is desirable and both are within reach. *Avoidance-avoidance conflict* (B) is more stressful. A person is motivated (M) to avoid each of two negative goals. Avoiding one of them requires approaching the other. In *approach-avoidance conflict,* (C), the same goal produces both approach and avoidance motives. *Multiple approach-avoidance conflict* (D) occurs when each of several alternative courses of action has pluses and minuses. Decision-making can be stressful—especially when there is no clear correct choice.

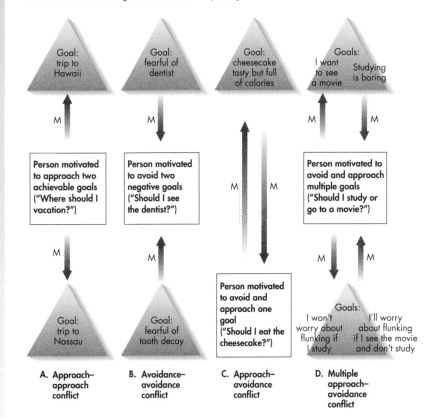

A. Approach–approach conflict
B. Avoidance–avoidance conflict
C. Approach–avoidance conflict
D. Multiple approach–avoidance conflict

LO2 Describe the impact of stress on the body.

The general adaptation syndrome, proposed by Selye, is a cluster of bodily changes that occur in three stages—alarm, resistance, and exhaustion. The alarm reaction is triggered by perception of a stressor. The reaction mobilizes or arouses the body. This mobilization is the basis for the instinctive fight-or-flight reaction. The alarm reaction involves bodily changes that are initiated by the brain and regulated by the endocrine system and the sympathetic division of the autonomic nervous system (ANS). If the stressor isn't removed, we enter the adaptation or resistance stage, in which the body attempts to restore lost energy and repair bodily damage. If the stressor isn't dealt with, we may enter the exhaustion stage—the body is depleted of the resources required for combating stress.

Stress suppresses the immune system. Feelings of control and social support can moderate these effects. The immune system has several functions that combat disease. One function is production of white blood cells (leukocytes). These cells recognize and eradicate foreign agents and

inflammation
increased blood flow to an injured area of the body, resulting in redness, warmth, and an increased supply of white blood cells

LO3 primary appraisal
evaluating a potential stressor as a positive, negative or neutral event

secondary appraisal
evaluating how to cope with a stressful event by using available resources

psychological hardiness
a cluster of traits that buffer stress and are characterized by commitment, challenge, and control

locus of control
the place (locus) to which an individual attributes control over the receiving of reinforcers—either inside or outside the self

LO4 health psychology
the field of psychology that studies the relationships between psychological factors (e.g., attitudes, beliefs, situational influences, and behaviour patterns) and the prevention and treatment of physical illness

pathogen
a microscopic organism (e.g., bacterium or virus) that can cause disease

biopsychosocial
having to do with the interactions of biological, psychological, and sociocultural factors

chlamydia
a sexually transmitted bacterial infection that is most commonly reported in young female adults

gonorrhea
a sexually transmitted bacterial infection that infects the penis, cervix, rectum, throat, and eyes; it is most commonly reported in young adults

HIV
human immunodeficiency virus; a sexually transmitted disease that attacks the immune system, typically progressing to AIDS (acquired immune deficiency syndrome) in which the body's immune system is weak and highly susceptible to infection and even death

unhealthy cells. Foreign substances are called antigens. The body generates specialized proteins or antibodies to fight antigens. Inflammation is another function of the immune system. This is increased blood supply, which floods the region with white blood cells. One of the reasons stress exhausts us is that it stimulates the production of steroids. Steroids suppress the functioning of the immune system. Persistent secretion of steroids decreases inflammation and interferes with the formation of antibodies. We become more vulnerable to various illnesses.

LO3 Identify the psychological moderators of stress.
Psychological factors can influence or moderate the effects of stress. Humour, laughter, and feelings of happiness may have beneficial effects on the immune system. On the other hand, there is a significant relationship between negative life events and stress scores, although the ability to predict a stressor apparently moderates its impact. Control and even the illusion of control can also moderate impact. Social support also seems to act as a buffer against the effects of stress. Sources of social support include emotional concern, instrumental aid, information, appraisal, and socializing.

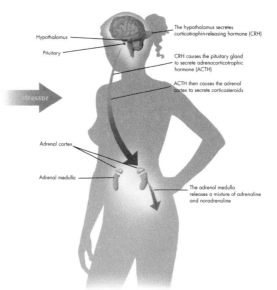

Hypothalamus
Pituitary

The hypothalamus secretes corticotrophin-releasing hormone (CRH)

CRH causes the pituitary gland to secrete adrenocorticotrophic hormone (ACTH)

ACTH then causes the adrenal cortex to secrete corticosteroids

Stressor

Adrenal cortex
Adrenal medulla

The adrenal medulla releases a mixture of adrenaline and noradrenaline

LO4 Explain the relationships between psychology and health.
The biopsychosocial approach to health recognizes that there are complex factors (biological, psychological, and sociocultural factors) that contribute to health and illness and that there is no single, simple answer. Biological factors such as pathogens, inoculations, injuries, age, gender, and a family history of disease may be the most obvious cause of disease, although genetics certainly plays a role. Coronary heart disease (CHD) is the leading cause of death in Canada. Risks for CHD include family history, physiological conditions, patterns of consumption, Type A behaviour, hostility and holding in feelings of anger, job strain, chronic fatigue and chronic emotional strain, sudden stressors, and a physically inactive lifestyle. Risks associated with certain forms of cancer—such as lung cancer—are often preventable. Cancer is characterized by the development of abnormal, or mutant, cells that may take root anywhere in the body. If not controlled early, the cancerous cells may metastasize—establish colonies elsewhere in the body. Risk factors for cancer include heredity and behaviours such as smoking, drinking alcohol, eating animal fats, sunbathing, and prolonged psychological conditions such as depression.

Chapter in Review

11

LO1

personality
the distinct patterns of behaviour, thoughts, and feelings that characterize a person's adaptation to life

psychoanalytic theory
Sigmund Freud's perspective, which emphasizes the importance of unconscious motives and conflicts as forces that determine behaviour

id
the psychic structure, present at birth, that represents physiological drives and is fully unconscious

ego
the second psychic structure to develop, characterized by self-awareness, planning, and delay of gratification

superego
the third psychic structure, which functions as a moral guardian and sets forth high standards for behaviour

identification
in psychoanalytic theory, the unconscious adoption of another person's behaviour

psychosexual development
in psychoanalytic theory, the process by which libidinal energy is expressed through different erogenous zones during different stages of development

oral stage
the first stage of psychosexual development, during which gratification is hypothesized to be attained primarily through oral activities

anal stage
the second stage of psychosexual development, when gratification is attained through anal activities

phallic stage
the third stage of psychosexual development, characterized by a shift of libido to the phallic region (from the Greek *phallos,* referring to an image of the penis; however, Freud used the term *phallic* to refer both to boys and girls)

Oedipus complex
a conflict of the phallic stage in which the boy wishes to possess his mother sexually and perceives his father as a rival in love

Electra complex
a conflict of the phallic stage in which the girl longs for her father and resents her mother

latency
a phase of psychosexual development characterized by repression of sexual impulses

LO1 Describe the psychoanalytical perspective and how it contributed to the study of personality.

Focus of Research
- Unconscious conflict
- Drives such as sex, aggression, and the need for superiority come into conflict with law, social rules, and moral codes

View of Personality
- Three structures of personality—id, ego, superego
- Five stages of psychosexual development—oral, anal, phallic, latency, genital
- Ego analysts—or *neoanalysts*—focus more on the role of the ego in making meaningful, conscious decisions

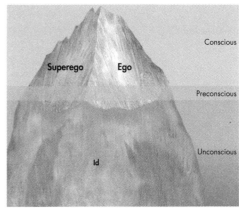

LO2 Explain the trait perspective and the "Big Five" trait model.

Focus of Research
- Use of mathematical techniques to catalogue and organize basic human personality traits

View of Personality
- Based on theory of Hippocrates and work of Gordon Allport
- Eysenck's two-dimensional model: introversion–extraversion and emotional stability–instability
- Current emphasis on the five-factor model (the "Big Five")—extraversion, agreeableness, conscientiousness, neuroticism, openness to experience
- Suggestion of sixth personality trait of honesty-humility

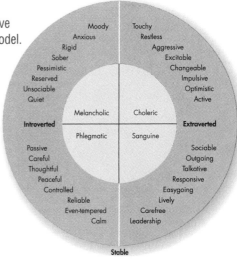

LO3 Identify the contributions of learning theory in understanding personality.

Focus of Research
- Behaviourists focus on situational factors that determine behaviour
- Social cognitive emphasis on observational learning and person variables—competencies, encoding strategies, expectancies, emotions, and self-regulation

View of Personality
- Watson saw personality as plastic and determined by external, situational variables
- Skinner believed that society conditions individuals into wanting what is good for society
- Canadian psychologist Bandura believes in reciprocal determinism—that people and the environment influence one another—and in the role of making conscious choices

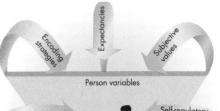
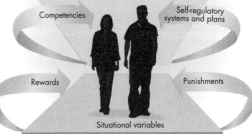

genital stage
the mature stage of psychosexual development, characterized by preferred expression of libido through intercourse with an adult of the other gender

analytical psychology
Jung's psychoanalytic theory, which emphasizes the collective unconscious and archetypes

collective unconscious
Jung's hypothesized store of vague memories that represent the history of humankind

inferiority complex
feelings of inferiority hypothesized by Adler to serve as a central motivating force

creative self
according to Adler, the self-aware aspect of personality that strives to achieve its full potential

individual psychology
Adler's psychoanalytic theory, which emphasizes feelings of inferiority and the creative self

psychosocial development
Erikson's theory of personality and development, which emphasizes social relationships and eight stages of growth

ego identity
a firm sense of who one is and what one stands for

LO2 trait
a relatively stable aspect of personality that is inferred from behaviour and assumed to give rise to consistent behaviour

introversion
a trait characterized by intense imagination and the tendency to inhibit impulses

extraversion
a trait characterized by tendencies to be socially outgoing and to express feelings and impulses freely

LO3 social-cognitive theory
a cognitively oriented learning theory in which observational learning and person variables such as values and expectancies play major roles in individual differences

gender-schema theory
a cognitive view of gender-typing that proposes that once girls and boys become aware of their anatomic sex, they begin to blend their self-expectations and self-esteem with the ways in which they fit the gender roles prescribed in a given culture

LO4 Describe the humanistic perspective of personality.
Focus of Research
- The experience of being human and developing one's unique potential within an often hostile environment

View of Personality
- People have inborn drives to become what they are capable of being
- Unconditional positive regard leads to self-esteem, which facilitates individual growth and development.

LO5 Describe the sociocultural perspective of personality.
Focus of Research
- The roles of ethnicity, gender, culture, and socioeconomic status in personality formation and behaviour

View of Personality
- Development differs in individualistic and collectivist societies
- Discrimination, poverty, and acculturation affect self-concept and self-esteem

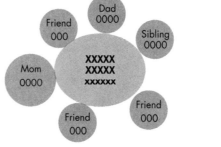

A. Independent view of self   B. Interdependent view of self

LO6 Describe the different kinds of tests psychologists use to measure personality.
The two most widely used types of personality tests are objective tests and projective tests. Objective tests present respondents with a standardized group of test items in the form of a questionnaire. Responses are limited to a specific range of answers. The MMPI is the most widely used objective test. It is usually scored for four validity scales and ten clinical scales. The validity scales suggest whether answers actually represent the person's thoughts, emotions, and behaviours.

In projective tests, people are shown ambiguous stimuli such as inkblots or drawings and asked to say what they look like. People project their own personalities into their responses. The Thematic Apperception Test (TAT) is an example of a projective test.

LO4 humanism
the view that people are capable of free choice, self-fulfillment, and ethical behaviour

self-actualization
in humanistic theory, the innate tendency to strive to realize one's fullest potential of perceptive clarity, peacefulness, simplicity, a sense of mission, sensitivity to the needs of others, being comfortable alone, a healthy sense of humour, and moments of profound emotional experience

unconditional positive regard
a persistent expression of esteem for the value of a person, but not necessarily an unqualified acceptance of all of the person's behaviours

conditional positive regard
judgment of another person's value on the basis of the acceptability of that person's behaviours

conditions of worth
standards by which the value of a person is judged

LO5 sociocultural perspective
the view that focuses on the roles of ethnicity, gender, culture, and socioeconomic status in personality formation, behaviour, and mental processes

individualist
a person who defines herself or himself in terms of personal traits and gives priority to her or his own goals

collectivist
a person who defines herself or himself in terms of relationships to other people and groups and gives priority to group goals

acculturation
the process of adaptation in which immigrants and native groups identify with a new, dominant culture by learning about that culture and making behavioural and attitudinal changes

LO6 validity
in psychological testing, the degree to which a test measures what it is supposed to measure

reliability
in psychological testing, the consistency or stability of test scores from one testing to another

standardization
in psychological testing, the process by which one obtains and organizes test scores from various population groups, so that the results of a person completing a test can be compared to those of others of his or her sex, in his or her age group, and so on

objective tests
tests whose items must be answered in a specified, limited manner; tests whose items have concrete answers that are considered correct

response set
a tendency to answer test items according to a bias—for example, to make oneself seem perfect or bizarre

projective test
a psychological test that presents ambiguous stimuli onto which the test-taker projects his or her own personality in making a response

Chapter in Review

LO1

seasonal affective disorder (SAD)
depressive mood disorder that manifests during the winter months, marked with increased eating, sleeping, weight gain, and a depressed mood

psychological disorders
patterns of behaviour or mental processes that are connected with emotional distress or significant impairment in functioning

hallucination
a perception in the absence of sensory stimulation that is confused with reality

ideas of persecution
erroneous beliefs that one is being victimized or persecuted

flat affect
a severe reduction in emotional expressiveness, found among many people with schizophrenia or serious depression

predictive validity
in this usage, the extent to which a diagnosis permits one to predict the course of a disorder and the type of treatment that may be of help

LO2

delusions
false, persistent beliefs that are unsubstantiated by sensory or objective evidence

affect (AFF-ekt)
feeling or emotional response, particularly as suggested by facial expression and body language

schizophrenia
a psychotic disorder characterized by loss of control of thought processes and inappropriate emotional responses

stupor
a condition in which the senses, thought, and movement are dulled

positive symptoms
the excessive and sometimes bizarre symptoms of schizophrenia, including hallucinations, delusions, and loose associations

negative symptoms
the deficiencies among people with schizophrenia, such as flat affect, lack of motivation, loss of pleasure, and social withdrawal

paranoid schizophrenia
a type of schizophrenia characterized primarily by delusions—commonly of persecution—and vivid hallucinations

disorganized schizophrenia
a type of schizophrenia characterized by disorganized delusions, vivid hallucinations, and inappropriate affect

catatonic schizophrenia
a type of schizophrenia characterized by striking motor impairment

---

LO1 Define psychological disorders and describe their prevalence.

Psychological disorders are characterized by unusual behaviour, socially unacceptable behaviour, faulty perception of reality, personal distress, dangerous behaviour, or self-defeating behaviour. The American Psychiatric Association groups disorders on the basis of clinical syndromes and factors related to adjustment. About half of us will experience a psychological disorder at one time or another.

Past-Year Prevalences of Common Psychological Disorders

	Anxiety Disorders	Mood Disorders	Substance Use Disorders
Men	3.6%	3.8%	4.4%
Women	5.8%	5.9%	1.6%

Sources: Source: Statistics Canada, 2003.

Note: The data in this table are based on a nationally representative sample of 36 984 Canadian residents aged 15 and above. Respondents could report symptoms of more than one type of disorder. For example, anxiety and mood disorders are often "comorbid"—that is, go together. Anxiety and mood disorders are discussed in this chapter. Substance use disorders include abuse of, or dependence on, alcohol or other drugs, as described in Chapter 4.

Adapted from Statistics Canada, *Canadian Community Health Survey* - Mental Health and Well-being (Highlights section), 82-617-XIE2003001, 2004. http://www.statcan.gc.ca/bsolc/olc-cel/olc-cel?catno=82-617-X&lang=eng.

LO2 Describe the symptoms, types, and possible origins of schizophrenia.

Schizophrenia is characterized by disturbances in thought and language, perception and attention, motor activity, mood, and social interaction. Schizophrenia is connected with smaller brains in some people, especially fewer synapses in the prefrontal region, and larger ventricles. A genetic vulnerability to schizophrenia may interact with other factors, such as stress, complications during pregnancy and childbirth, and quality of parenting, to cause the disorder to develop. People with schizophrenia may also use more dopamine than other people do. According to the biopsychosocial model of schizophrenia, people with a genetic vulnerability to the disorder experience increased risk for schizophrenia when they encounter problems such as viral infections, birth complications, stress, and poor parenting.

LO3 Describe the symptoms and possible origins of mood disorders.

Mood disorders involve disturbances in expressed emotions. Major depression is characterized by persistent feelings of sadness, loss of interest, feelings of worthlessness or guilt, and inability to concentrate. Bipolar disorder is characterized by mood swings between elation and depression. Genetic factors may be involved in mood disorders. Research emphasizes possible roles for learned helplessness, attribution styles, and underutilization of serotonin in depression. People who are depressed are more likely than other people to make internal, stable, and global attributions for failures. Most people who commit suicide do so because of depression.

LO4 Describe the symptoms and possible origins of six types of anxiety disorders.

Anxiety disorders are characterized by feelings of dread and sympathetic arousal. They include phobias, panic disorder, generalized anxiety, obsessive–compulsive disorder, and stress disorders. Some people may be genetically predisposed to acquire certain fears. Cognitive theorists focus on ways in which people interpret threats.

LO5 Describe the symptoms and possible origins of somatoform disorders.

People with somatoform disorders display or complain of physical problems, although no medical evidence for them can be found. They include conversion disorder, hypochondriasis, and body dysmorphic disorder. Somatoform disorders may reflect the relative benefits of focusing on physical symptoms or features rather than life problems that most people would consider to be more important.

waxy flexibility
a feature of catatonic schizophrenia in which people can be moulded into postures that they maintain for quite some time

mutism
refusal to talk

LO3 major depressive disorder (MDD)
a serious to severe depressive disorder in which the person may show loss of appetite, psychomotor retardation, and impaired reality testing

psychomotor retardation
slowness in motor activity and (apparently) in thought

bipolar disorder
a disorder in which the mood alternates between two extreme poles (elation and depression); also referred to as *manic-depressive disorder*

manic
elated, showing excessive excitement

rapid flight of ideas
rapid speech and topic changes, characteristic of manic behaviour

neuroticism
a personality trait characterized largely by persistent anxiety

learned helplessness
a model for the acquisition of depressive behaviour, based on findings that organisms in aversive situations learn to show inactivity when their actions go unreinforced

attribution style
the tendency to attribute one's behaviour to internal or external factors, stable or unstable factors, and so on

LO4 specific phobia
persistent fear of a specific object or situation

claustrophobia
fear of tight, small places

acrophobia
fear of high places

social phobia
an irrational, excessive fear of public scrutiny

agoraphobia
fear of open, crowded places

panic disorder
the recurrent experiencing of attacks of extreme anxiety in the absence of external stimuli that usually elicit anxiety

generalized anxiety disorder
feelings of dread and foreboding and sympathetic arousal of at least six months' duration

obsession
a recurring thought or image that seems beyond control

compulsion
an irresistible urge to repeat an act or engage in ritualistic behaviour such as hand washing

post-traumatic stress disorder (PTSD)
a disorder that follows a distressing event outside the range of normal human experience and that is characterized by features such as intense fear, avoidance of stimuli associated with the event, and reliving of the event

acute stress disorder
a disorder, like PTSD, that is characterized by feelings of anxiety and helplessness and caused by a traumatic event; acute stress disorder occurs within a month of the event and lasts from two days to four weeks

LO6 Describe the symptoms and possible origins of dissociative disorders.
Dissociative disorders are characterized by sudden, temporary changes in consciousness or self-identity. They include dissociative amnesia, dissociative fugue, and dissociative identity disorder (multiple personality). Dissociative disorders may help people keep disturbing memories or ideas out of mind, especially memories of child abuse.

LO7 Describe the symptoms and possible origins of personality disorders.
Personality disorders are inflexible, maladaptive behaviour patterns that impair personal or social functioning. Genetic factors may be involved in personality disorders. Antisocial personality disorder may develop from some combination of genetic vulnerability (less gray matter in the prefrontal cortex of the brain, which may provide lower-than-normal levels of arousal), inconsistent discipline, and a cynical worldview.

LO5 somatoform disorders
disorders in which people complain of physical (somatic) problems even though no physical abnormality can be found

conversion disorder
a somatoform disorder in which anxiety or unconscious conflicts are "converted" into physical symptoms that often have the effect of helping the person cope with anxiety or conflict

la belle indifférence
a French term descriptive of the lack of concern for their (imagined) medical problem sometimes shown by people with conversion disorders

hypochondriasis
a somatoform disorder characterized by persistent belief that one is ill despite lack of medical findings

body dysmorphic disorder
a somatoform disorder characterized by preoccupation with an imagined or exaggerated physical defect in one's appearance

LO6 dissociative disorders
disorders in which there are sudden, temporary changes in consciousness or self-identity

dissociative amnesia
a dissociative disorder marked by loss of memory or self-identity; skills and general knowledge are usually retained

dissociative fugue
a dissociative disorder in which one experiences amnesia and then flees to a new location

dissociative identity disorder
a disorder in which a person appears to have two or more distinct identities

or personalities that may alternately emerge

multiple personality disorder
the previous term for *dissociative identity disorder*

LO7 personality disorders
enduring patterns of maladaptive behaviour that are sources of distress to the individual or others

paranoid personality disorder
a personality disorder characterized by persistent suspiciousness, but not involving the disorganization of paranoid schizophrenia

schizotypal personality disorder
a personality disorder characterized by oddities of thought and behaviour, but not involving bizarre psychotic behaviours

schizoid personality disorder
a personality disorder characterized by social withdrawal

borderline personality disorder
a personality disorder characterized by instability in relationships, self-image, mood, and lack of impulse control

antisocial personality disorder
the diagnosis given a person who is in frequent conflict with society, yet who is undeterred by punishment and experiences little or no guilt and anxiety

avoidant personality disorder
a personality disorder in which the person is unwilling to enter relationships without assurance of acceptance because of fears of rejection and criticism

Chapter in Review

13

LO1 **psychotherapy**
a systematic interaction between a therapist and a client that brings psychological principles to bear on influencing the client's thoughts, feelings, or behaviour to help the client overcome abnormal behaviour or adjust to problems in living

asylum
an institution for the care of the mentally ill

LO2 **psychoanalysis**
Freud's method of psychotherapy (also the name of Freud's theory of personality)

catharsis
release of emotional tension, as after a traumatic experience, that has the effect of restoring one's psychological well-being

free association
in psychoanalysis, the uncensored uttering of all thoughts that come to mind

resistance
the tendency to block the free expression of impulses and primitive ideas—a reflection of the defence mechanism of repression

transference
responding to one person (such as a spouse or the psychoanalyst) in a way that is similar to the way one responded to another person (such as a parent) in childhood

wish fulfillment
a primitive method used by the id to attempt to gratify basic instincts

psychodynamic therapy
therapy based on the principles of psychoanalysis, but less time-consuming as the therapist takes a more directive role

interpersonal psychotherapy (IPT)
a short-term dynamic therapy that focuses on clients' relationships and direct alleviation of negative emotions such as anxiety and depression

LO3 **client-centred therapy**
Carl Rogers's method of psychotherapy, which emphasizes the creation of a warm, therapeutic atmosphere that frees clients to engage in self-exploration and self-expression

Gestalt therapy
Fritz Perls's form of psychotherapy, which attempts to integrate conflicting parts of the personality through directive methods designed to help clients perceive their whole selves

LO4 **behaviour therapy**
systematic application of the principles of learning to the direct modification of a client's problem behaviours

systematic desensitization
Wolpe's method for reducing fears by associating a hierarchy of images of fear-evoking stimuli with deep muscle relaxation

LO1 Define psychotherapy and describe the history of treatment. Psychotherapy uses psychological principles to help clients overcome psychological disorders or problems. Throughout most of history it has been generally assumed that psychological disorders represent possession, and cruel "treatment" methods such as exorcism have been used. Asylums, mental hospitals, and community treatment are relatively recent innovations.

LO2 Describe traditional psychoanalysis and short-term psychodynamic therapies. The main method of a Freudian psychoanalysis is free association, but dream analysis and interpretations are also used. Modern approaches are briefer and more directive, and the therapist and client usually sit face to face.

LO3 Define humanistic therapy and contrast its two main approaches. Rogers' client-centred therapy uses nondirective methods: The therapist shows unconditional positive regard, empathy, and genuineness. Perls's directive method of Gestalt therapy provides exercises aimed at helping people integrate conflicting parts of their personality.

LO4 Define behaviour therapy and identify various behavioural approaches to therapy. Behaviour therapy relies on principles of learning to help clients develop adaptive behaviour patterns and discontinue maladaptive ones. These include systematic desensitization and modelling. Virtual therapy is a new method for desensitizing patients to fears. Operant conditioning methods include token economies, successive approximation, social skills training, and biofeedback training.

LO5 Define cognitive therapy and describe Beck's approach and REBT. Cognitive therapy aims to give clients insight into irrational beliefs and cognitive distortions and replace them with rational beliefs and accurate perceptions. Beck notes that clients may develop depression because they minimize accomplishments and catastrophize failures. Ellis originated rational emotive behaviour therapy (REBT), which holds that people's irrational beliefs about events shape their responses to them. Cognitive-behaviour therapy links behavioural and cognitive therapy action based techniques with the focus on changing current beliefs and behaviours.

LO6 Identify advantages, disadvantages, and types of group therapy. Group therapy is more economical than individual therapy. Moreover, group members benefit from the social support and experiences of other members. However, some clients cannot disclose their problems to a group or risk group disapproval. Specialized methods include couple therapy and family therapy.

hierarchy
an arrangement of stimuli according to the amount of fear they evoke

modelling
a behaviour-therapy technique in which a client observes and imitates a person who approaches and copes with feared objects or situations

aversive conditioning
a behaviour therapy technique in which undesired responses are inhibited by pairing repugnant or offensive stimuli with them

rapid smoking
an aversive conditioning method for quitting smoking in which the smoker inhales rapidly, thus rendering once-desirable cigarette smoke aversive

eye-movement desensitization and reprocessing (EMDR)
a method of treating stress disorders by having clients visually follow a rapidly oscillating finger while they think of the traumatic events connected with the disorders

token economy
a controlled environment in which people are reinforced for desired behaviours with tokens (such as poker chips) that may be exchanged for privileges

successive approximations
in operant conditioning, a series of behaviours that gradually become more similar to a target behaviour

biofeedback training (BFT)
the systematic feeding back to an organism of information about a bodily function so that the organism can gain control of that function

self-monitoring
keeping a record of one's own behaviour to identify problems and record successes

behaviour rehearsal
practice

feedback
in assertiveness training, information about the effectiveness of a response

LO5 cognitive therapy
a form of therapy that focuses on how clients' cognitions (e.g., expectations, attitudes, beliefs) lead to distress and may be modified to relieve distress and promote adaptive behaviour

rational emotive behaviour therapy (REBT)
Albert Ellis's form of therapy that encourages clients to challenge and correct irrational expectations and maladaptive behaviours

cognitive-behaviour therapy (CBT)
an approach to therapy that uses cognitive and behavioural techniques that have been validated by research

LO7 meta-analysis
a method for combining and averaging the results of individual research studies

LO7 Explain whether psychotherapy works and who benefits from it.
Statistical analyses such as meta-analysis show that people who obtain most forms of psychotherapy fare better than people who do not. Psychoanalytic and client-centered approaches are most helpful with highly verbal and motivated individuals. Cognitive and behaviour therapies are probably the most effective. People from various cultural backgrounds may profit from different kinds of treatment.

LO8 Describe methods of biological therapy and their benefits and side effects.
Antipsychotic drugs help many people with schizophrenia by blocking the action of dopamine. Antidepressants help many people by increasing the action of serotonin, and light therapy regulates the production of melatonin. Lithium often helps people with bipolar disorder. The use of antianxiety drugs for daily tensions is controversial because people build tolerance and do not learn to solve their problems. ECT, another controversial treatment, induces a seizure and frequently relieves severe depression. The prefrontal lobotomy attempts to alleviate agitation by severing nerve pathways in the brain but has been largely discontinued because of side effects.

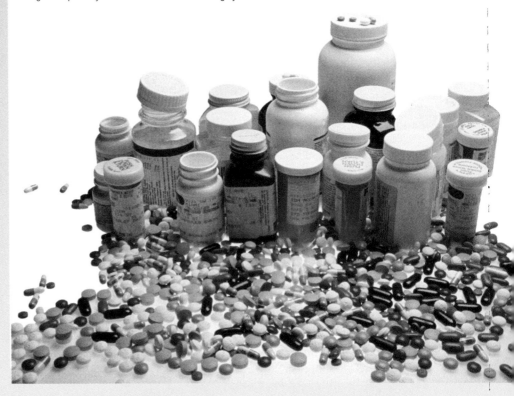

specific factors
those factors in psychotherapy that are specific to a given approach, such as free association in psychoanalysis or systematic desensitization in behaviour therapy

nonspecific factors
those factors in psychotherapy that are common to many approaches, such as the "therapeutic alliance" with the client

LO8 rebound anxiety
anxiety that can occur when one discontinues use of a tranquilizer

antidepressant
acting to relieve depression

selective serotonin-reuptake inhibitors (SSRIs)
antidepressant drugs that work by blocking the reuptake of serotonin by presynaptic neurons

light therapy
treatment for SAD in which the person sits in front of intense lights for several hours to regulate melatonin production

electroconvulsive therapy (ECT)
treatment of disorders like major depression by passing an electric current (that causes a convulsion) through the head

sedative
a drug that relieves nervousness or agitation or puts one to sleep

psychosurgery
surgery intended to promote psychological changes or to relieve disordered behaviour

prefrontal lobotomy
the severing or destruction of a section of the frontal lobe of the brain

Chapter in Review

14

situationist perspective
the view that social influence can goad people into doing things that are inconsistent with their usual behaviour

LO1 social psychology
the field of psychology that studies the nature and causes of people's thoughts and behaviour in social situations

LO2 attitude
an enduring mental representation of a person, place, or thing that evokes an emotional response and related behaviour

A–B problem
the issue of how well we can predict behaviour on the basis of attitudes

elaboration likelihood model
the view that persuasive messages are evaluated (elaborated) on the basis of central and peripheral cues

fear appeal
a type of persuasive communication that influences behaviour on the basis of arousing fear instead of rational analysis of the issues

reciprocity
a powerful social convention that dictates returning a favour for a favour

door-in-the-face
a persuasion technique where an initial large request (that is expected to be denied) is followed by a more reasonable second request (what the asker initially wanted)

selective avoidance
diverting one's attention from information that is inconsistent with one's attitudes

selective exposure
deliberately seeking and attending to information that is consistent with one's attitudes

cognitive-dissonance theory
the view that we are motivated to make our cognitions or beliefs consistent

attitude-discrepant behaviour
behaviour inconsistent with an attitude that may have the effect of modifying the attitude

low-ball
sales technique based on the buyers cognitive-dissonance when the seller suddenly requests a larger amount than what was originally negotiated

effort justification
in cognitive-dissonance theory, the tendency to seek justification (acceptable reasons) for strenuous efforts

stereotypes
beliefs about the attributes of individuals who belong to a group

attraction
an attitude of liking

LO1 Define social psychology. The situationist perspective studies the ways in which people can be goaded by social influences into doing things that are not necessarily consistent with their personalities. Social psychology studies the nature and causes of behaviour and mental processes in social situations. Topics covered in social psychology include: attitudes, conformity, persuasion, social perception, interpersonal attraction, social influence, group conformity, and obedience.

LO2 Define attitude and discuss factors that shape it. Attitudes are comprised of cognitive evaluations, feelings, and behavioural tendencies. A number of factors influence the likelihood that we can predict behaviour from attitudes: specificity, strength of attitudes, vested interest, and accessibility. Attitudes with a strong emotional impact are more accessible. People attempt to change other people's attitudes and behaviour by means of persuasion. According to the elaboration likelihood model, persuasion occurs through central and peripheral routes. Repeated messages generally "sell" better than messages delivered once. People tend to respond more to fear appeals than the purely factual presentation. Persuasive communicators tend to show expertise, trustworthiness, attractiveness, or similarity to the audience.

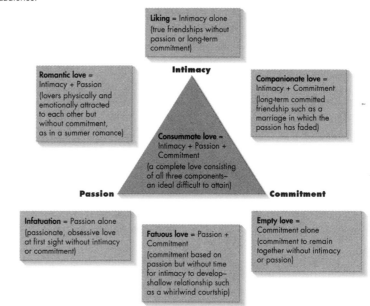

Liking = Intimacy alone (true friendships without passion or long-term commitment)

Romantic love = Intimacy + Passion (lovers physically and emotionally attracted to each other but without commitment, as in a summer romance)

Companionate love = Intimacy + Commitment (long-term committed friendship such as a marriage in which the passion has faded)

Consummate love = Intimacy + Passion + Commitment (a complete love consisting of all three components—an ideal difficult to attain)

Infatuation = Passion alone (passionate, obsessive love at first sight without intimacy or commitment)

Fatuous love = Passion + Commitment (commitment based on passion but without time for intimacy to develop—shallow relationship such as a whirlwind courtship)

Empty love = Commitment alone (commitment to remain together without intimacy or passion)

Intimacy / Passion / Commitment

LO3 Define social perception and describe the factors that contribute to it. The primacy effect refers to the fact that we often judge people in terms of our first impressions. The recency effect appears to be based on the fact that recently learned information is easier to remember. The attribution process is the tendency to infer the motives and traits of others through observation of their behaviour. In dispositional attributions, we attribute people's behaviour to internal factors. In situational attributions, we attribute people's behaviour to external forces. According to the actor–observer effect, we tend to attribute the behaviour of others to internal, dispositional factors, but we tend to attribute our own behaviour to external, situational factors. The fundamental attribution error is the tendency to attribute too much of other people's behaviour to dispositional factors.

triangular model of love
Sternberg's view that love involves combinations of three components: intimacy, passion, and commitment

intimacy
close acquaintance and familiarity; a characteristic of a relationship in which partners share their inmost feelings

passion
strong romantic and sexual feelings

commitment
the decision to maintain a relationship

consummate love
the ideal form of love within Sternberg's model, which combines passion, intimacy, and commitment

romantic love
an intense, positive emotion that involves sexual attraction, feelings of caring, and the belief that one is in love

LO3 social perception
a subfield of social psychology that studies the ways in which we form and modify impressions of others

primacy effect
the tendency to evaluate others in terms of first impressions

recency effect
the tendency to evaluate others in terms of the most recent impression

attribution
a judgement concerning why people behave in a certain way

dispositional attribution
an assumption that a person's behaviour is determined by internal causes such as personal attitudes or goals

situational attribution
an assumption that a person's behaviour is determined by external circumstances such as the social pressure found in a situation

actor–observer effect
the tendency to make attributions based on where our attention is (e.g., dispositional factors for others and situational factors for ourselves)

fundamental attribution error
the assumption that others act predominantly on the basis of their dispositions, even when there is evidence suggesting the importance of their situations

self-serving bias
the tendency to view one's successes as stemming from internal factors and one's failures as stemming from external factors

LO4 social influence
the area of social psychology that studies the ways in which people influence the thoughts, feelings, and behaviour of others

foot-in-the-door technique
a method for including compliance in which a small request is followed by a larger request

LO5 social facilitation
the process by which a person's performance is increased when other members of a group engage in similar behaviour

LO4 Explain why people obey authority figures and conform to social norms.
Other people and groups can exert enormous pressure on us to behave according to their norms. In fact, classic experiments have demonstrated that people influence others to engage in destructive obedience or conform to social norms. For example, the majority of subjects in the Milgram studies complied with the demands of authority figures, even when the demands required that they hurt innocent people by means of electric shock. Factors contributing to obedience include socialization, lack of social comparison, perception of legitimate authority figures, the foot-in-the-door technique, inaccessibility of values, and buffers between perpetrator and victim. Asch's research in which subjects judged the lengths of lines suggests that most people will follow the crowd, even when the crowd is wrong. Personal factors such as desire to be liked by group members, low self-esteem, high self-consciousness, and shyness contribute to conformity. Group size also contributes.

Overbearing experimenter

"Teacher" with "aggression" machine

"Learner" who appears to be receiving shocks

LO5 Describe how and why people behave differently as group members than as individuals.
The concept of social facilitation refers to the effects on performance that result from the presence of other people. The presence of others may facilitate performance for reasons such as increased arousal and evaluation apprehension. Anonymous group members, however, may experience diffusion of responsibility and performance may fall off, as in social loafing. Social psychologists have identified several decision-making schemes, including the majority-wins scheme, the truth-wins scheme, the two-thirds majority scheme, and the first-shift rule. Group decisions tend to be more polarized and riskier than individual decisions, largely because groups diffuse responsibility. Group decisions may be highly productive when group members are knowledgeable, there is an explicit procedure for arriving at decisions, and there is a process of give and take.

evaluation apprehension
concern that others are evaluating our behaviour

diffusion of responsibility
the spreading or sharing of responsibility for a decision or behaviour within a group

social decision schemes
rules for predicting the final outcome of group decision making on the basis of the members' initial positions

groupthink
a process in which group members are influenced by cohesiveness and a dynamic leader to ignore external realities as they make decisions

deindividuation
the process by which group members may discontinue self-evaluation and adopt group norms and attitudes

social role
a group position that is accompanied by norms for behaviour

altruism
unselfish concern for the welfare of others